The Miegunyah Press
at
Melbourne University Press

This is number thirty-four in the
second numbered series of the
Miegunyah Volumes
made possible by the
Miegunyah Fund
established by bequests
under the wills of
Sir Russell and Lady Grimwade

'Miegunyah' was the home of
Mab and Russell Grimwade
from 1911 to 1955

The COLONIAL EARTH

The
COLONIAL EARTH

Tim Bonyhady

The Miegunyah Press

MELBOURNE UNIVERSITY PRESS
PO Box 278, Carlton South, Victoria 3053, Australia
info@mup.unimelb.edu.au
www.mup.com.au

First published 2000
Reprinted 2001

National Library of Australia Cataloguing-in-Publication entry

Bonyhady, Tim, 1957– .
The colonial earth.

Bibliography.
Includes index.
ISBN 0 522 84915 6.

1. Environmentalism—Australia—History. 2. Environmental management—Australia—History. 3. Environmental law—Australia—History. 4. Environmental protection in art. 5. Environmental protection in literature. 6. Environmental policy—Australia—History. I. Title.

333.720994

FOR NICHOLAS

CONTENTS

ACKNOWLEDGEMENTS

IN 1966 the Australian National University broke with conventional academic structures and established a multi-disciplinary Urban Research Program. In 1999 the University closed what had become the Urban and Environmental Program. I was one of the last beneficiaries of this remarkable intellectual environment; *The Colonial Earth* is one product of the great opportunities I enjoyed there.

All big books take time. But the Urban Research Program was also an exceptionally stimulating workplace in which thinking and writing across established disciplines was not so much encouraged as expected. Patrick Troy, a member of the program from its inception and its head throughout my time there, was primarily responsible. This book owes a lot to him.

It also owes a lot to Anne Bonyhady, Nicholas Brown, Peter Christoff, Peter Cochrane, Richard Grove, Jenny Lee, Humphrey McQueen, Andrew Sayers and Claire Young. All helped me shape the manuscript. Anne Bonyhady, Nicholas Brown, Peter Cochrane, Jenny Lee, Humphrey McQueen and Claire Young all read the text. Peter Christoff stopped me putting it aside to write another book; Andrew Sayers took me to Tower Hill in 1987 and then again in 1997. Nicholas Bonyhady and Claire Young kept me happy.

INTRODUCTION

IN JANUARY 1993 I visited Hobart, drawn south by an exhibition of paintings at the Tasmanian Museum and Art Gallery. William Charles Piguenit had long been recognised as the first colonial artist of any consequence who was born and trained in Australia, and as the last major Australian romantic landscape painter. More recently, he had begun acquiring a new conservationist identity as a wilderness painter and 'nineteenth-century environmentalist'.[1] I wanted to investigate whether Piguenit was an early advocate of environmental protection or was simply celebrating and promoting Tasmania's scenery.

My interest in this question grew out of working both as a curator at the Australian National Gallery and as a lecturer in environmental law at the Australian National University. When not writing about Australian landscape painting, I had written about the way in which the law both assisted and impeded modern conservationists. The obvious connection between the two was land. But otherwise I could have been two people, sometimes wearing the hat of art historian, sometimes that of lawyer. Piguenit offered the opportunity to begin bridging the gap between art history and environmentalism, if not art history and law.

My initial intention was to write an essay exploring when Australian artists had begun expressing conservationist ideas in paint. If Piguenit had not done so in his early landscapes from the 1870s and 1880s, I thought I might have to jump to Arthur Streeton's late landscapes from the 1920s and the 1930s. But before long, I was not only looking past Piguenit, into the early and mid-nineteenth century, but also beyond Streeton towards the present. By mid-1993, I was writing a book about the significance of art and aesthetics to environmentalism in Australia, using a painting or photograph, print or drawing, as the starting point for each chapter.

As I soon realised, this Australian story was all the more significant because it was part of a much larger international story about the environmental aesthetic, which had rarely been explored except in the most piecemeal fashion.[2] Across the Old World and the New, nineteenth-century artists—ranging from Alfred Sharpe in New Zealand to George Catlin in the United States, William Morris in England, Theodore Rousseau in France and Edmund Kanoldt in Italy—took up a wide array of environmental causes. While they generally expressed these concerns in essays and pamphlets, lectures and letters, they also occasionally conveyed them through their art.[3]

Yet I soon found myself back in the law library, because I did not just want to examine how European artists in Australia had shaped and communicated aesthetic values in relation to the Australian environment; I also wanted to explore what had become of those values. As I worked to examine the relationship between environmental ideals, policy and practice, I realised that the law was crucial, both as an embodiment of society's commitment to protecting particular places and species and as a vehicle for securing that protection. More than ever, I could see a connection between the two halves of my writing.

The opportunity to bring these halves together was irresistible. Rather than focusing on the environmental aesthetic, I decided to take the law as seriously as art, exploring how these very different expressions of society, each with its own traditions, vocabularies and audiences, had responded to a new environment. At the same time, I sought to bridge the gap between art and law, writing across the culture as a whole. While I was eager to traverse a big environmental canvas—including pastoral lands and forests, native animals and pollution, the city and the bush—my premise, then as now, was that it was largely through the detail of what Australians depicted, said and did that one could see how they occupied the land, both imaginatively and physically.

Several years later, this book provides an answer to the question that initially took me to Hobart—although, as it turns out, the answer lies more in Piguenit's paintings of western New South Wales from the 1890s than in his earlier views of western Tasmania. *The Colonial Earth* also encompasses Streeton, as his environmental concerns were already manifest in the 1890s. But it starts in 1788 with the arrival of the First Fleet. Except for occasional forays forward, particularly to explore how Eugene von Guérard's *Tower Hill* began leaving its mark on the landscape a century after he painted it, this book stops in 1900. The twentieth century will, I hope, be the subject of another.

The standard view of the colonial period is that the invaders wreaked havoc on their new environment—both gratuitously and as an inevitable part of the process of settlement. This idea had its genesis in the 1820s and 1830s when occasional colonists rebuked their contemporaries for 'wanton', 'over-zealous' axework. By the 1870s and 1880s, local critics were deploring the 'murder' of Australia's trees, the 'war' against the continent's forests. The visiting English essayist J. A. Froude reckoned that colonial society was antithetical to environmental protection. The issue for Froude was one of 'sentiment'—the capacity to put emotion before practicality. He concluded: 'Sentiment belongs to leisure, and in the colonies, just now, they have none of either'.[4]

Soon it was a commonplace that the invaders were not simply untroubled by their destructiveness but rejoiced in it, so great was their alienation from their new surroundings and their eagerness to turn the land to new uses. When W. K. Hancock published his *Australia* in 1930, he famously declared that 'the invaders hated trees'. In *The Australian Ugliness*, published in 1960, Robin Boyd blamed Australia's 'arboraphobia' on its enduring 'pioneering cult'. Six years later, Jock Marshall provided a 'Guide to Anglo-Australian Cupidity, Wickedness and Waste' in *The Great Extermination*, declaring:

> The bush, to our great-grandfathers, was the enemy: it brooded sombrely outside their brave and often pathetic little attempts at civilisation; it crowded in on them in times of drought and flood. It, not they, was alien.[5]

The 1990s brought more of the same, as the work of Bill Lines and Tim Flannery overshadowed the more subtle, reliable environmental histories written by Joe Powell, Geoffrey Bolton and others.[6] In *Taming the Great South Land*, Lines maintained that 'Australia's pioneers felt no emotional ties to the land' but saw it simply as 'potential wealth' to be exploited. When a few colonists belatedly began criticising this ethos in the 1890s, they 'confined their concern to waste and . . . expressed no remorse for the loss of natural and indigenous life forms and landscapes'. Flannery went further in *The Future Eaters*. Blind even to the existence of the critics identified by Lines, he claimed nineteenth-century settlers showed 'no concern at all about wastage of timber', so confident were they that Australia's forests were superabundant.[7]

The reality was very different. While many colonists were alienated by their new environment, others delighted in it. The standard test is the settlers' response to the gum tree. The cliché would have it that the invaders saw the eucalypt as a symbol of everything that was different—and wrong—about their new home. In fact, many members of the First Fleet lauded the gum tree for its distinctiveness. Even from the 1820s, when the cliché has more substance, the eucalypts had champions. When the landscape painter

John Glover arrived in Tasmania in 1831, he reckoned them a 'painter's delight'.

Other aspects of the colonial landscape, particularly the continent's giant tree ferns, excited only admiration because they eclipsed those of Europe. In 1852 Godfrey Mundy, the deputy adjutant-general of the British military forces in Australia, recorded his delight in how tree ferns just twenty feet tall—less than half the size of the tallest reported—dwarfed the 'little microscopic varieties' that 'fern-mad' English gardeners nursed 'with vast anxiety and expense'.[8]

Some species of eucalypt also acquired global significance. The Tasmanian blue gum was acclaimed internationally as a 'tree of the future' because of its remarkably rapid growth and apparent capacity for countering malaria. From the 1860s it was a major Australian export, introduced in dozens of other countries. The Victorian mountain ash was acclaimed as a 'wonder of the world' after the Government Botanist, Ferdinand von Mueller, announced in 1866 that it was probably the tallest tree on earth, eclipsing the giant sequoias of California.

Colonists also came to feel deep affection for particular places that satisfied their taste for the picturesque and the sublime. Rural settlers identified with fern gullies, waterfalls or mountains in their local areas, but the places that excited most colonists were all within easy access of the cities. Port Jackson was pre-eminent. From the 1880s it was frequently referred to as 'Our Harbour' or, more often, as 'Our Beautiful Harbour', suggesting that Sydneysiders not only delighted in its beauty but also saw it as common property enjoyed by all.

The settlers' attachment to the colonial landscape was matched by their desire to preserve it. The protection of the continent's native fauna and flora, pollution of its rivers, degradation of its pastoral lands, planning and improvement of its cities, preservation of beauty spots, retention of public reserves and access to the foreshore were all major issues in the colonial era. Even climate change—perhaps the environmental issue most often thought of as modern—excited attention as early as 1795, when the magistrate Richard Atkins speculated that the weather was changing 'in consequence of the country opening so fast'.

Whitehall did little to encourage these concerns. When the First Fleet sailed from Portsmouth in 1787, British officials instructed Captain Arthur Phillip to preserve the livestock he was carrying with him so that they might become the basis of new herds in Australia, but gave him no comparable instructions in relation to Australia's native flora or fauna. Whitehall's order that Phillip reserve timber fit for naval purposes when granting land was designed not to protect the trees, but to ensure that the Crown enjoyed the exclusive right to exploit them. Whitehall forgot town planning; Phillip sailed with no instructions about how to lay out the first settlements.[9]

Yet the first colonial officials acted with remarkable speed. While Richard Grove has shown how a form of 'Green Imperialism' was practised by French officials on Mauritius from 1725 and the British officials responsible for St Vincent from the 1760s, these attempts at environmental protection started after these islands had already been devastated by years, if not decades, of settlement.[10] Australia—perhaps more than anywhere else—began with a form of colonialism alive to the importance of environmental protection and planning.

The first environmental laws—starting in April 1788, when Lieutenant Philip Gidley King protected plantain or banana trees on Norfolk Island, just four days after discovering them[11]—were predictably utilitarian. One of the objects of these laws was to ensure that the natural environment provided an enduring source of food, particularly when the invaders' imported supplies ran short. Another goal was to protect public health by maintaining the purity of drinking water. A third was to preserve timber, which rapidly became scarce around the new settlements.

John Hunter was one official who followed King in recognising the urgency of these measures. Within a month of becoming Governor of New South Wales in September 1795, Hunter prohibited pollution of the Tank Stream, which provided Sydney's main source of water. He also threatened to have adjoining landholders' houses pulled down if they kept pigs or opened new paths to the water. In December he prohibited the felling of cedar on public land along the Hunter River in order to stop its being 'indiscriminately cut' and either 'wasted or applied to purposes for which timber of less value might have answered'.[12]

By 1804 such laws were the norm. When Lieutenant-Governor David Collins established Hobart, he immediately 'cautioned' his subjects against polluting the stream that provided their fresh water, and 'positively forbade' them from 'going into, or destroying the underwood adjacent to the water'. Then he banned the felling of 'any timber, whether young or old, near the Encampment' without the approval of his chief carpenter. A fortnight later he prohibited the settlers from molesting black swans because he feared that 'the resource which they might have otherwise proved will totally fail, unless some steps are taken to prevent it'.[13]

This interest in resource protection was soon the stuff of private discussion and public debate. Already in 1802, both the French explorer Nicolas Baudin and the former Assistant Surgeon of New South Wales, James Thomson, privately warned Philip Gidley King that the seals of King Island would be destroyed unless he exercised his new power as Governor of New South Wales to protect them. In 1803, the *Sydney Gazette*—the settlement's only newspaper—carried the first public call for official action: 'A Well-wisher to POSTERITY' warned that settlers were compromising their children's future through the 'general massacre' of the seals, which could be 'a constant source of enterprise and emolument' if 'properly managed'.[14]

Yet the colonists' environmental concerns were not simply utilitarian, even in the most difficult circumstances. When Robert Ross succeeded King as commandant of Norfolk Island in 1790, the settlers faced the worst crisis of their 'starvation years'. But Ross was not just concerned to ensure a continued supply of food when he restricted the taking of birds on the island. Nor was he just mimicking existing metropolitan or colonial practice. His laws included what was probably the world's first prohibition of cruelty to animals.

The French artist Charles-Alexandre Lesueur exhibited the same moral concern while sailing with the Baudin expedition in 1802. When Lesueur visited King Island, he manifested his sympathy for its sea elephants by drawing them anthropomorphically, with humanoid faces. Five years later, he turned these drawings into an engraving, which was used to illustrate a text by his friend, the zoologist François Péron. Péron condemned the slaughter of sea elephants, not only because it would destroy 'the source of a valuable commerce' but also because he abhorred the cruelty with which English crews killed these 'gentle and peaceful' animals.[15]

Sydney's first plan, which Arthur Phillip completed in mid-1788, also had utilitarian, aesthetic and symbolic aims. Phillip wanted to make the new town's principal streets 200 feet wide to allow 'a free circulation of air' and so protect public health. He planned to prohibit the construction of more than one house per block in order to impose order and uniformity on the new town. He sought to give physical expression to his own authority and the broader power of the colonial state by placing Government House, the Law Courts and Barracks on high ground, above all his subjects.[16]

This plan was remarkably ambitious. Far from conceiving of the new settlement as just a temporary dumping ground for convicts, Phillip laid out Sydney so that it would be, as he put it, a future 'Seat of Empire', with grand streets almost the equal of Pall Mall in London and Unter den Linden in Berlin. A year later, Erasmus Darwin put this vision into verse. In a prefatory poem to *The Voyage of Governor Phillip*, Darwin imagined Sydney as a refined Georgian town, where 'broad streets [would] their stately walls extend, / The circus widen, and the crescent bend'.[17]

As colonial governments expanded, an array of officials began pursuing these environmental goals. Although the first colonial surveyor of timber, master shipwright Thomas Moore, was appointed by King in 1803 simply to secure naval timber for the British government,[18] most of Moore's successors had much broader concerns. These surveyors, land commissioners, botanists, foresters and engineers were keen to prevent waste and to ensure a continued supply of valuable resources. They were alive to larger environmental risks, particularly that of climate change as a result of deforestation. Their calculus too was not simply utilitarian. In 1837 Tasmania's Surveyor-General, George Frankland, sought to prevent quarrying in a fern gully known as Salvator Rosa's Glen on Mount Wellington—possibly the first time a colonist had argued for protection of a particular place on aesthetic grounds.[19]

Private citizens also began looking to give institutional expression to their concerns by establishing Australia's first environmental groups. The earliest, wealthiest and most enduring were the various colonial societies for the prevention of cruelty to animals. Other groups addressed an array of issues, ranging from Sydney's League for the Prevention of Pollution of Air and Water, which opposed the piping of untreated sewage out to sea at Bondi, to Melbourne's Kalizoic Society, which aspired to create the environmental conditions for 'beautiful life' in Victoria.

The press was even more significant in identifying and pursuing environmental issues. While many colonial newspapers regularly stimulated environmental debate, the most active was Melbourne's daily *Argus*, the pre-eminent conservative newspaper in Australia.

From the 1860s to the 1930s, the *Argus* probably provided more extensive and sharper reportage and analysis of environmental issues than any Australian newspaper before or since. Between 1879 and 1886 the monthly *Victorian Review* was also a regular forum for essays exploring environmental issues—whether its contributors were pursuing the possibilities of a distinctively Australian 'Climatic Architecture' or asking 'Is the Earth Becoming Bald?' as a result of deforestation.

These issues were championed disproportionately by men and women who straddled the art–environment divide, several of whom knew each other despite the distances separating them. For more than forty years, the artist–author Louisa Anne Meredith was the most significant Tasmanian advocate of environmental concerns. The art critic James Smith championed all manner of environmental causes as an editorial writer with the *Argus*, and was probably also responsible for the environmental focus of the *Victorian Review* as its *de facto* editor.[20] The pastoralist James Dawson first commissioned Eugene von Guérard to paint Tower Hill in Victoria's Western District, then became the most prominent advocate of its protection.

Art also assumed a new significance as a medium for changing how Australians looked at their environment. Eugene von Guérard's *Ferntree Gully in the Dandenong Ranges* not only put his subject on the map in 1857 but probably excited some colonists to want to preserve it. Within a decade of Louis Buvelot's setting up as an artist in Melbourne in 1864, his paintings were said to have led colonists to see the beauty of the once 'derided' gum tree. In 1893 Archibald Campbell and R. S. Sugars used their lantern slides to try to preserve the Dandenong State Forest from being thrown open to selection by smallholders. Both Piguenit's *The Flood in the Darling, 1890* and Streeton's *Cremorne Pastoral*—the two pictures of the year in Sydney in 1895—were recognised as part of major environmental arguments.

Colonial courts and tribunals equally revealed their potential as forums for challenging government. When a local landowner opposed the sale of part of Melbourne's Albert Park in 1875, the Victorian Supreme Court dismissed his suit, yet he still succeeded in exposing the Victorian government's lack of due process so that it abandoned its plans. Two residents of North Sydney persuaded a mining warden in 1895 that the Sydney Harbour Collieries Company should not be allowed to acquire the foreshore from Cremorne to Mosman. Then the New South Wales Land Appeal Court condemned the proposed colliery as 'a hideous blemish on the people's inheritance'. Eventually the colonial government refused to grant the final permission that the company required to start sinking pits.[21]

The breadth of this culture of environmental concern—embracing both the 'sentimental' and the practical—has profound implications for how we see Australian history. Just as it is heartening to know that some of the invaders were troubled by the morality of their dispossession of Australia's Aborigines,[22] so it is heartening to know that some colonists also wanted to conserve their new environment for aesthetic and moral as well as economic reasons—and that they sometimes succeeded in doing so. The combination of environmental concern and regard for Aboriginal interests is a powerful counter to the simple equation of invasion with exploitation, of colonisation with despoliation. The settlers' own language in the second half of the nineteenth century is most indicative. As they increasingly put it, their new environment was a 'heritage', if not 'national estate'.[23]

Yet this environmental regard was not always an unqualified good. Then as now, the pursuit of environmental protection often had inequitable social consequences. The siting of industry was one issue where colonists repeatedly divided on class lines. The revocation of reserves and state forests so that land could be opened to selection was another. What members of the middle class typically opposed because of its environmental impact, members of the working class generally welcomed because it provided their only avenue for obtaining land or keeping in work. Far from foiling the Sydney Harbour Collieries Company's plans to mine under Port Jackson, the colliery's opponents simply succeeded in shifting its operations from middle-class Mosman to working-class Balmain.

As 'conservation' became professionalised, it also bore less and less relation to environmental protection. Far from simply being a means of ensuring a continued supply of scarce natural resources, as it was in the first years of colonisation, it became a form of intensive resource exploitation predicated on radical interference with the environment. So Australia's first water conservators aspired to large-scale irrigation, and the first conservators of forests aspired to replace natural diversity with plantations that would produce 'crops of trees' for sawmillers on thirty-year rotations.

The colonists' environmental concerns often also came to nothing, starting in 1788, when Arthur Phillip abandoned his plan for Sydney within three months of making it. The first officials were unable to enforce their laws, despite their purportedly autocratic powers. John Hunter could not even police the Tank Stream—a relatively simple task, given its central location. Having first legislated to protect the stream in 1795, Hunter was forced to reiterate this order in 1796, to his manifest irritation. 'When an Order is given', he vainly declared, 'it is to be obeyed'.[24]

The official enthusiasm for industry was also inimical to environmental protection. Sealing in Bass Strait constituted the first major test because it exploited, as Philip Gidley King put it, 'the most considerable among the very few natural productions of this country that can be esteemed commercial'. After Nicolas Baudin and James Thomson called on King to intervene, he reconsidered his initial ambition to 'encourage' sealing 'as much as possible'. In 1803 he advised Whitehall that it would be 'expedient to restrain Individuals from resorting there in too great numbers, and to fix certain Times for their visiting these places'. But King made no attempt to do so, most likely because he put short-term economic advantage before long-term sustainability.[25]

The failure of government to order the repair of environmental damage already done also had profound consequences. So King recognised in 1803 that the clearing of riverbanks by landholders on the Hawkesbury River had increased the damage caused by floods. As a result, he prohibited the clearing of cedars on private land abutting the river, and 'earnestly recommended' that occupiers of this land replant these trees. But King's sense of the sanctity of private property rights—or perhaps his reluctance to antagonise his subjects—kept him from ordering the landholders to do so.[26]

The dangers of challenging such economic interests were demonstrated most dramatically when King's successor as Governor, William Bligh, sought to regulate the use of land in Sydney to preserve open space and secure orderly development in the burgeoning town. By 1807 Bligh's attempt to do so was a central issue in colonial politics—the stuff of public conflict. When the New South Wales Corps ousted Bligh a year later, their rebellion was a result not just of his suppression of the colony's rum economy, but also his assertion of the government's right to protect the urban environment.

Later, more democratic governments struggled to create enduring environmental regimes. By the late nineteenth century, it was a commonplace that colonial governments were incapable of implementing their environmental ideals because of their vulnerability to electoral pressure from colonists concerned with short-term advantage rather than their long-term collective interests. Because of the state's unwillingness to appoint an adequate number of rangers and inspectors, most environmental laws had little effect. In the rare cases where government launched prosecutions or private landowners invoked their property rights to preserve the natural environment, the courts were typically unsympathetic.

For all the passion of individual colonists who advocated environmental protection—the Sydney bookseller J. W. R. Clarke claimed in 1898 to have 'written nearly one thousand letters to the Australian press' about the need to preserve native flora and fauna[27]—they often did no better. Louisa Anne Meredith was just one of many who struggled to put her ideals into practice. Almost the only legacy of the Kalizoic Society—the one collective attempt at environmental protection by a broad cross-section of colonial experts in the visual arts—was that 'kalizoic' briefly entered the language as a byword for fashion.

These failures are all the more disturbing because of the very richness of Australia's history of environmental concern. In ignorance of this history, the destructiveness of colonial society has been explained away as the work of invaders antagonistic to their new landscape and blind to its limits. The difficulties experienced by modern governments in securing effective protection have similarly been seen as a product of a society just beginning to take its environment seriously. The history traversed in this book does not allow us this comfort. It suggests that the environmental aesthetic is as deeply embedded in the culture as is resistance to putting environmental ideals into practice.

SYDNEY BIRD PAINTER *A YOUNG MOUNT PITT BIRD* C. 1790

CHAPTER ONE

BIRDS OF PROVIDENCE

It is worthy of Remark that these Birds were coming in when our sad and melancholy Catastrophe happened, and were very scarce at the arrival of the relief. Nothing could have been better timed, and though rather paradoxical, everything happened as favourably as could be.

George Raper, Letter, August 1790

THE INVADERS LOVED BIRDS. Their letters, despatches and books attest to their delight in the 'astonishing variety' and 'uncommonly beautiful' plumage of Australia's novel species. Although some settlers reckoned that these birds lacked 'a pleasing note', others found them 'most melodious'. Colonial artists shared this enthusiasm. Between 1788 and 1800, birds were their favourite subject. Ornithological drawings possibly even outnumbered all other subjects combined—the new European settlement, Aborigines, mammals, reptiles, fish and plants. In the early 1790s there were at least three artists, now known as the 'Sydney Bird Painters', who seem to have drawn nothing else.[1]

The Mount Pitt Bird of Norfolk Island was the stuff of several of these drawings, despite its bland plumage. The Sydney Bird Painters depicted it at least three times. Another anonymous artist drew it twice. So too did Midshipman George Raper, one of a number of naval officers with the First Fleet who took up natural-history illustration in the colony. Captain John Hunter thought he had drawn it, but in fact probably depicted a wedge-tailed shearwater—an astonishing blunder for someone who lived on this petrel for four months.[2]

The Sydney Bird Painters depicted the petrel both as a chick and as an adult, something rarely done for other Australian bird species in the late eighteenth century.[3] *A Young Mount Pitt Bird*, which was most likely drawn from a skin or a poorly stuffed specimen, shows a chick standing at an age when it could not have done so. It also reveals the chick's legs, although only its toes would have protruded

MOUNT PITT BIRD C. 1790

JOHN HUNTER
BIRD OF PROVIDENCE, OR MOUNT PITT BIRD, NORFOLK ISLAND C. 1790

from its feathers. But it provides an accurate record of the petrel's head and ball-like body and shows how, when frightened, the chick would try to rear up with beak open, chattering away and trying to bite. Another drawing reveals why this species was so popular. An inscription on this drawing reads: 'These birds came to Norfolk Island to lay eggs on Mt Pitt. Their presence saved the people from famine.'

Lieutenant Ralph Clark's journal provides the best record of these events. Despite its poor grammar and worse spelling, Clark's journal has all the power of a daily log never rewritten for publication. His interest in the birds was partly professional. As acting quartermaster on Norfolk Island in 1790, Clark was not only responsible for the stores that the colonists brought with them but was also keenly interested in how they found additional supplies on the island. For more than three months, Clark's journal became a record of environmental destruction. He concluded almost every entry with a tally of the number of birds killed by the colonists. At first he kept separate counts of the number killed by the marines, soldiers and convicts. Later he only recorded a single daily figure.[4]

Clark began on 10 April, when the count was 625 birds. The following day he recorded 614. By late April, the number was over 1500. When he started keeping a running tally at the end of the month, it came to 15 368. Through May he recorded an average of 2700 each day, with more than 4000 on seven days. The highest daily figure was 6125 on 5 June. During July his count dropped to just a few hundred a day, until he abandoned his tally on 16 July because the colonists stopped bringing their bags to the guard house at the main settlement on Sydney Bay. By then his 'grand total' was 172 184 birds.[5]

The actual number must have been greater, because Clark started counting late and stopped early. He began about three weeks after the petrels had arrived on Norfolk Island for their annual breeding season, and a week after the colonists had begun catching them. He stopped at least a fortnight before the surviving petrels quit the island.

Clark also failed to record the total number of birds killed while he was keeping his tally. Most likely, the colonists did not always tell him the full extent of their bags. Clark also made no entries at all on nine days and acknowledged that his figures were incomplete on six days in April and May, as well as another twenty days from 28 June until 16 July. During this last period Clark recorded only the number of birds taken by the fifty colonists stationed with him at Charlottefield in the north-west of the island. He wanted to obtain the tally from Sydney Bay but the sergeant there did not keep his promise to record it.[6]

The actual tally may have been close to 300 000, if not higher. In February 1791 Clark wrote to one of his fellow officers at Port Jackson:

> You will hardly believe me when I inform you that from the latter end of April until the Middle of July no Smaller a number on a very moderate Computation than five thousand was Kild a night—I have often know Seven and Eight thousand, particularly on the Sunday Evenings brought into Camp by the Sailors, Marines and Convicts (male and female).[7]

Such figures are hard to believe, given that each petrel had a body about the size of a plucked pigeon, and almost every female taken in May was carrying a single egg larger than that of a hen. Because there were just 498 men, women and children on the island, the colonists would have had five birds each if the catch was evenly divided on the evenings when they caught 2500 birds. There would have been ten birds each when they caught 5000, and sixteen each if they ever caught 8000.[8]

The petrels were also not the colonists' only food. The provisions they had brought from Sydney included flour, rice, salt beef and pork. Jacob Nagle, a sailor with the First Fleet, recalled that the colonists caught other birds, including pigeons and a type of gannet 'as big as a goose'. They also harvested vast numbers of 'cabbages', as they dubbed the white heart of the tip of the native cabbage palm, and brought in 'plentiful' fish on the rare occasions when they could get a boat through the surf.[9]

Yet other contemporary accounts confirm Clark's daily log, if not his later letters. Major Robert Ross, the commandant of the settlement during 1790, recorded that 'for six months' there were 'as many birds as all the men on the island could take away with them'. Captain John Hunter, another eyewitness, noted that from April there were not 'less taken than from two to three thousand birds every night'. Governor Arthur Phillip reported from Sydney that the colonists killed 3000 and 4000 petrels a night. The master of the *Supply*, David Blackburn, heard they sometimes took over 5000.[10]

Such big catches were possible only because of the petrels' extraordinary abundance. On 30 April Clark recorded 'the[y] are coming in very fast about Sun Set the[y] come in So thick that they darken the place much Sooner than it otherwise would'. On 2 May, when his servant killed 193, the birds were like 'a Shower of hail' after sunset. Clark himself caught more than 200 in one and a half hours on 3 June, when 'the Air was as thick with them as knats are in a fine Summers Evening in England'. George Raper later wrote that at night the 'whole Horizon (in the Woods) was . . . covered with them, and there was no walking without kicking them before you'.[11]

The birds were also easy to catch. Although no one described the petrels as 'tame'—the standard characterisation of animals that lived on previously unpeopled islands and had no fear of humans—the colonists still found it simple to kill the petrels at Mount Pitt, the island's highest point. This 300-metre hill, which the first commandant of the settlement, Philip Gidley King, named after the British Prime Minister, was covered by the closed canopy of a subtropical rainforest, pierced by Norfolk Island pines. When King first went there in October 1788, he recorded that the forest floor was so 'full of very large holes' made by the petrels that he 'fell into one of them at every step'. Jacob Nagle confirmed that it was 'entierly underminded' by the petrels. John Hunter reckoned it 'as full of holes as any rabbit warren'.[12]

The colonists began by catching the petrels during the daytime, grubbing some out of their roosts with hoes and frightening others out with terriers. But they soon found that it was much easier to wait until the petrels returned to their roosts at nightfall, after feeding at sea during the day. As Nagle recounted:

> We would first get pine nots, which was plentiful, and split the pine for torches, one small one to seek the birds with when on the Mount, and one large one to bring us home with. We would go out in the afternoon and reach the Mount by dusk, I suppose about 4 or 5 miles up hills and down steep vallies, having the trees marked all the way.[13]

The settlers' fires helped to attract the birds. Hunter described how the petrels would 'drop down out of the air as fast as the people can take them up and kill them'. The birds could not escape, because 'the length of their wings prevents their being able to rise, and until they can ascend an eminence, they are unable to recover the use of their wings'. Nagle recalled how the settlers also lured many petrels from their roosts by mimicking their calls:

> The more we hollowed 'ho, ho, ho', the birds would come runing, crying out 'ke, ke, ke', thinking it was their mate or their young, and by that means every man would take home what he thought sufficient in his knapsack, which would be from twenty to thirty at least if not more.[14]

Because the petrels were such easy pickings, the colonists frequently returned 'loaded' to Sydney Bay by 8 p.m. after just a couple of hours in the field. But under the laws made by Robert Ross they could remain on Mount Pitt until 10 p.m. and, when they did, had a long day of it. As Nagle recalled:

> When completed, every man would light his torch and set out homewards, all in a line, as the path was small, and in this season of the year was heavy rains. By the time we got to town, [it] would be about 11 or 12 o'clock at night, all wet and muddy. Coming down the hill, it was equal to a lumenation, forty or fifty torches all in rotation, one after another, until we descended to the foot of the hill into the town and disappeared.[15]

THE 'DIVINE HAND OF PROVIDENCE'

The petrels of Norfolk Island were not the only birds that once filled the skies. In 1614 a settler in Virginia recorded seeing passenger pigeons 'three or four houres together flockes in the Aire, so thicke that even they have shadowed the Skie from us'. A Pennsylvanian poet rhymed in 1729:

> *Here in the fall, large flocks of pigeons fly*
> *So num'rous, that they darken all the sky.*

The great American bird man, John James Audubon, recorded seeing a flock in Henderson, Kentucky in 1813 so big 'the light of noonday was obscured as by an eclipse'.[16]

When Americans slaughtered these pigeons to extinction after the Civil War, it was a matter of choice, not necessity, and the waste was immense. As David Quamman has described:

> The birds were gathered like apples from an orchard, with hundreds left to rot on the ground . . . Barrels full of salted or iced pigeons were sent back to eastern cities, sold there for as little as a nickel a bird. When an occasional glut hit the urban markets, the price fell even further and passenger pigeons were given away or fed to hogs.[17]

The situation on Norfolk Island was very different. In March 1790, Governor Phillip moved more settlers to the island. His decision was influenced by the failure of the first crops in New South Wales, and by King's exaggerated accounts of the island's natural bounty. Phillip's plan was that John Hunter use the *Sirius* and *Supply* to take another 280 men, women and children to the island—more than doubling its population—then sail to Canton for extra provisions. But the *Sirius* was wrecked while landing stores on the island, leaving the *Supply* as the First Fleet's only link with the outside world.

This accident made the prospect of new provisions even more remote and further increased the population of the island, because Hunter and his crew were forced to remain there. King's replacement as commandant, Robert Ross, responded by immediately putting everyone on half rations. But the colonists feared for their survival partly because they did not realise that the petrels had returned for their annual breeding season. Ralph Clark manifested this ignorance on 30 March 1790, his birthday, which he judged 'the Worst that I ever Saw from the dreadful prospect before me that of Starving if Some thing dont come to our Relief or if we dont all exert our Selfs in clearing Ground for to put Corn or potatoes in'.[18]

The settlers knew little of the petrels because they had only been to Mount Pitt, which was their main rookery, outside their breeding season. While King reported in May 1788 that the petrels had afforded his party 'many fresh meals', he probably had not seen much of these birds, since he mistakenly thought they never quit their holes until sunset, whereas they typically fed at sea through the day and returned at dusk. When King first climbed Mount Pitt and stumbled on their roosts in October 1788, the petrels were gone. He saw little or nothing of them in 1789, because his subjects did not cut a road from Sydney Bay to Mount Pitt until the end of the year.[19]

This ignorance led the colonists to look on the petrels as little short of miraculous when they discovered their vast numbers in April 1790. Clark observed that the way in which these birds descended would 'make the Old Storry of Moses being in the Wilderness be a little more believed Respecting the Shour of quails'. Lieutenant William Bradley credited 'the Divine Hand of Providence'. John Hunter dubbed the petrels 'Birds of Providence'.[20]

Still the colonists remained in dread. While they knew it would be months before their crops were ready for harvest, they did not know how long the petrels would last. In May, Clark wrote, 'god knows what would become of [us]' were it not for the birds 'being So plenty as the[y] are'. By June he was hoping some of the convicts would die and relieve the pressure on their stores. To his regret there were 'very few Sick and only one of them in danger'. He wished 'the almighty would be So Kind . . . as to take a few of them for we could doe much better without them at present as we h[av]e So little to give them to eat now'.[21]

By mid-July the colonists' situation was even more precarious, prompting Ross to declare it:

> absolutely Necessary that as long as the Birds at Mt Pit are to be had in Such abundance and as the Season of the year is approaching for the Boat to be Employd in fishing that there Should not be any more Salt Beef or Pork Issued from the Store until those most Valuable Resources fail us.

But the number of petrels fell away almost immediately. To make matters worse, big surfs on the reef repeatedly stopped the colonists from getting their boats out, and when there was no surf, they returned almost empty-handed. On 31 July Clark noted, 'I am affraid the fish are leaving'.[22]

Had Ross remained true to his order, he would have increased the colonists' rations, but their imported supplies were too few for him to do so. Instead the colonists ate less. From the beginning of August, the men and women who went to Mount Pitt usually brought in just six or eight birds, but sometimes found none. On most days, they also caught no fish. The arrival of a new species of seabird, which the settlers dubbed 'flying Sheep', because it tasted like mutton when boiled, failed to make up for the departed petrels.[23]

All the settlers could do was to wait for relief to come by sea or for their crops to grow. According to George Raper, 'a most excellent Garden', which he started with two other officers, offered 'a good prospect of digging upwards of 30 bushels of Potatoes, picking vast quantities of fresh beans, and cutting many fine heart Cabbages and Lettuces'. But the colonists had little capacity for tending vegetables. John Hunter recorded that 'The people in general were now reduced so low in bodily strength for want of sufficiency of food, that much work could not be expected of them'.[24]

When two ships were sighted on 4 August, then disappeared to the colonists' intense disappointment, Ross cut their rations again. He maintained that two pounds of flour, one pint of rice and half a pint of caravances or chickpeas per week was the 'largest proportion' that could be issued until the settlers' potatoes and corn were ready. He also threatened to issue no more food to those who did 'not to the utmost of their power and strength contribute their share of labour to the general clearing and cultivating of land so essentially necessary to the good of the whole'.[25]

Twelve weeks provisions remained at this new 'most reduced allowance', but the settlers still despaired. Jacob Nagle later made much of the colonists' predicament. He recalled that on 6 August:

> Our last provisions was to be served out, which was but one half barrel of flower, to be served out amongst 700 souls. The birds ware destroyed, the cabbage tree likewise all gone, and as for fish, it was very uncertain.

The following day the *Surprize* and *Justinian* arrived with supplies. The same night a strong wind laid waste to most of the settlers' crops.[26]

Little wonder that the colonists on Norfolk Island attributed their survival to the petrels. According to Clark, these birds had been the 'greatest friends' the colonists had known. Without them, 'the greatest part of [us] would have been in our Graves before the Arrival of the above Ships'. Ross maintained that 'if Providence had not worked a miracle in our favour there would have been but few of us found alive when those ships arrived to our relief'. Nagle concurred: 'These birds, seemingly as God would have it, was the saving of us'.[27]

Colonists on the mainland similarly saw the hand of God in the 'most merciful relief' provided by the birds. In March 1791, Elizabeth Macarthur confided that the settlers' survival had strengthened her faith. When she recalled 'the pitiable situation of the inhabitants of Norfolk':

> a chill seems to overpower my faculties; my mind has so truly entered into their distresses that a dread comes over me which I am unable to describe, but it is succeeded by so firm a reliance on the merciful dispensations of an Almighty, whose hand I think we may here trace without presumption, that I can only admire in silence.[28]

PENAL DEMOCRACY?

If the story of the bird of providence stopped there, it would still be worth telling. There are few places in the world where the slaughter of a species in the immediate wake of European settlement is so well documented. But the petrel's story is of even more interest because the colonists not only caught these birds in extraordinary numbers but also sought to conserve them. While Philip Gidley King had introduced Australia's first environmental law on Norfolk Island in April 1788, ordering his twenty-two subjects not 'to cut down or destroy' any of the island's banana trees, Robert Ross's attempt to conserve the petrels provided the first major test of whether the law could limit the colonists' impact on their new environment.[29]

Ross has generally been represented as one of the ogres of Australian history. His horror of New South Wales has always riled Australian nationalists. In 1788 he declared:

> In the whole world there is not a worse country . . . All that is contiguous to us is so very barren and forbidding that it may with truth be said that here nature is reversed; and if not so, she is nearly worn out.

Ross was also difficult. Not long after the First Fleet landed, Ralph Clark reckoned him 'without exception the most disagreeable commander I ever knew'. The New South Wales Advocate-General, David Collins, harboured 'inexpressible' hatred for him. Amalgamating these traits, Robert Hughes dismissed Ross as 'a choleric, whining martinet who hated Phillip and the colony equally'.[30]

Yet Ross had a more attractive side. In August 1790 Ralph Clark declared him 'remarkably kind'. At the same time George Raper maintained that the crew of the *Sirius* had 'great right to remember with gratitude the kindness of our good Friend Major Ross . . . who spared no pains to make us comfortable in our situation, and was ever ready to serve us'. More recently, Alan Atkinson has argued that Ross was a capable administrator, alive to the latest ideas about land use, scientific agriculture and citizenship, who not only thought he could increase production by allowing convicts to grow their own grain and keep their own livestock, but also 'first considered how choice might be negotiated among the subject people'.[31]

Ross began his term as commandant of Norfolk Island following the wreck of the *Sirius* by declaring martial law. But because his commission did not authorise this action, he did not act unilaterally. First he consulted several of his officers. Then he obtained the written agreement of all his officers at a meeting at Government House. Finally, on 22 March, he gathered all the colonists together at Sydney Bay. After a proclamation declaring the new regime was read out, Ross explained why it was necessary and asked the colonists to indicate their consent by passing under 'the King's colours at the flagstaff, and between the colours of the detachment' as 'there was not time to administer an oath to everybody'.[32]

This process would have been remarkable whatever the nature of the law. As Alan Atkinson notes, it may have been the only instance before the introduction of universal suffrage when an entire Australian community—men and women, guards and convicts—took part in such 'a fundamental act of government'. But this process was even more remarkable because Ross wanted the convicts to agree that, rather than being sent to Port Jackson for prosecution, as had been the case while King was commandant, they could be tried on the island and put to death for stealing from the public stores. As John Hunter put it, Ross hoped to ensure that 'some of the worst characters ever sent from Great Britain should fear the commission of any crime here, more than they had ever done under the laws hitherto established in this settlement'.[33]

Just as Atkinson implies that this process was genuine, so did the officers of the First Fleet. Ross himself reported that there was 'ready and cheerful compliance'. According to Hunter, the ceremony was conducted 'with a degree of solemnity, and at the same time an apparent cheerfulness through the whole'. King claimed that everyone gave three cheers after Ross spoke; Clark wrote that 'every body most chearfully agreed'. Yet what else could the soldiers and marines do—let alone the convicts? They did not have the freedom of a secret ballot, but had to accept or reject Ross's new regime in public. Ross and Hunter were first to pass under the King's colours; the rest of the colonists could hardly refuse to follow.[34]

The settlers' lack of choice is confirmed by Jacob Nagle, the only non-officer on Norfolk Island to describe the imposition of martial law. Rather than remembering Ross as a democrat, Nagle declared him 'a merciless commander to either free man or prisoner'. Nagle recalled that Ross:

> laid us under three different laws: the seamen were still under the naval laws, the soldiers under the military laws, besides the sivel laws and a marchel law of his own directions, with strict orders to be attended to for the smallest crime whatever or neglect of duty.[35]

Control of food was central to the new legal regime. Probably after consulting his council of officers, Ross tried to stop the over-exploitation of the petrels. His goal was simply to ensure a steady harvest of the birds for as long as possible. He probably was not looking beyond the next few weeks or months. John Hunter recorded that because the 'singular advantages' offered by 'this vast resource . . . could only be for a season, we reflected, with pain, that they must have an end . . . in all probability . . . before we got relief'. In late March or early April Ross limited each colonist to three birds, twice a week, in order to stop overkilling.[36]

Ross was unfettered in making this law. As Richard Grove has observed, 'the absolutist nature of colonial rule made it possible to introduce interventionist forms of land management that would have been very difficult to impose in Europe'. Yet the significance of these new forms of land management depended on their implementation, and colonial authorities often lacked the authority to enforce them. In some cases, as Grove notes, there was significant indigenous resistance.[37] In other cases, the colonists proved at least as non-compliant.

Norfolk Island is a telling example. Even in a penal society of 498 people on an island of only 3450 hectares, Ross could not enforce his new law—and the convicts were not the only transgressors. As part of the larger rivalry between the services, the marines blamed the sailors as well. Clark reckoned it 'impossible to prevent the Sailors and convicts from killing the Birds when the[y] pleased'. Most likely, as Clark noted in another context, there was 'no difference between Soldier Sailor or Convicts'. All flouted the law. On 18 April Ross's guards apprehended a convict with sixty-eight birds in his haversack.[38]

If Jacob Nagle's journal is any guide, opposition to Ross's order was intense. When he came to write up his journal in the 1820s or 1830s, Nagle mistakenly recalled that Ross prohibited the killing of all petrels, apart from those taken daily by his own convict servant. Yet Nagle's resentment at Ross's attempt to control the taking of these birds rings true. As Nagle recounted it, a seaman who flouted Ross's order by killing two or three birds was punished with two dozen lashes. To Nagle, Ross's attempt to conserve the birds exemplified his 'tyrannical behaviour'.[39]

When Ross was unable to compel his subjects to obey this law, despite his use of the lash, he reconsidered. Once again he purported to be consensual. Rather than imposing a new law on the island, he made what George Raper described as a 'conditional Order' on 19 April in which he proposed that the colonists could take more birds so long as they each gave up half a pound of salt meat a week, one-seventh of their rations. While Ross may simply have taken this order to a council of his officers, it is possible that he put it to all the colonists for their endorsement.[40]

The exact nature of this new dispensation remains unclear. Clark noted on 20 April 'the Privalige being granted to kill Birds the Restriction on birds being taking off'. Raper recollected that Ross suggested they 'might kill and bring home as many Birds from the Mount as they pleased (as long as it did not interfere with their Work)'. According to Bradley, Ross initially proposed that everyone could take three birds a day. In his account, it was not until 14 May, when Ross met with his council of officers to consider 'the very exhausted state of the provisions' and reduced the weekly ration of meat to one-and-a-half pounds, that he proposed allowing everyone to 'bring in as many as they thought proper'.[41]

Whether Ross acted in mid-April or mid-May, taking one step or two, Australia's first significant conservation law was a failure, lasting less than two months. Because Ross could limit the rate at which Clark issued provisions from his storehouse but could not control what happened on Mount Pitt, he removed the controls on taking the birds and replaced them with unrestricted killing. According to Raper, the resulting 'slaughter and nightly havoc' was 'beyond Description'. Clark recorded that the number of birds killed jumped from between 600 and 800 a day to between 2000 and 3000.[42]

THE CONSERVATIONIST

There were literally no 'conservationists' in the eighteenth and nineteenth centuries. The term was coined only in the twentieth century. Yet, as Keith Thomas has shown, many of the key ideas that underpin modern environmentalism already had keen champions in England by the late eighteenth century, when an increasing number of people came 'to find man's ascendancy over nature increasingly abhorrent to their moral and aesthetic sensibilities'. According to Thomas:

> The growth of towns had led to a new longing for the countryside. The progress of cultivation had fostered a taste for weeds, mountains and unsubdued nature. The new-found security from wild animals had generated an increasing concern to protect birds and preserve wild creatures in their natural state.[43]

So too for the urban environment. In August 1788, just seven months after the First Fleet sailed into Port Jackson, the Director of the Society of Antiquaries, Richard Gough, called for systematic protection of England's ancient buildings, not only because they provided a key to national history by revealing 'the mode of life which prevailed in the ages wherein they were erected' but also because neither words nor pictures were an adequate substitute for the original. According to Gough, this goal could be achieved in a manner that was 'neither violent nor burdensome, by suggestion, and not by compulsion'. If only a group of noblemen, Members of Parliament and other men of rank and taste would explain that it was often cheaper to quarry new stone than to demolish old buildings for their materials, Gough reckoned many would be preserved.[44]

During the twenty months Ross served as commandant on Norfolk Island, he demonstrated an interest in conservation that extended far beyond trying to limit the taking of petrels. He started in May 1790, when he learnt that John Hunter intended to take a party of sixteen men to Mount Pitt to cut down trees for new houses. Recognising the folly of destroying the petrels' habitat, Ross declared that no trees should be felled there without his permission. Clark observed in his diary that Ross 'very properly' stopped this axework, because:

> the great part of our present Subsistence we get from there from the Birds that Resort to that place and . . . Cutting the trees down there might be the means of making them leave the Island much Sooner than the[y] otherwise would.[45]

Ross imposed further controls in the summer of 1790–91, after the extra supplies brought by the *Surprize* and *Justinian* began to run out. Even though Clark was forced to breakfast on dry bread and coffee made from burnt wheat, he again applauded Ross's decision that only 'the people who the Surgeon thinks are in want of them' would be permitted to take petrels. Clark described the birds as 'the only fresh thing that will make a little weak Soup for the Sick', and suggested that 'if every body was at liberty to kill them when the[y] thought proper ther would Soon not be a pidgeon left on the Island'. A convict who breached this order received fifty lashes.[46]

Ross also reconsidered the clearing of the island's forests. Both he and King had initially prided themselves on their success in removing trees because of the colonists' need to grow crops. When the island was first settled, 'every foot of ground was covered with trees' and it was 'impossible to walk four yards without encountering an almost impenetrable net-work . . . of a kind of supple-jack, or vine'. King considered that clearing fifty-four acres was one of the major achievements of his first two-year term as commandant. After Ross replaced King, he boasted that he had opened almost three times this area in half the time, clearing another 150 acres within a year.[47]

The best evidence of this destruction is one of George Raper's watercolours. Like his *View of the East Side of Sidney Cove* (1789, page 44), Raper's *Chief Settlement on Norfolk Island* (1790) shows the colonists' most substantial buildings surrounded by tree stumps. Raper recorded these stumps because they were there. As a result of his limited artistic training, he was a literalist who rarely if ever thought to reorganise his subjects to make them more picturesque. But Raper probably also delighted in the stumps as a marker of civilisation. His drawings are a celebration of both the settlers' architecture and their axework.

The destruction Raper depicted on the hill above Sydney Bay, the chief settlement on Norfolk Island, started in 1788, when King made a vain attempt to turn the hill over to agriculture. The following year, after King was warned that convicts were planning a rebellion, he sought to make it harder for his soldiers to be taken by surprise by ordering the felling of all trees in and immediately around the settlement. He had barely done so when a hurricane blew down almost all the remaining trees.[48]

This destruction was compounded by James Cook's prediction that the island's pines would provide an ideal source of masts for the British navy. While King initially perpetuated this misconception, maintaining that the pines were superior to any trees he had ever seen, by mid-1789 even he had accepted that most of the big pines were too rotten to serve as masts. Yet Governor Phillip still asked for more samples for testing in Europe, so the felling of the pines continued. To obtain just seven spars, John Hunter's sailors had to cut down thirty-four trees. The other twenty-seven were defective.[49]

Ross attempted to limit this axework in two ways. Because the colonists at Sydney Bay were finding it difficult to obtain fuel, he ordered that 'in future whenever any trees are felled, instead of the heavy timber being burnt on the ground, it shall be cut into

GEORGE RAPER
CHIEF SETTLEMENT ON NORFOLK ISLAND 1790

convenient lengths and stacks for firewood'. Because he recognised that the pines were particularly useful as a local building material, he also decided to control the practice that Americans then called 'girdling' and Ross called 'barking'—killing trees by cutting through their sapwood. In January 1791 Ross ordered that 'the pine-trees shall on no account whatever be cut down, barked, or in any manner damaged or destroyed, but by order of the commandant of the island'.[50]

WANTON CRUELTY

Ross departed from this utilitarian calculus in May 1790 when he found that some of his subjects were taking only the petrels' eggs because they preferred them to the birds' flesh. Although George Raper reported that the petrels were 'very fine eating, exceeding fat and firm . . . as good as any I ever eat', John Hunter was probably speaking for more of the settlers when he observed 'they had a strong fishy taste, but our keen appetites relished them very well; the eggs were excellent'. Because the birds were superabundant, there was no market for them, but there was a limited market for their eggs. Raper recorded that they were 'bartered at a very cheap rate'.[51]

This preference led some colonists to release birds that were not carrying eggs. When they found birds carrying eggs, they would sometimes even cut the eggs out, leaving the petrels 'to become a nuisance round the hills'. Ross must have found this waste obnoxious in view of the settlers' dearth of provisions. He probably also thought the practice barbarous. When Clark first learnt of it, he reckoned it 'one of the Crueles[t] things which I think I Ever herd' and hoped 'Some of them will be caught at this Cruel work for the Sake of making ane example of them'.[52]

This revulsion was probably something Clark brought with him to Australia. When the First Fleet sailed, it was already a commonplace in England that abuse of animals could be the first brutalising step on the road to callousness, sadism, even murder. More radically, some Englishmen regarded cruelty to animals as wrong, whether or not it had human consequences. On this view, animals deserved moral consideration in their own right. As part of God's creation, they should not be hurt gratuitously.[53]

Clark's concern for these birds is all the more striking because he otherwise was occupied administering a penal regime. Although Norfolk Island under Ross was not as brutal a place as it was after 1829, when it became a site of secondary punishment, convicts on the island in 1790 were still ordered to work in iron collars and leg irons, and flogging was the primary form of punishment of marines, sailors and convicts alike. Did Clark see no contradiction between his revulsion at the cutting out of the petrels' eggs and his ready acceptance of a soldier's receiving 400 lashes for telling an officer 'a wicked and Malicious Lie'? Did he not realise that there was a growing conviction in Britain that such physical punishments were cruel as well as ineffective?[54]

Clark was blind to these issues. Although he was passionate about puppies and protective of petrels, he had little regard for the men and women under his control. En route to New South Wales with the First Fleet, he damned the female convicts aboard the *Friendship* as 'troublesom whores', 'a disgrace to ther Whole Sex'. When thirty sheep took these women's place at Cape Town, he predicted that the sheep would be 'much more agreable ship mates'.[55]

Clark showed similar contempt for convicts after the wreck of the *Sirius*. When a male convict who could not swim pulled Clark off his raft and held on to him so that he almost drowned, Clark was so angry that, although the convict was 'almost dead' when they reached the shore, he took a stick to him the moment he recovered. Clark recorded, 'I . . . gave him a damd thrashing for pulling me of the Raft with him—he better have been drown for I will give him the Same every day for this month to come that I meet him'.[56]

While Clark soon took a convict mistress, Mary Branham, his journal suggests that he had little affection for her, or perhaps was embarrassed to record his feelings when he was already married and his wife Alicia and son Ralph were waiting in England. Whereas he began his journal by repeatedly addressing Alicia as 'his dear heavenly Woman', 'the most tender best and Beautifulest of her Sex', 'the best of wives the most Sincerest friend and the kindest of Mothers', he never mentioned Mary. He equally made much of his 'dear Sweet Boy' Ralph, while ignoring the daughter he had with Mary on the island. As a mark of his emotional confusion, he called this daughter Alicia.[57]

Other officers shared Clark's antipathy to cruelty to animals. A day after he railed against the convicts' practice of cutting out the petrels' eggs, Ross and his council not only changed the law but also sought to underline its significance by mustering all the convicts and reading it out to them. This new law made it easier for Ross and his officers to control the killing by prohibiting the settlers from going after the birds before 3 p.m. and requiring them to be back by 10 p.m. It also forbade them from taking 'Dogs, tools or Implements and distroying the Birds there Cruely and Wantenly'.[58]

According to Bradley, this prohibition was unusually effective. He recorded, 'the practice of destroying and throwing away the Bird having been put a stop to, they seldom brought in any but those with the Egg in them, letting the others go again after taking them'. As a result, the colonists probably released many more birds than they kept. When Clark made a rare visit to Mount Pitt in June, he noted: 'I Caught above two hundred of them but as I only wanted them that had Eggs I let them all goe Except 27 who were with Eggs'.[59]

Like King's order protecting the bananas on Norfolk Island and Ross's order protecting its pines, this law against cruelty anticipated similar measures at Port Jackson. But this law was not just significant in an Australian context; like many other environmental measures introduced on island colonies in the late eighteenth century, it was of global consequence. As Richard Grove has shown, the visibility of the devastation wrought by European settlers on small islands and the dearth of opportunities to ignore this destruction while despoiling new areas prompted metropolitan officials and colonial administrators to unprecedented attempts at systematic forest conservation, pollution control and fisheries protection.

Both British and French colonies were the sites of such initiatives. In 1764 the British government issued a proclamation that required its Commissioners for Trade in the Colonies to reserve woodlands on St Vincent and Tobago, not only 'to answer all public services as may require the use and expense of timber' but also 'to preserve the seasons so essential to the fertility of the islands'. Four years later, the commissaire-general of Mauritius ordered that a quarter of all landholdings be kept timbered, all forests within 200 yards of water be protected and all denuded areas be reforested.[60]

Ross's attempt to protect the petrels was equally innovative because it anticipated the first measures against cruelty to animals in England, which in turn led Europe on this issue. For all the criticism of cruelty in England in the late eighteenth century, the first Bill to outlaw bull-baiting was introduced only in 1800, and failed to pass. The first British law against cruelty to horses and cattle was enacted in 1822—more than thirty years after Ross's measure on Norfolk Island.[61]

A CONTINUING RESOURCE

After all this destruction of the petrels, their eggs and young, some colonists did not expect the birds again in such numbers, if they returned at all. Before leaving the island that February, William Bradley observed: 'The Birds . . . cannot again be expected for some years, from the vast number of Eggs and young Birds that were destroyed and the ground in which they burrowed being torn up'. Bradley thought that at most the birds might eventually assist 'a small number of Inhabitants', providing 'a resource in case of accident happening to a Ship with supplies or other failure'.[62]

Yet such was the colonists' need for extra food that they again looked for the birds within a few weeks. The catalyst was the climatic phenomenon we now know as El Niño. Both Arthur Phillip and David Blackburn described Sydney as suffering a 'Great Drought' from July 1790 until August 1791. According to the Reverend Richard Johnson, many of the creeks entering Port Jackson ran dry, the crops failed, the remaining water was bad and great numbers of birds, 'unable to bear the heat, . . . dropped from the trees and expired'. In similar vein, David Collins reported that many flying foxes 'dropped dead while on the wing'. On Norfolk Island the crops also failed.[63]

Ralph Clark sent two convicts to Mount Pitt on 23 March 'to See if the Birds were come in'. When they returned with twenty-three petrels, Ross immediately stopped issuing salt provisions. For the next three days Clark tried to resume counting the number of birds taken, but could not obtain the necessary figures. Meanwhile, he was relieved to hear that the marines and convicts saw 'no difference in the birds'—they were 'as numorous as ever'; a week later they were 'remarkably plenty'. When Clark went to see for himself in mid-April, he found the air 'full of them'. Just as he had the year before, he compared their arrival to 'a Shour of hail which lasted for about half ane hour'. Clark killed fifty-three within a radius of three yards, but reckoned he could have killed four times as many had he wished.[64]

Clark concluded his remarkable record of the petrels just before returning to Port Jackson with Mary Branham and Alicia in November 1791. On two successive evenings Clark went to Mount Pitt in order to conduct the first bird-marking experiments in Australia. When birds that he marked the first night returned to the same hole the following night, they confirmed his hypothesis that each bird had a 'particular hole'.[65]

Philip Gidley King, who returned to Norfolk Island in November 1791 in order to succeed Ross as commandant, began his second term by also taking a keen interest in the petrels. When the crops failed again, leaving flour on the island 'very short', King looked out for the birds, which arrived on 21 March 1792. Because the colonists caught between 800 and 1600 each night, King immediately reduced their rations and also changed their hours of work 'so as to leave off work at Four in the Afternoon, when everyone had it in their power to be at the Mount before dark'.[66]

King expected this arrangement to allow everyone on the island to have 'an equal chance of availing themselves of this providential resource'. It would only penalise the 'naturally indolent'. But he soon realised that it also prejudiced his overseers and watchmen, who were not free to go to Mount Pitt, and the 'many poor objects among the convicts' who were 'unable to procure birds for themselves'. As a result, King required colonists who went to Mount Pitt to give up one in ten birds they caught.[67]

As with so many of Ross's laws, this arrangement also did not last. King was forced to modify it when he discovered that some of his subjects were gaining an advantage over their fellows by going to Mount Pitt in the daytime and letting their dogs destroy the birds. Because these colonists were 'depriving those who were working, of that advantage, and would in the end deprive the Island of that resource', King prohibited anyone from going to the mountain before 4 p.m. He also made it an offence to 'wantonly destroy' the petrels. Most significantly, he directed that the petrels 'should in future be considered as game', which is how certain animals such as hare and pheasant, partridge and grouse were designated in England.[68]

The English laws that designated animals in this way were notorious for restricting hunting to those with an annual income of £100 from a freehold estate. As the great jurist William Blackstone put it in his *Commentaries on the Laws of England*, these laws required 'fifty times the property . . . to enable a man to kill a partridge as to vote for a knight of the shire'. King's order may have been contentious because the language of 'game' was so closely identified with class privilege. But in practice King's law was more democratic. It applied to convicts, soldiers and freemen alike, although soldiers and freemen were simply to be 'punished or fined', whereas convicts were to be 'severely punished'.[69]

According to King, this designation of the petrels as game put an 'effective stop' to the use of dogs. But the convicts soon embarked on another form of wanton destruction. Relying most likely on a report from King, David Collins recorded in September:

> The convicts, senseless and improvident, not only destroyed the bird, its young, and its egg, but the hole in which it burrowed; a circumstance that ought most cautiously to have been guarded against; as nothing appeared more likely to make them forsake the island.[70]

By then the ordinary migratory pattern of the birds would normally have had them away from the island, but Collins suggested the colonists' over-exploitation of the petrels was to blame. He recorded:

> The great havoc and destruction which the reduced ration had occasioned among the birds frequenting Mount Pitt had so thinned their numbers, that they were no longer to be depended upon as a resource . . . The convicts . . . wore a very unhealthy cadaverous

> appearance, owing, it was supposed, not only to the spare diet, but to the fatigue consequent on their traversing the woods to Mount Pitt, by night, for the purpose of procuring some slender addition to their ration, instead of reposing after the labors of the day.[71]

At least the drought was over. In September 1792 King reported that the settlers' crops were 'very thriving'. When they enjoyed their first good harvest in early 1793, King was confident their stores of wheat and maize would last them into 1794. But the 'starvation years' had taught King caution, and he looked forward to the petrels' return. On 21 March 1793, exactly a year since their arrival in 1792, he recorded: 'The Mount Pitt birds made their annual appearance, upwards of two thousand have been caught this night'. When the petrels continued in 'very great numbers', he again reduced the settlers' allocation of meat.[72]

King only became more confident the following year, when an even better season enabled the colonists to produce their first surplus of grain. After they harvested three times as much maize as the year before, King offered to sell 5000 bushels to Lieutenant-Governor Grose at Port Jackson. When Grose refused, the island suffered a glut. As a result, King did not bother either to record the petrels' arrival in March or to force the colonists to harvest them. When he finally noticed the birds in May, King was amazed to find them 'as Numerous as ever'.[73]

So it continued in 1795. With every barn full and 4000 pounds of freshly cured pork in the island's storehouses, King could look on the petrels as a 'curiosity'. Intrigued by how the petrels always arrived in late March, he asked colonists who frequented Mount Pitt 'to observe the exact time of their Coming in, as Nearly as Possible'. Although he thought it improbable that the birds could arrive on the same day each year, King's informants confirmed they did. Until 21 March, it was 'with some difficulty they could catch Two or Three Birds'. But on the twenty-first they 'came in great Numbers; Each Man catching in the Course of an Hour from 20 to 25 Birds, on that and some Succeeding Nights'.[74]

How many birds were killed during these years? Although the colonists' need for extra food in 1791, 1792 and 1793 was not as acute as during the winter of 1790, it was still great and the population on the island was much larger, particularly in 1792 and 1793, when it rose to more than a thousand. As a result, even if each of the colonists ate fewer birds, the total may have been much the same. King was possibly not exaggerating in 1794 when he reckoned that 'upwards of Two Hundred Thousand have been killed yearly'.[75]

By then the population of petrels had probably been reduced by the slaughter of so many adult birds and their young, as well as the harvesting of their eggs. Compared with 1790, when Ralph Clark caught over 200 petrels in an hour and a half, 25 birds in an hour was nothing. But, as King observed, few colonists bothered to 'avail themselves of that Resource'. The petrels had become of 'little consequence' as a result of the 'great Profusion of all kinds of Provision, and Stock' on the island; because they were 'now uninterrupted', King expected their numbers to 'keep increasing'.[76]

THE GREAT PIGSTY

King was wrong. Far from recovering once hunting stopped, the petrels continued to decline, because the colonists cleared the natural vegetation of the island and destroyed the birds' habitat. Although King reissued Ross's order of January 1791 requiring his permission before pines were felled, he continued granting land on the island. By 1796 about 45 per cent of the island had been alienated, including a number of blocks on the slopes of Mount Pitt.[77]

Exotic animals—particularly pigs—probably had even more impact on the petrels, just as they played a major role in the extinction of the dodo on Mauritius by eating their young and eggs. The colonists needed to find some use for their glut of maize, so they turned it into pig food. By 1796 the number of swine on the island had swelled to 4800; by 1804 there were more than 6000. In 1805 the convict poet John Grant reckoned the colonists had made the island 'a great pigsty'.[78]

The demise of many other species is well documented. The last two great auks were killed—and their single egg smashed—on 3 June 1844 at Eldey Island off Iceland by two fishermen employed by the Icelandic bird collector Carl Siemsen. The last passenger pigeon, a female known as Martha, was found dead on the floor of her cage in the Cincinnati Zoological Gardens at 1 p.m. on 1 September 1914. But no one recorded what happened to the petrels on Norfolk Island. Because they were no longer significant as a 'resource', they were ignored. The last reported colonial sightings of 'Mount-Pitt birds' were in 1798–99, when Matthew Flinders reported them at several sites in Bass Strait, although it may be that he was referring to a different 'sooty-coloured petterel'.[79]

More than a century later, Arthur Francis Basset Hull belatedly asked what had become of the petrels. Having ignored them when he published the first major scientific study of the birds of Lord Howe and Norfolk Islands in 1909, Hull published a supplement a year later in which he reported that he had climbed Mount Pitt in November 1909 and found no trace of any burrowing bird. Hull also reported that his collector had found neither birds nor burrows when he made a further inspection in August 1910. Hull figured that if the petrels still inhabited the island, there should have been signs of them. He concluded that 'the insatiable demands of the convicts resulted either in the complete extermination of the colony or in its removal to some more secure breeding ground'.[80]

The breeding ground Hull had in mind was Lord Howe Island, 800 kilometres south-west of Norfolk Island. He suggested that the Mount Pitt Bird might be identical to another species of petrel, which two staff members of the Australian Museum had first found on Mount Gower on Lord Howe Island in 1908. These birds had once occupied the lower slopes of Mount Gower, but pigs had driven them to less accessible spots higher up the mountain. Even so, they survived in significant numbers. Hull recognised that John Hunter's description of the Mount Pitt Bird fitted the bird on Mount Gower, except that he had described the bird as 'rusty black' rather than brown.[81]

Hull wondered whether they could be the same. This question could have been resolved easily for most species. Hull would simply have compared one of the petrels from Lord Howe Island with a specimen collected in the eighteenth century from Norfolk Island. But, while Ralph Clark sent at least two Mount Pitt birds to England in 1790,[82] and was almost certainly not alone in doing so, none of these specimens appear to have survived in English collections.

Because of this complication, Hull sent an example of the bird from Lord Howe Island to England, where the noted Australian expatriate ornithologist Gregory Mathews was working with his secretary Tom Iredale on what became his twelve-volume *Birds of Australia*. After extensive archival research, in which early Australian ornithological drawings were a key source of evidence, Mathews confirmed in 1912 that Hull was right. The brown-headed petrel on Mount Gower was the bird of providence. For Mathews, the rediscovery of this 'long-lost' bird was 'one of the most interesting events in the annals of Australian ornithology'.[83]

Yet Mathews remained uncertain whether the bird of providence might still breed on Norfolk Island. This question was finally resolved in 1921, when Mathews and Iredale confirmed that the petrel was no longer to be found there. Seven years later Iredale speculated that it might have disappeared from Norfolk Island by 1800, a date that has been widely accepted, although Iredale arrived at it under the misapprehension that the birds were not recorded after 1792, when David Collins discussed their destruction.[84]

The other major outstanding issue was when the petrels had begun breeding on Lord Howe Island. Mathews maintained that 'the persistent persecution of the early colonists forced them to abandon [Norfolk Island] and take refuge on Lord Howe Island instead'. The noted Sydney ornithologist K. A. Hindwood responded that it was at least as likely that the petrels had been breeding on Lord Howe for hundreds of years, 'long before historical times'.[85]

JOHN HUNTER
NORFOLK ISLAND GROUND-DOVE c. 1790

Whatever the date of its demise on Norfolk Island, the bird of providence may not have been the first bird to die out on the island as a result of European settlement. Pycroft's petrel also disappeared. So too did an endemic ground-dove, which was painted by John Hunter but otherwise was neither depicted nor described by the first colonists, causing its very existence to be doubted until 1984, when archaeologists found bones matching Hunter's drawing. Yet another petrel was not even painted or described by the first colonists and is known only from the archaeological record.[86]

Other species also soon died out. The last recorded Norfolk Island kaka—a large parrot that was perhaps the most spectacular bird found on the island—died in captivity in London in the 1850s. A sub-species of the New Zealand pigeon that was also unique to Norfolk Island was extinct by 1900. A combination of further clearing and the introduction of cats and other exotic animals led to the demise of the white-faced stormpetrel, long-tailed triller, Norfolk Island starling, grey-headed blackbird and flightless rail, so that eight of Norfolk Island's sixteen endemic species or sub-species of bird are now extinct, while another three are endangered.[87]

Such destruction has occurred on many small islands over the past four centuries in the wake of European settlement. According to T. R. Halliday, 200 of the 217 species and sub-species of bird that have become extinct since the start of the seventeenth century were confined to islands. Jared Diamond puts the figure at 155 of 171. Either way, the proportion is over 90 per cent—a figure that is even more remarkable when one considers that only 20 per cent of the world's bird species live on islands.[88]

Yet, having escaped extinction, the bird of providence has extended its habitats. In 1985 the Australian National Parks and Wildlife Service discovered a small colony on Philip Island, just six kilometres south of Norfolk Island. Although the island was once a treeless waste, devastated by years of foraging by pigs, goats and rabbits, the removal of these feral animals now makes it a safe breeding ground for seabirds, including the petrels. Probably the only reason that these birds have not returned to Norfolk Island itself is the persistence of these predators. If they could be removed, the national park now declared on Mount Pitt would provide an even more attractive habitat, containing as it does the principal surviving stands of natural or near-natural forest on the island. After an absence of two centuries, the birds of providence could return there to breed.[89]

Governor Bligh under the Bed c. 1808

CHAPTER TWO

NO PERSON SHOULD HAVE TWO HOUSES

I told him I could not allow any thing of the kind, as it would interfere with the plans which I had formed for the improvement of the town of Sydney. No man could build in the town of Sydney without permission: if every man was allowed to build as he thought proper, there would be no streets or regularity of building in the town.

Governor William Bligh, testifying at the court-martial of Colonel George Johnston, June 1811

ON 26 JANUARY 1808, the New South Wales Corps could have been celebrating the twentieth anniversary of the British invasion of Australia. By one account, 26 January was already an occasion for spontaneous feasting, especially among successful emancipists. But no colonial governor had yet attached sufficient importance to Australia's European history to commemorate Arthur Phillip's arrival in Port Jackson. The calendars published in the first *New South Wales Almanacks* for 1806 and 1808 identified 25 January as the date of the conversion of St Paul, and 27 January as the birthday of the Duke of Cambridge. They left the date in between blank, as if it had no consequence.[1]

The New South Wales Corps was also busy. Late in the afternoon, led by Colonel George Johnston, accompanied by the regimental band and followed by 200 onlookers, 400 soldiers marched on Government House in Sydney to arrest Governor William Bligh. As the mutineers marched up Bridge Street, John Macarthur, the architect of the coup, was confident the twenty-sixth was about to acquire new significance. Macarthur shouted: 'My Boys, the Memorable day shall be the most Glorious day the New South Wales Corps ever experienced'.[2]

Bligh's arrest was not as easy as the mutineers expected. They thought he would be waiting when they reached Government House, but he had gone into hiding. Bligh hoped to destroy documents to keep them from the mutineers, then flee to the Hawkesbury, where he claimed the 'whole body of the people' would defend him. After rummaging vainly through Government House for an hour or two—inspecting its outhouses, checking its grounds and using 'many bad expressions'—the soldiers concluded he had eluded them.[3]

Then Sergeant-Major Thomas Whittle decided to search the first floor of the building again, and Sergeant John Sutherland and Lance-Corporal Michael Marlborough found the Governor almost immediately. By all reports, he was in an inner bedroom normally occupied by his steward. Bligh maintained he was on the far side of the bed, bending down to tear up papers. Sutherland claimed he was under the bed, but promptly contradicted himself by recounting how he had helped Bligh over it. Marlborough testified that, after finding Bligh under the bed, he caught him 'by the collar, and dragged him out'.[4]

Within a day or two, the mutineers had turned to art—recognising, as one private in the New South Wales Corps put it, that pictures could 'exasperate the Inhabitants to hatred & contempt against the Governor'. As well as burning effigies of Bligh and his provost-marshal, William Gore, as the high point of their public celebrations of the mutiny,[5] the rebels made Bligh under the bed the subject of a small watercolour, a canvas and a large paper transparency lit from behind so that it could be seen at night. While Colonel Johnston initially informed his superiors in London that Bligh had been found 'in a situation too disgraceful to be mentioned', these paintings revealed what Johnston temporarily refrained from describing. They showed, as Watkin Tench put it, that Bligh was 'not only a tyrant, but a poltroon'.[6]

More paintings followed. John Macarthur took advantage of his new position as colonial secretary to grant liquor licences to his supporters, who adorned their public houses with signs celebrating the mutiny. One showed 'the figure of a Highland soldier emblematic of Major Johnston, with one foot on a snake and his sword thro' it, to whom a female figure is in the attitude of presenting a cap of liberty'. Another depicted Charles II hiding in the oak after his defeat at the battle of Worcester in 1650—an ignominious refuge in view of Charles's royal office. Both signs were displayed under the legend 'The ever-memorable 26th of January 1808'.[7]

All this art had environmental underpinnings in the causes of the mutiny. Although Bligh's overthrow was triggered partly by his suppression of the local rum economy, as H. V. Evatt famously argued in his *Rum Rebellion*, Bligh's unpopularity owed as much to his commitment to town planning. Already in 1807 Bligh's attempts to implement Arthur Phillip's last plan for Sydney had prompted several of his subjects to protest to London. In the immediate aftermath of the rebellion, members of the New South Wales Corps and their allies continued to challenge the propriety of Bligh's actions. They were still doing so in 1818 when the Lieutenant-Governor of Tasmania, William Sorell, refused to let one of the mutineers, Anthony Fenn Kemp, build on a block of land that he had been occupying without a formal grant or lease. When Kemp saw Sorell's secretary in the street in Hobart, he threatened another rebellion. Was Sorell's secretary aware, he asked, 'that Govr. Bligh had been arrested and deposed for matters connecting with Land?'[8]

The key issue underlying this aspect of the mutiny was public control of private property—an issue fundamental to environmental protection. When Bligh sought to regulate the use of land in Sydney, the affected landholders responded with the first major Australian statements about the inviolability of private property. In turn Bligh was first to warn of the chaos caused by uncontrolled private development and argue that government had a responsibility to regulate and even resume land in the public interest in order to secure a more ordered environment and a more equitable distribution of land. As he memorably put it, 'In a rising colony it is of some importance . . . that individual convenience should sometimes yield to general regularity and public utility'.[9]

GOVERNOR PHILLIP'S LEGACY

Town planning was common practice in the late eighteenth century. Arthur Phillip was just one of many enthusiasts. Within five months of arriving in Port Jackson in 1788, he laid out a great avenue leading from the harbour to a rise near what is now Wynyard Square. Phillip envisaged that this hill would become the site of his permanent Government House, so that he and his successors would sit both physically and symbolically above their subjects. The area north of this hill, towards Sydney Cove, would remain a public preserve. The area to the south would be alienated as private land but remain

GEORGE RAPER
VIEW OF THE EAST SIDE OF SIDNEY COVE 1789

JAMES HEATH
A View of the Governor's House at Rose Hill in the Township of Parramatta
c. 1795

subject to public control. If Whitehall agreed, Phillip wanted each grant subject to a clause that would 'ever prevent more than one house being built on the allotment' in order to 'preserve uniformity in the buildings'.[10]

Phillip probably still intended to follow this plan when he decided to build a temporary three-room house where the Museum of Sydney now stands. Then, finding his convict builders more competent than he expected, he extended this house to six rooms and two storeys and began thinking of it as his permanent residence. He went on to contravene his plan by relocating several other buildings from his grand avenue to the immediate vicinity of his new Government House. His first streets were not even parallel. Little wonder that the Spanish explorer Alexandro Malaspina thought Sydney's houses 'gathered together . . . in disorder'.[11]

Phillip conceived Parramatta—his second town in New South Wales—much like Sydney. Again he opted for a great avenue leading from the Parramatta River to a small rise, where he planned a second Government House. But Parramatta grew as Phillip planned. Already in 1791, one visitor declared its plan 'the most regular of any yet laid down at this place'. In 1792 another colonist characterised Parramatta as 'the grand settlement' with its 'one large street nearly one mile long':

> The houses are all separate from one another, space being left to enlarge them when necessary. There is a large hospital, church, storehouses, &c. The Governor has a house upon Rose Hill, a most delightful spot.

An engraving published a few years later in David Collins's account of the colony reveals that Parramatta still conformed to this plan.[12]

Phillip made his last attempt to control Sydney's development on 2 December 1792, just nine days before he returned to England, when he established a boundary line for the city stretching from the head of Darling Harbour to the head of Woolloomooloo Bay. In his accompanying memorandum, Phillip declared it 'the orders of Government that no Ground within the Boundary line is ever granted or let on Lease and all houses within the Boundary line are and are to remain the property of the Crown'. Apparently fearing that Francis Grose would claim he knew nothing of this plan when he took charge of the colony as Lieutenant-Governor, Phillip annotated the map recording his boundary lines: 'of this the Lieutenant Governor was informed before I left the Country'.[13]

Phillip probably made this order because he wanted the state to benefit when the town grew and land within it became more valuable. He signalled this aspiration in July 1790 in a despatch to Whitehall. Phillip explained that the convicts who occupied the huts that lined the main street of Parramatta would remain there only a few years; then the government would move them to cultivate lands further afield, leaving settlers to build houses along this street. But the state wold profit because, just as with Sydney, Phillip intended that land in and around Parramatta would remain the property of the Crown.[14]

Yet Phillip immediately breached his own order prohibiting the alienation of land in central Sydney. Although he had only nine days to do so, those nine days were also his last opportunity to bestow patronage in New South Wales, and land was the biggest gift in his command. The temptation was too great. On 8 December Phillip not only made five grants of land immediately outside Sydney's new boundaries, but also granted another four blocks within his own line. The only way in which he continued to treat Sydney as special was by granting these nine blocks as fourteen-year leases, not as freehold. As a result, the Crown could still take this land back into public hands or let it out at a higher rent when the leases expired.[15]

Given that Phillip had flouted his own order, it is little wonder that his successors also ignored it—though they showed some respect for Phillip's conception of Sydney by only issuing leases within his boundaries while granting freehold outside. Francis Grose issued fourteen leases during his term as Lieutenant-Governor between 1792 and 1794. Captain William Paterson—who had himself received one of the first four leases granted within Sydney by Phillip in 1792, and then received the second lease granted by Grose in 1794—issued two more leases when he was briefly the colony's administrator in 1795. John Hunter issued another twenty between 1795 and 1800.[16]

Grose and Paterson also departed from Phillip's vision of Sydney when they began recognising that convicts had at least some right to the land on which they built their huts. Whereas Phillip had expected that his successors would be able to remove these huts at will, Grose and Paterson issued each convict with a 'slip of paper' on which they typically wrote 'A. B. has my permission to settle'. Although the extent of the rights granted in this way was never properly determined, the recipients of these 'letters of occupation' enjoyed some security, so there was soon a buoyant market in this land.[17]

Nepotism led John Hunter to flout Phillip's order fundamentally. Having failed to secure a post for his nephew, Lieutenant William Kent, despite recommending him twice for appointment as Lieutenant-Governor of Norfolk Island, Hunter looked for other ways to help him. Kent was not entitled to an official residence because he was not part of the Governor's retinue, but Hunter gave him the first grant of freehold within Sydney on condition that he build on it. Kent promptly complied, spending £1500 on 'a handsome, large and commodious mansion-house', which was Sydney's 'best', rivalling if not eclipsing Government House.[18]

Philip Gidley King, who succeeded Hunter, tried to reassert the Crown's rights over central Sydney. In June 1801 he issued an order that began by providing that 'the grants and leases of all buildings erected at the expense of the public in this colony' and 'the grants and leases of all grounds allotted by Governor Phillip for public purposes' were to revert to the Crown. It concluded by providing that the 'same regulation' was to apply to 'the Crown lands (marked out as such by Governor Phillip)'.[19]

King's Surveyor-General, Charles Grimes, later claimed that the first part of this order was directed at just two houses built by the Crown for two of its senior officials. But this part of King's order was expressed in such general terms that it applied to all buildings erected at public expense and all land that Phillip had dedicated to public purposes. The second part applied to land within the city boundaries marked out by Phillip in 1792. King probably wanted all leases within this area to revert to the Crown, as Phillip originally had intended.[20]

This plan was compromised from the outset. Although King acted as if he could override earlier grants and leases, he sought to diminish public opposition to his stance by indicating that he could (and, by implication, would) allow the holders of these buildings and lands to continue to occupy them. In similar vein, King promptly retreated from his assertion of the Crown's rights over central Sydney and implicitly revoked Phillip's order by declaring that the land in the central city could henceforth be leased for five years.[21]

King was probably cautious because he was in a much more difficult position in 1801 than Phillip in 1792. Whereas Phillip's contemporaries had no reason to expect that he would grant leases within Sydney, by the time King became Governor this expectation was firmly established. King also understood that in Sydney, as on Norfolk Island, his power was far from absolute; he knew the costs of trying to impose unpopular decisions on his subjects. After King prohibited the unauthorised landing of rum in order to break the New South Wales Corps' monopoly and traffic in spirits, John Macarthur persuaded his fellow officers and their wives to ostracise the Governor and his wife. The surgeon D'Arcy Wentworth declared King 'a tyrant who was universally execrated'.[22]

King enjoyed some success in breaking the rum economy, if only because he soon rid himself of Macarthur, who had challenged every Governor since he arrived in Sydney in 1790 as a lieutenant in the New South Wales Corps, yet had still become one of the colony's biggest landowners through government grants. But even after King sent Macarthur to London in late 1801 to be court-martialled for flouting his authority, the Governor struggled to impose his will. Time and again he complained about the 'disappointment and concealed revenge', 'the censure and marked opposition', 'the assassinating and dark attacks' he suffered in performing his 'arduous and unpopular task'. Soon King was displaying what the botanist George Caley described as 'weakness . . . beyond belief'. According to Surgeon Edward Luttrell, 'a few interested individuals . . . bore all the sway in the colony, and . . . under the imbecile government of Governor King were actually the governors of the colony'.[23]

As King weakened, he abandoned his attempt to assert the Crown's rights over land in Sydney. The only five-year lease he issued was in 1802, when he granted his commissary John Palmer more than three acres on the west side of Farm Cove, in what is now Woolloomooloo. But even then King acted contrary to the spirit of his own order, promising Palmer that this lease would be renewed every five years for a total of twenty-one years. Otherwise King followed Hunter in making only one grant of freehold. In 1802 he bought William Kent's house, turned it into a Female Orphan Institution and, possibly because of its charitable status, granted it to the new asylum's trustees. King's seventy-five other grants within Sydney were all fourteen-year leases.[24]

When King stepped down as Governor in 1806, he had alienated more land in Sydney than any of his predecessors. The only difference was that in 1803 he quadrupled the annual rent for city leases from two shillings and sixpence to ten shillings per acre in recognition of the radical rise of property values. But this new rent was still too modest to discourage applicants for land such as the emancipist merchants and sometime business partners James Underwood and Simeon Lord, who acquired their first leases on the same day in May 1804 and promptly used them to erect buildings that underlined their commercial pre-eminence. While Underwood aspired to Sydney's most architecturally ambitious building, Lord spent £15 000 erecting the city's biggest, three times as large as either Government House or the new Orphan Institution.[25]

A LIGHT TOUCH?

When William Bligh arrived in Sydney in August 1806 accompanied by his daughter, Mary Putland, he was just as cavalier as his predecessors in his first dealings in land. Although Whitehall had upped the Governor's salary from £1000 to £2000 at the insistence of his mentor, Sir Joseph Banks, Bligh looked for even greater fruits of office. According to the official register, King granted Mary Putland 600 acres near what is now St Marys in January 1806. He also granted Bligh three parcels of land outside Sydney totalling 1340 acres just four days after Bligh reached the colony. Bligh returned the favour in January 1807 by granting King's wife Anna a 790-acre property, which Bligh appropriately called 'Thanks'.[26]

The date of at least the first of these entries was fictitious, as Philip Gidley King did not even know Mary Putland was coming to New South Wales until July 1806, six months after he purportedly issued her grant. King probably also did not make his three grants to his successor on 10 August, as Bligh could not have had his grants measured or known anything about their location when he had just reached Sydney. Instead, King and Bligh probably discussed all five grants some time after Bligh arrived, and implemented them much later.[27]

Whatever the dates, this exchange was improper if not illegal. Both King and Bligh were empowered to make grants only to emancipated convicts, free immigrants and members of the military, and then only so long as the grantee intended to settle in the colony and cultivate the land. King's and Bligh's official instructions also required them to obtain the approval of the Secretary of State before making grants of more than 150 acres to married free settlers. The grants to Bligh and Mrs King were both over this minimum. Neither Bligh nor Mrs King fitted into the specified classes of grantees. Nor could they claim any intention to settle: Mrs King was about to leave New South Wales permanently, and Bligh planned to return to his wife Betsy, who had remained in London because of her fear of sea travel.[28]

Bligh had every reason to be cautious when determining his policies in relation to the rest of his subjects. As Surgeon Luttrell recorded, he found 'an opposition formed against his government' when he arrived in New South Wales. By early 1807 the Reverend Samuel Marsden was warning Bligh that if he tried to break the rum economy, he would 'meet all the Odium, Contempt and Opposition that Interest, Pride and Passion can possibly invent'. By the end of the year Mrs Bligh was distressed by rumours in London that her husband was 'being superseded in his Government'. In a letter to Sir Joseph Banks, she reported that Bligh's opponents were 'making every effort to recall and ruin Bligh in his character'. She warned her husband: 'you have a great many enemies'.[29]

Bligh saw diplomacy as the solution. In November 1806 he observed, 'I have many difficulties to encounter both as to the ways and manners of the inhabitants, all of which must be touched on so lightly that they cannot perceive it until the reform is accomplished'. But Bligh's record was otherwise. His notorious 'bad language' not only provoked the mutiny on the *Bounty* in 1789 but also lay behind his court-martial in 1805. Sir Joseph Banks advocated his appointment as Governor of New South Wales, not because of his light touch, but because he was 'not subject to whimper and whine when severity of discipline is wanted'.[30]

True to form, Bligh abruptly put an end to the rum economy. Although he recognised that he would 'meet with the marked opposition of those few who have so materially enriched themselves by it', he decided not only to prohibit the importation of rum without a licence, as Whitehall had instructed, but also to prohibit its barter, which had, he reckoned, 'added to its pernicious effects . . . beyond all conception'. In February 1807 he put a 'total stop to . . . the exchange of spirits or other liquors as payment for grain, animal food, labour, wearing apparel, or any other commodity whatever'.[31]

Bligh was in a very different position when deciding what to do about land in Sydney, because he had arrived without specific instructions from the Colonial Office. But he had to confront this issue, if only because he arrived almost fourteen years after Arthur Phillip had granted the first four leases. Although Governor Hunter had already resumed one of these leases and extended the other three, John Palmer's five-year lease was due to expire in the first half of 1807, as was the first lease granted by Francis Grose. Several more were due to expire in 1808. The holders of these leases must have been anxious about their status and keen to know whether their rights would be extended.[32]

What type of town did Bligh find? While the only contemporary paintings of Sydney by the convict artist John Eyre are characteristically picturesque, these views taken from The Rocks give little sense of what it was like inside the town. Contemporary accounts also cast little light on the nature of most of the buildings, streets and public spaces. The closest statistics, those for 1804, are only a little more revealing. They indicate that there were 678 houses and 3200 people in Sydney and its immediate area. Although the soldiers could live in the town proper, most were concentrated in a military district, where there were 160 houses.[33]

JOHN EYRE
VIEW OF SYDNEY FROM THE WEST SIDE OF THE COVE
C. 1806

Bligh saw Sydney as being in both physical and legal disorder. His solution was not just to refuse to grant new leases; he also decided to try to reassert the Crown's rights, starting next to Government House, with the area then known as either Government Farm or the Domain. Arthur Phillip had originally conceived this area as the Governor's private ground, but it was probably rarely if ever the Governor's exclusive preserve. The first settlers were quick to use it as a common for grazing stock, quarrying stone and removing loam. Philip Gidley King not only allowed a row of private houses to be built there under informal letters of occupation but also granted a lease over three-quarters of an acre to his clerk, the emancipist David Dickinson Mann, whom he wanted near him.[34]

Bligh fixed on the Domain because he believed that it was—or should be—Crown property, having been improperly dealt with by King. He was also encouraged to act because the Domain still contained at most ten houses, which his Superintendent of Convicts, Nicholas Divine, reckoned were all 'temporary'. In similar vein, Bligh's commissary, John Palmer, dismissed them as 'very bad indeed, thatched buildings, . . . good for nothing' occupied by 'very loose characters'. Mann was the only exception. In 1807 he was working as a clerk for Palmer, who was widely seen as one of Bligh's 'confidential friends'—his 'next in comand' after Palmer's brother-in-law, the merchant Robert Campbell. By Mann's account, his house cost £400.[35]

Bligh began in time-honoured fashion in January 1807—exercising the landowner's power of exclusion by enclosing the Domain with a new ditch and embankment so that it became a 'no thoroughfare'. Then he gave the householders within this area six months to quit and remove or sell the materials of their houses. Bligh encouraged these householders to move by offering them alternative allotments, so long as the blocks they chose were 'not materially wanted for Government, or occupied by any other individuals'. He later claimed he even offered to grant this land as freehold—although if it lay within Phillip's boundaries, he too would then have been in breach of Phillip's order.[36]

Bligh had even more reason to be restrained when John Palmer's lease over more than three acres of the Domain expired in March 1807. Not only were Bligh and Palmer friends, but Palmer had also erected 'two windmills and a bakehouse of considerable value'. Had Bligh been as generous to his supporters as his opponents claimed, he would have renewed Palmer's lease for another five years, as Governor King had promised. Instead Bligh combined principle with pragmatism. He wrote to ask Whitehall what he should do, but let Palmer retain possession of his land in the interim. This action gave substance to his supporters' claim that Bligh ruled for all instead of just serving the colonial elite. As his steward described it, Bligh spent his days 'receiving the petitions & complaints of the people—free or bond, rich or poor—without exceptions'. Robert Campbell applauded Bligh for 'subjecting the rich as well as the poor to the laws of their country'.[37]

When some occupiers of the Domain ignored his order, Bligh did not expel them. Instead he published a notice in the *Sydney Gazette* in July giving them until November to quit, and again offered to grant them unoccupied land to build elsewhere in the town. Bligh also went out of his way to justify his actions. Probably because he recognised that the removal of these houses was controversial, Bligh publicly explained that they were causing 'great annoyance' to Government House and fell within both the Domain and Phillip's boundaries for Sydney. Although Phillip had made his original order without consultation with London, Bligh sought to enhance its status by claiming that Phillip had made it under 'instructions from His Majesty's Ministers'.[38]

Bligh was equally cautious when he finally acknowledged David Dickinson Mann's special position. In October 1807 Bligh sent a despatch to Whitehall by the *Duke of Portland*, asking what he should do about Mann, given that his lease was 'close to Government House and a great annoyance' and had been granted by King for fourteen years contrary to both Phillip's order prohibiting any alienation of land within central Sydney and King's own order limiting leases to five years.[39]

Meanwhile Bligh employed his characteristic bad language in challenging other landholders outside the Domain. William Blakemore, a member of the New South Wales Corps, may have been the first. He later maintained that Bligh asked

> if the hut opposite my own dwelling was mine. I answered, yes. His Excellency asked why I had not his liberty to build it. I told His Excellency that it was built two years before he came to the colony. He then asked who gave me liberty to build it. I answered, Major Johnston. His Excellency then damned Major Johnston.

Bligh ended their conversation by emphasising his concern for equity. 'No person should have two houses', he declared, 'and others go without'.[40]

By October 1807 Bligh had probably also threatened John and Gregory Blaxland, who were among the first settlers with substantial capital to choose to emigrate to New South Wales. The Blaxlands soon spent £900 buying a house and shop stretching over two allotments in the city. As described by John Blaxland, Bligh 'several times repeated we should never hold them after the lease expired, which has only eleven years to run'. Bligh may have done so partly out of anger at the Blaxlands' extravagant demands for convict workers and land elsewhere, as well as their suggestion that he allow them to establish a distillery, in which they offered him a share. But Bligh again probably wanted to see land in central Sydney distributed more equitably. According to Lieutenant William Minchin, Bligh directed his assistant engineer to divide the Blaxlands' land into three portions so that 'the next two settlers who came out, that wanted a place in the town, should have each a part'.[41]

Bligh also questioned the validity of another eight leases granted by King outside the Domain. Although Colonel Johnston claimed that Bligh acted out of 'mere malice and love of oppression', Bligh maintained that the land covered by these leases was all 'eligible and wanted' for public purposes. One lot was leased to John Macarthur, who had returned to New South Wales in 1805, having resigned from the army in order to pursue his scheme for a colonial wool industry. Bligh protested that it was 'within the limits' of St Phillip's, the only church in Sydney and the building he had done most to improve. Bligh argued that another lot, leased to Colonel Johnston, 'should have been for the use of the unfortunate prisoners' in the jail next door. A third leased to the Government Surgeon, John Harris, was 'detrimental to the parade'.[42]

While Bligh awaited instructions from Whitehall, he also imposed a moratorium on building on the five leases that were still vacant. This decision was even more ambitious than his actions in the Domain, because the land in question was not seen as being the Governor's particular province. Whatever the legality of King's actions, the holders of these leases also had paper title to their land—and they included some of the most powerful men in the colony, led by Macarthur and Johnston.[43]

A REVOLUTION WILL SHORTLY HAPPEN

The response of the 'very loose characters' in the Domain to Bligh's attempts to evict them is recorded only at second hand. According to two of Bligh's witnesses at Johnston's court-martial, Ferdinand Meurant was 'perfectly satisfied' when he moved from the Domain to a new site. As a result, he refused to testify against Bligh, despite being 'solicited repeatedly' by Johnston's supporters. Another of Bligh's supporters testified that Thomas Austin, a watchmaker, accepted that the proximity of his tenement to the Governor's garden made it 'certainly rather a nuisance', and he too was 'perfectly satisfied' with the Governor's promise to help him build another house on a new allotment.[44]

The response of the powerful is much better documented—and not just through their testimony at Johnston's trial. When the *Duke of Portland* sailed for London in October 1807 carrying Bligh's request for advice on what he should do about leases in Sydney, it also carried several letters from his opponents written in a concerted attempt to secure his removal. The recurrent complaint in this correspondence was the Governor's interference with private land.

The former colonial magistrate, John Harris, whom Bligh dismissed after he failed to seize two illegally imported liquor stills, was most outspoken in the separate letters he wrote to Philip Gidley King and his wife Anna. Harris maintained that 'Caligula himself never reigned with more despotic sway'; Bligh had instituted another 'Reign of Terror'. With obvious relish, he recounted how one local satirist had looked for a repeat of the mutiny on the *Bounty*, pleading: 'Is there no CHRISTIAN in New South Wales to put a stop to the tyranny of the Governor?' He told Mrs King: 'He destroys and makes away with all private property'. He informed her husband: 'It is strange that the governor will . . . meddle with private property, which ever was and ought to be sacred'.[45]

John Blaxland put his case to Whitehall in an attempt to secure the Blaxlands' investment in the city by persuading the Colonial Office to extend their lease for another term. He claimed the brothers' premises were not required for any public purpose, because they were 'at the upper part of the town, and not near any Government buildings'. More damningly, he cast Bligh as an intolerable despot:

> He openly laughs at the laws of England, and has been heard to say, 'What does he care for them; he will make laws for N.S. Wales which every son of a bitch shall obey.'[46]

Bligh's Deputy Commissary, Robert Fitz, who arrived in Sydney at the same time as the new Governor, was even more convincing when he too wrote to Whitehall. Unlike Harris and Blaxland, Fitz had not been directly disadvantaged by Bligh. Fitz also admitted that he was 'not upon the best terms' with the governor—then neatly made Bligh seem capricious by adding that he had no idea why they had fallen out. Not least, Fitz declared that he did 'not act an invidious part' and that everything he related would 'be founded upon facts alone'.[47]

According to Fitz, 'The first unpopular act of his government was directing people to quit their houses—built within certain lines'. Far from recognising the Crown's legitimate interest in retaining this part of the Domain, Fitz suggested that Bligh had unfairly forced the occupiers to 'quit their dwellings without the least remuneration' because he was not satisfied with having 150 acres to graze his horses. Fitz also maintained that the 'evil' of Bligh's actions affected all landholders because it rendered 'the tenure of property very insecure':

> For if one governor can do away the act of a former one, all property of whatever nature must be uncertain. This has been verified, as the value of property has considerably fallen since these Orders have been published.[48]

Had it not been for Philip Gidley King, Bligh might have been in trouble in London. But even though John Harris had claimed that Bligh had damned King and worked to overturn everything he had done as Governor, King recognised Harris's rancour as an expression of the former magistrate's own disappointments. More generally, King's advice to Whitehall drew on the difficulties he had faced as Governor:

> The private accounts from that colony, as far as they reflect and animadvert on the conduct of those in trust, ought to be received . . . with much caution; because there is no society where the clashing of duty and interest between the Governor and the governed are more violent than in New South Wales, and more particularly so if the Governor does his duty.[49]

Bligh himself first acknowledged the opposition to his rule in a despatch to Whitehall in October 1807. Bligh reported that he was being opposed by 'a very few who have been in the habit of turning everything to their own interest'. His daughter was more open. In a letter to her mother, she explained that Bligh was

> dreadfully harassed by business and the troublesome set of people he has to deal with. In general he gives great satisfaction, but there are a few that we suspect wish to oppose him; as yet they have done nothing openly; tho' it is known their *tools* have been at work for some time; that is, they are trying to find something in Papa's conduct to write home upon; but which, I am sure, from his great circumspection, they will not be able to do so with honour to themselves. Mr McArthur is one of the party, the others are the

> Military officers, but they are all invited to the house & treated with the same politeness as usual.[50]

If Bligh needed further warning of the risks he was taking, David Dickinson Mann probably advised him through his employer John Palmer as well as the Commissary's deputy, James Williamson, who was another of Bligh's 'most intimate friends'. According to Mann, he repeatedly warned Palmer late in 1807 that the Governor was in jeopardy. Mann claimed to have told the Commissary that 'the inhabitants were in a state of great ferment' and that 'unless steps were taken to conciliate the people, a revolution . . . would shortly happen'.[51]

Bligh was conciliatory in relation to the Domain, where his subjects were weak. When a number of the occupiers named in his notice in the *Sydney Gazette* failed to move to another site by 1 November, Bligh left them undisturbed. Although he characteristically abused David Dickinson Mann when they met, Bligh let him retain possession of his house until 1 January 1808, when Mann informed Bligh that he wanted to buy a block near by and build a brick house on it. When Bligh agreed, the only question left unresolved was how much compensation the government would pay for Mann's old house.[52]

Bligh was much more aggressive when confronting the many powerful landholders outside the Domain. While Bligh did not deprive any of these colonists of their holdings, he flaunted his power, declaring 'that his verbal permission to occupy land was better than a lease, for *that* he could take away'. He also threatened Simeon Lord, who remained one of Sydney's wealthiest merchants, and possibly Thomas Whittle, who occupied an influential position as the representative of 'the Non-commissioned Officers and Rank and File at head-quarters' of the New South Wales Corps.[53]

Bligh threatened Lord in December 1807 after the merchant bought a lease with eleven years to run over a vacant block in Bridge Street adjoining his own house. As with the Blaxlands, it may have been Bligh's other confrontations with Lord that prompted the Governor to warn the merchant that his lease would not be renewed if he built on this site. Writing to Sir Joseph Banks in November, Bligh dubbed Lord 'a very nefarious party' and claimed he was an 'intimate' of John Blaxland. But Bligh also maintained that he warned Lord because his building would have interfered 'with the plans that were in agitation for the improvement of the town'. Bligh claimed 'a right of preemption for Government, as the storehouse was very near, and that ground was wanted for Government'.[54]

Bligh may have threatened Thomas Whittle in December 1807 after discovering that he too was a multiple landholder. In addition to a public house, Whittle had a private dwelling in Sydney's 'Military District', which was on a lease with six or seven years to run and was worth at least £500. As Whittle told the story in April 1808, Bligh declared 'in a violent passion, that neither house or ground should be mine; that it was his, but that I might remove the materials of the house off the ground as soon as I pleased'. Whittle responded by making his house and land over to Colonel Johnston in order, as he put it, 'if possible, to save it for my young family (six children)'.[55]

According to Johnston, other colonists did the same. During his court-martial, Johnston claimed that Bligh's actions created such insecurity that the 'lower class' was 'in the habit of requesting some person of respectability and character to accept a friendly assignment of their leases'. Yet Whittle was the only soldier whom Johnston was able to identify as having assigned his lease. More significantly, Whittle collapsed after contradicting himself under cross-examination as to when this episode occurred. As Bligh described it:

> The soldiers gave the most atrocious falsehoods in proof of my arbitrary character, and stuck at nothing to lessen Johnston's guilt. One of the soldiers, . . . when in the midst of his zeal and falsehood against me, was suddenly seized with a fainting fit like the stroke of death and was taken out of Court.[56]

Bligh's opponents were also responsible for heightening the conflict over land in Sydney. John Harris claimed in October 1807 that he had already ignored Bligh's order not to build on his lease. But if he was not indulging in characteristic hyperbole and had actually breached Bligh's order, Harris did not turn it into a direct challenge to Bligh's authority. Macarthur was very different. In January 1808, he employed a group of off-duty soldiers to sink postholes so that he could fence his lease. Macarthur later claimed that he did so because he wanted to build a house for his family in Sydney. But since he was about to be tried for sedition and was liable to be imprisoned or sent to England if he was found guilty, it is hardly likely that he suddenly wanted a new home. Rather, it seems he wanted to challenge Bligh's authority.[57]

Bligh again was conciliatory, informing Macarthur that if he did not want to wait until Whitehall ruled on the status of his lease, he could exchange it for a block of the same size. Macarthur, however, asked for a smaller, more valuable block on the waterfront reserve. Bligh refused, but offered an alternative site, which Macarthur rejected because it was 'where the common gallows had stood' and was 'surrounded by all the vile and infamous characters of the town of Sydney'. Bligh then reiterated that Macarthur should not build until Whitehall had responded. Bligh's Superintendent of Convicts, Nicholas Divine, confirmed that he would remove any post that Macarthur put in. When Macarthur immediately began fixing one, Divine 'pulled down the post, declared he did it by order of the Governor, and added, in a very emphatic tone, "when the axe is laid to the root, the tree must fall"'.[58]

LIBERTY AND PROPERTY

Property rights loomed just as large in late January 1808 immediately before the rebellion. When John Macarthur was tried for sedition on 25 January, he warned the six officers on the bench: 'You have the eyes of an anxious public upon you, trembling for the safety of their property, their liberty, and their lives'. When he drew up a requisition calling on Colonel Johnston to oust Bligh on 26 January, he declared:

> The present alarming state of this colony, in which every man's property, liberty, and life, are endangered, induces us most earnestly to implore you to place Gov. Bligh under an arrest, and to assume command of the colony.[59]

The mutineers continued to dwell on this issue after ousting and imprisoning Bligh. On 27 January, they issued a proclamation promising that under the new regime 'no free man shall be taken imprisoned, or deprived of his house, land, or liberty, but by the law'. When Macarthur justified the rebellion to Whitehall in April, he began by fixing on Bligh's threats to private property:

> One act of oppression was succeeded in a progressive course by a greater, until a general sensation of alarm and terror prevailed throughout the settlement. Several inhabitants were dispossessed of their houses, and many others of respectable characters, or who had become opulent by trade, were threatened with the Governor's resentment if they presumed to build upon or alienate their own lands.[60]

The same argument was put by Sarah Wills who, significantly, was not directly involved in the mutiny. In a letter to her mother in May, she accused Bligh of taking 'every shameful advantage of those that lay in his power'. As she described it:

> From some he took good houses and gave them bad ones—from others he took their houses and turned them into the street and made them no recompense whatever. Some he stopped building. Others he made make improvements against their inclinations and on the whole endeavoured to crush every person as much as possible.[61]

Yet Wills was probably not impartial. The vehemence of her letter suggests that she and her emancipist husband Edward had been harmed by Bligh. Perhaps rum had formed part of their business as importers and retailers in Sydney. Another possibility is that they were frustrated by Bligh's refusal to grant new leases in Sydney; they had to wait until after his overthrow for their first grant. Whatever the explanation, Sarah and Edward were on close terms with the mutineers. Major Edward Abbott described Edward as 'a man of very large property, and a very respectable man'. When the rebels decided to send John Macarthur to England so that he could explain their grievances to Whitehall, Wills agreed to contribute £30, the sixth-largest subscription.[62]

Colonel Joseph Foveaux, who became acting Governor in July 1808, was particularly unconvincing. Foveaux had been absent on Norfolk Island throughout Bligh's administration, but he described the situation as if he had witnessed Bligh's abuse of private property at first hand. In a private letter to Whitehall in September 1808, he declared:

> It was a constant and familiar expression of his, when any of the injured persons complain'd, 'It is all my own.' The consequence was

> that no man looked upon his property as secure, altho guaranteed to him by the strictest forms of the law, or the most solemn assurances of the Government, and the improvement of the colony, either in building or in agriculture, must have been totally obstructed had so ruinous a system been persevered in.[63]

The first independent test of these allegations in 1809 favoured Bligh. When the British government submitted the correspondence of Bligh, Johnston and Foveaux to one of its legal advisers for an opinion about the merits of their conduct, he found that, while Bligh had 'sometimes used improper and unguarded language', he had never acted on his threats by depriving anyone of a lease. Overall, Bligh's administration had been 'just and vigorous'; by contrast, Johnston bore 'the highest degree of criminal responsibility' for the mutiny.[64]

Yet Bligh's threats to land remained a major issue when Johnston was finally court-martialled in 1811. At the beginning of the case Bligh was cross-examined intensely:

> Was not the house of John Shee, a fisherman, pulled down by your order? . . . Was not the house of Frederick Meurant pulled down by your orders? . . . Do you recollect whether William Kimber was another? . . . Was not David Dickinson Mann ordered by you to pull down his own house, built on his own leasehold land? . . . Did you not order Thomas Whittle, sergeant-major of the 102d regiment, to pull down his house on his own leasehold at a few hours' notice?

One after another, members of the New South Wales Corps testified that Bligh's challenges to private property had affected not just landholders but the whole society. As they put it, Bligh's 'threats to dispossess people of their leaseholds, the interruptions he threw in their way of improving upon them, and his orders to pull down houses' all 'excited the greatest alarm', causing a 'sensation'.[65]

The former Judge-Advocate Richard Atkins lent credence to this view. Although compromised by his overriding concern to shield himself from responsibility, Atkins was the only witness with any claim to impartiality, having been asked to testify by both sides. He recalled that:

> The inhabitants of the town of Sydney . . . complained very much . . . of the invasion of private property; as far as the buildings were concerned, they were under apprehensions that Gov. Bligh would order their buildings to be taken down . . . [W]henever I went along the streets, the people were talking about those houses having been pulled down by order of the Governor; and I have heard men say, 'My turn will be next.'[66]

This view was rejected by Charles Grimes, whose evidence was at least as compelling. Not only was Grimes a longstanding ally of John Macarthur, having sided with him in his earlier disputes with William Paterson and Philip Gidley King, but he had also fallen out with Bligh over the latter's attempts to stop the rum economy. Having often communicated Bligh's threats to landholders in his capacity as Surveyor-General, Grimes maintained that they were a spur to mutiny only for the landholders affected. Otherwise, he testified, they were not 'particularly mentioned' by most colonists.[67]

Perhaps the most significant aspect of the court-martial was the rebels' attempt to show that Bligh had acted illegally both within and outside the Domain. In his concluding address, Johnston maintained that Bligh had acted unlawfully when he ordered the removal of the houses on the Domain, because Arthur Phillip's designation of this area as the Governor's private ground had been negated by his successors' decisions to permit and even invite building there. In any event, Johnston argued, Bligh 'should have proceeded in a very different manner':

> The Surveyor of the colony should have estimated the value of the houses to be removed; the party to be affected should have had the election of a new situation, and every compensation which liberality could suggest, ought to have been made,—for property is too sacred to be taken away without form or process, and merely at the will of a Governor, announced by a proclamation in a newspaper.[68]

Both John Macarthur and Charles Grimes argued that Bligh had acted unlawfully in imposing a moratorium on building, let alone resorting to force to stop Macarthur erecting a fence around his allotment next to St Phillip's Church. Their argument turned on the standard clause in Sydney's leases stipulating that they were granted 'for the express purpose of erecting buildings upon'. Grimes maintained that this clause imposed an obligation to build. John Macarthur declared that, until Bligh became Governor, he 'never knew an instance of persons being prevented from building, if they thought proper, upon their own leaseholds'.[69]

Bligh replied that he had acted properly when ordering occupiers of the Domain to move their houses because this area remained Crown land. More generally, Bligh justified his attempt to regulate building on existing leases within Sydney by reminding the court that his successor, Lachlan Macquarie, had promptly asserted his power to regulate land that was already in private hands. As part of trying to ensure that all buildings within the town followed 'a regular plan, so as to Combine Convenience with ornament', Macquarie prohibited anyone from erecting 'any house or dwelling in the town of Sydney, whether on *leasehold* ground or otherwise, without previously obtaining his permission'.[70]

Bligh was equally sharp when he reminded the tribunal that unregulated 'improvement', as development was typically then called, was not always a public good. Bligh declared: 'if every man was allowed to build as he thought proper, there would be no streets or regularity or building in the town'. He also recognised the risk of urban sprawl, warning that 'if some attention was not paid to these things in Sydney, the town would be so scattered as to take up ten miles in space'.[71]

The significance of these issues was recognised by at least one member of the court. 'Improvident grants of land are the ruin of colonies', he observed, 'It comes to a question of right, whether the Governor had the power of revoking grants of land made by former Governors.' But the advocate-general persuaded the court to leave this issue to 'a future stage of this investigation', and characteristically its members failed to return to it. When the court delivered its judgement in July 1811, it made no findings about the witnesses' many assertions and counter-assertions. Instead it found Johnston guilty of mutiny, then effectively exonerated him by deciding he should simply be cashiered.[72]

Meanwhile, Macquarie achieved much more than Bligh as he continued town planning in both New South Wales and Tasmania with unprecedented enthusiasm. As part of redesigning Parramatta, Windsor and Hobart in 1811, Macquarie ordered that no new buildings—whether houses, outhouses or offices—were to be erected on existing leases until the local commanding officer had approved their plans. He was even more intent on controlling what happened on new leases. Despite the manifest inconvenience, he required all applications for allotments in these towns to be sent to him in Sydney. In both cases Macquarie, like Bligh, assumed that he could and should regulate private land. While John Macarthur was able to oust Bligh, he could not stop his successors pursuing much the same policies.[73]

JOHN GLOVER *A VIEW IN MILLS PLAINS* c. 1835

CHAPTER THREE

A PAINTER'S DELIGHT

He is delighted with this country, assures me that nature is not less singular and essentially distinguished in her landscape than in her animal creation—although I might not at present see it.

G. T. W. B. Boyes describing John Glover,
20 April 1831

JOHN GLOVER was an unlikely emigrant. When he quit England for Van Diemen's Land in September 1830, he was sixty-three and his wife Sarah sixty-nine, both far beyond the age when most Englishmen and women chose to become colonists. London had also treated Glover well. While his landscape paintings had probably been as much derided as applauded, he had grown rich as an 'English Claude', who emulated the seventeenth-century French artist Claude Lorrain. When he arrived in Hobart in April 1831, Glover informed local authorities that he had established two local bank accounts containing more than £4000 and had 'several other Thousands left in England which may be called for if necessary'. According to one English source, he was worth £60 000.[1]

Glover's financial success and reputation helped him to establish a new life for himself and his family in Van Diemen's Land. Assisted most likely by one of his three sons, all of whom had emigrated before him, Glover soon bought 'two improved Farms' at Tea-tree Brush near Brighton, where the 'rich and beautiful plains' were renowned for being 'thinly covered with timber', 'plentifully watered' and covered with 'the finest grass growing upwards of three feet high'. Glover also applied for a free grant of land. Because these applications were determined according to wealth, he was eligible for the largest possible holding. By late May the colonial Land Board had recommended that 'the celebrated Landscape Painter of England' receive 2560 acres at Mills Plains near Deddington, which Glover expected to be even better for cattle. By August he had bought five farms, including two more totalling 3600 acres at Mills Plains, sold another at a profit and begun painting.[2]

Glover was Australia's first farmer–artist, though by local standards his combined holding of 6160 acres at Mills Plains was modest. In 1832, the year Glover settled at Patterdale, as he dubbed his property, one of his fellow settlers estimated that there were more than fifty colonists who held over 18 000 acres. Hundreds more held between 8000 and 10 000 acres, and almost every landholder had at least 4000. Yet because Glover was not dependent on a local market for patronage and initially looked to sell his paintings in England, he was free to give Patterdale disproportionate significance in colonial art. As one critic noted in 1835, when Glover held his only major exhibition of Tasmanian paintings in London, here was an artist who could 'settle on, and cultivate a mountain side, and sit down to paint it afterwards in a style which few can surpass'.[3]

Glover's paintings are remarkable for his enthusiasm for the gum tree. When he arrived in Van Diemen's Land, the eucalypts had loomed large in colonial writing since 1788 without obtaining a comparable place in colonial art. While the invaders had always been more or less enthusiastic about land dotted with trees, rich in grass and free of undergrowth, by the 1830s gum trees were generally thought to be as ugly as they were monotonous. Glover transformed colonial art by putting eucalypts at the centre of his canvases; his Tasmanian landscapes were the first great celebration of the gum tree in painting, poetry or prose.

Glover also expressed the colonists' satisfaction in transforming their new environment. If he was conventional in his aspiration to turn at least part of his property into a little England, the image he projected in his paintings suggests rare achievement of this ambition. His pictures celebrating the house he built, the garden he planted and the corn he harvested at Mills Plains convey his pride in having successfully civilised the colonial landscape.

The relationship between these two aspects of Glover's art—his delight in what he found on his land and what he made of it—is all the more significant because it took the partial destruction of one to create the other. When Glover acquired his land, the colonists' appetite for clearing and cultivating was tempered by increasing recognition of the aesthetic and economic benefits of retaining native trees. Patterdale provides an illustration of how a colonist who was unusually enthusiastic about gum trees, and probably exceptionally conscious of the ugliness of most clearing, resolved this tension.

A key question in considering these issues is the extent to which the colonists were influenced by the eucalypts' appearance. The usual assumption is that the invaders reviled these trees for being different from those of Europe. Yet the first colonists delighted in the distinctive attributes of the gum tree. While later settlers were not as enthusiastic, their response was similar to that of colonists and visitors in other settler societies such as Canada and the United States, where the oaks and elms were much more like British trees.[4] The similarities suggest that colonists were probably at least as influenced by the abundance of trees in the New World as by how they looked.

EVERGREENS

When the First Fleet sailed from Portsmouth in 1787, there was unprecedented enthusiasm for trees in England. According to the Reverend William Gilpin, the great champion of the new aesthetic of the picturesque, it was 'no exaggerated praise to call a tree the *grandest*, and most beautiful of all the products of the earth'. This rapture may have been inspired partly by the new dearth of woodland in England—as trees became scarcer, they were valued more highly. But officers of the First Fleet maintained it in Australia, despite finding more gum trees at Port Jackson than they would have liked.[5]

Surgeon George Worgan was one enthusiast. In the journal he kept following his arrival in Port Jackson in 1788, Worgan admired the 'gentle risings & Depressions, beautifully clothed with variety of Verdures of Evergreens, forming dense Thickets, & lofty Trees appearing above these again'. Although Worgan noted that the Australian landscape was 'delusive' because it was much harder to cultivate than it first appeared, he rejoiced that the eucalypts retained their covering during his first Australian winter. He boasted to his brother: 'We *have*, and *shall* have all through the Winter green Trees in abundance to look at, that is more than you can say in your Winter Master Dick'.[6]

Worgan's fellow officers concurred, not only when they had just arrived in New South Wales and everything was excitingly new, but also when they had been there a number of years. On reaching Port Jackson, Surgeon Arthur Bowes recorded: 'The tallest and most stately trees I ever saw in any nobleman's grounds in England, cannot excel in beauty those which nature now presented to our view'. When Captain Watkin Tench published his first book about the colony in 1789, he admired how these 'large spreading trees' afforded 'a succession of leaves in all seasons'. They were one of the reasons Tench reckoned the 'face of the country . . . certainly pleasing'. In his second book, published in 1793, Tench echoed Worgan's joy in how gum trees flourished in winter with 'tropical luxuriancy'. For Tench, 'evergreen' was a term of praise. He was delighted that the eucalypts did not assume the 'sickly autumnal tint, which marks English trees in corresponding circumstances'.[7]

The first women free settlers in New South Wales agreed, most likely encouraged by their situation at Parramatta, where the landscape was generally thought much more attractive than at Sydney. In one of her first letters to England, written after settling at

Parramatta in 1790, Elizabeth Macarthur reckoned that 'all the beauty' of the countryside was 'literally on the surface'. The luxuriant soil produced 'fine Shrubs, Trees, and Flowers which by their lively tints afford a most agreeable landscape'. Eliza Marsden, who settled at Parramatta in 1794, shared her friend's judgement, exclaiming that the country was 'very romantic, beautifully formed by nature'.[8]

Many men—both convict and free—who arrived in New South Wales in the 1790s were similarly enthusiastic. One soldier reported that the country surrounding Parramatta was another 'Botany Bay', abounding in 'the most beautiful shrubs and evergreens that produce very fragrant flowers'. The magistrate Richard Atkins lamented that the timber of the gum trees was 'of no value but for burning', yet saw beauty in their 'lofty and wide spreading branches'. Even the convict artist Thomas Watling, who declared Australia unpaintable because of its dearth of 'bold rising hills' and 'azure distances', delighted in the majesty and variety of the trees 'wreathing their old fantastic roots on high: dissimilar in tint and foliage; cumbent, upright, fallen, or shattered by lightning'.[9]

EVERBROWNS

Thirty years later, most writers condemned the eucalypts. Far from delighting in their difference, colonists and visitors judged them against an English standard and found them wanting in ever more extravagant terms. This stance demonstrated the writers' enduring civilisation and good taste. It also differentiated them from the native-born 'currency' youth, who appear to have admired the gum trees but rarely recorded their own responses because of their lack of education.

One criticism of the gum trees was that they were monotonous. Although 100 species had already been identified, many observers treated eucalypts as if they were all alike—a fundamental failing for devotees of the picturesque, to whom variety was crucial. Already in 1807 William Bligh lamented that the 'face of the country' was 'very much covered with trees of a dark, and sombre hue, without any variety of tinge to relieve the eye'. In 1818 Elizabeth Macarthur 'admitted that the beautiful green of the English trees, far surpasses, particularly when the leaves are young, the verdure of our unchanging ever greens', though she continued to 'enjoy the beauty of each in their season'. By 1820 the New South Wales Surveyor-General, John Oxley, was protesting:

> One tree, one soil, one water, and one description of bird, fish, or animal prevails alike for ten miles and for one hundred. A variety of wretchedness is at all times preferable to one unvarying cause of pain and distress.[10]

The gum tree was also dismissed as ugly. Commissioner Thomas Bigge, who arrived in Sydney in 1819 to review—and damn—Lachlan Macquarie's administration of the colony, twisted 'evergreen' into 'everbrown', a term that passed into common usage even though Bigge did not put it into print. When Edward Curr published an emigrants' guide to Tasmania in 1824, he declared that nothing could 'be more unsightly than the generality of the tree, thinly clothed with leaves, and the trunks and huge branches covered with long, shaggy strips of dead bark'. To Curr the eucalypts were symbols of 'desolation and decay, rather than of life and verdure'.[11]

Barron Field was more influential. A one-time drama critic for the London *Times*, friend of Coleridge and Wordsworth, and sole judge of the Supreme Court of New South Wales from 1816 until 1823, Field had a profound influence on Australian law, but his impact on Australian literature was even more enduring. His poem 'The Kangaroo' and the discussion of the gum tree in his *Geographical Memoirs* are among the most significant expressions of the notion that Australia is a land of antipodal inversion.

Like Thomas Watling, Field began by considering whether the gum tree could be the stuff of art. 'What can a painter do', he asked, 'with one cold olive-green?' His answer extended beyond the monotony of the eucalypts' colouring to their failure to provide a mass of shade and to express the changing seasons, which in Europe were a source of 'all the dearest allegories of human life'. Although his travels in the colony did not extend beyond Bathurst, Field declared there was not 'a single scene' in New South Wales 'of which a painter could make a landscape, without greatly disguising the character of the trees'.[12]

Field admired colonial scenery only when he thought it 'English'. When he crossed the Blue Mountains, he was happiest when the 'harsh trees' about Blackheath and Wentworth Falls were replaced by 'downs, meadows and streams' and there were 'no side scenes of eucalyptus'. The one occasion when he looked fondly on the 'eternal eucalyptus'—and thought them paintable—was on the Bathurst Plain, where the wooded hills were so far away that the peculiarities of the individual trees were invisible, and the sunset transformed their colouring into 'that golden-blue or purple which landscape-painters love'.[13]

These criticisms soon became clichés. Henry Widowson of the Van Diemen's Land Agricultural Society maintained in 1828 that the island's 'trees and forests . . . rather diminish than add to the beauty of the country, where they are thinly spread; the tops grow extremely ugly, and bear not the slightest resemblance to the worst of our oak and elm'. In 1832 John Henderson declared that the 'dull sombre tints of the foliage' in New South Wales and Tasmania were 'calculated to produce melancholy sensations', and suggested that artists use 'brighter colouring' in their landscapes in order to stimulate 'pleasing ideas'.[14]

So it continued in many influential books. When the New South Wales Surveyor-General Thomas Mitchell published his *Three Expeditions into the Interior of Eastern Australia* in 1839, he restated that 'the poverty of the foliage of the eucalyptus' afforded 'little of mass or shadow', while its trunk and branches rarely added 'anything ornamental to landscape'. Charles Darwin damned the 'peculiar pale green tint' of the 'never-failing Eucalyptus family', derided the gum trees' bark as 'desolate and untidy' and lamented the fact that the colonists were deprived of 'the first bursting into full foliage of the leafless tree'. When he crossed the Blue Mountains, the only areas Darwin found 'pretty' were treeless valleys.[15]

AS GOOD AS ART

Other colonists expressed both horror and delight at the gum trees. When G. T. W. B. Boyes, the new deputy assistant commissary-general of New South Wales, described his first experiences of Sydney and Hobart in a letter to his wife Mary in 1824, he judged the eucalypts as an accomplished amateur artist well schooled in the picturesque. The trees about Port Jackson appalled him. He abhorred their 'stunted ragged and frightful appearance'. Yet Boyes reckoned that the trees on the Derwent River in Van Diemen's Land not only eclipsed anything he had seen in nature but rivalled their finest idealisations in art. In these trees, Boyes found 'forms that till lately I thought were to be found nowhere but in the imagination of the painter'.[16]

The Austrian traveller Baron von Hügel also had a very mixed reponse to the eucalypts when he spent a year in Australia in 1833–34.

After making his way to the Macarthurs' property at Camden, Hügel recorded: 'One can honestly say that one often rides through the woods without seeing a single tree which would be allowed to remain standing in a park in Europe'. He found the trees around Sydney so ugly that he empathised with colonists who cleared every tree around their houses. But Hügel also declared it 'extremely one-sided and foolish' to treat gum trees as if they were all alike; in other parts of New South Wales and Tasmania he had seen trees that 'could compare with any in the world'.[17]

Thomas Shepherd was even more enthusiastic, although as owner of Sydney's biggest nursery he had a commercial interest in promoting exotic plants, which were the stuff of his business. In a lecture prepared for the Sydney Mechanics' School of Arts in 1835 (but not delivered, due to his sudden death), Shepherd observed that 'some gentlemen may probably dislike our gum trees', but he questioned their taste. While he accepted that the 'length and nakedness of trunk' of old gum trees might not appeal to everyone, he claimed they looked 'as well as the old ornamental trees in an ancient English park'—and no one could 'venture to say that a young gum tree does not look handsome'.[18]

The Scottish ship's surgeon Peter Cunningham was the first author to write at length about the native-born 'currency' youths. As part of elaborating on the commonplace that the 'currency' believed Australia 'unsurpassable', Cunningham recounted in 1827 how one youth blindly asserted that 'Big Cooper's' in Sydney was better than any 'splendid shop' on London's Ludgate Hill. Another thought the 'choicest Newmarket racers' neither as beautiful nor as fast as 'Australian turf pedigree'. As for their appreciation of nature, Cunningham reported:

> The very miserable-looking trees that cast their annual coats of bark, and present to the eye of a raw European the appearance of being actively *dead*, I have heard praised as objects of incomparable beauty![19]

Cunningham implied that he thought this praise misplaced. In similar vein, he repeated the standard criticism of the gum tree for providing 'no rustlings of the fast-falling leaves, nor burstings of the buds into life and loveliness in the spring'. Yet he went on to speculate that the '*evergreen* state' of Australia's forest trees might be responsible for the colonists' good health, because it spared them the usual 'vegetable putrefaction' of autumn. More significantly, Cunningham admitted that his own aesthetics were changing. After two years in New South Wales, he was beginning to look 'pleasurably' on the eucalypts.

Cunningham explained his new appreciation by suggesting that new arrivals in Australia soon acquired the local aesthetic, which was very different from that of the metropolis. 'Our ideas of beauty', he declared, 'are, in truth, less referable to a *natural* than an *artificial* standard, varying in every country according to what the eye has been habituated to, and fashion prescribes'. This statement is significant because Cunningham is likely to have gained his values not from the 'currency' youths but from other colonists of his own class. If so, there may have been many settlers in New South Wales who looked on the eucalypts much more positively than the standard literary image suggests.[20]

THE CHANGING FOREST

When the natural-history collector George Caley reported on his explorations of the Blue Mountains in 1804, King recognised that he would need to explain Caley's language if his superiors in London were to understand what he had seen. The invaders had begun by following English usage in equating 'forest' with 'wood', but King explained that their terminology had since changed. The new colonial term for a dark, impenetrable thicket was 'brush'. A 'forest' was open grassland, the only type of area fit to graze. Even without this gloss, Caley's preferences were clear. He explained that when he and his companions emerged from the 'brush', 'the first sight of forest land had great effects upon our minds, which had the appearance of a *Paradise*, in comparison to that which of late we had been accustomed to'.[21]

Caley's preference for open landscapes over densely wooded country was widely shared. Tasmania was commonly presented as more attractive to settlers than New South Wales because of the relative dearth of trees in some parts of the island. In particular, the country between Hobart to Launceston was so open that Lieutenant Charles Jeffreys drove a barouche from one town to the other when there was still 'not more than twenty miles of what could be termed a road'. Yet the colonists' response is difficult to interpret because they described very diverse landscapes as 'forests'. In 1812 Lieutenant Edward Lord explained that Tasmania's 'forest land' had only one tree for every ten in the 'forests' of New South Wales. Governor Macquarie equated 'forest' with grassland, 'brush' and even 'thick brush', including one area 'full of bogs or swamps'.[22]

This loose usage was probably less frequent from the 1820s, when it became a commonplace that forests were distinguished by both the presence of trees and the lack of undergrowth. James Atkinson explained that it was 'always to be understood, that forest means land more or less furnished with timber trees, and invariably covered with grass underneath, and destitute of underwood'. Thomas Mitchell reiterated that a 'forest' was 'an open wood, with grass'. Charles Wilkes, who commanded the United States Exploring Expedition that visited Australia in 1839, explained to his American readers that the 'forests' of New South Wales consisted of gum trees 'so widely scattered that a carriage may be driven rapidly through them without meeting any obstruction'.[23]

Colonists continued to have good reason to appreciate these 'forests' because of their economic potential. Baron von Hügel maintained:

> A painter or a curious traveller would find little or nothing there to repay his trouble, but an Australian feasts his intoxicated eyes on this stretch of country—so ideal for raising sheep—unable to comprehend how one could fail to be enchanted by it.

Granville Stapylton, who went to 'Australia Felix' in 1836 as Thomas Mitchell's second-in-command, was just one colonist who viewed the landscape as Hügel suggested, repeatedly applauding 'forests' as 'fine' or 'fertile' because of their utility as grasslands.[24]

Yet just as individual gum trees were dismissed as monotonous if not melancholy, so Australia's forests were increasingly derided. Already in 1819, W. C. Wentworth declared that the 'vast forest' between Sydney and the Blue Mountains was 'gloomy'—devoid of 'diversity, beauty and sublimity'. Edward Curr was even more critical in 1824, describing the 'woody tracts' called 'forests' in Tasmania as areas of 'dreary, uninteresting sameness'. In 1830 Robert Dawson of the Australian Agricultural Company invoked one of the new clichés about the New World when he dismissed the 'forests' of New South Wales as 'interminable'.[25]

THE NATURAL PARK

Australia's 'parks' were a rare constant in the affections of European explorers and settlers from 1770 when the artist Sydney Parkinson first conceived the Australian landscape in this way in his account of James Cook's first voyage. After the First Fleet arrived in 1788, many of the invaders followed Parkinson's lead. George Worgan likened the western reaches of Port Jackson to 'a Beautiful Park'. Elizabeth Macarthur was even more expansive in 1798, declaring that 'the greater part of the country is like an English park'. When Lieutenant Bowen established the first European settlement on the Derwent in 1803, he described the river's western bank as 'more like a nobleman's park in England than an uncultivated country'.[26]

Colonists such as Edward Curr, who used this analogy carefully, applied it to land that not only offered a 'variety of wood and lawn' but also 'rising ground and water'—all essential ingredients of the 'parks' created by the English landscape gardener, Lancelot 'Capability' Brown, in the 1750s and 1760s. But some writers identified parks where there was no water. Mrs G. R. Porter, who in 1830 published one of the first novels set in New South Wales, had her protagonist identify a park in a 'beautiful undulating prospect,

AUGUSTUS EARLE
JUNE PARK, VAN DIEMEN'S LAND 1825

with just enough of wood about it to fill up the enchantment of the scenery'. Other visitors and colonists found parks where there was neither undulating ground nor water. In 1825 the artist Augustus Earle described one of his Tasmanian watercolours depicting such terrain as 'perfect Park scenery'.[27]

The most striking aspect of this analogy is that English writers generally thought of 'parks' as distinctively British—part of 'Capability' Brown's great legacy. According to William Gilpin, the park was 'one of the noblest appendages of a great house'. Nothing gave 'a mansion so much dignity'. While Brown's parks were carefully constructed, they appeared natural compared with the formal surroundings of great houses in continental Europe, with their 'regular cascades, spouting fountains, flights of terraces, and other achievements'. Gilpin boasted that 'in England alone the model of nature is adopted'.[28]

This nationalistic embrace of 'parks' could have led the English to mourn their absence overseas. Instead they were soon identifying parks across the globe. By using this familiar term, they not only explained the unfamiliar but also emphasised the attractions of open country, which appealed to them for reasons part psychological, part utilitarian, part aesthetic. Explorers and colonists were more comfortable in country dotted with trees than in thickly wooded terrain; they were pleased that these areas were ready for immediate grazing, if not always cultivation; and the clumps of trees satisfied their taste for the picturesque. Whereas the utilitarian and the aesthetic parted company in late eighteenth-century England, so that, as Keith Thomas has written, 'what was useful was most likely to be regarded as ugly', the connection between economics and aesthetics in Australia remained direct, as Baron von Hügel recognised in 1834.[29]

Class also fuelled this enthusiasm. In England, 'parks' were the domain of the gentry and aristocracy. Not even the wealthiest colonist could hope to acquire such an estate at 'home'. But in Australia such landscapes were more accessible. Elizabeth Macarthur best conveyed the settlers' sense of elevation on acquiring such land—or even just living surrounded by it. Like her husband John, Elizabeth came from a family of no social rank or political consequence in Britain but aspired to head a new gentry in Australia. According to Elizabeth, the trees on Australia's parks created 'the appearance of a wilderness or shrubbery, commonly attached to the habitations of the people of fortune'.[30]

Race also influenced how these landscapes were viewed. As early as 1793, John Hunter described how Aboriginal fires were intended to clear the country of brush or underwood. When George Augustus Robinson began working as storekeeper on Bruny Island in 1829, he learnt that Aborigines deliberately beat out the fires they had lit in order to create clumps or copses of trees across the plain, forming 'a beautiful picturesque scenery'. Yet most colonists failed to take the next, obvious step and explicitly acknowledge that at least some of Australia's 'parks' were an Aboriginal creation.[31]

This failure probably resulted from colonists' conception of parks as products of civilisation. As 'Capability' Brown's great successor Humphry Repton put it, landscape gardening distinguished 'the pleasures of civilised society from the pursuits of savage and barbarous nations'. If colonists credited Aborigines with making these landscapes, they would implicitly be recognising them as civilised. Instead Australian settlers repeatedly declared the parks 'natural'—a significant conclusion not just because of its denial of Aboriginal agency and ownership but also because it suggested that, at least in this respect, Australian nature was comparable to British culture.[32]

CUTTING, GRUBBING, GIRDLING, BURNING

The invaders' own transformation of the landscape started on 27 January 1788, the day after Governor Phillip landed at Sydney Cove and took possession of New South Wales. As described by George Worgan, 'all the Artificers & an 100 of the Convicts were landed, carrying with them the necessary utensils for clearing the Ground and felling the Trees'. According to Worgan, the 'principal business' of the settlers between then and May 1788, when he wrote to his brother, was 'the clearing of Land, cutting, Grubbing and burning down Trees, sawing up Timber & Plank for Building'.[33]

As George Raper recorded in his *View of the East Side of Sidney Cove* in 1789 (page 44), the settlers' usual practice in early New South Wales was to fell trees about a metre from the ground and then burn off the fallen timber, leaving the stumps. Both William Bradley and Surgeon John Harris thought that to characterise this practice as 'clearing' was a misnomer, but the colonists often could not do more. In 1793 Watkin Tench suggested that what looked like 'slovenly husbandry' was 'probably necessary' in a country where 'immediate subsistence is wanted'. In 1819 John Oxley explained to Commissioner Bigge that it rarely cost more than fifty shillings per acre to fell and burn off timber, but cost at least twice as much to grub out the stumps.[34]

Colonial officials sought to facilitate this work by providing landholders with cheap labour. Phillip initially wanted every settler on a farm of 500 to 1000 acres to have at least twenty convicts. In practice, he was even more generous, giving officers such as John Macarthur ten men to clear and cultivate their initial grants of 100 acres. Sir Thomas Brisbane put even more men in the field, offering clearing gangs of thirty convicts to favoured landowners at a nominal rate. In 1822 Brisbane had 'a Thousand men employed in clearing the Country of its excess of Forest Timber and Brushwood'. In 1824 he boasted that these gangs had already cleared 11 500 acres in just two years, compared with only 55 000 acres in the first thirty years of settlement.[35]

Colonial officials also made clearing a matter of legal obligation. In 1805 George Paterson advised Governor King that settlers in Van Diemen's Land should be required to cultivate part of their land grants for five years. In 1811 Lachlan Macquarie implemented such a scheme, hoping to curtail the widespread practice of obtaining grants

> for the sole purpose of selling them, whereby the Lands were transferred from one to another in the rude uncultivated state in which they had been originally granted, and continued unproductive to the general Interest and Supplies of the Colony.

The standard requirement in Van Diemen's Land was to 'clear and cultivate' a modest five of every hundred acres within five years.[36]

These provisions had little effect, at least partly because the vagueness of the requirement to 'clear and cultivate' made it hard to enforce. In 1819 John Oxley testified to Commissioner Bigge that the Crown had never even threatened to resume land for breach of this condition, let alone actually done so. When Tasmania's Land Commissioners embarked on a survey of the island in 1826, they inspected a property where the owners had neither 'cleared ten acres, nor . . . expended ten pounds on improvement'. They considered it a 'remarkable circumstance that the Government should . . . grant lands under certain restrictions and covenants . . . merely for the purpose of being laughed at and set at defiance'.[37]

Colonial officials responded not only by stipulating a minimum level of investment but also by being much more specific in requiring clearing and cultivation. From 1828 the standard provision in Van Diemen's Land gave grantees seven years to spend at least as much on 'improvements' as the land was worth at the time it was granted. Allotments in suburban Hobart had to be 'effectually cleared of all trees (except such as may bona fide be reserved for ornament), stumps and roots of trees within twelve months'. The ground also had 'to be properly broken up by the spade or plough, and a crop . . . sown within the second twelve months'.[38]

While some colonists persisted in flouting these requirements because they treated their landholdings as speculative investments, others needed no encouragement to fulfil the grant conditions. Even when they could obtain convict labour, these settlers often employed free men for the more difficult tasks such as grubbing out stumps. Once Brisbane's successors stopped supplying clearing gangs, landowners had no choice but to hire axemen or do the work themselves. By 1829, when Henry Widowson published his emigrants' guide, the usual mode of clearing in Tasmania was to employ one or two men at a set rate per tree plus rations.[39]

As in other parts of the New World, colonists and visitors took pleasure in the fruits of this process because it both created a new physical space and secured them symbolic possession of their new environment. At the end of her first year in Ontario, Catherine Parr Traill reported:

> We cannot help regarding with infinite satisfaction the few acres that are cleared round the house and covered with crops. A space of this kind in the midst of the dense forest imparts a cheerfulness to the mind, of which those that live in an open country, or even a partially wooded one, can form no idea. The bright sunbeams and the blue and cloudless sky breaking in upon you, rejoices the eye and cheers the heart.[40]

In similar vein, Traill's Australian counterparts delighted in their 'victories' over the gum tree and the pleasures of finding 'immense and useless forests of Eucalypts' replaced with substantial buildings and gardens enriched with European fruit trees. Joseph Lycett's

JOSEPH LYCETT
BURWOOD VILLA, NEW SOUTH WALES, THE PROPERTY OF ALEXANDER RILEY ESQ 1824

Views in Australia singled out Alexander Riley's property, Raby, as an illustration of 'those striking contrasts which agreeably surprise the traveller in the forests of this country, on suddenly coming in view of the vast openings cleared by the industry of man'. It presented Riley's Burwood as 'a remarkable instance of how speedily the Forest in NEW SOUTH WALES can be cleared of its superfluous timber, and rendered contributable to the comforts and luxuries of man'.[41]

Colonists gave this clearing even larger significance by casting it as part of 'The Course of Empire' in which wild woods were replaced first by pastoralism, then agriculture and finally commerce. In 1819 W. C. Wentworth dwelt on the 'cheering prospect' of 'what is now one vast and mournful wilderness, becoming the smiling seat of industry and the social arts: to see its hills and dales covered with bleating flocks, lowing herds, and waving corn'. James Wallis announced in 1821 that the engravings in his *Historical Account of New South Wales* would

> serve to show and convince . . . from what slender beginnings, and in how few years, the primeval forests . . . may be converted into plains

> covered with bleating flocks, lowing herds, and waving corn; may become the smiling seats of industry and the social arts, and be changed, from a mournful and desolate wilderness, into the cheerful village, the busy town, and the crowded city.[42]

The enduring assumption was that trees were an 'encumbrance'. In his *Letter from Sydney*—written from Newgate Prison in 1829 without any direct experience of Australia—Edward Gibbon Wakefield made much of how the trees on his imaginary land grant of 20 000 acres were not an asset, as they would have been in England, but an obstacle. Although he described his land as thinly wooded—with trees 'scattered over the . . . property, as in an English park'—Wakefield maintained that he would be even better off if only he could afford the cost of clearing. He observed: 'It seems droll, does it not, that an English hundred-and-fifty-thousand-pounds-worth of any thing should, any where, be a dead loss of fifteen thousand pounds? It is true, however'.[43]

In this context, the cheapest mode of clearing was a major issue. One method, often discussed because of its beguiling simplicity, was to

> chop a row of trees fully half through, then fell a heavy one at the end of the row, so that it may fall against the second, which snapping at the chopped part of the stem, falls in like manner against the third, and so on until the whole row of trees is beaten to the ground.

Henry Widowson reckoned this 'the general mode of clearing' in Tasmania, despite describing the island as lightly timbered. Peter Cunningham was more honest when he acknowledged that such clearing was rarely practicable because the trees in Australian forests were generally too far apart.[44]

'Sapping'—otherwise known in the 1820s and 1830s as 'girdling', 'disbarking', 'ringing' or 'ringbarking'—was still more controversial. James Atkinson rejected the practice, arguing that when settlers tried to burn the rung trees, a great many stumps remained and required 'as much or more trouble to be got rid of, than the whole tree would in the first instance'. Thomas Shepherd endorsed disbarking as 'the most expeditious, effectual and cheapest' form of clearing, so long as the trees were killed in summer when the sap was up. Peter Cunningham reckoned that the dead trees burned like tinder if they were left standing for three years, and it was then relatively simple to dig around and set fire to the stumps. In his view, 'mere girdling', without even removing the dead trees, improved the pasture 'a full fourth; it becoming sweeter from not being exposed to the droppings of the leaves, and more luxuriant from the nourishment formerly taken up by the trees being now applied to the grasses'.[45]

THE PROPRIETY OF CLEARING

When the prolific travel writer Anna Jameson wrote her *Winter Studies and Summer Rambles in Canada* after spending nine unhappy months in Ontario in 1836–37, she lambasted the settlers for failing to recognise even the 'most magnificent timber trees' as either 'useful or ornamental'. With characteristic flourish, Jameson declared: 'A Canadian settler *hates* a tree, regards it as his natural enemy, as something to be destroyed, eradicated, annihilated by all and any means'. She also dwelt on how her horror at the settlers' destructiveness cast her as an outsider:

> The pity I have for the trees in Canada, shows how far I am . . . from being a true Canadian . . . I cannot look on with indifference, far less share the Canadian's exultation, when these huge oaks, these umbrageous elms and stately pines, are lying prostrate, lopped of all their honours, and piled in heaps with the brushwood, to be fired—or burned down to a charred and blackened garment—or standing, leafless, sapless, seared, ghastly, having been 'girdled' and left to perish.[46]

Jameson's contemporary, Catherine Parr Traill, provided an explanation of this gulf between visitor and colonist, which was also evident in the United States. Traill reported that at first she was appalled by all the 'horrid black stumps', but she soon recognised that labour was so expensive that it could be devoted only to 'indispensable work'; 'new beginners' could not afford to engage in such 'pretty improvements' as clearing away stumps. After two years in Ontario, Traill became so attached to the country that her aesthetics changed. She reported:

> The very stumps that appeared so odious, through long custom seem to lose some of their hideousness; the eye becomes familiarized even with objects the most displeasing, till they cease to be observed.

In similar vein, one emigrants' guide to Tasmania suggested that the stumps dotting most of the farms did 'not appear very agreeable to a new-comer, but the eye soon gets habituated to them'.[47]

James Macarthur, son of Elizabeth and John, distinguished between the different stages of clearing. A great admirer of Australian nature, Macarthur declared:

> The first steps towards forming a home amidst the wilds are not only toilsome, but in some degree disheartening. Even those natural beauties, which may have influenced the settler in his selection of a site, are converted into deformity. The forest must be hewn down; and, in its immediate effects, nothing can be more desolating than this operation.

But Macarthur emphasised that this desolation was only temporary: as the felled timber and stumps were gradually burned off, they were replaced by 'the charms of culture and civilization', which offered 'fresh attractions, of a more pleasing and permanent character' than those destroyed.[48]

Others were not as forgiving. Many observers were not only alive to the excesses of the colonists' axework but also appalled by how stumps remained an enduring blight on the land. As they elaborated their objections, clearing became the subject of the first sustained critique of the settlers' impact on their environment. Even more remarkably, this criticism was not just expressed by visitors or newly arrived settlers. Long-standing colonists were at least as ready to condemn their fellows' degradation of the Australian landscape.

As in North America, the initial basis of this criticism was aesthetic. William Neate Chapman, an occasional artist who arrived in New South Wales in 1792, observed that Sydney Cove was 'not so beautiful as the entrance of the Harbour on account of the trees being cut down'. A similar aesthetic may have led Thomas Watling to elide the signs of clearing in his art. While most of his contemporaries in New South Wales simply sought to record what they found, Watling was confident that he could improve on it, believing himself a 'genius in bondage'. As Jane Lennon has observed, even Watling's wash drawings of Sydney from the mid-1790s are notable for the relative scarcity of stumps. Possibly he excluded them because they violated his sense of the picturesque. His oil painting

A North View of Sydney Cove is even further removed from fact: Watling framed it with his own arboreal creations, making up for the trees that had been felled.[49]

When John Hunter, Philip Gidley King and David Collins began to control clearing, their motivation was utilitarian. They wanted to stop waste of valuable timber, turn the trees into a source of public revenue by imposing a royalty on them, and preserve firewood as close as possible to centres of population. But by 1815 official policy also had an aesthetic underpinning. In a Government Order published in the *Sydney Gazette* and read in all the churches, Lachlan Macquarie rebuked the 'lower Order of Settlers' for failing to make the most of their farms, particularly along the Nepean and Hawkesbury Rivers. As part of calling on his subjects to 'adopt a new System of Industry', the Governor deplored 'the fallen Trees and dead Stumps still remaining unburned', which 'at once disfigure the appearance of the Country, and present the greatest Impediment to every Thing like Neatness, or lucrative Cultivation'.[50]

Other colonists expressed similar sentiments. In 1824 Edward Curr lamented that Tasmanian farms were 'studded over with large stumps of trees . . . impressing the mind with the painful sensation of incommodiousness and half civilization'. A year later G. T. W. B. Boyes puzzled over the 'unfeeling spirit' that led settlers in New South Wales 'to give so many noble trees so wantonly to the axe and to the flame'. Once again, this criticism had a class dimension. Boyes admitted that to reproach the lower orders 'for want of taste would be absurd, few of them ever heard of such a principle'. He also recognised that precedent was against him when the Surveyor-General of New South Wales, John Oxley, had cleared 'every tree' from nearly 2000 acres of his own land. But Boyes still thought 'a sense of interest might have struck them forcibly—that to leave timber upon part of their property which they had no intention to cultivate would be the highest economy'.[51]

James Atkinson's criticisms were even more significant, because his *Account of the State of Agriculture and Grazing in New South Wales* was a practical manual, awarded a gold medal by the Agricultural and Horticultural Society of New South Wales in 1827. Economics and aesthetics were both part of his case. Atkinson rebuked 'over-zealous improvers' for clearing all the trees on their land, thereby depriving their stock of shade and leaving themselves short of firewood at a time when timber was already growing scarce in the areas Europeans had settled first. He lamented that the vast quantities of wood left on the ground gave the country 'a littering and slovenly appearance', injured the pasture and tore the fleeces of the sheep. He argued that the stumps of felled trees were a blight on the land because of their 'unsightly appearance' and 'the inconvenience of working among them'.[52]

A succession of Tasmanian colonists added to this criticism. In 1829 Henry Widowson deplored this 'miserable system' of clearing, which meant that 'at every seed-time, a plough is broken, and the space left round the stump, becomes choaked up with weeds and rubbish'. He concluded that the axework of many of Tasmania's first settlers had 'rather added to, than disrupted, the uncivilised appearance of the country'. In his *Hobart Town Almanack for 1832*, James Ross similarly deplored the 'heedless' destruction of trees and shrubs, which were 'useful as shelter in winter [and] necessary (to say nothing of ornament) as shade in summer'. A year later Augustus Prinsep reiterated that 'with the usual hastiness of settlers', the immediate vicinity of Hobart had been 'cleared of all trees . . . not even one, for beauty or for shade, has been spared'.[53]

The same was true in New South Wales. Baron von Hügel was particularly critical of Sir John Jamison, Australia's first titled settler and one of the wealthiest men in New South Wales. Hügel recorded acidly that Jamison had won 'a great gold medal' from the local Agricultural Society in 1833 for inventing a new method of destroying stumps. A contemporary drawing by Conrad Martens and an engraving by William Wilson suggest that Jamison applied his invention to Regentville, his property near Penrith. But, like Thomas Watling in his drawings and paintings of Sydney in the 1790s, these artists probably made Regentville appear more picturesque by clearing their views of stumps in a way Jamison had not bothered to do himself. Hügel, who visited Regentville in 1834, railed that it was notable for 'the greatest number of stumps to be seen in front of any planter's residence in the whole colony'. Had Jamison, he wondered, actually 'discovered a method of preserving the stumps from decay'?[54]

Thomas Shepherd was even bolder when he delivered the first of his lectures on landscape gardening at Sydney's Mechanics' School of Arts in 1835 before a large audience, which probably included many wealthy landowners. Far from trying to flatter these potential clients into patronising his nursery, Shepherd lambasted them. He was particularly dismissive of Sydney's first suburb of Woolloomooloo, where Governor Darling had made another attempt at town planning in 1827. Woolloomooloo's status as the town's most fashionable address owed much to Darling's regulations, which required landowners to erect only one villa costing a minimum of £1000 on each allotment, secure approval of their plans before they started building and site each villa facing Sydney and at least sixty yards from the road. But Shepherd remained unimpressed by the suburb's formal villa gardens. He railed:

> When you, gentlemen, first got your estates, your ground was well furnished with beautiful shrubs. You ignorantly set the murderous hoe and grubbing axe to work to destroy them, and the ground that had been full of luxuriant verdure, was laid bare and desolate, and the prospect was ruined.[55]

THE ARTIFICIAL PARK

One alternative to such wholesale clearing was to try to convert woodland into parks by leaving occasional clumps of gum trees. The Reverend Richard Johnson was among the first colonists to combine the two approaches. As well as completely clearing 200 acres, he selectively cleared 80 acres, which he divided into four twenty-acre enclosures for cattle. Watkin Tench applauded Johnson's handiwork when he first visited Parramatta in 1790. Just as he delighted in Johnson's big clearing, because he had not seen 'an opening of such extent' since leaving England, so he admired his enclosures for their 'very park-like and beautiful appearance'.[56]

When other colonists tried selective clearing, its effectiveness became an issue. James Atkinson reckoned it an aesthetic failure because 'lofty naked trees, with a few branches and scanty foliage at the top' would 'never be very elegant or beautiful objects'. He considered it of no practical use because these trees could 'afford no shade or shelter to the stock' and, having 'grown surrounded by others in a thick forest', they invariably became 'sickly . . . when exposed and left by themselves . . . their limbs continually dying and falling off, till in a few years nothing is left but bare leafless trunks'. Atkinson maintained that colonists would be more successful if they started anew by clearing 'the old forest entirely away' and then planting 'small clumps' of exotic or native trees.[57]

This view was widely held, not just in Australia. When Anna Jameson asked why Canadians did not 'leave groups of the finest trees, or even single trees, here and there, to embellish the country', she was told that it was 'impossible—for the trees thus left standing, when deprived of the shelter and society to which they have been accustomed, uniformly perish'. Catherine Parr Traill tried to preserve 'a few pretty sapling beech-trees' from the 'choppers', but the only one they spared was killed by fire. She came to look on it as 'a melancholy monument of the impossibility of preserving trees thus left'. Traill also soon concluded that, if settlers left just a few trees, they were liable to fall in storms. Like Atkinson, she advised that it was best to clear all existing trees—then plant new ones which, freed of competition, would 'take deep root and spread forth branches the same as the trees in our parks and hedge-rows'.[58]

The most notable Australian opponent of these arguments was Thomas Shepherd, who tried to persuade his fellow colonists that landscape gardening could have economic as well as aesthetic benefits. In particular, Shepherd argued that if colonists created new parks, the charms of their estates would make them more readily saleable, prompting 'gentlemen of taste and fortune' from other countries to pay 'considerably advanced prices' for them. Shepherd also emphasised that, while the owners of parks in England incurred substantial losses growing grass where crops would be more profitable, there was no such demand for agricultural land in Australia and the new grasslands created within the parks would provide a valuable source of pasture 'for many years to come'.[59]

A key plank of this argument was that parks could be created in Australia 'at a comparatively trifling expense'. Where the owners of English and Scottish estates spent vast sums planting new trees to embellish their parks, Shepherd maintained that colonists should simply thin out existing forests by 'disbarking'. At most he suggested adding a few exotic trees 'to take off the sombre appearance and monotony of our native woods' and some young gum trees, which he so much admired, 'to blind the naked stems of the old trees'.[60]

The two Sydney estates that Shepherd described as fitting his prescriptions were Dr James Bowman's Lyndhurst in Glebe and Alexander Macleay's Elizabeth Bay House. Shepherd noted that the native trees at Lyndhurst had been preserved and were 'as pleasing as if a new assortment of trees had been planted, and had grown up in their place'. He applauded Macleay for having

> never suffered a tree of any kind to be destroyed, until he saw distinctly the necessity of doing so. He thus retained the advantage of embellishment from his native trees, and harmonised them with foreign trees now growing. He also obtained the benefit of a standing plantation which it otherwise might have taken twenty or thirty years to bring to maturity.[61]

This praise was perhaps self-serving: Shepherd may have been involved in planning the grounds of Lyndhurst, if not also Elizabeth Bay House. Even so, he was exceptional in recognising that the natural environment needed little if any modification. Shepherd cast Lyndhurst and Elizabeth Bay House as proof that:

> The country could . . . at a very small cost, and with less labour than is required by the indiscriminate destruction of our native trees, present an exterior to the eye of the stranger, and the resident in the Colony, such as no other country in the world I believe could furnish.[62]

THE NEW LANDSCAPE

If John Glover read the likes of Edward Curr and Henry Widowson when he considered emigrating, they did not influence his view of his new environment. When Glover prepared to quit England in 1830, he 'delighted' in 'the expectation of finding a beautiful new world—new landscapes, new trees, new flowers, new animals, new birds'. On his arrival in Van Diemen's Land in 1831, he was quick to declare that it fulfilled all his expectations, although he also acknowledged that he found its difference a challenge. '[T]here is a trilling and graceful play in the landscape of this country', he observed, 'which is more difficult to do justice to than to the landscapes of England'. As a means of coming to terms with this difference, he executed 300 drawings in his first six months.[63]

Glover's enthusiasm was reinforced by his good fortune in acquiring a grant at Mills Plains, where most of the land was free of undergrowth and rich in grass—probably as a result of Aboriginal burning. Even in a 'thickly wooded part' of Mills Plains, he remarked, it was 'possible almost everywhere, to drive a Carriage as easily as in a Gentleman's Park in England'. He thought Mills Plains made for

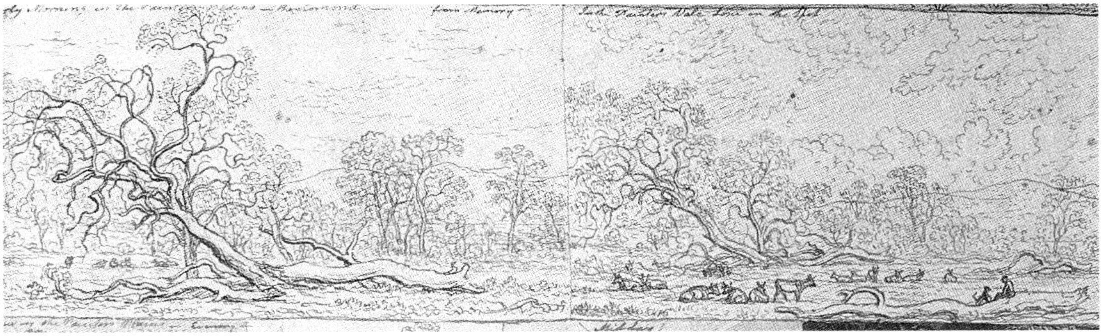

JOHN GLOVER
EARLY MORNING ON THE PAINTER'S PLAINS AND *IN THE PAINTER'S VALE* 1832

art: he identified the subject of one of his sketches as the 'Painter's Vale' and another as the 'Painter's Plains'.[64]

Gum trees were the subjects that occupied Glover most. To begin with, he drew one tree portrait after another. Like Thomas Shepherd, he delighted in big, old trees. One particularly revealing page in his 1832 sketchbook is divided into eight drawings—all recording the eucalypts' great twisting branches. Glover's paintings gave even more powerful expression to this enthusiasm. Whether presenting Tasmania as an Aboriginal or a pastoral Arcadia, his pictures are always dominated by gum trees. *A View in Mills Plains* (page 66) combines everything he admired in his new landscape, celebrating a particularly majestic tree, its park-like surrounds and its immediate suitability for grazing.[65]

Glover started out with the grandest social and political ambitions for these paintings. According to G. T. W. B. Boyes, Glover told him in April 1831 that he intended to use his pictures

> to reform the Convicts/ no trifling labour/ and to direct the views and regulate the conduct of the rest of the population till they have arrived at such estate of moral advancement that will make the idea of human perfection no longer Utopian.

By August he was hoping to use the gift of a painting to William IV as a pretext for 'writing to him to state the grievances of the country, to beg for a House of Parliament here to make our little rulers feel themselves responsible to the people'.[66]

Although nothing came of these schemes, Glover probably still hoped his paintings would lead his British contemporaries to look more favourably on Australia. He expected that the packet of pictures he sent to his daughter Emma in mid-1831 would give her 'a more perfect idea of the beauties of this country than has yet been shown in England'. He probably saw the two Tasmanian landscapes that he sent for exhibition in London in 1832, and the thirty-six that followed in 1835, as a rebuttal of critics of the gum tree such as Barron Field and John Henderson. These paintings were his attempt to demonstrate that eucalypts could be the stuff of art without being portrayed in brighter colours.[67]

The public response in 1832 was mixed. While the *Hobart Town Courier* claimed that Glover's paintings attracted 'great attention', not all this attention on the 'self-exiled' artist was favourable. One English critic maintained:

> With his motives for transportation at three score, and in an easy circumstance, we have nothing to do, but we think he could not have 'gone further and fared worse', or made us fare so badly, if he had stayed at home. If they are as like the views in Vandiemen's Land as they are like Glover, they should have remained where they were, for they lose in us the admiration they might have excited in an assembly of Kangaroos, Connoisseurs, Amateurs, and Patrons, doubtless very little inferior to many here.[68]

Three years later, the response was more enthusiastic, although Glover still failed to persuade English critics of the beauty of the gum tree. The *Morning Post* followed him in admiring how these trees preserved 'to the artist the enviable privilege . . . of viewing the distant landscape on every side through their bare serpent-like branches and delicate foliage', but it still cast the trees as not just 'novel' but 'fantastic'. *The Times* repeated the cliché that Australia's trees were

> neither so delicate nor so umbrageous as the trees of Europe: they are not so well adapted to the beauties of landscape as the oak, the elm, the beech, and the poplar of this country; there is, moreover, a sameness of appearance about them, which deprives their representation of interest.[69]

The colonial response to Glover's work was more favourable. Not only were his fellow colonists more inclined to look up to Glover as a great artist, but their own direct experience of the colonial landscape allowed them both to judge and to appreciate his success in recording it. Although G. T. W. B. Boyes observed tartly that

Glover's trees were 'designed with hideous fidelity to Nature', J. Massingberd Campbell described Glover's trees as 'incomparable', and George Augustus Robinson exclaimed:

> The sombre and various hue of the foliage and character and scenery in nature the beautiful combination of form . . . could not be described by any other means. All attempts at verbal description would fail.[70]

MY HARVEST HOME

Glover's eagerness to transform his new landscape matched his enthusiasm for what he found there. When he embarked from Gravesend in 1830, Glover sailed with a good supply of potted plants, seedlings, seeds and songbirds. In Hobart, where he stayed before moving to Mills Plains, he delighted in his English garden. The plot he depicted in *Hobart Town, taken from the Garden where I lived* was only half-tamed, its grass roughly cut, its paths made of dirt. Yet Glover fixed on its bounty, boasting that his geraniums, roses and other flowers were evidence of 'what perfection Gardens may be brought [to] in this Country'.[71]

Glover's appetite for improvement at Mills Plains far exceeded his legal obligation to spend a sum equal to the land's unimproved value within seven years. One of his predecessors had already built a house,

JOHN GLOVER
HOBART TOWN, TAKEN FROM THE GARDEN WHERE I LIVED 1832

only to 'dispense' with it and erect another, which still stood in 1831, but Glover judged it inadequate and sent his son James to superintend the building of a third house and a weatherboard 'men's hut'. Because this third house was not ready when Glover himself settled at Patterdale in 1832, his entire party repaired to the hut. John senior and Sarah occupied one bedroom. Their son Henry shared the other with his wife, who was 'in some expectation of being confined'. Meanwhile, John junior slept in the stable, which initially had no roof, and the men slept in the loft.[72]

Glover hoped to move into his own house before the start of winter in 1833, but in September he was still living in the men's hut and using a small tent at the top of his garden as his studio. There was more progress on Glover's 'other purchased and back grants', where he 'deemed it expedient to establish a settlement' and Henry set 'to work to build a house and commence clearing'. Because he 'had a sawyer at constant work' preparing timber, he could 'draw off such quantity as he found convenient, and he soon made up his house [and another men's hut] in the weatherboard style'.[73]

When Glover's own house was finally ready, its two-storey, shingle-roof and stone construction, adjoining studio with skylights and low, glass-paned hot-house probably contrasted sharply with the houses already on Patterdale. Glover painted one of the old dwellings and his new one as part of the larger autobiographical dimension of his art, which saw him return to his old English sketches to paint his birthplace in Leicestershire, as well as using much more recent sketches to paint his first house in Hobart and first farm near Brighton. One of the pictures that he sent to England in 1835 was *An Old Farm House, Mills Plains*; another was *A View of the Artist's House and Garden, Mills Plains.*

Glover's painting of his new house and garden conveys his pride in how he was transforming the colonial earth. Most of the plants had been introduced by Glover, though a few—including the willow by the pond—may have been started by one of his European predecessors. When the Quaker missionary James Backhouse visited Patterdale in 1833, he recorded that Glover took 'much interest in his garden. He brought a number of trees from England which are thriving with him.' By the summer of 1834–35, when Glover painted this landscape, it had been cleared of almost all native vegetation. The only possible exceptions are the fronded trees in the middle distance—most likely tree ferns, which Glover may have

JOHN GLOVER
A VIEW OF THE ARTIST'S HOUSE AND GARDEN, MILLS PLAINS C. 1835

transplanted from neighbouring valleys, if they did not originally occupy the area.[74]

Close inspection reveals that Glover's primary practical goal in undertaking all this work was to establish a significant vegetable plot and an orchard. Much of the middle ground of *A View of the Artist's House and Garden* is occupied by small, evenly spaced fruit trees. But the painting is dominated by the introduced flowers in its foreground, including the roses and geraniums he had made much of in Hobart, as well as hollyhocks, mullein, Chinese hibiscus, heather, broom, madonna lilies and laurustinus. Glover showed these flowers all blooming together, out of their proper seasons, in order to heighten the impression of bounty, but otherwise his painting appears to be an accurate record of how much he had achieved at Mills Plains in just a few years.[75]

Glover also took intense pride in his success as a farmer. In his *Account of Van Diemen's Land*, Edward Curr maintained that:

> In our Australian paradise, our highest aim is to exhibit on a small scale something like the beauties which rise at every step in the land to which we have bade adieu, well content if we can here and there

JOHN GLOVER
MY HARVEST HOME 1835

produce a corn-field surrounded by a post and rail fence, or a meadow of English grasses clear of stumps.

By September 1833 Glover already had his third crop of corn growing in a paddock that had been 'broke up' before he bought it. If this paddock had not been entirely cleared by Glover's predecessors, he soon did so. By 1835, when he depicted what was probably a gang of assigned convicts hard at work in *My Harvest Home*, all this paddock needed to meet Curr's ideal was a post-and-rail fence. But Glover did not feel this want: this record of 'the day the harvest was all got in' is one of his most ecstatic Tasmanian paintings.[76]

Another view of Mills Plains from the mid-1830s depicts a brilliantly lit band of trees beyond a dark foreground of fallen trunks and branches. Just one tree in this middle band has been felled, opening a vista to the hill behind. Since Glover generally omitted any signs of clearing from his paintings, it may be that this stump is part of his larger emblematic treatment of landscape. Just as the rainbow in his *Mount Wellington with Orphan Asylum* (1837) is probably a mark of divine protection of the children, so this stump may symbolise the

JOHN GLOVER
TASMANIAN LANDSCAPE
C. 1835

necessity of axework to create a path for colonists from the present into the future, out of the darkness into the light.[77]

Glover's impact on Patterdale during his first years there otherwise appears to have been slight. Although he could have afforded to embark on extensive clearing, his sketches and paintings do not suggest he did so; nor do John Glover junior's surviving letters. Glover's art may be poor evidence, because his attachment to the picturesque probably meant he had little appetite for depicting clearing, but John Glover junior's letters provide stronger testimony, because he had an abiding concern with land use at Patterdale. Most likely, John senior's delight in the gum tree, as much as the widespread recognition of the benefits of retaining at least some trees as a source of firewood and shade, initially led him to leave much of his land intact.

The Glovers gradually cleared more land in the second half of the 1830s. While James Glover was the family's 'chief farming manager', he had a 'natural bias' towards running sheep and cattle, but continued to prepare more land for corn. In 1839, John junior characterised clearing as one of their 'common occupations of ordinary employment'. As if the Glovers had already established a rhythmical pattern of work akin to a natural rhythm, young John wrote:

> We sow, plant, fence, and break up new ground in progressive order, and our crops, thank Goodness, turn out equal to most; our wheat in particular often surpasses most of our neighbours.[78]

After Henry Glover became manager of Patterdale in 1839, he worked even harder to turn more land over to crops, which were his primary interest. As John junior recorded, Henry was 'very successful . . . in the cultivating line, plowing, sowing &c'. As if it were something of a novelty on Patterdale, John explained that Henry 'employed men to grub up and burn off trees on new ground, altogether one of the most laborious and expensive undertakings'. As a result, 'many acres' which were 'a cattle and sheep run and a growing forest' when Henry started, were 'clear, plowed and green with rising corn' by December 1840.[79]

Something of this clearing is manifest in Glover's last known *View of Mills Plains*, which from the relative looseness of its

JOHN GLOVER
A VIEW OF MILLS PLAINS
C. 1840

paintwork was probably executed around 1840. It reveals a vast, vacant field stretching beyond the line of trees behind Glover's buildings towards the hills in the far distance. Yet this painting also shows how Glover's plantings had flourished. The fruit trees that he had first depicted small in *A View of the Artist's House and Garden* were now a vast orchard, rich in blossom, running across the picture from his house. Most significantly, this painting shows that Glover had deliberately opted to retain gum trees where it probably mattered most to him, immediately around his own home.[80]

EUGENE VON GUÉRARD *FERNTREE GULLY IN THE DANDENONG RANGES* 1857

CHAPTER FOUR

FERN FEVER

We very much regret that the woodcutters are busy cutting down the Fern Tree Gully, and that a considerable number of trees have been felled. We trust that a stop will be at once put to such a barbarous proceedings, that the gully may be left in its integrity, and that timber may be sought for in some less romantic spot.

ARGUS, 23 NOVEMBER 1861

OUR MUSEUMS and art galleries are full of ferns. You can see them pressed into albums, etched onto porcelain, adorning epergnes and rising from the octofoil bases of silver-mounted emu eggs, as well as stencilled on furniture and celebrated in nature prints, lithographs, photographs and paintings. Colonial buildings, from

J. H. Steiner
William Thurston Testimonial Epergne
c. 1877

butchers' shops to ballrooms, were equally full of ferns. When colonists did not want them inside for 'pot culture', table decorations or housing in Wardian glass cases, they put them outside in ferneries or 'bush houses'.[1]

The Anglican clergyman–scientist William Woolls explained that ferns were so popular because of 'the extreme elegance and extraordinary diversity of their forms, as well as the facility with which many species can be procured and dried'. Queensland's Government Botanist, F. M. Bailey, thought it was simply because ferns were 'the most beautiful order in the whole range of the Vegetable Kingdom'. Either way, as George Augustus Robinson put it, ferns were 'exceedingly romantic'.[2]

This enthusiasm was part of the colonists' baggage. According to David Elliston Allen, ferns first became fashionable in Britain in the late 1830s; the craze for them peaked in the mid-1850s, particularly among women, and ran until the late 1860s. In fact this enthusiasm was manifest in England from the 1790s, when William Gilpin declared the fern 'the most picturesque' of 'all minuter plants' because of 'the form of its leaf—its elegant mode of hanging—and its dark-brown polished stem'. This appetite reached new heights in the last

Chest of Drawers c. 1890

quarter of the nineteenth century, when ferns were found in the homes of 'hard-working mechanics' as well as of the middle class, and fern-robbing became widespread.[3]

Australia was much the same. In the 1790s Elizabeth Macarthur and her friend Elizabeth Marsden ranked ferns among the most beautiful native plants. In the late 1850s a Melbourne nurseryman began listing Australian species for sale. Twenty years later, the back streets of working-class Collingwood had potted specimens in the windows, while some of Victoria's great mansions boasted spectacular ferneries. According to F. M. Bailey, it was 'almost impossible' to find a house where ferns were 'not to be met with either living or dead'.[4]

This 'pteridomania'—as the fern craze was known from the 1850s in both England and Australia—was fuelled by the size of Australian ferns, which convinced colonists and visitors alike of the 'comparative insignificance' of their English counterparts. A rare dissentient was the Irish botanist W. H. Harvey, who failed to satisfy his sister's 'fern fever' while visiting Tower Hill in Victoria's Western District in 1855. But the fault lay with Harvey. Had he made his way from the outer banks of the volcanic crater to the islands in its middle, as James Bonwick did two years later, he would have found 'gigantic ferns' forming 'delightful bowers and alcoves'.[5]

For some colonists, the size of Australia's ferns evoked a 'far distant tropical region'. For others, ferns were 'emblematic of Australia, or of this colony', as the Melbourne artist Nicholas Chevalier put it when designing a fancy-dress costume for Lady Barkly, wife of the Victorian Governor. James Smith of the *Argus* predicted in 1893 that when 'a man of genius' arose among Australian architects, he would probably

> find in the tree fern the 'leit-motif' of a new style of architecture, which will reflect the genius loci as faithfully as the form and colours of Egyptian architecture reflected the climate and natural features of the Valley of the Nile; as the pagodas of India and China recall the old Tartar tents of skins, with the corners of their coverings uplifted by spears . . . and as the Gothic cathedrals of Northern Europe were reproductions of the far receding aisles and vaulted roofs of immemorial German and Scandinavian forests.[6]

Much of this enthusiasm was inevitably directed at fern gullies close to the colonies' main cities. When Eugene von Guérard first

NICHOLAS CHEVALIER
FANCY COSTUME
EMBLEMATIC OF AUSTRALIA
(DETAIL) C. 1860

exhibited his *Ferntree Gully in the Dandenong Ranges* in 1857, he alerted many Melburnians to the beauty of his subject. Before long, the Dandenongs were under exceptional pressure, not only from timber-getters but also from professional fern collectors and excursionists with an appetite for fern-gathering. But while the government took some steps to preserve the area, its protective laws had little effect. The colonists' fernmania became the gullies' curse.

THE MAKING OF FERNTREE GULLY

The gullies of the Dandenongs attracted few visitors until the mid-1850s. Forty kilometres east of the city centre—a three-hour ride for those with good horses—they were too far off for a day trip 'except for robustious persons'. The only alternative was to camp out overnight, and few colonists bothered. When a small group of tree ferns was displayed at the Victorian Exhibition of 1854, the Dandenongs' gullies were 'but partially known'. In 1857 they were still considered 'inaccessible'.[7]

Von Guérard unwittingly put Ferntree Gully on the map. When he sketched there, it was known locally as Dobson's Gully after Thomas Dobson, who had established a timber camp near by in 1854. Von Guérard still used that name ten years later, but few people would have known what he meant, such was the impact of his picture. As a local history of the Dandenongs noted in the 1880s, von Guérard 'was pleased to call the painting Fern Tree Gully, on account of the handsome fern trees, and that name has clung to the place ever since'.[8]

Von Guérard's painting had this effect partly because the Gully was a place waiting to be better known. But *Ferntree Gully* was also recognised immediately as the 'most masterly' work of Victoria's 'greatest landscape painter'. Unlike most colonial pictures, *Ferntree Gully* did not disappear from view after its first exhibition. Instead, it remained on show in 1858–59 in the most public of places—a shop window in Collins Street—and was an object of public discussion for much of this time.[9]

This enthusiastic response owed much to James Smith, Australia's only art critic of any substance from the mid-1850s until the mid-1880s. Smith was so excited by *Ferntree Gully* that he wanted it sent to Europe as testimony to the quality of colonial nature and culture. According to Smith, *Ferntree Gully* deserved 'a place in one of the royal or national galleries of Europe, both as a specimen of colonial art and as a faithful transcript of some of the most remarkable features of colonial scenery'. By the end of December 1857 he had found seven other admirers of the picture willing to start a subscription to buy it for presentation to Queen Victoria. Their plan was that forty colonists give five guineas each, thereby raising the £210 that von Guérard wanted.[10]

Others were not so colonial: they argued that it would be better to start a National Gallery of Victoria with *Ferntree Gully* than consign it to 'some out-of-the-way corner in one of the palaces'. Perhaps because of this debate, Smith succeeded in raising only £60, leaving von Guérard no choice but to sell *Ferntree Gully* privately. Having already refused one offer, he sold it to the businessman Frederick Dalgety, who took it to England. When Dalgety lent it to the Victorian Court at the London International Exhibition in 1862, the organiser of the Victorian display reported that he could have sold it at once. An 'eminent artist in London', quoted gleefully by the Melbourne press, preferred *Ferntree Gully* to 'the feverish Turner Gallery'.[11]

No other painting by von Guérard created such interest. Of the hundreds of sites he painted, Ferntree Gully was the one he made famous; the scene where he 'immortalized' the tree fern; the reference point for other art depicting the Gully. *Ferntree Gully* was also quick to entice excursionists from Melbourne, starting with a party organised by one of von Guérard's artist friends, Julie Vieusseux. While Vieusseux had intended to visit the Gully before von Guérard first exhibited his painting in 1857, this idea may have come from talking to von Guérard or looking at his sketches. His painting appears to have prompted her to go there on New Year's Day 1858.[12]

Disaster followed when Vieusseux's 8-year-old son disappeared, and a fourteen-day search failed to find him. Two years later his bones were found in a hollow log. One of those who looked hardest for him was Alfred Howitt, better known for his part in the search for Burke and Wills. In a letter written in January 1858, Howitt described not only the search for the boy but also the earlier part of the excursion, when he climbed from Dobson's hut to the top of the range, where a surveying party a few years before had created a 'One Tree Hill' as a trigonometric reference point by clearing the summit of all but one tree.[13]

This part of the letter conveys the same wonder and excitement that animated von Guérard's painting. Howitt wrote:

> The ferntrees increase in number—from scattered clumps to stand so close together that their broad ferny leaves form a perfect roof so shady that the temperature becomes instantly cooler when you enter it—among their roots runs the coolest, clearest stream you can imagine and on each side an almost impenetrable musk scrub covers the side of the range. It would be almost impossible to give you an idea of the strange effects of light and shade in the gully. The fern trees seem to form a living grotto. Their rough mossy stems are the columns, their arching fronds are the roof . . . It is one of those tropical looking spots one would rather expect to find in the south seas than in Australia . . . We ought to have been a thousand miles away from Melbourne instead of twenty, so wild and solitary was the scene.[14]

THE VOICE OF CONSERVATISM

Richard Grove has dubbed the 1860s an 'environmental decade' because of the 'unprecedented wave of environmental concern' in many parts of the world, from India to the United States. This concern was particularly evident in Victoria. But, while elsewhere many of the great nineteenth-century advocates of environmental protection were social reformers, if not radicals, in Melbourne a conservative newspaper was most outspoken. Although the daily *Argus* had a much smaller circulation than the rival *Age*, its readership was recognised as 'very influential'. For at least seventy years, the voice of Victorian conservative politics and the voice of conservation were one and the same.[15]

When timber-getters began working in Ferntree Gully in November 1861, the *Argus* immediately called for an end to this destruction. Within a few days, the government had nailed up placards warning timber-getters not to work there, but it did not formally prohibit logging. The *Argus* responded with an editorial deploring the attack on the Gully as just one instance of the 'wholesale and indiscriminate destruction' of Victoria's trees.[16]

This editorial was probably the work of James Smith, who served not only as art, theatre and literary critic but also as a leader-writer in a period when the paper often carried four leaders and sub-leaders each day. Smith was unusual for the breadth of his environmental concerns. The destruction of forests was the issue that occupied him most, but he also wrote powerfully about the urban environment and was alive to the folly of overcropping, attacking South Australian farmers for effectively 'living off their capital, with the fatal results that usually follow such a course'.[17]

Smith prided himself on his role in persuading the Victorian government to establish the colony's first permanent forest reserves. In a series of editorials for the *Argus*, he warned of the perils of soil erosion and siltation if hills were stripped of their protective covering. In addition, he privately approached the Surveyor-General, Charles Ligar, who was one of the Victorian officials responsible for the creation of Crown reserves. According to Smith, Ligar 'promptly grasped the situation, and induced the Ministry of the day to proclaim large areas of our forest lands permanent reserves'.[18]

Smith may have started with the *Argus* editorial in November 1861. His case was partly utilitarian. Drawing on examples from Greece to the Sandwich Islands, he argued that the continued fertility of the soil depended largely on 'the preservation of the woods in certain localities'. Closer to home, he predicted there would soon be a shortage of timber, because trees were disappearing 'in a rapidly widening radius' around all Victoria's centres of population. But Smith also emphasised the importance of aesthetics:

> A certain portion of woodland is . . . essential . . . to the beauty of the landscape. It is the main and, indeed, in most of our districts, the sole ingredient of the picturesque, and we should be deficient in the ordinary good taste supposed to be characteristic of a civilised people, if we were insensible to the necessity of improved care and judgment in protecting and enlarging our reserves of the kind.[19]

Smith argued that the timber-getters' axework at Ferntree Gully—'one of the few really delightful bits of scenery' near Melbourne—exemplified the need for new controls. While he welcomed the government's attempt to stop a repetition of the 'vandalism' at the Gully, placards on trees would not stop timber-getting. He urged the government to establish reserves where 'the cutting of timber should be altogether prohibited in our time, and if at any future time permitted, it should be placed under . . . rigid restrictions and regulations'.[20]

Smith also emphasised the need for strict enforcement of the law. The *Argus* had just reported that the park land of Richmond Paddock had been illegally stripped of at least one tree each fortnight for six months. In the whole city, there was scarcely a park that had remained untouched over the past two years. Why was it, Smith asked, that the caretakers of these parks failed to 'exercise a proper surveillance'? What was their function if not 'to look after and preserve the trees'? And what hope was there for Ferntree Gully when such destruction continued unchecked in the city 'under the eyes of the citizens and under the very hands of the park-keepers themselves'?[21]

The government took just three months to implement the first of Smith's proposals. In February 1862 it established Victoria's first reserves 'for the purpose of affording splitting timber and firewood' for local residents. By the end of the year over 35 000 acres near the goldfields had been gazetted as 'firewood' and 'timber reserves'. But while the surveyor John Hardy recommended that the government designate Ferntree Gully as Victoria's first scenic reserve, it refused to protect any areas in this way.[22]

When the government finally established a Dandenong State Forest in 1867, including Ferntree Gully, it sought to ensure a continuing supply of timber by prohibiting the felling of all trees less than eighteen inches in diameter. But otherwise it allowed splitters to fell an unlimited quantity of timber in return for an annual licence fee, which peaked at only £5, and required sawmillers to pay a royalty of just a shilling for every thousand feet. In any event, enforcement of the new restrictions was lax because the government relied on the honorary services of the local publican, Thomas Grimwood. The waste was also immense: splitters generally took the very best timber and left the rest.[23]

What was the result? Accounts of Ferntree Gully published from the mid-1860s could be describing two places—one vandalised, the other pristine. These differences depended partly on whether the writer was independent or had been employed to promote the place. They also depended on whether the writer was looking at the bottom of the Gully, which was more degraded, or higher up the hill, which was more intact. But the different accounts of the Gully also give force to the truism that what we see depends on what we know. The degradation of the Gully was seen by colonists who knew what it had once been like. Those who went there for the first time admired its beauty and could not imagine it had ever been more wondrous.

The *Illustrated Australian News* published the most powerful witness to the Gully's 'considerable defacement' in 1865. This wood engraving showed a splitter's hut with a large clearing in front and a wall of giant dead eucalypts behind. A bank of tree ferns still rose above the hut, but the *News* explained that they were just a fraction of what had once stood there. Because of the 'havoc' caused by the splitters, the remaining ferntrees failed 'to give an adequate idea of the enchantment which their graceful frondage [once] lent to the scene'.[24]

Other contemporary writers who described this transformation used *Ferntree Gully in the Dandenong Ranges* as a yardstick, even though it had been out of Victoria for several years. At least one visitor in 1866 was disappointed to discover that nature no longer resembled art. Another recalled how in the late 1850s:

> That pretty spot, buried deep in the ranges of Dandenong, which von Guérard's pencil sketched so faithfully, was yet simply as nature had formed it. The sawyer and the wood-splitter, with their scathing industries, had not yet marked it for their own, and the few Melbournites in the habit of visiting it rejoiced in a scene than which some of them . . . knew no lovelier.[25]

The Wood-Splitters' Hut in the Fern Tree Gully
1865

Yet visitors new to the Gully continued to find it beautiful. When Thomas Grimwood opened a hotel there in 1866, it became even more attractive for those who wanted to stay overnight and were 'averse to gipsying'. The first *Guide for Excursionists from Melbourne*, published in 1868, described the Gully as a 'gem amongst the jewels of nature's scenery'. When Victoria received a visit from 300 naval officers of the English Flying Squadron in 1869, their excursion to the Gully enhanced its reputation as 'one of the great show places of Melbourne', a site visitors were 'obliged to see'.[26]

Excursionists usually made their way up the Gully to One Tree Hill, just as Alfred Howitt had done in 1858. The ascent was 'steep and full of obstacles'. The summit itself was hardly welcoming: the 'One Tree' was 'all bare and branchless' and the ground was still covered with the trees felled by the surveyors, making it 'troublesome for ladies'. But it was a cliché that the view stretching from Gippsland to Westernport was worth the climb. The officers of the English Flying Squadron reckoned they had 'witnessed nothing like it on their voyage, except at Madeira'.[27]

THE LIMITS OF LAW

The Victorian government showed some concern for the environment of the Dandenongs in 1870 when it introduced special regulations for the 'care, protection and management' of the state forest. The most significant of these regulations made it an offence to 'cut down or remove . . . any indigenous shrubs or fern trees, or remove the fronds of fern trees' without a 'special order' from the Board of Land and Works. The government also appointed a salaried bailiff based at Ferntree Gully—a significant advance on relying on the voluntary services of Thomas Grimwood.[28]

Yet the bailiff had so many other duties that the time he devoted to the forest was 'absurdly small' and the new controls still went unenforced. When the government introduced a new set of Crown Land regulations three years later, it failed to improve the old system of 'indiscriminate licensing' of timber-getting in state forests; worse, it repealed all additional controls, including those protecting the Dandenongs. W. E. Ivey, the Secretary of Victoria's Central Forest Board, considered that 'no more effectual method of legalizing the destruction of timber could have been devised'.[29]

Meanwhile, excursionists kept coming to the Gully in ever greater numbers. According to one account, the Gully was 'pre-eminently the scenery outing of Melbourne' because it offered 'the best glimpse of what is most characteristic in Australian scenery' at the 'smallest expense of time and distance'. Melburnians wanting to escape the summer heat looked to the Dandenongs for 'pure oxygen' to invigorate the soul, and 'mountain ozone' to cleanse the blood. Ferntree Gully was more fashionable, if not more popular, than Brighton, Sorrento or Queenscliff. It was 'the paradise of picnickers', a 'refreshing retreat' during the hottest months.[30]

More clearing resulted. By the early 1880s, the old picnic area near the base of the Gully was a camping ground invaded by 'masses of sweetbriar'. Around Christmas it was 'covered by drags, waggonettes, and coaches' and populated by 'groups of merry people . . . crowned with sprays of ferns and creepers'. Several species of fern had begun to disappear. In 1881 the naturalist Charles French noted that the 'very handsome' *Lomaria lanceolata* was found 'now very sparingly in the Dandenong and Macedon gullies'; the small raspfern *Doodia caudata* was 'confined to a few of the less frequented spots, such as Sassafras and other back gullies'.[31]

Amateur collectors were not the only culprits. Professional collectors supplied a flourishing trade in tree ferns, both in Australia and overseas. Their trunks were exported to Europe and North America as 'ornamental pedestals'; their stems were planed into walking sticks and polished into ornaments. Closer settlement intensified the pressure after 7500 acres of the original Dandenong State Forest around One Tree Hill were thrown open for settlement in 1878.[32]

Local bailiffs made a rare attempt to stop this traffic in 1881 when they prosecuted a Melbourne man, William Bucknall, for taking fern trees from Ferntree Gully. Bucknall's conviction would have been straightforward under the special regulations introduced in 1870, because they expressly prohibited the cutting of ferntrees in the Dandenong State Forest. The repeal of these regulations meant that Bucknall had to be charged under the general law requiring anyone taking timber from Crown Land to have a licence. This charge raised the issue: were fern trees 'timber'? The local justices at Dandenong decided they were and fined Bucknall £5, but he appealed to the Supreme Court.[33]

The prosecution's case was uninspired. It invoked English precedent to argue that ferntrees were timber because they were used for building purposes, but Victoria's Chief Justice, Sir William Stawell, rejected this test on the basis that grass or moss would not be treated as timber just because they were used for building. Alexander Wallis, Victoria's Secretary of Agriculture, testified that 'botanically speaking, the stem of the fern-tree was timber, although it was not the timber of commerce', but the court dismissed his evidence because counsel for the prosecution could not explain what he meant.[34]

The judges' rulings were barely more cogent. Justice Holroyd acquitted Bucknall on the basis that he had taken '"tree ferns", not "fern-trees"'. Chief Justice Stawell maintained that the licensing provision in the Land Act was 'intended to protect the revenue'—a conclusion hardly supported by the risible licence fee. Perhaps encouraged by Wallis's affidavit, Stawell also mistakenly assumed that there was no revenue to be raised from the cutting of ferntrees.

Rather than appeal to the Privy Council in London, the government promised it would immediately take 'other steps to conserve the fern trees in the district'. But it failed to do so. While a deputation of local residents led by Thomas Grimwood persuaded the Minister for Lands to set aside 412 acres at Fern Tree Gully in 1882 as a temporary reserve for public recreation, the Minister conferred no new protections on the Gully's ferntrees, which were the subject of an immediate 'rush' by excursionists and professional pickers.[35]

A year later, the government finally made it an offence to 'cut, remove, injure, damage, or in any way interfere with the ferns . . . growing within or upon Dandenong State Forest'. Yet even then, enforcement remained lax. While the ranger kept watch on fern-takers over holiday periods, he simply 'relieved' them of the fronds they carried rather than prosecuting them for breaching the law. One of Australia's most popular gardening guides continued to advise excursionists from Melbourne that they could 'easily make a nice selection' of ferns on their 'holiday rambles' in the Dandenongs. A local guidebook advised excursionists always to carry a trowel 'for taking any desired fern'.[36]

TELEMACHUS

The lack of a railway to Ferntree Gully was the area's primary protection in the mid-1880s. While coaches went there twice each weekday and three or more times a day in summer, colonists had developed such a taste for train travel that many regarded the drive as 'equivalent to an impassable mountain barrier'. Mount Macedon, twenty kilometres further from Melbourne, was more accessible, because the train took just one and three-quarter hours. Although its ferns had also been depleted by more than twenty years of amateur and professional collecting, a good day trip there could yield a dozen or more varieties and still leave ample time to spare.[37]

When the government finally acceded to local demands to extend the railway in 1888, Francis Myers, alias Telemachus, was quick to acknowledge its significance in the *Argus*. By one account, Myers' weekly essays about the Victorian countryside were 'simply rushed for the instant' they appeared, and 'Saturday's talk' among 'literary folk' was 'usually of Telemachus' latest'. Another of Myers' admirers thought him the equal of the most famous colonial writers—Henry Kendall, Adam Lindsay Gordon and Marcus Clarke.[38]

Myers called on the colonial government to protect the remaining 20 000 acres of unalienated land in the Dandenongs as either a 'national estate' or a 'national park'. He was probably inspired to do so by J. B. Gregory of Victoria's Field Naturalists' Club, who was proposing the same protections for all 123 000 acres of Wilson's

Promontory. Gregory's initial idea was to garner 'scientific' support from the Royal, Geographical and Zoological Societies in order to stop the Promontory's being opened to settlement. When the zoologists refused, he persuaded the Victorian Academy of Art to participate instead. In February 1888 a combined deputation was 'well received' by Victoria's Minister for Lands, who sent a party of officials to the Promontory ten days later in order to assess the deputation's claims.[39]

Myers conceived the 'forest park' of the Dandenongs as a counterpart to the 'ocean park' at the Promontory. Victorians, he declared, had a choice: they could create 'a park unique in Australia and unsurpassed for natural beauty in the world', or allow the area to be destroyed by 'more nibbling here of selectors under various pretences, or of sawmillers, or seekers after gold which will not pay Chinaman wages for the labour of winning it'. While the Dandenongs remained a state forest, a 'needy Minister' could open the land for settlement. But as a 'national estate' or 'national park', the area would be preserved for all time and become increasingly valuable as Melbourne grew and land became scarcer. 'Why', Myers asked, 'should not this generation, and the next and the whole of our posterity . . . have ocean and woodland mountain and meadow playgrounds?'[40]

Myers envisaged a national park that was both developed and protected: he wanted government to make 'its beauties accessible', while 'in no sense and in no instance destroying them'. He hoped new roads would be cut and a few acres of scrub cleared and replaced with couch grass lawns. He also wanted a ranger appointed with one or two assistants who would erect 'a few rustic bridges . . . to help people over existing bog tracks', build 'a few simple walls where plentiful supplies of cool sweet water would always be stored', and banish the cows, which were then roaming over the gullies, 'trampling the springs into mudholes, killing out the tender young ferns, [and] rubbing the delicate orchid and lichen and moss growths' from bigger tree ferns.[41]

Myers' overriding concern was that the park be a place 'for the people'. While he could see that many parts of the Dandenongs were destined to become a retreat of the wealthy who would build summer houses in the hills, Myers wanted the park 'for the hundreds and hundreds of thousands' who could only get 'their recuperation, and health, and purifying country influences, in brief gulps'. Myers believed the masses wanted such access to nature. Like James Smith and many other contributors to the *Argus*, he also believed that it would save the working class from the corruption of urban living. He maintained:

> They look from the city to the foliage-embowered hills, and feel that in this new world they also should have some heritage there. And the feeling is right and should be gratified. Open the parks and forests, run out the railways on all Sundays and holidays and there will not through nine months of our year be many people spending their leisure in slums, and bars and taprooms.[42]

Sunday travel was the nub of the issue, because Sunday was the only free day of the week for most workers in Melbourne and hence their primary opportunity to educate and amuse themselves. For years debate raged over how the Sabbath should be observed. Should trains run? Should the National Gallery and Public Library open? The train to Ferntree Gully was just one part of this debate, but the arguments in favour of it were particularly strong because the Railway Commissioners had already opened lines to the bay at Brighton, Mordialloc and Frankston to secure additional revenues. There was also a strong sniff of selfishness about the stance of the Presbyterians of the Lord's Day Observance Society, who would deny others access to the Gully on Sundays when they were mostly members of the upper class who could enjoy the Gully whenever they pleased.[43]

Myers' arguments came to nothing. Although government officials commonly referred to the Gully in the 1890s as a 'national park', it remained a recreation reserve under the control of local trustees, who were hamstrung by a lack of funds.[44] Such was the power of the Lord's Day Observance Society that when the railway opened in 1889 it ran only six days a week. As a result, Melbourne's artisans had few opportunities to take the train, which brought the Gully within an hour and a half of the city. Except for public holidays, the Gully remained a middle-class preserve.

CHEAP DAY RETURNS

By the time the train arrived, only the upper part of Ferntree Gully was more or less intact. According to a local guide book, it offered:

> [A] vast profusion of fern trees . . . ranging from a foot to thirty feet in height[;] . . . a great wealth of pink and white epacrids; hazel and musk trees, a large number of kinds of acacia, and an infinite variety of shrubs with no common names recognisable to the general mass of visitors.

Although One Tree Hill was still renowned for its vistas, the view towards Melbourne was often dulled by pollution. The bottom of the hill, where von Guérard had painted *Ferntree Gully*, had been 'vandalized', its 'phenomenal vegetation . . . removed or sacrificed', leaving it more or less bare.[45]

As the *Age* observed, this degradation left another part of the Dandenongs—Sassafras Gully—as 'the real attraction of the locality'. But while Ferntree Gully itself was more than a mile of rough travel away from its railway station, and the scenery along the road from the station was 'not very attractive', Sassafras Gully was even harder to reach. As a result, only a few colonists explored its 'unspoiled beauty'.[46]

The diary of L. E. Hervey, an English tourist on his way round the world, also suggests that Ferntree Gully offered some excursionists more than enough challenges. Hervey thought the Gully as pristine as it was dangerous. He recorded that at its entrance the 'blazing sun' was replaced by shade, and 'in many place the ferns were so thick over head that the sky was not visible . . . It was very beautiful, a very rapid stream running at the bottom of the gully, with a sort of track along one side'. Whereas a local guide book described the climb up the Gully as 'a very easy one, even for ladies and children', Hervey found it treacherous: 'In places the track was so steep that it was a case of clamber with tooth and nail, and swinging oneself up by the trees. There were any amount of snakes, and one we saw was a most venomous sort.'[47]

The impact of the new train travellers first became an issue in 1890, when Melbourne's 'hordes' exploited one of their few opportunities to take cheap day returns to the Gully on the Prince of Wales's birthday. The *Argus* had expected nature to be an improving influence that would 'inspire the denizens of the cities . . . with high thoughts and with reverence for the Power that had created such beauty', so that the artisan 'would return to his home better fitted to battle with the world than before'. Instead the *Argus* discovered that the artisan's 'uppermost thought' was 'to rip and tear the ferns to pieces, to purloin the wild flowers, and to scatter broadcast bottles, jam tins and waste paper, and other articles not calculated to improve the scenery'.[48]

This account was jaundiced by class bias. Middle-class excursionists had been despoiling the Gully in much the same way for years, but the *Argus* treated such destruction as new:

> The natural enemy to the landscape is the railway . . . for not only do the lines and culverts and bridges disfigure the hills and valleys, but they are the means of conveying to beauty spots persons who take a savage delight in destroying what they ought to admire and preserve. The latest railway, which is not a national blessing in every sense, is the extension to Ferntree Gully which has been opened barely twelve months. Ferntree Gully was the delight of the lover of nature, for its picturesqueness and richness were almost unsurpassed. Perhaps it might be said that even now it is beautiful, notwithstanding the violation to which it has been subjected, but its beauty is rapidly vanishing, and may very soon become a thing of the past unless steps are taken to protect it.[49]

Victoria's new Forestry Department, headed by George Perrin, manifested the same bias. Having taken no action against middle-class fern-gatherers in its first two years of operation, the department threatened to prosecute working-class 'delinquents' who uprooted large numbers of ferns. The department declared that unless 'strong measures' were taken, Ferntree Gully would 'soon be stripped of its beauty, and . . . cease to be a place of attraction for the residents of Melbourne on holidays'. The *Argus* concurred, as did the local council, which called for at least a few offenders to be fined heavily as an example to others. But, though one of the department's inspectors had taken the names of thirty offenders, it charged none of them.[50]

The Victorian Railways further increased the opportunities for middle-class travel in February 1893 when it offered a special Saturday excursion to the Gully as a means of boosting its revenue in the midst of the prevailing depression. To mark the occasion, the *Argus* published an essay on Melbourne's 'Mountain Playground' by the 73-year-old James Smith, who simply cannibalised his old accounts of the Gully and wrote as if it still resembled von Guérard's painting:

> You move through the sinuous cloisters in a green twilight . . . in the midst of a stillness that is wonderful . . . broken only at intervals by the tinkling chime of falling water in the dark, moist ravine below, or by the faint rustle of leaves, so high overhead that they seem to belong to some other region.[51]

Encouraged by this article, almost 700 Melburnians, including 500 women, took advantage of the first cheap fare to the Gully. When they returned at the end of the day, 'almost every lady' was carrying 'bunches of maiden hair, handfuls of green ferns or bundles of the tall grasses'. But the Forestry Department's inspectors were invisible. Far from calling for enforcement of the law, the *Argus* merely observed that in the women's 'simple trusting minds' the ferns seemed to have 'been produced for the ornamentation of suburban drawing-rooms'. But then, as the *Argus* itself emphasised, these excursionists were not suburban youth but respectable members of 'the gentler sex' who usually travelled first class, not second, and hence were above the law.[52]

THE POOR MAN'S FARM

Protests by the unemployed peaked in Melbourne in April 1893, when the depression was at its worst. Although 28 per cent of trade unionists were out of work, James Patterson's government refused to provide unemployment relief and private charity proved woefully inadequate. On 10 April the unemployed 'assembled in force' outside Patterson's office, 'bailed up' Ministers as they went in and out, and declared 'in a threatening manner' that they would have 'to get bread . . . some way'. That night, the Unemployed Workers' Association staged its first meeting outside the Richmond Town Hall, and the crowd of 1500 relished the news that Patterson was 'undoubtedly frightened' by their protests.[53]

Patterson responded that it was for private enterprise to provide work for the unemployed, while the government simply ensured that 'well behaved citizens did not starve'. He also refused to create relief works in Melbourne because he was intent on removing the unemployed from the city. But he promised to facilitate 'reproductive works' outside Melbourne that would produce food or some other 'salable and convertible commodity'. The government's goal was to 'find some place in the country where they could say to any man who said he was starving, "There is a place where you can go and earn food."' One of the first areas it targeted was the Dandenong State Forest, which it claimed was ideal for market gardens and orchards because of the area's good soil and proximity to Melbourne.[54]

John McIntyre, the Minister for Lands, looked forward to opening part of the Dandenong State Forest for selection in five- or ten-acre blocks by workingmen with a little capital, while providing land for 'a poor man's or labour farm' for 'the relief of starving men' above Ferntree Gully near One Tree Hill. Otherwise the government planned to have nothing to do with this 'labour colony', which was a rural version of the urban workhouse. Instead, Melbourne's Charity Organisation Society would attract donations to pay for rations, which would be all the unemployed received until they proved themselves 'reasonably proficient as farm labourers'. They would then become entitled to a small wage, although the Charity Organisation Society would not pay it until they quit the labour colony.[55]

Ferntree Gully was never threatened by this scheme. Because of its popularity and status as a recreation reserve, McIntyre immediately announced that the government would make a national park of a 'large area' around it. But this 'large area' proved to be only 1000 acres—one-twentieth of that sought by Francis Myers in 1888—and it formally remained part of the Dandenong State Forest. The area designated for settlement grew from 5000 to 7000 acres, almost half of what remained of the original state forest. From the outset, it included Sassafras Gully, which had become more accessible in the early 1890s after George Perrin cut a track through it.[56]

The outcry was immediate, particularly from members of the middle class. Melburnians wanted to retain the state forest as their recreation ground. Existing residents of the Dandenongs did not want the tone of their district lowered. Yet opposition to the government's plan was not confined to the bourgeoisie; nor was it just a matter of self-interest. A key part of the argument against the government's plan was that small selectors with little capital could never succeed in the forest. Opponents of the plan also maintained that future generations of all classes had an interest in keeping the city's 'great lungs' intact.

George Perrin was first to protest against the 'sacrifice' of his state forest. If the government continued to act in this fashion, he warned, Victoria would become dependent on imported timber and 'the foreign producer' would have the colony 'entirely at his mercy in regard to price'. But the Minister proceeded. After again being 'besieged for several hours' by unemployed artisans on 19 April, he announced that men could go to the Dandenongs 'at once and peg out their blocks'. McIntyre acknowledged that he was 'breaking away from the strict letter of the law', because the Victorian Land Act provided that existing reserves could not be sold, leased or licensed, but he predicted that Parliament would support his action. By the end of the day, a rush on the forest had started.[57]

The radical *Age*—the one Melbourne daily to display genuine concern for the plight of the unemployed—responded by declaring it 'an act of cruelty to encourage impecunious or inexperienced persons to begin work that must end in disaster, and render their condition worse than it now is'. Although sawmillers and splitters had taken the best timber from the Dandenongs, the area was still heavily treed and the cost of clearing it 'entirely beyond the resources of the unemployed'. The only way to do the work was with horse or bullock teams, and it would be at least two years before the selectors could hope for a payable crop. Meanwhile the selectors' only source of income would be 'from the sale of ferns smuggled and sold in Melbourne'.[58]

This argument had history on its side. As the field naturalist J. B. Gregory reminded readers of the *Argus*, they only had to look at what had become of the area around One Tree Hill since it was opened to selection in the late 1870s. Far from becoming home to dozens of small farmers who worked their land productively, One Tree Hill was covered with 'ruined huts and fences, and orchards running wild', while much of the land had fallen into the hands of speculators who had bought it for just £1 an acre. Gregory predicted that selectors around Sassafras Gully would suffer the same fate.[59]

The government's decision also came under attack because the forest was the watershed that supplied Lilydale, Nunawading and Moorabbin. Others argued that the Dandenongs were important as a recreation ground. One field naturalist maintained that, even if the government had to find land for the unemployed, it should exempt the nearest state forest to Melbourne because the 'growing metropolis' needed 'all the breathing room possible'. The president of the local shire council agreed that the 'heavily timbered, deep, steep, and abrupt gorges' of the Dandenongs were 'useful for recreation purposes and none other'. When McIntyre visited the Dandenongs on 20 April to inspect the land he had just thrown open, he was greeted as 'the angel of devastation who was to convert a mountain Eden into a plain ploughed field'.[60]

This opposition also took a more organised, institutional form. A group of Trades Hall delegates who visited the Dandenongs declared it 'totally unfitted' for agriculture. At his second attempt, J. B. Gregory persuaded the Field Naturalists' Club to call on McIntyre to reverse his decision, though many of the club's middle-class members remained loath to impede the government's efforts to help the unemployed. Gregory found it much easier to lead the more upper-class members of the Royal Society of Victoria 'from the safe road of science into the pitfalls of politics' and join the Field Naturalists' deputation. The Dandenong, Moorabbin and Nunawading Councils formed their own deputation, though some councillors from Dandenong looked on the revocation of the state forest as 'a good thing' because it would 'open up a country which was not producing any revenue'.[61]

McIntyre responded by announcing that he would take 'every precaution' to preserve Sassafras Gully, which to him simply meant creating a reserve two or three chains wide on either side of the creek, or a chain beyond the fern groves on each bank. Otherwise McIntyre defended his decision, claiming that the water supply of Lilydale and Dandenong was protected and that the 'best proof' that the land was suitable for small farmers was that it was being 'rushed by practical men' who were under 'no compulsion to go there'. At the same time McIntyre went on the attack, accusing local residents of seeking to monopolise the 'extreme beauty' of the area where they lived. According to the Minister, 'all patriotic persons' needed to make 'every effort' to assist the government to achieve its 'national purpose' of settling people on the land rather than 'throwing difficulties in the way'.[62]

Two prominent field naturalists, Archibald 'Beaky' Campbell and R. S. Sugars, hit on a new medium for pressing their case. Instead of protesting in print through letters to the *Argus* or in person through deputations to the government, Campbell and Sugars turned to the lantern slides they had taken over the previous three years. Although they had sought simply to celebrate the Dandenongs' beauty when taking these slides, Campbell and Sugars saw the political potential of these images—perhaps the first time anyone in Australia recognised how photography could stimulate public interest in protecting the

ARCHIBALD CAMPBELL
SASSAFRAS GULLY 1891–92

environment. Their lecture on the 'Beauties and Wonders of the Dandenong State Forest' filled the theatre of Melbourne's Working Men's College. According to the *Argus*, their pictures were 'silent but telling protests against the intention of the Minister of Lands'.[63]

THE FRUITS OF SELECTION

Ferntree Gully was subject to ever greater pressure from December 1893 because the government finally overcame its 'religious scruples in favour of commercial principles' and decided to run Sunday trains there. When the first train reached Bayswater, one stop before Ferntree Gully, the station was decorated with a large sign celebrating this onset of 'healthy Christianity'. More than 700 tickets were sold, yielding the department a profit of £100.[64]

The trustees of the recreation reserve had neither the means nor the wit to manage the Gully so that it could withstand such invasions. The government refused to contribute except when the Gully's 'devastation' was seriously interfering with revenue from the railway line. As a result, colonists familiar with the Gully again lamented what had become of it. One recorded that, while there was still 'much of the beautiful' about the Gully, it had been 'much knocked about by careless tourists during the last few years', leaving it only 'a shadow of its former self'. Another found it 'weary and careworn', not nearly as picturesque as in the 1870s, though even then it bore little relation to von Guérard's *Ferntree Gully*.[65]

Meanwhile, the opening of the Dandenongs proved a disaster both for the environment and for the selectors who had rushed to take up McIntyre's offer. Sassafras Creek was soon a scene of 'ruthless destruction', because the government revoked the Dandenong State Forest without establishing its promised reserves. The unemployed were not simply competing among themselves; wealthy colonists used 'dummies' to pick out many of the best blocks, including much of the area initially intended for a labour colony.[66]

Still the alienation of the state forest continued. In September 1893 McIntyre secured the passage of a new Settlement on Land Act providing for the establishment of 'village settlements' for more of Melbourne's unemployed. In all, more than 5000 additional acres were excised from the Dandenong State Forest for three village settlements, which attracted colonists even less equipped for life on the land than the free selectors who had preceded them. According to one account, the residents of the first settlement near Monbulk were Melbourne artisans and tradesmen who had been 'starved out of town'. Some of them had not the 'least idea of even erecting a bark hut', let alone felling the big trees that remained in the forest, and were 'sleeping on the ground and living generally in a manner that would disgrace a blackfellow'.[67]

When McIntyre visited the Dandenongs in March 1894, the free selectors appeared to be doing much better than the village settlers. Aided by their better blocks, some of the selectors had built 'comfortable slab and weatherboard houses'. Others, McIntyre noted with approval, had demonstrated their pioneering spirit by constructing huts of tree-ferns lined with bracken. Nearly all had an acre or two of vegetables growing 'luxuriantly'. Meanwhile the village settlers were struggling with soil so 'poor, sour and generally unprofitable' that their crops turned out 'dead failures' and McIntyre had to promise to allow them to move nearer to Ferntree Gully.[68]

In fact, the lot of the free selectors was often no different from that of the village settlers. Both groups battled to 'subdue the monarchs of the forest, and turn their holdings from its primeval useless state into reproductive little homesteads'. Even when they did so, it was often difficult to get their crops to market because there were no made roads, and they sometimes had to use sleds to carry their produce over the mud. In any event, the price for berries, their staple crop, was often low. The common experience was one of exchanging urban poverty for rural misery.[69]

In some respects the village settlers were better off than the free selectors. Not only were the settlers entitled to payment from the government for 'improvements' to their blocks, but they were also entitled to preference when the government created jobs improving local roads. Perhaps most significantly, they had less stake in their land and hence were relatively free to quit it, as most of them soon did. But the selectors had invested their little capital and hence had to cling to their blocks despite the appalling conditions. Their first opportunity to sell out at 'fancy prices' came in the early 1900s when, as Francis Myers had predicted, well-to-do Melburnians began looking for 'mountain sites for country residences'. Then those who did best were often not those who had struggled hardest to clear their land, but those who had preserved its natural beauty by leaving it studded with blackbutt, hazel and ferntrees.[70]

LOUISA ANNE MEREDITH *GUM FLOWERS AND 'LOVE'* 1860

CHAPTER FIVE

LOUISA

Can you imagine that anyone of my habits and pursuits could bear the estrangement from all the many delights afforded them by living in a civilized (pardon the word) country . . .? Where would my literature be in Van Diemen's Land? Writing sonnets to whales and porpoises, canzonets to kangaroos, madrigals to 'prime merinos' and dirges to black swans, illustrated by portraits of the engaging and lovely natives?

LOUISA ANNE TWAMLEY TO GEORGE MEREDITH, 18 MAY 1833

LOUISA ANNE TWAMLEY had already begun establishing herself as an artist and writer in Birmingham when her uncle George Meredith invited her to Tasmania to be his children's governess. The 20-year-old Twamley's 'usual occupation' was, by her own account, 'miniature portrait painting', but she had also contributed poems and reviews to the radical *Birmingham Journal* and was looking forward to the publication of her first book of verse, illustrated by six of her own etchings. In order to build on these precocious foundations, Twamley reckoned she needed 'all the literary papers, periodicals, new music, new engravings' Birmingham could offer. Tasmania, she implied, would be her ruin. If she ever needed the £100 a year her uncle offered, she could obtain it as a teacher in England.[1]

Twamley made the most of her decision. Six years later she had exhibited twenty-six paintings, primarily miniatures, with the Royal Birmingham Society of Artists. She had also published a landscape annual on the Wye Valley, illustrated with engravings after established English landscape painters such as Copley Fielding and David Cox, and had produced four sentimental flower books, which, as Wilfred Blunt put it, combined her own 'charming—if inaccurate—pictures' and 'delightfully awful verse'. Twamley's contemporaries revelled in these limitations. By one account, she was 'well known to the flower-loving world as the most graceful expositor of English botany'. Another admired her 'pretty verses' and 'yet pleasanter prose'.[2]

Then marriage intervened. Having been spurned by William Lewis, who edited the *Birmingham Journal*, she was courted by her cousin, Charles Meredith, and married him in April 1839. Six weeks later, Louisa was bound for Sydney and unprecedented literary success.

Louisa's new environment improved her writing by giving her more to say. When *Notes and Sketches of New South Wales*, her first book without plates, was published in London by John Murray in 1844, it delighted readers and reviewers in England and Australia—except for the *Sydney Morning Herald*, which was infuriated by Louisa's unusual willingness to criticise colonial society. In seven years it ran through four editions, making it one of the most successful titles in Murray's 'Home and Colonial Library'.[3]

Louisa was slower to make much of her art in Tasmania. In 1845, and then again 1846, she failed to contribute to the first major art exhibitions held in Hobart. *My Home in Tasmania*, which first appeared in two volumes in London in 1852 and New York in 1853,

Louisa Anne Meredith
Weeping Gum-Trees and Old Forge 1852

included thirteen vignettes after her own drawings, but the four full-page engravings were after drawings by Francis Robert Nixon, the first Anglican Bishop of Tasmania. Louisa thanked Nixon for allowing her to present some of Tasmania's 'lovely scenes . . . in a form so well worthy of their own beauty', while dismissing her own 'trifling sketches' as interesting only on account of their accuracy. For once, she was not indulging in excessive modesty. Much like John Glover, she admitted to finding the difference of the gum trees a challenge. As she put it, they 'demanded far greater care in their delineation' than she was 'at first . . . disposed to accord them'.[4]

Over the next forty years Louisa not only published more than a dozen books in London and Hobart but also reverted to being their primary illustrator, whether she needed botanical or zoological pictures or landscapes. She also exhibited flower paintings, which to her delight won prizes at intercolonial and international exhibitions in London, Melbourne, Sydney and Calcutta. On the back of her medal from the Melbourne exhibition of 1866–67 she recorded: 'Only fifty of these "silver" medals were struck. I am the only *woman* to whom one was awarded for art combined with literature.'[5]

Yet these successes did not pay and her financial situation was often precarious, so Louisa had to look for other employment. When she visited Melbourne in 1860, she was keen to find work at the *Argus* alongside her old acquaintance James Smith, whom she admired and often quoted as 'an eloquent writer of descriptions'. From the mid-1860s she began seeking a royal pension on account of her literary service. When Queen Victoria refused, Louisa turned to the Tasmanian Parliament. Its grant of £100 per annum in 1884 as a mark of her contribution to 'the cause of Science, Literature and Art' made her Australia's first cultural pensioner.[6]

Throughout this period Louisa did not just quietly celebrate nature, as she had been in England, but robustly defended it. Like many of her contemporaries, she had a clear environmental hierarchy topped by animals, which she thought second only to human beings among God's creations. Cruelty to domestic species was her greatest concern. Then came the extinction of native animals. Plants mattered less to her, though she loved ferns and railed against their destruction on Mount Wellington outside Hobart. As one schooled in the picturesque, she deplored large-scale clearing.

Louisa brought these issues before all conceivable audiences through children's stories and lavish illustrated folios, a popular tourist guide and travel books. But she did not just criticise her fellow colonists. She also played a key role in establishing a Tasmanian Society for the Prevention of Cruelty to Animals. Not least, she helped to secure some of Tasmania's first environmental legislation through Charles, who served more than twenty years in the colony's Parliament, including four terms as Treasurer and one as Minister for Lands.[7]

This activism was part of the larger international rise in environmental concern in the second half of the nineteenth century. Louisa's sense of how attitudes were in flux was manifest in 1860 when she observed: 'The revolting outrage of bull-baiting was pleasant to our savage ancestors; but the legislature of our day has abolished it utterly'. At the same time, she emphasised that even greater change was possible, asking: '[W]hy should not the small things be protected as the large?'[8]

Louisa's closest colonial counterpart in pursuing these environmental issues was Louisa Atkinson, another precocious woman artist–author, who began contributing articles and drawings to the *Illustrated Sydney News* in 1853 aged nineteen. Like Meredith, Atkinson lamented the wanton destruction of Australian fauna. Unlike Meredith, she warned that deforestation could have climatic consequences. But Atkinson's early death in 1872, at the age of thirty-eight, stopped her pursuing these issues at length, let alone ever working to see her environmental values enshrined in law.[9]

Yet Louisa Anne Meredith is significant not only for what she did but also for what she did not do. As part of developing the personalised voice expected of women writers in the mid-nineteenth century,[10] she articulated her environmental priorities and the limits of the expanded sense of moral concern that led her to campaign so strongly to protect animals. More than any other colonial advocate of environmental protection, she revealed her environmental values and the difficulties of putting these principles into practice.

A MORAL PESTILENCE

If Norfolk Island led England when Robert Ross ordered his subjects not to cut the eggs out of the providence petrel, from the 1820s England drew far ahead of its Australian colonies in trying to prevent cruelty to animals. The first British legislation in 1822 elicited no response in New South Wales and was followed in Tasmania only in 1836. The creation of a Society for the Prevention of Cruelty to Animals in London in 1824 engendered no Australian counterparts, even when Queen Victoria elevated this flourishing group into a Royal Society in 1840.[11]

According to Keith Thomas, England led the world in this arena because of its high degree of urbanisation and industrialisation. As animals became increasingly marginal to processes of production, the new middle class gradually came to look on them not as working livestock but as subjects of moral concern. In doing so, these townspeople fundamentally reassessed their own place in the world, rejecting the view that humans were free to dispose of animals in any way they wanted. Instead, they accepted that it was wrong to kill animals or cause them to suffer unnecessarily. The big question was what forms of killing and suffering were necessary.[12]

Louisa was at the forefront of exploring these issues in Australia, though her stance was far from radical. She accepted that human beings were entitled to domesticate animals and kill them, so long as their deaths were as painless as possible. As she explained in 1861:

> I am no Quixotic visionary, desiring or dreaming that animals, useful to man's lawful labour and also 'good for food', should be left

> unused or uneaten. *We* are no Vegetarians, but have our own beautiful sheep and oxen killed for the sustenance of our family and establishment; they are well kept during their present lives; and instant death comes to them, unheralded by terrors and torments.[13]

Consistent with this position, Louisa accepted that wild animals could be killed if they were pests or were needed for food. She recounted with pride how Charles had once killed nine seagulls with a single shot when shipwrecked in Bass Strait and had sometimes fed his family in Tasmania by bringing in a dozen wattlebirds for breakfast. She thought the Cumberland Hunt in New South Wales 'certainly useful' when it went after the 'destructive native dog or dingo'; she saw at least some justice in the 'war' that colonists waged against possums because of their 'sad ravages among the young corn'.[14]

Yet Louisa opposed the pursuit and killing of animals for mere sport. As early as 1844 she recounted how she pleaded with her fellow passengers on the voyage from England to stop massacring the 'harmless and really beautiful' cape pigeons out of 'mere wanton love of destruction'. In 1852 she raged at how the few introduced deer in Tasmania were chased to exhaustion only to be rescued 'for future torments . . . by the noble and Christian worthies who enjoy the cruel sport'. It was no defence that 'deeds quite as cruel' were encouraged 'at home': there was no reason why 'all the bad habits of an old country should be scrupulously transplanted to a new one, whilst so many of the good ones remain forgotten'.[15]

Although the targets of these criticisms were all men, Louisa looked on cruelty as a 'moral pestilence' that touched all sections of society. In her view, it was almost as much a sin to ignore cruelty as to engage in it:

> Men, women, and children may commit, or connive at, or leave unpunished, crimes and cruelties towards the animal creation; but it is my fixed belief, that so surely as there is a hereafter, even so surely will all such wickedness be visited upon our souls; and that not one in such sin of wanton cruelty against the smallest living thing will pass without its judgment, or be '*forgotten before God.*'

Louisa was most caustic about her fellow women, particularly their implication in the plumage trade, which burgeoned from the 1860s, attracting international criticism. In her children's book *Tasmanian Friends and Foes* (1880), Louisa used the voice of one of her male characters to pronounce:

> I should advocate and insist on total abstinence in the matter of feather ornaments—birds' wings, and all such Red-Indian-squaw paraphernalia of the present silly and most cruel fashions. From the Arctic seas to tropical forests is now waged woman's war of extermination against the whole bird creation. Millions on millions of lovely, harmless—ay, more than harmless, *useful*—happy lives are sacrificed every year to gratify the depraved fancies of vain, idle women, who, if they cared to realise *our* ideal of the sex, would be too humane and gentle to endure the thought that a single sparrow should be destroyed for their pleasure.[16]

INVARIABLE EXTERMINATION

Louisa's interest in the fate of Australia's native fauna was more limited. While she looked on cruelty as a human failing, she regarded extinction as an inevitable consequence of colonisation. On finding no emus at Emu Plains on the Nepean River east of Sydney in 1839, she reflected: 'as civilised, and therefore doubly destructive man advances in a new country, he invariably exterminates or scares away the timid creatures that have for ages dwelt there undisturbed'.[17]

Like many early travellers across the Blue Mountains, Louisa initially believed that the animals most in danger were kangaroos, particularly the biggest species, popularly known as 'foresters'. When Barron Field saw his 'first and only kangaroo' at Bathurst in 1822, he predicted they would soon be extinct. A decade later Charles Darwin agreed after failing to see even one there. In similar vein, Louisa reported in 1844 that she did not see a kangaroo, and her Charles had never 'met with more than half a dozen. So effectually is the race being exterminated'.[18]

The colonists may not have been to blame. Eric Rolls has suggested that kangaroos were relatively rare on the mainland at the time of European settlement. They may have only become abundant around 1860, after Aboriginal hunting came to an end, grasses suited to kangaroos spread and there was a decline in the number of dingoes, which had traditionally been their main predators. But the standard explanation from the 1820s blamed the settlers. Field declared, 'The stockmen hunt them, and the cattle and sheep supplant them'. Darwin thought the colonists' greyhounds were the kangaroos' doom.[19]

These observations were not intended as criticisms. For example, Field was no more troubled by the possible disappearance of the kangaroo than he was by that of the beaver and wild deer in North America. He thought such extinctions just part of the process by which 'man necessarily advanced from the hunter to the pastoral state'. When Louisa wrote *Notes and Sketches of New South Wales*, she was so unconcerned by the fate of the kangaroo that she dismissed it in a footnote.[20]

Gradually, however, colonists began taking this issue more seriously. In 1846 the Tasmanian surveyor N. L. Kentish called for an end to the wholesale slaughter of kangaroos. He wanted new laws to be introduced and rigorously enforced to prevent the extinction of this 'beautiful species'. Louisa came to share this concern; in 1852 she lamented how Tasmania's police magistrates issued hunting licences so indiscriminately that the great grey kangaroo was 'in all the inhabited districts an extinct animal'.[21]

By then, Louisa was just as concerned about Tasmania's black swans. In 1804 David Collins had made one of the colony's first environmental laws to stop the settlers feasting on swans' eggs. Louisa feared the swans' extinction and was disturbed by the brutality with which her fellow colonists extracted the 'soft, thick white down'. As she described it:

> The general custom was, to take the birds in large quantities in the moulting season, when they are most easily captured and extremely fat; they were then confined in pens, *without any food*, to linger miserably for a time, till ready to die of starvation, because, whilst they are fat, the down can neither be so well stripped off, nor so effectually prepared. Troops of people make a trade in the eggs, taking these in immense quantities from all the known haunts of the swans, so as very nearly to exterminate them.

Twenty-five years later, Louisa was even more outspoken in her children's book *Tasmanian Friends and Foes*. Many of her contemporaries would have known whom she meant when her autobiographical character Mrs Merton identified 'a captain in the army, stationed at a central point on the east coast as a police magistrate' as the 'pioneer and ringleader' of the 'wretched hucksters' who carried out the 'greedy, sordid, cruel trade' in the eggs of black swans. With characteristic irony, she wrote:

> This gallant, noble officer had a boat and crew allowed him for the public service, and these he employed in a systematic raid upon the swans' nests, far and near, round the bays and lagoons . . . Hundreds and thousands of dozens of eggs were taken every season and sent up by him in the Government boats for sale in Hobart. Humbler, but equally greedy traders, following Captain M—'s example and continuing the traffic for a long series of years, . . . nearly succeeded in wiping the black swans from the face of the waters.[22]

Louisa was also alive to the impact of introduced animals on native species. In *Walch's Tasmanian Guide Book* for 1871, which she wrote anonymously, she railed at the destructiveness of feral cats, blaming them for the decline of indigenous quails. She declared:

> Let all sportsmen destroy bush cats, that game may increase; let all farmers destroy them, that their best friends, the bright little birds, may live, to devour the grubs, flies and caterpillars which will otherwise infest their grain and crops; and let all naturalists and lovers of nature destroy them, because every cat-life taken causes the saving of countless, beautiful, innocent, joyous creatures, which outweigh the value of a ferocious, skulking, treacherous beast of prey in an incalculable ratio.[23]

A TEMPLE IN THE WILDERNESS

The only plants Louisa valued almost as much as animals were ferns. In England, she rhymed:

> *The green and graceful Fern,*
> *How beautiful it is!*
> *There's not a leaf in all the land*
> *So wonderful, I wis.*

Louisa was even more excited by Australian ferns—particularly the tree ferns that Charles discovered in a valley near Port Sorell in the mid-1840s. Over the next forty years, Louisa celebrated this valley in poetry and prose, fiction and non-fiction. Each time, she cast it in religious terms. It was her 'temple in the wilderness'—'an ancient vaulted crypt'. Of all the places she described in Australia, it alone had 'almost a sacred character'.[24]

Because of this valley's remoteness, it remained more or less intact, but the fern gullies on Mount Wellington were very vulnerable because of their proximity to Hobart. When Louisa first made the despoliation of these gullies a public issue in 1852, she identified art as a cause, blaming sketching parties for littering the gullies with empty champagne bottles, corks and greasy sandwich papers. Twenty years later many of these areas had been destroyed. In *Walch's Tasmanian Guide Book* Louisa implicitly accepted the destruction caused by 'the increase of the town, and the yearly extending cultivation of its environs'. She was less forgiving of 'the exceedingly tasteless and senseless custom of cutting down long fronds or even whole fern trees to be conveyed into town, and set up or nailed up in . . . churches, ball rooms, flower shows, butcher's shops, and others'.[25]

Louisa's outrage was heightened by her sense that the ferns were sentient. It was 'an act of cruelty', she declared:

> to hack, to cut it down, to abase and crush its glorious symmetry, bruise and break its delicate transparent pinnules, cart it away through drying sun and wind, and dust, and set it up, withering, fading, limp, and melancholy in the corner of a room or staircase as an *ornament*.

Such fern-getting was wasteful and selfish: 'for the short-lived gratification of a depraved taste, the person who thus robs of their beauty these exquisite nooks of the mountain forest deprives all his fellows of their rightful legitimate pleasure therein'. What was commonly conceived as 'decoration' she dismissed as 'Goth-like barbarity'.[26]

Within a few years, other colonists were making similar protests. In his presidential address to the Royal Society of Tasmania in 1876, the Governor, Sir Frederick Weld, called for the slopes of Mount Wellington to be 'preserved to future generations as a noble public forest and park' in order to protect their ferns and trees. Although large parts of the mountain had already been alienated, Weld argued that these holdings should be reacquired immediately because 'any difficulty that might at present be incurred in dealing with private rights would be increased tenfold as years went by, whilst the injury already done was incalculable, and was going on from day to day'.[27]

By 1879 Louisa could look back on how she had 'protested earnestly, both with tongue and pen, for long years past' against 'the sin of destroying such scenes of loveliness'. But her ambition to see Mount Wellington's remaining fern valleys 'spared, and securely protected from destruction' remained unrealised, as did Weld's larger ambitions. Louisa suggested that if the popular botanical writer Francis George Heath, who had conceived England as *A Fern Paradise*, ever saw 'an untrodden, unspoiled Tasmanian fern-valley', he would realise that 'he had applied the epithet too soon'. But these valleys survived only in 'remote nooks' as 'the greedy Vandalism, which covets and destroys at a blow' had 'desolated near all the fern-groves near Tasmanian towns'.[28]

THE PROBLEM OF THE GUM TREE

Louisa always had less sympathy for gum trees. When she visited the conservatory of the Birmingham Botanic Gardens before leaving England, Charles introduced her to 'a scrawly, straggling little tree'. It was Louisa's first sight of a blue gum, and she was unimpressed. As she later noted, 'the miserable aspect of the poor exile did not lead me to anticipate much pleasure in seeing forests of its relatives here'.[29]

Louisa maintained this view in Australia. Like Barron Field, whose work she knew, she began by presenting the eucalypts as a symbol of all that was 'topsy-turvy' in the antipodes, because they were evergreen and lost their bark instead of being deciduous and losing their leaves. The only species she praised in New South Wales were those that struck her as more or less '*English*-looking'. One was the blue gum, which Meredith picked out because the bloom of its leaves provided 'a pleasing contrast to the dark olive-green tint of the commoner kinds' reviled by Field. The other was the peppermint, which even satisfied the conventional test of art, she maintained, because its leaves were brighter and thicker. She reported seeing 'some old ones that an artist would delight to sketch'.[30]

By 1852, when Louisa published *My Home in Tasmania*, visiting scientists had begun rejecting the cliché that Australia's flora was monotonous. Charles Wilkes of the United States Exploring Expedition had recognised that the number of Australian species rivalled that of Brazil, which was already renowned for its tropical diversity. The Polish polymath Paul de Strzelecki had observed that 'on near examination' the 'unvaried mantle of olive-green' covering Australia's forests possessed:

> much gracefulness in form both of species and of individual trees, and many delicate or minute shades of verdure, which, combined with the ever changing ash-grey colour of the shedding bark of the *Eucalyptae*, the undulating and often broken surface upon which it thrives, and the resplendent sky above, present a world of interest and attraction.[31]

Louisa disagreed. Like many other colonists, she felt herself 'some degrees nearer home' in Tasmania than New South Wales because the island was 'so much more English', but she still damned Tasmania's forests as 'monotonous'. To her, there was nothing 'more thoroughly wearisome both to mind and body' than 'a slow progress through these dreary-dark' domains. Again England provided her point of reference. These 'huge, tall, gaunt, bare half-dead trees' were 'as different from the verdant leafy, shadowy depths of an English wood as a decaying mis-shapen skeleton is from a perfect human form in vigorous life'. The thicker the forest, the more she railed against the 'universal gum trees'.[32]

Yet Louisa showed more discrimination than Godfrey Charles Mundy, whose two-volume account of Australia also appeared in 1852. Whereas Mundy took derision at the 'everlasting' gum trees to new extremes, Louisa maintained the conventional distinction between gum trees growing in ones and twos on grassland, which she admired, and dense forests, which she abhorred. Describing her arrival at Port Sorell in 1844, she exclaimed:

> Gigantic gum-trees rose on every side, and in every variety that such tall, straight, bare, gaunt things can exhibit; for handsome as *single* gum-trees frequently are, and thick-foliaged and massive in their sombre hues, those which grow clustered in the forests are almost invariably ugly.[33]

By 1860, the island's blue gums were exciting much more acclaim. Since the 1820s these trees had been recognised as exceptionally tall, fast-growing and suited to boat-building, but now the Royal Society of Tasmania and local businessmen began elaborating these utilitarian

LOUISA ANNE MEREDITH
TITLE-PAGE OF *OUR ISLAND HOME: A TASMANIAN SKETCHBOOK* 1879

arguments in an attempt to persuade the British government to turn to the blue gums for naval timber. One of Louisa's friends, the artist Mary Morton Allport, observed in her diary that 'nothing in the world is so graceful as the whitey-blue gums, except the English Birch, and that has not the lovely colour'.[34]

This new enthusiasm informed Louisa's children's book *Loved and Lost!* Twenty-one years after arriving in Australia, Louisa no longer thought of herself as English. While her view of the gum trees

LOUISA ANNE MEREDITH
BUCKLAND CHURCH AND PARSONAGE, PROSSER VALLEY
1879

remained equivocal, they had become 'our grand *Eucalypti*'. She explained:

> They are usually thought ugly by English people, and very many are undeniably so; but in some parts of the colony, where they seem to flourish as if they enjoyed themselves, many of the species attain an enormous size, and are truly magnificent trees. The blossoms, like great myrtle-flowers full of honey, are of different sizes, those of the blue gum being as large as a crown-piece, and the peppermint gum bearing clusters of little ones that would each hardly cover a threepenny piece.[35]

Louisa attached even greater significance to the blue gum in her lavish folio of lithographs, *Some of My Bush Friends in Tasmania*, which also appeared in 1860 and, like *Loved and Lost!*, included only her own plates. In the text accompanying one of her finest lithographs, 'Gum Flowers and "Love"'(page 126), she brought together all the arguments in favour of these 'noble' trees. The blue gum, she wrote, deserved to be considered as Tasmania's 'emblem-tree' because of its 'grandeur and giant proportions', 'the beauty of its great starry flowers', and 'the durability and value of its timber . . . for many uses equal, and for some, even preferable to oak'.[36]

Louisa was even more enthusiastic in her second lavish volume of lithographs, published in 1879. The increasing international interest in the blue gum's medicinal properties led her to put Tasmania's 'noblest tree' on her title page. At the same time, she lamented the loss of the park-like landscapes she had delighted in for forty years. Describing the Prosser Valley north of Buckland, where the Merediths had lived between 1855 and 1864, she complained that 'severe "utilitarian" improvement' was destroying the native trees. Were she to draw this scene again, 'the new drawing would probably make a worse picture than the old'.[37]

THE ROMANCE OF RUINS

Louisa's appreciation of the Australian landscape was even more affected by its dearth of places associated with what she regarded as significant historical events. In her landscape annual about the Wye Valley, published before she quit England in 1839, Louisa's primary concern was to contemplate 'the deeds and people of former times, as associated by History, and Tradition with the present'. Her enjoyment of the scenery of the Wye was fuelled by her knowledge of its human past. As she listened to the river, she imagined hearing 'the voices of "men of olden days", who dwelt, fought, or died within its sound'.[38]

Could Australia compare? Lieutenant Daniel Southwell, a member of the First Fleet, addressed this issue in 1788 when he fancied what colonists might make of Port Jackson. He imagined the harbour as the site of 'charming seats' and 'superb buildings' erected according to the latest fashion. More remarkably, his romantic sensibility led him to look forward to a time when the first great buildings erected by Europeans in Australia would be decaying and colonists could enjoy the sight of the 'grand ruins of stately edifices'.[39]

Fifty years later, at least the occasional visitor thought that Sydney already boasted old buildings of real interest. When the English businessman John Hood arrived in 1841, the first Government House was set to be demolished. Although Hood believed the building had just 'one good room in it', he felt it was worth preserving for its links

> with all the earlier associations of the colony—which some may possibly say it would be as well to forget, but not so I; on the contrary, I would value it, were it merely as being the scene of Governor Bligh's siege in this his own castle . . . In a word, I have a fancy for old things—old friends—old wine—and old houses.[40]

The clergyman–scientist William Woolls found the historical associations of the Australian landscape at least as rich. In his *Miscellanies in Prose* (1838), the first volume of essays published in Australia, Woolls accepted that there was some truth in the constant criticism that New South Wales was 'deficient in those interesting scenes which contribute so much to enliven and dignify the histories of other countries'. Yet Woolls maintained:

> Australia is not uninteresting to the lover of antiquity, for we may truly say that many of its scenes are calculated to awaken the most pleasing recollections. Can the admirer of classical lore survey the numerous flocks, which are now seen sporting over our plains, and be forgetful of those primitive ages when kings and queens tended their flocks, and valued them as their chief possessions? Can he behold the vine and the fig spreading luxuriantly over the land, and be unmindful of the beautiful passages in ancient writing which speak of them as the attendants of peace and plenty? And can he traverse the wide-spreading plain, climb the summit of the lofty range, or wander 'by gushing fount, wild wood, and shadowy dell', without calling to mind the inimitable descriptions of ancient poetry?[41]

James Martin identified very different associations in his rival *Australian Sketch Book*, which appeared a week after Woolls's volume. Martin, who was just eighteen years old, declared that he particularly enjoyed the conjunction of 'some historical incident . . . with a beautiful and romantic spot'. He detected an 'air of antiquity and veneration' at Bedlam Point on the Parramatta River, and was especially attracted by Captain Cook's landing place at Botany Bay, where the Philosophical Society of Australasia had erected a brass plaque to mark its own establishment in 1822. According to Martin, Botany Bay was the one spot in the colony 'hallowed by the memorable incidents of by-gone days, and rendered sacred by the transactions of illustrious men'. Although most colonists neglected it, Martin was not alone in his taste; he reported there was no spot 'more frequently visited by the lovers of the picturesque and the grand'.[42]

Still other colonists viewed giant trees as a link to a pre-European past, equating the trees' great size with great age. For Godfrey Charles Mundy, the 'few patriarchal trees that have survived storm and fire and axe' were Australia's only 'antiquities'. When another Anglican clergyman–scientist, William Branwhite Clarke, arrived in Sydney in 1839, he looked on the big old trees which surrounded the harbour as a symbol of a lost Golden Age. They were, he declared, 'relics of the forest as it was in the days of its primeval dignity when the lords of the soil roamed at will and were not branded as savages by comers from the other end of the globe'. Had Clarke had his way, these trees would have been preserved. As he put it, 'These are old trees and I would not cut them down'.[43]

Louisa's initial response was more conventional. In describing the 'fantastic forms' of Hassan's Walls in the Blue Mountains in 1844, she declared, 'Had I been travelling in an old country, I should at once have decided that these were truly the ruins of some mighty mountain-fortress of former days'. Had she been travelling 'in a romantic or legendary country', she would have identified 'loop-holes, arches, battlements, and buttresses'. But Louisa declared it impossible to entertain such ideas in New South Wales. '[N]one who know and have felt the leaden influence of its ledger and day-book kind of atmosphere', she wrote, 'would believe it guilty of suffering' from poetry or imagination.[44]

Louisa still found the Tasmanian landscape almost as devoid of history more than thirty years later. One of the few buildings to have satisfied her taste for the old and picturesque was a 'moss-grown wooden water-mill' near Perth, south of Launceston, which was 'as full of exquisite colour, and as innocent of perpendicularity in any line about it, as any artist-beloved old ruin in the most primitive Yorkshire dale'. Louisa found this mill 'specially precious and delightful' because it was 'so very rare, as looking really ancient and venerable in a young land'. But by the time she celebrated this 'treasure' in print, a flood had destroyed it.[45]

THE LIMITS OF COMPASSION

From the late eighteenth century, many campaigners against cruelty to animals championed an array of other causes on behalf of other-wise despised and disadvantaged human beings. In England William Wilberforce worked to end slavery as well as to outlaw bull-baiting and to found the Society for the Prevention of Cruelty to Animals. The same expanded moral concern was at work in the United States, where Harriet Beecher Stowe and Lydia Maria Child campaigned first against slavery, then to succour animals.[46]

Louisa failed to champion Australia's Aborigines in this way partly because of the Merediths' involvement in Tasmania's Black War in which at least two of their servants were killed and several others were harassed and speared, their horses killed and huts plundered. Most likely, the Merediths were largely to blame for these attacks. According to George Augustus Robinson, who embarked on his 'friendly mission' to conciliate the Aborigines in 1829, they committed 'many aggressions' on the Aborigines. But Charles cast them as innocents, dwelling instead on 'the horrors, and terrors, and hairbreadth escapes of his younger days in the colony when every bush within spear-throw of the house was a source of danger'.[47]

Louisa's views must also have been shaped by the killing of Charles's brother George by South Australian Aborigines in 1835 or 1836. According to Robinson, who investigated George's death for Governor Arthur, Meredith had seized Aboriginal women from Point Nepean and Port Lincoln on the Australian mainland and sold them to sealers in Bass Strait. The Aborigines who killed Meredith had done so as 'a just retribution' for the injuries done to them. But the *Hobart Town Courier* maintained that George had been 'barbarously murdered'—a verdict echoed by a host of later South Australian accounts.[48]

Louisa's understanding of these events was probably formed by what she was told by Charles and other members of his family. Having arrived in Hobart well after Tasmania's Black War ended, Louisa may have known little or nothing of the Merediths' aggression against the island's Aborigines. She may also have been ignorant of George's business as a slave trader in Bass Strait since he had probably broken with his family when he embarked on this venture and Robinson's report to Governor Arthur was never published. But it may also be that Louisa suppressed this side of the Merediths' colonial experience in order to preserve their reputation.[49]

The closest Louisa came to expressing concern for Australia's Aborigines was in *Notes and Sketches of New South Wales*, where she claimed to have 'strong misgivings as to the equity' of the dispossession of native peoples. But Louisa still cast the European settlement of New South Wales as the 'least objectionable' in all 'the cruel annals of colonization' because it had generally been 'peacefully effected' and 'the scanty aboriginal population' continued to enjoy 'a superfluous abundance . . . of both land and sustenance'. She castigated Aboriginal men as 'always tyrannical, and often brutally cruel' to their wives. She lampooned their malnourished children, likening their 'naked, long-armed, large-stomached, little bodies' to 'a new sort of spider'.[50]

When Louisa returned to these issues in *My Home in Tasmania*, it was a commonplace that Europeans were to blame for the Black War. Charles Darwin had 'no doubt' that 'this train of evil and its consequences originated in the infamous conduct of some of our countrymen'. The explorer John Lort Stokes declared the destruction of the Tasmanian Aborigines a 'national crime' for which the whites bore 'moral responsibility'. Godfrey Charles Mundy attributed the Aborigines' ferocity to 'the outrages received by them from the brutal convict population'. Louisa dismissed this view, maintaining that nothing could be 'further from the truth' than to blame the violence on 'unprovoked acts of aggression and violence on the part of the whites'.[51]

The challenge for Louisa was to explain why hostilities had flared after settlers and Aborigines had lived together for twenty years in relative peace. Most likely the conflict was a result of intense competition over land caused by pastoral expansion. But relying on Charles, whom she quoted at length, Louisa rejected this explanation, maintaining that:

> The quantity of land occupied by the English . . . was comparatively speaking so small, as not to be felt by [the Aborigines] as a deprivation, even had they not gained rather than lost by the change, in the food given them by the settlers.[52]

Louisa and Charles fixed instead on an external agent—a New South Wales Aborigine known as 'Musquito' or 'Mosquito' who was transported to Tasmania in 1813 but promised repatriation in return for tracking bushrangers. When his efforts went unrewarded, Mosquito turned against the settlers. For nine months in 1823–24, before he was captured and hanged, he was at the forefront of Aboriginal resistance to European settlement. With a Tasmanian Aborigine known as Black Jack, he led the Laremairremener people in killing five stockkeepers. Louisa and Charles suggested much greater bloodshed, claiming that Mosquito had initiated 'a war of extermination, both of man and beast'. The Aborigines 'spared neither age nor sex; the aged woman and the helpless child alike fell victims to their ferocity'.[53]

The one exception admitted by the Merediths was that Aboriginal women 'would often steal away from the tribe, and give notice of an intended attack'. But there was no such recognition of Aboriginal humanity in the Merediths' account of the dearth of Aboriginal children. Louisa declared:

> The disappearance of the young children among the natives compels us to the inference that they were destroyed; doubtless on account of the difficulty of conveying them about in the rapid flights from place to place which the blacks now practised in the perpetration of their murders. No white people ever found or killed any children that I am aware of, and few after this time were seen with the tribes; the dreadful conclusion seems therefore unavoidable.

Louisa either did not realise or would not admit that the kidnapping of Aboriginal women and the ravages of gonorrhoea were primarily to blame.[54]

Over the next forty years, Louisa reiterated her views on Aborigines ever more vehemently, as did her friend, the former Surveyor-General James Calder, who contributed to her *Tasmanian Guide Book* in 1871 and shared her outrage at cruelty to animals. In 1869 the St David's Literary and Musical Society in Hobart heard Louisa recite a new ballad about the killing of a family of colonists by 'black devils'. In 1880 she not only maintained that the Aborigines had benefited from European settlement because the settlers had given them 'food and blankets and other things', but argued that the Aborigines were incapable of understanding how the colonists' occupation of the country would ultimately affect them because they were 'the very lowest type of humanity; the ugliest, least intelligent, and least teachable of savages'.[55]

Louisa's anger was most apparent in 1891 in her last book of lithographs, *Bush Friends in Tasmania*. Although she presented it as just a volume of 'Native Flowers, Fruits, and Insects', Louisa went out of her way to defend the reputation of 'pioneers' like Charles against the commonplace that they had 'slaughtered' the Aborigines

Louisa Anne Meredith
Wooden Fruits 1891

to make room for sheep and cattle. In a section nominally about the 'Wooden Fruits' of protaceae, she declared:

> I have lived in the colony fifty years hearing with eager interest the tales of adventure, trial, and peril which so many had to relate; but not one of these contained a single incident implying wrong or hurt to a native or—and this is peculiarly significant—do any of the wholesale assertions as to the settlers' 'cruelty' give one detailed narrative of the murderous or cruel acts, nor mention any names of individuals accused.

According to Louisa, the pioneers led 'lives of noble labour and privation' and 'deserved better of posterity . . . than to have cruel slanders spoken about their graves'.[56]

PRINCIPLE INTO PRACTICE

Hunting was one issue on which the Merediths were divided. What Charles looked on as 'sport', Louisa thought a 'murderous diversion'. Yet when Charles needed help with a little pigeon shooting, Louisa gave way. With remarkable candour, she admitted: 'I must not deny being an accomplice for, by walking up the lands of the field, I put up the birds, whilst he shot them as they flew over towards the scrub'.[57]

Louisa wrote at length about her own appetite for ferns. In *My Home in Tasmania* she recounted how, when Charles showed her the 'enchanted' valley near their home at Port Sorell, she made 'a collection' of small ferns new to her. In her first volume of *Bush Friends*, she described how, 'as usual', she collected 'ferns, leaves, flowers, grasses, moss' on an excursion to Mount Wellington. She reported more fern-gathering on the mountain in her *Guide Book*.[58]

How could Louisa be untroubled by this collecting, yet protest so vehemently at the destruction wrought by others? Most likely, she believed that collections like her own had a valuable educative function, unlike those taken for purely ornamental purposes. She probably also believed that small-scale fern-gathering by her family and friends had an insignificant impact. She did not consider how it defiled the 'primeval beauty' she valued so much, nor how its cumulative impact could be just as destructive as the decorators' depredations.

The greatest test of Louisa's values was in relation to clearing. In *Notes and Sketches of New South Wales* she joined the international chorus of criticism of settlers in the New World. Like Anna Jameson in Ontario, she wrote from the perspective of a visiting Englishwoman. Without bothering to consider what might have prompted settlers to take up their axes with such vigour, she declared:

> The system of 'clearing' here, by the total destruction of every native tree and shrub, gives a most bare, raw, and ugly appearance to a new place. In England we plant groves and woods, and think our country residences unfinished and incomplete without them; but here the exact contrary is the case, and unless a settler can see an expanse of bare, naked, unvaried, shadeless, dry, dusty land spread all around him, he fancies his dwelling 'wild and uncivilized'.

Louisa was equally judgmental when she described how colonists treated the rest of their land. As she put it with characteristic spleen, 'ugly blackened and burned stumps' covered so much of the island that it resembled 'a large and closely occupied graveyard'. Like Anna Jameson, Louisa was horrified by ringbarking. Just as Jameson described 'ringing' as producing 'a ghastly forest of tall white spectres', Louisa declared that the 'huge leafless skeletons' of ringbarked trees had 'an indescribably dreary and desolate appearance'.[59]

Louisa began by being one of the rare colonists to put different values into practice. Whether knowingly or not, she and Charles followed the prescriptions of the Sydney nurseryman Thomas Shepherd by retaining some native trees on their first Tasmanian farm at Oyster Cove. When the Merediths established their garden, they marked a 'singularly handsome' blackwood 'for preservation, amidst the doomed throng of less eligible residents'. Although they removed most of a grove of wattles from in front of their house, they retained 'a few handsome groups or single trees . . . for ornament'. Other trees 'adorned the unploughed marsh and sheep-run', and there were 'fine belts of trees' along the two rivers that ran through their property.[60]

Yet, as Louisa herself described it, the Merediths' life at Oyster Cove remained an 'ever-recurring' sequence of digging, clearing, grubbing, ploughing, sowing and reaping. When Charles was clearing around their house, Louisa 'enjoyed lending a helping hand' and delighted in the fruits of their work. Her satisfaction at their first harvest matched that of John Glover almost a decade before in *My Harvest Home*. She wrote:

> Heavy and luxuriant were the crops our new land yielded us, and most pleasant it was to see wide fields of golden grain waving in the sunshine, and rows of sturdy reapers busily plying their gleaming sickles, where, only the year before, we had with difficulty threaded our tortuous way through scrub and forest.[61]

The Merediths were no different from their neighbours when it came to creating new fields for agriculture. They even sometimes resorted to ringbarking, which remained an 'experimental' form of clearing during the 1840s. While Louisa sought to preserve at least a few trees, applying the same aesthetics to the fields as to the garden, she could not persuade Charles, who looked on this domain in purely utilitarian terms. Louisa recorded:

> I often vainly interceded for the life of some noble tree, which, as its tall kindred fell all around it, looked so grand and ornamental, and so pleasing an object in the general clearance, that I would have gladly preserved it; but the harbour which trees in the middle of fields afford to the opossums, and the destructive, but most beautiful little parrots which abound here, was always urged against me, and the death-doom rarely averted, even by most eloquent pleading . . .[62]

Louisa and Charles were forced to leave this property in 1844, when Charles's incompetence as a farmer was compounded by a severe economic depression. Their new home was a rough timber cottage in a small clearing near Port Sorell on Tasmania's north coast. Louisa dubbed it a 'Castle Dismal'. Before long she came to understand why colonists were so eager to create open space around them. Although she did not withdraw her previous indictment of the settlers' axework, she confessed that one of her 'few amusements' at Port Sorell was burning 'victim-trees'. For a good evening's entertainment, the Merediths would 'fire-stick' five or six trees, delighting in the blaze and the extension of their clearing.[63]

THE LEGISLATOR

The year 1860 was a turning point for both Louisa and Charles when it came to environmental protection. While Louisa began expressing her concerns with unprecedented force in *Loved and Lost!* and *Some of My Bush Friends in Tasmania*, Charles used his position as a member of the Tasmanian Legislative Assembly to introduce a Bill protecting black swans' eggs. Charles also unsuccessfully tabled a petition calling for the protection of kangaroos. One of the petitioners' goals was to ensure an enduring supply of game for sport, which Louisa reviled, but she would have applauded their desire to preserve the kangaroos from 'utter extermination'.[64]

While Louisa privately deplored the government's unwillingness to incur any expense preserving native fauna, both Charles and Louisa liked to see the Black Swans Act as Tasmania's first legislation to protect endangered species and as an effective means of doing so. They were proud that Charles had persisted in trying to protect the swans despite intense criticism. In a letter to James Calder in the late 1860s, Louisa described how when Charles 'introduced his bill . . . he was jeered and ridiculed but he *passed it*—to my great joy'. In

1874 Charles similarly reminded the Legislative Assembly of 'the abuse, the ridicule which he received for attempting to protect [the] black swans'. In 1884 Louisa echoed, 'The first effort made to protect them was received in a manner calculated to daunt one less determined; but, undeterred by scoff and jeer, Mr Meredith persevered session after session until he carried his point'.[65]

In fact, the Tasmanian Parliament was not the obstacle that Louisa remembered. The Black Swans Bill was enacted at Charles's first attempt, just six weeks after he introduced it in late July. A Native Game Act—which was introduced by Thomas Lloyd Gellibrand and established a closed season for wild ducks, teal, quail, plover, bittern, emus and bronze-winged pigeons—was enacted with even greater ease in less than a fortnight in September 1860.

Yet Louisa did not exaggerate the 'scoffs and jeers' that the Black Swans Bill excited. When Charles introduced his Bill, the *Launceston Examiner* exclaimed:

> For our part we are unable to conceive of any argument in favour of the measure, and when the notice first appeared on the paper we thought it a brainless hoax. Of what special use are black swans to the colonists of Tasmania that the legislature should be asked to throw over them the shield of its protection? Neither the sportsman nor the epicurean would give a pin for a gross of them, and although the skin is covered with a beautiful white down it is rendered almost valueless from the difficulty of removing the overlying black feathers.

The *Examiner* went on to argue that legislative intervention was pointless, as the black swan and many other species were doomed to extinction. Sixteen years before Trucanini died, it declared:

> The primitive human denizens of our forests have been extirpated, and all the lower tribes of animals that refuse to yield allegiance to civilised man must share a similar fate. But we do not apprehend that this event, however distressing to zoologists, will be attended with very alarming consequences to the colony . . . Tasmania will still exist, and perchance prosper too, when the black swan, like the Dodo, shall live only in the history of the past.[66]

This abuse may have intimidated Charles. Over the next eight years, he failed to introduce or support any other animal protection legislation, and then simply endorsed a new Native Game Act introduced by the Attorney-General, William Dobson. Another eight years elapsed before he supported legislation establishing a closed season for brush and forest kangaroos—a move favoured by members of the Southern Hunt Club.[67]

Charles only re-emerged as a significent advocote of environmental protection in 1879, just before ill-health forced him to quit the Tasmanian Parliament. On one remarkable day in May, he began by seeking the establishment of a select committee to examine the best means of preserving and propagating oysters. As an allied measure, he introduced a Bill to protect seagulls from wilful destruction. He then called for another select committee to examine how Huon pines could be preserved. A little later he moved that a licence be required to carry guns on unalienated Crown land and proposed that, in the interests of 'religion and humanity', licensed vehicles drawn by animals be prohibited from operating in all Tasmanian towns on Sundays. Finally, he introduced a Bill to strengthen the colony's Prevention of Cruelty to Animals Act, which William St Paul Gellibrand had introduced in 1877.[68]

Yet when the Assembly appointed Charles to chair both the select committees he wanted, he made little of these positions. Each committee met just twice and examined only three witnesses whose testimony, as the *Launceston Examiner* recognised, was 'singularly inconclusive and in some respects contradictory'. While Charles and Louisa's fourth son, Owen, maintained that there was only one remaining forest of Huon pine, one of the other witnesses testified that pine grew along nearly all the rivers in Tasmania's south-west. Rather than hear further evidence, Charles predictably agreed with Owen; his committee concluded that 'in accessible places, the full-grown trees are all cut down, and trees only one foot in diameter are being sacrificed' and recommended that 'the felling of Huon pine be prohibited, save under regulations to be made by the Governor-in-Council'.[69]

This recommendation had no more impact than most of Charles's other measures. The Assembly rejected his claim that gun licences would stop 'wanton destruction of game and add thousands of pounds to Treasury coffers'. Charles's fellow parliamentarians equally dismissed his attempt to invoke the Fourth Commandment as a basis for banning the use of horse and bullock-drawn vehicles on Sundays. When he argued that seagulls should be protected because they ate a species of crab which was the 'great enemy' of oysters, his Bill failed to receive a second reading.[70]

Charles's Bill amending Tasmania's Cruelty to Animals Act was his one success. In addition to widening the Act so that it covered animals carried by hand as well as those in vehicles, this Bill recognised the Tasmanian Society for the Prevention of Cruelty to Animals, which Louisa had played a key role in establishing a year before. Charles ensured that the society would receive the entire penalty for any successful prosecution it instigated under the Act, and half the sum where someone else was the informant. These provisions gave his wife's new society a vital source of revenue.[71]

'MY DEAR HUSBAND'

What was Louisa's contribution to this legislation? Her involvement in Charles's public career is suggested by one of her letters to Henry Parkes, who had become an admirer of her writing in England when she was contributing to the *Birmingham Journal*. In most unladylike fashion, Louisa tried to use her influence to secure Charles an official position in New South Wales. She wrote:

> I have been wondering if your colleagues might not have some office in which my dear husband's clear sense and ability combined with his so long intimate knowledge of colonial affairs of *every* kind might be valuable? He *found* our Tasmanian official business in almost chaotic confusion—he left it so straight and simple that his subordinates declared their work was not half what it used to be.[72]

Even stronger evidence of Louisa's influence emerged after her death in 1895. According to one of her obituaries, Louisa 'aided and sustained' Charles 'in his public career by the vigour of her own intelligence, which was almost masculine in some respects'. More than thirty years later, Margaret Swann credited Louisa with using 'her strong powers of organisation in connection with his election campaigns, though 'this was done as unobtrusively as possible' because of the 'prevailing prejudice against women taking part in politics'. In 1979 Louisa's biographer, Vivienne Rae Ellis, presented Charles as a cipher for Louisa, particularly when it came to environmental causes.[73]

Yet Charles's political reputation, while mixed, suggests he was a significant figure in his own right. When he quit Parliament in 1879, the Hobart *Mercury* declared:

> It may be safely said of him that he never made of a political opponent a friend, that he has scarcely ever had a political friend who he has not made an opponent; and he has done more than any other Tasmanian politician to lower the dignity of Parliamentary debate.

By contrast, an obituary in the *Town and Country Journal* in 1880 judged him

> the very Rupert of debate—fearless, earnest, honest, truthful, witty, and withal uncompromising . . . His enmities were political. He did not make them personal . . . Even those who most suffered under the withering sarcasm of his scathing tongue, whilst they feared honoured the man and paid tribute to his dauntless nature.[74]

Another of Louisa's surviving letters also suggests that her influence over Charles's legislative agenda was far from absolute. In response to a request from James Calder for help securing parliamentary action to protect mutton birds, Louisa advised Calder to approach the Attorney-General, William Dobson, who had just secured a new Native Game Act. Louisa wrote: 'From what I read of Mr Dobson's good intents touching ducks and other water birds, I think *he* would be a good champion to enlist. I would *try him*.' Louisa also indicated that her 'good husband' would support Calder in his 'mutton bird crusade', but she declined to 'bring the matter before the master'.[75]

Louisa also wrote very different accounts of the Black Swans Act. In a letter to Calder in the 1860s and her memoir about Charles in the 1880s, she wrote as if he had been solely responsible for this legislation. Yet Louisa's advocacy of such a measure in *My Home in Tasmania* suggests that she was also behind it. Louisa implied as much in *Tasmanian Friends and Foes*, where she had Mrs Merton tell her children: 'how all of us who dared to advocate such an unheard-of measure were ridiculed and assailed with all manner of abuse, perhaps your father and I know best'.[76]

THE ART OF THE POSSIBLE

By 1878 there were societies for the prevention of cruelty to animals in Victoria, New South Wales and South Australia, but not Tasmania. Then a group of boys set their dogs on a cat in a Hobart street and the local *Mercury* made the most of the story. According to its initial report, when the dogs failed to kill the cat, the boys lit a fire 'and flung the poor half-killed cat into it, roasting it slowly to death'. Although the 'cries of the animal and the fiendish delight of the perpetrators of this atrocity' were 'something dreadful', no one intervened.[77]

Until then, there had been just one prosecution under Tasmania's Cruelty to Animals Act in the nineteen months it had been law. By one account most members of the public did not realise that the Act had been passed; even 'the subordinate members of the police force generally were unaware of its existence'. The *Mercury*'s protests prompted the police to charge one of the boys, who would have been jailed for three months had not his milkman father paid his £5 fine.[78]

Louisa and Mary Selena Gellibrand, William Gellibrand's niece, looked to secure more lasting benefits from this outcry by establishing a local Society for the Prevention of Cruelty to Animals. Their activism probably reinforced the view that 'there was something effeminate in having regard for the sufferings of the lower order of animals'. In England women probably always comprised a majority of members of the Society for the Prevention of Cruelty, and in the 1870s they finally began occupying its formal offices; the Tasmanian society was created by women. After 'an incredible amount of work' by Louisa and Mary Selena, the new society was instituted at a public meeting in Hobart, with Louisa its honorary secretary.[79]

One immediate issue was whether the Tasmanian society would try to put an end to hunting and coursing, which were widely believed to cause animals 'unnecessary fear'. A correspondent of the *Mercury* even suggested that coursing constituted 'aggravated cruelty, because of probable greater intensity of suffering, in the agonising terror and tragic death of the hounded hare'. Yet the new society's president, the Governor, Sir Frederick Weld, promptly warned it against taking such 'extreme positions'. As 'an old sportsman' and patron of several hunt clubs, Weld refused to countenance any criticism of hunting.[80]

The obvious implication was that Weld wanted the new society to engage in class discrimination—a long-standing charge against such groups. A decade earlier, John Stuart Mill had declined the vice-presidency of the English Society for the Prevention of Cruelty because it confined itself 'to the offences committed by the uninfluential classes of society'. In similar vein, an anonymous correspondent of the *Mercury* protested:

> For blackguards, ignorant and debased, to maltreat dogs in upper, or cats in lower Goulburn street is cruelty to be dealt with by the lash; not so, however, should gentlemen in scarlet or broadcloth urge poor horses over a four-mile course, plying spur and whip with increasing energy as they perceive the strength of their miserable victims failing them; not so, should gentlemen chase a timid hare or deer over hill and dale, which flying vainly for its life, is ultimately dragged down and rent to death by their fierce, swift dogs; not so if gentlemen liberate birds from traps that, falling around, shattered and maimed, they may afford sport to a fashionable, vice-regal Society, pledged to do away, by the lash if necessary, that foul blot on a civilised and Christian community, 'cruelty to animals'.[81]

Louisa probably sympathised with this view. In her books she condemned the cruelty of both the lower and upper classes. But pragmatism probably persuaded her to heed Weld's strictures. As the *Mercury* explained, the new society 'would not carry public opinion with it' if it attacked hunting and hence 'would be powerless for good'. According to the *Mercury*:

> All the societies in Christendom will not succeed in putting a stop to hunting, coursing, fishing, and such like sports. Why, therefore, peril the possible by attempting the impossible. Because the Society cannot do all it might desire is no reason why it should do nothing.[82]

Over the following year, much of the society's work was educational. It published sections of the Cruelty to Animals Act on placards and handbills and gave them to cab-drivers. It encouraged schoolmasters to enrol their students as members of the society's 'scholars' branches', offered Christmas prizes for children's essays and distributed 500 copies of an address by Louisa to 'Young Australia' on the treatment of domestic pets. It also confronted offenders—sending more than fifty letters of remonstrance to colonists who reportedly had ill-used animals and shaming many others by publicly describing their wrongdoing at its meetings and hence in the columns of the *Mercury*.[83]

The society also invoked the law, either directly or indirectly, aided by several honorary inspectors, an honorary veterinary surgeon and an honorary legal adviser as well as a full-time inspector whose position was funded out of subscriptions and donations. Under some public pressure, the society extended its operations to horseracing and persuaded the Tasmanian Race Club Committee to punish any jockey 'found guilty of whipping or spurring a horse after the winning post has been passed, or using a whip or spur after all chance of winning had been lost'. The society also encouraged the Hobart police to bring prosecutions and succeeded in twenty-five of the thirty prosecutions it initiated itself in its first year.[84]

Governor Weld duly congratulated the society on 'wisely . . . not attempting the impracticable', but except for one prosecution at Spring Bay on Tasmania's east coast, it seems the Act remained unenforced outside Hobart until mid-1879, when Launceston's Superintendent of Police instituted a series of prosecutions for cruelty to horses. At the same time, another case of cruelty prompted Launceston's Benevolent Society to consider whether it should expand its activities beyond the welfare of the poor to the well-being of animals. Soon the town's *Examiner* was calling for local action.[85]

Louisa made the most of this opportunity. As secretary of the Tasmanian society in Hobart, she possibly did not even wait for an invitation before sending a 'large package of information' to the Benevolent Society. When she arrived in Launceston, where Charles had just been appointed police magistrate, Louisa played a key role in persuading a public meeting that it should establish a branch of the Tasmanian society rather than create a separate association. Having previously agreed to become secretary of the Launceston society once she had resigned her position in Hobart, Louisa then became honorary secretary to the new, enlarged society.[86]

Although Mary Selena Gellibrand soon took over most of her work, Louisa remained as ready as ever to express her concerns. As late as 1893, aged eighty, she wrote to the *Mercury* twice in four days condemning the 'inhuman process' by which sheep and cattle were shipped from New South Wales to Tasmania, and also asked her old friend, Sir Henry Parkes, to see whether he could exercise his 'weighty influence' in New South Wales 'in getting the cruel mischief remedied'. When she died in 1895, few other women had done so much to promote environmental protection, in Australia or elsewhere. Neither had any other colonial author or artist, male or female.[87]

Louis Buvelot *Gisborne Hill from the Slopes of Mount Macedon* 1875

CHAPTER SIX

THE MASTER OF THE GUM TREE

He was the first to point out how admirably the despised gum, box, peppermint, and stringy-bark trees will lend themselves to pictorial treatment when judiciously handled. He studied their physiognomy, and he reproduced every feature of it—stem, bough, branch and leaf—with conscientious accuracy, but without elaboration of detail. For all artistic purposes, indeed, he may be said to have discovered these trees. Previously, people looked upon them as containing so many tons of firewood.

JAMES SMITH, 'THE BUVELOT LOAN EXHIBITION',

ARGUS, 10 JULY 1888

ARTISTS HAVE LONG been credited with changing the way we look at nature. In 1823 John Constable declared that Richard Wilson had shown 'to the world the hidden stores and beauties of Nature . . . what exists in nature but which was not known till his time'. Fifty years later colonial critics were making the same claim for Louis Buvelot, who took just a few years to establish himself as Melbourne's leading artist after emigrating from Switzerland in 1864. For much of the 1870s and 1880s, Buvelot was recognised as the one Victorian artist whose work rose 'beyond mediocrity'; he was also the only landscape painter who had commissions 'always largely in advance of his productions'.[1]

Buvelot made his reputation with a few large canvases, but he maintained it with pictures that combined modest scale with modest subject matter. What excited his contemporaries about Buvelot's paintings was his ability to find poetry in the prosaic, transforming the ordinary and accessible, rather than searching out new romantic subjects in the most remote parts of Victoria as Eugene von Guérard and Nicholas Chevalier had done. Part of this transformation of the commonplace was Buvelot's treatment of gum trees in paintings such as *Gisborne Hill from the Slopes of Mount Macedon* and *Near Lilydale*. Time and again, Buvelot's contemporaries credited these pictures with leading them to stop 'despising' the eucalypts and instead to see that they were at least the equal of the oak, the ash and the elm.

This claim is a radical one. If Buvelot's admirers were right and colonists suddenly came to admire the gum tree in the 1870s and 1880s, this shift would be comparable to the revaluation of 'mountain gloom' as 'mountain glory' in eighteenth-century Europe. Although Raymond Williams has argued that this shift was just an addition to fashionable taste in which mountains and forests became new 'objects of conspicuous aesthetic consumption', it has more commonly been seen as a revolutionary change in the way Europeans looked on wild nature. If Buvelot led his contemporaries to see the gum tree differently, his achievement would be equally profound.[2]

One problem with this argument is its premiss that the great majority, if not all, colonists despised the eucalypts when Buvelot arrived in Australia. Another problem is in establishing that many colonists came to look more favourably on the gum trees while Buvelot was painting in Melbourne, let alone that this shift in values was due to his work. When W. K. Hancock famously declared

LOUIS BUVELOT
NEAR LILYDALE 1871

'The invaders hated trees', he was thinking of the second half of the nineteenth century when, as he recorded, 'tree-murder by ring-barking devastated the country on a gigantic scale'.[3] Could colonists' aesthetic preferences have been at such variance from what they did to their environment, or did Buvelot's admirers exaggerate the extent of his influence?

THE DOCTRINE OF WASTE

Thomas Power lives through the law reports. He was the first landowner in Australia to resort to court to stop clearing. Power acted in 1856 when Charles Bedford, a tenant on his land at Booroondara near Melbourne, persisted in felling trees for sale as firewood without grubbing up the stumps. Power's complaint was that Bedford was stripping the land of valuable trees without rendering it suitable for cultivation. He sought an injunction to stop Bedford's axework, and damages for the loss he had already suffered.[4]

Like many legal proceedings, Power's action provides a window into contemporary life and values. His case is significant not only for what it reveals about colonial attitudes to clearing but also because it tested whether the law should be the same in Australia as in England. Much as colonial artists born and trained in Europe needed to adapt to the novel environment, Australian judges had to decide whether and when they should depart from established English law in order to develop new doctrines arguably more suited to colonial conditions.

Power's case raised these issues because Bedford argued—and Power did not deny—that in Victoria, unlike England, it was 'the usage and custom of the country . . . to cut and dispose of the trees without restriction'. Four adjoining landholders called by Bedford confirmed that the way in which he felled trees and left their stumps was 'the usual mode' of cultivation. They testified that, just as in New South Wales in the first years of settlement, 'it was not the usage to grub trees on a bush farm. That the expense would have been too great, and no tenant would have undertaken a farm on such terms.'[5]

Yet the fact that Power brought this case—and other landlords instituted similar actions in the late 1850s and early 1860s[6]—reflects the increased value of timber in Victoria after the gold rushes. Justice Molesworth emphasised this point when he held that he had to judge the agreement between Power and Bedford according to attitudes prevailing in 1849, when the lease was entered into, rather than those applying in 1856.[7] At the same time, the limited success of landlords in these cases is a mark of how Justice Molesworth, who heard them all, continued to look on eucalypts as a burden on the land.

One issue in Power's case concerned the applicability of the English doctrine of 'waste', which restricted and sometimes prohibited tenants from felling trees. When American courts considered this doctrine soon after Independence, they recognised the local enthusiasm for clearing by modifying the common law. In general, they held that waste was not committed if clearing allowed land to be cultivated and improved the value of the estate. These decisions allowed tenants to destroy some, but not all, timber on their land, because the courts held that wholesale clearing would 'essentially and permanently diminish the value of the inheritance'.[8]

The colonial status of judges in nineteenth-century Australia led them to be much slower to develop their own common law, regardless of whether English precedents suited Australian conditions. In this case, however, Justice Molesworth indicated that the novel environment might warrant novel law. As he put it, 'there is a great difference in the state of things in Victoria and England;

timber here being superabundant and not of value, as at home'. He also made plain that aesthetics should not constrain colonial land use, declaring that the English doctrine protecting 'ornamental' timber did not apply where there were no buildings on the land, and that 'mere huts' were 'not to be protected as mansions'. But because he found that Power and Bedford had entered into a special agreement, he did not have to decide whether to apply or reject the English rules. According to Molesworth, both parties had agreed that 'the very felling of the trees, leaving stumps, improved the pasturage, and was for the benefit of the land'.[9]

MAN AND NATURE

The idea that clearing could change climate was first explored in classical Greece by Theophrastus of Eresus, and attracted renewed attention in Europe after Theophrastus's work was republished during the Renaissance. In Australia, it was a cause of concern from the first years of European settlement. Already in 1795, Richard Atkins wondered whether the colonists' clearing was to blame for 'excessive cold showers' when 'every year before this we had hot weather'.[10]

This concern increased during the nineteenth century, although colonists held radically different views about the consequences of clearing. Barron Field and the Reverend Robert Knopwood speculated in the 1820s that it had led the temperature to drop in New South Wales and Tasmania. William Charles Wentworth similarly observed:

> The coldness of the climate keeps pace with the progress of agriculture. In the more contiguous and cultivated districts, the natural grass becomes every year more affected by the influence of the frost.

By contrast, the Polish scientist Paul Strzelecki maintained in 1845 that the colonists' destruction of scrubs and forests 'must have necessarily rendered the climate . . . both drier and hotter'.[11]

This fear that the dry continent would become even drier reached unprecedented levels in the 1860s. Initially, however, it failed to increase regard for native trees, because the colonists who were convinced that deforestation caused desiccation were all keen acclimatisers. One of the most prominent was Edward Wilson, the proprietor of the *Argus*, which welcomed the clearing of native forest in 1860 even as it lamented that most Victorians were not sufficiently alive to how rainfall decreased as land was denuded of timber. The *Argus* adopted this stance partly on the basis that Australia's native timber was 'neither useful nor ornamental'. Echoing Barron Field, it declared that the cabinet-maker could apply the gum tree 'to no purpose' and the landscape painter could 'do nothing with such unpromising materials'. But the *Argus* also argued that colonists had nothing to fear because planting of exotic deciduous trees 'would more than counteract the ill effects to be anticipated from the constant destruction of our native timber'.[12]

Wilson and the *Argus* became even more concerned about climate change in 1863–64 after nearly all the gum trees died in a twenty-mile belt in Victoria's Western District and patches of dead and dying trees were discovered from Hamilton to Geelong. But while the *Argus* emphasised the importance of preserving the surviving forests as an interim measure, its primary concern remained the identification of 'superior' exotic trees 'really adapted to the country and susceptible of successful plantation'. The *Argus* maintained that the 'noble' oak and elm failed this test. While recognising the 'general wish' to introduce these trees from 'the old country', the *Argus* feared they would 'degenerate' in Australia's very different climate. Because they were deciduous, it also rejected them on aesthetic grounds, arguing that they would be 'inharmonious' with the Australian winter landscape. The solution, it maintained, lay with evergreens from countries with climates similar to Australia, such as Italian stone pines.[13]

When El Niño caused another drought soon after Buvelot arrived in 1864, it heightened appreciation of Victoria's native trees. As the Government Astronomer, Robert Ellery, observed a few years later, the effect of forests on rainfall only pressed 'on the *public* mind in times of . . . water famine'. The Government Botanist, Ferdinand von Mueller, argued that large-scale tree-planting would 'exercise a marvellous effect on the increase of rain, on the retention of humidity, and on the mitigation of burning winds'. The weekly *Australasian* maintained that every existing tree felled unnecessarily was 'a positive loss to the community' because of the loss of moisture to the ground. If timber-getters were left 'to work their own sweet wills upon the forests', Victoria would become another Sahara. 'The thing must be stopped', it declared, 'and stopped summarily'.[14]

These arguments were strengthened by George Perkins Marsh's *Man and Nature*, which was published in New York and London in 1864 and reached Victoria a year later. Marsh recognised that, 'of all organic beings', man alone was 'essentially a destructive power' who turned the 'harmonies of nature . . . to discord'. He argued that extensive clearing would result in a shortage of timber as well as erosion and floods and the loss of plants and animals. He feared climate change because he recognised that good tree cover conserved moisture and provided a safeguard against extreme temperatures. According to Marsh, Australia was perhaps the only place where the impact of deforestation on rainfall might be fully investigated, because large areas of forest were still being cleared and the colonies enjoyed the wealth from gold to conduct the necessary scientific research.[15]

Although this suggestion came to nothing, Marsh's influence was immediately apparent in a 'Report on the Advisableness of Establishing State Forests' prepared in 1865 by Charles Ligar, Clement Hodgkinson and R. Brough Smyth, who were Victoria's Surveyor-General, Assistant Commissioner for Lands and Secretary for Mines. These senior officials advised the government to protect existing forests around Victoria's mining centres and to establish plantations on the treeless basalt plains. While they suggested that the plantations include 'more valuable kinds' of eucalypt, their preference was for exotic species. They wanted all 'overgrown' trees in existing forests replaced with a combination of deciduous species and the best timber-producing conifers.[16]

Hodgkinson immediately acted on this report by setting aside state forests, which he expected would be a permanent part of the public estate. He also designated more timber reserves, which he expected would be sold off once miners and settlers had exploited their trees. These actions excited the *Australasian* to unprecedented optimism about the preservation of native forests. On 1 September 1866, the day James Smith first noticed Buvelot's pictures in the *Argus*, the *Australasian* declared:

> We have passed the pioneer period when aesthetic considerations had no weight. The importance of trees, both in the utilitarian and aesthetic sense, is now as fully recognised here as in Europe. The necessity of preserving large tracts of forest in various districts throughout the country, because of their climatic influence, is acknowledged, and will soon be practically attended to.[17]

THE MOST UNPROMISING MATERIALS

Buvelot's reputation owed a great deal to James Smith, who prided himself on being the artist's discoverer, championed his work in the *Argus* and became his amanuensis. When Buvelot fell out with the Victorian Academy of Arts in 1874, Smith wrote to the *Argus* on his behalf because of Buvelot's 'imperfect acquaintance with our language'. After the artist's death in 1888, Smith wrote tributes not only for the *Argus*, the *Australasian* and the *Australasian Sketcher*, which all had the same proprietors, but also for the rival weekly *Table Talk*.[18]

What initially excited Smith was Buvelot's ability to transform the familiar. In 1867 he applauded Buvelot's capacity

> for ennobling common subjects, and revealing the picturesque elements which are to be found in the most unpromising materials. Nothing is too mean and trivial for his pencil; but directly he has touched it, it ceases to be mean and trivial.

A few years later, Smith picked out one of Buvelot's scenes near Prahran. It consisted of just 'a stagnant pool, an agroupement of gum-trees, a distant mountain, and some tea-scrub in blossom'. The only 'relief' came from 'the yellow withered grass and the parched-up arid ground'. Yet Smith also saw it as proof of how much an artist could make out of 'unconsidered trifles'.[19]

Other writers followed suit. In 1874 the *Illustrated Australian News* applauded Buvelot for his capacity to take 'the simplest materials in the way of landscape—a few gum trees, a water-hole, and a distant mountain-range' and 'produce a picture at once truthful and pleasing'. In 1881 the dramatist Garnet Walch praised Buvelot for investing 'the most prosaic subject with poetic feeling, without any sacrifice of fidelity to nature'.[20]

Buvelot's focus on one or two trees was unexceptional in a European context. From the late eighteenth century many English artists had begun painting tree portraits. John Glover brought this practice to Tasmania in the 1830s. But otherwise it was unusual among colonial artists—hence Smith's excitement. The 'irregular and fantastic forms of Australian trees', he wrote, had captivated Buvelot; every tree in his paintings was 'distinctly individualised'; each tree had 'its own character, physiognomy, and expression'.[21]

Some colonial critics regarded these tree portraits as the best that could be made of a bad job. Smith himself started in 1866 by viewing

Buvelot's 'treatment of our unmanageable foliage' as an illustration of what could be done by 'judicious massing to conceal the ugliness which it so often presents in detail'. In 1875 another critic reluctantly concluded: 'We cannot do otherwise than accept the gumtree as the permanent type of Australia. Our rocks and mountains, our pastures and creeks, are always characteristic; but the eucalyptus is the most characteristic of all'. In 1888 the *Age* applauded Buvelot for idealising his subjects, making the gum trees 'more picturesque' than they were.[22]

Already in 1872, however, the anonymous author of an essay on the fine arts in Victoria argued that, far from hiding the gum trees' ugliness, Buvelot was

> first to reveal . . . the special picturesqueness, and wonderful variety of form and colour presented by the commonly-despised trees of Australia, and to show that, whether in isolation or in combination, these ragged and rugged members of the eucalyptus family are no less beautiful than the more symmetrical and umbrageous elm, oak, beech and birch of the mother country.

Within a year, Smith was applauding Buvelot for showing

> how undeserving our indigenous vegetation is of the disesteem into which it has fallen in the estimation of those whose eyes have been educated, and whose tastes . . . have been formed or disciplined by long familiarity with the more symmetrical, compact, leafy, and well-balanced trees of Great Britain.[23]

When Buvelot died, Smith acclaimed him as 'both a realist and an idealist'. According to Smith, Buvelot's realism lay in his accurate portrayal of the gum trees. He was the first to 'prove' they had 'a beauty of their own'. His idealism was to have invested the eucalypts 'with a charm not previously recognised. He saw in them more than the ordinary observer could; but the latter saw the same after looking at them through the artist's eyes.'[24]

THE STRANGER AND THE RESIDENT

Smith made these claims from personal experience. Before Buvelot settled in Victoria, Smith admitted, he 'never learned to admire the

LOUIS BUVELOT
WATERPOOL NEAR COLERAINE, SUNSET 1869

contorted forms and ragged foliage of so many of our Australian trees'. In a characteristic review in 1860, he expressed his distaste for Victoria's 'dingy greens and dirty browns'. When he first called for protection of native forests, it was despite their appearance rather than because of it. Smith's environmental concerns and his aesthetics only fell into line when Buvelot showed him the gum trees' 'fantastic beauty'.[25]

We will never know how many other colonists enjoyed similar conversions. But Buvelot's paintings were seen by many of his fellow colonists. From 1870 three of his landscapes—*Summer Evening at Templestowe*, *Winter Evening at Heidelberg* and *Waterpool near Coleraine, Sunset*—were on more or less permanent display in the National Gallery of Victoria. Buvelot's paintings also occupied a prominent place in the big intercolonial and international exhibitions held in Melbourne in 1866, 1872, 1875 and 1880, and his work was frequently engraved in the illustrated press. A special commemorative exhibition of his work opened at the Victorian Gallery six weeks after his death in 1888.

Yet if there was a reappraisal of the gum tree while Buvelot was painting, it partly happened independently of him. One example is the British novelist Anthony Trollope, who set out for Australia in 1871 expecting to find the eucalypts 'displeasing to the eye' because that was the accepted impression 'at home in England'. As Trollope put it, the 'eternal gum-tree' had become 'an Australian crest, giving evidence of Australian ugliness'. But Trollope found that, even if the eucalypts were not the 'loveliest' of trees, they also were not the 'ugliest', while Australian scenery equalled that of 'any part of the world'.[26]

The English essayist J. A. Froude had much the same experience a decade later. Like Trollope, Froude admitted that he expected to find the 'universal eucalyptus . . . grey and monotonous', but he was surprised to discover 'a proteus in shape and colour' that often resembled English trees. Sometimes the eucalypt branched 'like an oak or cork tree'; sometimes it was 'feathered like a birch'; sometimes it glowed 'like an arbutus, with an endless variety of hue—green, orange, and brown'. The 'huge twisted trunks and spreading branches' of old gum trees looked 'exactly like oaks at a distance', while blackwoods 'might have passed for yews'.[27]

These responses give the lie to Howard Willoughby's claim in 1886 that the rejection of Australian vegetation as monotonous was 'the criticism of the stranger, and not of the resident'. Willoughby, who was best known to his contemporaries as the political columnist 'Timotheus' of the *Argus*, argued that:

> An acquaintance with the bush soon dispels the notion of monotony. The eucalypts are found to differ one from another; the handsome Banksias, the curious Casuarinas . . . the graceful acacias, all claim attention and individualise the scene.

Yet for all his thirty years in Victoria, Willoughby could not match Froude's enthusiasm, confessing that he found the 'average gum' 'scraggy' compared with the oak or elm.

Nor was Willoughby exceptional in this regard. John Stanley James, alias Julian Thomas, the 'Vagabond', who was Francis Myers' predecessor at the *Argus*, failed to adjust to the gum tree in his first ten years in Australia. Even though he must have become familiar with Buvelot's paintings and often read Smith's views on the significance of his treatment of the gum trees, James was glad to escape them. 'Any tree not eucalyptian', he declared after visiting the beech forest of the Otways in 1885, was 'a welcome addition to Australian scenery'.[28]

Despite his emphasis on the revelatory power of Buvelot's paintings, Smith himself never suggested that the eucalypts were the equals of English trees. When he made his one return visit to England in 1882, he was struck by the 'beauty of outline and redundancy of foliage' of the trees, and by how they resolved 'themselves everywhere into pictures that delight the eye'. Although he cast this trip as a 'holiday' rather than a return 'home', Smith revealed his attachment to his original landscape when he declared:

> Each has its distinctive and peculiar charm—the plume-like elm, the gnarled oak, the weeping larch and pensile birch; the beech, with the exquisite curves of its horizontal branches . . . it is impossible to look at these without envying England the possession of such elements of loveliness in her landscape scenery, and contrasting them with the gumtree, the peppermint, the honeysuckle, and the she-oak of Australia—greatly to the disadvantage of the latter.[29]

TREES OF THE FUTURE

The enthusiasm for the gum tree in the 1870s and 1880s also rested on the nexus between the utilitarian and the aesthetic. In 1877 the Queensland Government Botanist, F. M. Bailey, observed:

> If we look back some thirty years we can scarcely now believe that it was often then said that the Australian flowers were without beauty or fragrance, yet nevertheless such was the cry . . . Of timber trees also we were said to possess but few, just Gums and wattles, the wood of which was thought to be too heavy and hard ever to be brought into much use. But now what a change has taken place. Our Eucalypts and a few others of our timber trees are sought after for planting in all parts of the Globe, where there is the least chance of their succeeding. Tree after tree is now being brought into use, and as each becomes better known, growing the more appreciated.[30]

This revaluation started with *Eucalyptus globulus*, the blue gum that so excited Louisa Anne Meredith. In 1863 it became one of the first species of gum tree advertised by an Australian nurseryman. By the early 1870s it was renowned internationally not just for its rapid growth, the value of its timber and the beauty of its flowers but also for its contribution to public health. In a period when malaria was still thought to be spread by miasmas rather than mosquitos, blue gums were thought to purify the atmosphere. Their leaves were also mistakenly declared a powerful therapeutic agent. With much greater reason, blue gums were celebrated for their capacity to dry out marshlands, although scientists did not realise that the shade they provided often created a rich breeding ground for mosquitos.[31]

While blue gums attracted champions around the world, French scientists played a key role in promoting them as therapeutic agents. In 1870 a Dr Gimblet of Cannes reported his success in using their leaves to treat intermittent neuralgia. A year later Professor Gubler of Paris created even more excitement with two papers suggesting that *Eucalyptus globulus* cured malaria where quinine had failed. According to one of Gubler's Spanish correspondents, the leaves of the blue gum produced 'marvellous and almost incredible results'. Another advised:

> If you could see the crowds who come to seek this remedy from me, and the despair of those to whom I cannot give leaves because my trees have already been completely stripped, your doubts would quickly be dispelled.[32]

A spate of articles followed. An Austrian doctor reported that when he used eucalypts to treat 432 sufferers from intermittent fever, 310 were completely cured, 202 of them by a single dose. A Scottish doctor called for the blue gum to be introduced into southern England because there was 'no reason why British enterprise should be backward in extending the area of growth of a tree of such undoubted beauty and economic value, and probably also of great medicinal importance'. Soon blue gums were being planted as far north as the Isle of Arran in the Firth of Clyde, and there was a 'craze' for them in California. They were even renamed. In some quarters, they became the 'Fever Trees', in others the 'Trees of the Future'. According to Ferdinand von Mueller, not even the English oak had ever excited so much attention.[33]

Colonists were amazed by this international enthusiasm. In 1872 the weekly *Australasian* admitted its surprise that this 'familiar' tree possessed medicinal and environmental virtues 'we Australians never expected'. In 1880 a Melbourne nurseryman echoed that the 'once despised Blue Gum tree' had risen 'transcendently above many other plants, if not above all plants, in hygienic importance'. Its most celebrated success was in the Pontine Marshes of the Roman Campagna. A typical account in the *Sydney University Magazine* trumpeted that the blue gum was achieving what 'the Caesars and the Popes had failed to accomplish':

> Large sums of money and centuries of labour were spent in draining the malarious region but almost in vain. The acclimatisation and extensive propagation of an Australian tree will do what money and science failed to bring about.[34]

Mueller was one of the great Australian champions of the blue gum, distributing its seeds internationally at every opportunity. So great was his identification with this species that he chose it for his baronial arms and was duly dubbed 'blue gum'. The pharmacist Joseph Bosisto, who established Australia's first large-scale eucalyptus-oil distillery, was just as significant. In a paper delivered to the Royal Society of Victoria in August 1874 and widely quoted internationally, Bosisto asked 'Is the Eucalyptus a Fever-destroying Tree?' His evidence of its environmental benefits led the *Argus* to wonder whether the growth of miasmatic diseases in Victoria was due to the wholesale clearance of native timber in and around the colony's towns and cities.[35]

The *Australasian Sketcher* first linked the aesthetic and hygienic reassessments of the gum tree a few weeks later. As well as carrying a summary of Bosisto's lecture and a column deploring the destruction of the eucalypts, the *Sketcher* published an article on the annual exhibition of the Victorian Academy of Art in which James Smith observed:

> Until very recently, most of us, entertaining a vivid recollection of the redundant leafiness of English trees, the beauty of their flowing outlines, and the richness of their verdure, have been accustomed to despise the irregular forms, the more sombre tints, and the more ragged foliage of the Australian eucalypts; just as we undervalued, or rather were entirely ignorant of, its immense value as a hygienic agent. But M. Buvelot has shown us the immense capacity of our sylvan antocthones for pictorial treatment. A group of gnarled gum trees, a few charred stumps, some living and dead brush-wood, and a

> water-hole—these, when transferred to his canvas, become a source of permanent delight to the eye.[36]

Three years later the *Daily Telegraph* again made this connection after a week of 'unwholesome fogs' had resulted in an outbreak of bronchial diseases in Melbourne and a new report from Algeria had credited the eucalypts with making areas 'previously unfit for human habitation . . . healthy and tenable'. As this report described, much of Algeria had been 'almost uninhabitable, owing to the prevalence of fever and the plague of mosquitos' when the first consignment of 60 000 gum trees arrived from Australia in 1866. A decade later the country had been transformed by a million and a half eucalypts: 'the morbid influences of the exhalations from the marshes' had almost vanished, while Algeria acquired the makings of a valuable timber crop.[37]

The *Telegraph* responded by identifying gum trees as Australia's most valuable gift to the Old World. It also questioned whether colonists should be replacing the eucalypts with 'alien vegetation', which was 'probably modifying the climate in a manner altogether detrimental to its healthfulness'. Not least, the *Telegraph* wondered why British colonists had been so blind to the virtues of the eucalypt: why it had been left to French scientists 'to discover and promulgate the amazing value of the eucalyptus as a sanitary agent' and a Swiss artist, Buvelot, 'to reveal to us the picturesqueness of the gnarled form and ragged foliage of the forest giant; to show us the tender beauty of the blue bloom on the leaves of the sapling'?[38]

A PREY TO ALL COMERS

This revaluation did not translate into better protection of Victoria's forests while Buvelot was painting. Instead, the rate of clearing in Victoria and the other Australian colonies accelerated through the 1870s and 1880s, creating a new sense of crisis. The *Australasian* maintained that the shortage of wood caused by this 'war upon live timber' was the 'most urgent question' facing 'the human race as a whole at the present time'. One of the instigators of South Australia's first Forestry Act, F. E. H. W. Krichauff, lamented the destruction of 'many thousands, no, millions of tons of useful timber . . . to make room for the plough'. John La Gerche, a Victorian Crown Lands bailiff, deplored the forests' continuing 'slaughter'. The Sydney clergyman–scientist William Woolls thought it 'murder' to kill trees without using them.[39]

The South Australian Parliament tried hardest to counter this destruction. In 1873 it offered £2 per acre to anyone who planted at least five acres with either native or exotic species so long as the area was fenced and stock excluded from it. This sum was twice the bonus offered under the equivalent legislation in New Zealand, but the South Australian government received just four applications and approved only one. Consequently, it considered making tree planting mandatory. As Krichauff recognised, this obligation would be 'of incalculable value to the whole Colony, . . . especially to the farmer himself . . . in after years', but he feared that it would drive colonists across the border. As a result, the Forest Board decided in 1878 to make trees more accessible by giving away its surplus plants.[40]

One of the rare occasions when the Victorian government acted was in 1869 when a group of wealthy Melbourne lawyers, politicians and businessmen, including the owner of the *Age*, David Syme, used goldfields regulations to select land in the Macedon State Forest. Because this land had already been cleared of timber fit for sawmilling, the district surveyor recommended—and the Assistant Commissioner of Crown Lands stipulated—that the applicants be required to plant at least fifty conifers on their twenty-acre blocks. But this condition was intended not just to secure reafforestation but also to be discriminatory, precluding 'ordinary applicants' from securing more land in the forest. The entire process was an abuse, as Syme and his associates simply wanted to establish exclusive summer residences.[41]

The legislation that governed land selection through the 1870s was particularly destructive. The champions of this legislation saw it as a means of 'unlocking the land' from wealthy squatters—as pastoral lessees were generally known—by entitling selectors to take up smallholdings without prior survey or down payment. Yet most of the nine million acres alienated over the next eight years were taken up by squatters who were already leasing the land. Genuine selectors typically had no option but to begin clearing their small blocks of 640 or 320 acres if they were to have any chance of making a living. In any case, they were required to do so as part of their statutory obligation to 'improve' the land by turning it over to cultivation.[42]

While the selectors' destruction of trees was an easy target for conservatives already opposed to this democratisation of landholding, the Reverend Julian Tenison-Woods was one critic of deforestation who struggled with the politics of selection. Tenison-Woods was no friend of the squatters, but he believed the Crown should protect the colonies' forests and manage them in the interests of both present and future generations. He was reluctant to oppose one of the great liberal causes of his time, but felt obliged to condemn the immense waste produced by the selectors.[43]

This criticism intensified when governments revoked Victoria's state forests so that they could be turned over to settlement. While the opening of the Dandenongs in 1893 was particularly controversial, it had many precedents. Most notably, in 1879 the Berry government revoked 150 000 acres of state forest in the Otways, leaving just 35 000 acres protected, and threw open 12 000 of the 15 000 acres reserved at Mount Macedon. But as a rare sop to colonists who feared that deforestation produced droughts—a commonplace in Victoria, while South Australians were more attached to the idea that 'rain follows the plough'—the government required selectors at Mount Macedon to plant ten trees per acre on fifty twenty-acre residential blocks. More remarkably, the government belatedly set aside just 500 acres 'for climatic reasons in connexion with the growth of timber'—perhaps the first and only time land was expressly reserved on this basis in Australia.[44]

The revocation of the Macedon State Forest provoked outrage, because the land was generally recognised as unfit for agriculture—a view confirmed when most of the selectors walked off their blocks within two years. Colonists who attributed droughts to deforestation were particularly concerned because Victoria had been drought-stricken since 1878. When the climate was already so bad, these colonists feared for a future in which there would be even fewer trees. They found no solace in the government's tree-planting requirement, because they knew it would not be enforced. They also wondered how a government that showed so little regard for Victoria's forests could simultaneously decide to plant at least 60 000 trees in the Wimmera in 1879 and 'some hundreds of thousands' there in 1880.[45]

The answer was political expediency. As the *Argus* recognised in 1879:

> In this colony a popularity-hunting Executive is so fearful of endangering the re-election of a single supporter in the Legislative Assembly, that it lends a favourable ear to propositions for throwing open any forest reserve to the axe of the splitter or the occupancy of

> the speculator, provided some political gain is to be made out of so reprehensible a proceeding.

While the *Argus* acknowledged that absolute monarchies had not succeeded in protecting forests, the Victorian government's weakness prompted it to query whether democracies would do better. In similar vein, the destruction of kauri across the Tasman led J. A. Froude to reflect that New Zealand 'must suffer something for the honour of being governed by a Parliament'.[46]

James Smith, who may well have written the *Argus* editorial, pursued this question in the monthly *Victorian Review*, which ran from 1879 until 1886 and displayed a keen interest in all manner of environmental issues. Having read far beyond the copy of Marsh's *Man and Nature* that he bought after it went into a second edition in 1874, Smith asked in 1880: 'Is the Earth Becoming Bald?' His answer was that deforestation in all temperate regions was 'a peril of unparalleled magnitude' that threatened to turn the earth into a 'sterile wilderness'. He foresaw disaster for Victoria if the colonial government continued to revoke state forests. With manifest fury, he predicted:

> Pressure will be brought to bear upon the representatives of the districts by men whose importunities cannot be disregarded because their electoral power is considerable. The unfortunate members . . . yield, and the Government for the time being is solicited to cancel the reservations of the coveted timber. Perhaps the continuance of the administration in office depends upon the support of a small majority, which the secession of the applicants would transform into a minority; and, therefore, the Government cannot afford to say 'No'. The reservations are abolished; and the work of destruction soon commences and goes merrily on.[47]

So it proved. But even where state forests escaped this fate, their survival was often of little consequence because government failed to protect them. While it had the power to prohibit timber-getting, it was rarely willing to provoke the fierce protests that ensued. Instead it relied on the weakest of regulatory systems, which failed to secure government revenue, ensure a long-term supply of timber or prevent waste by individual timber-getters or large sawmillers, who sometimes tried to put each other out of business by destroying the timber in each other's informal 'territory'. In one episode in the Bullarook forest, a sawmiller led a gang of thirty-five men into another's usual area. When his rival responded in kind, more than 600 of the finest trees were felled within a few days and their timber wasted.[48]

While the scale of this destruction made it the stuff of news, the government proved powerless to act, because both sawmillers had authorities entitling them to fell as many trees as they chose regardless of whether they required them. Smaller abuses were too numerous to attract attention, and the government did little to stop them in the 1870s and 1880s. At most, it employed twenty-four bailiffs for all Victoria's reserves and state forests. As a result, not even the most diligent bailiff, patrolling a forest on his own, could prevent extensive theft and destruction. When the bailiffs caught offenders, they also struggled to obtain convictions because the forest regulations were often poorly drafted and many local magistrates were aligned with the mining industry, which was the main consumer of timber. Even when prosecutions succeeded, magistrates typically imposed derisory fines.[49]

Successive governments failed to act, not only because timber interests were too powerful but also because public land was popularly equated with public access. As the *Argus* regretfully acknowledged, colonists looked on the trees in state forests not as Crown property but as 'the property of anyone who might choose to appropriate them'. When the McCulloch government introduced a new Forests Act in 1876, it simply formalised the existing unsatisfactory system of local forest boards. Three years later the Berry government abolished these boards because they were more concerned with immediately satisfying local demand for cheap timber than with ensuring a long-term supply. Otherwise, governments invoked lack of parliamentary time as an excuse for inaction. In 1880 'the condition of public business would not allow a Forest Bill to be introduced this session'. A private member's Bill, widely circulated for public comment in 1881, was never debated. In 1883 'the many large and important measures on the paper' made it impossible for the government to say when its own Bill would be submitted. Characteristically, it never was.[50]

Because of this failure, Victoria's forests were probably as mismanaged when Buvelot stopped painting in the mid-1880s as when he started twenty years before. The colony's Carriage Timber

Board reported in 1884 that 'waste on a gigantic scale' was permitted, if not encouraged, by the existing licensing system. For just £5 a year, a splitter was entitled to range across Victoria's forests and fell as many trees as he could. When Frederick Vincent of the Indian Forest Service inspected Victoria's forests for the colonial government in 1887, he found that their administrative arrangements were 'quite puerile and so ill-conceived that they can scarcely be seriously discussed'. Because most splitters continued to fell much more than they removed, thousands of trees could be found rotting in state forests, silting up rivers and being reduced to embers in Victoria's recurrent bush fires.[51]

THE MANIA FOR RINGBARKING

The gap between Buvelot's celebration of the gum tree and what happened on the ground is demonstrated even more clearly by the adoption of wholesale ringbarking. In 1858 James Bonwick knew of only one instance of such clearing—by a Tasmanian pastoralist who had more than doubled the carrying capacity of his land in this way. Two years later, Tasmania's Surveyor-General, James Calder, reported that 'very heavy forests', which would once have seemed 'insuperable obstacles' to settlement because of the cost of the 'old processes' of felling, grubbing and burning off, were 'not *now* looked on as such very serious impediments to settlement' because of 'the present cheap and comparatively easy style of clearing'. About the same time, Thomas Hungerford began large-scale ringbarking in the Hunter Valley of New South Wales.[52]

By 1865 the 'Yeoman' page of the *Australasian* was advising its readers that the best time of year for ringing was in autumn and winter, when the sap was down, and that it was essential not just to 'bark' the trees but to cut through the sapwood. Before long, as William Woolls sarcastically noted, the country weeklies were carrying 'elaborate papers, and even learned controversies on the best methods of ring-barking'. Yet the question of timing was a real one: contrary to the advice first proffered by the *Australasian*, it eventually became conventional wisdom that the best time for ringbarking was 'when the sap was well up, generally after good late summer rains'.[53]

Ringbarking transformed the colonial landscape. Because Europeans disdained such low-paid, tedious work, it became a Chinese preserve, at least in New South Wales, with gangs of up to seventy Chinese ringbarkers working on some properties. In 1880 one pastoralist estimated that three-quarters of the privately owned land in the Hunter Valley had been ringbarked, along with a 'very considerable' proportion of Crown land. Many other parts of New South Wales, Victoria and Tasmania were probably much the same, as selectors found ringbarking the easiest way of meeting their statutory obligation to improve their blocks and the quickest way of turning them over to cultivation.[54]

The wheat-breeder, William Farrer, was one champion of this large-scale ringbarking. After a series of wet years when large numbers of sheep succumbed to footrot and liver fluke, Farrer advocated ringbarking in 1873 as a means of drying the soil and doubling if not quadrupling the carrying capacity of 'ordinary bush'. But he also warned that 'excessive' ringbarking had caused many parts of Victoria 'to suffer from want of rain to an alarming extent'. Like Thomas Shepherd, he consequently advised that pastoralists should 'here and there . . . leave for ornament any well-shaped trees, or any trees that are valuable for their timber' so that Australia could once again appear 'wooded like an English park'.[55]

Other scientists were much more critical. Ferdinand von Mueller deplored this 'reckless' practice in a lecture at Melbourne's Industrial Museum in 1871. The clergyman–scientists William Woolls and William Branwhite Clarke went further in papers to the Horticultural and Royal Societies of New South Wales in 1876, condemning ringbarking for wasting valuable timber, disrupting the water cycle and marring the landscape. Clarke could not understand how gentlemen 'far above the hungry and uneducated selector' could 'deliberately leave acres of unfelled timber, bare of foliage, barkless and broken by winds'. He reckoned it 'suicidal' to ring the 'wonderful *Eucalypti*' that the 'All-wise Creator' had planted in the 'great Australian garden'.[56]

These arguments excited immediate debate in the Sydney press, particularly from Leopold de Salis, a pastoralist, member of the Legislative Council and member of the Royal Society. While acknowledging that it was an 'abuse' to ring 'well-growing trees', de Salis contended that ringbarking must be beneficial because it was carried out by 'a shrewd practical class of citizens'. He maintained that experience at Lake George, where ringbarking had been 'more thoroughly carried out' than anywhere else in New South Wales, showed that clearing did not necessarily reduce rainfall. Perhaps most notably, de Salis found aesthetic benefits in ringbarking, arguing that it revealed an 'extended variety of background', more than offsetting 'the temporary disfigurement of foreground'.[57]

Ringbarking continued to be debated for years, both inside and outside the Royal Society. In 1878 the Jesuit Julian Tenison-Woods joined his Anglican counterparts in condemning its waste of valuable timber. W. E. Abbott responded in 1880 with the first significant Australian empirical evidence about the impact of clearing on the water cycle. Having observed the impact of ringbarking on his own property in the Hunter Valley for eleven years, Abbott concluded that, far from causing creeks to dry up through evaporation or decline in rainfall, it led to a permanent increase in stream flow. But Woolls was unconvinced. In paper after paper, he continued to decry indiscriminate ringbarking because of its effect on 'the rainfall and health of the country'.[58]

This debate had almost no political influence. Although the New South Wales government introduced new regulations in 1875 prohibiting lessees of Crown land from ringbarking unless they obtained ministerial consent, it imposed no controls on freeholders who owned their land. Moreover, some squatters did not even bother to seek ministerial permission as required by the new law governing Crown land. Others obtained it only to ignore the standard conditions requiring them to leave all 'useful timber'. Still others complied only to find that they could not re-create the park-like landscape that Farrer hoped for. Even when they left large clumps of trees for ornament, shade or timber, these trees died almost as soon as those that had been ringbarked.[59]

These laws became the stuff of controversy in 1881, not because of their environmental impact but because they threatened to put a stop to free selection. Although Parliament had simply intended squatters to be compensated for structural improvements such as dams and fences, a local magistrate held that the legislation extended to ringbarking, and that selectors had to pay for ringing, not according to its cost, but according to the increase in the value of the land. In the case before him, the selector had to pay five shillings an acre for work costing only a shilling. A group of selectors and their parliamentary representatives immediately donated the money for an appeal to the Supreme Court.[60]

This case was heard by James Martin, the precocious author of the 1838 *Australian Sketch Book*, who had gone on to become

Attorney-General, Premier and then Chief Justice of New South Wales. As a Member of Parliament, Martin had pursued a variety of environmental causes, ranging from cruelty to animals to protection of native trees on Crown land. As Chief Justice, he founded a League for the Prevention of Pollution of Air and Water and canvassed a wide range of aesthetic, economic and environmental arguments in a vain attempt to stop Sydney's untreated sewage being piped out to sea at Bondi. But Martin believed that ringbarking was justified on both economic and aesthetic grounds. Although he nodded towards the separation of judicial and political functions by declaring that it was for Parliament to determine whether ringbarking was in the public interest, Martin promptly ignored his own prescription. He led the court in concluding that ringbarking not only could be 'exceedingly valuable in causing the land to be turned to useful purposes' but also could be 'an improvement in the way of taste'.[61]

The New South Wales legislature also endorsed ringbarking. While not all Members of Parliament went as far as Leopold de Salis, who dismissed gum trees as 'gigantic weeds' that prevented the growth of grass, they generally assumed that ringbarking increased land values. Environmental and aesthetic concerns had no place in their calculus. Their overriding concern was to ensure that selection remained possible. Debate was dominated by tales of how squatters who served as magistrates had begun fixing the value of ringbarking at twenty-five shillings an acre, encouraging their fellows to employ 'perfect armies of Chinamen' to ring their land so that it would become prohibitively expensive.[62]

The new legislation enacted by Parliament provided that only lessees who had obtained ministerial permission would be entitled to compensation, which was fixed at one shilling and threepence per acre. This provision was little constraint. Although the government's foresters typically refused to allow ringbarking of timber 'fit for sawing or splitting purposes', by 1884 the government had authorised the ringing of almost four million acres. By 1888 it had approved another four million acres under new regulations requiring a permit only for trees that were twelve inches in diameter four feet from the ground. Elsewhere ringbarking did not even become a major political issue. Victorian legislation in 1884, requiring pastoral lessees to obtain permission before ringbarking, was both too late and too limited, as selectors were exempted.[63]

A French colonist, Edmund Marin la Meslée, thought the consequences 'terrifying'. After visiting the Victorian side of the Murray in 1876 and finding 'immense' tracts of forest where 'not a leaf or a piece of living bark' was 'to be seen on the trees', he observed:

> Nothing can give any idea of the infinitely sad and desolate air of these dead forests. One might suggest a page, torn from a portfolio by Gustav Doré, showing a part of Dante's *Inferno*. It is the vision of Ezekiel: and the forest resembles a multitude of skeletons raising their long, fleshless arms to the sky.

The Warrnambool artist Daniel Clarke seems to have been the only colonial landscape painter in the 1870s and 1880s to depict something of what la Meslée so vividly described—and Clarke probably did so only because he had no choice. To satisfy local interest in the remarkable geology of the volcanic landscape at Tower Hill, Clarke could not help but record the devastation of the crater island by large-scale ringing. Other minor colonial artists such as William Tibbits and H. L. van den Houten simply included occasional ringbarked trees in their work. But Buvelot failed to do so. His work does not even reveal that these trees existed, let alone that they dominated much of the colonial landscape.[64]

THE FIRST CONSERVATION GROUP IN THE WORLD

As colonists prepared to celebrate the centenary of European settlement in Australia in 1888, the publisher William Frederick Morrison blamed artists for the gum trees' bad reputation. Referring most likely to Sydney's landscape painters, Morrison maintained: 'Artists have with ridiculous unanimity pronounced it unpicturesque, and have decried its glory. They assume to say it is positively "ugly".' Morrison suggested that 'the difficulties that confront the artist when he undertakes to paint it' were 'the latent and unexpressed reason for his condemnation of the tree. The artist cannot paint it—it is above his art, and remains a subtle beauty that eludes his grasp and laughs to scorn his futile efforts to produce its form: and hence the eternal war.'[65]

James Smith continued to see things very differently. When the retrospective of Buvelot's paintings was held in July 1888, Smith repeated his standard account of Buvelot's influence. Once colonists had looked on the 'despised' gum tree simply 'as containing so many tons of firewood'. Then Buvelot had revealed its beauty and, by implication, colonists had come to realise that it was good for more than burning. Perhaps they even had discovered that gum trees were worth retaining in the ground—a view given some credence by the Victorian government's decision to appoint the colony's first Conservator of Forests.[66]

When the New South Wales government of Sir Henry Parkes had looked to appoint its first Inspector of Forests within the Department of Mines in 1881 at an annual salary of £350, the applicants included a forester trained in India. Instead Parkes chose the poet Henry Kendall, who had acquired a knowledge of Australian trees from working for a large timber merchant in northern New South Wales for five years. Parkes intended Kendall's appointment as a sinecure, just as the Cowper government had made Conrad Martens its Assistant Parliamentary Librarian in 1863. But where the ageing Martens found a comfortable billet in the library, Kendall was in no health to traverse the colony inspecting forests in return for an extra £1 a day in travelling expenses. A year after taking up his position he was dead, having achieved nothing of his plans for the reservation of 'beautiful scenery . . . for the aesthetic wants of the future'.[67]

The Victorian government of Duncan Gillies took the office of conservator more seriously, publicly advertising its post in March 1888 with a salary of £650. According to one critic, even this salary was inadequate; it was not enough to lure Australia's most experienced forester, J. Ednie Brown, from South Australia. But it succeeded in attracting George Perrin, who had worked with Brown before becoming Tasmania's first Conservator of Forests in 1886. Just two years later, Perrin had lost political support in Tasmania, the colonial government was preparing to retrench public servants, and the island's powerful mining industry wanted unrestricted access to timber. As a result, he was happy to move to Melbourne.[68]

One of Perrin's boasts was that in South Australia he had been responsible for the only three state forests to return a profit. As part of this utilitarian concern, Perrin abhorred large-scale ringbarking; he wanted to restrict logging to trees marked by his staff and charge a royalty on all trees. At the same time, he wanted all trees to be felled when they were mature, by which he meant thirty to thirty-five years old. His ambition was to turn mixed forests into stands of straight saplings—ideal for supplying pit props to the mining industry—with blocks of uniform age and size always coming on for the sawmiller.[69]

The Northern District Forest Conservation League, which was established in August 1888 after a 'very enthusiastic meeting' in Bendigo, and soon stretched to the Murray, had similar goals. Local miners were prominent in the new League because they saw forest conservation as a means of securing a reliable supply of timber for fuel and pit props. The many sawmillers who joined the League aspired to work with the colonial government in 'forming new forests, replanting old ones, and conserving existing plantations, for the use of the people of Victoria'.[70]

This League may have been the first 'conservation' organisation in the world, anticipating Gifford Pinchot's Conservation League of America by twenty years. Its formation in Bendigo exemplifies how conservation in Australia in the late nineteenth century was as much a rural concern that struggled to get a hearing in the city as an urban concern imposed on the country. While the members of the League were primarily men with an immediate interest in using timber, excessive clearing affected the entire local community. As the *Argus* reported, Bendigo had 'suffered terribly' from droughts and floods, which were 'all largely and justly attributed to the denudation of the old hill forests, which left the earth's surface rather as a hot metal plate than an all-absorbent sponge'.[71]

The new League demonstrated its naivety when it accepted the government's assurance that legislation for 'improved forest management' would be introduced before the end of the year. In October 1888 the Minister for Lands John Dow still maintained that 'nothing would give him greater pleasure' than to introduce this Forests Bill. In early November he announced he would proceed 'at the first opportunity'. But within a week he had reverted to the stock excuse that the government's legislative program allowed no time for this Bill so that at most it could introduce new regulations.[72]

Although the government increased its funding of Perrin's State Forests Branch, it impeded his work by providing him with neither clerical assistance nor a suitable office. When it sent him to Stawell to investigate whether local selectors were ringbarking valuable trees or 'mere scrub', his visit triggered even more axework by selectors who were intent on clearing their land before Perrin could secure new controls. By the time Perrin had reported the 'wanton destruction of highly useful timber', the selectors had wasted much of Victoria's best ironbark country.[73]

One of Perrin's supporters was Francis Myers, who had long been using his weekly essays in the *Argus* to decry the 'havoc and waste' caused by splitters, prop-getters, sawmillers and settlers. As Myers put it, 'Progress for the people, destruction to our forests' was an 'almost universal Australian motto'. Myers applauded Perrin for trying to initiate a system which would yield Victoria 'noble revenues' and 'save for posterity the magnificent heritage nature prepared for us in our forest lands'. He also displayed exceptional realism about the difficulty of Perrin's position. Just two months after Perrin started work in Victoria, Myers declared that the conservator was

> in worse plight than the Israelites who were set to make bricks without straw. He must have public sympathy and practical legislation to help him and these will only follow a realisation on the part of the polity of the importance of the matter which is placed under his control.[74]

Perrin needed all the help he could get. By late 1888 'a good many people' were looking 'ugly' at him. Not only was he confronted by what Myers described as an 'almost universal sentiment against the trees'; he was also opposed by the colony's sawmillers, who 'bitterly resented' the 'slightest hint of regulation' after being 'allowed to run riot in the forests' for years. At a public meeting in Echuca, the centre of red-gum logging on the Murray, timber-getters argued that the requirement that all trees for logging be identified by the Conservator would be 'disastrous' for their industry as 'trees might be marked which would be utterly unfit for the mill'. If the new regulations were introduced without fair notice, the sawmillers claimed they would have to breach their contracts, throwing 'large numbers of men' out of work.[75]

As often since when new environmental controls have been mooted, these arguments were baseless. When Myers visited the Murray with Perrin early in 1889, he saw

> tremendous stacks of sawmill logs, enough . . . to serve the mills at Echuca for six months to come, and to render absurd that cry about

> the stoppage of the mills which was raised against the new regulations.

Had Perrin been allowed to implement his new regime, he reckoned he could have put 500 men to work immediately and solved 'the unemployed question at once if it ever turned up again'. But the government gave way to the sawmillers. It started by deferring the new timber regulations for a month—a relatively small concession when Victoria's forests 'had been abandoned to the spoilers for thirty years'. Then it exempted sawmillers with long-term contracts.[76]

The Northern District Forest Conservation League looked as if it might be more successful when it tried to influence the political debate during Victoria's 1889 election. Like the Woman's Suffrage Society, it circulated a questionnaire for all candidates. The first question was whether they would support legislation for the preservation and conservation of Victoria's forests 'early in the session'. The second was whether they would favour funding local bodies to fence and plant waste lands within their boundaries. The third was whether they would support subsidies to private individuals to plant forest trees, as was already being done in South Australia.[77]

Whereas the *Argus* derided the Woman's Suffrage Society for the impracticality of its ambitions, it applauded the Conservation League's questionnaire as a means of ensuring that all candidates were 'properly tested and sifted' on a 'matter of great and increasing importance to Victoria and Australia'. The *Argus* hoped that the questionnaire would force the candidates, most of whom were ignorant of forestry issues, to educate themselves. In the weeks leading up to the election, dozens of parliamentary candidates responded by discussing conservation. The Premier, Duncan Gillies, maintained that, since forests constituted a vital water catchment for Melbourne, it was nonsense to suggest that 'city people did not care as much for the protection of our forests as the people of the country did'.[78]

Yet Gillies also emphasised the difficulty of securing new legislation when there were 'powerful interests at work for the purpose of getting all they can out of the forests, destroying them as they may'. He declared:

> Unless the public of Victoria—who have a far larger interest in the preservation of these forests than a few individuals have—will set

> their faces . . . against the destruction of these forests, this private influence which is constantly brought to bear to prevent the Government doing the right thing will have its own way yet.

So it proved when Gillies was returned as premier and, for at least the third time, broke his promise to introduce forests legislation.[79]

THE NATIVISTS' CONCEIT

While Buvelot's paintings changed how some colonists looked on the gum tree, this new sympathy did not translate into conservation on the ground. Nor did Buvelot's influence last long after his death. In 1890 an anonymous critic still lamented that no artist since Buvelot had been 'properly to the front with gumtrees'. James Smith continued to maintain that Buvelot 'first taught us the picturesqueness of Australian trees'. But other colonists both old and young were soon talking and writing as if Buvelot's revelation of the eucalypts' beauty had never happened.[80]

Henry Laurie, Professor of Philosophy at Melbourne University, typified this attitude. Having lived in Victoria for twenty-five years, Laurie could have been expected to follow Smith in lauding Buvelot as the colonial artist most successful at depicting the gum tree. Yet in a lecture to the Victorian Artists Society in 1889, Laurie ignored Buvelot, maintaining that a new generation of artists was just beginning to interpret 'the beauty which had been missed by unaccustomed eyes. They had to teach us that even gum trees were not all alike, but that each had its peculiar habit in trunk, and branch, and leaf, and in the thick masses on scanty sprays of its foliage'.[81]

Other commentators soon followed suit. An essay published in 1901 by both the *Age* and the *Bulletin* declared: 'The great eucalypts are only today coming into their artistic heritage'. Its anonymous author maintained that Australian painters had only started discovering

> the lovely quality of colour in our gum trees, a quality that could not but escape the attention of those who brought to Australia young affections already pledged to sweeping willows, trim hedges, and the positive greens of the English landscape.

In 1910 the art chronicler William Moore contended that Buvelot had 'failed to suggest the real atmosphere of Australia'.[82]

The alias adopted by the Ballarat-born poet and sketch-writer Nathan Spielvogel suggested that he shared this inter-generational conceit. Far from calling himself 'Telemachus' or even 'The Vagabond', Spielvogel was 'The Gumsucker', as the native-born were commonly called. Writing in the early 1900s, he assumed that foreign birth had tainted colonists' views of the gum tree:

They sailed the sea to the bush king's realm,
His groves for their crops they cleared,
They thought of oak, and of ash, and elm,
They looked at the gum and sneered . . .
They said his limbs were of sombre hue,
Too mean to provide them shade,
They sniffed his scent, when the breezes blew
And sighed for a primrose glade.

Spielvogel believed only gumsuckers like himself could see the beauty of Australia's 'own great tree' and look on it with pride.[83]

If Spielvogel was right to emphasise the nexus between native birth and appreciation of native vegetation, delight in the gum tree would by then have been widespread. By 1901, the native-born made up 77 per cent of what the new Commonwealth's census dubbed the 'immigrant races'. But Spielvogel's sweeping characterisation of the response of foreign-born colonists to the eucalypts was not just bad history; it also failed to explain the present. Spielvogel made no allowance for Hans Heysen, who was no gumsucker, having come to Australia from Germany aged seven, yet from 1908 became the next artist to be hailed as first to catch 'the spirit of the Gum Tree'.[84]

Charles Walter *Our Artist* 1873

CHAPTER SEVEN

ARTISTS WITH AXES

After fixing our points of view and holding a council of war in reference to the execution of some trees which obstructed the view in one or two directions, and which we decided should be lowered on the morrow, we returned to the camp, and the evening was devoted to a grand clothes drying match.

J. H. Harvey, *Australian Photographic Journal*, 1895

THE ENGRAVING SHOWS 'Our Artist'. Charles Walter was a German from Mecklenberg who settled in Victoria in the 1850s. When not collecting specimens for Ferdinand von Mueller, Victoria's Government Botanist, Walter worked as a 'Country Photographic Artist'. Most of his patrons seem to have been local landholders, to whom he offered 'Views of Residence Seats and Scenery', but Walter also contributed to the monthly *Illustrated Australian News*, which made something of an identity of him. Hence the engraving, published by the *News* in 1873 as one of nine illustrations to an article by Walter about a trip to Cape Otway, south-west of Melbourne.[1]

The engraving shows Walter with a box on his back, a tent over his shoulder, a tomahawk in hand. The box contained his photographic equipment—camera, glass plates, processing trays and chemicals, which he needed to process his plates because the emulsion was sensitive to light only when wet. The tent was Walter's portable darkroom. But what of the tomahawk?

Contemporary accounts of Walter's work as a photographer describe how he cleared his path to places rarely, if ever, visited by his fellow colonists. On a trip to Mount Buller in 1868, he 'penetrated to places inaccessible to vehicle or horse, and only penetrable to human foot, after considerable clearances had been effected in the thickets'. When he went to Cape Otway in 1873, he had to cut his way 'through a dense undergrowth of scrub from six to eight feet high' with 'tomahawk in hand'.[2]

In the *News's* engraving, however, Walter's tomahawk had another function: it was a symbol of the larger difficulties he encountered on his expeditions, which the *News* liked to present as a public service. Its image of Walter—like that developed around other peripatetic landscape painters and photographers—was that of the selfless artist who risked life and limb, travelling alone and sleeping where he could, so that his fellow colonists could discover 'the romantic and the picturesque', which nature had scattered 'so lavishly' around them.[3]

This quest for the romantic and picturesque did not always involve a corresponding respect for nature, at least of the type we know today. As well as carrying tomahawks and axes to clear their paths, many photographers—or their patrons and assistants—used them for view-making in the most literal sense. When they were not moving bushes or branches in order to enliven their foregrounds, they were felling trees in order to expand the horizon. Some landscape painters probably also created their views in this way, or had others do so for them.

This restructuring of nature was in line with the widespread use of tomahawks and axes in the nineteenth century. As late as the 1880s, tomahawks were part of the excursionist's basic kit.[4] Axes were a prominent feature in almost every view of big trees by Nicholas Caire, who abandoned haircutting for photography in the mid-1860s. Whether the foregrounds of Caire's prints show swagmen, picnic parties or his companions busy with tape measures, they generally include an axe, not just because it was an essential tool but also because it symbolised the colonists' capacity to shape their environment.

Yet while the number of trees felled in the service of art was trivial when set against the great swathe of forest that colonists cleared for grazing and cultivation, the destruction of these trees is still significant because it undermines the assumption that nature is immovable. Nineteenth-century photographers are often thought to have been limited to seeking out subjects that happened to conform to the compositional conventions established by landscape painters. In fact, they also cut and pasted their subjects to satisfy these conventions. While they could not move mountains, they could fell, uproot and transplant trees.

The photographers' axework also undermines the stereotype of the romantic artist in awe of nature; it violates the assumption that celebration of nature involves respect for it. Not least, it raises questions about the limits of environmental concern in the nineteenth century—particularly because most of the documented examples of such axework were by artists and patrons otherwise identified with environmental protection.

THE ARTISTS' CAMPS

Artists' camps in Australia will always be associated with Box Hill, where Tom Roberts, Arthur Streeton and Frederick McCubbin worked from 1886 until 1888; Heidelberg, where Roberts, Streeton and Charles Conder painted from 1888 until 1890; and Little Sirius Cove on Sydney Harbour, where Roberts lived on and off from 1891 and Streeton from 1892. But the first artists' camps were held already in 1875, in the Grose Valley beneath Govett's Leap in the Blue Mountains. Although generally discussed as examples of the nexus between art and tourism,[5] these camps are at least as noteworthy for their axework.

The organiser of these camps was Eccleston du Faur, who worked as a draughtsman in the New South Wales Surveyor-General's Office from 1863 until 1866, then became Chief Draughtsman in the Occupation of Crown Lands Office. Over the next fifteen years du Faur initiated a systematic survey of pastoral New South Wales that identified land available for selection and helped to resolve boundary disputes. Probably because of the contacts and expertise he acquired in this capacity, du Faur quit the public service in 1881 to establish his own pastoralists' agency.[6]

This work might suggest that du Faur was interested only in the opening of the land. Yet colonial survey departments accommodated powerful advocates of the environmental limits of development. The South Australian Surveyor-General, George Goyder, played a key role in confining wheat-growing to areas with reliable rainfall. In 1870 he successfully opposed plans to throw open all land in the colony to selection, partly because it would offer 'a premium to the exhaustion of the soil by giving new or virgin soil in exchange for worked out land'. Charles Ligar, whom James Smith approached over the establishment of forest reserves, was Goyder's Victorian counterpart.[7]

Du Faur manifested his interest in environmental protection in 1892, when he began campaigning for the New South Wales government to create a national park for northern Sydney, just as Australia's first National Park had served the city's south since 1879. When Ku-ring-gai Chase was gazetted as a park in 1894, du Faur became its managing trustee and 'devoted the greater part of his time to it'. As well as making the Chase a recreation ground, du Faur had what he regarded as 'a higher mission': he 'aimed above all at the fullest preservation of natural flora and at the establishment of an area over which marsupials and other Australian fauna might roam and breed in safety'.[8]

Du Faur was also a great champion of institutional support for art in New South Wales. In 1871 he became a founding member of the colony's Academy of Arts, and then in 1872 its honorary secretary. Over the next few years he twice saved the Academy 'from premature dissolution by his voluntary self-sacrifice of his time, and the undertaking of personal financial responsibility in its behalf'. In 1876 he also became de facto director of the new Art Gallery of New

South Wales and, as president of its trustees, was the Gallery's chief policy-maker for almost forty years.[9]

Du Faur first sought to establish an artists' camp at Govett's Leap in the late 1860s. As an incentive, he offered free transport and accommodation. But a professional photographer refused because 'it was not likely to pay', while an amateur declined 'owing to the press of business'. Du Faur decided to try again in 1874, when he returned to Govett's Leap. His goal was to bring the scenery of the Grose Valley 'home to those who were less fortunate in being able to visit it, or who lacked the information as to its being worth a visit'. He wanted to show the world that the Grose Valley compared favourably with the 'celebrated' Yosemite Valley in California.[10]

Photography was the obvious medium because of its success in promoting Yosemite. The work of the Californian photographer Carleton Watkins had not only helped to persuade the United States Congress to make Yosemite a State Park in 1864, but had also reached an international audience. In 1871 the National Gallery of Victoria had bought twenty of Watkins's giant plates—up to 18 by 22 inches—including seven views of Yosemite. With other photographs, engravings and panoramas, as well as published accounts, these plates had made it a cliché in Australia that Yosemite was unmatched for compressing 'so much varied grandeur and beauty . . . into so small a scale'.[11]

While du Faur issued an open invitation to professional and amateur artists in New South Wales to attend his camps in 1875, he was most concerned to attract an accomplished photographer who might emulate Watkins's giant plates. As a result, he persuaded his own Academy and the Commissioners responsible for the New South Wales display at the Centennial Exhibition in Philadelphia in 1876 that they should employ the Sydney photographer, Joseph Bischoff. At 12 by 16 inches, Bischoff's plates were only about half the size of Watkins's images, but they were twice the size of most Australian colonial photographs. It took five men just to carry them.[12]

Landscape painting was less significant as a promotional medium, but it had greater cachet. Because it was at a low ebb in New South Wales, du Faur invited W. C. Piguenit, who shared his own professional background, having worked from 1850 until 1874 as a draughtsman in the mapping office of Tasmania's Survey Department. While du Faur and Piguenit may not yet have met, du Faur had boosted Piguenit's reputation in April 1875, when he successfully organised a subscription to buy Piguenit's *Mount Olympus, Lake St*

JOSEPH BISCHOFF
THE VALLEY OF THE GROSE
1875

Clair, Tasmania as the first step towards establishing an Art Gallery of New South Wales.[13]

By July 1875 du Faur was preparing for the arrival of his artist guests. As he soon discovered, the only track to the floor of the Grose Valley was 'overgrown, encumbered by fallen trees, and obliterated in part by landslips'. The 'density of the scrub and forest timber' in the valley also meant that there were few places from which 'the abruptness of the cliffs' could 'fairly be appreciated'. Du Faur's solution was to hire a gang of axemen to reopen the old track and clear 'views to be taken by pencil and camera' at sites he selected.[14]

Piguenit was the first artist to arrive. For ten days in mid-September, he worked on his own in the valley without engaging in further clearing. Then du Faur joined him, along with Bischoff and a party of senior schoolboys from Sydney Grammar and the King's School. Du Faur and the schoolboys promptly created new views at their second camp, at the junction of the Grose River and Govett's Leap Creek. Three days later they renewed their axework closer to Govett's Leap Falls. By October 'a large number of trees' had been felled at the first camp, and 'several points' had been 'cleared and marked for taking' on the way to the second.[15]

Bischoff struggled to make the most of these opportunities. Some of his photographs suffered as a result of damage to his chemicals when they were carried into the Grose Valley. He also underexposed many of his views 'in fear of losing detail in the distance', and had to photograph the selected spots 'irrespective of light or weather' because the Academy and the Exhibition Commissioners failed to pay him adequately. But Bischoff left the most vivid record of this destruction when he constructed a panorama from the first camp, looking from the north-east through to the south towards Mount King Gorge. Bischoff aimed to photograph the cliffs, but he also recorded the stumps and felled tree trunks in the foreground, where du Faur had cleared a strip several metres wide to open the view beyond.[16]

Many colonists probably remained as blind to the crudity of this clearing in the 1870s as they had been in the 1830s. Contemporary descriptions of photographs by Nicholas Caire overlook the stumps in the foreground for the 'beautiful and romantic' scenery behind. But Ernest Docker, one of Bischoff's fellow photographers at the camps, recognised the ugliness of this axework. While acknowledging that it opened 'to view some grand crags with broken and picturesque skyline', Docker deplored the 'very inartistic foreground' it produced and turned with relief to other spots marked for taking by du Faur, where the stream rushed 'over rocks, with quiet pools here and there, giving nice foregrounds'.[17]

Bischoff also appears to have delighted in spots that remained intact. His *The Valley of the Grose*, with its rocks and pools in the foreground and cliffs looming faintly behind, is among the most compelling colonial landscape photographs. It is also his only view of the Valley to have gained some currency as a result of its publication by the New South Wales Government Printer. Bischoff seems to have found no market for the photographs he took through du Faur's clearings. Only one set is known to exist.

Du Faur thought more axework the solution. While he proudly noted that his party 'properly cleared' views of the two main waterfalls in the gorge, he lamented that he had opened only a partial panorama of the surrounding cliffs. With manifest regret, he recorded that just 'a few days' more work would have 'opened up the sky . . . all round the compass, forming a view of cliffs of 2000 feet high all round, not easily to be surpassed'. He felt the strength of his party was 'altogether inadequate for making the clearings in timber and scrub, without which many of the finest views could not be favourably reproduced by photography'.[18]

Yet even if Bischoff had been able to stay longer, his chemicals had remained intact and du Faur had felled every tree he wanted, his ambition to establish the Grose Valley as another Yosemite was fanciful, as du Faur himself should have known. The highest waterfall in the Grose Valley is 520 feet, whereas Yosemite Falls are over 2000 feet high and carry incomparably more water in spring. Although the cliffs of the Grose Valley rise 2000 feet from the valley floor, the highest peaks at Yosemite rise more than 4000 feet, and the Grose Valley cannot match the great glaciated forms of North Dome, South Dome and Half Dome.[19]

THE PHOTOGRAPHER'S FRIEND

Du Faur was not alone in taking an axe to places he valued so that they could be celebrated better by art. Such clearing was probably the norm among photographers in the Old World and the New, amateur and professional. In describing his third and last expedition through the western Himalayas in 1866, the British photographer Samuel Bourne recorded how he created a foreground by 'sawing down

Joseph Bischoff
The Valley of the Grose
1875

several birch trees'. An essay in the *Philadelphia Photographer* in 1873 advised readers that 'a good axe' was 'a friend in need' when it was 'desirable to cut a small tree or remove a branch that would otherwise obscure some important point of your view'.[20]

The photographer to make most of his axework was Eadward Muybridge, who went to Yosemite in 1872. While the federal government had entrusted Yosemite to the State of California for its 'constant preservation', California was yet to appoint a guardian to care for the valley. As a result, Muybridge was free to create new views that would distinguish him from Carleton Watkins. He later boasted that he not only 'had himself lowered by ropes down precipices to establish his instruments in places where the full beauty of the object to be photographed could be transferred to the negative'; he also had gone 'to points where his packers refused to follow him'; not least, he had 'cut down trees by the score'.[21]

Amateurs such as J. H. Harvey, the honorary secretary of the Victorian Amateur Photographic Association, were also ready to use axes to open new views, though they did not have the same commercial incentive. When Harvey and another 'leading and pioneering' amateur visited Kanangra Walls in the Blue Mountains in 1894, they began by selecting views to take when the weather cleared. A number of trees obstructed their view in 'one or two directions', so they decided on their 'execution'. After 'a grand clothes drying match', they 'lowered' these trees the following morning and started photographing.[22]

Yet three days later Harvey was appalled to discover that 'vandals' had destroyed Dante's Glen, a fern gully that had been 'a real beauty spot' when he first visited it in the early 1880s. Harvey declared it 'shameful' that the rough barricade of stakes that had protected the Glen on his first visit had been removed to allow tourists 'to roam about any portion of the gully', ruining its 'luxuriant vegetation'. One explanation of this apparent inconsistency may be that, like many of his fellows, Harvey valued fern gullies more than gum trees; it may also be that he put art before nature.[23]

Photographers found another use for their axes when their foregrounds were empty and hence devoid of interest according to the conventions of the picturesque derived from eighteenth- and nineteenth-century landscape painting. The only remedy was to introduce vegetation into the foreground to lead the eye into the view. But photographers taking stereographs also needed to fill their foregrounds, because the depth of field that made stereographs so popular depended on there being an immediate reference point in the foreground from which the middleground and background could be measured.[24]

This type of rearrangement of nature was encouraged in 1896 by the British critic Alfred Wall, who advised readers of his *Artistic Landscape Photography* that it was sometimes desirable to plug spots that were 'too startlingly conspicuous . . . by moving a bush, the trunk of a felled tree, some broken or displaced boughs, . . . in some naturally suggestive way'. A year later, a Hobart audience received similar advice from J. W. Beattie, who was Tasmania's leading landscape photographer as well as one of the island's great advocates of scenery preservation and the dedication of national parks. Beattie explained that he always carried an axe so that he could 'soon remedy any faulty composition'. His favourite targets were pandanus or 'grass trees', because they were 'so handy for foregrounds', as one can see in his photographs of Lake Emily in the Hartz Mountains and Lake Marion and Mount Gould, north-west of Lake St Clair.[25]

All this evidence of artist–axemen opens new ways of looking at *Bridge over the Delegate at Quedong*, an engraving that the *Illustrated Australian News* published in 1871 after a photograph by Charles Walter. Although an early member of the Field Naturalists' Club, which made many attempts to protect Victoria's natural environment, Walter may have used his tomahawk not just to clear his path but also to construct his views. The double stump in the left foreground, if not also the one behind, was probably his handiwork, opening his view of the river and the bridge.[26]

J. W. Beattie
Lake Marion and Mount Gould c. 1880

AFTER CHARLES WALTER
BRIDGE OVER THE DELEGATE AT QUEDONG 1871

The pandanus in *Mount Ida, Lake St Clair*, a stereoscope by Morton Allport taken in Tasmania in 1862, is equally suspicious. This grass tree not only looks as if it is propped up by the log in front of it; it is also perfectly positioned to satisfy the conventions of the picturesque. Already in 1863 the Tasmanian monthly, *Walch's Literary Intelligencer*, declared this stereograph 'the most beautiful and artistic' of Allport's photographs. More recently, Ann-Marie Willis identified it as one of Allport's few photographs to take 'full advantage of the stereoscopic effect because it has . . . a clearly defined foreground (a large grass tree), middle distance (bushes and a man in a boat on the lake) and background (mountain)'.[27]

Carleton Watkins and William Henry Jackson were probably at least as quick to refashion the landscape, despite being the two American photographers most often identified with the rise of environmental concerns because of the role played by their work in the protection of Yosemite and Yellowstone. When Watkins made his second trip to Yosemite with the California State Geological Survey in 1865–66, he had one tree trimmed of its branches to open what he

MORTON ALLPORT
MOUNT IDA, LAKE ST CLAIR
1862

regarded as the 'best general view' of the valley. In Oregon in 1867, he repeatedly felled trees so that he could secure new views of the Columbia River.[28]

HOW EUGENE VON GUÉRARD GOT HIS VIEW

Landscape painters did not have the same need to shape their views in this way. They could shift position—making a foreground sketch from one spot while sketching their middle ground and distance from another. They could invent their foregrounds, omitting obstructions and introducing trees to frame their views and figures or animals to enliven them. In 1792 the Reverend William Gilpin declared:

> I hold myself at perfect liberty . . . to dispose the *foreground* as I please; restrained only by the analogy of the country . . . I pare a knoll, or make an addition to it. I remove a piece of paling—a cottage—a wall—or any removable object, which I dislike.

Not least, Gilpin boasted, 'I take up a tree here, and plant it there'.[29]

Comparison of preliminary drawings and finished paintings reveals that Australian colonial artists similarly manipulated their foregrounds so that they would satisfy the conventions of the picturesque and contain more 'typical' local content, which appealed particularly to a foreign audience. The situation was much the same in the United States. As Barbara Novak has observed, Thomas Cole thought it kind 'to let the ancient trees stand, altering them at will in composition, or imposing Claudian pastorales on them when the mood demanded. The artist made the necessary changes on canvas. Nature remained intact.'[30]

Yet artists could not always obtain the views they wanted by working around nature. In 1811 the English landscape painter Joseph Farington congratulated a landowner for directing his steward not to allow any trees to be felled near Lodore Waterfall in the Lake District. But because 'the trees had grown so abundantly as to intercept every good view' of the falls, Farington also told the landowner that 'much improvement might be made under judicious direction'. To Farington's manifest delight, the landowner responded that he could take charge: 'He said that should *I* go there again He wd. rather leave this to my taste & direction than to that of any other person'.[31]

The colonial artist who opened most views was Thomas Mitchell, who had a gang of convicts under his command. In 1828, when Mitchell made a One Tree Hill of Mount Jellore near Mittagong, he spent more than two days sketching the panorama. Other colonial artists simply had their own axes or tomahawks. On a trip from Ferntree Gully to the Baw Baw plateau in 1858, Eugene von Guérard carried 'a big knapsack, in front a roll of blankets—a sketchbook in a leather case at his side—round his waist a hunting knife—a tomahawk—a tobacco pouch'. Nicholas Chevalier carried an even greater armoury: 'shot and powder—knife and tomahawk in belt—gun on shoulder'.[32]

The artists needed these tomahawks to clear their paths, but they probably also occasionally used them to open new views. One example may be von Guérard, who made his preliminary sketches for *Ferntree Gully in the Dandenong Ranges* (page 100) while timber-getters were hard at work, cutting tracks and searching out the tallest, straightest mountain ash to reduce to palings and shingles. As one contemporary account put it, the only Europeans to go to the Dandenongs were 'the woodman, who repairs thither to fell their gigantic timber' and 'the adventurous artist, who visits them for the purpose of transferring to his canvas the marvels of their scenery'.[33]

The potential for conflict between the artist and the timber-getter is illustrated by *The Picturesque and the Practical*, a cartoon in

ATTRIBUTED TO
NICHOLAS CHEVALIER
THE PICTURESQUE AND THE PRACTICAL 1858

Melbourne Punch in 1858, drawn most likely by Nicholas Chevalier, who knew something of both activities, having come out to Australia in 1854 partly to inspect his father's sawmill at Beechworth. 'The Picturesque and the Practical' shows how easily a colonial landscape painter could lose his subject. 'Having made a pleasing sketch of a picturesque gum tree', the artist 'returns two days afterwards to complete the picture, but finds the aspect of his subject has materially changed in the interval'. The tree has become a stack of palings.[34]

No such conflict divided von Guérard and Thomas Dobson in the Dandenongs. As well as sketching Dobson's hut, von Guérard stayed with him, probably more than once. The two also had an identity of interest so far as certain clearing was concerned. Dobson needed to turn the trees into railway sleepers, piles and palings. Von Guérard needed them cleared to create a view within the forest. When James Smith first reviewed *Ferntree Gully*, he noted that it was only because of 'the felling of some timber' that von Guérard could 'obtain a fore-ground sufficiently clear of obstructive objects' to allow him to include 'the distance in his range of vision'.[35]

Who was responsible for this axework? Von Guérard may simply have exploited a view already opened by Dobson as part of his

EUGENE VON GUÉRARD
CABBAGE-TREE FOREST, AMERICAN CREEK, NEW SOUTH WALES C. 1867

ordinary timber-getting. But it may be that von Guérard asked Dobson to fell these trees for him or even took up an axe himself, drawing on his experience on the Ballarat goldfields, where his only surviving diary records that he spent days 'felling trees, sawing the trunks into lengths, and splitting these into planks'.[36]

This diary suggests that when von Guérard arrived in Australia he had little concern for his new environment. If he came to regret the 'stretches of fine forest transformed into desolate-looking bare spaces, worked over and abandoned', his reason was not so much the devastation of the landscape but that, for all their toil, so many miners left the diggings no richer and sometimes even poorer than when they started. Had he been more successful, he might well have thought this destruction justified.[37]

The letter-press accompanying von Guérard's lithographed *Australian Landscapes*, published between 1866 and 1868, casts little more light on his environmental values. While von Guérard contributed information about his subjects, he could not have written the text, as the English was too good. In any event, it too was ambivalent about environmental change. Most significantly, the text accompanying his *Cabbage-Tree Forest, American Creek, New South*

Wales gloried in the diversity of the Illawarra's 'magnificent forests', but it accepted that the 'progress of settlement' necessitated their destruction because they hid 'a rich chocolate soil of especial value to the farmer'.[38]

Whatever its origins, the axework at Ferntree Gully did not trouble James Smith, who delighted in the 'sylvan solitude' of von Guérard's subject, 'the magnificent group of fern-trees with their curving feathery frondage' and the 'swelling amphitheatre beyond'.[39] While Smith was a powerful advocate of environmental protection from the early 1860s, he may not have yet developed these concerns when he first reviewed von Guérard's painting in 1857. Alternatively, he may have remained unconcerned because Ferntree Gully continued to appear intact in von Guérard's painting, although the axework could not have been far off to allow him to get his view.

Smith probably also thought the clearing in a good cause—assisting Art. Even if von Guérard had been involved, he had done no more than put into practice the prevailing theory that it was the artist's job not just to record nature but to improve it. As another colonial critic observed, it was 'heresy' to suggest that artists should confine themselves to reproducing the 'beautiful in nature . . . presenting the most beautiful objects in the most favorable aspects'. The common 'conceit', which Smith embraced, was that it would 'not do to paint nature exactly as she appears'; there was always a 'redundancy to be omitted, or deficiency to be supplied'.[40]

AIN'T THEM TREES IN YOUR WAY?

Arthur Streeton was another landscape painter to encourage axework, although the circumstances were more bizarre. As Streeton recalled in his unpublished 'Personal Narrative', he was working on the Hawkesbury River in 1896, painting what became *The Purple Noon's Transparent Might*, when a local roadmender called Ned Hogan accosted him carrying an axe. Hogan had threatened Streeton when they had met earlier at the local hotel, but this time he was friendly. He asked, 'Ain't them trees in your way?' Streeton replied, 'Yes, they are, they spoil the view.' Hogan then 'advanced to the trees . . . His axe rose with mighty sweeps, and with a few blows the trees crashed down the precipice and unveiled a perfect view.'[41]

More usually, landscape painters benefited from clearing but took no part in it. One of Eccleston du Faur's companions, who helped

ARTHUR STREETON
THE PURPLE NOON'S TRANSPARENT MIGHT 1896

with the axework in the Grose Valley, recorded that their object was to clear views not just for the photographer but also for 'the sketcher', W. C. Piguenit. Elsewhere landscape painters must have often taken advantage of views accidentally opened by timber-getters, just as excursionists often used routes created by splitters.[42]

The need for such view-making was already recognised in 1846 when an excursionist to Mount Wellington called for 'some of the trees [to] be taken away to show a clearer view of the Falls'. Forty years later, a contributor to the *Argus* called for axework in the Upper Yarra country between the Black Spur and Marysville, north-east of Melbourne:

> Another way in which art might be made to assist nature would be to cut down trees and so disclose to view scenes of beauty which are now hidden from the eye. It is disappointing, to say the least of it, to climb some thousands of feet and find oneself hemmed in by timber. The trees, doubtless, are magnificent, and much to be admired, but

the absence of a few here and there would make all the difference between a grand view and none at all.[43]

One Tree Hill above Ferntree Gully was one spot that provided such a view for many years because of the axework of the surveyors who made it a trigonometrical survey point in the 1850s. In the late 1880s it was a commonplace that 'no painting, were it even photographically executed, could possibly convey the faintest idea' of the view towards the city. But regrowth soon threatened this vista. While a local guide book applauded the 'good sense' of those who had opened new views by clearing along the road from Ferntree Gully, James Smith called for more axework at One Tree Hill itself so that excursionists could enjoy an unobstructed view of the city.[44]

Smith's colleague at the *Argus*, Francis Myers, also advocated selective viewmaking, but in the interests of art, not tourism. While travel writers commonly invoked landscape paintings as a yardstick for their descriptions, Myers was exceptionally interested in art. Sometimes he discussed European works in Australian collections, but more often he invoked paintings of the scenes he was describing, even though some of these pictures could not have been known to his Victorian readers. When Myers described himself as sitting on the 'very spot' where W. C. Piguenit had painted 'a very great picture of the Murray Valley', he implicitly underlined his own good taste, helping to justify his extended word pictures.[45]

Myers was a friend or associate of many landscape painters and was quick to promote their work, often presenting an alternative to James Smith's view of contemporary art. In one of his first essays for the *Argus* in 1887, Myers described how John Ford Patterson had been painting around Bacchus Marsh for weeks, preparing 'material, as he hopes for pictures which will do a little to interpret the scenic mysteries of Australia, and not appeal in vain to patrons of Australian art'. When Tom Roberts was in the Riverina in 1891, Myers indirectly boosted his work by calling for an artist to paint what became Roberts's *A Break Away!* At the same time, Myers championed the work of Arthur Streeton, whom he recognised as the only artist to make a 'serious attempt to paint the face of Australia's summer' and achieve 'a true, if crude, conception of the summer's heat'.[46]

Another of Myers's themes was the profligacy of colonial pastoralists. In a characteristic account of the Riverina, he deplored the 'pitiful . . . crazy work' that saw tens of thousands of seedlings and saplings destroyed along the Murray annually. He lamented 'the waste and the unthrift, and the utter disregard of our obligations to posterity which our perpetual work of deforestation betrays and proclaims'. He was no less appalled that in good seasons, when there was 'grass enough to spare', pastoralists did nothing to conserve it. When he asked about ensilage, they replied 'Well, yes', but took 'no practical steps in that direction'.[47]

Myers was equally shocked by the pastoralists' acceptance of pests on their land. When he came on a 'crop' of thistles in the Riverina 'miles broad and very high', the landholders explained that clearing them was 'too much trouble, no labour, wouldn't pay'. When he asked about the locusts 'coming out of the soil in millions', local 'optimists' maintained that there was 'grass enough for sheep and locusts too' until the locusts went away of their own accord. But Myers sensed that things were profoundly awry. As he put it:

> These plagues and pests, coming on us unexpectedly, inexplicable as sudden strokes from the mace of fate, are possibly in the nature of reminders from something very great and perfectly unassailable and slightly reverenced, and often madly flouted and not very well understood.[48]

Myers' sense that colonists were violating the laws of God—or at least the 'Balance of Nature'—turned him into a powerful advocate of environmental protection. But, like Eccleston du Faur and J. W. Beattie, he also wanted more 'views', even if trees had to be felled to reveal them. In writing about the country between Marysville and the Black Spur, Myers lamented that such clearing was 'in the category of nobody's business':

> A few judicious axe strokes are badly wanted here . . . toppling two or three trees by the roadside right over into the gorge, where the scrub growth would speedily bury them. If three trees were so removed, an uninterrupted view would be obtained of a valley and mountain which were designed by nature to prompt and gratify the painter's art. Just exactly suited to a moderate canvas.[49]

Elsewhere views were opened by a combination of private and public action. One of the primary objects of the trustees responsible for the National Park south of Sydney was to open new roads and walks and clear old ones so that all visitors, 'including ladies and young children', could enjoy the 'excellent views' and 'charming vistas' with 'ease and safety'. In the Blue Mountains track-cutting became a matter of competition between local boards, trusts and Progress Associations at Lawson, Wentworth, Hazelbrook and Katoomba. Local residents named Mount Piddington near Katoomba after the former Colonial Treasurer, who not only had tracks opened to the mountain but also had many trees on its summit felled so that visitors could enjoy an uninterrupted view of the country.[50]

SHOOTING, SHOOTING, SHOOTING

The use of the axe in view-making was equalled, if not surpassed, by that of the gun in natural-history illustration. While some animals were trapped and then killed in the studio, either by suffocating them or piercing their hearts with a steel pin, most were shot in the field. When the natural-history painter John Lewin sailed for New South Wales in 1799, his kit included 'A Long barreld gun 6 feet in the Barrel'.[51] The great trick of the illustrator was to restore life to his specimens through art.

The embodiment of the marksman–artist was America's most famous bird man, J. J. Audubon, who was not only a remarkable watercolourist but also an accomplished hunter. His field equipment included a shotgun, pistol, Dakota Indian war club, pipe-tomahawk and gun-shaped war club of the Mandan Indians. All major portraits of Audubon show him with rifle rather than portfolio in hand. So eager was he to present himself as a great hunter that in one of his watercolours he depicted himself as trapper, with a gun and dead bird slung over his back and a tomahawk in his right hand, even though the golden eagle in the picture was one he had bought rather than caught.[52]

Audubon's appetite for hunting extended far beyond his own art. While he railed against the 'brutal propensity' of the Labrador 'eggers', whose object was 'to plunder every nest' and 'kill every bird' that came their way, his own narratives reveal that he delighted in 'rare sport', often going out in the field simply for the enjoyment of the chase and the kill. He recognised that certain types of hunting were 'probably too well understood and too successfully practised in the United States', but hoped to 'induce' his readers to take to the woods with their guns.[53]

This passion for hunting is clearest in Audubon's account of his expedition to the Florida Keys, an area rich in ibises, godwits, flamingos, frigate pelicans and fish-crows. When Audubon first approached Indian Key, his 'heart swelled with uncontrollable delight' at so many new birds and he 'longed to make a more intimate acquaintance with them'. His method of doing so was crude:

> Each of us provided with a gun, posted himself behind a bush, and no sooner had the water forced the winged creatures to approach the shore, than the work of destruction commenced. When at length it ceased, the collected mass of birds of different kinds looked not unlike a small haycock.[54]

Photography promised an alternative mode of 'shooting' that would leave the target intact instead of destroying it. In 1882 one of the French pioneers of photography of birds in flight invented a new camera, which he called a 'photographic gun'. At much the same time, the idea of 'sport' was re-cast so that the challenge became that of pitting one's skill against the natural shyness of the animal. In another word-play, the new breed of field naturalist–photographer delighted 'in obtaining a big "bag" without harm to a single creature'. When R. S. Sugars delivered a lecture to Victoria's Field Naturalists in 1891, he took obvious delight in making much of the 'weapons' he carried on a field trip, only to reveal they were 'nothing more murderous than two cameras'.[55]

In practice, the shift from one type of shooting to another was neither simple nor swift. Collectors had to work hard to persuade themselves that it was better to have a photograph than a stuffed bird or blown egg. Instead of cameras replacing guns, the two coexisted for many years. Sugars often carried both 'in the event of finding anything interesting'.[56] But gradually the gun became a last resort; the camera supplanted it as the primary, then the only tool.

Sugars' friend Archibald 'Beaky' Campbell embodied this shift in values. When Campbell first went to the Dandenongs 'in quest for game' in 1869, aged just sixteen, his appetite for hunting would have impressed even J. J. Audubon. As Campbell recalled without apparent embarrassment in 1883:

> We had not travelled far before we came on to a stringy-bark flat, which abounded with Bronze-wing pigeons. We diminished their

> ranks by several braces, and likewise bagged a good many Wattle-birds and King Parrots. This finished the morning's work. In the afternoon we went in search of bears, shot one or two, skinned them, and returned to camp. In the evening we did a little 'possum shooting. Next morning more Bronze-wing shooting, and home was the cry of the afternoon.

Yet Campbell also made plain that such slaughter was no longer acceptable. As part of his argument that the killing of birds could be justified only 'to prove some portion of their economy for scientific knowledge', he called for Victoria's Game Act to be strengthened and enforced. It was 'shameful', he declared, that many of Australia's 'useful and beautiful birds' were shot or hunted in a 'wanton and ruthless manner', 'often under the cognisance of the police'. He urged the Field Naturalists' Club and the Zoological Society to work together to persuade the government 'to have the Game Act more stringently carried out, and likewise amend it by adding thereto many of our gay-plumaged birds'.[57]

By 1884 Campbell was not only calling for the list of protected species to be increased sixfold—from 39 to 239—but also warning that the retention of native forests and protection of wetlands were at least as significant as law enforcement. When the Australasian Association for the Advancement of Science held its inaugural meeting in 1888, Campbell took the opportunity to press for uniform bird protection legislation across the continent, and promptly became the Victorian representative on the new Association's Protection of Native Birds and Animals Committee. Campbell maintained that it made little sense to protect species in one colony when they could be killed with impunity across the border. As he put it, the question of bird protection added 'another string to the bow of Federation'—perhaps the first time anyone suggested that the creation of the Commonwealth could result in better environmental protection.[58]

Campbell probably had many reasons for turning to photography in the 1880s, initially asking Nicholas Caire to take occasional pictures for him, then doing so himself. With the invention of dry plates, photography offered a means of catching movements too fast to be followed by the eye. It was also the cheapest means of producing plates for reproduction, facilitating the publication of Campbell's two-volume *Nests and Eggs of Australian Birds* in 1900 with 131 illustrations. Photography also enabled birds to be recorded alive—a key issue for someone with Campbell's increasingly preservationist values.[59]

Photography therefore worked both for and against preservation of the environment. So far as the landscape was concerned, the new technology was destructive where the old had been relatively benign. But when it came to natural-history illustration, photography facilitated nature preservation, allowing animals to be recorded without even trapping them. Under Campbell's editorship, the Australian ornithologists' journal, the *Emu*, began carrying a regular column on 'Camera Craft' in 1915. According to the *Emu*, the number of ornithologists abandoning the rifle for the camera was 'steadily on the increase'. It was 'becoming recognised' that the work of the naturalist who could 'bring living animals before the eyes of others' was 'of higher value than the work of the collector of specimens'.[60]

By 1919 there was a Nature Photographers' Club of Australia. A year later, when the nature writer Charles Barrett edited a book of their work, he made much of how 'hunting with a camera' satisfied the 'instinct for the chase' that lurked 'in every man' without causing destruction, which was 'hateful to all lovers of Nature'. Part of 'The Bird-Lovers' Pledge' sung by members of the Gould League ran:

To hurt them is not manly
Nor is it any fun
So we'll shoot them with a camera
But never with a gun.

Yet, were it not for the gun's continuing attraction, these lines would have been redundant.[61]

OF HEROES AND VILLAINS

The enthusiasm of artists for the axe and the gun has been overlooked, and not just in Australia. How else could George Bird Grinnell, editor of the American monthly *Forest and Stream*, have chosen the 'Audubon Society' as the name for a new Society for the Protection of Birds in 1886? How else can it be that, for most of the last forty years, American photographers such as Carleton Watkins and William Henry Jackson have been presented as key figures in the emergence of a new respect for nature?

In a rare environmental critique of artists working on the American frontier, the American art historian Nancy Anderson has berated artists such as Sanford Gifford, Albert Bierstadt and Thomas Moran for failing to depict the despoliation of the environment. She has also accused them of implying that there was little or no conflict 'between the spectacular natural beauty of the land . . . and the inevitable changes that accompanied the conversion of minerals, forests, and water'. According to Anderson, these artists were just like all the other carpetbaggers who flocked to the West, 'mining' the landscape 'for the raw materials from which they fashioned studio paintings'.[62]

If the celebration of the artist as conservationist went too far—elevating an avid gun-man into the namesake of one of America's most significant environmental organisations—this revisionism is also too extreme. While landscape painters presented a manifestly selective image of the American frontier, there is still a large gap between their celebrations of nature and the devastation wrought by miners and loggers. Where miners and loggers laid waste, artists on the whole left the environment intact.

Other recent criticisms of nineteenth-century painters also beg the question of how much one can expect of artists working on the frontier. For example, Paul Fox and Jennifer Phipps have indicted Australian colonial painters for their adoption of the picturesque, which they characterise as an agent of dispossession 'born of the eighteenth century enclosure movement and the subsequent construction of the gentleman's park from communally used land'.[63] Yet even if one accepts this account of the picturesque, is it reasonable to imply that artists should have quickly invented a new visual language for a new place or, just as difficult, adopted one not identified with the rich and powerful?

The economic situation of artists working on the frontier is also an issue. Had artists sought to expose environmental destruction, as Anderson suggests, they would have found no market for their paintings, at least in the mid-nineteenth century, and probably not even in the 1880s or 1890s. Perhaps most significantly, Anderson fails to take account of the way in which artists most closely resembled miners and loggers—when they took up axes and guns in the pursuit of their art. If one wants clear examples of the painter or photographer treating the natural environment as a resource ripe for exploitation, it is the trigger-happy, axe-ready artist.

Augustus Earle
A Bivouac of Travellers in Australia c. 1838

This destructiveness is of no consequence if we recognise that many colonial landscape painters and photographers were happy to see the wilderness opened as part of the advancement of European settlement. Consider, for example, what Augustus Earle had to say about his visit to the Illawarra in 1827, which resulted in *A Bivouac of Travellers in Australia*, the only Australian subject he exhibited at the Royal Academy in London. While Earle delighted in the subtropical vegetation, he also treated the forest as something to be exploited:

Such tangled thickets now we passed, such mighty trees we saw,
Such giants of Australian growth, now fill'd my mind with awe,
They seemed to say in future times, we'll guard our native shore
Such Navies shall grow out of us, as ne'er were seen before.[64]

The realisation that artists were axemen matters a great deal, however, if we start from the premise that celebration rests on appreciation and respect. The artist's use of the axe and the gun breaks this nexus. This rupture is disturbing enough when the work of art includes some sign of what has gone on. While we may not know who felled the trees in Joseph Bischoff's panorama of the Grose Valley, at least there is tangible evidence of something awry. We have a chance to recognise the basis of the celebration offered. The breakdown between celebration and conservation is even more disturbing where the work itself gives no hint of what has gone on and only the written record may reveal how the art was produced.

This problem is most acute in relation to a work such as von Guérard's *Ferntree Gully*, which seems to treat nature as cathedral—the fern gully as a sacred place. Because this view of nature is so close to that of contemporary environmentalism, it is easy to presume a complete identity of values. We should beware. The painting may not be what it seems. We need to accept the possibility that the Australian colonial artist who, perhaps more than any other, seems to have valued nature in all its detail, may have been happy to destroy it just to be able to present this view.

THE BEGINNING.

"IN THE MORNING OF LIFE, WHEN THE BEAUTIFUL MARRIED THE TRUE, THEIR OFFSPRING WAS THE KALIZOIC SOCIETY."—*Adapted from the President's Address.*

THOMAS CARRINGTON *THE BEGINNING* 1884

CHAPTER EIGHT

THE KALIZOIC BROTHERHOOD

It may truly be said of the Kalizoic Society that till it was started the existence of the Beautiful was unknown among us. Advertisements covered our walls, houses were ill built and ugly, and the clothing of both men and women was hideous and unsuitable. Most of can remember the time when the Fitzroy, the Flagstaff, and other public gardens were howling wastes filled with the sweepings of the streets and the rubbish from back yards; while the Government offices scattered over the city were a disgrace to civilisation and a heartbreak to people of an aesthetic turn of mind. Our streets were unplanted and undrained, our beautiful Yarra a common sewer, our theatres refuges for fleas and traps for catching draughts and bad smells, and the young men of Melbourne and its suburbs were about as unlovely a lot as ever offended the eye of the artist. How all this is changed is now a matter of history.

MELBOURNE PUNCH, 21 AUGUST 1884

WHO NOW REMEMBERS the Kalizoic Society? Who even knows what 'kalizoic' means, or would think of it as an Australianism? 'Jumbuck', 'billabong' and 'matilda', yes; but not 'kalizoic'. It sounds too highfalutin. Yet 'kalizoic' was at least as Australian as ringbarking, although it was a product of the city not the country—a word that arose not from opening up unfamiliar country but from attempting to beautify the urban environment.[1]

Like many colonial organisations, the Kalizoic Society was based on a British model. Its inspiration was the Kyrle Society, which was formed in London in 1875 and had a similarly cryptic name. But, as with all such transplants, the new institution did not simply mirror the old. Where the Kyrle Society was devoted to assisting the deserving poor, the Kalizoics were at least as interested in improving Melbourne's most fashionable suburbs.

The society's instigator was Louis Henry, a German doctor who arrived in Melbourne via London in 1879 and promptly set about establishing a local branch of the British Medical Association. Five years later Henry wrote to the *Argus* calling for a 'Kalizoic Society'—from the Greek *Kalos* or beauty and *zoe* life. As he described it, the new society would be devoted to 'the encouragement and cultivation of the beautiful'. It would make 'a systematised effort to improve' Melbourne.[2]

Henry's letter was followed immediately by an editorial from the *Argus* and another letter from that 'Victorian Virtuoso', James Edward Neild, who was not only Melbourne's leading pathologist but also one of its most interesting art and theatre critics. Neild was ripe for the kalizoic enterprise. Like Keats, he believed in a 'religion of beauty'. At times he even suggested that beauty become a substitute for religion.[3]

This support was enough to give life to Henry's idea, though most colonists still needed to be told that 'kalizoic' had 'not much to do with geology, and still less with a medical preparation similar to Eno's fruit salt'. Within eight weeks the Kalizoic Society had a constitution and a committee led by the *Argus*'s own James Smith. In the hothouse of Melbourne's literary world, Smith had earlier gone from being a witness at Neild's wedding to a target of his nastiest prose. Neild falsely accused Smith of accepting bribes in return for favourable theatrical reviews. With more reason, he declared Smith a plagiarist. But by 1884 the two men had made up, allowing them to collaborate in the kalizoic cause.[4]

The new society was one of Australia's first environmental organisations. Its only predecessor of any longevity in Melbourne was the Australian Health Society, which the unitarian preacher and feminist Martha Turner had founded in 1875. By staging 'Meetings for Wives and Daughters' in working-class suburbs and public lectures by the likes of James Smith on the benefits of sunlight, the Society sought to persuade the 'respectable poor' to practise 'sanitary economy'. Its premise was that individual action could secure public health.[5]

Henry's emphasis on the beautiful gave his venture a very different complexion. While the weekly *Australasian* maintained that 'very few nowadays' questioned that the beautiful was 'as essential a factor in progressive intellectual life as the useful or the moral', *Melbourne Punch* could not resist the target Henry offered. Although *Punch* regularly illustrated what was wrong with Melbourne's environment, the Kalizoics' concern with the beautiful was exactly the kind of high-minded sentiment it liked to deflate. When James Smith gave the society's inaugural address, *Punch* devoted almost two pages to mocking the Kalizoics in print, while its chief cartoonist, Thomas Carrington, ridiculed the new society's beginnings in a full-page cartoon.[6]

This ridicule proved warranted: the actions of Melbourne's experts in aesthetics bore no relation to their rhetoric. But 'kalizoic' acquired a life of its own. It became a byword for fashionable taste in interior decoration—the name of an emporium that, thirty years later, still claimed to be Melbourne's 'most up-to-date warehouse for art furnishings and furniture'.[7] It also entered general usage in both Melbourne and Sydney, when the degradation of the urban environment was being challenged on aesthetic grounds.

COLOUR, SPACE AND MUSIC

The Kalizoic Society might never have existed without Octavia Hill, one of the many women who changed the shape of nineteenth-century philanthropy. While other philanthropists were 'polluted', as she saw it, by 'a depraved hunger for rags, sharp need, and slums', Hill devoted herself to improving the physical and moral well-being of England's 'industrious thrifty working people'. Of all the major Victorian housing reformers, she alone regarded aesthetic questions as essential to her work, she fought to ensure that 'colour, space and music' were enjoyed by those who had 'least of them'.[8]

Hill began acquiring her first houses in London in 1865, using capital lent to her at nominal interest by John Ruskin, who had just come into his inheritance. The big model tenements then being built in London involved large-scale demolitions and evictions. Hill, by contrast, bought small blocks, renovated them and let them at low rents, either without displacing the original tenants or by accommodating them in her other houses. By the 1880s she was managing £70 000 worth of property—a remarkable sum for someone who had no independent means. But, while she may have had as many as 6000 tenants, this number was insignificant given the shortage of housing in London.[9]

Hill was always concerned for her tenants' broader environment. Whereas the big model blocks were notoriously drab and forbidding, Hill wanted to develop a 'love of beauty' among her tenants and bring 'joy and beauty in their lives'. At her first model dwellings she created a playground, which Ruskin's gardener maintained and planted with trees. She also began holding singing classes for married women and older girls, gave them bunches of flowers and taught them the art of flower arrangement. At least once a year she organised 'intervals of bright joy' so her tenants could experience the countryside at first hand.[10]

The Kyrle Society generalised this work. A few devotees of Alexander Pope's verse probably recognised that John Kyrle was the model for Pope's 'Man of Ross', who established a public park and planted elms in Ross-on-Wye. Octavia's sister Miranda characterised the new organisation more accessibly as a 'Society for the Diffusion of Beauty'. In 1883, the year before the Kalizoic Society was established, the Kyrle Society was flourishing with branches in Manchester and Liverpool. Its open spaces committee devoted the bulk of its funds to buying three disused burial grounds for conversion into public gardens. Its musical branch performed forty-five oratorios and concerts in churches, hospitals and workhouses. It also gave flowers to the poor and pictures to benevolent institutions.[11]

PUBLIC HEALTH AND ARTISTIC CULTURE

Melbourne did not need a Kalizoic Society to tell it that the beautiful was integral to the physical and moral quality of colonial life. Already in 1879 James Smith had written an essay for the weekly *Australasian* in which he called for 'a mission for beautifying the land we live in' so as to improve 'individual and national character'. Smith's ambition was to make the Australian countryside more English. For all his new appreciation of the gum tree, he still called for rural landowners and townspeople to join together in a 'Flower Mission', sowing the seeds of English wildflowers such as primroses and pansies along colonial hedgerows within easy distance of Victoria's major towns and cities. His goal was to emulate English lanes, which he reckoned 'one of the most beautiful objects in the world'.[12]

The journalist George Bicknell was much more wide-ranging in 'A Plea for Sanitation', published in the *Victorian Review* in 1882. According to Bicknell, aesthetics, public health and public morality were inseparable. He maintained that it was imperative to give society both 'the means for cleanliness and the cultivation of a taste for beauty'. 'Fresh air, cold water, soap, paint, pictures, sculptures, books, flowers, trees' were all 'regenerative influences' that tempered 'foulness and vulgarity'.[13]

Bicknell was so sure the 'longing for beauty' was a great virtue that he even endorsed the 'aesthetic cult' led by Oscar Wilde and James McNeill Whistler, with its 'knee-breeched youths and limp-skirted damsels'. While acknowledging that it was impossible not to smile at 'the aesthete contemplating sunflowers and lilies', Bicknell still applauded such a commitment to beauty. He bracketed the 'fierce tones of the apostle of art' and 'the mincing delicacy of the apostle of aestheticism' with the 'really valuable', 'common-sense' aestheticism of sanitary reformers and evangelists who were taking gutter children out of the city into the countryside.[14]

Bicknell partly looked to government to advance this work. He called for the appointment of a Minister for Health with wide-ranging environmental and cultural responsibilities, including:

> the administration of a Building Act; the important business of sewage; the enforcement of all health statutes and by-laws; the prevention of such terrible barbarisms as stream pollution and forest destruction; the encouragement of tree-planting; the advancement of technology and art studies; and the general oversight of all cognate matters of importance to the public health and artistic culture.

Bicknell predicted such a Ministry would 'work a revolution in society', but he maintained that anything the state could do, private effort could do 'invariably better'. His ideal was 'an association of capitalists, urged by philanthropic motives'.[15]

Melbourne was the first Australian city to boast such associations—probably because of its exceptional wealth as much as its mass of poverty. Its mayor and town clerk, Thomas McPherson and Edmund FitzGibbon, provided a catalyst in 1871, when they led a tour of the city's lodging houses, which, the *Australasian* excitedly reported, were 'so close and poisonously stinking that most of the visitors had to puff incessantly at cigars or pipes'. The inhabitants were 'nearly all of the loafer class—dirty, ragged, greasy, bleary-eyed'—hardly surprising, since the inspection took place between 11 p.m. and 2 a.m. They also were 'vicious-looking'. Yet even this sensationalism provided a corrective to the myth that everyone in Melbourne had enough to live on. FitzGibbon used the occasion to call for a model lodging house as a first step towards preserving the city from 'some deadly epidemic'.[16]

The response was immediate. The Victorian government granted the necessary land in King Street in the city. The Society for the Promotion of Morality took the lead in raising £5000 for the building, which was intended to provide overnight lodging 'for the poorer classes at an almost nominal sum, and yet sufficient to make the institution self-supporting'. In practice, the hostel was more commercial than charitable. The rent of sixpence a night was the same as that in common lodging houses. But at least this was less than the ninepence and then a shilling a night charged by the model lodging house established a decade later in Sydney, which consequently served more affluent working men, and even the lower middle class, rather than those most in need.

By 1882, when Bicknell wrote his essay, the Society for the Promotion of Morality had also helped to establish a Retreat for Fallen Women in Collingwood, a Prisoners' Aid Society and a Society for Prevention of Cruelty to Animals. A Women's Model Lodging House Company was also almost ready to call tenders and start building. But there were no colonial counterparts to the big model tenements or Octavia Hill's small blocks of houses, which provided permanent accommodation for the poor.[17]

To Bicknell's delight, this need looked as if it might finally be met. The idea was developed in the correspondence columns of the *Argus*. First an anonymous correspondent called on Melbourne's philanthropists to raise funds to close some of the public houses in the city's slums. Soon the Presbyterian radical Charles Strong was calling for a new company to buy slum tenements for demolition and reconstruction. Within a fortnight, this cause had been taken over by the Society for the Promotion of Morality, which also aspired to educate 'gutter children' and mitigate 'the terrible evils of prostitution and its exposure in the public streets'.[18]

Over the following weeks the *Argus* fuelled public concern by sending one of its journalists, along with 'the usual police guide', to gather material for another exposé of 'The Back Slums'. The Baptist clergyman Samuel Chapman added to the moral fervour with two 'manlike and spirit-stirring discourses' about the evil of these areas. The society issued a report in March 1883 calling for legislative reform so that the government could condemn existing buildings and control the plans of new ones. But neither public nor private action followed.[19]

THE TWO DOCTORS

Like George Bicknell, Louis Henry believed that private initiative was superior to government action, although he too wanted government help. When he first advanced the kalizoic idea in January 1884, Henry presented it primarily as a means of compensating for the dearth of 'taste and interest' among Melbourne's local councils when it came to beautifying parks and streets. He hoped a government grant would supplement private subscriptions, enabling the new society to turn Melbourne's 'many wildernesses' into gardens.[20]

Yet Henry also had broader concerns for the public domain. He took St Kilda as an example partly to show that there was work awaiting the new society across the entire city. If this 'fashionable watering place' was blighted by as many 'abominations' as Henry described, Melbourne's poorer suburbs could only be much worse off. But St Kilda was also the type of suburb from which Henry expected to attract most support, and he wanted to make clear that the 'better class of citizens' would benefit directly from the society's work.[21]

Henry declared that, whenever he took visitors to St Kilda, he was 'humiliated' by all the 'outrages upon the senses of sight and smell'. One problem was St Kilda's architecture, particularly the 'hideously designed bathing establishments'. Another was the ugliness of the esplanade, which was 'bleak, bare, comfortless and unsuggestive of any one pleasant idea'. A third was the degradation of the once-beautiful tea-tree scrub, which had become a dumping ground for 'all the broken bottles, old boots, disused pickle jars, empty sardine tins, and other domestic refuse of the neighbourhood' as well as the site of 'a noisome drain, and a reeking abattoir'.[22]

James Neild wanted to take the Kalizoic Society in a different direction. His primary concern was the destructiveness of the pupils at Melbourne's government schools, whom he declared 'absolute savages' because of their appetite for breaking branches off trees and tearing flowers from plants in public gardens. The solution, he believed, lay in incorporating the kalizoic ideal into public education. He was not against religious instruction in state schools, but he thought it more important that 'some of the finer kinds of morality' be instilled in children, particularly 'a reverence for the beautiful'.[23]

Neild also had a much wider agenda in mind. While Henry discussed only public space, Neild hoped to see similar improvement of Melbourne's front and back yards. Whereas Henry's first thoughts were of the city's well-to-do suburbs, Neild also wanted to improve its slums. He maintained that the Kalizoic Society would find 'an unlimited field for its operations' and should 'not by any means be limited to the precise lines laid down' by Henry's opening letter.[24]

The *Argus* was both bemused and impressed. It accepted the importance of improving Melbourne's parks and gardens, but it also suggested that the new 'kalizoic brotherhood' clean up the Yarra, which had been notoriously polluted for more than thirty years. While the colonial government had legislated in 1855 'to prevent the further pollution' of the river, this Act could never achieve this ambition because it did not apply to the Yarra's tidal reaches. It also went unenforced from the early 1860s, when its legitimacy was destroyed by attacks from advocates of new industry in working-class suburbs such as Richmond and Collingwood.[25]

Readers of the *Argus* were quick with other suggestions for the new society. One correspondent wanted the Kalizoics to superintend the design of all new buildings and add to the joys of fashionable society by taking charge of 'the laying out of promenades, . . . the placing of seats in the most charming spots, and the building of kiosks for the sale of coffee and light summer drinks'. Another wanted the Kalizoics to preserve the rivers of rural Victoria from the 'poisonous sludge' produced by the colony's mines.[26]

No voluntary organisation could have done everything asked of the Kalizoic Society. Some of the functions suggested for it required legislative support. Others were only possible with substantial funds. But such considerations did not worry Henry and his supporters, who decided to take up all the ideas mooted in the press and more. At the head of the new society's objects came 'the encouragement and cultivation of the beautiful'. Last was the enlistment of 'the sympathies of the professional and general public . . . by the creation of an artistic taste, and by constituting every citizen a custodian of our gardens, trees, and birds'.[27]

In between was something for everyone, rich and poor. One object was 'the placing of seats in suitable spots' and 'the erection of kiosks for light refreshment and shelter'. A second was 'the purification of the back slums' and 'the removal of all dwellings unfit for habitation'. Then came 'the encouragement of window, cottage or front gardening', 'the prevention of the pollution of our streams and reservoirs', 'the planting of trees and flowers' and 'the mitigation of the dust nuisance'. Finally there was 'the diffusion of correct principles of decoration', the application of 'the true principles of constructive art to domestic architecture' and 'the promulgation of objects of the society among the pupils of all the schools . . . so as to induce the young to become the natural guardians of whatever is intended for public enjoyment'.[28]

THE AESTHETICIANS

By March 1884 the Kalizoic Society had a committee embracing a broad cross-section of Melbourne's experts in aesthetics. Earlier organisations of colonial artists had included architects, just as the architects' institutes had included artists. The Kalizoic Society went much further. Its president was James Smith, who by then was a trustee of the National Gallery of Victoria as well as the *Argus*'s art critic. One of its vice-presidents was George Folingsby, Eugene von Guérard's successor as Director of the Gallery and Master of its Art School. Its committeemen included W. R. Guilfoyle, the renowned landscape gardener in charge of Melbourne's Botanic Gardens; George C. Gordon, the acclaimed 'scenic artist' at Melbourne's Theatre Royal; C. S. Patterson, the city's most fashionable exponent of 'interior ornamentation'; and Alexander Fletcher, who had become Melbourne's most successful art dealer at least partly because he showed just the odd Australian work amid endless consignments of European pictures.[29]

This array of aesthetic talent was supplemented by two architects. Nahum Barnet was just beginning to make a name for himself, having won the commission to design Melbourne's Workingmen's College, later the Royal Melbourne Institute of Technology. Although one would never know it from his prize-winning design, Barnet was a significant advocate of a 'vernacular', even 'indigenous', architecture suited to 'the exigencies of climate'. Joseph Reed was more established. Not only was he responsible for many of Melbourne's major public buildings, including the Town Hall, the Exhibition Building and the first section of the Public Library, but, as James Smith put it, he had contributed to a 'remarkable improvement' in the architecture and interior decoration of Melbourne houses.[30]

The other committeemen were more diverse. Patrick Moloney was another doctor. Henry Gullett was editor of the weekly *Australasian*. Ephraim Lamen Zox was the Member of Parliament for East Melbourne, president of the Melbourne Hebrew congregation and a pillar of many charitable causes. Edmund FitzGibbon had effectively ruled the City Council from 1856, using his position as Melbourne's town clerk to play a key role in defending the city's parks from attack and pressing for sanitary reform. The schoolmaster Alexander Sutherland had written a series of fables for the Australian Health Society.[31]

A public call for ladies to support 'so good a scheme' produced almost no response. Whereas seven of the twenty members of the Australian Health Society's first committee were women, the Kalizoic Society included just four on its committee of twenty-four, and it is likely that only two of these women were there in their own right. The others, Mrs James Smith and Mrs James Neild, were included because of their husbands' leading roles.[32]

ART AND INDUSTRY

Melbourne Punch was the one Victorian illustrated newspaper to share the Kalizoics' concern at the despoliation of the city's environment. In a typical cartoon in 1882, Thomas Carrington marked the forty-seventh anniversary of John Batman's exploration of the Yarra by depicting what Melbourne's founder would have

THOMAS CARRINGTON
NOW AND THEN 1882

discovered had he returned to the once 'pellucid stream'. Holding his nose under a sky blackened by smokestacks, Batman pulls his way through water 'so thick that it could be cut with a knife'.[33]

The rest of the illustrated press wanted only to show the progress of Australia's cities. When these newspapers depicted industrial subjects, the smokestacks symbolised the productiveness of colonial manufacturing, not damage to the environment.[34] Landscape painters were interested only in the Beautiful. Either they ignored industry when selecting subjects or they suppressed its adverse consequences—a common feature of views of the Yarra valley, which was one of the main painting grounds of Melbourne artists from the 1850s.

James Smith was prompted to consider this issue by Julian Ashton's first major series of Australian paintings—a set of watercolours on the Yarra between Brander's Ferry and Cole's Wharf. Already in 1872 Smith had deplored the 'disgustingly depraved and polluted' state of the Yarra as it crawled through Collingwood and beyond. Seven years later, he maintained that nothing could be 'more

JULIAN ASHTON
EVENING—MERRI CREEK
1882

unpromising for artistic purposes' than this 'foulest and ugliest part of the river'. But Smith went on to acknowledge that Ashton had succeeded in presenting this 'huge sewer' in a new light.[35]

This success made Smith think of Louis Buvelot. Just as the Swiss artist had 'revealed all sorts of previously unnoticed beauties in our indigenous timber and foliage, and . . . caused us to look upon our sylvan scenery with something like a new sense of vision', so Ashton had 'proved that under certain aspects of sky, and at particular periods of the day, the Yarra and the most prosaic objects on its banks' could be presented 'on paper, in such a way as to charm the vision, without any sacrifice of accuracy to pictorial effect'. But Smith had missed the difference between the two. Whereas Buvelot had prompted some of his fellow colonists to re-evaluate the natural, Ashton had found beauty in the degraded.[36]

When artists began painting *en plein air* in oils on the Yarra and its tributaries, the immediacy of this type of painting was not accompanied by a corresponding sensitivity to the state of the environment. One example is Ashton's 1882 view on Merri Creek, which he later claimed as the first oil painting executed out-of-doors in Australia. This landscape suggests nature undisturbed, but the reality was very different. Just a year before, members of the Health Committee of the Melbourne City Council had found that this creek was an 'abomination', fouled by the sewage and drainage of Coburg, East Brunswick and Northcote.[37]

Yet not all subjects were susceptible to such treatment in paint, which suppressed the nuisance more effectively than the law was able to do. Nahum Barnet identified these limits in January 1884 when he suggested that a kalizoic artist paint Melbourne's rubbish tip for the next exhibition of the Victorian Academy of Art. Barnet dwelt on how 'still life' was 'prettily represented by a score of obsolete boots [and] gracefully-grouped heaps of vegetables and flowers'; on the 'atmosphere' offered by 'the scourings of a thousand-and-one back yards'; and on the 'beautiful' that might be discovered by 'the dozen dilapidated urchins of questionable parentage . . . actively prodding amongst the rubbish'.[38]

Barnet did not expect any of Melbourne's painters to take up this challenge. He knew that the tip was too ugly; if any colonial artist followed his prescription, the result would be a picture that 'for realistic treatment, colourful effect, and breadth of tone' would surpass even that 'home of terrible realism in art—the Paris Salon'. But *Melbourne Punch* characteristically responded. Its next issue, published just two days later, included a cartoon of the tip captioned 'No Kalizoic Society wanted here. No "reaching out for the beautiful" needed.'[39]

THOSE FUNNY PEOPLE

Melbourne Punch showed the Kalizoics no mercy. Although James Smith had been its editor from 1857 until 1863 and James Neild one of its first contributors, *Punch* manufactured one excuse after another to lampoon the new society almost every week from January 1884. This reversal of roles was not one the former humorists enjoyed. More than a decade later, Neild was still bitter at how 'the distressingly funny people made poor jokes' about the society.[40]

The Corporation 'Tip' 1884

THE CORPORATION "TIP."

No Kalizoic Society wanted here. No "reaching out for the beautiful" needed.

One of these jokes started with a fist-fight in the anteroom of the New South Wales Legislative Assembly between two parliamentarians, Alexander Wisdom and David Buchanan. This fight had nothing to do with the Kalizoics, but *Punch* quipped that the way in which Wisdom ornamented Buchanan's eyes was 'a distinct violation of all Kalizoic rules, and would make any man of taste tear his hair out in frenzy'. According to *Punch*, Wisdom needed to be 'taught at once number 5 article of the Kalizoic synopsis—*i.e. "The diffusion of correct principles of decoration in all its branches"*'.[41]

A KALIZOIC SOCIETY AND ITS WORK.

[A correspondent of the *Argus* suggests that a "Kalizoic Society" be established to secure a "beautiful life" for the cities of Australia.]

1. *Their first operation will be on the Premier of N. S. W. They will Kalizoic him into a professional beauty.*

2. *The next attempt will be on that extraordinary growth at the centre of the back of our fashionably-dressed ladies. The Kalizoic pruning knife will cut remorselessly away the boil, or whatever it is.*

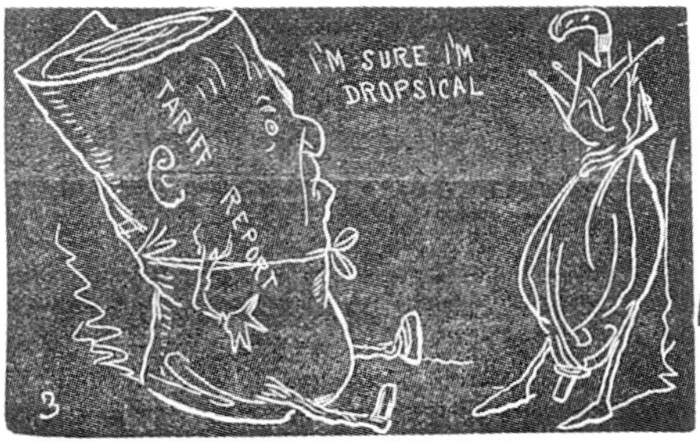

3. *That Tariff Report and that umbrella will both be brought under the influence of the Kalizoic people. Let us hope it will reduce their bulk and general un-Kalizoic appearance.*

4. *The* magnum opus *of the Society—To Kalizoic the larrikin and the gentleman who makes money by furnishing houses in the suburbs on time payment.*

A Kalizoic Society and its Work 1884

Punch had similar sport a fortnight later, when it claimed that the first task of the women on the committee of the Kalizoic Society would be to improve the crinolette—the reduced form of crinoline that excited such outrage in the early 1880s. *Punch* predicted that the women would 'be divided, one for continuing the tail, and two against its modification or abolition'. With characteristic mischief, *Punch* announced that the society had given its leader-writer permission to be present at the ladies' first meeting so long as he 'behaves himself and does not poke any fun'.[42]

The *Melbourne Bulletin* was at least as effective in making fun of the Kalizoics. One of its weekly women's letters from Gladys to Belle ran:

> You remark, dear, on the singularity of the fact that, with four exceptions, (three of them ladies), personal beauty among the Executive of the Kalizoic Society is conspicuous only by its absence.

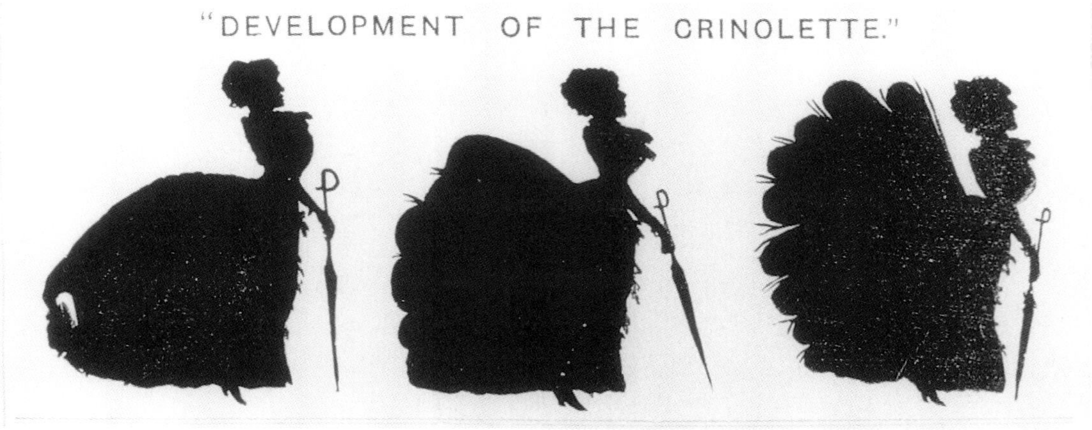

Development of the Crinolette 1884

> Why, you dear, innocent old goose, that's not strange at all. The choice was made designedly. It is intended that they commence at once on themselves, just to show the public what may be done with an unpromising subject. You must admit, dear, that the slightest improvement there would strike the most careless observer and . . . be a 'cheap ad'.

Even the Sydney *Bulletin* could not resist this new target. It quipped that the new society had established its head office in a former fellmongering establishment in Footscray, Melbourne's most industrialised suburb, which was notorious for its 'stinks'. According to the *Bulletin*, the Kalizoic Society would also be establishing branches on Collingwood Flat by the Yarra and in Little Bourke Street, Melbourne's most infamous slum. There was even a 'prospect of affiliation' with Sydney's 'own Kalizoic Club in Kent-street', notorious for its 'many wretched hovels'.[43]

The reputation of the society was further damaged in April 1884 by a very Victorian correspondence about 'The Coinage of New Words' in the *Argus*. This debate was started by a Melbourne physician, William Cutts, who noted archly that there was 'nothing beautiful in bad spelling'. An anonymous correspondent added that 'Greeks of the best period' preferred to make compounds from the noun 'kallos', not the adjective 'kalos', and hence the new society should be called 'Kallozoic'. When Henry justified his spelling by reference to 'calisthenic' and 'caligraphy', the response was that these words were 'simply as badly spelled as "kalizoic" itself, and should not be imitated'. All Henry could do was dismiss the debate as the stuff of pedants, but it still helped to make the society a laughing-stock.[44]

WHEN THE TRUTHFUL WOOED THE BEAUTIFUL

The Kalizoic Society's inaugural meeting and concert in May 1884 attracted a 'large and fashionable gathering' including Members of Parliament, judges, clergymen, doctors, solicitors, architects and artists. But the size of the crowd did not indicate support for the Kalizoic cause. The meeting was a place to look and to be seen. Probably as many people went out of curiosity—or to ridicule—as out of sympathy with the new society's ideals. The mood was best suggested the day before by Gladys of the *Melbourne Bulletin* in one of her regular letters to Belle:

> What a question to ask. Now, is it at all likely that I would miss such a swell affair as the Inaugural Concert of the Kalizoic Society? Everybody of note is sure to be there dressed in their most Kalizoic clothes. The musical part has been well catered for, and the best talent engaged, so that alone will be quite a treat, to say nothing of the change one is sure to see in the personal appearance of the promoters of this idea.[45]

Most of the evening was occupied by an address by James Smith, who countered the ridicule of the Kalizoics over the previous four months by emphasising the difficulty of what they had undertaken. Smith declared that since 1847, when Thackeray wrote 'In the Morning of Life the Truthful wooed the Beautiful, and their offspring was Love', it had 'demanded more than ordinary courage on the part of any writer or speaker to spell the word beautiful with a capital B'. To 'project a society which should dedicate its efforts to the cultivation of that sentiment in daily life' amounted 'almost to an act of audacious heroism'.[46]

Smith devoted the rest of his lecture to explaining the Kalizoic cause. As usual, he was 'exhaustive', but his lecture was not just a patchwork of famous authors, as was often the case. He argued that many of Melbourne's social problems were due to the separation of the urban population from nature. He reminded his audience of the 'barbarism', 'brutality' and 'ruffianism' lurking in the city; of how they were pained by 'the merely animal pleasures' in which certain sections of the population indulged. But, he went on:

> Do we ever ask ourselves to what extent the ugly, squalid, repulsive environments of these people are responsible for such habits and enjoyments; and whether, in fact, these men and women could be other than they are, while exposed to daily contact with everything that is physically and morally depressing, degrading and debasing.[47]

Smith called on property owners, local government, artists and architects to support the society in a 'crusade against ugliness'. He wanted the slums made 'sweet and wholesome', and 'neglected backyards' to be converted into 'miniature ferneries'. Like Octavia Hill, Smith also aspired to improve the morals of the residents of these areas. Whereas the Kyrle Society trusted in music, Smith looked to art as a compensation for the loss of nature in the city, offering an escape from 'dust and mire'—and from 'the dusty purposes and miry doings' of its inhabitants.[48]

The problem, Smith recognised, was to make art accessible. While members of his audience could cover their walls with oil paintings that reproduced 'the inexhaustible charm and infinite variety' of nature, this pleasure was 'the privilege of the few'. Smith wanted to see beauty in service 'for the sake of the many'. The answer lay in reproduction. Just as he supported the purchase of casts of classical sculptures for the National Gallery of Victoria, so he looked forward to seeing the bare walls of Melbourne's hospitals, benevolent asylums and orphanages covered with 'bright and cheerful' prints 'to relieve the eye, engage the attention, and occupy the thoughts of the sick; to dissipate the listlessness of old age; and to stir the imagination of friendless or forsaken childhood'.[49]

The great benefit Smith looked forward to was social cohesion. He was not just concerned for the plight of the urban working class; he also feared their capacity for violence, even revolution, an issue he had written about at length after visiting England in 1882–83. Smith maintained that the popularisation of a love of the beautiful would assist the 'levelling-up movement', which was 'the most effective antagonist to the anarchical tendencies of society in the older countries of the world'. He concluded:

> The more cheerful and beautiful life can be rendered for those who perform the manual toil of civilised races, the more firmly we weld together the different classes of the community by the sympathies which spring from common tastes and common enjoyments, common subjects of interest, common sentiments, common methods of looking at things that are both elevating and delightful, the more solid and durable will be the social edifice.[50]

TALK OF BEAUTY WITH A B AND CULTURE WITH A C

Smith's talk was grist to the mill of *Melbourne Punch*, which promptly identified the Kalizoic Society with the Aesthetic Movement, itself a constant butt of jokes. Although Smith dismissed Whistler's one painting to reach Melbourne as 'eccentric' and 'unintelligible', and was probably at least as contemptuous of Wilde's dandyism, *Punch* was able to make this connection because the Kalizoics and the Aesthetes were both preoccupied with the Beautiful. They also appeared similarly impractical.[51]

Punch was at its cleverest when it modelled a ditty on the best-known song from Gilbert and Sullivan's comic opera *Patience*, which premiered in London in April 1881 and was still showing there in July 1882, when the Williamson Opera Company brought it to Melbourne. *Patience* ridiculed and, ironically, also popularised the Aesthetic Movement. When it opened in Melbourne, the local *Bulletin* observed that, while the aesthetic dresses worn by the chorus were 'intended as caricatures', they were 'tasteful and becoming'. Soon 'everybody' was asking 'How do you like *Patience*?', 'Haven't you been to *Patience*?'[52]

Gilbert had written 'If you're anxious for to shine in the high aesthetic line as a man of culture rare, / You must get up all the germs of the transcendental terms, and plant them everywhere'. *Punch*'s variant ran:

> *If you're anxious for to shine in the Kalizoic line as a man of culture rare,*
> *You must get a lot of ferns, and with statuettes and urns, just plant them everywhere;*
> *Talk of beauty with a B and of culture with a C in a kind of complicated sort of way,*

And shudder at the taste of tins and bottles placed as an ornamental fringe around the bay.
And every one will say
As you walk your flowery way,
'If that's not good enough for him which is good enough for me,
Why what a cultivated kind of youth a Kalizoic youth must be.'

The accompanying full-page cartoon by Thomas Carrington (page 218) took Smith's opening quotation from Thackeray about the marriage between the beautiful and the true, and twisted it so that the Kalizoic Society became their offspring. Consistent with *Punch*'s ditty, Carrington showed the Kalizoics as Aesthetes with flowing locks and knee-breeches, sunflowers and lilies. Building on the *Melbourne Bulletin*'s running joke about the Kalizoics' looks, Carrington showed James Smith as 'The True', wonderfully transformed in his hand-mirror, more handsome than in life.[53]

ROTTEN ROW

Such criticism could not be answered by more talk. Lucy Gullett, a member of the Kalizoic Society's committee who wrote for the weekly *Australasian* as 'Humming Bee', recognised that the Society needed to 'justify its name'. She reported in July that, if it succeeded, a kindred society would probably start in New South Wales because the Kalizoic idea held a 'lively interest for Sydney folks'. But while the Kalizoic Society received 180 expressions of interest in Melbourne, it attracted just 60 subscribers at a guinea each, and the Victorian government refused to give it a grant.[54]

The Kalizoic Society's only attempt to do something for Melbourne's poor was to secure pictures for charitable institutions, as Smith had suggested. When the secretary of Melbourne's Women's Model Lodging House requested a 'little tasteful decoration', Lucy Gullett called on the readers of her column to give generously. But while a 'number of ladies and gentlemen' offered pictures, none of these offers was made good, so the society had to buy what it wanted. By the end of 1884 the society had given Melbourne Hospital just five 'choice oleographs' imported from Europe, depicting subjects such as *The African Embassy at Rome* and *After Mass*. Three months later the society provided similar decorations for the Benevolent Asylum, where they reportedly 'added much to the cheerfulness of the inmates'. Then the society stopped.[55]

The Kalizoics' only other work was at Albert Park, south of the city. The colonial government had established many public reserves by the mid-1850s, so Melbourne did not need a Kyrle Society to bring private land into public ownership. But because the government soon threatened to turn many of these parks to other uses, the city depended on groups and individuals to defend them. In 1856 the *Argus* declared:

> We should be glad to find the principle firmly established that our public parks are sacredly dedicated to the future wants of Melbourne city, and are not to be perverted from their true uses to supply even considerable monetary conveniences. In a new place like this, park reserves constitute an important public trust held by the present generation for the benefit of the next.[56]

The Kerferd government put the park at the centre of Victorian politics in 1875 when it tried to sell its St Kilda Road and Fitzroy Street frontages. Henry Pollard Palmer, a partner in a firm of importers and warehousemen in the city, responded by resorting to the Victorian Supreme Court on behalf of other wealthy local residents in an attempt to protect their sea breezes and views of Port Phillip Bay. The local member for St Kilda, Murray Smith, adopted Octavia Hill's line that parklands were a 'garden for the poor'. Henry Wrixon, who was elected to the Legislative Assembly as a radical land reformer, followed the conservative *Argus* in maintaining that 'all public reserves, parks, and gardens, and every piece of land of the kind should be securely tied up in the hands of the Government for the use of the people. They belong to everybody and they ought to be kept for everybody'.[57]

Justice Molesworth dismissed Palmer's action. While Molesworth acknowledged that the value of neighbouring land was enhanced by its 'agreeable views' and found that the government had flouted due process by failing to give due public notice of its plan to revoke the park, he applied conventional English doctrine in holding that Palmer did not have a sufficient interest to bring his action because the common law did not recognise 'a right to a prospect or view'. After almost two days of debate in Parliament, Kerferd escaped censure only by elevating the issue into a vote of no confidence. Yet such was

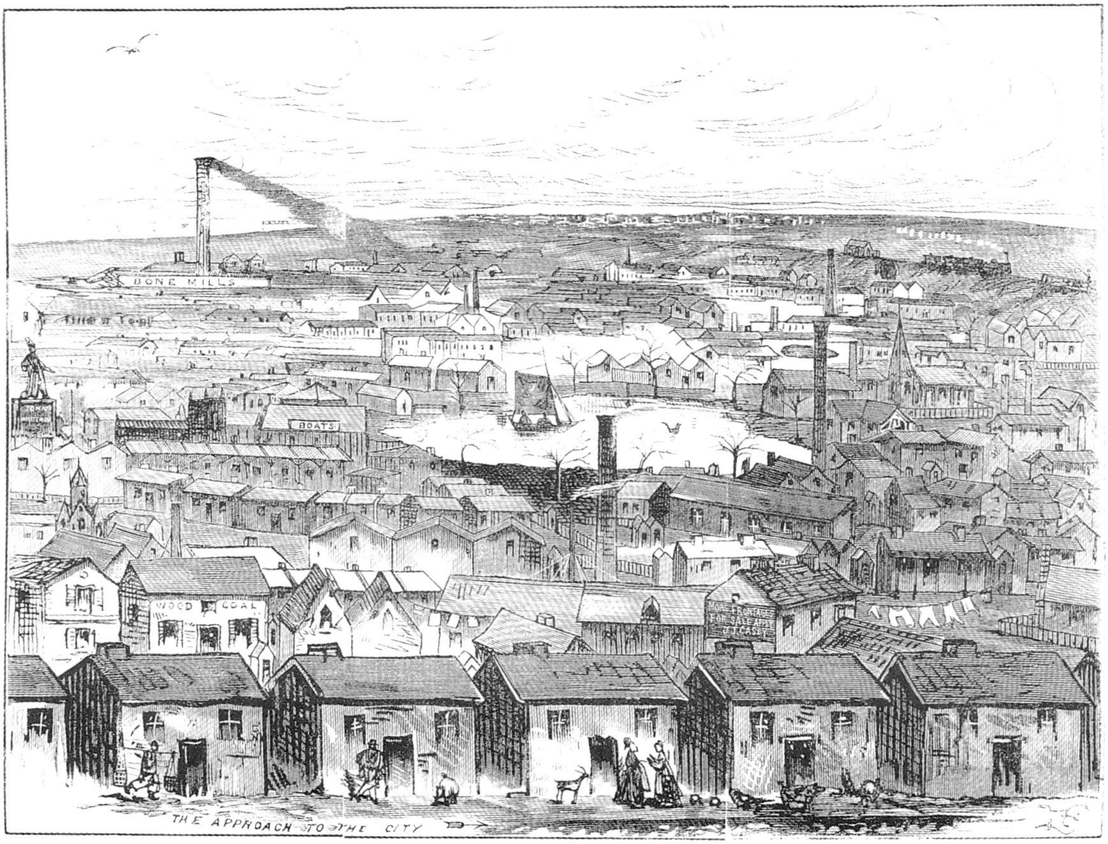

THOMAS CARRINGTON
BIRDS-EYE VIEW OF ALBERT PARK (AS IT VERY SOON WILL BE) 1875

the government's embarrassment at Molesworth's finding that it withdrew the Fitzroy Street frontages from sale and vested what remained of the park in the Board of Works and the St Kilda and South Melbourne councils.[58]

Many colonists still wondered what would become of the park. Thomas Carrington drew a cartoon in which the entire park had been sold off and turned over to smokestacks and workingmen's cottages, but these fears were not realised. By the early 1880s the park was one of Melbourne's 'pleasantest places of resort', and a group of 'influential gentlemen' wanted to make it even more fashionable by constructing a carriage drive along the lines of 'Rotten Row' in London's Hyde Park. When the government refused to contribute, these men inaugurated a Friday afternoon drive, hoping that the money would come later.[59]

The first drive in December 1884 was graced by the Victorian Governor and his wife, Sir Henry and Lady Loch. Many 'ladies and gentlemen well known in social circles' took the opportunity to show off their equipages and horses, 'their pretty slim figures and their good riding'. Herr Plock's eighteen-piece band delighted those present with 'appropriately stirring marches' and 'dreamy waltzes'. The only misfits were one or two families who mistakenly associated Rotten Row 'with a rural picnic, and . . . complacently ate huge sandwiches and drank startling quantities of gingerbeer before the astonished gaze' of Melbourne's high society.[60]

This new opportunity for display fitted Louis Henry's conception of the Kalizoic Society as an organisation that would serve Melbourne's better class of citizens. In similar vein, a correspondent of the *Argus* identified establishing a 'Rotten Row' as the type of 'practical development' the new society should undertake. But after visiting England in 1882, James Smith singled out the 'languid beauty . . . cantering upon a two-hundred guinea horse' in Hyde Park as an example of the conspicuous consumption that threatened to bring on revolution. When he addressed the Kalizoic Society's first meeting, Smith was concerned for the poor, not the rich.[61]

Henry's conception prevailed, however, when the Friday afternoon drive was instituted in Albert Park and a subscription was started to pay for Herr Plock's band, improve the drive and embellish the grounds. As Gladys observed ironically in the *Melbourne Bulletin*, the Kalizoics jumped at this 'splendid chance . . . to distinguish themselves'. By Christmas they had contributed five guineas to the fund for the band. By the New Year they had begun providing seats, which Gladys archly hoped would 'not be used by picnic parties'.[62]

A PREFERENCE FOR SHAKSPEARE

One reason for the Kalizoic Society's abysmal record was that its leading members were distracted by other enthusiasms. The most immediate was the creature of E. E. Morris, who became a Kalizoic soon after taking up the chair of modern languages at Melbourne University in January 1884. Just a week after Smith gave his inaugural address, Morris wrote an essay for the *Argus* on 'Shakspeare', as he insisted on spelling the Bard. Morris's goal was a society devoted to 'the production and publication of essays on Shaksperian subjects, critical and aesthetical'. A fortnight later, Smith himself promoted the new society. By then a Melbourne Shakspeare Society had already been constituted, with Smith and James Neild on the committee.[63]

The new society's links with the Kalizoics extended beyond their common leadership. The Shakspeare Society held regular meetings at the Hawthorn home of Lucy Gullett. Neild organised the new society's biggest entertainment in 1885 to mark the anniversary of Shakespeare's presumed birthday. George Gordon provided a backdrop depicting the Stratford-on-Avon parish church. W. R. Guilfoyle offered to provide greenery from the Botanic Gardens, but was prohibited from doing so by the Minister for Lands.[64]

The Shakspeare Society met some of the same ridicule as the Kalizoics. *Australian Tit-Bits*, another Melbourne satirical magazine, cast the two societies as equally superfluous in September 1884. But *Tit-Bits* blundered when it suggested the Shakspeare Society would 'die a sudden death'. Partly because it drew on a large number of Morris's university students, who had already begun gathering for play readings, the Shakspeare Society soon had 200 members, more than three times the number attracted by the Kalizoics.[65]

By 1893 Neild, who had succeeded Morris as President of the Shaksperian Society, could proudly reflect that 300 papers on Shaksperian topics had been delivered at the society's first 100 meetings. The society had also staged regular Shaksperian entertainments, started a Shaksperian library and instituted an annual examination in Shaksperian literature, attracting 250 candidates. After Neild stepped down as president in 1898, James Smith remained active, 'always ready to offer a paper . . . when outside contributions fell short'. When Smith died in 1910, at the age of eighty-nine, he was still the society's vice-president.[66]

THE BEAUTIFUL LIFE

The failure of the Kalizoic Society to attempt anything of substance did not stop Melburnians invoking the term 'kalizoic' when the city's physical environment was a matter of public debate. One such issue was the appearance of the city's schools—'even the Church of England Grammar School' on St Kilda Road—because of children throwing 'luncheon papers about in the most careless manner'. Another was the theft of flowers from Kew Cemetery. A third was the destruction of eucalypts in Melbourne's streets and parks, which aroused increasing protests late in 1884.[67]

A typical letter of outrage came from a resident of Hawthorn—the suburb where Smith lived—who signed himself 'Eucalyptus' and declared that he might have been a 'Kalizoist' all his life without knowing it. The local council, it transpired, had felled 'a grand old gum tree', mistakenly thinking it 'decayed and dangerous' when it 'might have served as an ornament and a landmark for a century or more to come'. 'Eucalyptus' reckoned that when the gum trees were all gone, the area would have lost its 'Australian character'; 'the tardy and perfunctory planting' of exotics could not compensate. He declared that at the next election he would only support candidates who pledged themselves to 'conserve and protect all the sound and still beautiful "remnants" of the Australian forest'.[68]

At the same time, 'kalizoic' also took on a life of its own in relation to interior decoration—one of many areas that the society itself intended but failed to pursue, apart from inviting 'the manufacturers and importers of art works' to send samples to its meetings. Miss L. Pearce, a practitioner of 'art needlework', was the opportunist who saw potential in this new label for the 'beautiful life', despite all the ridicule it provoked. By November 1884, just a few months after arriving in Melbourne from England, she had opened a 'Kalizoic' shop in suburban Windsor and another in the Collins Street building occupied by C. S. Paterson.[69]

The Kalizoic sold table centres and fireplace curtains, chair-backs and handkerchief sachets, Parisian and Viennese fans. Customers could choose either finished objects or materials for embroidery, stamped with Pearce's 'latest art designs'. Pearce advertised extensively in the weekly *Australasian*, which rewarded her by puffing that the Kalizoic offered a wealth of serges and silks, fringes and cords previously unavailable in Victoria, all 'in harmony, every colour artistic, every shade perfect'. After similar inducements, *Table Talk* declared it 'impossible . . . to do justice to the most beautiful and artistic work' on view at the Kalizoic.[70]

Soon the Kalizoic was one of Melbourne's most fashionable shops. Its main lines in 1886 included Indian rugs, carpets, portières and curtains. It also imported fans ranging from ostrich feathers to dyed birds' feathers and was an outlet for Liberty's of London, which had supplied the 'art fabrics' used in the London production of *Patience*. Alongside Liberty's 'art cottons intended for library and morning-room dados', the Kalizoic offered 'art silks admirably adapted for draping bronzes, pictures, and mirrors' and 'Roman sheeting and plushes and serge or diagonal cloth . . . in all the art colours'.[71]

This success prompted Miss Mable Lane, another exponent of art needlework, to open a 'Kalizoic and Art Needle Work' depot and warehouse in St Kilda. Her claim to have 'The Beautiful in Every Variety at less than Melbourne Prices' was a direct challenge to Pearce, who responded by advertising that her shops had no connections with the St Kilda Kalizoics. But Pearce did not have to worry for long; within two years she again had the Kalizoic label to herself.[72]

WHEN HEALTH SPURNED BEAUTY

As the *Argus* knew all too well, its readers were given to 'taking up matters with enthusiasm, and dropping them in haste'. So it proved with the Kalizoics. By early 1885 they were trying to amalgamate with the Australian Health Society, which had a much bigger, more active membership, thanks to the efforts of the women on its council. But after what *Punch* described as a protracted 'flirtation', Health spurned Beauty. While acknowledging that its objects were similar, the Health Society announced in May 1885 that a 'careful examination' of the Kalizoic Society's 'scope and methods of workings' revealed amalgamation was 'impracticable'.[73]

Two years later, the Kalizoic Society tried again to append itself to another institution. This time it turned to the Australian Artists' Association, which had held its first exhibition in 1886 in opposition to the Victorian Academy of Art. One of the founders of the Artists' Association was Tom Roberts, whose family doctor was James Neild. Another was Frederick McCubbin. The participants in its first exhibition included Arthur Streeton, who already knew McCubbin as his drawing master at the art school of the National Gallery of Victoria and appears to have become friends with Roberts in late 1886, when they met at Mentone. By early 1887 Streeton was painting with Roberts and McCubbin at Box Hill.

The new association initially aimed to be a society of artists, but in January 1887 Roberts persuaded his fellows to open it to all colonists so as to increase its membership and finance its exhibitions. One of the first to take advantage of this opportunity was Louis Henry, who soon took a leading role in organising the Association's smoke nights and increasing its membership. Another Kalizoic to join was Joseph Reed, who sent a drawing to the Association's autumn exhibition in March 1887. James Neild and the picture dealer Alexander Fletcher followed.[74]

This overlapping membership brought the Artists' Association closer to the Kalizoic Society, but otherwise the two groups had little in common. The Artists' Association had manifested no interest in the urban environment. Its members, led by Tom Roberts, feared that chromolithographs, which the Kalizoics had tried to institutionalise, would become cheap substitutes for paintings. Yet Roberts introduced Henry and Neild to explain the goals of the Kalizoic Society at a meeting of the Artists' Association in May 1887. Ten days later, the Artists' Association agreed to amalgamate with the Kalizoic Society and to establish a Kalizoic Committee once a sub-committee including Roberts drew up its rules and regulations.[75]

Henry and Neild probably initiated this amalgamation because they remained committed to their Kalizoic ideals and wanted to give them a new institutional form, but the artists' reasons for agreeing remain obscure. With few if any funds or members, the Kalizoics had little to offer. Did the artists think local benevolent institutions would acquire their work instead of imported chromolithographs? Were they hoping for a colonial counterpart to Octavia Hill, who had commissioned twelve mural designs from Walter Crane in 1886 for her block of houses in Red Cross Street, Southwark?[76]

Whatever the reason, the Artists' Association also did not last. Six months later it amalgamated with the rival Victorian Academy of Art to form the Victorian Artists' Association. During this period, the only link between the Kalizoics and the Artists' Association was that Nahum Barnet and Joseph Reed contributed to the Artists' Association's last exhibition. None of Melbourne's artists showed any interest in depicting what was wrong with Melbourne's environment. Nor did the Artists' Association attempt to continue the Kalizoic Society's work of embellishing the walls of Melbourne's benevolent institutions.[77]

Soon the key figures in the Kalizoic Society were returning to the Australian Health Society. Neild delivered the first of several lectures for the Health Society in 1888. James Smith resumed a year later. Henry was the society's president in 1900. But Tom Roberts maintained close links with former Kalizoics. One of his patrons was C. S. Paterson, who bought his *Reconciliation*, commissioned

Roberts to paint his portrait and, from 1888, was his landlord at the new Grosvenor Chambers, which included six studios specifically designed for artists. As president of the new Victorian Artists Society, Roberts was probably also responsible for inviting Neild to officiate at one of the society's conversaziones in 1889. Both Roberts and Streeton were friends of George Gordon, whose portrait Roberts painted in 1893.[78]

Roberts and his followers were even closer to Pearce's Kalizoic warehouse and its fashionable array of aesthetic wares. Both Roberts and Charles Conder decorated their studios with Liberty silks and fans of the type stocked by Pearce. When Roberts, Conder and Streeton held their 9 by 5 Exhibition of Impressions in 1889, they hung red Liberty silk 'drawn, knotted and looped' among their paintings. This look was so closely identified with Pearce's shop that one reviewer described the paintings as being 'deftly set off by hangings and other accessories in the Kalizoic fashion', even though the artists had obtained their decorations from a rival supplier, Cullis Hill & Co.[79]

Before the year was out, Pearce had staged a 'Special Show of Art Materials For Decorations and Furnishings. Style, Louis XIV, XV, et XVI'. While Cullis Hill had been importing Louis XIV furniture since it opened in 1884, Pearce boasted that this collection from the Paris Universal Exposition of 1889 was 'the choicest and only assortment of the kind in Australia'. The *Australasian* advised its readers that, if they wanted to discover 'the newest idea at home for modern household decoration', they should 'visit the Kalizoic without fail'.[80]

The Kalizoic retained this reputation for the 'ultra-fashionable' through the early 1890s. After inspecting a new consignment of counterpanes, table covers and chair backs made from silks in 'all the brightest and most Oriental-looking shades', the new weekly *Bohemia* was grateful that the 'awful' sampler and the 'more recent' crochet work had disappeared, thanks to 'the spread of culture and the aesthetic movement'. *Bohemia* saw the Kalizoic as a local embodiment of the '*fin de siecle*', and shopping there as the only way 'to be quite up to date'.[81]

Yet 'kalizoic' was not just an early example of the transformation of environmental concern into fashionable consumption. The original association with environmental improvement persisted through the 1890s. In Melbourne Neild called for the revival of the Kalizoic

Society in a series of articles about the importance of the city's parks and gardens and the 'savagery' of its state-school children. The *Sydney Morning Herald* used 'kalizoic' as a term familiar to all its readers when 'aesthetical' questions involving the degradation of Sydney Harbour became subjects of debate. If Henry and Neild changed nothing on the ground, at least they briefly added to Australian English.[82]

NICHOLAS CAIRE *GIANT TREE HOUSE, GIPPSLAND* C. 1885

CHAPTER NINE

UNCLE SAM, THE BARON AND KING EDWARD VII

Without doubt in future years scientific men in all parts of the world, when studying varied aspects of plant life, will come across references to the giant trees which once existed in Victoria, and will send to our grandchildren, or maybe our great grandchildren, for authentic records of the same. Finding that they can get no satisfactory information, they will naturally conclude that the so-called giant trees existed only in our imagination, and originated in the early days, from stories told us by the aboriginals.

NICHOLAS CAIRE, 'NOTES ON THE GIANT TREES OF VICTORIA', 1904

IN THE MID-1880S Nicholas Caire took one of his biggest series of photographs at Wynstay, the property of Thomas Davies in the Strzelecki Ranges in South Gippsland. Davies's main income seems to have come from a small raspberry patch on his standard selection of 320 acres, so he was probably too poor to pay Caire. But Caire did not mind. Wynstay's immense mountain ash were sufficient compensation. For more than twenty years, Caire pursued these trees with a fervour unmatched by any other colonial artist, naming them and writing evocatively about them as individuals. By the time he died, he 'knew all the giant trees of Gippsland and could talk interestingly of their age, height, dimensions and family history'. Probably no other colonist was as passionate about what Caire called 'Giant Land'.[1]

The mountain ash excited Caire partly because he mistakenly believed that they were not just 'the oldest inhabitants of the land' but among the oldest living things on earth. Extrapolating from dates for the giant redwoods of California, Caire once speculated that the biggest Victorian trees were 3500 years old.[2] But the mountain ash also excited Caire because he believed that the tallest Victorian trees topped the tallest redwoods. We will probably never know for certain whether he was right. Almost all the big trees that created such excitement in the second half of the nineteenth century have either been felled or lost their tops. The height of trees on both continents

NICHOLAS CAIRE
THE TREE AND THE HOUSE BUILT OUT OF IT C. 1885

NICHOLAS CAIRE
TALL DEAD GIANT TREE, GIPPSLAND C. 1885

was probably exaggerated. Yet the mountain ash may well have been the tallest trees in the world in the 1860s, when colonists first measured them, even if they had lost this status by the 1880s because timber-getters always took the biggest trees first.

Caire's photographs of Wynstay convey his awe. Some show Davies with neck craned in amazement looking up at big, standing trees. Others show him astride the buttress of 'Hercules', the biggest tree on Wynstay, which Caire described as 'a monster, growing in red volcanic soil', 'supposed to have been the largest . . . in Australia'. Still others show the giant stumps Davies left when he cleared his block.

But the common feature of all these photographs is that the trees are dead. The standing trees were charred and leafless. 'Hercules' had fallen after a fire. In the few years Davies had owned Wynstay, he had turned it into a graveyard of big trees. Its giants were, as Caire titled one of his prints, 'Heroes of the Past'.[3]

That sniff of nostalgia is the closest Caire came to expressing regret. Otherwise Caire implicitly accepted the destruction. His most revealing photograph is *The Tree and the House Built Out of It*, which in fact includes just a stump, not a tree. Next to it is the first house built by Davies and his family. Possibly just two rooms, at most four, the house symbolises the productive use of timber, though the photograph can equally be interpreted as an example of how so much can be turned into so little.

Caire's response and the Davieses' delight in their neat, new house are readily understood if one looks at another of Caire's photographs of the family's first home at Wynstay—a hollow tree that they felled, roofed and used as a dwelling, with five people spread between three windowless 'apartments' over two storeys.[4] To move from this hollow to a timber home was good reason for pride. More generally, it would be naive to think there might have been anything other than large-scale clearing of the giant trees. Because the mountain ash covered great tracts of Victoria, it was to be expected that clearing would be the norm.

Yet not all the giant mountain ash had to fall. As colonists well knew, in 1864 President Lincoln had protected the Mariposa Big Tree Grove, an area of just two square miles near Yosemite. By 1872 one of Carleton Watkins's photographs of the Grizzly Giant—the most famous tree in the Mariposa Grove—was on display at the National Gallery of Victoria.[5] If Victorians valued their big trees similarly, all they had to do was follow or expand on this precedent.

HALF A THOUSAND FEET!

David Boyle was a footsoldier of natural history. An amateur botanist, Boyle never published what he found in the Dandenongs in the 1860s and 1870s. Instead he gave his discoveries to Ferdinand von Mueller, who repaid him by naming one *Cyathea boylei*. Another of his discoveries was a giant eucalypt that Boyle found in 1866 after Mueller called on colonists to identify big trees. Boyle measured this tree at 392 feet, but its top had been broken off. When Boyle compared his tree with others still intact, he concluded that it must have once reached 420 feet, just 30 feet short of the tallest reported redwood.[6]

Mueller could easily have seen this 'stupendous' find for himself and checked the accuracy of Boyle's measurements. A day-trip from Melbourne would probably have been enough. But Mueller does not appear to have embarked on this kind of fieldwork until the mid-1870s, when he went to the Upper Yarra for a few days and measured 'some gigantic Eucalypts, getting many angles showing a greater hight [sic] than that properly recorded of any Sequoia'. Meanwhile, he relied on a specimen Boyle had brought him to identify his big tree as *Eucalyptus amygdalina*, the 'Peppermint' or 'Drooping Gum' of Tasmania, and called for more 'actual' measurements to see if even taller eucalypts might be found.[7]

The response was immediate. By early 1867, Mueller was able to announce 'some astounding data, supported by actual measurements', demonstrating the 'marvellous height of some Australian trees'. Mueller reported *Eucalyptus amygdalina* had been measured 'repeatedly' in the Dandenong Ranges, at 420 feet. One tree on the Black Spur was 480 feet—30 feet more than the tallest redwood. Another near Berwick had a base eighty-one feet in circumference four feet from the ground and possibly attained 'a height of half a thousand feet'![8]

Some of these measurements were probably inaccurate because most tall trees were surrounded by forest, and the standard method of triangulation by theodolite depended on a clear line of sight to both the top and bottom of the tree. In practice, as one surveyor noted, 'if the butts could be seen the tops were invisible, and *vice versa*; hence the impossibility of measuring their heights accurately'. The only solution was to clear around the tree—a task beyond most individuals.[9]

Yet Mueller had good reason to trust his informants. Boyle's tree had fallen, enabling him to measure it 'with a tap line'. The tree with a girth of 81 feet, possibly 500 feet high, had been reported by 'a most trustworthy surveyor', G. W. Robinson. Another tree, 365 feet high with a circumference of 41 feet, had been recorded by Mueller's own assistant, E. B. Heyne, who had measured not just 'the out & in but the real circumference'. Little wonder that Mueller concluded it was 'by no means unlikely' that Victoria enjoyed 'the most elevated trees of the Globe'.[10]

THE REGNANS

For Mueller the immensity of the mountain ash confirmed not only that the products of the New World eclipsed those of the Old but also that nature was greater than culture. The height of California's big trees had initially been conveyed by equating them with the top of St Paul's in London. Mueller invoked the spire of the Munster of Strasbourg, the world's tallest cathedral, and the great pyramid of Cheops, one of the Seven Wonders of the Ancient World. The highest eucalypts, Muller boasted in 1867, topped both these triumphs of civilisation.[11]

Three years later, Mueller underlined the significance of the mountain ash by renaming them. Whereas British and American scientists argued for years over whether the proper scientific name of the redwoods was *Wellingtonia gigantea* (after the Iron Duke) or *Sequoia gigantea* (after the Cherokee who invented his tribe's written language), Mueller had the big Australian trees to himself. As a matter of convention, he should have presented substantial scientific grounds when first identifying the mountain ash as a distinctive form of eucalypt. But Mueller did not always heed the established rules of botanical nomenclature. Without bothering to define the new species, something he only attempted in the late 1880s, he identified them as the kings of Australia's forests—*Eucalyptus regnans*.[12]

This promotion of the eucalypt was unwelcome in the United States. Having turned the height of the redwoods into a symbol of national greatness, Americans were intent on retaining their pre-eminence. The simplest way was to redefine the competition. Because the mountain ash stopped Americans claiming the world's highest tree and the baobab stopped them boasting the tree of greatest girth, they claimed that the sequoia was still the largest tree in the world because of its combined thickness and height. But Victorians would not change their measure. As Howard Willoughby observed in 1886: 'It pleases Australians greatly that their country contains the "tallest tree in the world"'. They took particular satisfaction that the mountain ash dented America's reputation as 'the country of big things'.[13]

Many English travellers probably also enjoyed this besting of the Californian giants by a loyal British colony. During Anthony Trollope's visit to Victoria in 1872, the colony's Inspector of Forests, William Ferguson, measured a tree on the Watts River at over 400 feet. Trollope thought Ferguson's report so significant that he republished it in full in his two-volume *Australia and New Zealand*.

A decade later, when the English essayist J. A. Froude, visited California, he infuriated his American hosts by declining to visit the giant sequoias because he had seen taller trees in Victoria.[14]

Yet the height of the mountain ash was not all that appealed to its admirers. They also delighted in how it rose 'straight and tapering as a ship's mast' in contrast to the gum trees' usual 'grotesque and tortuous growth'. They placed even greater store in it as a link with a distant past, equating its great size with great age, so that the mountain ash became a natural substitute for medieval or classical ruins, a time-line into Australia's aboriginal past.

This view was widespread. As Tom Griffiths has observed, 'when Europeans ventured into landscapes that were barren of recognisable history and culture, they often turned to the natural environment rather than the uncertain human past for temporal depth'. Yet Griffiths has still defined the 'antiquarian imagination' as 'a historical sensibility particularly attuned to the material evidence of the past'.[15] This definition undervalues the importance of the natural environment. Through the 1870s and 1880s into the early 1900s, the most powerful speculations about the deep past in Australia were inspired by the 'patriarchs' of the forest.

The giant red gums in Louis Buvelot's *Waterpool near Coleraine* (page 168) inspired Marcus Clarke to 'sad reflection' on 'the vanished past which saw them bud and blossom'. In an essay initially published by the National Gallery of Victoria and reused in Clarke's famous preface to the poetry of Adam Linday Gordon, which soon went through ten editions, Clarke cast these trees as 'emblems of the departed grandeur of the wilderness'. He also considered them 'a monument of the glories of that barbaric empire upon whose ruins the ever-restless European has founded his new kingdom'.[16]

The giant mountain ash similarly excited William Woolls. On reading Mueller's first reports of David Boyle's discovery in 1867, Woolls speculated that many of Australia's 'primeval forests' were not just hundreds of years old but 'of older standing than the sable race which was found roaming amongst them'. A decade later, he made even more of the 'antiquity' of these trees. He asked, 'What a history could these gum trees unfold, if they had the faculty of speech?' He answered:

> They might tell of races of animals and vegetables which have been extinct for ages; of floods and droughts with which those of recent

> periods cannot be compared; of the gradual preparation of this continent for the abode of men; of the mysterious landing of the aboriginal races; and lastly, but of yesterday, the advent of Captain Cook, and the disappearance of the black man before the power, diseases, and luxury of what is called civilization.[17]

By 1882 Douglas Sladen, whose anthologies of Australian poetry are deservedly better known than his own verse, was also using Australia's giant trees as a vehicle for speculating about the continent's deep past. Excited by G. W. Robinson's discovery of another immense mountain ash on Mount Baw Baw in Gippsland, Sladen asked:

What have you witnessed in your long existence
On remote ranges in the Gippsland distance?
Have you seen native empires rise and fall,
And stories tragical?
Did some black Dido, flying from her lovers,
Found a new kingdom, happy in thy covers,
Until a Maori Aeneas came
And lit the cursed flame?
Or a dark Robin Hood devote his leisure
To stealing skulls, and take a savage pleasure
In making what Blacks have by way of priests
Uneasy at their feasts?[18]

A FOREST HERITAGE

Ferdinand von Mueller was quick to recognise the vulnerability of the giant mountain ash. Already in 1866 he predicted that the 'most stately' trees were 'generally certain to sink first' because of the value of their timber. He even suggested that these trees might be in danger of 'annihilation'. Yet Mueller could hardly call for their protection, even if he wanted to do so, because it was not clear where the tallest trees grew. Instead he simply asked that they be measured before they disappeared.[19]

Four years later, Mueller dwelt on the suitability of the mountain ash as an 'industrial plant' while lecturing on applied botany at Melbourne's new Industrial Museum. Always keenly interested in the economic potential of nature, Mueller explained that just half the wood from the tree measured at 480 feet on the Black Spur would yield 17 780 railway sleepers or 23 miles of three-rail fencing. Reduced to one-inch planks, it would yield 426 720 superficial feet of timber and cover almost ten acres. If the whole tree was burned, it would yield 17 950 bushels of charcoal, 227 269 gallons of vinegar, and 2 tons, 11 hundredweight of potash.[20]

Yet Mueller also called for the tallest mountain ash to be protected. He argued that 'Some feelings of veneration and reverence should also be evinced towards the native vegetation, where it displays its rarest and grandest forms'. It was 'lamentable that in all Australia scarcely a single spot' had 'been secured for preserving some relics of its most ancient trees to convey to posterity an idea of the original features of our primeval forests'. While implicitly blaming government, Mueller also lambasted individual landholders for their 'vandalism', which he contrasted with the 'respect' for nature shown by the 'uncivilised inhabitants of many a tropical country'.[21]

Mueller called for greater exploitation and greater protection of Australia's forests when he gave another lecture at the Museum in 1871. While reiterating that colonists were far from making the most of the forests' economic potential, Mueller also asked his audience to 'contrast the magnificence of a dense forest, before the destructive hand of man has defaced it, with the cheerless aspect of wide landscapes, devoid of wooded scenery'. In keeping with his belief that nature was greater than culture, Mueller declared that 'no settlement, however princely—no city, however great its splendour, brilliant its arts, or enchanting its pleasures' could arouse the same veneration as 'an undisturbed noble forest region'.[22]

Mueller looked for a popular movement to give effect to this environmental aesthetic. Just as Victoria had societies devoted to the prevention of cruelty to animals and the protection of introduced game species, he called for 'a strong and widely-spreading league . . . for the saving of the native forests'. In concluding his address, he identified the forest as a 'heritage' worth preserving—perhaps the first time anyone in Australia had seen part of the environment in these terms:

> I regard the forest as a heritage given to us by nature, not for spoil or to devastate, but to be wisely used, reverently honoured and carefully maintained. I regard the forests as a gift, intrusted to any of us only for transient care during a short space of time, to be

> surrendered to posterity again as an unimpaired property, with increased riches and augmented blessings, to pass as a sacred patrimony from generation to generation.[23]

This lecture reached far beyond Mueller's initial audience. The *Argus* and *Australasian* published it immediately. By late 1871 it was available as a pamphlet and in a collection of essays delivered at the Museum. In 1872 it was republished twice in London. In 1876 it was republished in the United States. In 1879 Mueller himself reused large sections of it in another essay in which he argued that Australia should emulate Japan, where forests were 'revered almost with sanctity, and allowed to remain in the freshness of their virgin-splendour'. The only species he singled out was the *regnans*, which he declared 'must forever be counted . . . among the wonders of the world'. Colonists should 'approach it with veneration, and shield and guard it against unholy hands'.[24]

Possibly the first tree identified as satisfying this test was at Neerim in Gippsland. Although only about 200 feet high, this tree was 67 feet in circumference 5 feet from the ground. When one of the *Australasian*'s rural essayists visited Neerim in 1882, he recognised that it was unlikely anyone would fell the tree 'for amusement', but feared it might be injured accidentally when the surrounding scrub on the township reserve was burned. He wanted it protected because, when the railway line from Melbourne to Neerim was completed, 'Such a tree would be handy for the purpose of being shown to distinguished visitors from America and elsewhere'.[25]

Soon visitors and colonists were identifying forests that deserved protection. In 1886 J. A. Froude declared that the 'unique' mountain ash of the Black Spur ought to be preserved. In 1888, Francis Myers suggested that the giant trees of the Dandenongs also be 'sought out, and made approachable, but preserved from mutilation with all care'. A year later a contributor to the *Australasian* called on the government to preserve at least a few square miles of Gippsland's big tree country:

> The grand forest could remain in its natural condition, with the glorious wealth of scrub plants underneath, to be a joy for the tired workers in our cities for all times to come. The native birds and animals could be preserved in this people's park . . . The plan has worked well in America: why should it not be as successful here?[26]

THE WOODMAN DOES NOT SPARE THE TREE

These arguments had no effect. Just as Americans felled some of the biggest sequoias for display in international exhibitions, so Victorians felled a mountain ash recorded at 430 feet high for the Paris Exhibition of 1878. Many more were ringbarked and then burned by colonists eager to convert forest to farmland. Some were killed and left to rot standing after splitters cut large chips out of their sides in order to discover if their grain was straight enough for splitting. Others were felled by timber-getters and selectors, who soon learned the folly of trying to cut through the mountain ash's great buttresses. Instead they erected scaffolding and left giant tree stumps up to twenty or even thirty feet high scattered across the countryside, as one can see in another of Nicholas Caire's photographs of Wynstay, *Giant Tree Gate Posts*.[27]

The timber-getters began by taking the tallest trees because there was more money in them. G. W. Robinson believed that the 'longest barrelled trees' were already gone when he began working in the Dandenongs in 1854. Robinson helped to take out many giants over the next eight years, including one he measured at 360 feet, but he had 'no doubt . . . that some of the earlier cut down trees would have measured quite 400 feet'. In 1886 Howard Willoughby noted that 'in all accessible parts, the fine specimens are doomed to early destruction . . . The woodman does not spare the tree. The more huge the round, straight, polished, and beautiful stem, the more likely he is to mark it as his own.'[28]

The tallest trees reported in the 1870s were no longer standing. One was the tree on the Black Spur that Trollope brought to international notice. When measured by William Ferguson in 1872, it was 435 feet 'from its roots to the top of its trunk', but Ferguson speculated it must originally have been over 500 feet because it had been severely burnt. The other was the tree that Douglas Sladen celebrated in verse. According to first accounts, this tree was 471 feet. A few years later, it was described as 480 feet with its top broken off, making it possibly 520 feet in all.[29]

Surveyors rarely made such measurements. John Hardy, who mapped the Dandenongs in the mid-1860s, explained why. It was not just that his survey was 'strenuous work'; nor that his weekly rest day was always filled with 'washing and mending clothes, cleaning and general over-hauling of equipment, transcription of notes, and posting-up of the progress plan'. Hardy was also deterred by Mueller's first reports. As he put it, 'what was to be gained by measuring trees approaching 400 feet, when there was much talk of trees approximating 500 feet'?[30]

Timber-getters had no interest in these records. According to G. W. Robinson, splitters looked on him 'with pity' when they saw him 'scrambling about over logs and fallen branches to measure a fallen giant'. When he explained that he was measuring the tree for Mueller, 'they regarded us both as daft'. But the splitters competed to find the biggest trees, using their own measures. Sometimes they employed their means of production. In 1891 Mueller recorded repeated 'reports of trees seven axe-handles in diameter'. More often, they measured their product. By one account, an 'average' tree yielded 4000 five-foot palings. Another reckoned 'a good average' 12 000. The biggest trees turned out over 20 000.[31]

UNCLE SAM AND BIG BEN

When the Acting Tasmanian Governor, Sir John Lefroy, and his wife Charlotte made an official visit to Geeveston in 1880, they were most impressed by a stringybark that was 200 feet high and had a 40-foot girth 6 feet from the ground. Sir John recorded that he hoped to make 'arrangements' to preserve it 'for posterity'. Lady Charlotte achieved this goal with a plaque:

> This Giant of Tasmanian Woods is at the special request of Lady Lefroy to be preserved as long as Nature shall spare it, to show posterity what the forests of Tasmania were in the days when 'A man was famous according as he lifted up axes upon the thick trees'. Psalm lxxiv, v.

In Victoria, however, the most done for any of the giant trees was to name them. This identification probably contributed to their survival. Just as 'Lady Lefroy's Tree' escaped the axe in Tasmania, so none of Victoria's named trees were felled for their timber. But, whereas many of California's big trees were named after wartime heroes such as General Sherman and General Noble, Presidents such as Andrew Jackson and literary greats such as Bret Harte and Mark Twain, none of the names bestowed on Victoria's mountain ash bolstered national identity. The Victorians' sense of their big trees' gender was also different from the Californians'. While many of the redwoods were looked on as female, starting with 'The Mother of the Forest', the first sequoia stripped of its bark for public display in 1854, the only mountain ash thought of as female were the 'The Sisters' on top of the Dandenongs. All the others given gendered names were identified as male, just as they were described collectively as 'patriarchs'.[32]

Nicholas Caire probably initiated this naming near Fernshawe, halfway up the Black Spur, which became a popular destination for excursionists from Melbourne in the early 1870s. Some came for the ferns that gave Fernshawe its name, others to fish, particularly for trout, which Victoria's Acclimatisation Society introduced in 1872. Lyrebirds, both living and dead, were another attraction. While their tails decorated 'many a metropolitan parlour', their bodies could be served as pheasant if carefully cooked. But what made Fernshawe 'unique' was its proximity to the Black Spur and its big timber.[33]

The first tree Caire named was a blackbutt on the road up the Black Spur. Although it was only about 250 feet high, having lost its top, and just 40 feet in girth, it became 'an object of public interest' because Cobb and Co.'s coaches travelled past it every day. The second tree Caire named was a mountain ash about a mile and a half away, which again was only about 250 feet high but had a circumference of 57 feet. Caire called the first tree 'Uncle Sam' in deference to the United States and its sequoias; he looked to England for the second, calling it 'Big Ben'.[34]

OLIVER WENDELL HOLMES REQUESTS

It took an American to spur Victorians to be more systematic in recording the tallest mountain ash. Oliver Wendell Holmes Senior—father of the famous Supreme Court Justice—was a renowned essayist with an 'intense, passionate fondness for trees'. His collection, *The Autocrat of the Breakfast-Table*, first published in 1858, included 'A Talk on Trees', in which he wrote of his 'enthusiasm' for forest giants in general and 'romantic attachments to certain trees in particular'. Holmes was also a great champion of photography—coining the term 'stereoscope' in an essay in the *Atlantic Monthly* in 1859.[35]

These interests came together for Holmes in 1861, after the *Boston Evening Transcript* published an article by the renowned preacher-cum-lecturer Thomas Starr King celebrating the sequoias. Holmes promptly asked Starr King whether 'love or money' could procure him photographs of the 'great pines'. Starr King in turn approached Carleton Watkins, who sent Holmes twelve stereographs. Before long, Holmes had brought Watkins's work to national attention through another essay in the *Atlantic Monthly*, in which he singled out the 'Grizzly Tree' of Mariposa as one of the 'most interesting' subjects 'in the whole realm of Nature'.[36]

Twenty-five years later, Holmes wanted comparable Australian material. In a letter to Frank Stanley Dobson, a Melbourne lawyer and politician who was also a fellow of the Linnaean Society and former President of the Victorian Field Naturalists, Holmes asked for photographs of Australia's giant gums. Dobson could have met this request simply by sending him some of Nicholas Caire's work, but he was more ambitious. Probably encouraged by the Victorian government's decision to hold an international exhibition in 1888, he decided to organise a systematic survey of Victoria's biggest trees in order to check their height and record them for posterity. While some colonists privately doubted the accuracy of the measurements published by Ferdinand von Mueller, Dobson was confident his survey would find trees at least 400 feet high, eclipsing the tallest sequoia, which had been re-measured at 325 feet.[37]

By mid-1888 Dobson had persuaded the Victorian Lands Department to contribute £400 for photography, his fellow trustees of the Public Library had given £100 and the Commissioners of the Exhibition a further £100. But Caire was less co-operative. Although he asked just £250 in return for photographing 25 trees over 70 feet in girth, Caire declared that, because these trees were found 'in most out-of-the-way places, and extremely difficult of access', he would need five years to locate them. The Commissioners could not wait, so they sought to divide the work between Caire and J. Duncan Peirce, a civil engineer-cum-photographer otherwise known only for his views of the Broken Hill Silver Mine in 1887. When Caire rejected this division of labour, the job went to Peirce and a Melbourne surveyor, C. R. Cunningham.[38]

Meanwhile the Exhibition Commissioners considered other possibilities. Samuel Willis, a resident of suburban Prahran, offered a section of an actual tree with a circumference of 70 feet for just £25. James Dawson, a pioneer settler of Victoria's Western District, responded that it would be both 'an imposition' on the public to exhibit this tree when larger trees existed, and 'vandalism' to destroy such 'a splendid specimen'. Instead, he proposed that the Commissioners send an artist to make a drawing of Victoria's largest tree, which could then be used as the basis for a full-sized model for permanent display in the exhibition grounds.[39]

While these possibilities were debated, the Centennial Exhibition opened in July 1888 without the giant mountain ash being properly represented. Here, if ever, was confirmation that colonists did not value their big trees. With the world coming to Melbourne—or so Victorians hoped—they failed to show off the biggest manifestation of local nature. To the Commissioners' embarrassment, the Victorian display included just a small slab of mountain ash three feet in diameter. There were no photographs—an omission highlighted when the sequoias, including the Grizzly Giant, were 'worthily' illustrated in the American photographic court.[40]

This omission was partially remedied when Samuel Willis came good with his offer of the butt of a hollow mountain ash 72 feet in circumference from Menzies Creek in the Dandenongs. But Peirce lagged behind. He reportedly was an indifferent bushman with little liking for wet scrub. Caire also refused to assist him, while some other colonists wanted to be paid for divulging what they knew. Peirce's main problem, however, was that the 'fabulous heights' of the trees he was told of always vanished when his assistants cleared a base line and Cunningham measured them with his theodolite. Consequently, the Vegetable Products Committee decided to offer a reward of £20 for any tree 400 feet high, with an extra £3 for every additional five feet. In a letter to the *Argus*, Peirce challenged Caire to reveal what he knew, emphasising that he would receive £80 for just one 'monster' 500 feet high.[41]

This reward enticed more colonists into the field. 'The Present Position of the Gippsland Populace', a cartoon in *Melbourne Punch* in mid-November, showed representatives of all classes trying to claim the reward, with a colonist up every tree and all the tall timber dead, most likely ringbarked. Yet there were still no takers, so the chairman of the Vegetable Products Committee, James Munro, used his own private fortune to raise the stakes. Although Munro displayed no regard for the mountain ash on his country estate at

The Present Position of the Gippsland Populace
1888

Narbethong, where he had a gang felling up to thirty trees an hour, he offered an additional £100 to anyone able to claim the Committee's prize.[42]

No one claimed these rewards. When Peirce finally gave up the hunt at the end of 1888, just a few weeks before the Centennial Exhibition closed, the tallest tree he had found was on a spur of Mount Baw Baw in Gippsland. At just 326 feet, it fell far short of the

J. DUNCAN PEIRCE
EUCALYPTUS AMYGDALINA REGNANS, NEERIM TOWN RESERVE 1888

heights first announced by Mueller, though it was still one foot taller than the highest known sequoia. The tree with the greatest circumference was the one at Neerim brought to public notice by the *Australasian* in 1882. None compared with the estimated height of Willis's mountain ash, which was said to have been 400 if not 430 feet, although it must have lost its top before Willis discovered it or else he would have claimed at least £120.[43]

THE BARON

Peirce's photographs made him an object of derision. When they went on display in January 1889, the Vegetable Products Committee rebuked him for failing to find 'the largest possible trees' and misleading 'visitors from abroad as to the real size of our vegetable giants'. David Boyle, who had put the mountain ash on the map in 1866, attacked both Peirce and the Committee in the *Argus* for ignoring a mountain ash he had named 'The Baron' after Mueller. According to Boyle, this tree had been 525 feet high when he had first measured it in the late 1870s. In late 1888 it had lost its top but was still 466 feet high. While Boyle was careful not to divulge the location of 'The Baron', he declared it 'a great mistake that such large trees . . . should be unknown to the public'.[44]

Nicholas Caire, whom Boyle took to photograph 'The Baron', was even more contemptuous. After sending a print of this photograph to the exhibition, Caire reminded readers of the *Argus* that the tree at Neerim—the most impressive photographed by Peirce—had been 'known to thousands of people for years past'. According to Caire, timber-splitters who had seen Peirce's photographs declared that the trees he had discovered were 'mere whipsticks'. Caire himself dismissed Peirce's specimens as 'simply the youth and offspring of the patriarchs' of the forest which were 'the tallest in the world, reaching 500 ft in a few instances'. After 'a great waste of public money', he lamented that it remained 'for private enterprise to represent . . . the true dimensions of our giant eucalypti'.[45]

Over the following weeks, Peirce attacked Boyce and Caire for having hidden what they knew. An anonymous contributor to the *Argus* suggested that colonists 'clear this matter up, and having found our largest trees, . . . make some endeavour to preserve them for the admiration of posterity from the fire and axe of the selector'. The *Australasian* showed its readers how to make 'A Simple Tree-Measurer' from two bamboo tubes. Meanwhile, Caire returned to Neerim in search of even bigger trees, and implicitly recognised the significance of Peirce's work by also going to Mount Baw Baw to photograph the 326-foot tree. Mueller added that 'steps should be taken to fence and protect the giant trees of the colony'. Otherwise, he distanced himself from the debate, explaining that the tallest tree he had seen 'measured about 400 ft', but he gave this figure with reserve as he had 'to trust his memory'.[46]

The task of resolving this dispute fell to Victoria's Conservator of Forests, George Perrin, who probably found it a pleasant diversion from the conflicts over his attempts to reform forest management. While Caire would not disclose the location of 'The Baron', in May 1889 Boyle took both Perrin and Peirce to the tree, which was in Sassafras Gully in the Dandenongs surrounded by thick brush. For two days Perrin's four assistants laboured with axes, cutting 'a channel through the scrub from the station of the theodolite to the bole of the tree' so that he could measure it. The result was a

J. DUNCAN PEIRCE
THE 'BARON' 1889

J. DUNCAN PEIRCE
THE 'BARON' 1889

remarkable discrepancy. What Boyle had claimed to be 466 feet, Perrin measured at 220 feet. The tallest tree discovered by Perrin in the Dandenongs was 271 feet.[47]

How could Boyle have blundered so badly? As Francis Myers explained it in the *Argus*, Boyle had

> set up a stick in the ground, or got his assistant to hold up a stick, and then himself, creeping bellywise, obtained a position wherefrom

> he could bring his own eye at ground level, the top of the stick, and the top of the tree in line.

This method would have been accurate

> if the ground were perfectly level, and the stick held exactly perpendicular, and if, also, the tree was upright and absolutely straight, and if the eye were exactly on the ground line, and the [many] calculations were made without any error.

But the ground was never level, the stick never perpendicular, the tree never straight.[48]

Like other collectors, Boyle was also driven by a search for the novel, and the glory to be won from discovering the world's biggest tree was a powerful spur to exaggeration. His fellow colonists similarly wanted to believe such boasts. As Myers again described it, Mueller had been first to be misled:

> [T]he big trees . . . looked enormous to him, and he accepted the gauging of amateurs who desired to make them more enormous still. They grew in the Baron's vision in the first place, in his imagination in the second, and at length they so grew in us all, that we, as a people, were prepared to hold our own against the world, if not the universe. We might feel dwarfed in the matter of mountains when Himalayas or Andes or Alps were mentioned, but when any boast was made of Wellingtonia gigantea, or giant red trees, or primeval elms or oaks, the enthusiastic Australian had but to mention Eucalyptus amygdalina and his self-possession returned. Three hundred, four hundred, five hundred—we shot well above five hundred in our faith—and actually deemed that if we could look out from the crown of our tallest eucalypt we could overlook the world.[49]

Myers was not alone in taking Boyle's blunder and the findings of Peirce and Perrin as proof that mountain ash over 400 feet had never existed. Many other colonists doubted or dismissed all the other figures published by Mueller. Yet, as several *Argus* correspondents noted, the issue was far from clear-cut, because Mueller had relied primarily on reports from licensed surveyors and government scientists, whose measurements were of 'great authority'. These men had also recorded fallen trees, so their findings were more likely to have been accurate; but their measurements could not be tested, because these trees no longer existed.[50]

Meanwhile other colonists were 'seized with a desire to see some of these forest giants, and perhaps discover some new ones'. When one group of Melburnians visited Neerim, they photographed and measured the 'Monarch' on the town reserve, then found another 'prince of the forest' that was apparently unknown to local residents, though it was just a short distance from the main road. The leader of this party, John Barker, recognised that measurement and preservation of the mountain ash could be incompatible. In a letter to the *Argus*, he acknowledged that the most 'effectual means' of destroying these trees was to clear around them. Yet he and his companions cleared the scrub and saplings so that they could 'immortalize' the tree's measurements.[51]

Caire was even more cavalier, albeit just in print. He suggested that one of the tallest mountain ash should be felled because of continuing doubts about the accuracy of their measurements when standing. While he deprecated 'the idea of destroying any of our giant trees', Caire hoped to 'prove by actual tap measurement' that there were still 'a few rare specimens' in Victoria 400 feet high.[52]

Mueller also was unwilling to leave the big trees alone. While reiterating his call for these 'wonders of the empire of plants' to be 'retained as state property, duly protected by law' so that 'the next generation may yet enjoy a view of these living wondrous structures of centuries', he thought the best way of achieving this end was to clear around them, fence them off and cut tracks 'for easy approach of visitors'. If government was unwilling to proclaim such spots 'the people's inalienable property', private philanthropy might secure them. As he put it:

> Should someone in opulence desire to build himself one of the most lasting monuments, it would be by the bequest of an isolated primeval forest, ever untouchable, for the free enjoyment of the orderly portion of the public.[53]

THE DESTRUCTOR OF FORESTS

The preservation of the mountain ash finally became a political issue in late 1888 when sawmillers began making 'prodigious efforts' to increase their access to the forests of the Black Spur. James Munro, who was then the leader of the opposition in the Victorian Parliament as well as chairman of the Vegetable Products Committee, declared it would be 'an act of vandalism to allow the cutting down of trees in one of the chief show grounds of the colony'. Sawmillers responded that they would not injure 'the beautiful parts of the forest'. The *Australasian* predicted that the Gillies government would give the sawmillers what they wanted unless public opinion was 'forcibly expressed'.[54]

A year later the deal was done. The new Yea River Company undertook to spend £100 000 on sawmills and tramways and pay 2s 6d for every 1000 superficial feet of timber felled. In return, the government agreed to grant exclusive rights over 5000 acres of state forest and 14 000 acres of adjoining land close to the Black Spur for twenty-one years, with a right of renewal for the same period. The promoters of the new company looked forward to annual profits of £20 000 on its capital of £150 000; for his part, Perrin saw this agreement as a first step towards introducing a more general timber royalty and better management. If logging were done by a single company, he argued, it would be easier 'to fix the responsibility of destroying saplings and immature timber'. The result would be a proper financial return to the state and an end to indiscriminate logging by 'paling men', who left two-thirds of what they felled in the bush, often taking just one length of timber from trees 250 to 300 feet high.[55]

In this calculus, Perrin looked on the great age and size of the mountain ash as a reason for their destruction. Time and again, he emphasised that colonists needed all 'the old timber out'. He had 'no intention of keeping a single matured tree from the saw-miller' because 'every year it stands the tree is deteriorating through decay' and 'is simply occupying the ground to the detriment of its successors'. With manifest pride, he informed his Minister that the new agreement marked 'an important epoch in the history of forest management in Victoria . . . likely to result in a permanent revenue, conserve the forest and put a stop to the fearful and careless destruction going on everywhere'.[56]

When the *Argus* revealed this agreement in November 1889, there was an 'immediate explosion' in Parliament. Over the next two days it was debated twice in the Legislative Assembly. It also provoked a stream of editorials and articles in the press, a parliamentary inquiry, and then another parliamentary debate in October 1890. As a result, the agreement did not proceed, but neither did Perrin's attempts to secure a better economic return from the forests. When Victoria introduced a royalty on timber in the early 1900s, 'after strenuous opposition to change was experienced at every turn', it was the last Australian jurisdiction to do so.[57]

The agreement was controversial partly because it appeared to violate the Victorian Crown Lands Act, which sought to stop the creation of monopolies in Victoria's forests by barring the Crown from leasing them. Consistent with this prohibition, the radical *Age* attacked the agreement as anti-democratic. Meanwhile, the conservative *Argus* impugned it on economic grounds. It argued that, while the state should secure sufficient revenue from timber licences to employ rangers to protect its forests, Perrin was wrong to try to turn the colony's forests into a source of profit to the Crown.[58]

The environmental impact of the agreement was most contentious. The Parliament divided on whether Perrin was living up to his responsibilities as 'conservator' of Victoria's forests. Jonas Levien, who had been responsible for Victoria's forests from 1883 until 1886 as Minister for Agriculture, applauded Perrin for ensuring 'the permanency of the forests' by ridding them of their 'large timber'. Like Perrin, he believed that the 'proper way of conserving the forests was to cut down the trees when they reached maturity'. The radical goldfields representative John Woods, who had worked to keep questions of forest conservation before Victoria's Legislative Assembly through the 1880s, responded by branding Perrin 'the destructor of forests'.[59]

A minor issue in this debate was the government's failure to require the Yea River Company to replant what it felled. The major ground of attack was that the mountain ash should not be logged at all. As the *Argus* put it in November 1889:

> The Black Spur forest is one of the beauty spots of the colony. Its magnificent timber, its sassafras and myrtle gullies, are only now beginning to be appreciated. Travellers who come ten thousand miles are charmed with the fairy spectacle which we have too much neglected. It would be nothing short of a crime now to hand over to the destroyer giant eucalypts and natural fern bowers, which could never be replaced.[60]

Aesthetics were central to this case. When James Munro declared it 'disgraceful to talk of destroying such a beautiful forest', the Minister for Lands, John Dow, interjected that the colony was 'not going to keep a forest for the sake of ornament'. In turn, Munro asked, 'Were they not? . . . Surely they were not going to destroy every beauty spot in Victoria. Surely they would leave some parts of the colony for ornament.' According to Munro, the Black Spur 'ought to be reserved by Act of Parliament, so that no-one should destroy it'.[61]

The *Argus* supported this position. 'A Plea for Beauty' by one of its occasional essayists, Edwin J. Hart, identified Victoria's mountain forests as 'one of the few things of beauty' that colonists could point to with pride. Hart acknowledged that the Black Spur could be turned into 'a perennial source of revenue' by replanting it with trees, but he argued that 'deprived of its kings' the Black Spur 'would lose all distinctive feature and descend to a commonplace tree grown waste'. He also argued for protection on utilitarian grounds, because the beauty of the forest could rejuvenate mankind 'morally and physically'. Not least, he questioned the type of civilisation that would engage in such destruction, reminding his readers that even a Goth or Vandal would have

> regarded the forest with a half affectionate, half superstitious veneration, and held his despoiling hand from its beauties . . . In such woods as clothe the slopes and long ravines of the Black Spur, and plume the steep sides of high-crested Juliet, the barbarian would have seen a living temple, where we, or those who are supposed to represent us, see naught but an unproductive waste.[62]

Yet was the forest as intact as Hart implied? The government argued that the area to be granted to the Yea River Company had already been worked over and hence was 'not really virgin forest, as had been stated'. Gillies claimed it had 'been in the hands of the splitters ever since 1881'. Perrin maintained that 'the bulk of the land' had 'been culled of its splitting timber over and over again for the past 30 years'. James Munro responded that 'only a small portion' had been worked.[63]

The age and longevity of the forest were also issues. The government and its supporters contended that the mountain ash in the area were less than forty years old, because all the trees in the area had been killed by the bushfires of Black Thursday in 1851. They also suggested that the timber would be wasted if these trees were not felled soon. While mountain ash grow rapidly, sometimes reaching 130 feet in twenty years, Jonas Levien claimed that they were of 'mushroom growth', reaching 300 feet within 35 years and then decaying just as rapidly. If the trees were 'locked up'—perhaps the first usage of this formulation in an Australian environmental context—Levien predicted 'they would very quickly go to ruin'.[64]

Like several members of the Assembly, the *Argus* was unconvinced. It ridiculed the idea that trees '75 feet in circumference and hundreds of feet in height, could have attained their enormous proportions during the life of men . . . still young'. But even if the mountain ash were as 'wonderfully recuperative' as Levien claimed, the *Argus* declared thirty-five years too long 'for a beauty spot to remain as an object-lesson of greed and carelessness'. According to the *Argus*, the Black Spur was Victoria's 'wonderland—a spot to be held semi-sacred'. It was one place where colonists could not 'serve nature and mammon'.[65]

Still the colonial government did nothing to protect Victoria's tallest trees—not even the mountain ash that Peirce had recorded on Mount Baw Baw. When paling-getters began working there in the early 1890s, they felled this tree and split it into 6000 six-foot palings. They also found much higher trees—a relatively simple task, as Peirce had been satisfied with measuring one close to his camp—and felled and split them too.[66]

'The Baron' was also soon in jeopardy as a result of the Patterson government's revocation of much of the Dandenong State Forest in 1893. When members of the Victorian Field Naturalists went on an excursion to Sassafras Gully four years later, the surrounding hills were covered with the skeletons of giant trees and the tree ferns were dying as the upper storey of eucalypts disappeared. They advised other field naturalists to visit 'The Baron' before it shared its neighbours' fate.[67]

Neerim's 'Monarch' or 'Giant' was no less vulnerable, as the local Buln Buln Council was well aware. Recognising that this tree had made the district 'famous', the council urged George Perrin to protect it from fire. When he eventually visited Neerim in 1894 on one of his regular visits to Gippsland, the local *Guardian* reported that he 'at once recognised it to be a thing of national importance' and promised to organise the removal of the surrounding scrub, which had been cut and was 'lying all around the tree, endangering its life'. But Perrin came too late. Within a fortnight of his inspecting the tree, it was ravaged by a bushfire.[68]

Neerim's tree survived for only a few more years. In 1895 it was 'bigger looking than ever', having been cleared of whatever undergrowth had survived the fire. It also was more of an attraction for visitors, because it was clearly visible from the main road. Perrin responded by establishing a four-acre reserve and building a fence around the tree—the first time a mountain ash was safeguarded in this way. But by 1901 the fence had fallen into disrepair and by 1904, as Caire recorded, the tree itself had been 'reduced to ashes'.[69]

ROUND THE WORLD 'TREE HUNTING'

John Muir was the greatest American champion of national parks from the 1870s until his death in 1914. In more than sixty years in the United States, the Scottish-born Muir made just one trip abroad—a 'round the world "tree hunting"' expedition in 1903. Where Oliver Wendell Holmes satisfied himself with photographs, Muir wanted to see all the 'tree friends' he had read about and to establish that the redwoods were the world's tallest trees. From Manchuria he wrote 'I haven't found any big trees yet but I have seen some pretty tall Cryptomerias'. Having measured 'some of the noblest of the much vaunted Deodars' in India, he was pleased to find that none compared with America's 'largest second growth Sequoias'.[70]

Muir had to visit Australia because colonists continued to boast that their 'great trees' were at least 'rivals of the mammoth trees of the Yosemite Valley'. For all his ridicule of David Boyle, even Francis Myers maintained that there were trees 400 feet high in the 'Big Bush' above the Black Spur. Other writers went further, repeating Ferdinand von Mueller's old line that the mountain ash reached 480 feet and eclipsed Strasbourg Cathedral. At a meeting of the Royal Society of Victoria in 1890, one of the most dependable nineteenth-century witnesses, Alfred Howitt, reported that he had found a 350-foot fallen eucalypt, and several 'reliable authorities' had told him of a 415-foot tree.[71]

In Muir's twenty-seven days in Australia, he 'began botanical studies over again with all the wildness and enthusiasm of youth'. He started in Perth, where he met Bernard Woodward, director of the Western Australian Museum and the first advocate of permanent flora and fauna reserves in the west, and set out 'to see if these wonderful old Eucalyptus trees down here were really the largest vegetation in the world'. Muir arrived at his next stop, Melbourne, on 23 December and went to the Botanic Gardens the following morning. To his disappointment, William Guilfoyle, the director of the gardens, was ill. But one of Guilfoyle's assistants informed Muir that he had never seen a eucalypt over 300 feet, though he believed some were near 400. He also encouraged Muir to visit Caire, who declared that any tree forty feet in circumference was a giant, a far cry from the seventy feet he had insisted on in the 1880s.[72]

Muir spent more than seven hours on Christmas Day travelling by train and coach to what he called 'Lindtland'—the home of J. W. Lindt, who was Caire's closest photographic associate and major competitor. Between 1882 and 1892 Lindt sold 25 000 prints of the Black Spur area (including a series of photographs of 'Giant Eucalypti' such as 'Uncle Sam'). When the depression forced him to close his city studio, he decided to quit Melbourne for the summit of the Black Spur, where in 1894 he bought thirty-two hectares and built a 'Hermitage', which served not only as his own home and studio but also as a 'pleasure resort'.[73]

When Lindt promoted the Hermitage, he made much of how it combined 'the comforts of a refined house with the romance of the Primeval Forest' that surrounded it. Despite his enthusiasm for the vegetation of the Black Spur, Lindt retained just a few 'giants' on his block so that he could use them as tree houses. He replaced the rest with an elaborate garden of introduced species, including several sequoias. From this exotic environment, Lindt offered to guide his visitors to big trees. The largest he knew was a mountain ash sixty-four feet in girth near the summit of Mount Monda. On Boxing Day 1903 he took a party of his guests, including Muir, 'through the best of the great forest hereabouts', although not, it seems, to Mount Monda.[74]

This excursion was the highlight of Muir's Australian visit. In a letter to his wife, Muir exclaimed that he had seen:

> an ideal Australian forest such as I have dreamed of for many years but hardly hoped to see. Should I see no more of Australia and the sky about the Southern Cross I would be repaid for my long journey many times over.

Yet Muir was relieved that the eucalypts were neither as big nor as old as the sequoias:

> The great trees Eucalyptus amygdalina are about 200 feet high average—a few 250—a very few 20 or 30 feet taller. Mr Lindt who says he has spent forty years in 'The Bush' does not believe a single

tree on the continent exceeds 300 feet in height. The rings are very indistinct on large trees. The few I was able to count showed that even the very large trees are not very old, say 200 years or 300.[75]

Muir's last Australian stop was Sydney, where he visited Joseph Maiden, the director of the Botanic Gardens. Maiden had initially accepted Mueller's claims for the mountain ash, but by 1904 Boyle's mistake had led Maiden to conclude that there were no 'Eucalypts in Australia much if any over 300 ft in height' and that 'all the stories attributed to Baron Mueller were false or gross exaggerations'. This evidence strengthened Muir's case for protecting the redwoods as the world's tallest trees, just as it implicitly weakened the case for preserving the mountain ash. When Muir arrived in San Francisco, he promptly announced that 'stories that he had been told of eucalyptus trees being 400 or 500 feet in height he found to be untrue, none of the genus reaching a greater height than about 300 feet'.[76]

JOHN MUIR'S LEGACY

Is it a coincidence that, within a few months of Muir's visit to Melbourne, Caire was taking his photographs of newly discovered big trees straight to the press? That a few months later Caire delivered his first and only paper to Victoria's Field Naturalists on 'The Giant Trees of Victoria'? Or that by the end of the year Lindt and Caire had published a guidebook to the Black Spur area including a section on 'Giant Trees'? Most likely not. While the photographers' actions were prompted partly by the discovery of two new big trees in the Cumberland Valley near Marysville, Caire and Lindt were probably also inspired by Muir, who was a great publicist.

The two trees in the Cumberland Valley were exceptional for their girth rather than their height. The first, promptly dubbed 'The Cumberland Giant', was a white manna gum, 58 feet in girth six feet from the ground, but only 180 feet high having lost its top. The second, found a quarter-mile away and soon named 'Edward VII' in a typical show of Imperial loyalty, was even bigger. By one account, it was 70 feet in girth at a height of 6 feet. By another its girth was 112 feet at its base and 80 feet at a height of 10 feet. Either way, it not only surpassed the Neerim Giant but eclipsed a new sequoia Muir had just claimed as 'the largest tree in the world'.[77]

These new trees were made for the camera. Whereas photographers always found it difficult to convey the great height of

NICHOLAS CAIRE
EDWARD VII 1904

the mountain ash—even when they had a clear line of sight—they could capture their great buttressed bases. Within days of the discovery of 'The Cumberland Giant' and 'Edward VII', Caire was pioneering a new form of photo-journalism—recording the giant girth of these trees for immediate publication by the Melbourne *Leader*, which recognised the public appetite for such 'forest wonders'. These photographs, particularly that of 'Edward VII', succeeded more than any of Caire's other work in conveying the immensity of the giant trees.[78]

When Caire gave his illustrated address to the Field Naturalists a few months later, he argued for preservation of the giant trees primarily because of their age, not their height. One of Caire's friends had counted 1200 rings on the stump of the tree sent to the Paris Exhibition in 1878. In the same year Julian Tenison-Woods had suggested that eucalypts do not always put on a ring of wood for each year of growth. But Caire applied the standard old-world rule of one ring for each year of growth and concluded that the mountain ash reached 1200—if not 1500—years before decay and shrinkage set in. Having raised the issue with an 'American expert', most likely Muir, Caire suggested that such trees had probably been saplings 'when the people of England were semi-barbaric'.[79]

Caire made plain his attachment to the giant trees and his grief at their destruction. He introduced 'Big Ben' as the 'parent of the Black

Spur forest, a splendid specimen of *E amygdalina*, with a solid trunk, without a sign of decay, 57 feet in girth'. 'Poor "Ben" was unprotected', Caire lamented, 'and was caught in the great bush-fires of 1902, and killed'. The Neerim Giant and Hercules at Wynstay were just two of the other trees he included in a long list of the dead, evoking a diminished landscape where giant trees were 'few and far between'.[80]

Caire recognised that individual settlers were partly responsible. Perhaps thinking of Thomas Davies and Wynstay, Caire painted 'the selector' as 'a rough and ready man, with but little poetry or sentiment in his otherwise sturdy character', and 'blind as to the origin or history of these great plants, his one desire being to see his land cleared and grass growing for the sustenance of his stock'. Caire was even more critical of government for having failed to prevent 'the wholesale destruction of our forests'.[81]

Caire had little hope for the big trees. He despaired that Victoria's giants were still 'regarded as so much firewood'. But he consoled himself that his photographs might stop sceptics of later generations concluding that the big trees had never existed. Although Caire predicted that the giant trees would soon all be dead, he hoped that if they became better known, it might provoke 'an effort to conserve and protect some of the finest specimens'.[82]

This faith in public awareness—combined with rank commercialism—probably inspired Caire and Lindt to produce their illustrated *Companion Guide to Healesville, Blacks' Spur, Narbethong and Marysville*, which ran through several editions starting in 1904. Caire and Lindt encouraged their readers to admire 'Uncle Sam' as they made their way beyond Healesville on the main road up the Black Spur, and to employ a guide at Marysville in order to discover the giant trees of the Cumberland Valley. As an inducement, they included Caire's photograph of 'Edward VII'. Like Louisa Anne Meredith in *Walch's Tasmanian Guide Book* in 1871, Caire and Lindt also used their popular tourist guide to encourage a mass audience not just to enjoy but to cherish their excursion grounds. They declared:

> If only a love and admiration of the beautiful can be instilled into the minds of the rising generation, then and only then will it be possible to hand down to those who are to follow us the glorious heritage of the bush, with all its innumerable beauties and features unimpaired. If such a spirit can be assured, then one of the main ideas in the publishing of this book will be fulfilled.[83]

W. C. Piguenit *The Flood in the Darling, 1890* 1895

CHAPTER TEN

THE FLOOD IN THE DARLING

I drown dry gullies and lave bare hills,

I turn drought-ruts into rippling rills—

I form fair islands and glades all green

Till every bed is a sylvan scene.

I have watered the barren land ten leagues wide!

But in vain I have tried, ah!, in vain I have tried

To show the sign of the great All Giver,

The Word to a people: O lock your river.

HENRY LAWSON, 'THE SONG OF THE DARLING RIVER', 1899

W. C. PIGUENIT DID MORE to advance environmental exploitation than most colonial artists. The maps he produced as a draughtsman with Tasmania's Survey Department from 1850 until 1873 provided a basis for settlement and subdivision. His final map showing all the tracks across western Tasmania, which he prepared for the department in 1876 as a supplement to his new career as a professional landscape painter, proved of 'inestimable value' to prospectors. The cuttings in his scrapbook suggest a keen interest in how the colony's timber could be best exploited.[1]

Yet Piguenit was also unusually close to questions of resource conservation from at least 1871, when he made his first major sketching trip through Tasmania's south-west with his friend, the explorer–politician James Reid Scott. On their return to Hobart, Scott warned that Huon pine was being overcut. In a letter to the *Mercury*, he predicted that if the piners around Port Davey went unregulated, they would take out all the marketable trees, depriving the colony of 'the finest timber in the world'. It was 'a ruinous policy', he maintained, to allow forests to be felled, unless they were replanted or turned over to agriculture.[2]

Piguenit would also have been familiar with questions of nature preservation through Colonel W. V. Legge, who accompanied him on at least one of his Tasmanian sketching expeditions and frequently acted as his host at his property near St Marys. A noted ornithologist, Legge was appalled by the slaughter of native birds. From the late 1880s he championed the protection of endangered species. In the early 1890s he became the most prominent advocate of a Tasmanian national park.[3]

Piguenit himself, however, never discussed these issues in print or brought them into his Tasmanian pictures. If he saw his landscapes as having a practical purpose, it was to promote tourism. When five of his views of Mount King William, King Gell and Frenchman's Cap were on show in Hobart in 1887, Piguenit looked forward to improved 'facilities' making these peaks 'as attractive to the tourist as the famed Blue Mountains of New South Wales or Sounds of New Zealand'. The address he gave to the annual meeting of the Australasian Association for the Advancement of Science in 1892 was an illustrated tour guide to Tasmania's 'Western Highlands'.[4]

Piguenit looked very differently on the landscape of western New South Wales, where one of his brothers-in-law conducted two surveys of the Darling and a nephew spent several years on the river.

Piguenit's scrapbook suggests that he was alive to the importance of conserving native plants in this region because of their importance as fodder during droughts.[5] Like many other colonists, including the poets Henry Lawson and 'Banjo' Paterson, he was a keen advocate of water conservation. Most likely he intended his finest painting, *The Flood in the Darling, 1890*, as an argument for conserving water in the west against times of drought.

THE MORAL OF THE FLOODS

When colonists first came upon the Darling, it was very different from the river it is now. Every three to four years, floodwaters spilled over its banks and stretched far and wide across the surrounding plains. While flash floods caused by local rain dispersed almost as rapidly as they appeared, rainfall hundreds of kilometres away in the river's vast catchment sometimes produced floods that lasted for weeks.[6]

In between, colonists found that 'droughts' were almost as common as 'good seasons'. But this characterisation was hardly scientific. The New South Wales Government Astronomer and unofficial meteorologist, H. C. Russell, began recording rainfall on the Darling only in 1871, and then only at Bourke. Most settlers judged the seasons by economics as much as meteorology. The language of drought expressed not just the quantity of rainfall but the use to which the land was put—and that intensified as pastoralists stocked the land with ever more sheep. Whereas there were 350 000 in the western third of the colony in 1860, there were 3 million twenty years later.[7]

Members of the Royal Society of New South Wales were quick to question the impact of this pastoralism. In 1880 W. A. Dixon, an instructor in chemistry at the Sydney School of Arts, suggested that colonists had neglected to study native fodder plants because it was

> too much in the interest of every one to let the sheep and cattle of to-day eat the best there is, even if they destroy it off the face of the earth, without regard to what those of to-morrow will do.

In a prize-winning paper to the society two years later, Andrew Ross deplored

> the gradual but wholesale destruction of the native grasses and herbage all over the country, resulting from the practice . . . of grazing immense flocks of sheep year after year on the same pasturage, without giving any rest to the land.[8]

This use—or abuse—of the land excited general attention after the rains failed in 1883–84 and the Darling became unnavigable, leaving ninety steamers aground on its banks. Pastoralists, who were carrying unprecedented numbers of stock, could neither ship wool from their sheds nor bring in fodder. Many sheep died of thirst; probably even more starved to death. According to J. W. Boultbee, who went on to head the water conservation branch of the New South Wales Department of Mines, the 'actual loss and decrease in the number of sheep' in the Western Division was 6 million. H. C. Russell put the number for New South Wales at 9 million.

Could such losses be justified? One view—still championed by the geographer R. L. Heathcote in the mid-1960s—was that pastoralists had no choice. They had to stock heavily so that they would make as much money as possible while good seasons lasted, even if they then lost most of their stock when bad seasons came. According to Heathcote, this exploitation of the good seasons was a model of 'opportune use', applicable far beyond the semi-arid plains of Australia.[9]

Many colonists were troubled by this practice because of their sense of responsibility for animals in their care. Although primarily concerned with the economics of stock losses, even the New South Wales Royal Commission on Water Conservation invoked 'the unutterable anguish of the many thousands of animals, which in a period of drought perish by slow degrees from hunger and thirst'. Francis Myers accused pastoralists on the Darling of flouting their humanitarian obligations. Having been there in the mid-1880s, when the land 'stank with carrion', he declared:

> No man has a right to gamble for a quick fortune with the lives of 100 000 living creatures for counters. He is bound by every tie of duty and humanity to look forward and make provision. It is clear it can be done, and it should be done.[10]

The destruction of native plants and grasses by overstocking also became a topic of general debate. In a typical essay, Myers predicted that saltbush would soon be 'killed out' from the Murray to the Darling:

> Another decade or two and myall and boree would be gone also; shrubs and trees would also be utterly destroyed, and half the plains barren, through the gnawing out of the very roots of the grass.

With a characteristic flourish, he observed, 'God Almighty did not conserve Australia for the nineteenth century that it should be treated in such a fashion as that'.[11]

One obvious response was for pastoralists to run fewer stock so that they could feed them through dry seasons. In 1885 the 'father of Bourke', E. J. Bloxham, argued that stock numbers on the Darling should be cut by two-thirds. But most colonists looked for ways of maintaining high stocking levels without incurring losses in droughts. Artesian bores provided an increasingly significant source of water from the early 1880s, but the areas they could irrigate remained modest despite their great volume; a bore that yielded 2.7 million gallons a minute could water just 750 acres. Consequently, the conservation of flood waters was always the focus of debate.[12]

Despite the similar language, this water 'conservation' meant something quite different from forest conservation. Where forest conservation was an antidote to the profligacy of man, water conservation sought to harness the profligacy of nature. Rather than seeing nature as a product of an all-wise Creator in which everything was perfect for its purpose, advocates of water conservation believed nature was imperfect and ripe for improvement. Far from affirming the 'economy of nature', they set out to remedy 'waste in nature', as South Australia's Deputy Surveyor-General, Edward Sanger, titled an essay in the *Victorian Review* in 1883.[13]

The common law was one obstacle to water conservation. Even landowners with water frontages had only limited rights of abstraction under the common-law doctrine of riparian rights, so legislation was necessary to authorise large-scale diversion of water. The cost of major waterworks was also an issue. In 1885 the New South Wales royal commission recommended that flood waters on the Darling should be trapped in the river's many lakes, lagoons and anabranches, but reluctantly accepted that irrigation was uneconomic because the flow of water on the river was too small and uncertain to justify the cost of constructing irrigation canals. The problem was that farmers in other parts of the country could grow crops more cheaply. As E. J. Bloxham had testified, irrigation might increase the value of the land fivefold, but to do so 'might cost ten times its present value'.[14]

While the New South Wales government waited to see the effects of Victoria's Water Supply and Irrigation Act, which was enacted in 1886 in response to a Royal Commission chaired by Alfred Deakin, the Darling oscillated between drought and plenty. After flooding in 1886, it was almost dry again two years later during the 'centennial drought', when rainfall for much of Australia was the lowest on record. By the end of 1888, five million sheep had died in New South Wales. A drover who started from Wilcannia with 15 000 sheep reached Hay with 3000. The owner of a station near Albury cut the throats of 25 000 sheep to preserve feed for more valuable stock.[15]

The worst flood on record followed in 1890. Half a million sheep died on the flood plains of the Barwon, Culgoa and Narran Rivers when unprecedented general rain over much of New South Wales and Queensland was compounded by heavy local falls. Yet public attention was fixed on town, not country. Bourke was the 'capital of the west', the biggest stock and wool-loading centre in Australia, with a population of 2500 and property worth a million pounds. When its residents called for help, the government voted £750, then another £1000 and eventually an additional £2000 as well as sending 700 labourers to build an embankment around the town. At first the local residents looked primarily to their own property, erecting crude walls of galvanised iron and bags of earth around their houses, stores and hotels. They only began helping the paid navvies when they realised that collective protection of the entire town was more likely to save them.[16]

Many colonists did not wait to see what the floods would bring. Two hundred took free rail passes to Nyngan, though to do so they had to declare themselves paupers. Another hundred travelled at reduced rates. The government emptied the Bourke jail and sent its inmates to Bathurst. Meanwhile, colonists who lived outside Bourke looked for safety in town. The Governor and his wife, Lord and Lady Carrington, made a brief visit from Sydney to applaud the townspeople's efforts to keep out the water. Francis Myers was among dozens of journalists, artists and photographers who descended on Bourke to report what happened.[17]

Had Bourke been better sited, it would have been safe, but the town was built on low ground by the river, and the Darling rose

BURSTING OF THE EMBANKMENT 1890

higher than expected. By late March, it had submerged the Bourke wharf which usually sat twenty-five feet above the water. By mid-April it had risen another twenty feet. 'No spot in Australia' attracted so much attention. As the water rose, 'all Australia' watched Bourke's 'long and courageous struggle'. Would the embankment hold? Had the Darling peaked, or was a wall of water six feet high still descending the Culgoa?[18]

The embankment failed. Although the navvies succeeded in making it ten feet high and thirty feet wide by ploughing the town common and the main street, one section was so sandy that it gradually became saturated. Then water began oozing through, despite the navvies' efforts to sheath it with galvanised iron and bind it with bushes. Finally, a sixty-foot section gave way. Volunteers 'rushed almost shoulder deep into the tide, and endeavoured to form a living dam of their backs', but the entire town was soon under three feet of water.[19]

LIVINGSTON HOPKINS
THE MORAL OF THE FLOODS
1890

This inundation made the flood even bigger news. The *Argus* reckoned there had been no calamity equal to it 'since Australia was colonised'; the weekly *Australasian* lamented that the 'enemy' had 'taken possession of the town'. This story, which was conveyed in both words and pictures, had two sides. One was the residents' 'gallant efforts': their 'heroic resistance to the watery invader' was 'as fine as anything recorded of Dutch struggles at the dykes'. The other was the impact of the flood on Bourke. As the town's streets became canals, its hotels became islands and then began collapsing when private embankments also failed. Before long, damage ran to at least £50 000.[20]

When colonists looked beyond this immediate threat to life and loss of property, they fixed on water conservation. Even before he set out from Melbourne, Francis Myers criticised the New South Wales government for failing to impound 'tens of thousands of acres of water' by throwing barriers across the Darling's billabongs and anabranches. Sydney's *Daily Telegraph* reiterated this argument when the embankment failed, while the front page of the weekly *Bulletin* carried a cartoon by Livingston Hopkins titled *The Moral of the Floods*, in which Aquarius explained that he was simply providing enough water to see colonists through the next drought—though they were wasting it 'as usual'.[21]

Some colonists responded that it was still possible to dam the flood waters so that, when the 'drought fiend' returned, the 'Bourke devastator' would become 'Wilcannia's boon, Menindie's joy, and even Broken Hill's eternal but watery salvation'. Others thought that it would be 'unwise in the extreme' to trap the overflows of the Darling, as dams would only increase the size of future floods. The *Herald* acknowledged the 'risk in interfering with the larger operations of nature where the possible consequences are not closely studied . . . especially . . . interference with the regimen of great rivers, and the water system of an extensive tract of country'.[22]

The government not only refused to act; it promptly dismembered its Water Conservation Commission, which had been measuring the storage capacity of the various depressions along the Darling with a view to using them as dams. One reason was probably the cost. Another was that irrigation in Victoria was becoming synonymous with large, irrecoverable state expenditure. But as a sop to the many advocates of irrigation in rural New South Wales, the government appointed an engineer, Hugh McKinney, to head a new Water Conservation and Irrigation Branch in the Department of Public Works.[23]

McKinney believed in his profession. He not only asserted 'the prerogative of the engineer to speak with authority about broad, legal, administrative and policy matters'; in his view, no one was 'more entitled to be heard'. One of McKinney's ambitions was to transform the Darling into a reservoir 1344 miles long so that it would be permanently navigable and could irrigate native grasses and lucerne on the rich alluvial soils of its 'great river-valley'. The one constraint he recognised was the risk of salinity. Unlike most of his contemporaries, McKinney knew from India that 'irrigation should not be allowed in places where soil is much impregnated with salts or where the subsoil drainage is defective'.[24]

In the early 1890s, however, there was no drought plain on the Darling to transform 'into an inspiring picture of prosperity'.

According to H. C. Russell, the period from 1889 to 1893 in New South Wales saw the five best consecutive years of rainfall on record. A contributor to the *Australasian Pastoralists' Review* observed in 1895 that the Darling had 'rolled along its channel in almost continuous flood' for six consecutive years. As the number of sheep rose to an all-time high of fourteen million, the wool clip set new records. So did the wheat harvest, leading to calls in 1892 for a Sunday to be set aside 'for general praise and thanksgiving'.[25]

McKinney blamed the weather for his lack of success. Not long after he was appointed in 1891 he complained that the 'extreme wetness' was responsible for a lack of public enthusiasm about irrigation. Two years later, he was even more vexed that the good seasons had 'produced a short-sighted luke-warmness as to the importance of water conservation and irrigation'. Addressing an agricultural conference in February 1895, he reiterated that those who had farmed western New South Wales since 1889 had done so 'under exceptionally favourable circumstances'.[26]

McKinney's only success came in April 1895, when the government announced that it would build an experimental lock and weir on the Darling at Bourke as the first step towards locking the river as far as Brewarrina. But even then the government was less interested in the navigability of the river or water conservation than in creating jobs for those thrown out of work by the 1890s depression. The plan to lock the entire river ran into immediate problems. Because each lock would cost around £20 000, the scheme had to be reviewed by the Parliament's Public Works Committee, which approved only the lock at Bourke.[27]

PRAYING FOR RAIN

By 1895 western New South Wales was in economic turmoil. While wool prices had been falling since the 1870s, they dropped by a further third between 1890 and 1894, more than offsetting the record production of wool during these years. The rabbit plague, which reached the Darling in the mid-1880s, added to pastoralists' woes, as did the shearers' strikes of 1891–92 and 1894. Because many pastoralists could not repay their debts, they were reduced to managing their properties for the banks and finance houses that took over their leases.[28]

At least the pastoral outlook was 'very encouraging', bolstered by 'splendid rains' in January and February 1895. A good lambing season appeared assured. But when there was no rain in March, the *Australasian Pastoralists' Review* feared 'an approaching drought' would cause 'considerable losses'. By April drovers in the west and north-west were shifting stock wherever pastoralists could find agistment or had 'change country' of their own. Where stock could not be shifted, scrub-cutters were busy lopping branches off native shrubs to keep the sheep alive. The only benefit of the dry weather was that it was forcing the 'rabbit pest' to resort to poisoned waters.[29]

By May 'desolation' reigned on the Darling, the Paroo and the Barwon. The lack of rain since February was 'painfully evident by the bare paddocks and, in some districts, by the dying sheep'. The only grass left in the back country had been eaten by starving rabbits, which were dying in thousands. Many pastoralists were 'looking anxiously for a break-up of the drought in time to save the winter herbage'. Others recognised that it was too late: even if good rain fell immediately, the frosts would kill everything that sprouted.[30]

So it proved. While rain in June–July excited reports that the drought was over, these falls were too light to add much to the water supply and too late to yield a good growth of winter feed. By September 1895 the Darling was too low for river traffic, and the country west of Bourke was 'as bare as a Sydney Street'. As rising meat and dairy prices brought the drought home to the city, the metropolitan press ran one drought article after another, and H. C. Russell announced that in some parts of New South Wales the drought was already the worst on record.[31]

This turnabout was more or less expected. In one of many attempts to identify the frequency of good and bad seasons, Thomas Heney concluded in 1891 that severe droughts afflicted the Darling every three years. Hugh McKinney warned in 1893 that the low price of wool and the destruction caused by rabbits had left western New South Wales more vulnerable to drought than ever before. All 'practical and experienced men' agreed that the plains' carrying capacity had plummeted by 20 or even 30 per cent, as cattle, sheep and rabbits compacted the soil and destroyed the best native shrubs and grasses.[32]

Yet pastoralists neither set aside fodder nor attempted to preserve native vegetation. Frederick Turner, the Chief Botanist with the New South Wales Department of Agriculture, called for the conservation, if not active cultivation, of native grasses so that their seeds could be redistributed to areas where they had disappeared, but nothing was done. Anyone wanting to buy saltbush seed had to send to California, where the Agricultural Experiment Station at Tulare had built up stocks from seeds sent to them by Ferdinand von Mueller in the 1880s.[33]

Still pastoralists maintained that their predicament was 'a grievance gratuitously put upon them by an unkind Providence'. The Cardinal of Sydney, Patrick Moran, also looked heavenward. In early September he called on his own clergy to pray for rain when saying Mass. Together with other church leaders, he persuaded George Reid's government to fix a day of 'general humiliation and prayer' so that everyone could call on the Almighty to mitigate or remove the 'very serious calamities' afflicting the colony.[34]

These formulas were old; colonists had used them for years. But the response had become increasingly negative. James Moorhouse, Anglican Bishop of Melbourne from 1877 until 1886, was partly to blame. In February 1882 there had been a 'water famine' in Victoria for over a year, particularly in the north-western wheat belt. The township of Donald was down to one tank of fresh water. Wedderburn was dry. The government responded by providing water trains, which carried supplies for domestic purposes free of cost. It sent augers and boring machines to the Wimmera, East Loddon, Echuca and Shepparton. Melbourne's Catholic churches contributed prayers for rain on the last Sunday of the month. But Moorhouse, who had been an advocate of irrigation since the drought of 1879, refused to join them.[35]

'Don't pray for rain, dam it' is the quip Moorhouse will always be remembered for, though he later admitted to lacking the wit to say it. Instead he declared that, while all Anglican clergymen were free to use the 'prayer for rain' in the Book of Common Prayer, it was 'absolutely impious to cry to God' when colonists had neglected 'his own providential indications of his will' that they conserve the water sent to them. Moorhouse also issued a new prayer:

> Forgive us, O Lord, that we have so indolently and irreligiously broken Thy natural laws, and despised the indications of Thy will in the time past, and give us grace, we beseech Thee, so to lay to heart Thy present and grievous and most just chastisement, that we may bestir ourselves to conserve and employ Thy precious gift of water,

> to the fertilising of our fields, the relief of our necessity, the replenishing of our land with prosperous and happy people, and the glorifying of Thy holy name . . .[36]

The response was immediate. The Catholic and Wesleyan weeklies condemned Moorhouse's stance, but the daily press endorsed it. The *Age* saw no reason to ask God to change 'the order of nature' simply because a few hundred farmers had taken up land in a dry district without constructing dams. When rain followed the Catholics' prayers, the *Argus* explained it away, noting that it usually rained in Victoria in February.[37]

Moorhouse provoked even more controversy when he went to Kerang in March to see the drought for himself. As he described it, the plains near Kerang were 'almost as bare of green grass as the high road'; there were 'vast stretches . . . without trace on them of man or beast'. Moorhouse also invoked religious imagery to evoke this devastation. The country, he declared, looked 'as if it had been blasted by the breath of some destroying angel'. But he still maintained that the solution lay with man, not God.[38]

In his first public address in Kerang, Moorhouse elaborated on his reasons for refusing to issue a special prayer. He argued that the Old Testament God who punished with famine and pestilence did so as a result of His 'peculiar relation' with the people of Israel. The anointing of the sick in the New Testament was similarly limited to an 'age of miracles' long past, when 'miraculous healing was a common gift'. While God could and would change the course of nature 'given a sufficient reason, such as the authentication of the mission of His Divine Son', he otherwise regulated the weather by 'unchanging laws'. The object of prayer was to seek 'spiritual blessings rather than material requirements'.[39]

Two days later, Moorhouse identified irrigation as the only answer to drought, and political action as the one way to achieve it. 'You don't agitate enough, you don't organise enough . . . Above all you don't bring sufficient pressure to bear upon your local members', he admonished the people of Kerang. His advice was to 'Organize, agitate, cry out, send up deputations'.[40]

These lectures made praying for rain *the* test of the response of Christianity to contemporary science. For weeks, Moorhouse happily defended himself in the letters columns of the *Argus*, arguing about doctrine with a host of fellow clerics led by the Roman

Catholic Archdeacon, P. J. Slattery, who condemned him for denying divine agency and the efficacy of prayer. When the Melbourne Presbytery designated the second Sunday in April for further prayers for rain, the Anglicans still did not join them. Nor did the debate stop when the drought broke in April–May. Moorhouse's stance was a butt of jokes for years to come; a subject of discussion in every drought; a keystone of almost every argument for water conservation.[41]

As Stuart Macintyre has noted, this debate marked a decisive change in Victoria's religious temper. Henceforth 'the Protestant denominations were beset by doubt and anxious argument'. New South Wales was also affected, as became clear in 1895 when the government called for prayers for rain. Rather than set aside a weekday, as was conventional, the government chose a Sunday, perhaps because it was uncertain that its proclamation would otherwise be observed. At least one clergyman admitted that 'had a week day been proclaimed as a holy day the opportunity for picnic excursions would have been seized and God would have looked down on the mockery of His name'.[42]

The Sydney press was scathing. The flood on the Darling of 1890 was the local example invoked by those who believed that praying for rain was 'a foolish attempt to substitute religion for irrigation'. While nature had 'sent as much water down the Darling as would irrigate enough land to make the colony independent of rain for years to come', settlers had let it run to waste. The obvious solution was for the government to put the unemployed to work constructing dams. The *Australian Star*, a constant critic of the Reid government, suggested that the Premier's only reason for fixing a day of prayer was 'to keep sweet with the Evangelical party'.[43]

Still most of the churches responded as if Moorhouse had never existed. As the *Star* noted, 'Anglicans and dissenters, church and conventicle, Little Bethel and Cathedral' agreed that local drought was a punishment for local sin, which could be expiated by due humiliation. The only dissentient was a Unitarian Minister, George Walters, who acknowledged that there was scriptural authority for the efficacy of praying for rain, but declared that 'those were things that few reasonable people credited nowadays'. Walters maintained:

> The time had come to say frankly that they could not believe all they read in the Bible. They must read it and criticize it as they would

ordinary literature, and not bend their reason to the crude ideas and fancies of men who lived in an unscientific age.[44]

A key issue was whether praying for rain worked. The Reverend William Martin, an Anglican minister at St Barnabas's Church in the city, cited some 'very remarkable figures' to demonstrate its success. After public prayers on 19 October 1882, it had rained on 21 October. Further prayers on 27 February 1884 had been followed by rain on 10 March. Prayers on 7 June 1885 had been followed by rain on 10 June. Prayers on 24 June 1888 had been followed by rain on 21 July.[45]

The nexus between prayers and rain in 1895 was stronger than ever. Not only was the gap just two days, but it rained so hard over most of New South Wales that there were claims the drought had broken. As Sydney was deluged, a group of Salvationists 'divested themselves of their boots and socks . . . and . . . waded and splashed through the waterways and channels in the streets . . . exclaiming vociferously that "God had answered their prayers"'.[46]

Not everyone was convinced. The gaps between order and delivery of rain in both 1884 and 1888 were too long. The rain in July 1888 was also so slight that prayers for rain were repeated in Sydney in August and the drought broke only in December–January. John Tebbutt, the eminent astronomer who doubled as president of the Windsor branch of the British and Foreign Bible Society, suggested that the only way to test the efficacy of prayer was for those who prayed to specify the time, place and quantity of rain they wanted. No one took up his challenge.[47]

When the rain persisted in September 1895, both church and state were triumphant. By the end of the month the Anglican Primate of Sydney and George Reid had already discussed designating a day of thanksgiving. At the synod of the Anglican Diocese of Sydney, the Almighty was thanked for sending the rain as a 'direct answer' to the people's prayers. Four days later the government issued a proclamation fixing the following Sunday for the special prayers and made much of its God-fearing credentials in what the *Bulletin* derided as a naked attempt to catch the 'pious' vote.[48]

Yet once again there was no cause for celebration. The September rains proved too light to have any lasting effect, and El Niño continued to hold sway through to the end of the century and beyond. When colonists held another round of services in thanksgiving for rain in September 1902, their optimism was again misplaced, as 1902 proved to be the worst year of what became known as the Long Drought. When conditions finally improved in 1903, the number of sheep in western New South Wales had been cut by two-thirds.[49]

THE IRRIGATION POET

'Banjo' Paterson and Henry Lawson are usually paired for their differences rather than their similarities. Paterson romanticised rural Australia; Lawson saw it through a dark glass. But they agreed about water conservation and irrigation. Both men saw the watering of the inland as essential to the development of western New South Wales, and both worked to promote it, although for Paterson water was just an occasional subject, while for Lawson it was a lifelong concern.

Paterson was first into print. In his one and only political pamphlet, published before the New South Wales election in 1889, he declared the colony should develop irrigation works and artesian water in the country rather than erecting a bridge across Sydney Harbour. As a journalist with the *Sydney Morning Herald*, he promoted what became the Burrinjuck Dam on the Murrumbidgee River. His 'Song of the Artesian Water' of 1896, written more than a year into the Long Drought, treated bores as cure-alls. Paterson started by rejecting prayers for rain:

> *Now the stock have started dying, for the Lord has sent a drought;*
> *But we're sick of prayers and Providence—we're going to do without;*

He finished with a characteristically optimistic account of the 'million-gallon flow' bringing 'hope and comfort':

> *To the tortured thirsty cattle, bringing gladness in its going;*
> *Through the droughty days of summer it is flowing, ever flowing.*[50]

The Bourke flood prompted Lawson to begin promoting water conservation. In a piece of 'Straight Talk' he contributed to the *Albany Observer* in May 1890, on a visit to Western Australia, he wrote:

> When we left New South Wales a few weeks ago its driest and hottest towns were being washed off the land, and rescue boats were being sent up by the dozen right to the centre of that imaginary 'Great Australian Desert' of our grandfathers.

With the confidence of youth, he predicted: 'The rising generation will yet see their inland seas of flood waters curbed and stored in great artificial lakes, reservoirs, and canals'.[51]

Like Paterson, Lawson developed his ideas when he had barely seen western New South Wales. He wrote 'Borderland' in mid-1892 as if had just returned from 'up the country'; in fact, he had been in Sydney for the previous eighteen months. After implicitly rebuking Paterson for romanticising the bush, turning 'thirsty gutters' into 'shining rivers', he concluded:

> *I believe the Southern poets' dream will not be realized*
> *Till the plains are irrigated and the land is humanized.*
> *I intend to stay at present, as I said before, in town*
> *Drinking beer and lemon-squashes, taking baths and cooling down.*

Paterson later claimed this attack was contrived: Lawson had suggested that the two poets 'write against each other' to advertise themselves. If so, the game got out of hand. A fortnight after the *Bulletin* published 'Borderland', the solicitor–poet replied from his chambers in Bond Street:

> *You had better stick to Sydney and make merry with the 'push',*
> *For the bush will never suit you, and you'll never suit the bush.*

A week later, Lawson was back in print:

> *It was pleasant up the country, Mr Banjo, where you went*
> *For you sought the greener patches and you travelled like a gent . . .*[52]

Ten days after J. F. Archibald of the *Bulletin* put an end to this poetic warfare, Lawson was on the train to Bourke with £5 and his ticket west. The result was one of his formative experiences. Within less than a year, Lawson gathered much of the material for *While the Billy Boils*, his first collection of stories published in 1896, and for almost everything he subsequently wrote about the outback. Lawson himself treated what he saw as typical of the country. 'If you know Bourke', he wrote, 'you know Australia'.[53]

As chance would have it, Lawson went west during the one dry spell in the long wet. Had he set out a year earlier or a year later, he might have developed a different image of the outback. But he arrived in Bourke in September 1892, just as the *Australasian Pastoralists' Review* reported that the pastoral outlook was 'very dispiriting'. Thousands of sheep were dying 'in the wool' and those that survived were too weak to muster, so that some pastoralists had to shear at their outstations.[54]

These conditions confirmed Lawson's prejudices. While 'agreeably disappointed' to discover that Bourke was 'a much nicer town' than he had expected, he was relieved to have his assumptions about the outback confirmed. In his first letter east, written on the day of his arrival in Bourke, he crowed: 'The bush between Bathurst and Bourke is horrible. I was right and Banjo wrong'.[55]

The conditions hardly improved for most of the time Lawson was out west. While light rain allowed several of the Darling sheds to resume shearing in September and saved 'many in the back country from despair', feed remained scarce. Falls in November were again insufficient to carry pastoralists 'through the season'. By the end of 1892 the number of sheep in western New South Wales had dropped from fourteen million to less than twelve million. By May 1893 less than four inches had fallen for the new year, 'a miserable insufficiency'; many stations had lost between ten and twenty thousand sheep; some had lost sixty thousand.[56]

Lawson struggled in this new environment. Within hours of arriving in Bourke, he 'took a stroll out to find' the Darling but, as he told his aunt, failed to find it.[57] Was he joking? The Great Western Hotel, where he was staying, was just three blocks from the river. Perhaps this letter was Lawson's first attempt at his recurrent theme about rivers that could not be found. Alternatively, it may be just a mark that he was an inept 'new chum'.

Lawson barely adjusted over the following months. When he headed north after Christmas with a companion, they found no work and little food. As he described it in another letter, they 'lived mostly on Johnny cakes and cadged a bit of meat here and there at the miserable stations'. When they reached Hungerford on the Queensland border, he was 'a beaten man'. 'You can have no idea of the horrors of the country out here', he wrote:

> Men tramp and beg and live like dogs . . . We walk as far as we can—according to the water—and then lie down and roll ourselves in our blankets. The flies start at daylight and we fight them all day till dark—then mosquitoes start.

A few weeks later, he complained again from Bourke, 'It's as hot as hell here—too hot to think or write'. All he wanted was to return to Sydney 'never to face the bush again'.[58]

Lawson finally quit Bourke in mid-1893—most likely in June—exploiting a 'dodge' in which he received a free train ticket back to Sydney in return for taking nominal charge of five cattle trucks. Just before he headed east, there was 'a good wide-spread downpour'. One report after another confirmed 'that the earth is thoroughly saturated; that tanks are full, and water everywhere plentiful'. Yet this abundance of water caused its own problems. With the Barwon and the Darling in flood, the sheep could not be brought in until September.[59]

Lawson did not see this flood, just as he never saw the Darling run dry. But he had experienced the flux of bad and good seasons, and hyperbole was his stock in trade. When he came to write about the Darling in the mid-1890s, he described it as 'either a muddy gutter or a second Mississippi'. With characteristic audacity—or blindness—he also ignored his own penchant for exaggeration while deriding others for romanticising the bush. Adopting the royal plural, he proclaimed, 'We wish to Heaven that Australian writers would leave off trying to make a paradise out of the Out Back Hell'. In his own voice, he lampooned a fictional companion:

> I watched a mate of mine sit down in camp on the parched Warrego—which was a dusty gutter with a streak of water like dirty milk—and write about 'the broad, shining Darling'. The Darling when we had last seen it, was a narrow streak of mud between ashen banks with a barge bogged in it. Two weeks later this mate was sitting in a dusty depression in the surface, which he alleged was the channel of a river called the Paroo, writing an ode to 'the rippling Warrego'.[60]

Lawson drew the moral: 'Let us irrigate'—or forget 'talk of settling people on the land'. He put this argument most passionately in his 'Song of the Darling River', first published in the *Bulletin* in

1899, in which he assumed the voice of the river and begged to be locked and contained:

I want no blistering barge aground,
But racing steamers the seasons round;
I want fair homes on my lonely ways,
A people's love and a people's praise.

A year later Lawson instructed readers of the weekly *Worker*:

> Every spare penny should be spent on water conservation and irrigation, in sinking tanks and putting down bores, in locking our thousands and thousands of miles of rivers—almost at sea level—where oceans of water waste away after each flood time. To attend to these things is a national work, for the benefit of the whole nation; to neglect them is a national crime—it is suicidal.[61]

To Lawson's disappointment, the State government initially failed to act. In 1904, he recalled:

I wrote of the unlocked rivers, in the days when my heart was full,
And I pleaded for irrigation where they sacrifice all for wool.

His excitement was equally palpable a year later when the government held a Water Conservation and Irrigation Conference, which resulted in legislation authorising the building of the Burrinjuck Dam and the creation of the Murrumbidgee Irrigation Area. Lawson trumpeted:

And now the glorious scheme's afoot,
Our country to deliver
From drought and earth on blazing waste,
By long neglected river.

He delighted at reports that 'hundreds of boys in Australia long to be engineers'.[62]

By 1915, Lawson was able to construct himself as someone with a *curriculum vitae* in drought and water conservation. When the Water Conservation and Irrigation Commission offered him a job as publicist for the Murrumbidgee Irrigation Area—a position created by the premier, William Holman, to rescue him from drunkenness and destitution—Lawson replied:

> Anyone who has read my works and known something of my earlier life would know that I'm quite qualified for the work suggested. We were drought-ruined on a selection in the Mudgee district to begin with . . . afterwards I saw the great possibilities for water storage on the Darling River and wrote about it for years.

When Lawson took up the job in Leeton in 1916, he styled himself 'Government Irrigation Poet'. 'Australia's greatest hope', he declared, had 'always been the conservation of water, and irrigation'.[63]

THE IRRIGATION ARTIST

Like Lawson, W. C. Piguenit was slow to see the Darling. During his first ten years in New South Wales, he visited western New South Wales only once, in 1883–84, and even then he went only as far as Dubbo. Piguenit was also slow to make much of the outback in his art. The one western landscape he exhibited with the Art Society of New South Wales was his *Cattle Droving*. While he made several sketches recording how the Macquarie River had been reduced to small waterholes, he did not turn them into canvases, most likely because the drought was alien to the sensibility for well-watered landscape he had developed in Tasmania.[64]

Piguenit learnt about the Darling from his brother-in-law, Gerald Halligan, who was chief engineer in the Harbours and Rivers Section of the New South Wales Department of Public Works. After conducting a survey of the river in 1885, Halligan returned during the centennial drought in 1888. His official function was to investigate how the Darling could be made more navigable, but he could not stop himself reporting on the great opportunities for conservation and irrigation that could turn 'thousands of square miles on the river lying idle . . . into a garden'. Hundreds of lakes, lagoons and billabongs, Halligan wrote, were 'filled by flood waters from the river entering by a narrow channel'. He advised that 'a few thousand, and in some cases a few hundred pounds expended in the construction of flood gates at the entrance to these lakes would conserve very large quantities of water'.[65]

Piguenit discussed these issues in January 1889 in a letter to his English cousin Fanny. By then, the drought had ended over most of Australia, breaking, like many El Niño-related droughts, in late December and early January. But Piguenit was interested only in the Darling, the one part of New South Wales where the drought continued. He explained:

> We are now in the height of our summer and experiencing exceedingly hot weather, more especially in the western or interior parts of the Colony where the thermometer last week for several days ranged from 108 to 116 degrees in the shade. Unfortunately this excessive heat has been accompanied by extremely dry and scorching winds, with little or no rain, and the result has been a terrible amount of suffering on the part of sheep and cattle on the back runs, and of course an accompanying loss on the part of pastoralists. These droughts, which are of frequent occurrence, form the worst feature in the climate of N.S.Wales and inflict great loss upon almost every interest and especially those engaged in pastoral pursuits. My nephew . . . tells me that during the drought of 1883–4 the sheep station on which he was engaged lost upwards of 90,000 sheep while an adjoining station lost 130,000.

Piguenit maintained that the fluctuations from abundance to scarcity of water were 'unmistakable evidence' of 'the necessity of a comprehensive system of water conservation being established in the country'. He was delighted that the government had begun recognising this need, and that Halligan's survey had contributed to 'the contemplated work of conservation and irrigation'.[66]

Piguenit returned to this theme in his next letter on 26 April 1890, the same day as Livingston Hopkins's 'The Moral of the Floods' was on the cover of the *Bulletin*. Once again Piguenit was particularly concerned for his nephew, who escaped the flood but suffered 'still further losses' when 'the incessant rain destroyed all his tobacco, and a great part of his maize crop', leaving him 'very dispirited'. Piguenit reported:

> [T]errible floods . . . have occurred both in Queensland and N.S.Wales . . . indeed old residents say that they surpass in severity anything that has been recorded since white man first settled in Australia. The Darling River which averages in ordinary seasons

> from 100 to 200 yards in width is now in some parts from 30 to 40 miles. The town of Bourke is at the present moment inundated . . . Fortunately owing to the Authorities having removed most of the people few lives have been lost, but the destruction of stock has been enormous and a large number of settlers have been entirely ruined.[67]

A few days later, Piguenit was on the train west. Characteristically, he was not interested in Bourke and its inhabitants: figure subjects were never his forte. Instead he wanted to paint 'the country while in its flooded state', 'so entirely covered with water as to resemble the sea'. Piguenit was probably attracted by the pictorial possibilities of such a large mass of water because of his taste for wet landscapes; perhaps he saw it as sublime. He may also have wanted to convey 'The Moral of the Floods' in a medium more substantial than a cartoon.[68]

When Piguenit arrived on the Darling there were insects and snakes everywhere. While vast numbers of rabbits had been killed by the flood, thousands of others had taken refuge up trees and could be seen along the river banks as the water receded. Pastoralists tried to make the most of this opportunity by driving the rabbits into yards made of wire netting and beating them to death with sticks. Even so, the new growth that followed the flood was consumed by grasshoppers and the surviving rabbits, leaving 'the outlook in the West . . . gloomy in the extreme'.[69]

Piguenit ignored these consequences of the flood, focusing instead on the submerged plain, which Francis Myers described as 'a great, smooth, shining sea, dotted with clumps of bushes . . . everything reflected and still'. By September Piguenit had completed two landscapes, which he exhibited as contemporary reportage, titling them *Out West during the Floods of 1890*. One showed Mount Oxley, the only piece of land still visible to the east of the town when the flood peaked; the other offered a similar view south to the Gunderbooka Range.[70]

These paintings gave no hint that anything was awry. At the annual exhibition of the Art Society of New South Wales in September 1890, they were acclaimed as 'beautiful scenes', particularly notable for their treatment of light. The view towards the Gunderbooka Range was applauded for its 'fine sky, with its masses of purple clouds just touched by saffron tints, the beauty of the golden light which gilds the desolation of the far-stretching tide, and the luminous touch which characterises the whole'.[71]

W. C. PIGUENIT
OUT WEST DURING THE FLOODS OF 1890—THE GUNDERBOOKA RANGE 1890

Five years later, Piguenit embarked on *The Flood in the Darling, 1890*, which was acclaimed as the one outstanding entry in the annual exhibition of the Art Society of New South Wales in September–October 1895. Although one carping critic found 'a little too much glare in the water' and questioned Piguenit's decision to ignore the Bourke people's 'gallant fight for their town', even he recognised that Piguenit had excelled himself with a 'great picture' of 'an event of national interest'. The Trustees of the Art Gallery of New South Wales, led by Eccleston du Faur, bought the painting immediately for 150 guineas.[72]

Piguenit's reasons for painting the Darling again in 1895 were mixed. As with his first paintings from 1890, *Flood in the Darling* was in part a study of clouds and light, water and reflections. But Piguenit had larger ambitions, which led him to work on a bigger canvas. No longer was he practising contemporary reportage, or even depicting a conventional view with an identifiable mountain backdrop. While he still worked from a sketch done in the field, the precise location of his subject was no longer significant. Most likely, he conceived *Flood in the Darling* as a history painting with a moral, as Sir Joshua Reynolds had envisaged when he designated history painting the highest form of art.[73]

D. H. Souter cast *Flood in the Darling* in these terms when he wrote the most important contemporary essay about Piguenit in 1905. While best known for his cartoons in the Sydney *Bulletin*, Souter was also a prominent journalist who co-edited *Art and Architecture* and wrote for the *Stock and Station Journal* and *Country Life*. Manifesting his interest in rural issues, he interpreted *Flood in the Darling* as both a record of the past and as an argument for more intensive development of the west. To Souter, Piguenit's painting preached 'a perpetual sermon on the possibilities of water conservation, which should strongly impress our State economists'.[74]

Souter was not alone in maintaining this faith in water conservation through the Long Drought. In 1896 Piguenit's brother-in-law, Gerald Halligan, dwelt on 'the immense possibilities of water conservation' in western New South Wales. According to Halligan, even 'the most casual observer' who travelled through the Darling country 'was struck with the wonderfully luxuriant growth, where water was judiciously applied to apparently useless soil'. In 1901 Hugh McKinney's successor, L. A. B. Wade, continued to maintain that it would pay to build large dams on the Darling between Bourke and Wentworth so long as they were used not just for watering stock but to support agriculture.[75]

The cry for state aid was insistent when the New South Wales Minister for Lands and the first Chairman of the Western Lands Commission went on a tour of inspection of the Darling in 1902. 'Stop the flood waters from rushing away to the sea', cried the leaseholders. 'Fill the lakes and lagoons and billabongs', 'Lock the Darling'. Even after seven years of drought, they maintained that had the government built weirs on the river, 'hundreds of thousands of acres . . . would be covered with magnificent sheets of water, . . . creating splendid water frontages . . . valuable for stock . . . as well as for irrigating small areas devoted to the growth of fodder crops'.[76]

The Long Drought led other colonists to reconsider the possibilities of water conservation and irrigation in New South Wales. Edward Millen, a pastoralist, journalist and politician, was a key figure in this revaluation. Through most of the 1890s Millen was an ardent advocate of watering the inland, maintaining that it was 'the fresh vivifying agency . . . required to stimulate the industrial life of Australia' and the most effective means of saving the £1 million worth of sheep that New South Wales lost on average each year through

ATTRIBUTED TO
D. J. McLEAN
MULGA TREE ON YANTARA STATION, NEAR MILPARINKA
C. 1900

droughts. But by the summer of 1899–1900, Millen had radically revised his views.[77]

In a seven-part report for the *Sydney Morning Herald*, republished immediately as a pamphlet, Millen argued that overstocking and rabbits, aided and abetted by droughts, had permanently degraded western New South Wales. As he described it, the western plains had been 'churned up as though they had been rich

CHRISTOPHER BRANDIS
COBHAM LAKE HOMESTEAD, NEAR MILPARINKA 1901

alluvial diggings worked by a myriad army of eager miners'. As if explaining two of the first photographs of this erosion published in 1901 by a royal commission into conditions in western New South Wales, he wrote:

> Where the butts of salt and other bushes remained they served to keep a little soil around them, but between the wind had cut down to the underlying cement-like clay, leaving them elevated on precarious and gradually disappearing pedestals.

On one station 'the sheepyards had to be excavated before shearing could start'; at another 'the manager advised against letting the buggy horses go into the horse-paddock . . . as in places the fence was so sanded up that they might get out'.[78]

Millen maintained that the only solution was for pastoralists to reduce their flocks and for the government to reduce estimates of the area's carrying capacity and hence the rent it charged pastoral lessees. Water conservation was useless in extended droughts. The crux of his argument was that, although the Long Drought was 'widespread, remorseless, prolonged', it was unexceptional. As Millen put it, colonists had made a 'fundamental error' in regarding the normal condition of the west 'as one of fair seasons punctuated with occasional drought' when in fact it was 'one of drought . . . punctuated with occasional moist seasons'.[79]

ARTHUR STREETON *CREMORNE PASTORAL* 1895

CHAPTER ELEVEN

CREMORNE PASTORAL

The long tree-covered slopes of Mosman, Athol and Bradley's Head were lovely in the late afternoon; amber and gold lighting up the myriads of eucalypts, light echoing upon light, and the surface of the bay below like a robe of intense blue satin. A coaling company was formed, and in some clever way acquired permits to bore for coal. One day the thousands of gum trees had been cut down. The multitude of trees lying low was a shocking sight.

ARTHUR STREETON, *ARGUS*, 15 SEPTEMBER 1934

IN 1895 SYDNEY HARBOUR was set for mining. The New South Wales government had granted most of the land under the harbour to a colliery company, paid half the cost of a test bore, and leased the company a prime water frontage near Bradleys Head. All the company needed was another lease so that it could erect a wharf to ship its coal. A prudent company would only have started preparing to put down its shafts after the government had granted this lease. But not the Sydney Harbour Collieries Company. It immediately began stripping Bradleys Head of vegetation.

Arthur Streeton had particular reason to value this part of the harbour. It was both his home and his prime painting ground. As Streeton later recounted, he was one of many who spoke out against the mine. His *Cremorne Pastoral*—his largest painting celebrating the harbour and its foreshores—also became part of the argument against the mine when he first exhibited it with Sydney's new Society of Artists, a day before W. C. Piguenit's *The Flood in the Darling, 1890* went on display at the rival Art Society of New South Wales.

The reception of these contemporary paintings had much in common. Like *Flood in the Darling*, *Cremorne Pastoral* was widely acclaimed, often reproduced and bought immediately for 150 guineas by the Art Gallery of New South Wales. But whereas *Flood in the Darling* was seen as an argument for greater environmental exploitation, *Cremorne Pastoral* was interpreted as an argument against mining Sydney Harbour. At a time when it was still common to talk of the 'picture of the year', the two great rival paintings for 1895 were subject to fundamentally different environmental readings.

OUR BEAUTIFUL HARBOUR

Mining was on the cards in Sydney from 1847, when the Reverend W. B. Clarke first suggested that the coal found at the surface in the Hunter Valley and the Illawarra was part of the same measure and hence must underlie the city. Over the next thirty years a succession of geologists agreed with Clarke's prediction but disagreed as to how deep the seam might be—a crucial issue, because if the seam were too deep, extraction would not be viable.[1]

Speculators began testing Clarke's hypothesis in 1878. A year later the colonial government granted R. D. Adams, a Sydney businessman and sometime poet, the right to mine 10 000 acres under Port Jackson, Middle Harbour and the Parramatta River. By one account, Moore Park was soon 'as full of holes as a cullander'. But none of the first five bores struck coal, though the deepest was almost 2200 feet. Two others at Liverpool and Sutherland struck seams too thin to mine at 2300 and 2600 feet. Most colonists dismissed Clarke's idea as 'the wildest of wild cat ventures'.[2]

Harper Brothers, a firm of Sydney consulting engineers, persevered. In 1890 they established the Sydney and Port Hacking Coal Company, which acquired Adams's rights to the harbour and then used the government's diamond drill to put down the deepest bore yet sunk in Australia. It struck a seven-foot seam 2800 feet beneath Cremorne Point, confirming Clarke's prediction. But volcanic intrusions had reduced the coal to valueless cinder.[3]

The company might have got no further on its own, because its capital was almost exhausted. But the government decided that 'the future value to the State of workable seams of coal beneath Sydney could scarcely be overestimated', so it gave the company even more help. First Edgeworth David, a geological surveyor with the Mines Department, determined that there was no reason why valuable coal might not be found close to the initial bore. Then Edward Pittman, the government geologist, fixed the most promising site, just a quarter of a mile away. Finally the government lent its diamond drill and the officials to work it, and met half the actual costs of boring, leaving the company to raise only another few thousand pounds.[4]

When this bore struck coal 2900 feet beneath Bradleys Head in November 1893, Edgeworth David's excitement knew no bounds. Writing in his new capacity as professor of geology at Sydney University, David declared that, although the first bore had found 'only quite local' coke, the norm was 'a magnificent seam of steaming coal'. Within three days, seven speculators had applied for authorities to mine under another 10 000 acres beneath or near the harbour, while another company had applied for the right to mine 8000 acres under the Pacific Ocean. The *Sydney Morning Herald* made so much of this 'new source of wealth and public benefit' that the *Australian Mining Standard* reckoned it read like a 'promoter's prospectus'. Because of the stimulus to local manufacturing, the *Herald* expected that the harbour's foreshores would 'at no great remoteness of time be covered with hives of busy industry' and Sydney would enjoy 'a peerless position in the South Seas' as 'a commercial entrepot'—the only metropolitan city 'in the whole world . . . with a coal mine in operation, virtually within its town boundaries'.[5]

The Cremorne Coal Bore 1893

This embrace of the colliery discounted its impact on Port Jackson, the city's pride and joy. In the early 1870s, Anthony Trollope had observed that Sydney people were 'by no means indifferent to the beauty of their harbour' but they talked about it with a certain diffidence. There was 'something of shamefacedness, a confession of provincial weakness, almost an acknowledgement that they ought not to be proud of a thing so insignificant'. By the early 1880s this diffidence had gone, encouraged by Trollope's judgement that the harbour was 'so inexpressibly lovely' that it made a man consider moving 'to the eastern coast of Australia, in order that he might look at it as long as he can look at anything'. According to James Inglis, the creator of Billy Tea and former President of the Sydney Chamber of Commerce, the first question Sydneysiders asked visitors was 'what do you think of the harbour?'[6]

By the early 1890s, Port Jackson was 'Our Harbour', or even 'Our Beautiful Harbour'. This declaration of common enjoyment—if not common ownership—was no fiction. The harbour was accessible to most inhabitants of the city, because the bulk of its population still lived within walking distance of its shores. Relatively short hours of work and Saturday half-holidays also meant that both 'the Middle-class and the People' could take advantage of it. The harbour was of 'real use' rather than something 'merely to blow about'.[7]

The *Herald* was so excited by the colliery that it invoked 'Our Beautiful Harbour' only to dismiss it. Those 'more than ordinarily susceptible to the aesthetic' would lament 'the rearing of great smoke-stacks, and the heaping up of piles of coal debris'. But so long as the shafts were confined to Cremorne, this solitary example of 'black country' would not be a blot on the scenery. At worst, the *Herald* contended, the colliery would be 'a foil to the matchless charms of Port Jackson', at best 'a special feature, lending itself even to the picturesque'.[8]

Harper Brothers were equally confident when the *Daily Telegraph* questioned them about siting the colliery 'upon one of the prettiest and, as yet, most solitary eminences of the harbour'. What of the 'rows of stunted cottages devoid of foliage surroundings, and often grotesquely ugly, the bare streets trodden in with coal-dust, the swarms of ill-clad children, and the gangs of grimy men'? Harper Brothers replied that 'a good wharf . . . a few huge bunkers, and the gear that ordinarily surmounts a miners' shaft, would be about the only surface indications of the grimy business going on in the depths below'. While the miners' cottages would 'have to go up somewhere', there was no reason why they 'should be an eyesore any more than the home of any son of toil'.[9]

A. B. Piddington—the future parliamentarian, chair of the Inter-State Commission, Industrial Commissioner and head of several royal commissions—disagreed. Aged just twenty-three in 1893, Piddington was combining working at the bar with teaching English literature at Sydney University. As described by Michael Roe, Piddington's close friendship with the poet Christopher Brennan was indicative of 'his semi-Bohemian and modernist leanings. His culture included art and music, as well as literature.'[10]

From his chambers in Phillip Street, Piddington wrote to the *Daily Telegraph* ridiculing the notion that the disfigurement of the harbour would be 'only a little one'. Piddington predicted that within a few years Sydney would 'transact its business under an atmosphere like that of London'; its southern suburbs would 'have their wonderful glories of light and colour dimmed with a pervading infusion of gloom' and enjoyment of the city's eastern parks would be 'permanently impaired'. Not least, the harbour itself, 'the peculiar pride and glory of the community', would be 'invisible under a constant irruption of colliers, tugs, and barges, either approaching, or loading, or departing from the great central canker at Cremorne'.[11]

Before allowing such an 'irreparable' transformation of Port Jackson, Piddington argued, local residents had to consider not just their own interests but those of the nation; not just the interests of the present generation but those of the future. The harbour and its foreshores were the stuff of a public trust, a heritage worth preserving:

> We in Sydney are the trustees for all Australia and of all time of that national heritage of beauty which gives to us our pride of place amongst the capitals of this continent and endows these with a reflected glory amongst the people of all nations who visit us.[12]

Piddington cast this argument as part of a universal tradition that put aesthetics before commerce. All 'thoughtful men', he declared, knew 'from history and human nature that a reverence for beauty . . . in nations as in individuals' was 'the hall mark of worth and character and sense'. He also set preservation of the harbour's beauty within a local tradition in which the encouragement of culture and protection of the environment were all of a piece. Perhaps unaware that the Art Gallery of New South Wales had itself been sited in the Domain only after keen debate about its occupation of park land, Piddington declared:

> If we discern any greatness of soul in the spirit that has led to the foundation of our university, the endowment of our admirable art gallery, the maintenance of our public parks and gardens, the establishment of our museums, the vigilance exercised over our

Livingston Hopkins
King Coal at Cremorne
1893

centres of national beauty, such as the Jenolan Caves, then let our generation be the equal of its predecessors in this great quality.[13]

The proper way of securing this goal was for government to stop the mine proceeding while rewarding its promoters for their enterprise. Piddington maintained that it would be 'scandalous' for the state to treat citizens who had 'shown such pluck and tenacity of purpose in any but the most liberal way'. The government should meet all the miners' outlays and give them a 'generous return' for the risks they had run. Just as Edward Hargraves had been rewarded for his discovery of gold in 1851, so the Coal Company should receive a 'national reward' for making a discovery that could 'one day, say in such a crisis as war, prove of incalculable value'.[14]

These arguments made some Sydneysiders think again. In an editorial on 'City Desecration', the *Daily Telegraph* agreed that utility 'in the strict commercial sense' was not everything; if mining would blight Sydney, 'it would be better, at any loss possible, to leave the coal unmined'. The *Bulletin* protested that the harbour would be 'disfigured by huge, gaunt poppet-heads, and its waters . . . blackened by coal dust'. Its cartoonist, Livingston Hopkins, who had established one of the first artists' camps on Port Jackson at Edwards

C. H. HUNT
A GLIMPSE OF THE FUTURE: CREMORNE 10 YEARS HENCE
1893

Beach, showed 'King Coal' emerging from the bore to tell 'Mr Shindykit': 'Well, yes it is a Beautiful Harbour, but we'll soon change all that'.[15]

'Hop' and the *Bulletin* were even more critical of the 'Private Enterprise Government' of George Dibbs for having 'fooled away' what might prove 'the grandest mineral concession in New South Wales'. Instead of doing its own prospecting and then selling the coal by public tender, the government had parted with the coal for the 'miserable royalty' of sixpence per ton, which was the minimum prescribed by statute. To make matters worse, the government had also paid for most of the prospecting even though 'a few bulbous capitalists' were to get all the profit. If the government gave any more coal concessions at sixpence per ton, the *Bulletin* declared it 'should be smashed at once'.[16]

The new Australian Labor Party also raised the issue in Parliament through Henry Newman, its member for Orange in central New South Wales, who otherwise was a successful mine owner and manager. Newman pressed the government to extract a better price for the coal if mining proceeded. He also identified the larger public interest in preserving the harbour intact. But the Minister for Mines, Thomas Slattery, was dismissive, replying that it was 'not clear how the state would be served by locking up this seam of coal'.[17]

When C. H. Hunt, who had been a member of an artists' camp on Middle Harbour in the late 1880s, pictured the impact of the mine for the *Illustrated Sydney News* at the end of the year, he showed Cremorne Point stripped of all its vegetation and given over to mining. Yet Hunt may not have intended his engraving as a criticism of the colliery; he presented the mine as a model of good order, which blighted neither Mosman in the foreground nor the flourishing centre of Sydney across the harbour. Although one of the *News*' items about the bore lamented that coal had become the property of a few capitalists rather than belonging 'to the world at large', another article quipped that Cremorne boasted 'one of the few classes of "bore"' that was 'tolerated and even welcomed to a district'.[18]

THE PEOPLE'S DOMAIN

The controversy stopped there, most likely because the mine seemed a long way off. While the company began trying to raise the capital it needed to develop the mine, and even suggested it might be sinking its first shaft at Cremorne Point before Christmas, such talk fooled no one. The company itself acknowledged it needed to raise a quarter of a million pounds. Others reckoned it would need half a million—a vast sum when New South Wales was in the depths of depression, British investors were wary of sinking more capital into Australia after losing millions of pounds in the bank crashes of 1893 and it was unclear whether the mine would be viable.[19]

This question loomed large partly because there was already an oversupply of coal in New South Wales, the deep shafts would cost more to sink than those at any other colliery in Australia, and ventilation would be correspondingly difficult and expensive. It was also unclear which of the company's two bores would prove representative. One Sydney geologist argued that 'no limit' could be set on 'the range and destructive influences of the basalt'. The *Australian Mining Standard* maintained that, for all the scientific interest of the company's discovery, it was of no commercial value without hard evidence that the mine could yield a fair return on investment.[20]

James Inglis's public statements about Sydney Harbour suggest he should have opposed the colliery. In 1880 he had lamented the 'disfiguring evidence of man's presence' on and around the harbour—'the pollution of the city's drainage' and the 'smoke of steam-ships and factories, and all the ugliness of our utilitarian age of coal, iron, smoke, and steam'. But Inglis put these concerns aside when Harper Brothers learnt that he was going 'home' in January 1894 and asked him to try to float the new Sydney Harbour Collieries Company in London.[21]

Inglis was ideal for this job because of his extensive business contacts. In one address touting the new company in London, he maintained that its discovery was arguably the 'most momentous . . . of the century' so far as the mineral wealth of New South Wales was concerned. Like the *Sydney Morning Herald*, he hoped Sydney would become the first metropolis in the world with 'a coal mine in operation within its boundaries, and in such favourable position that the coal can be rolled down the shoots from the pit's mouth into the largest ocean-going steamers'. According to Inglis, 'scientific experts and practical coal-masters' figured that the harbour would yield 200 million tons of coal, 'worth well-nigh one hundred million pounds sterling'.[22]

Yet Inglis struggled to establish the company until late 1894, when a boom in mining stocks on the London exchange allowed dozens of syndicates to foist 'a great deal of rubbish' on the public. Most of the excitement focused on South African and West Australian mines, but it also boosted other colonial stocks. Although he raised only £128 000, less than half of what he aspired to, Inglis floated the company in March 1895.[23]

Meanwhile the colliery's managing director in Sydney, T. S. Huntley, sought a site for its operations. His requirement was a piece of foreshore relatively close to the second bore. Had he opted to buy a site on the open market, there would have been nothing to stop the company sinking its shafts. But Huntley looked to the government for a cheap site. In particular, he sought a mining lease because the colony's Mining Act prescribed a fixed rent of five shillings per acre for mining leases, regardless of whether the land was in the Riverina or central Sydney.[24]

Most of the harbour's foreshores were still Crown land—a rare case of environmental protection being instigated by Whitehall rather than by colonial officials. British Canada provided the model. Having already reserved all land within 100 feet of the high-water mark along its coast, the Colonial Office instructed Governor Darling in 1828 to do likewise in New South Wales. But after just three years the Colonial Office weakened this protection, authorising the Governor to sell this reserve for commerce or navigation, and public access to the harbour was further jeopardised by adjoining landowners illegally fencing in the remaining Crown land.[25]

This privatisation of the foreshore became increasingly controversial from the mid-1880s as part of the larger colonial debate about alienation of the public domain. In 1886, after the government had sold forty harbour-front lots in five years, George Reid introduced a Bill to stop any further sales around the harbour. The Minister for Lands, Henry Copeland, imposed a moratorium, declaring that 'if all the applications . . . in the Lands Office were granted there would not be a square foot of frontage for the people'. But the government failed to make time to debate Reid's Bill, and Copeland lifted his moratorium after just five months, allowing sales to continue.[26]

The 100-foot reserve around Cremorne, where the Collieries Company had sunk its bore, was one of the areas most at risk throughout this period. The main threat came from a local landowner, James Milson, who repeatedly applied to have the reserve revoked so that he could buy it. Although the government refused him in 1877, 1879, 1880 and 1881, Milson persisted. In 1884 the Minister for Lands approved his application only to be overturned by Cabinet. In 1887 Milson proposed that, in return for being granted the frontage, he would give the Crown a single block of the same size on Robertson's Point, which he argued would be better suited to public recreation. Whereas the local St Leonards Council had previously opposed Milson's plans, it accepted this offer, as did the Minister for Lands and the Cabinet.

A former Mayor of St Leonards, George Ranken, explained the Council's about-turn in a bitter letter to the *Sydney Morning Herald.*

Ranken described how his council had maintained 'a desperate but generally fruitless contest' to save the frontages since he was first elected in 1885. He claimed the council had consistently opposed applications to buy this land—but they had 'never heard any more of it' until the sale was gazetted. Although the council's 'special anxiety' was to preserve the water frontage at Cremorne, its members agreed to Milson's proposal because 'all their experience' suggested that 'if they did not accept the terms offered by the syndicate, the whole of the frontage would be made away with . . . on the quiet at some favourable political juncture'.[27]

This view proved too pessimistic, because the Opposition made an issue of the exchange. When the Legislative Assembly debated the disposal of the colony's foreshores as a matter of public importance, it emerged that much of the Robertson's Point site that Milson proposed to give the public was of little benefit to him because it was 'too narrow for building purposes'. By contrast, the foreshore at Cremorne was not only one of the most beautiful spots in the harbour but the only remaining accessible area of any length on the North Shore left for public use. As a result, the government retreated, promising not to complete the sale without notifying Parliament—an outcome that the Opposition boasted would preserve 'to the people a magnificent heritage—a water frontage . . . unequalled in Port Jackson'.[28]

Still the reserve at Cremorne remained under threat. Having failed to persuade the government to grant it to him, Milson claimed the land by adverse possession, and began clearing and marking it out for sale. The Supreme Court of New South Wales decided against Milson in 1891, but he promptly appealed to the Privy Council in London. Ownership of this strip of land was consequently uncertain in 1893, when the Collieries Company began looking for a site to establish its plant. The company had to look elsewhere, even though this land was its first choice because of its proximity to the test bores.[29]

The company's second choice was the military reserve at Bradleys Head. Although marginally further from the bores, this reserve had a wharf that could accommodate the largest ocean-going steamers, and the coal could be reached by shafts 150 feet shorter than anywhere else. In addition, as the company belatedly emphasised, Bradleys Head was an area with 'but little population', so relatively few people would be exposed to pollution from the mine. According to the company, it had 'no wish to open the works in the immediate vicinity of a thickly populated suburb'.[30]

The council of the new Borough of Mosman—already among 'the most exclusive' of Sydney's suburbs—saw things differently. When the company applied for a mineral lease over twenty-four acres in March 1894, the council protested that the colliery would 'prove an eyesore' and 'deface the natural beauty' of the area. When the company also claimed that its operations would increase the value of adjoining land, the council replied that people who had built 'comfortable homes' in Mosman in 'anticipation of the borough becoming a leading residential suburb', would be 'disgusted to find themselves in a colliery village'. In September 1894 the government refused to lease or sell the reserve at Bradleys Head.[31]

The company's third choice was to reclaim land around Kurraba Point at Neutral Bay, where there was no 100-foot reservation. But in February 1895, while this application was proceeding, the Privy Council rejected Milson's appeal in the Cremorne foreshore case. As a result, the Collieries Company was finally free to apply for the land it had always wanted most. For twenty acres of harbour frontage between Mosman and Neutral Bay, it looked forward to paying just £5 a year.[32]

This application jeopardised what was at stake in the Crown's successful assertion of ownership of the reserve against Milson. The underlying issue in this litigation was a competition between a few private individuals and the Crown acting for all members of the public. When the case first came to trial in 1891, Sir Julian Salomons opened by emphasising that he was acting 'on behalf of the Crown, or rather the public'. In summing up, he asked whether a stretch of foreshore worth perhaps £100 000 could have fallen into private hands. His conclusion was that 'the land . . . belonged to the public'.[33]

BY THE MEREST CHANCE

Opposition to the company's application depended on the Mining Act's provisions for public notice, which required would-be miners to advertise their intention on the land in question, and to post notices outside a post office and a mining registrar's office. These provisions were notoriously flawed. As one commentator put it in the late 1880s, promoters commonly posted notices in places that were invisible to passers-by and put advertisements outside offices miles away, where they would be 'plastered one over another in a heterogenous mass of waste paper . . . in many instances carried away by the wind before the paste . . . had time to dry'.[34]

It was therefore by 'the merest chance' that the local Member of Parliament, E. M. Clark, and a local alderman, William Anderson, happened to see a public notice of the company's application posted at the Mines Department. Had they not seen this notice, the company's application would have been uncontested and most likely would have succeeded. Having seen it, Clark and Anderson could take advantage of the Mining Act's provision for objections to mining applications to be heard in the mining warden's court. This court had been created to resolve disputes between competing miners or between miners and landowners, but any members of the public could participate in its hearings. Clark and Anderson lodged their objection with an hour to spare.[35]

Like Henry Newman, who had questioned the mine in 1893, Clark was one of the first Labor Members of Parliament. A manager of a brickworks, he twice stood unsuccessfully for Parliament as an independent free trader in the 1880s. Then a strong branch of the Labor Electoral League was established in North Sydney in 1891 but could not find a suitable candidate. Clark made the most of this situation, offering to support the platform of the League, press for eight-hour legislation and sit on the cross-benches. When elected, he more than kept his word: he joined the Labor Party, gained admission to its first caucus, and continued generally to support Labor until the end of the decade.[36]

If Anderson was mainly concerned about the mine's impact on local landowners, Clark articulated the broader public interest. He argued that, if the company succeeded, members of the public would be excluded from a prime area where the Privy Council had just upheld their rights. Clark also deplored the way in which the case had arisen, arguing that mining under the harbour was too important to be decided without proper public notice. He was appalled that to exercise his right he had to pay £5, as much as the company expected to pay annually in rent, even though he was acting 'in the public interest, and had no personal motive to serve'.[37]

The local arguments against mining were further articulated at a protest meeting chaired by Mosman's mayor in the council's chambers. According to one local landholder, the mine 'would prove the ruination of Mosman and North Shore'. Another deplored its effect on their 'beautiful and growing suburb', and especially on those who 'had paid a high price for land and houses in the belief that the Government reserve [around the foreshore] was secure from the hands of the spoiler'. These landowners were not opposed to coal mining—just to mining in their suburb. They called for the coal to be mined from other 'more secluded and less peopled shores'.[38]

The company's managing director, T. S. Huntley, put this protest in perspective by explaining that the meeting had attracted only 30 or 40 of the 1500 householders in Mosman. Huntley maintained that 'those who earn their daily bread by the labour of their hands' would support the company's application. He also sought to reassure residents that they had little to fear. The company would ensure that the works were 'as sightly and as unobjectionable as possible'. They would 'consume their own smoke, and make no more dust than . . . made by bunkering steamers in the ordinary way'.[39]

A correspondent of the *Herald*, John Cunningham, added that the government was in no position to stop the company when the naval base on Garden Island was just as 'unsightly' as the proposed mine. Cunningham also maintained that there was no legitimate basis for denying the company its lease when land use was generally unregulated in the colonies. Because there were no planning or zoning laws, no one could stop him 'from erecting a foundry . . . on a freehold property of mine at Cremorne and facing our harbour'. Why then, he asked, should a different rule apply to this new 'national industry'?[40]

The mining warden disagreed. Having inspected the Cremorne foreshores for himself and heard Clark's advocacy of the public interest, he advised the government to refuse the company's application, or at least defer it until the company had completed negotiations to buy land that was already in private hands. Other miners who lost cases in the wardens' courts often used their political influence, or allegedly resorted to bribery, to try to persuade the Secretary of Mines to ignore the wardens' recommendations. But if the Collieries Company tried to do so, it failed. Ten days after receiving the warden's advice, the government rejected the colliery's application.[41]

Clark and Anderson were only lucky once. While their case was proceeding, the company was applying for another lease over a disused part of the military reserve at Bradleys Head. This application was advertised in the *Government Gazette*, and notices were posted in the mining warden's office, at the nearest post office and on the land itself. But Clark and Anderson did not object, most likely because they did not see the notices. As a result, the government granted the company a forty-year lease over six-and-a half acres with a water frontage between Athol Gardens and Bradleys Head at a rent of less than £1 a year.[42]

All the company still needed was a wharf so that it could ship its coal. In early August the only sticking point seemed to be price. The Land Board recommended that the government grant a wharfage lease subject to a rental of £400 a year and a royalty of a halfpenny a ton; the company thought this sum too high. But it did not bother to wait for its appeal to be heard, let alone for the government to grant the lease. Instead it set eighteen men to work felling the trees on Bradleys Head.[43]

E. M. Clark responded immediately in Parliament, but he struggled to extract any information from the Reid government. When he asked the Colonial Secretary on 15 August whether boring for coal or sinking shafts had begun at Bradleys Head, the Colonial Secretary replied that he knew nothing of the issue and Clark should put his question to the Secretary for Mines. Clark remained none the wiser when Parliament next sat on 20 August because the Secretary for Mines gave the strictly accurate answer that neither boring for coal nor sinking shafts had begun. When Clark tried again on 28 August, the government finally admitted that the company was 'clearing a portion of that area for sinking pits'.[44]

It was only then that Sydneysiders began to realise what was happening. On 30 August the *Sydney Morning Herald* published the first letter protesting against the mine. 'A Citizen' described the leasing of Bradleys Head as 'a matter of great importance' that had to 'be sifted to the bottom'. The Minister had given the company 'use of the most prominent and beautiful point in the harbour . . . still owned by and reserved for the public', and had allowed much of the timber on the headland to be cut down. When the company began sinking its shafts, the headland would become the dumping ground for an 'enormous quantity of debris'.[45]

Other Sydneysiders remained oblivious, not realising that the company had raised the capital it needed and was preparing to sink its shafts. The *Bulletin* put this ignorance into print. On 31 August it informed its readers:

> No further tidings as to the attempted flotation of the Cremorne . . . colliery having transpired, it is presumed that the project has been abandoned for the present. Some people in England were lately asking why did not Australians partly finance the scheme if it was such a good thing.[46]

STREETON'S SHRIEK

As Arthur Streeton told the story, he played a critical role in turning the mine into a public issue. On 19 August 1895 he returned to Sydney from six weeks in Adelaide and Melbourne. Travelling with him was Tom Roberts, who had been away all year, painting *Bailed Up* near Inverell in northern New South Wales. Both artists returned to Curlew Camp on Little Sirius Cove, just a few hundred yards from Bradleys Head—the artists' camp that had been Roberts's intermittent home since 1891 and Streeton's most reliable address since 1892.[47]

If any artist might have been expected to protest against the mine it was Roberts, who had secured the amalgamation of the Kalizoic Society and the Australian Artists' Association, and had also ventured beyond art to broader aesthetic questions in his occasional journalism. In a characteristically pugnacious piece in 1893, he had deplored Melbourne's architecture:

ROBERT CHERRY
ARTHUR STREETON PAINTING A LITTLE ROTTER (OIL SKETCH) AT CURLEW, C. 1893

> What is good . . . is hidden or lost, and where men might have raised buildings to be a delight to the eye and mind, the architect has unworthily helped the client to rear edifices which reflect perfectly the period of their making, and whose note is expensive vulgarity . . . the styles are like the money that made them—borrowed.[48]

Streeton, by contrast, had never tried journalism; his few ventures into public debate were confined to art, and in one of his rare letters to the press had claimed authority only to judge painting. Yet Roberts was silent about the mine whereas Streeton seems to have spoken out. He recorded the episode twice: in an unpublished 'Personal Narrative' written in the mid-1920s, and in an article about Sydney Harbour for the *Argus* in 1934.

In his 'Personal Narrative' Streeton described how 'the community was indignant for a few days' after the trees were felled, but 'beyond murmurs and indignation from the citizens nothing was done'. Then Streeton intervened. As he put it:

> I was just leaving the harbour to go and paint my large picture ('Fires on') in the Blue Mountains and I composed a letter rapidly in the train, protesting against the vandalism which threatened our harbour, and posted it to the 'Daily Telegraph' office: when my letter appeared it was referred to as 'Streeton's Shriek', but it certainly aroused interest and alarm, was followed by other correspondence in the press and the coal mining proposal was abandoned.

His account in the *Argus* ran:

> A rapidly written protest appeared in the press. It pointed out that all the loveliness of the harbour just inside the Heads was likely to become obliterated by a mass of coaling hulks and machinery. This letter was referred to as 'Streeton's shriek'. But other protests followed, people woke up, and the infamous project came to an end.[49]

Both accounts are problematic. Despite the detail of his recollections, Streeton went to the Blue Mountains to paint *Fire's On!* in 1891, long before mining of the harbour was an issue, and the *Daily Telegraph* did not carry any letters about the mine in August or September 1895. Nor do any of the other Sydney newspapers appear to have carried a letter about the mine published under Streeton's name in this period.

Where might this letter be? One possibility is that Streeton wrote it anonymously. It could be the letter from 'Citizen' published by the *Sydney Morning Herald* on 30 August, although the voice seems wrong. Moreover, if he wrote anonymously, this letter could have become known as 'Streeton's shriek' only among his closest friends. Another possibility is that Streeton exaggerated his own significance. Perhaps he wrote to one of Sydney's newspapers in late 1893, when the coal mine was first an issue, or in late 1895 or even 1896. But that he protested seems clear. Otherwise he would not have remembered this incident so vividly forty years later. There also was no reason for Streeton to manufacture a pedigree of environmental concern in the 1920s and 1930s.

Streeton probably spoke out because, of all the artists at the camp in Little Sirius Cove, he was most affected by the operations of the Sydney Harbour Collieries Company. A coal hulk may already have been moored near Cremorne Point, as Streeton himself recorded in one of his undated paintings from the mid-1890s, but its environmental consequences were small. Mining at Bradleys Head would have destroyed the tranquillity he so enjoyed at the camp: the bay 'all asleep and so very peaceful', 'picnic parties pulling about quietly through the rare phosphorescence'. The colliery also would have blighted a subject that Streeton had made his own since moving to Sydney in 1892. Whereas Roberts painted only a few harbour views in this period, Streeton made himself a new reputation by painting little else. As the *Bulletin's* 'Red Page' had it in 1900, Streeton, not Captain Phillip, was 'the discoverer of Sydney Harbour'.[50]

Streeton's confidence to take this stance came with being recognised as 'the coming man', 'the rising star of Australian art'. The 9 by 5 Exhibition in Melbourne in 1889 had taught Streeton that artists could benefit from the occasional public confrontation. His opposition to the company's plans was also consistent with the view that artists were qualified to speak on any aesthetic question, inside the picture frame or out. As an anonymous correspondent of the *Sydney Morning Herald* put it, 'the hideous erections of various kinds . . . the grimy wharfs and barges, the general blackness and repulsiveness' would destroy the harbour's beauty. He hoped artists, journalists and clergymen—an unlikely triad—would use their 'ability and influence to arouse the ordinarily apathetic public to a full sense of the calamity . . . in store for them'.[51]

ARTHUR STREETON
SIRIUS COVE C. 1895

THE VALUE OF SENTIMENT

If Streeton helped to alert Sydneysiders to the hazards posed by the coal mine, E. M. Clark was responsible for turning it into a major political issue. By 4 September the *Evening News* had condemned the mine, the *Herald* had carried more letters of protest and Sydney's Amateur Sailing Club had deplored the lease of a public reserve to a private company. But the government continued to hide the basis on which it had granted the land until Clark moved that the Legislative Assembly debate the leasing of the headland as a matter of public importance. Over the next two days every Sydney newspaper editorialised against the colliery as the company's 'vandalism' in denuding Bradleys Head made them realise that mining was no longer a distant possibility but an immediate threat. At a big meeting in the Domain, the city's socialists called on the government to cancel the lease.[52]

Landowners in Mosman played only a small role in this outcry. The mine had become a significant issue for all Sydney if not New South Wales. As in 1893, many of the arguments were economic. The company claimed it would produce £15 000 a year in revenue for the Crown, perhaps £3 500 000 over the life of the mine. As well, there would be 300 jobs while it was sinking its pits and 1500 while it was mining. Its opponents responded that the company could only live up to this boast if it produced £40 million worth of coal, leaving it with a profit of over £20 million once it had met all its expenses. Moreover, there was no unmet demand for coal in New South Wales, so any revenue and jobs created by mining at Bradleys Head would be at the expense of the Hunter and the Illawarra, where there was already high unemployment and wages were under threat from falling coal prices.[53]

The privatisation of public property was also significant. The company contended that all it wanted was a 28-year lease, so there was 'no question' of alienating the foreshores. Its opponents recognised that such a long lease was little different from selling the land. The *Evening News* reported that 'people not involved in coal speculation' were 'pretty well agreed' that the Crown should retain all of Sydney's foreshores. One Member of the Legislative Assembly declared that the government should be preserving 'the rights of the people' instead of giving the foreshores 'to any company or syndicate to do what they like with'. According to another, 'Not one inch of the foreshore should be parted with'.[54]

The colony's need to attract foreign investment was another issue. Whenever someone attacked the mine, they were accused of 'driving capital out of the country'—'a very dangerous thing to do'. Even opponents of mining feared that New South Wales could not afford to play 'fast and loose' with its credit in England without 'disastrous' consequences for many companies or even the colony's national loans. But this prospect did not prompt them to abandon the headland. Instead they followed A. B. Piddington in arguing that, as a last resort, the government should compensate the company.[55]

The debate about the 'disfigurement' and 'defilement' of the harbour was particularly intense because Port Jackson's beauty was so important to many colonists. As Mark Twain observed when he arrived in Sydney just twelve days after the Legislative Assembly debated the coal mine, the harbour was 'the darling of Sydney'. Twain thought it 'not surprising' that the people were 'proud of it, nor that they put their enthusiasm into eloquent words'. This pride was vital to their sense of place in Australia. The reputation of the harbour as a 'wonder of the world' made them happier to be in Sydney.[56]

A key issue in this debate was whether 'sentimental' or non-utilitarian values had a place in a colonial society. The company's manager, T. S. Huntley, maintained that 'sentiment' was inappropriate in such a practical place and age. One 'might as well try to build a wall across the Sydney Heads to keep out the sea as try to stop the trend of commercial enterprise in a new country like this'. Opponents of the mine looked on 'sentiment' as an index of civilisation. As one of them put it:

> The desire to prevent the destruction of a beautiful picture probably is 'sentiment' but surely, even in this commercial age, the value of sentiment is recognised as a factor in the education and cultivation of the individual.[57]

This link between culture and environment was emphasised by J. G. Hay, a former officer of the Lands Department, who also linked the controversy over the coal mine to a Native Flora Protection Bill then before Parliament. One of the main objects of this legislation was to prohibit wildflower shows, which had become increasingly popular since the mid-1880s with disastrous environmental consequences, because many exhibitors pulled up entire plants rather than simply cutting their flowers. Lady Carrington, the wife of the New South Wales Governor, was so appalled by this destruction that she refused to be the patron of these shows. Charles Moore, Director of Sydney's

Botanic Gardens, lamented that they had become 'nothing more nor less than money-making games' to clear off church debts.[58]

Billy Hughes was just one of many parliamentarians outraged by the Native Flora Protection Bill, which was introduced by Frank Farnell, the Member for Ryde and a trustee of the National Park south of Sydney. Hughes branded Farnell an aesthete—a term of more than usual opprobrium in September 1895, because Oscar Wilde had just been arrested after losing his libel action against the Marquess of Queensberry. Hughes accused Farnell of currying favour with constituents 'of an exceedingly aesthetic turn of mind' and wanting 'to pose before an astounded world as an art critic and as a man who cultivates a love of the beautiful'.[59]

What Hughes derided, J. G. Hay applauded. In a letter to the *Herald*, he asked:

> Why are we building up a national gallery? For what reason are we striving to foster the fine arts? Why are some among us striving at the eleventh hour to save our glorious flora? Are we to measure everything by the yard-stick of syndicates and companies?

According to Hay, if Bradleys Head became 'a dirty, grimy colliery township', the colonists would 'rightly be the execrated of all the world'.[60]

This outcry was one of the first occasions when an Australian government was caught out encouraging resource development only to find public opinion powerfully against it on environmental grounds. George Reid sought to escape the furore by arguing that all his ministry had done was to carry through processes set in train by its predecessors. He also declared that his sympathies were 'entirely' with those who objected to mining; if he could honourably stop the company proceeding, he would do so. As a result, Clark opted not to press the issue further. But had he insisted on a vote, the *Bulletin* reckoned the government might have fallen—the first time an environmental issue would have had such an impact in Australia since John Macarthur ousted William Bligh in 1808.[61]

PICTURES AT AN EXHIBITION

The first exhibition of Sydney's new Society of Artists opened in late September 1895 at the city's ice rink. Like the Australian Artists'

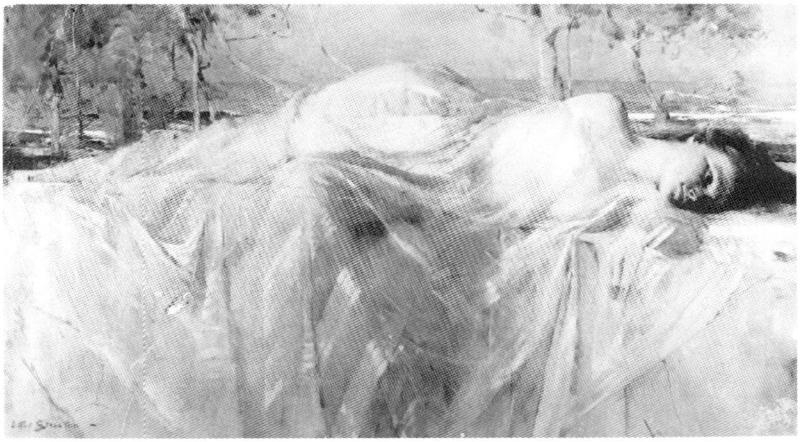

ARTHUR STREETON
OBLIVION C. 1895

Association in Melbourne almost a decade before, the society was formed by artists wanting to control the display and sale of their own work. A group of younger artists, led by Frank Mahony, Henry Fullwood and Livingston Hopkins, decided to establish a society run by a committee elected only by exhibiting members. In just six weeks they attracted 115 members, including all of Sydney's best painters except for W. C. Piguenit. When Roberts and Streeton returned to Sydney in mid-September, Roberts became the society's president, Streeton one of its councillors.[62]

Roberts's major picture in the society's first exhibition was *Bailed Up*—one of the weakest of the series of big paintings of bush life he executed in the 1880s and 1890s. While Roberts reworked *Bailed Up* in the 1920s, it is still clear why Julian Ashton, who was the *Telegraph*'s critic as well as a member of the new society, reckoned that one of Roberts's horses was as wooden as a rocking-horse. The *Herald* observed that Roberts's figures were 'not entirely convincing'; the *Bulletin* echoed that the work had 'less life and vigour than might have been expected'.[63]

Streeton received more acclaim for his *Oblivion*, which took lines from Tennyson's 'Lotus-Eaters' as its excuse for depicting a thinly clad girl lying on a marble slab. Streeton's fellow artists reportedly thought it the pick of the exhibition. Ashton declared:

> The drapery and the barely suggested landscape are done to perfection, and the gradual transition from the snow-white robes to the delicate flesh tints of the bust and the crimson ... in the lips, is one of the most poetic schemes of color that we have seen for a long time.

But then, as 'Sappho Smith' of the *Bulletin* already knew, such 'women-pictures' were 'painted for men'.[64]

The painting that attracted most attention, however, was Streeton's *Cremorne Pastoral*—the biggest picture he had painted of Sydney Harbour. While Ashton recognised that *Cremorne Pastoral* lacked the appeal of some of Streeton's smaller panels of Sydney Harbour, he maintained that its size, workmanship and general 'importance' still made it 'perhaps the best landscape ever painted in New South Wales'. His fellow trustees of the Art Gallery of New South Wales agreed, selecting it as their major acquisition from the new society's exhibition.[65]

Cremorne Pastoral probably started out as just another celebration of the harbour. It depicted the view from the footpath between Old Cremorne Wharf and Cremorne Point, looking across to Rose Bay—a favourite with Tom Roberts, who had already painted it in 1894 and returned to it in 1895 and 1896. Streeton probably began working on *Cremorne Pastoral* before July 1895, when he went to Melbourne, oblivious to any possibility that the harbour would be mined. But by September, the controversy over the coal mine had given *Cremorne Pastoral* new meaning. In its review of the exhibition, the *Australian Star* declared that future generations might have to thank Streeton for having preserved 'a fair representation of the place as it existed before the invasion of the colliers'.[66]

Yet neither Roberts nor Streeton took advantage of the exhibition to speak against coal mining. Roberts chaired the society's inaugural supper, but when he spoke on behalf of his fellow artists, he confined himself to promoting the society, announcing that it would welcome the work of architects, decorators, medallists and 'even' poster designers in its exhibitions. Having just had *Cremorne Pastoral* bought by the Art Gallery of New South Wales, Streeton spoke for himself when he congratulated the Gallery's trustees on buying 'the best Australian work that could be obtained in the colony'.[67]

THE LONG ARM OF THE LAW

The government's opportunity to stop the mine came four weeks later, when the Land Appeal Court heard the company's appeal against the Land Board's recommendation that it pay an annual rent of £400 plus half a penny per ton of coal shipped for a wharfage lease near Bradleys Head. The company argued that the Board could only set a fixed rent, not a royalty, and that the 'exorbitant' conditions which it recommended were also 'incompatible with the moral obligations imposed on the Executive to aid rather than hinder the Company in carrying out . . . an undertaking of national importance'.[68]

In a landmark ruling, the Land Appeal Court turned the popular political rhetoric about trusteeship of the public domain into a matter of legal obligation. The Court held that the Crown occupied

> a position in relation to public lands something in the nature of a trustee under an obligation to dispose of or alienate those lands, whether permanently or temporarily, only in the interest and for the benefit of the people of this Colony.

The Crown was therefore obliged to obtain the best possible price for the wharf. The Court recommended that it ask for a flat annual rent of £1500, not £400, regardless of the amount of coal shipped.[69]

The court's jurisdiction beyond this issue was unclear. According to one account of argument in the case, counsel for the Crown called on the court to consider whether the lease should be granted at all, even though this question was not under appeal. Another report claimed the lawyers for both sides agreed that the court's only function was to consider the conditions on which the lease should be granted. Its President accepted that the court had 'judicially nothing to do with the question as to whether the lease should be granted or not'. But the court still addressed this issue, exercising its advisory function 'according to judicial forms'.[70]

Although the arguments presented by the court were not new, few Australian tribunals have ever been so critical of a development proposal. The court found that the company had applied to the government simply because it 'expected to obtain a lease of public land on much easier terms than one of private land'. The government should prevent this exploitation of the public domain by refusing to part with it until 'all available privately-owned sites had been exhausted'. While land for Sydney's expansion north and south was 'practically unlimited', the foreshores were a finite resource for which there would be increasing demand as Sydney's population grew, making it something the government should resume, not alienate.[71]

The court also considered the economics of the mine. It emphasised that the royalties to be paid by the colliery company were not what they seemed, as the government would lose revenue from the mines in the Hunter and the Illawarra. In any event the court regarded the beauty of the harbour as something beyond monetary value. The coal mine, it predicted, would be 'a permanent eyesore', 'a hideous blemish on the people's inheritance'. 'No consideration in the nature of rent', it declared, 'could afford any compensation or consolation for the disfigurement of a harbour' that all Australians had 'been taught to cherish as one of nature's choicest masterpieces'.[72]

The company cried foul. The court had exceeded its jurisdiction, it claimed, and the colliery would be unfairly prejudiced by a refusal of the wharfage lease. The company maintained that, having received a memorandum from the Minister for Lands in favour of granting of the lease, it had ordered machinery worth £10 000. It also claimed to have entered into a binding contract to have its shafts sunk for £60 000—a lie, as within three months the company was reassuring its shareholders that they had benefited from the delay caused by the controversy because the company had received a better offer of £44 000.[73]

The pressure from London was equally intense. The British end of the syndicate began working the cable for all it was worth. A typical telegram ran:

> A strong feeling has been excited in the City by rumours that the New South Wales Government intend to cancel the leases for foreshores granted the Sydney Harbour Collieries Company. The company are relying upon the Government to carry out promises made, as they have already expended large sums of money on the strength of those promises.

Yet the company did not appeal to the colony's Supreme Court—most likely because, even had it succeeded and the Land Court been forced to confine its decision to the question of rent, the Minister for Lands would still have been entitled to refuse to grant the wharfage lease. As it was, the strength of the Land Court's decision made it easier for George Reid to keep his promise. At the end of the year, his government announced that it had rejected the company's application.[74]

THE WORKINGMEN'S SUBURB

As so often with environmental disputes, the company did not accept this decision. At its annual general meeting in London, its chairman claimed that the government was in breach of promise and that he 'could not conceive that any British colonial Government could be guilty of bad faith'. When James Inglis returned from London to Sydney, where he promptly became president of the New South Wales Chamber of Mines, he declared that the feeling at 'home' was one of 'intense surprise' at the government's actions. Had such 'sentimental objections' been put in London or Cardiff against similar big works, the 'common sense of the people' would have laughed them 'out of countenance'. He could not understand how anyone who valued 'the supremacy of Port Jackson' could have opposed 'such a splendid commercial enterprise'.[75]

Opponents of the mine were quick to rebut these arguments. One reader of the *Herald* asked:

> Will such a grimy institution not absolutely divest that especial part of the harbor of its pristine beauty? And if so, how much money expended in wages, how many dividends sent home to England, will compensate this country for so grand an act of vandalism?

In his view, all the company's talk about investment simply heralded the 'bold and barefaced exploitation of the people's rights'. The key question was not one of 'production of further wealth' but 'of the distribution of the abundant wealth now existent'.[76]

The government also held firm, denying that it had promised to grant the lease, but it gave the company every opportunity to find another site. While it suspended the conditions in the mining lease and authority to mine, which required the company to employ at least eighteen men at all times, the company looked for another location. To avoid further controversy, it wanted one that was still close to the coal but was not controlled by the colonial government. It also wanted a site away from 'the fairway of the harbour', where all passenger traffic passed, and hence not as open to criticism on aesthetic grounds. Not least, it looked for an area where the local residents were more welcoming—or less able to defend themselves.[77]

This compromise was probably as much as most opponents of the mine had hoped for. Because the company already had its lease over the harbour, the chances of stopping it mining had always been low. The big question had been where it would sink its shafts, not whether it would do so.[78]

The company took only a few weeks to identify an alternative site in Balmain, once one of Sydney's most exclusive suburbs, which had become a largely working-class domain dominated by shipyards, sawmills and some of Sydney's biggest chemical and boiling-down works. Rather than applying for another piece of Crown land or approaching private landowners as recommended by the Land Appeal Court, the company went to the local council. Its choice was Elkington Park—six acres on the foreshore near Long Nose Point that offered 'every facility for coaling ships of any size'.[79]

Councils in working-class areas sometimes limited the excesses of industry or even tried to stop noxious trades setting up in their municipalities. More often they welcomed industry, deliberately compromising public health and environmental quality in order to achieve higher land values, greater municipal revenue, additional employment and increased local trade. Most notoriously, the businessmen who dominated the Collingwood Council in Melbourne looked on the Yarra as a sewer for local industry and wanted it 'thrown open to manufacturing enterprise'. As well as campaigning for the repeal of the Yarra Pollution Act of 1855, the council dismissed inspectors who were too zealous in enforcing sanitary laws.[80]

Balmain was especially susceptible to the company's offer of a fixed rent, plus a royalty on the coal raised, because the council's finances were in crisis. In 1894 it had decided to seek a special Act of Parliament authorising it to mortgage its town hall as security for a debt of £9000. Over the following year the council's bankers had agreed to substitute Elkington Park as security for the mortgage. But 'technical difficulties' stopped the passage of the special Act in September 1895, leaving Elkington Park ripe for the taking by the colliery.[81]

Balmain's mayor, Alexander Milne, was keen to accommodate the company in order to ensure that Balmain did not lose this opportunity 'to earn a good round sum'. Although the park had been described just a few years before as 'a popular place of resort', Milne reckoned it was not 'sufficiently patronised to warrant them sacrificing such an opportunity to lease the park on favourable terms'. One alderman responded that it would be a mistake for Balmain to lose 'one of the prettiest parks in Australia' and that, if the syndicate was serious, it could always buy land elsewhere in their suburb. Instead the council agreed, by a majority of ten to two, that the question be put to a plebiscite.[82]

Such votes about industrial location were relatively commonplace in the late nineteenth century—part of a larger embrace of 'direct democracy' at the local level that faded in the early 1900s and only began re-emerging in the 1970s. But this 'democracy' was always compromised by the franchise, which typically restricted the vote to ratepayers and allowed plural voting by wealthy landowners. Almost the entire working class and even many middle-class colonists could not vote. The electoral rolls were limited to a small minority of the adult population.[83]

When these polls were held in working-class suburbs, local artisans and working men were often among the most enthusiastic campaigners for industry despite their disfranchisement, because they feared that suppression of industry would mean 'starvation for themselves and their families'. In 1883, when ratepayers in the Melbourne suburb of Footscray opted to give local factories time to remedy the nuisances they were causing, rather than have them prosecuted for polluting, the decision was greeted with cheers by 200 local workmen who had 'waited anxiously during the day'. In vain the *Age* argued that this issue was of more than local concern because the atmosphere was 'the property of every man who inhales it, whether he be a ratepayer of the malodorous borough or a mere wayfarer'.[84]

When the poll about Elkington Park was held early in 1896, Balmain's ratepayers voted two to one in favour of granting the park to the colliery. By the end of the year the company had erected wharves on its lease. Because Balmain was three miles from Cremorne, the prudent course would have been for the company to put down another bore. But it was short of funds, having been floated with insufficient capital, and its geological advisers saw no need for a third test. Consequently, the company began sinking two shafts, each 2800 feet deep, 18 feet in diameter and lined with bricks. The cost was immense, the result a disaster: the seam was not worth working, because it was split by a band of shale.[85]

The company's only option was to drive east towards Cremorne. To the company's relief, the shale gradually became thinner and was replaced by 'excellent' coal, 'second to none for steaming purposes'. But this seam soon turned so poor that the company's operations became uneconomic. One investor in the company in this period was Tom Roberts's new wife Lillie, who could have watched the colliery's progress for herself from east Balmain, where she and Tom lived from 1897 until 1901. Attracted by the prospect of a return of 6 per cent when banks were paying just 2 per cent, Lillie bought debentures in the colliery in 1906. But two years later it had already shut down and, though the mine reopened, it never paid its way.[86]

Eugene von Guérard *Tower Hill* 1855

CHAPTER TWELVE

THE TEMPLATE

We found [the painting] in a little old stairway where it was very dark. We suddenly realised . . . here was Tower Hill with trees all over it. We could see that this was what we would like it to be.

MAX DOWNES, 1992

COLONIAL ARTISTS are not bad tourist guides. With their taste for the picturesque and the sublime, you can be sure they knew a good view. But the differences between what they painted and what we can see now are often dispiriting. Take the Basin Banks, a crater lake near Camperdown in western Victoria, which was lined with eucalypts when Eugene von Guérard painted it in 1857. Stripped of all trees, it now looks like a dam. Or look down from Mount Arapiles to the north, as von Guérard did in another of his landscapes painted in 1874. The Mitre Rock and Lake are still there, but again most of the surrounding trees are gone.

Woodlands, a two-storey Italianate mansion near Ararat, tells a different story. When von Guérard painted it in 1869, the 'shepherd king' John Wilson could afford to employ as many servants as he wanted to maintain his new home. Von Guérard showed three men at work in its year-old garden, complete with elaborate waterworks. When I saw Woodlands a few years ago, the conifers Wilson planted had grown huge and fallen, the fountain was empty, the artificial lake dry, the house deserted—a symbol of the squatters' unsustainable vision of growing fat on the land.

Ferntree Gully is equally depressing. Although it has been a national park since 1928, its ferntrees are so scarce that its name makes little sense. Even the site of von Guérard's painting is hard to find. Possibly it is outside the entrance to the national park where there is still a creek, though it is stagnant, infested with brambles and surrounded by more or less cleared fields. More likely it is within the national park; but where the hills on the horizon line up just as von Guérard painted them, there is only bitumen. Von Guérard's Gully, it seems, has become a carpark.

Tower Hill in western Victoria was even more despoiled after von Guérard painted it in 1855. Its crater lake was immediately dammed, its islands and banks soon ringbarked, burnt, cleared, grazed and quarried—as recorded by the Warrnambool artist Daniel Clarke.[1] But the volcanic landscape remained so remarkable and the memory of its original flora so enduring that Victorians talked of restoring it from the 1890s, when it became the colony's first national park. For the next sixty years, their efforts were spasmodic at best. But once Tower Hill stopped being a national park in 1960, this ideal became a reality. Tower Hill was replanted in von Guérard's image as part of an attempt at environmental restoration unparalleled anywhere in the world.

DANIEL CLARKE
TOWER HILL, AN EXTINCT VOLCANO, NEAR WARRNAMBOOL 1878

THE PATRON AS PRESERVATIONIST

Like many successful pastoralists, James Dawson wanted paintings of both his own property near Port Fairy and the most notable feature in his local landscape—Tower Hill, which he described as 'one of the most beautiful and interesting specimens of an extinct volcano in all Victoria'. In 1855 he commissioned an oil painting from von Guérard and a duplicate in watercolours, which he sent to London to be lithographed. But Dawson's interest in Tower Hill was not exhausted by art. When he returned there in 1891 and discovered that it no longer resembled von Guérard's painting, he publicly protested. Tower Hill, he maintained, was 'intended by Nature to be a public park, and place of pleasure for the people of the district'.[2]

No other patron of colonial art acted this way, but Dawson was no ordinary colonist. Together with his daughter Isabella, he wrote the first major ethnographic study of the Aborigines of western Victoria. When Isabella would not let him publish it in her name, he sought the assistance of James Smith at the *Argus* to ensure that she was 'equally prominent in any credit awarded'.[3] Dawson was also a powerful champion of Aboriginal rights, a fearless member of the Victorian Society for the Prevention of Cruelty to Animals and a staunch advocate and defender of public reserves.

Dawson was exceptional for trying to articulate what Aborigines themselves wanted rather than what he thought best for them. In 1877 he testified to Victoria's Royal Commission on Aborigines that Aborigines were 'fully aware of the position the occupation of their country by the white man has placed them in, and of their strong claims on him for proper maintenance and protection'. Dawson endorsed the Aborigines' case: they had been 'ruthlessly driven from their hunting grounds', and had the 'strongest and most undeniable claims on the people of this colony for support and protection, without labour of any kind in return'.[4]

Dawson did his best to put his ideals into practice as local guardian of Aborigines at Camperdown from 1876. When he found that two local Aborigines were living in a waurn of 'the most miserable description', he built a 'comfortable hut' for them at his own expense. When they refused to live there, he was disappointed but recognised the limits of paternalism. Time and again he admonished his fellow colonists that the Aborigines should be allowed to live where they chose because of their attachment to specific pieces of land. The problem with reserves, he warned in 1877, was that the government required the Aborigine to 'leave his native land, his favourite hunting grounds and the home of his youth, so dear to the savage that many pine and die after removal'.[5]

Dawson went further when he returned from Scotland in 1884 to find that the last of his charges, Wombeetch Puyuun aka Camperdown George, had died and was buried in a swamp. Dawson began by transferring Wombeetch Puyuun's remains to a central plot in the Camperdown cemetery with his 'own hands'. Then he sought to raise money for a memorial. When local landholders refused to contribute and the editor of the *Argus* would not publish his letter condemning them, Dawson went for the editor with his umbrella. Finally, he proceeded at his own expense, erecting a six-metre obelisk that towered over all the memorials around it. He put the date '1840' on top of the obelisk to mark the beginning of the Aborigines' 'extirpation'.[6]

Dawson also championed the rights of animals. Like Louisa Anne Meredith, he looked on them as 'next to Man the noblest work of God'. On one occasion, this concern led him to protest that Aborigines at the Framlingham reserve were showing 'great cruelty . . . in the treatment of their horses'. Otherwise he policed his fellow colonists, despite the enmity it brought him. The annual Camperdown show was just one of his targets. When he discovered that local farmers were exhibiting unmilked cows in the hope of obtaining prizes, he drew attention to this 'barbarous, dishonest, and illegal' practice and threatened to prosecute the offending entrants in order to stop 'the cowardly abuse of the brute creatures'.[7]

Dawson's environmental interests included the protection of the platypus and Victoria's giant trees, but he was particularly concerned for public reserves. When the colonial government gazetted its intention to revoke the reserve at Mount Rouse, another of the Western District's volcanic craters, Dawson protested that it was 'impossible to overvalue the importance of public reserves as places of recreation for present and future generations'. Hence it was 'imperative on everyone having the interests of the community at heart' to stop the government selling this land 'to their friends at nominal prices'.[8]

Dawson was eighty-four and in ill-health when he returned to Tower Hill in 1891, but as ready as ever to put his views into print. In a letter to the *Camperdown Chronicle*, he declared it fortunate 'for future generations' that he had commissioned von Guérard's paintings, because Tower Hill no longer bore any relation to its 'primitive state', which von Guérard had recorded so 'faithfully and beautifully'. Dawson was 'amazed and disgusted to find everything altered, the fine trees on the cones and in the craters of the island all gone excepting half a dozen or so and the banks turned into a cabbage garden'. Even worse, the neighbouring town of Koroit had cut a drain to the lake, turning it into 'a seething, stinking mud-pool, full of fermenting, malarious matter, sufficient to poison the whole neighbourhood'.[9]

As Dawson must have expected, his letter was read in Koroit, where the local *Sentinel* admitted it knew nothing of von Guérard's painting, but otherwise accused Dawson of making 'not one true statement'. The *Sentinel* maintained that the trees on the islands had been destroyed by fire rather than felled. There also was 'not the slightest miasma from the lake': the drain simply carried stormwater, and the local council exercised the 'greatest care' to ensure 'no offensive matter' ran into it.[10]

By then, Dawson had gone direct to the colonial government. The clearing of Tower Hill probably struck him as irreparable, but he thought the pollution could be stopped if the government required the people of Koroit to get rid of their 'foul matter by its legal and natural course of drainage'. On a visit to Melbourne, he arranged interviews with the Secretary of Lands and the Secretary of the Board of Health, and persuaded them to investigate the lake.[11]

This activism came to nothing. Local health officers replied that the state of the lake was due to 'a natural drying-up process'; the drain carried only stormwater after heavy rain and no one living on the lake bank had suffered a serious illness in seven years. But within a few months local residents were also protesting about 'offensive matter' going into the drain. Later accounts make clear that the town's waste at least sometimes reached the lake, justifying Dawson's insistence that it was a 'seething swampy lagoon, supplied through two tunnels with the sewage of the town of Koroit, and the numerous farms of the district'.[12]

THE NATIONAL PARK

When the ownership of the *Sentinel* changed late in 1891, so did its contents. Its new proprietors made much of the 'beautiful natural monument'of Tower Hill because it was one of Koroit's 'most popular places of resort', and they fancied that it could assist Koroit to be chosen as the new national capital when Australia became federated. They also acknowledged that Tower Hill's 'beauty and loveliness' had, at least temporarily, been 'ruined': its wildfowl driven away by professional shooters, its trees 'cut down and burnt', its undergrowth 'almost completely destroyed'. They wanted professional shooting on the lake to be restricted, if not banned, and urged the local council to restore Tower Hill's trees.[13]

Six months later, the local member, Sir Bryan O'Loghlen, introduced a Bill to vest the lake and islands of Tower Hill in the council, which he hoped would 'restore the spot to its pristine beauty'. O'Loghlen underlined this idea by calling his legislation the Tower Hill National Park Bill. The press in Koroit and Warrnambool agreed that national parks were the only means of preserving 'the indigenous trees, shrubs and flowers of our island continent'.[14]

Yet the vesting of Tower Hill in the council was never likely to lead to its protection, let alone restoration, because Koroit was accustomed to exploiting it. Although formally a reserve for public recreation, in 1891 it served as a town common where every ratepayer could depasture five head of stock. When the *Sentinel* called for the replanting of Tower Hill, the council responded by setting fire to one of the islands. Its object was to remove the undergrowth, which reduced the feed available for grazing and was 'a great harbour for rabbits'. But the blaze left 'hundreds of burning stumps'.[15]

O'Loghlen's Bill was also flawed. Rather than defining a 'national park' as a place to be preserved or rehabilitated, it simply vested Tower Hill in the council 'as a public park for public recreation purposes'. The Bill also did not address how the restoration of Tower Hill might be paid for; the council's receipts from grazing on the islands were insufficient to pay for a ranger, let alone clear the islands of its rabbits, which had already survived fires, a Saturday shoot by local residents and furrows filled with poisoned grain.[16]

The council duly continued to exploit Tower Hill once it became Victoria's first national park. Although the 1892 Act stipulated that Tower Hill could be used 'for no other purpose whatsoever' than public recreation, the Council turned it into a quarry, using its scoria as 'road metal' and its tuff for gravel. Although there were many other deposits of scoria and tuff near by, Tower Hill became the main local source of material for road-making. By 1894, there were seven pits—three in the national park, the other four on private land—leaving great gouges in the crater and the islands.[17]

Koroit was probably also to blame for the disappearance of the lake on the eastern side of the islands. The water level in the lake started dropping almost as soon as the council began tapping the main spring in 1890; then the lake dried up for extended periods before finally disappearing altogether during the drought of 1914, allowing stock to graze unimpeded on the islands. These sheep and cattle, along with firewood collectors, an unprecedented number of rabbits and repeated burning by the council's ranger, destroyed most of Tower Hill's remaining native trees and shrubs. The only native animals that survived were eastern swamp rats, snakes and lizards.[18]

This degradation was exacerbated by the first significant attempt at tree-planting, which added Monterey pines to the crater's bank. After the town's United Friendly Societies' Committee persuaded the council to obtain trees from the State Forestry Commission, local schoolboys planted 600 pines in 1924, which flourished behind a protective fence. The schoolboys knew that 'when the early pioneers first came to settle near Tower Hill' it had been 'a real Australian wonderland', its banks covered with 'beautiful tree-ferns, hazel and musk bushes'. Despite their very different plantings, they saw themselves as recreating this 'well-wooded' past and enhancing the future. In an essay in the local school magazine, one of the boys declared, '[W]e shall watch their growth with interest . . . for we feel sure that what we are doing will be of great benefit to those who come after us'.[19]

Other local residents wanted native trees. P. E. O'Grady, a Warrnambool accountant, exclaimed in 1937, 'What a wonderful scene could be recreated if Tower Hill . . . was replanted with native timber!' He thought the Warrnambool Rotary Club would help because it was 'interested in all tree-planting schemes'. Two years later the Australian Natives' Association planted a stand of manna gums, the staple source of food for koalas in southern Australia. The Association wanted to establish a chain of koala colonies throughout Victoria, where the fur trade, habitat destruction and disease had reduced the koala population to perhaps 500 in 1925. But rabbits burrowed under the protective fence and killed almost all the trees within a year, so the council reverted to planting pines and willows.[20]

Meanwhile the State government allowed the council to approve a new quarry on the north side of the main island in 1939. Despite the war, there was such an outcry against this 'disastrous disfigurement' of the most prominent face of Tower Hill that the government was forced to institute an inquiry by Victoria's Land Board. When it convened in 1941, the council contended that this quarry offered the finest, most readily accessible scoria, would provide royalties necessary to pay for the cost of maintaining Tower Hill, and would be obscured behind a wall of pine trees. A solitary road-building contractor supported this stance. The Koroit Progress Association opposed it—along with the Warrnambool City Council, the Warrnambool branch of the Australian Labor Party, the South Western District Council of the Australian Natives' Association and numerous individuals—resulting in the quarry's closure.[21]

When the lake began returning after severe floods in 1946, the water became a natural barrier to stock, and some native species started to recover. Coots and grey teals, swamp hens, black ducks and black swans were among the waterbirds that visited the lake. Swamp gums also made the most of this opportunity. But African box-thorn, thistles and hemlock continued to blight the entrance. Two-thirds of the islands were dominated by South African capeweed and native bracken, a fireweed that colonises recently burned areas. Rabbits, foxes and mice were also rampant, there was still no resident population of ducks, the lake was so saline that it would support only salt-tolerant plants, and new excavating equipment was enlarging the quarries around the crater at an ever-increasing rate—particularly the Country Roads Board's pit at the entrance to the park.[22]

FOR ALL PEOPLE FOR ALL TIME?

The despoliation of Tower Hill made it notorious. From the late 1940s it was repeatedly invoked as an example of how Victoria's national parks were being mismanaged. The involvement of the Country Roads Board, a statutory authority, made this destruction all the more reprehensible. But all of Victoria's parks were being degraded because the State government confined its funding to recognised tourist resorts, and even then the sums were inadequate. The only way in which the honorary local committees responsible for the parks could raise revenue to manage them was to institutionalise their degradation. Some leased the grazing rights; others sold the timber, which may not have been unlawful as there was no statutory provision defining national parks as areas set aside for nature preservation.[23]

Conservationists began campaigning to stop these abuses in 1946. A key figure was Crosbie Morrison, editor of the monthly magazine *Wild Life* and presenter of a weekly radio programme on Australian natural history broadcast nationwide from Melbourne. J. Ros Garnet, a biochemist with the Commonwealth Serum Laboratories who was honorary secretary and then president of the Field Naturalists' Club of Victoria, also became a powerful voice for environmental protection through hundreds of newspaper features and letters to the editor. The solution that Morrison and Garnet looked for was State control of all parks, including Tower Hill. Their model was Queensland, which had the 'most enlightened policy towards national parks in Australia' because it alone used general revenue to fund a National Parks Authority.[24]

The State government, however, ignored these arguments, and the council further blighted Tower Hill by authorising a motorcycle racing track around its slopes. As similar abuses proliferated in other national parks, conservationists decided that, rather than simply working through organisations such as the Field Naturalists' Club, which had many other objects, they needed to form a Victorian National Parks Association. Morrison became the new group's first president, and Garnet its honorary secretary. Its inaugural public meeting in 1953 more than filled Melbourne's Town Hall. Its motto was 'The preservation of parks for all people for all time'.[25]

Even so, the conservationists might not have prevailed without Dewar Goode, chairman of the State and Federal Land Usage Committees of the Australian Primary Producers' Union. Like James Dawson, Goode was a Western District grazier who championed environmental protection. In 1955 he initiated a joint meeting with the Victorian National Parks Association, which finally prompted the Liberal–Country Party government of Henry Bolte to legislate. One of Goode's most effective arguments was that, with the Olympics coming to Melbourne in 1956, Victoria needed to improve administration of its national parks.[26]

The new Act improved on earlier legislation both by establishing a National Parks Authority and by defining national parks as areas set aside for preservation of native plants and animals and features of special scenic, scientific or historical interest. But the National Parks Authority was dominated by government departments more interested in development than conservation. The Act was also passed in such haste that the Authority was almost established with nothing to control; only a late amendment specified the areas to be entrusted to it. Even then, the Act omitted Tower Hill, because it was created under a special Act of Parliament rather than under the State's Lands Act, and there was no time to consult the Koroit Council.[27]

This omission left Tower Hill in an anomalous situation. As a matter of law, it remained a national park, but the new Authority had no control over it. What was to be done? Crosbie Morrison, who became the Authority's first director, maintained that its funds were so limited that it should 'in general . . . focus attention first upon bringing the parks under its control to the desired pitch of efficiency', a very economistic way of defining its role. But Morrison was keen to bring Tower Hill within the Authority's jurisdiction because it was the only existing park in south-western Victoria. Dewar Goode, who became a founding member of the NPA, agreed. He argued that the Authority should oversee Tower Hill immediately because 'it would be a pity if development by local bodies spoilt its significance' when it was 'obvious that at some future date it would come under the authority'.[28]

The Koroit Council initially welcomed State control. The economic significance of Tower Hill's quarries was declining as crushed rock was replacing scoria in road-making, and the council expected the Authority to bring more money into the district by 'improving' Tower Hill, which still lacked any provision for tourists. When Goode visited Koroit, the mayor declared that he would welcome an end to quarrying in order to stop the disfigurement of Tower Hill. Morrison also found 'support on every side' for Tower Hill's inclusion in what he grandly described as Victoria's 'National Parks System'. At the council's request, the Authority not only agreed to take charge of the area but also had its staff examine what private land should be added to the park.[29]

Meanwhile, a local farmer applied for grazing rights over the islands. Far from rejecting his application as incompatible with Tower Hill's existing status as a national park, four of Koroit's seven councillors were delighted at the prospect of no longer having to employ a ranger to police the area. Their one concern was that the farmer had offered only a nominal rent, claiming there was little feed because of all the bracken, cape ivy and thistles. The councillors believed they could do better and decided to call for tenders.[30]

Ross Robinson, the resident doctor at Koroit's district hospital, responded by seeking permission to plant 'suitable trees' on Tower Hill. While he expected to select mainly Australian natives, he also wanted to plant poplars, elms, willows and oaks with 'due regard to the formation of a balanced plant life in the area'. Having already helped to plant forty or fifty trees on the island as a child, only to see them destroyed by rabbits, Robinson did not want his efforts wasted again. A key part of his proposal was that the trees be protected from stock until they were established: hence the council should reconsider whether to allow new grazing over the island.[31]

The council turned to the State's main proponent of tree-planting, the Natural Resources Conservation League, which had distributed a million trees in Victoria over the previous decade. The League advised that only natives should be used 'in keeping with National Park ideas'. Having seen 'a painting of Tower Hill by a Frenchman of a hundred years ago'—most likely von Guérard's lithograph—one of its staff also explained that 'it was possible to get much information regarding the vegetation, flora and fauna'. But when the council allowed a group of local residents (including Robinson) to begin planting, they selected poplars and willows.[32]

At the same time, the National Parks Authority admitted that it could contribute little to Tower Hill. When Dewar Goode visited Koroit, he emphasised that it was 'a new body', 'had no money', 'would have to go slowly' and 'had a great deal of work to do to look after areas already gazetted'. The Authority proposed to delegate its power to the council, which would remain the Committee of Management for the park. The Authority's main function would be advisory: its 'body of highly trained men' would give the council 'every possible assistance' and stop it doing 'silly things'.[33]

The noted lyrebird expert L. H. Smith, who succeeded Crosbie Morrison as the Authority's director in 1958, was no more forthcoming. While he promised 'technical advice' to assist Warrnambool's new Field Naturalists' Club in replanting Tower Hill, Smith offered no financial support. As a result, Koroit Council had little reason to continue wanting the Authority to take charge of Tower Hill. Besides, there was a new claimant to the area.[34]

ALDO LEOPOLD COMES TO AUSTRALIA

Unlike John Muir, Aldo Leopold never crossed the Pacific, but he has had a much greater influence on Australian environmentalists. Above all, Leopold is renowned for his *Sand County Almanac*, first published in 1949, in which advocated a new 'land ethic' based on an expanded notion of community, including soils, water, plants, and animals. He maintained: 'We abuse land because we regard it as a commodity belonging to us. When we see land as a community to which we belong, we may begin to use it with love and respect'.[35]

Yet Leopold made his reputation not as an environmental philosopher but as an expert on *Game Management*, the title of his first book. As a professor in the Department of Agricultural Economics at the University of Wisconsin from 1933, Leopold looked on game as 'major forest products' or 'crops' to be maximised. A keen shooter, he aimed to produce a sustainable supply of animals for hunting for sport. Instead of the traditional emphasis on protecting game by rigorously enforcing close seasons, Leopold believed in actively managing species such as deer and quail in order to increase their numbers. A central part of this strategy was to establish refuges within forests and then improve habitat by 'deliberate and purposeful manipulation of the environment'.[36]

One devotee of Leopold's work was Max Downes, the first biologist appointed by any Australian government to examine native waterfowl. Downes's initial job with Victoria's Fisheries and Game

Branch in the early 1950s was to document and explain the declining numbers of game birds. But Downes was soon also looking for ways of maintaining, if not increasing, the existing duck population. At a time when most Australian biologists were looking to England, Downes read *A Sand County Almanac*. But what impressed him more was Leopold's *Game Management*, which persuaded him that preservation of habitat was the best means of producing as much game as possible.[37]

Victoria's Game Act did not further this goal. Although it prohibited shooting in 'sanctuaries', it did not require the owners of these areas to protect habitat and, as Downes soon discovered, most failed to do so. Even worse, Victoria's powerful Department of Agriculture was actively destroying swamps on Crown land, which had once provided prime breeding grounds for ducks. According to Downes:

> Virtually all were leased for agriculture, most were heavily grazed by cattle or sheep and the vast majority had severely deteriorated because of 'river improvement' and drainage works funded by the Victorian government for agricultural development.

Downes concluded that this loss of habitat was so great that it would not be enough for the Department of Agriculture to stop draining wetlands along the ducks' flight paths. The government would also have to turn the few swamps that remained into actively managed game reserves and restore swamps that had been cleared and drained. Like Leopold in the 1930s, Downes aimed to create conditions that would 'feed and breed the maximum harvest of wildlife'.[38]

This focus on habitat involved a major shift for the Game Branch, which had traditionally relied on law enforcement to protect wildlife, with the result that Victorian shooters looked on it as 'the enemy'. Yet Victoria was one of the States where hunting was most entrenched. Whereas the rest of Australia had stopped using the term 'game' by 1900 because it smacked of class oppression under England's draconian old laws, it persisted in Victoria in the 1950s, suggesting that the species classified in this way existed only for hunting.

Downes maintained that 'a well informed and co-operative public' would bring far greater benefits than rigorous law enforcement. Shooters were the prime group he wanted to win over. He first secured their co-operation in the early 1950s when he began a duck-banding programme. By establishing annual competitions with cases of cartridges as prizes, he lured up to 3000 shooters each year to send in the bands on birds they had killed. In 1958 he helped to establish the Victorian Field and Game Association, knowing that it would help his cause if the shooters became a more potent political force.[39]

This strategy bore immediate results when the State government introduced legislation requiring all duck shooters to hold an annual licence. Victorian shooters had previously resisted gun licences as an assault on 'the ordinary privileges of citizenship', but the new association supported this Bill because the £1 licence fee was to be used to establish and maintain a chain of game reserves along the ducks' flight paths. When the legislation came into force, it promptly yielded £34 000, ten times the amount previously available to the Fisheries and Game Branch. This revenue enabled the Branch to create Victoria's first reserves specifically set aside and managed for wildlife conservation. One area it fixed on was Tower Hill.[40]

LOCAL DEMOCRACY

Tower Hill became a centre of conflict in 1958 when local conservationists began seeking an end to duck shooting. By early 1959 they were confident of significant support. They advised J. Ros Garnet that the local member for Portland was 'a great Tower Hill park man'. The editor of the *Koroit Sentinel* had 'always taken a great interest in the Park and would be pleased to have it a Sanctuary'. Even the president of the local branch of the Australian Primary Producers' Union agreed.[41]

The Warrnambool Game Shooters' Club was so concerned that it responded with a petition calling on the State government to allow shooting to continue. Before long, it had attracted 742 signatories. But the shooters need not have worried, because the National Parks Authority still had no jurisdiction over Tower Hill and the council refused to protect the area's bird life while it retained charge of the park.[42]

This decision outraged local conservationists, led by Ross Robinson, who maintained that shooting was inconsistent with Tower Hill's status as a national park. The president and vice-president of the Game Shooters' Club replied that areas such as

Tower Hill were 'outdoor schoolrooms', which had proved vital in World War Two:

> A great deal of the Australians' natural ability at bushcraft and handling weapons was learned on the swamps, marshes and fields of this country. It came in handy, to say the least, at Kokoda and many other places. It could be handy again.[43]

Garnet inflamed this debate from Melbourne by accusing the shooters of violating the international code that recognised national parks as areas dedicated to nature preservation. Koroit's mayor warned Garnet to stay out of local affairs. According to the mayor, the Shooters' Club had prevailed because it was 'a powerful body, with a powerful following' and 'the publicity and letter writing that followed . . . did not help the cause at all'; 'it led to a clash of organizations and personalities that should never have occurred'.[44]

Over the following months, L. H. Smith of the National Parks Authority returned to Koroit to reiterate why Tower Hill should remain a park. Garnet persisted in arguing from Melbourne that Tower Hill's geology made it a place of much more than local interest. Warrnambool's Field Naturalists obtained an acre from the Koroit Council as a trial plot and began clearing it for planting with native trees grown by local schoolchildren. Their goal was not just to restore Tower Hill's natural beauty but to bring back its bird life and possibly even establish a koala colony. Their only rules for planting were to use a mixture of species and to avoid straight lines.[45]

Local shooters responded by branding national parks elitist. Although the only basis for this claim was that shooting was prohibited, they maintained that the National Parks Authority would turn Tower Hill into 'a museum-like area where only a small band of specialists' could find 'real pleasure'. The shooters also argued that Koroit would profit if Tower Hill became a game reserve, because the Fisheries and Game Branch had the resources necessary to develop it. Whereas the National Parks Authority had at most £20 000 to spend on the fourteen parks under its control, the Fisheries and Game Branch had just received £34 000 in the worst duck season in ten years and could expect to receive £70 000 in a good season.[46]

Although otherwise a keen supporter of national parks, Max Downes was even more persuasive in arguing that his Branch had the necessary expertise and resources to turn Tower Hill into a 'Show

Place of Victoria'. When the Koroit Council asked him to address one of its meetings, Downes explained that Tower Hill was ideally situated on the main flight path for waterfowl moving across Victoria, while the islands' isolation by water would facilitate control of predators and vermin. A game reserve would also offer something for everyone. Tower Hill's scenic beauty and geology would be 'fully preserved and developed', a koala colony could be established as the field naturalists wanted, and shooting could continue as its prohibition would 'achieve no conservation purpose'.[47]

The field naturalists' disadvantage in this contest was underlined in April 1959, just as Koroit was preparing to celebrate Anzac Day. While other Victorian towns prided themselves on the trees in their avenues of honour, the Koroit Council decided to fell its twenty-three memorial silver poplars because their suckers were reaching into private property and constituted a 'potential menace' to a new eight-inch water main. Local residents organised a protest meeting at the local RSL club, but the council's workmen pre-empted them. A few hours before the meeting started, the workmen ringbarked and poisoned all the trees.[48]

Downes's energy and enthusiasm were also vital. Whereas Smith was 'hopelessly vague' and ignored local conservationists when he visited Tower Hill, Downes spent a day with Ross Robinson, then an evening talking until midnight with Reverend Shrader of the Warrnambool Field Naturalists. Although both Robinson and Shrader deplored shooting, they were convinced that Downes was Tower Hill's 'only hope': he would put an end to quarrying, stop the council reopening the speedway track around the islands, and alone had 'the will and the resources to restore Tower Hill to what it ought to be'.[49]

When the council met in October 1959, economics determined its choice. One councillor maintained that the Game Branch had received £58 000 in 1958 and had just five reserves under its control. Another quoted Downes as promising that his department would spend £10 000 a year on Tower Hill. Even if this amount was exaggerated, the council expected the Game Branch to develop Tower Hill immediately, whereas the National Parks Authority would not spend £10 000 in ten years.[50]

This vote determined Tower Hill's future. Victoria's new State Wildlife Reserves Investigation Committee considered what should become of Tower Hill in January–February 1960, but its decision was never in doubt, as its function was to improve shooting in Victoria.

By May Cabinet had approved the transfer of Tower Hill to the newly renamed Fisheries and Wildlife Branch as Victoria's seventh Game Reserve.[51] Four months later this decision was law and Victoria's first national park no longer existed—but then in practice it never had.

THE MERITS OF MICROSCOPISM

The Koroit Council made the right choice. Although the proceeds from shooters' licences never rose above £41 000 and fell as low as £18 000, the Fisheries and Wildlife Branch was always better funded and staffed than the National Parks Authority, and more successful in securing its objectives. While new parks were sometimes established without reference to the Authority, the Fisheries and Wildlife Branch had such success in acquiring its preferred sites that it soon aspired to control a 'representative sample of all physical environments found in the state'. As Downes had promised, the Branch treated Tower Hill as 'a shop-window for the state's wildlife system', 'a working exhibit on how a natural area can be reclaimed'.[52]

The Branch immediately stopped quarrying and grazing within the reserve and appointed two bailiffs, who began poisoning foxes, eradicating noxious weeds such as boxthorn and thistles, and attacking the islands' rabbits, which were the primary obstacle to the growth of new trees. While an initial aerial drop of baits had immediate, spectacular results, some rabbits survived even after repeated poisoning and ripping into their burrows. As a result, the Branch still had to provide tree guards for each seedling in areas where infestation remained high or the plants belonged to species particularly attractive to rabbits.[53]

The Branch was also quick to try to control the use of private land both within and outside the crater. In 1961 it infuriated local councils and landowners when it persuaded the government to make an interim development order giving Victoria's new Town and Country Planning Board control over the area between Tower Hill and the ocean. While this order did not affect the quarries already operating on private land, it required the Board's consent for all new land uses, including subdivision and the opening of further quarries. At the same time, the Branch sought to buy up and close the existing quarries. By early 1962 it had acquired seventy-four acres on the crater's eastern banks; by 1966 only one quarry was still operating.[54]

The department was also quick to publicise its work. Even in 1960, before it actually took charge of the old national park, it published the first of a series of pamphlets by Downes in which he cast Tower Hill as 'a monument to . . . the destruction of vegetation and wildlife which resulted from settlement of Victoria by the white man' and emphasised 'the opportunity . . . to bring this area back to something approaching its original condition'. In 1962 the department worked with the Country Roads Board and the Tourist Development Authority to create a new lookout on the Princes Highway overlooking Tower Hill. In 1964 it re-established access to the islands by rebuilding the causeways, which had been submerged in the 1950s.[55]

Restoration of Tower Hill necessarily lagged behind. But local field naturalists continued helping to replant it even though it was no longer a national park. A key figure was Ross Robinson, who maintained that it was more important to restore Tower Hill than to continue worrying about who controlled it. While he still objected to shooting, Robinson applauded Downes for developing a 'very good plan embracing the eradication of vermin, revegetation, and the encouragement of native birds of all kinds, not solely game birds'.[56]

Downes's greatest problem was to determine what species to plant and where. Following Aldo Leopold, he believed the original vegetation would provide the best habitat for maximising the number and range of wildlife at Tower Hill. But what had Tower Hill been like before Europeans began degrading it? One guide was provided by its remnant vegetation. Early accounts of the area were also instructive, particularly James Bonwick's book about western Victoria from 1858. But von Guérard's view of Tower Hill proved most compelling. In 1959 a local resident presented a copy of his lithograph to the Warrnambool Council.[57]

While conservationists such as J. Ros Garnet were already familiar with von Guérard's print, the donation of the lithograph to the council was important because many local residents believed that Tower Hill had always been bare. As the local *Standard* immediately recognised, von Guérard's lithograph suggested that Tower Hill had been studded with islets, while the main island and the outer banks of the crater had been heavily wooded.[58]

Then Max Downes accidentally discovered that James Dawson's granddaughter, Mrs K. M. Winter, had the oil painting in Melbourne.

This discovery was even more significant. Here was an original, not a copy—a primary document made in Victoria, not a reproduction from London.

The only question was whether von Guérard could be trusted. His reputation was hardly encouraging. In 1960 von Guérard's paintings were known, if at all, for being 'un-Australian', and were omitted from almost all survey exhibitions of Australian art. The only State gallery that held his paintings was the National Gallery of Victoria—and then only because it had acquired them in von Guérard's lifetime. But just a little fieldwork by Downes cast von Guérard's work in a new light. When he took von Guérard's lithograph to Tower Hill, he found it fitted the topography with 'remarkable accuracy'.[59]

Von Guérard's depiction of the vegetation of Tower Hill could not be checked so easily. It required extensive archival research—something Downes did for all his wildlife reserves. By 1961 he had written a remarkable 95-page account of Tower Hill's history to 1892. This library work led Downes to conclude that von Guérard had accurately represented the general arrangement and types of vegetation—the communities of tea-trees, wattles, sheoaks, banksias and eucalypts towards the tops of the cones; the clearings on the eastern slopes of the island caused by poor soil and low rainfall; the reed beds and tussocks in the swampy water.[60]

But what of the individual species? When von Guérard began painting in Melbourne, he was applauded for his 'microscopism'. It was a commonplace that his landscapes could also serve as botanical or geological studies. Every tree, even every flower was said to be identifiable. When his erstwhile champion, James Smith of the *Argus*, derided him in 1870 for offering no more than this detail, von Guérard replied:

> If ever the artist in question could succeed to paint Australian scenes to make them delightful illustrations for treatises of botanical or geological features of the Colony then he would be convinced that for the future his paintings would have a greater value, where it will be doubtful if those which can be taken equally well for a misty English or an Australian landscape will have the same future.[61]

Had von Guérard achieved this goal when painting Tower Hill? In 1960 Downes showed his painting to J. Ros Garnet, who not only identified thirteen species but reported that 'no obvious inconsistencies were apparent in any of the trees or shrubs which could be recognised'. Six years later J. H. Willis, the Senior Botanist at Melbourne's Royal Botanic Gardens, was confident of identifying just ten species, of which Garnet had only identified the blackwoods and the southern grass tree or xanthorrhoea. Willis found the presence of the xanthorrhoea 'startling and unexpected'. He did not know if it occurred in any other volcanic area, and asked whether its inclusion could be artistic licence.[62]

We may never know. Scientists extrapolating from the present are often wrong about the past. But the xanthorrhoea was renowned in the mid-nineteenth century for adding a 'picturesque', even 'oriental' aspect to otherwise monotonous scenery. Von Guérard would have been tempted to introduce it to make his work more interesting. As Charles Wilkes commented when he visited New South Wales with the United States Exploring Expedition in 1839, the xanthorrhoea was particularly suited to 'the foreground of a picture'.[63]

Had such inconsistencies and doubts been raised in 1960, they might have diminished the impact of von Guérard's painting. But they took six years to emerge, and even then Willis's report was not published. As a result, Downes naturally concluded that 'the vegetation was drawn as accurately as the hills and [was] much as it was seen in 1855'. For the first time in almost a century, the detail of von Guérard's work became cause for appreciation, not derision. The painting became the most powerful testimony to how Tower Hill had been degraded by European settlement—and a template of how it could 'come into its own again'.[64]

ART INTO NATURE

Restoration of Tower Hill started in earnest in 1961. A group of Warrnambool field naturalists raised 1500 seedlings in their own small backyard nursery, using seeds they had gathered locally. Together with departmental officers, they planted tea-trees, paperbarks and blackwoods on the northern shore of the main island to provide shelter for waterbirds. They also began replanting the slopes of the main cone of Tower Hill and a gully leading up its eastern side, where they looked forward to establishing 'delightful bowers' of tree ferns under the shelter of blackwoods, as described by James Bonwick in 1858.[65]

TOWER HILL 1961

If von Guérard's painting was the primary basis for restoration of the north-eastern slopes of Tower Hill, Bonwick provided more guidance for the south-western slopes, which von Guérard did not depict. Further botanical advice came from Helen Alston of Melbourne's National Herbarium, who carried out surveys of Tower Hill and of similar areas where the original vegetation remained more intact. After comparing her findings with Downes's discoveries from the historical records, she identified seventeen trees and shrubs, as well as many herbs, reeds, sedges and ferns, either 'known to have been or very likely to have been constituents of the original flora'.[66]

None of these small plants were available from nurseries, but in 1964 the Branch discovered that a prison farm in Gippsland sold trees at one-fifth the price charged by the Natural Resources Conservation League. As a result, the Branch could increase its replanting, and looked for additional volunteers to help. As in 1924, it turned to local schoolchildren, who came in groups of up to fifty and planted ten trees each. One year 2200 children participated. The Warrnambool Field Naturalists, Shooters and Apex Club also contributed. By 1966 these volunteers had planted 24 000 trees. By 1971 the tally was 106 000, although you would hardly know it from photographs

ERIC WADSWORTH
TOWER HILL AND ONE OF ITS CRATERS 1972

taken at the time: they suggest a grassland dotted with conifers.[67]

Reintroduction of Tower Hill's original fauna was also slow. When the Branch put out nesting boxes for wild ducks in 1964, the boxes were probably too warm, having been made of old black chemical containers donated by ICI. They also were invaded by starlings, whose scent and lice discouraged ducks from following them. When the Branch started reintroducing mammals, it was properly cautious and tried just grey kangaroos, swamp wallabies, wombats, echidnas and short-nosed bandicoots.[68]

The Branch was also impeded by the Koroit Council, which continued to regard Tower Hill as its own. According to Gavin Cerini, the Branch's first game management officer at Tower Hill, the council still looked on the Branch's activities as a form of 'outside interference' in 1970, when it had been responsible for the reserve for ten years. In a letter to J. Ros Garnet, Cerini confided: '[O]ne must take a long term view of things in this community'.[69]

A decade later Cerini and his volunteers had removed all the pine trees from the islands and lake banks, and had planted almost 250 000 trees, half of which had survived. They had also erected artificial

ERIC WADSWORTH
NATURAL HISTORY CENTRE, TOWER HILL 1972

nesting boxes for possums and sugar gliders, which otherwise could not have survived, since none of the trees were old enough to have hollows. Birds had also begun returning: where local field naturalists had recorded 60 species in 1960, there were 164 by the early 1980s.[70]

Just as Tower Hill came increasingly to resemble von Guérard's canvas, so part of the River Stour in England was coming to resemble John Constable's *The Hay Wain*. The trigger was a proposal for a giant gravel pit, which the National Trust and the Stour Valley Preservation Society stopped by buying a large part of the area. The Trust then went on recreate Constable's landscape. As Michael Rosenthal has discussed, the Trust not only reopened Constable's vista of the meadow by clearing a line of trees but also excavated the dry dock where Constable's father used to construct barges, as Constable recorded in another painting.[71]

Yet the new cultural landscapes inspired by the two paintings were very different. The National Trust's attempt to impose the past on the present was an exercise in nostalgia. Its object was to create a static landscape, with just a surface similarity to Constable's famous painting. Downes, by contrast, wanted to create a viable new ecosystem. His test for Tower Hill was whether the new biota supported more wildlife, not only because they might serve as game, but also because they indicated a healthier environment. An alternative test suggested by a local scientist was what would happen if there was a major fire. Because of the new seed bed, he predicted the trees would return: the replication of von Guérard's painting had become self-generating.[72]

TOWER HILL 1985

Meanwhile, James Dawson's granddaughter, Mrs K. M. Winter, sought to make even more of Tower Hill. Excited by Max Downes's plans, she offered to give £100 in 1961 as a memorial to her grandfather. Downes decided to put it towards establishing a Museum or Natural History Centre, which would explain the restoration of Tower Hill and the larger system of game reserves in Victoria. At the suggestion of Neil Clerehan of the *Age*'s Small Homes Service, Downes approached Robin Boyd, the Melbourne architect with best credentials as a conservationist. Having denounced the hatred of trees which he dubbed 'arboraphobia' in *The Australian Ugliness*, Boyd was the obvious choice to participate in Tower Hill's restoration.

Boyd did not come cheap. Winter's £100 simply paid for his sketch plans. Another £400, which the Field and Game Association raised as a means of legitimising continued shooting by its members at Tower Hill, paid for Boyd to complete building plans. The State government agreed to pay £28 000 or two-thirds of the cost of the building so long as the public donated the remaining one-third. By 1968 the money had been raised, primarily outside the Warrnambool area, as Tower Hill increasingly became a general symbol of environmental restoration of more interest to Melburnians

TOWER HILL 1985

than residents of the Western District. By 1970 the centre was open with von Guérard's painting on display, another gift from Winter to what had become the Department of Fisheries and Wildlife.[73]

The Natural History Centre is one of Boyd's best buildings. As he explained it, 'a complete, one-piece, yet seemingly organic growth' was called for because the building was 'an artificial interloper in an area whose sole objective was to appear unspoilt by artificiality'. But photographs taken at the time suggest another motive. Boyd's design drew on the degraded landscape stripped of vegetation. The building's saucer-like roof echoed the tops of the bald cones rising behind—a resonance now partly lost as the tops of the hills have been revegetated.[74]

For six years, von Guérard's painting was the first thing visitors saw on arriving at the centre. But the Branch then decided that the centre was too insecure to house the painting which jumped in value in the 1970s as von Guérard came to be regarded as one of Australia's finest colonial artists. As a result, the Branch decided to loan it to the regional gallery in Warrnambool, where it was soon surrounded by new paintings of Tower Hill—the first for almost a century—inspired both by the revegetation and the post-modern appetite for quotation.

Before long von Guérard's *Tower Hill* had excited more contemporary art than any other colonial painting.[75]

THE TREE RABBITS

Given the complexity of restoring the ecosystem of even as small an area as Tower Hill, the Fisheries and Game Branch was bound to make mistakes. But nature kindly cured the Branch's first blunder: its corruption of the aquatic environment in order to give local anglers year-round fishing. Having already provided English perch, the Branch stocked the lake with 60 000 rainbow trout in 1962. These fish died when the lake dried up during the drought of 1967–68, and the Branch knew better than to restock it when the lake refilled.[76]

Mistakes on land have proved more enduring. Because provenance was widely disregarded in the 1960s, the Branch did not consider whether its seedlings from Gippsland were the same as those native to Tower Hill. In fact, there were significant differences. While the manna gums from Gippsland grew with tall straight trunks, those around Tower Hill tended to spread with multiple stems from the butt. The trees from Gippsland also failed to adjust to their new environment. Many of those planted on the higher, drier parts of Tower Hill died in dry seasons. Others failed to set seed.

The Branch always knew that it had planted the wrong wattle. Its problem was that nurseries in the 1960s did not sell the late black wattle, which was indigenous to Tower Hill. As a result, the Branch opted for the early black or green wattle from New South Wales, having been assured that the two were 'almost indistinguishable'. In all, it planted 25 000, which flourished, providing roosts for birds and wattle sap and seed for sugar gliders. But the early wattle, as its name implies, flowers at a different time of year from the late black wattle. Its branches also have a different configuration. Although the Branch switched to late black wattles in 1975, it may now be impossible to eradicate the early wattles because of their seed beds across the islands.[78]

The department also introduced koalas, which had defoliated one island after another since the 1920s, starting with French, Phillip and Quail Islands in Victoria and then Kangaroo Island in South Australia. Each time the koalas overbrowsed the trees which they found most palatable, destroying their own habitat. Many starved to death on Quail Island in the early 1940s. In order to avoid a repetition of these incidents, the department decided that koalas should be released only into areas of at least 4000 hectares, except for small patches of prime habitat adjacent to larger Crown forests.[79]

At just 144 hectares, the three islands of Tower Hill fell far short of the department's minimum. They also did not offer an adjacent forest into which the koalas could disperse. Yet the department ignored its own guidelines because it believed koalas would be a great attraction. By 1988 the original nineteen 'tree rabbits'—as one local ranger dubbed them—had become hundreds, if not thousands, and had eaten out the tops of many manna gums on Tower Hill. By 1992 they had caused such damage that rangers began relocating 500 to a much larger area of Crown forest in the Casterton area near the South Australian border. By the mid-1990s between two-thirds and three-quarters of the manna gums were dead, as were all the tree ferns planted in the early 1980s to recreate Bonwick's 'beautiful bowers'.

What to do? Further relocation within Victoria would simply transfer the problem elsewhere. In New South Wales and Queensland, koalas were suffering a critical decline; but relocation there was problematic because the introduced animals would probably interbreed with existing koalas, which are generally considered a different sub-species.[80]

In South Australia, where koalas were again defoliating Kangaroo Island, a special inquiry recommended culling by trained marksmen as cheap and humane. But it was a political impossibility because of the koala's iconic status. Neither State nor federal politicians were willing to risk an outcry or a loss in tourist trade by mounting a koala shoot, particularly after 1995, when the Goss government lost office in Queensland partly as a result of protests over its decision to construct a new motorway between Brisbane and the Gold Coast through the site of the State's biggest remaining koala population.[81]

The solution adopted in South Australia and Victoria was sterilisation, even though it did nothing to reduce the existing population or relieve overbrowsing in the short term, and the cost was immense compared with the States' small budgets for species actually at risk of extinction. The South Australian and federal governments spent almost $650 000 a year to have scientists experiment with vasectomies and tubal ligations on Kangaroo Island—almost as much as the State government spent on all endangered species. The Victorian government embarked on a three-year trial of two different hormone implants on sixty females on Tower Hill.

Meanwhile rangers at Tower Hill were busy felling dead manna gums and planting new ones. But the State government gave them no money to control pests on the reserve in 1994–95, just $1000 in 1995–96, and $2000 in 1996–97. As a result, they were unable to stop a rapid increase of invasive species including cape ivy, hemlock, teasel, sweet pittosporum, thistles and pine trees, which were rampant on the banks of the crater. By 1997 there were only two rangers with occasional contract help, compared with three rangers and three full-time field workers a decade before. Although Tower Hill was attracting 200 000 visitors each year, the total budget for the reserve was a derisory $117 000 including salaries.

This decline in public commitment to Tower Hill started when the Cain Labor government abolished the Department of Fisheries and Wildlife in 1984 and transferred its functions to a 'mega-department' including the old National Parks Service, Forests Commission and Department of Crown Lands. Shooting at Tower Hill remained lawful, but otherwise the new department managed it like a national park. The game reserves also lost their separate funding from shooters' licences. While all reserves suffered, Tower Hill was particularly affected because it lost its status as the showcase of the reserve system.

The consequences were profound. The department failed to implement its plans to lay pipes through the dam so that the lake could be flushed out, reducing its salinity and allowing aquatic life to return. The local council abandoned its planning controls on the northern side of Tower Hill and houses were built on the edge of the crater, destroying its integrity. When the department stopped planting trees in the late 1980s, it ignored a pilot study of the best way to begin re-creating the understorey, which Max Downes always intended as a key step towards re-establishing a normal forest community.[82]

These failures illustrate the difficulty of restoring even the smallest natural environments. A quarter-century of remarkable public enthusiasm and expenditure was undone by a decade of negligence. If the gap between art and nature narrowed dramatically in the 1970s and 1980s, it reopened wide through the 1990s. In the 1980s Tower Hill sported a sign identifying 'Von Guérard's Lookout', which encouraged visitors to stop and dwell on the increasing coincidence of place and painting. Now the sign is gone, and the one colonial painting to leave its mark on the environment is again a record of what Tower Hill was rather than an inspiration for what it might be.

CHAPTER ONE

Sydney Bird Painter, *A Young Mount Pitt Bird,* c. 1790, watercolour, 48.1 x 30.2 cm, Mitchell Library, State Library of New South Wales, Sydney.

Mount Pitt Bird, c. 1790, watercolour, 31.2 x 41.6 cm, laid onto sheet 31.5 x 51.5 cm, Mitchell Library, State Library of New South Wales, Sydney.

John Hunter, *Bird of Providence, or Mount Pitt Bird, Norfolk Island*, c. 1790, watercolour, 22.8 x 18.5 cm, from *The Hunter Sketchbook,* Rex Nan Kivell Collection, National Library of Australia, Canberra.

George Raper, *Chief Settlement on Norfolk Island*, 1790, watercolour, 32.6 x 48.5 cm, Natural History Museum, London.

John Hunter, *Norfolk Island Ground-Dove*, c. 1790, watercolour, 22.8 x 18.5 cm, from *The Hunter Sketchbook,* Rex Nan Kivell Collection, National Library of Australia, Canberra.

CHAPTER TWO

Governor Bligh under the Bed, c. 1808, watercolour, 23.7 x 37.0 cm, Mitchell Library, State Library of New South Wales, Sydney.

George Raper, *View of the East Side of Sidney Cove*, 1789, pen, ink and watercolour on laid paper, 27.0 x 43.0 cm, Natural History Museum, London.

James Heath, *A View of the Governor's House at Rose Hill in the Township of Parramatta*, c. 1795, wood-engraving, 17.6 x 24.8 cm, from David Collins, *An Account of the English Colony of New South Wales*, opp. p. 125, National Library of Australia, Canberra.

John Eyre, *View of Sydney from the West Side of the Cove*, c. 1806, watercolour, 36.0 x 67.0 cm, Dixson Galleries, State Library of New South Wales, Sydney.

CHAPTER THREE

John Glover, *A View in Mills Plains*, c. 1835, oil on canvas, 75.5 x 112.4 cm, Rex Nan Kivell Collection, National Library of Australia, Canberra.

Augustus Earle, *June Park, Van Diemen's Land*, 1825, watercolour, 24.2 x 40.3 cm, Rex Nan Kivell Collection, National Library of Australia, Canberra.

Joseph Lycett, *Burwood Villa, New South Wales, the Property of Alexander Riley Esq*, 1824, hand-coloured aquatint, 17.7 x 28.0 cm, from Lycett's *Views in Australia, or New South Wales and Van Diemen's Land*, London, 1824–25, National Library of Australia, Canberra.

John Glover, *Early Morning on the Painter's Plains* and *In the Painter's Vale*, 1832, drawing, Tasmanian Museum and Art Gallery.

John Glover, *Hobart Town, taken from the Garden where I lived*, 1832, oil on canvas, 76.0 x 152.0 cm, Dixson Galleries, State Library of New South Wales, Sydney.

John Glover, *A View of the Artist's House and Garden, Mills Plains*, c. 1835, oil on canvas, 76.2 x. 114.6 cm, Art Gallery of South Australia.

John Glover, *My Harvest Home*, 1835, oil on canvas, 76.2 x 113.9 cm, Tasmanian Museum and Art Gallery, Hobart.

John Glover, *Tasmanian Landscape*, c. 1835, oil on canvas, 76.1 x 114.0 cm, Dixson Galleries, State Library of New South Wales, Sydney.

John Glover, *A View of Mills Plains*, c. 1840, oil on canvas, 77.0 x 114.5 cm, Art Gallery of New South Wales, Sydney.

CHAPTER FOUR

Eugene von Guérard, *Ferntree Gully in the Dandenong Ranges*, 1857, oil on canvas, 92.0 x 138.0 cm, National Gallery of Australia, Canberra, Gift of Joseph Brown.

J. H. Steiner, *William Thurston Testimonial Epergne*, c. 1877, silver, glass and cedar, 46.0 x 23.5 x 25.0 cm, Art Gallery of South Australia.

Chest of Drawers, c. 1890, pine stencilled in black ink, 80.0 x 95.5 x 45.0 cm, National Gallery of Australia, Canberra.

Nicholas Chevalier, *Fancy Costume Emblematic of Australia*, detail, c. 1860, watercolour, 36.7 x 25.8 cm, Rex Nan Kivell Collection, National Library of Australia, Canberra.

The Wood-Splitters' Hut in the Fern Tree Gully, 1865, wood-engraving, from *Illustrated Australian News for Home Readers*, 23 December 1865, p. 8, National Library of Australia, Canberra.

Archibald Campbell, *Sassafras Gully*, 1891–92, photograph, 10.0 x 15.0 cm, Museum Victoria, Melbourne.

CHAPTER FIVE

Louisa Anne Meredith, *Gum Flowers and 'Love'*, 1860, lithograph, 37.4 x 27.4 cm, from Louisa Anne Meredith, *Some of My Bush Friends in Tasmania*, London, 1860, plate 5, National Library of Australia, Canberra.

Louisa Anne Meredith, *Weeping Gum-Trees and Old Forge*, 1852, wood-engraving, 7.0 x 7.0 cm, from *My Home in Tasmania*, London, 1852, vol. 1, p. 168, National Library of Australia, Canberra.

Louisa Anne Meredith, *Our Island Home: A Tasmanian Sketchbook*, 1879, autotype, 31.5 x 22.0 cm, title-page of *Our Island Home: A Tasmanian Sketchbook*, London, 1879, National Library of Australia, Canberra.

Louisa Anne Meredith, *Buckland Church and Parsonage, Prosser Valley*, 1879, autotype, 21.4 x 31.0 cm, from *Our Island Home: A Tasmanian Sketchbook*, London, 1879, National Library of Australia, Canberra.

Louisa Anne Meredith, *Wooden Fruits*, 1891, lithograph, 22.8 x 33.0 cm, from *Bush Friends in Tasmania*, London, 1891, plate 10, National Library of Australia, Canberra.

CHAPTER SIX

Louis Buvelot, *Gisborne Hill from the Slopes of Mount Macedon*, 1875, oil on canvas, 71.3 x 112.5 cm, Bendigo Art Gallery.

Louis Buvelot, *Near Lilydale*, 1871, oil on canvas, 46.0 x 69.0 cm, National Gallery of Australia, Canberra.

Louis Buvelot, *Waterpool near Coleraine, Sunset*, 1869, oil on canvas, 107.4 x 153.0 cm, National Gallery of Victoria, Melbourne.

CHAPTER SEVEN

Charles Walter, *Our Artist*, 1873, wood-engraving, 11.0 x 7.7 cm, from *Illustrated Australian News for Home Readers*, 31 December 1873, p. 212, National Library of Australia, Canberra.

Joseph Bischoff, *The Valley of the Grose*, 1875, photograph, 22.0 x 77.5 cm, La Trobe Library, State Library of Victoria, Melbourne.

Joseph Bischoff, *The Valley of the Grose*, 1875, photograph, 34.3 x 24.8 cm, National Gallery of Australia, Canberra.

J. W. Beattie, *Lake Marion and Mount Gould*, c. 1880, photograph, 9.8 x 13.8 cm, Tasmanian Museum and Art Gallery, Hobart.

after Charles Walter, *Bridge over the Delegate at Quedong*, 1871,

wood-engraving, 11.6 x 12.0 cm, from *Illustrated Australian News for Home Readers*, 17 June 1871, p. 125, National Library of Australia, Canberra.

Morton Allport, *Mount Ida, Lake St Clair*, 1862, photograph, 7.5 x 14.5 cm, Allport Library and Museum of Fine Arts, State Library of Tasmania.

attributed to Nicholas Chevalier, *The Picturesque and the Practical*, 1858, wood-engraving, 13.0 x 17.5 cm, from *Melbourne Punch*, 15 July 1858, p. 204, National Library of Australia, Canberra.

Eugene von Guérard, *Cabbage-Tree Forest, American Creek, New South Wales*, c. 1867, colour lithograph, 33.4 x 53.0 cm, from *Eugène von Guérard's Australian Landscapes*, Melbourne, 1866–68, National Library of Australia, Canberra.

Arthur Streeton, *The Purple Noon's Transparent Might*, 1896, oil on canvas, 123.0 x 123.0 cm, National Gallery of Victoria, Melbourne.

Augustus Earle, *A Bivouac of Travellers in Australia*, c. 1838, oil on canvas, 11.8.1 x 89.1 cm, National Library of Australia, Canberra.

CHAPTER EIGHT

Thomas Carrington, *The Beginning*, 1884, wood-engraving, 24.7 x 18.9 cm, from *Melbourne Punch*, 22 May 1884, p. 205, National Library of Australia, Canberra.

Thomas Carrington, *Now and Then*, 1882, wood-engraving, 13.1 x 17.6 cm, from *Melbourne Punch*, 8 June 1882, p. 224, National Library of Australia, Canberra.

Julian Ashton, *Evening—Merri Creek*, 1882, oil on canvas, 91.6 x 122.0 cm, Art Gallery of New South Wales, Sydney.

The Corporation 'Tip', 1884, wood-engraving, 11.1 x 8.8 cm, from *Melbourne Punch*, 17 January 1884, p. 27, National Library of Australia, Canberra.

A Kalizoic Society and its Work, 1884, wood-engraving, 13.7 x 17.6 cm, from *Melbourne Punch*, 10 January 1884, p. 19, National Library of Australia, Canberra.

Development of the Crinolette, 1884, wood-engraving, 11.1 x 8.8 cm, from *Melbourne Punch*, 17 January 1884, p. 27, National Library of Australia, Canberra.

Thomas Carrington, *Birds-Eye View of Albert Park (As It Very Soon Will Be)*, 1875, wood-engraving, 18.8 x 24.8 cm, from *Melbourne Punch*, 1 July 1875, p. 255, National Library of Australia, Canberra.

CHAPTER NINE

Nicholas Caire, *Giant Tree House, Gippsland*, c. 1885, photograph, 28.1 x 21.3 cm, National Library of Australia, Canberra.

Nicholas Caire, *The Tree and the House Built Out of It*, c. 1885, photograph, 21.6 x 28.1 cm, National Library of Australia, Canberra.

Nicholas Caire, *Tall Dead Giant Tree, Gippsland*, c. 1885, photograph, 28.1 x 23.1 cm, National Library of Australia, Canberra.

The Present Position of the Gippsland Populace, 1888, wood-engraving, from *Melbourne Punch*, 15 November 1888, p. 462, National Library of Australia, Canberra.

J. Duncan Peirce, *Eucalyptus Amygdalina Regnans, Neerim Town Reserve*, 1888, photograph, 42.0 x 29.0 cm, from *The Giant Trees of Victoria*, Melbourne, c. 1890. plate 2, National Library of Australia, Canberra.

J. Duncan Peirce, *The 'Baron'*, 1889, photograph, 42.0 x 28.8 cm, from *The Giant Trees of Victoria*, Melbourne, c. 1890, plate 7, National Library of Australia, Canberra.

J. Duncan Peirce, *The 'Baron'*, 1889, photograph, 42.0 x 28.7 cm, from *The Giant Trees of Victoria*, Melbourne, c. 1890, plate 8, National Library of Australia, Canberra.

Nicholas Caire, *Edward VII*, 1904, photograph, 20.9 x 27.8 cm, National Library of Australia, Canberra.

CHAPTER TEN

W. C. Piguenit, *The Flood in the Darling, 1890*, 1895, oil on canvas, 122.5 x 199.3 cm, Art Gallery of New South Wales, Sydney.

Bursting of the Embankment, 1890, wood-engraving, 14.0 x 18.1 cm, from *Illustrated Sydney News*, 10 May 1890, p. 16, National Library of Australia, Canberra.

Livingstone Hopkins, *The Moral of the Floods*, 1890, wood-engraving, 43.0 x 27.6 cm, from *Bulletin*, 26 April 1890, p. 3, National Library of Australia, Canberra.

W. C. Piguenit, *Out West during the Floods of 1890—The Gunderbooka Range*, 1890, oil on canvas, 76.0 x 127.7 cm, Queen Victoria Museum and Art Gallery, Launceston.

attributed to D. J. McLean, *Mulga Tree on Yantara Station, near Milparinka*, c. 1900, photograph, 11.8 x 8.0 cm, from 'Royal Commission to Inquire into the Condition of the Crown Tenants, Western Division of New South Wales', *Journal of the*

Legislative Council of New South Wales, 1901, vol. 63, part 2, Australian National University, Canberra.

Christopher Brandis, *Cobham Lake Homestead, near Milparinka*, 1901, photograph, 8.6 x 12.3 cm, from 'Royal Commission to Inquire into the Condition of the Crown Tenants, Western Division of New South Wales', *Journal of the Legislative Council of New South Wales*, 1901, vol. 63, part 2, Australian National University, Canberra.

CHAPTER ELEVEN

Arthur Streeton, *Cremorne Pastoral*, 1895, oil on canvas, 91.5 x 137.2 cm, Art Gallery of New South Wales, Sydney.

The Cremorne Coal Bore, 1893, wood-engraving, 16.5 x 11.5 cm, from *Illustrated Sydney News*, 25 November 1893, p. 2, National Library of Australia, Canberra.

Livingstone Hopkins, *King Coal at Cremorne*, 1893, wood-engraving, 8.5 x 10.4 cm, from *Bulletin*, 18 November 1893, p. 11, Australian National University, Canberra.

C. H. Hunt, *A Glimpse of the Future: Cremorne 10 Years Hence*, 1893, wood-engraving, 31.0 x 24.2 cm, from *Illustrated Sydney News*, 2 December 1893, p. 1, National Library of Australia, Canberra.

Robert Cherry, *Arthur Streeton painting a little rotter (oil sketch) at Curlew*, c. 1893, photograph, 7.7 x 10.2 cm, private collection.

Arthur Streeton, *Sirius Cove*, c. 1895, oil on wood panel, 68.8 x 16.8 cm, National Gallery of Australia, Canberra.

Arthur Streeton, *Oblivion*, c. 1895, oil on canvas 56.2 x 100.5 cm, private collection.

CHAPTER TWELVE

Eugene von Guérard, *Tower Hill*, 1855, oil on canvas, 68.2 x 122.0 cm, Department of Natural Resources and Environment, on loan to Warrnambool Art Gallery.

Daniel Clarke, *Tower Hill, an Extinct Volcano, near Warrnambool*, 1878, oil on canvas, 56.6 x 91.5 cm, Warrnambool Art Gallery.

Tower Hill, 1961, photograph, Tower Hill Natural History Centre.

Eric Wadsworth, *Tower Hill and One of its Craters*, 1972, photograph, 14.5 x 19.5 cm, National Library of Australia, Canberra.

Eric Wadsworth, *Natural History Centre, Tower Hill*, 1972, photograph, 19.5 x 14.5 cm, National Library of Australia, Canberra.

Tower Hill, 1985, photographs, Tower Hill Natural History Centre.

AGH	*Australian Garden History*
AGNSW	Art Gallery of New South Wales
AMS	*Australian Mining Standard*
APR	*Australasian Pastoralists' Review*
AS	*Australasian Sketcher*
ATCJ	*Australian Town and Country Journal*
BA	*Bendigo Advertiser*
BJP	*British Journal of Photography*
CC	*Camperdown Chronicle*
DA	*Dandenong Advertiser*
DT	*Daily Telegraph*
EN	*Evening News*
GT	*Gum Tree*
H	*Herald*
HRA	*Historical Records of Australia*
HRNSW	*Historical Records of New South Wales*
HTC	*Hobart Town Courier*
IANHR	*Illustrated Australian News for Home Readers*
IJA	*Illustrated Journal of Australasia*
IMP	*Illustrated Melbourne Post*
ISN	*Illustrated Sydney News*
JHA	*Journal of the House of Assembly (Tasmania)*
JPPPT	*Journals and Printed Papers of the Parliament of Tasmania*
JPRSNSW	*Journal and Proceedings of the Royal Society of New South Wales*
JRAHS	*Journal of the Royal Australian Historical Society*
KSTHA	*Koroit Sentinel and Tower Hill Advocate*
LE	*Launceston Examiner*
LTL	La Trobe Library, State Library of Victoria
MB	*Melbourne Bulletin*
ML	Mitchell Library, State Library of New South Wales
MP	*Melbourne Punch*
NLA	National Library of Australia
NSWGG	*New South Wales Government Gazette*
NSWLAV&P	*New South Wales Legislative Assembly Votes and Proceedings*
NSWPD	*New South Wales Parliamentary Debates*
PLNSW	*Proceedings of the Linnean Society of New South Wales*

PPRRST	*Papers, Proceedings and Reports of the Royal Society of Tasmania*
PPRST	*Papers and Proceedings of the Royal Society of Tasmania*
PRSV	*Proceedings of the Royal Society of Victoria*
RAHSJP	*Royal Australian Historical Society Journal and Proceedings*
SG	*Sydney Gazette*
SM	*Sydney Mail*
SMH	*Sydney Morning Herald*
SQM	*Sydney Quarterly Magazine*
SSR	*Southern Scientific Record*
TPRSV	*Transactions and Proceedings of the Royal Society of Victoria*
TT	*Table Talk*
VGG	*Victorian Government Gazette*
VHJ	*Victorian Historical Journal*
VHM	*Victorian Historical Magazine*
VN	*Victorian Naturalist*
VNPA	Victorian National Parks Association
VPD	*Victorian Parliamentary Debates*
VPP	*Victorian Parliamentary Papers*
VS	*Victorian Studies*
WHRDA	*Western Herald and Darling River Advocate*
WN	*Warragul News*
YAA	*Yeoman and Australasian Acclimatiser*

INTRODUCTION

1 See Bob Brown, *Lake Pedder*, p. 14; Dinah Dysart, 'William Charles Piguenit: Nineteenth Century Environmentalist'; Tim Bonyhady, 'Lake Pedder 1871'.
2 A notable exception is Hans Huth, in 'Nature and the American' and *Nature and the American: Three Centuries of Changing Attitudes*.
3 See, for example, Roger Blackley, *The Art of Alfred Sharpe*; Roderick Nash (ed.), *The American Environment: Readings in the History of Conservation*, pp. 100–1; Jack Lindsay, *William Morris: His Life and Work*, pp. 234, 243, 291, 356; Douglas G. Pearce and Gerard Richez, 'Antipodean Contrasts: National Parks in New Zealand and Europe', p. 56; Simon Schama, *Landscape and Memory*, p. 116.
4 James Anthony Froude, *Oceana or England and her Colonies*, p. 242; cf. James Bonwick, *Western Victoria: Its Geography, Geology and Social Conditions*, p. 68.
5 W. K. Hancock, *Australia*, p. 33; Robin Boyd, *The Australian Ugliness*, ch. 4; A. J. Marshall, 'The World of Hopkins Sibthorpe' in Marshall (ed.), *The Great Extermination*, p. 2; Vincent Serventy, *A Continent in Danger*, p. 205.
6 See particularly J. M. Powell, *Environmental Management in Australia 1788–1914*; Geoffrey Bolton, *Spoils and Spoilers: Australians Make Their Environment 1788–1980*.
7 William J. Lines, *Taming the Great South Land*, pp. 96–7, 133; Tim Flannery, *The Future Eaters*, p. 360.
8 Godfrey Charles Mundy, *Our Antipodes*, vol. 2, p. 27.
9 *HRNSW*, vol. 1, part 2, pp. 88–90.
10 See Richard H. Grove, *Green Imperialism: Colonial Expansion, Tropical Island Edens and the Origins of Environmentalism 1600–1860*.
11 Paul G. Fidlon and R. J. Ryan (eds), *The Journal of Philip Gidley King R.N. 1787–1790*, p. 70.
12 *HRNSW*, vol. 2, p. 326; *HRA*, series 1, vol. 1, p. 683; Powell, *Environmental Management*, pp. 18–20.
13 *HRA*, series 3, vol. 1, pp. 219–20, 264–5.
14 *SG*, 29 May 1803, p. 3.
15 François Péron, *King Island and the Sealing Trade 1802*, pp. 30–1.
16 *HRNSW*, vol. 2, p. 692.
17 Alan Frost, *Arthur Phillip 1738–1814: His Voyaging*, pp. 214, 268.
18 *SG*, 15 May 1803, p. 1; 12 June 1801, p. 1; 26 June 1803, p. 1; *HRA*, series 1, vol. 4, pp. 83, 105–6, 258.
19 Elizabeth de Quincey, *The History of Mount Wellington: A Tasmanian Sketchbook*, p. 61; Raymond Wright, *The Bureaucrats' Domain: Space and the Public Interest in Victoria*.
20 See Lurline Stuart, *James Smith: The Making of a Colonial Culture*, esp. p. 99.
21 *DT*, 31 October 1895, p. 3; *In re Sydney Harbour Collieries Company* (1895) 5 Land Appeal Court Reports 243, 259–60.
22 D. J. Mulvaney, *Encounters in Place: Outsiders and Aboriginal Australians 1606–1985*; Henry Reynolds, *This Whispering in Our Hearts*.
23 Tim Bonyhady, 'The Stuff of Heritage' in Tim Bonyhady and Tom Griffiths (eds), *Prehistory to Politics: John Mulvaney, the Humanities and the Public Intellectual*, pp. 144–62.
24 *SG*, 11 December 1803, p. 1; *HRNSW*, vol. 2, p. 326; vol. 3, pp. 10–11, 206, 518; David Collins, *An Account of the English Colony in New South Wales*, vol. 1, p. 450.
25 D. R. Hainsworth, *The Sydney Traders*, esp. pp. 130–1, 136–7.
26 *HRA*, series 1, vol. 5, pp. 67–8.
27 *Science of Man*, vol. 1, 1898, p. 244. See also Helen Irving, 'The Most Eccentric of them All: J. W. R. Clarke', in David Headon and John Williams (eds), *Makers of Miracles: The Cast of the Federation Story*, pp. 189–96.

CHAPTER ONE: BIRDS OF PROVIDENCE

1 *HRNSW*, vol. 1, part 2, p. 222; vol. 2, pp. 690, 744, 798; John Hunter, *An Historical Journal of the Transactions at Port Jackson and Norfolk Island*, p. 315; Watkin Tench, *A Complete Account of the Settlement at Port Jackson*, p. 175; George B. Worgan, *Journal of a First Fleet Surgeon*, pp. 20–1; C. M. Finney, *To Sail Beyond the Sunset: Natural History in Australia 1699–1829*, pp. 45, 53, 57; Richard Neville, *A Rage for Curiosity: Visualising Australia 1788–1830*, pp. 24, 28; Jane Lennon, 'Second Thoughts on First Views: The Port Jackson Circle 1788–1800', pp. 35–6.
2 *HRNSW*, vol. 1, part 2, p. 398; Paul G. Fidlon and R. J. Ryan (eds), *The Journal and Letters of Lieutenant Ralph Clark 1787–1792*, p. 282; John Calaby (ed.), *The Hunter Sketchbook*, pp. 9, 25, 208–9.
3 Neville, *A Rage for Curiosity*, pp. 23–4, 28.
4 Fidlon and Ryan (eds), *Lieutenant Ralph Clark*, pp. 129–47.
5 Fidlon and Ryan (eds), *Lieutenant Ralph Clark*, pp. 129–48.
6 Fidlon and Ryan (eds), *Lieutenant Ralph Clark*, pp. 134, 144–8.

[7] Fidlon and Ryan (eds), *Lieutenant Ralph Clark*, p. 292.

[8] John Hicks, 'The Natural History of Norfolk Island', in Raymond Nobbs (ed.), *Norfolk Island and its First Settlement 1788–1814*, p. 165.

[9] *HRNSW*, vol. 1, part 2, p. 399; Hunter, *An Historical Journal*, p. 182; William Bradley, *A Voyage to New South Wales*, pp. 199–200; Fidlon and Ryan (eds), *Lieutenant Ralph Clark*, p. 138; John C. Dann (ed.), *The Nagle Journal*, pp. 124–6, 361.

[10] *HRNSW*, vol. 1, part 2, pp. 419, 466; Hunter, *An Historical Journal*, p. 182; 'Letters of David Blackburn', p. 333. David Collins also recorded that the colonists often took between 2000 and 3000 a night, while more than thirty years after the event, Jacob Nagle put the count at 1200–1400. See David Collins, *An Account*, vol. 1, p. 151; Dann, *The Nagle Journal*, p. 125.

[11] *HRNSW*, vol. 1, part 2, p. 398; Bradley, *A Voyage*, p. 202; Fidlon and Ryan (eds), *Lieutenant Ralph Clark*, pp. 130, 131, 137, 139. See also Collins, *An Account*, vol. 1, pp. 150–1; *HRNSW*, vol. 2, p. 496.

[12] *HRNSW*, vol. 1, part 2, p. 400; Arthur Phillip, *The Voyage of Governor Phillip to Botany Bay*, p. 91; Hunter, *An Historical Journal*, pp. 183, 315–16, 333; Paul G. Fidlon and R. J. Ryan (eds), *The Journal of Philip Gidley King*, p. 46; Dann, *The Nagle Journal*, p. 124; Flannery, *The Future Eaters*, pp. 176–8, 189–93.

[13] Collins, *An Account*, vol. 1, p. 151; Dann, *The Nagle Journal*, p. 124.

[14] Hunter, *An Historical Journal*, p. 182; Dann, *The Nagle Journal*, p. 125.

[15] *HRNSW*, vol. 1, part 2, p. 398; Hunter, *An Historical Journal*, pp. 181–2; Collins, *An Account*, vol. 1, p. 151; Bradley, *A Voyage*, pp. 199–200; Fidlon and Ryan (eds), *Lieutenant Ralph Clark*, pp. 292–3; Dann, *The Nagle Journal*, p. 125.

[16] David Quamman, *The Song of the Dodo: Island Biogeography in an Age of Extinctions*, p. 308.

[17] Quamman, *The Song of the Dodo*, pp. 309–10.

[18] *HRNSW*, vol. 1, part 2, pp. 320, 381, 417; Fidlon and Ryan (eds), *Lieutenant Ralph Clark*, p. 125; Wright in Nobbs (ed.), *Norfolk Island*, p. 113.

[19] Hunter, *An Historical Journal*, pp. 183, 316; Collins, *An Account*, vol. 1, pp. 77, 96; Phillip, *Voyage*, p. 91; Bradley, *A Voyage*, p. 199; Valda Rigg, 'Convict Life: A "Tolerable Degree of Comfort"?' in Nobbs (ed.), *Norfolk Island*, p. 100.

[20] Hunter, *An Historical Journal*, pp. 182, 315; Collins, *An Account*, vol. 1, p. 151; Fidlon and Ryan (eds), *Lieutenant Ralph Clark*, pp. 131, 132, 137, 141, 284; Bradley, *A Voyage*, p. 205.

[21] Fidlon and Ryan (eds), *Lieutenant Ralph Clark*, pp. 137, 143.

[22] Fidlon and Ryan (eds), *Lieutenant Ralph Clark*, pp. 148–56, 293.

[23] Hunter, *An Historical Journal*, p.185; Fidlon and Ryan (eds), *Lieutenant Ralph Clark*, p. 293.

[24] *HRNSW*, vol. 1, part 2, p. 399; Hunter, *An Historical Journal*, pp. 185, 190.

[25] *HRNSW*, vol. 1, part 2, pp. 390–1, 416. This order could not be dated 7 August, as published in *HRNSW*, because the relief ships were spotted at dawn that day. More likely, the order was to take effect on 7 August.

[26] *HRNSW*, vol. 1, part 2, p. 400; Hunter, *An Historical Journal*, p. 185; Bradley, *A Voyage*, pp. 206–7; Dann, *The Nagle Journal*, p. 127.

[27] *HRNSW*, vol. 1, part 2, pp. 391, 402; Fidlon and Ryan (eds), *Lieutenant Ralph Clark*, pp. 141, 282, 284, 292; Dann, *The Nagle Journal*, p. 124.

[28] *HRNSW*, vol. 2, p. 496.

[29] Hunter, *An Historical Journal*, pp. 306–7.

[30] *HRNSW*, vol. 1, part 2, p. 212; Fidlon and Ryan (eds), *Lieutenant Ralph Clark*, p. 263; Robert Hughes, *The Fatal Shore*, pp. 95–6; John Ritchie, *The Wentworths: Father and Son*, p. 50.

[31] *HRNSW*, vol. 1, part 2, p. 399; Fidlon and Ryan (eds), *Lieutenant Ralph Clark*, p. 284; Alan Atkinson, *The Europeans in Australia: A History*, vol. 1, pp. 63, 72.

[32] *HRNSW*, vol. 1, part 2, pp. 319–20; Hunter, *An Historical Journal*, p. 386; Collins, *An Account*, vol. 1, pp. 104–5; Fidlon and Ryan (eds), *Lieutenant Ralph Clark*, p. 123; R. N. Dalkin, 'Norfolk Island—The First Settlement 1788–1814', p. 196; Fidlon and Ryan (eds), *Journal of Philip Gidley King*, pp. 343–5; Atkinson, *The Europeans*, vol. 1, p. 73.

[33] *HRNSW*, vol. 1, part 2, p. 381; Hunter, *An Historical Journal*, pp. 178–9; Rigg, 'Convict Life', p. 100; Atkinson, *The Europeans*, vol. 1, p. 73.

[34] *HRNSW*, vol. 1, part 2, p. 320; Hunter, *An Historical Journal*, p. 179; Fidlon and Ryan (eds), *Lieutenant Ralph Clark*, p. 123; Dalkin, 'Norfolk Island', p. 196.

[35] Dann, *The Nagle Journal*, p. 121.

[36] Hunter, *An Historical Journal*, p. 183.

[37] Richard Grove, *Ecology, Climate and Empire: Colonialism and Global Environmental History 1400–1940*, p. 40.

[38] Bradley, *A Voyage*, p. 202; Fidlon and Ryan (eds), *Lieutenant Ralph Clark*, pp. 128–9.

39 Dann, *The Nagle Journal*, p. 127.
40 *HRNSW*, vol. 1, part 2, p. 398; Fidlon and Ryan (eds), *Lieutenant Ralph Clark*, p. 128.
41 *HRNSW*, vol. 1, part 2, pp. 335, 398; Bradley, *A Voyage*, pp. 199, 201–3; Fidlon and Ryan (eds), *Lieutenant Ralph Clark*, pp. 128, 133.
42 HRNSW, vol. 1, part 2, p. 398; Fidlon and Ryan (eds), *Lieutenant Ralph Clark*, p. 128.
43 Keith Thomas, *Man and the Natural World: Changing Attitudes in England 1500–1800*, esp. pp. 15, 300–1. Compare Jack Goody, 'Man and the Natural World'.
44 *Gentleman's Magazine*, vol. 58, part 2, 1788, pp. 689–91; Michael Hunter, 'The Preconditions of Preservation: A Historical Perspective', in David Lowenthal and Marcus Binney (eds), *Our Past Before Us: Why Do We Save It?* p. 26.
45 Fidlon and Ryan (eds), *Lieutenant Ralph Clark*, p. 135.
46 Fidlon and Ryan (eds), *Lieutenant Ralph Clark*, pp. 179–80.
47 *HRA*, first series, vol. 1, p. 234.
48 *HRA*, first series, vol. 1, p. 141; Fidlon and Ryan (eds), *Journal of Philip Gidley King*, pp. 47, 91, 109, 133, 191–5, 201–3, 247, 251; Margaret Hazzard, *Punishment Short of Death: A History of the Penal Settlement at Norfolk Island*, p. 23; Alan Frost, 'The Growth of Settlement', p. 122.
49 *HRA*, series 1, vol. 1, p. 71; Collins, *An Account*, vol. 1, p. 77; Bradley, *A Voyage*, p. 221; M. L. Treadgold, *Bounteous Bestowal: The Economic History of Norfolk Island*, p. 21.
50 *HRA*, series 1, vol. 1, pp. 242–3; N. J. B. Plomley, *Friendly Mission: The Tasmanian Journals and Papers of George Augustus Robinson*, p. 264; Treadgold, *Bounteous Bestowal*, pp. 16–17.
51 *HRNSW*, vol. 1, part 2, p. 398; Hunter, *An Historical Journal*, pp. 182, 315–6; Bradley, *A Voyage*, p. 203; Fidlon and Ryan (eds), *Lieutenant Ralph Clark*, p. 136.
52 Bradley, *A Voyage*, p. 203; Fidlon and Ryan (eds), *Lieutenant Ralph Clark*, p. 136.
53 James Turner, *Reckoning with the Beast: Animals, Pain and Humanity in the Victorian Mind*, esp. p. 11; Thomas, *Man and the Natural World*, pp. 150–65, 279–80.
54 Fidlon and Ryan (eds), *Lieutenant Ralph Clark*, p. 220; J. B. Hirst, *Convict Society and its Enemies: A History of Early New South Wales*, p. 63; Rigg, 'Convict Life', p. 101; Hughes, *Fatal Shore*, pp. 114–18.
55 Fidlon and Ryan (eds), *Lieutenant Ralph Clark*, pp. xvi, 19, 22, 65.
56 Fidlon and Ryan (eds), *Lieutenant Ralph Clark*, pp. xvi, 122; Ritchie, *The Wentworths*, p. 56.
57 Fidlon and Ryan (eds), *Lieutenant Ralph Clark*, pp. 15, 18, 19, 20, 22.
58 Fidlon and Ryan (eds), *Lieutenant Ralph Clark*, p. 136.
59 Fidlon and Ryan (eds), *Lieutenant Ralph Clark*, pp. 136, 139; Bradley, *A Voyage*, p. 203.
60 Grove, *Green Imperialism*, esp. pp. 220, 271; Grove, *Ecology, Climate and Empire*, pp. 10–11.
61 Thomas, *Man and the Natural World*, pp. 143–4, 149–50.
62 Bradley, *A Voyage*, pp. 221–2. Ross was seemingly more optimistic. See *HRNSW*, vol. 1, part 2, p. 419.
63 *HRA*, vol. 1, p. 248; *HRNSW*, vol. 1, part 2, pp. 430, 470, 529, 533; Collins, *An Account*, vol. 1, pp. 137, 153–4, 162; 'Letters of David Blackburn', p. 333; George Mackaness (ed.), *Some Letters of Reverend Richard Johnson*, part 1, pp. 37–8; Fidlon and Ryan (eds), *Lieutenant Ralph Clark*, p. 189; Grove, *Ecology, Climate and Empire*, p. 143.
64 Fidlon and Ryan (eds), *Lieutenant Ralph Clark*, pp. 189, 190, 193. While David Collins reported from Sydney that the petrels were 'observed . . . to be quitting the island' in May 1791, Clark, who was actually on the island, suggests that they remained. See Collins, *An Account*, vol. 1, pp. 162–3; Fidlon and Ryan (eds), *Lieutenant Ralph Clark*, p. 200.
65 Fidlon and Ryan (eds), *Lieutenant Ralph Clark*, p. 200; Gilbert Whitley, 'The Doom of the Bird of Providence', p. 44.
66 Philip Gidley King, Despatch, 8 May 1792, CO201, vol. 9, no. 2, pp. 98–9; Collins, *An Account*, vol. 1, p. 177; Reg Wright, *The Forgotten Generations of Norfolk Island and Van Diemen's Land*, p. 69.
67 Philip Gidley King, Journal, March 1792, CO201, vol. 9, no. 2, pp. 98–9; vol. 10, no. 1, p. 290.
68 Philip Gidley King, Journal, March 1792, CO201, vol. 10, no. 1, p. 290.
69 An Act for Better Preservation of the Game within that Part of Great Britain called England 1770; William Blackstone, *Commentaries on the Laws of England*, vol. 4, pp. 175, 408–9; Philip Gidley King, Journal, March 1792, CO201, vol. 10, no. 1, p. 290.
70 Philip Gidley King, Journal, March 1792, CO201, vol. 10, no. 1, p. 290; Collins, *An Account*, vol. 1, p. 233.
71 Collins, *An Account*, vol. 1, p. 233.
72 Philip Gidley King, Despatch, 8 May 1792, CO201, vol. 10, no. 1, p. 308; *HRNSW*, vol. 1, part 2, pp. 658–9; Collins, *An Account*, vol. 1, p. 275; Treadgold, *Bounteous Bestowal*, p. 21.

[73] Philip Gidley King, Journal, May 1794, p. 145, MS70, NLA; Collins, *An Account*, vol. 1, pp. 363, 385.

[74] Philip Gidley King, Journal, March 1795, p. 198, MS70, NLA; Collins, *An Account*, vol. 1, p. 427.

[75] Philip Gidley King, Journal, May 1794, p. 145, MS70, NLA; Raymond Nobbs, 'Viewing the First Settlement', in Nobbs (ed.), *Norfolk Island*, p. 5.

[76] Philip Gidley King, Journal, March 1795, pp. 198–9, MS70, NLA.

[77] AJCP CO201/9/116; C0201/10/280; Wright in Nobbs (ed.), *Norfolk Island*, pp. 117, 120.

[78] W. S. Hill-Reid, *John Grant's Journey: A Convict's Story 1803–1811*, p. 121; Treadgold, *Bounteous Bestowal*, p. 21; Quamman, *The Song of the Dodo*, pp. 268–9.

[79] Matthew Flinders, *Observations on the Coast of Van Diemen's Land*, pp. 11, 26, 33.

[80] A. F. Basset Hull, 'The Birds of Lord Howe and Norfolk Islands', pp. 636–93; A. F. Basset Hull, 'Further Notes on the Birds of Lord Howe and Norfolk Islands', p. 784.

[81] Hull, 'The Birds of Lord Howe and Norfolk Islands', p. 650; Hull, 'Further Notes', p. 784.

[82] Fidlon and Ryan (eds), *Lieutenant Ralph Clark*, pp. 161, 282.

[83] Gregory M. Mathews, *The Birds of Australia*, vol. 2, pp. 141–9.

[84] Mathews, *Birds of Australia*, vol. 2, pp. 141, 148; Gregory M. Mathews and Tom Iredale, *A Manual of the Birds of Australia*, p. 34; Tom Iredale, 'Bird of Providence'. Cf Hughes, *Fatal Shore*, p. 101.

[85] Mathews, *Birds of Australia*, vol. 2, p. 148; K. A. Hindwood, *The Birds of Lord Howe Island*, pp. 41–2.

[86] Robert V. J. Varman, 'Material Life Including the Evidence from Archaeology' and Hicks, 'The Natural History of Norfolk Island', in Nobbs (ed.), *Norfolk Island*, pp. 157, 168; Calaby, *The Hunter Sketchbook*, p. 212.

[87] R. Schodde et al., *A Review of Norfolk Island Birds: Past and Present*, p. 83; Hicks in Nobbs (ed.), *Norfolk Island*, p. 169; Calaby, *The Hunter Sketchbook*, pp. 184, 188.

[88] T. R. Halliday, *Vanishing Birds: Their Natural History and Conservation*, p. 170; Jared Diamond, 'Historic Extinctions: A Rosetta Stone for Understanding Prehistoric Extinctions', in Paul S. Martin and Richard G. Klein (eds), *Quarternary Extinctions: A Prehistoric Revolution*, esp. pp. 838–9; Quamman, *The Song of the Dodo*, pp. 263–4.

[89] Schodde, Fullagar and Hermes, *A Review of Norfolk Island Birds*, p. 101; Neil Hermes, *Birds of Norfolk Island*.

CHAPTER TWO: NO PERSON SHOULD HAVE TWO HOUSES

[1] *New South Wales Pocket Almanack and Colonial Remembrancer for the Year of our Lord and Saviour 1806*, p. 1; Mr Bartrum, *Proceedings of a General Court-Martial . . . for the Trial of Lieut.-Col. Geo. Johnston . . . on a Charge of Mutiny*, pp. 81–2; K. S. Inglis, *The Australian Colonists: An Exploration of Social History 1788–1870*, p. 137. Cf C. M. H. Clark, *A History of Australia*, vol. 1, p. 218; Alan Atkinson, 'The British Whigs and the Rum Rebellion', p. 86.

[2] Atkinson, *The Europeans*, vol. 1, p. 289.

[3] *HRNSW*, vol. 6, p. 347; Bartrum, *Proceedings*, pp. 9, 25–6; George Mackaness, *The Life of Vice-Admiral William Bligh*, vol. 2, pp. 193–5.

[4] *HRNSW*, vol. 6, pp. lxv–lxviii, 575; Bartrum, *Proceedings*, pp. 26, 268, 371–3, 390–1.

[5] *HRNSW*, vol. 6, p. 692; Bartrum, *Proceedings*, pp. 114–17, 121–2, 137, 370; 'William Bligh's Chickens', p. 85.

[6] Bartrum, *Proceedings*, pp. 116, 121; H. V. Evatt, *Rum Rebellion*, ch. 31.

[7] *HRNSW*, vol. 6, p. 670; Bartrum, *Proceedings*, p. 120.

[8] *HRA*, series 3, vol. 3, p. 902. The significance of land to the rebellion has been recognised by Alan Atkinson, 'Taking Possession: Sydney's First Householders', in Graeme Aplin (ed.), *A Difficult Infant: Sydney before Macquarie*, pp. 72–3, 84–7; John Ritchie, 'Introduction' to *A Charge of Mutiny: The Court Martial of Lieutenant Colonel George Johnston for deposing Governor William Bligh in the Rebellion of 26 January 1808*, p. xvi. See also Ross Fitzgerald and Mark Hearn, *Bligh, Macarthur and the Rum Rebellion*, pp. 92–4, 120–1, 126; Atkinson, *The Europeans*, vol. 1, pp. xviii, 279–89. But Atkinson, Fitzgerald, Hearn and Ritchie have worked from the premiss that Bligh wrongfully invaded private property. For further discussion of the leasehold dimension of this question, see my 'Governor Phillip's Legacy' in P. N. Troy (ed.), *Equity, Environment and Efficiency*.

[9] Bartrum, *Proceedings*, p. 394.

[10] *HRA*, series 1, vol. 1, p. 48.

[11] *HRA*, series 1, vol. 1, p.143; Robert J. King, *The Secret History of the Convict Colony*, p. 135.

[12] *HRNSW*, vol. 2, pp. 775, 794.

[13] *HRA*, series 1, vol. 6, p. 714.

[14] *HRA*, series 1, vol. 1, p. 198; *HRNSW*, vol. 1, part 2, p. 359.

[15] *HRA*, series 1, vol. 6, p. 714; *The Beginnings of Government in Australia*, p. 16; Peter Bur-

roughs, *Britain and Australia 1831–1855*, p. 45; R. J. Ryan, *Land Grants 1788–1809*, p. 218.

16 *HRA*, series 1, vol. 6, p. 714; Ryan, *Land Grants*, p. 13; Atkinson, *The Europeans*, vol. 1, pp. 79–80.

17 *HRA*, series 1, vol. 1, pp. 667, 783; vol. 2, pp. 17–18; Brian H. Fletcher, 'The Hawkesbury Settlers and the Rum Rebellion', p. 48.

18 *HRNSW*, vol. 4, pp. 87–8, 113; 133, 135; Ryan, *Land Grants*, p. 233; James Broadbent, *The Australian Colonial House*, pp. 8–10. *HRA*, series 1, vol. 2, p. 742 suggests that 'it is probable that the grant was never validated, as it was contrary to Governor Phillip's ordinance that no grant should ever be made in the town of Sydney'. This argument is supported by the fact that in 1800 King seems to have agreed to compensate Kent only for his house, not the land. But the making of this grant is confirmed at *HRNSW*, vol. 3, p. 45; vol. 4, p. 113. It is also improbable that Kent would have erected a house at such cost without title to the land. Kent could also not have surrendered his grant if it had never been issued to him. The government register also noted when a grant was not executed. See Ryan, *Land Grants*, pp. 244–5.

19 *HRNSW*, vol. 4, pp. 402–3.

20 *HRNSW*, vol. 4, pp. 402–3; Bartrum, *Proceedings*, pp. 282–3. Compare Atkinson, *The Europeans*, vol. 1, p. 81.

21 *HRNSW*, vol. 4, pp. 402–3.

22 *HRNSW*, vol. 4, pp. 893–4; Ritchie, *The Wentworths*, pp. 84–8.

23 *HRA*, series 1, vol. 4, pp. 159, 243, 478; *HRNSW*, vol. 5, pp. 132, 530, 673; vol. 6, pp. 296, 687–8; Mackaness, *Life of Bligh*, vol. 2, p. 96; Clark, *A History*, vol. 1, pp. 161–5; George Parsons, 'The Commercialism of Honour: Early Australian Capitalism', in Aplin (ed.), *A Difficult Infant*, p. 113; Ritchie, *A Charge of Mutiny*, p. xiii.

24 *HRA*, series 1, vol. 6, p. 735; Ryan, *Land Grants*, pp. 152, 236, 243, 284–5; J. F. Campbell, 'Historical Notes on Government House Domain, Sydney', pp. 113, 116; Atkinson, *The Europeans*, vol. 1, p. 274.

25 Ryan, *Land Grants*, pp. 242, 244; Broadbent, *Australian Colonial House*, pp. 10–14.

26 Fletcher, 'The Hawkesbury Settlers and the Rum Rebellion', p. 234; Ryan, *Land Grants*, pp. 186, 190, 191.

27 Mackaness, *Life of Bligh*, vol. 1, pp. 96–7, 99; John Baalman, 'Gubernatorial Land Jobbing', esp. pp. 245–7.

28 *HRNSW*, vol. 5, pp. 638–9; Baalman, 'Gubernatorial Land Jobbing', pp. 244–5.

29 *HRNSW*, vol. 6, pp. 296, 417, 461–2; Mackaness, *Life of Bligh*, vol. 2, pp. 106–10, 150; D. R. Hainsworth, *The Sydney Traders: Simeon Lord and his Contemporaries*, p. 55; Atkinson, 'The British Whigs and the Rum Rebellion', pp. 73–90.

30 Mackaness, *Life of Bligh*, vol. 2, pp. 96–7, 131.

31 *HRNSW*, vol. 6, pp. 249–51, 153.

32 *The Beginnings of Government in Australia*, p. 16; Ryan, *Land Grants*, p. 218.

33 *SG*, 15 April 1804, p. 3; Atkinson, *The Europeans*, vol. 1, p. 393.

34 *HRNSW*, vol. 6, p. 347; Bartrum, *Proceedings*, p. 366; Mackaness, *Life of Bligh*, vol. 2, p. 96; Helen Proudfoot et al., *Australia's First Government House*, p. 103.

35 *HRNSW*, vol. 6, pp. 340, 343, 347; Bartrum, *Proceedings*, pp. 57, 59, 78, 134, 145, 188, 230, 236, 245, 364; Margaret Steven, 'Robert Campbell and the Bligh Rebellion', p. 350.

36 *HRNSW*, vol. 6, pp. 275–6, 347; Bartrum, *Proceedings*, pp. 59, 110, 126–7, 133–4, 393.

37 *HRNSW*, vol. 6, pp. 359; Mackaness, *Life of Bligh*, vol. 2, p. 152. See also *HRNSW*, vol. 6, p. 697.

38 *SG*, 26 July 1807, p. 1.

39 *HRNSW*, vol. 6, p. 360.

40 *HRNSW*, vol. 6, p. 589.

41 *HRNSW*, vol. 6, pp. 311; Bartrum, *Proceedings*, p. 245.

42 *HRNSW*, vol. 6, pp. 341, 346, 359–60, 612; Bartrum, *Proceedings*, pp. 147, 245.

43 *HRNSW*, vol. 6, pp. 359–60; Bartrum, *Proceedings*, pp. 386–7.

44 Bartrum, *Proceedings*, pp. 98–9, 107–8, 126–7.

45 *HRNSW*, vol. 6, pp. 339, 342–4, 347, 360.

46 *HRNSW*, vol. 6, pp. 311–12.

47 *HRNSW*, vol. 6, p. 305.

48 *HRNSW*, vol. 6, p. 305.

49 *HRNSW*, vol. 6, p. 656.

50 *HRNSW*, vol. 6, pp. 365, 372; Mackaness, *Life of Bligh*, vol. 2, p. 149.

51 Bartrum, *Proceedings*, pp. 145, 365.

52 *HRNSW*, vol. 6, p. 347; Bartrum, *Proceedings*, pp. 58–9, 364–7.

53 *SG*, 22 February 1807, p. 2; Bartrum, *Proceedings*, pp. 351, 363, 368; Mackaness, *Life of Bligh*, vol. 2, p. 149.

54 Bartrum, *Proceedings*, pp. 59, 276–8, 393–4; Mackaness, *Life of Bligh*, vol. 2, p. 183; Ryan, *Land Grants*, p. 242.

55 *HRNSW*, vol. 6, pp. 587–8; Bartrum, *Proceedings*, pp. 367–8; Atkinson, *The Europeans*, vol. 1, pp. 277–8.

56 Bartrum, *Proceedings*, pp. 148, 198–9, 228, 368, 371, 387, 394; Evatt, *Rum Rebellion*, pp. 187, 190.

57 *HRNSW*, vol. 6, p. 341, Bartrum, *Proceedings*, p. 180; Evatt, *Rum Rebellion*, p. 189.
58 *HRA*, series 1, vol. 6, pp. 424–5; Bartrum, *Proceedings*, pp. 168–9, 180–3, 228; Evatt, *Rum Rebellion*, pp. 188–9.
59 *HRNSW*, vol. 6, pp. 454, 468; Bartrum, *Proceedings*, p. 152.
60 *HRNSW*, vol. 6, p. 576; Bartrum, *Proceedings*, pp. 207, 389, 391.
61 Atkinson, *The Europeans*, vol. 1, pp. 272–3.
62 Bartrum, *Proceedings*, pp. 300, 356; Mackaness, *Life of Bligh*, vol. 2, pp. 272–3; Ryan, *Land Grants*, p. 261.
63 *HRNSW*, vol. 6, p. 751; Anne-Maree Whitaker, 'Joseph Foveaux: "A Gentleman of High Reputation"', p. 25. See also *HRNSW*, vol. 7, p. 237.
64 *HRNSW*, vol. 7, pp. 209–14.
65 Bartrum, *Proceedings*, pp. 57–9, 175, 186, 212–14, 217, 277, 298, 351, 365, 368, 371.
66 Bartrum, *Proceedings*, pp. 53, 175; J. M. Bennett, 'Richard Atkins: An Amateur Judge Jeffreys', p. 288; Atkinson, 'Taking Possession', p. 86.
67 Bartrum, *Proceedings*, p. 277.
68 Bartrum, *Proceedings*, pp. 386–7.
69 Bartrum, *Proceedings*, pp. 183–4, 207, 277–8, 280, 463.
70 *HRA*, series 1, vol. 7, p. 269; *HRNSW*, vol. 7, p. 403; Bartrum, *Proceedings*, pp. 57, 393–4.
71 Bartrum, *Proceedings*, pp. 58–9, 394.
72 Bartrum, *Proceedings*, pp. 184–5.
73 *HRA*, series 1, vol. 7, pp. 399–400, 460; series 3, vol. 1, pp. 512–13; *SG*, 11 May 1811, p. 1.

CHAPTER THREE: A PAINTER'S DELIGHT

1 John Glover, Application for Grant of Land, 1831, State Library of Tasmania.
2 Glover, Application; John Glover to Emma Lord, 26 August 1831, pc; *Godwin's Emigrant's Guide to Van Diemen's Land*, p. 10; Lloyd Robson, *A History of Tasmania*, vol. 1, p. 199.
3 *Morning Post*, 4 July 1835, p. 5; Robson, *A History of Tasmania*, vol. 1, p. 206.
4 Cf. T. M. Perry, *Australia's First Frontier: The Spread of Settlement in New South Wales 1788–1825*, p. 6.
5 William Gilpin, *Remarks on Forest Scenery and Woodland Views*, vol. 1, p. 1; Stephen Daniels, 'The Political Iconography of Woodland in Later Georgian England', in Denis Cosgrove and Stephen Daniels (eds), *The Iconography of Landscape*, pp. 43–4.
6 Worgan, *Journal*, pp. 9–10, 12, 23.
7 *HRNSW*, vol. 2, p. 392; Watkin Tench, *A Narrative of the Expedition to Botany Bay*, pp. 118–19; Watkin Tench, *A Complete Account of the Settlement at Port Jackson*, p. 130; Richard Neville, *A Rage for Curiosity*, pp. 17–18.
8 S. M. Onslow, *Some Early Records of the Macarthurs*, p. 30; A. T. Yarwood, *Samuel Marsden: The Great Survivor*, p. 46.
9 *HRNSW*, vol. 2, p. 817; Thomas Watling, *Letters from an Exile at Botany Bay to his Aunt in Dumfries*, p. 9; Bennett, 'Richard Atkins', p. 264.
10 *HRA*, series 1, vol. 6, p. 144; Robert Brown, 'General Remarks, Geographical and Systematical, on the Botany of Terra Australis', in Matthew Flinders, *A Voyage to Terra Australis*, vol. 2, p. 586; John Oxley, *Journal of Two Expeditions to the Interior of New South Wales*, p. 113; Onslow, *Some Early Records*, p. 312.
11 Edward Curr, *An Account of the Colony*, pp. iv, 14, 110; Robson, *A History of Tasmania*, vol. 1, p. 197; Mrs Charles Meredith, *Notes and Sketches of New South Wales*, p. 64; Peter Chapman (ed.), *The Diaries and Letters of G. T. W. B. Boyes: Volume 1, 1820–1832*, p. 219.
12 Barron Field, *Geographical Memoirs on New South Wales*, pp. 421–4.
13 Field, *Geographical Memoirs*, pp. 430, 443.
14 Henry Widowson, *Present State of Van Diemen's Land*, p. 175; John Henderson, *Observations on the Colonies of New South Wales and Van Diemen's Land*, p. 130.
15 *Geology and Natural History of the Various Countries visited by H. M. S.* Beagle, pp. 517, 518, 522, 525; Thomas Mitchell, *Three Expeditions into the Interior of Eastern Australia*, vol. 1, p. 318.
16 Chapman (ed.), *Diaries and Letters of G. T. W. B. Boyes*, pp. 169, 422, 431–2, 457.
17 Baron von Hügel, *New Holland Journal: November 1833–October 1834*, pp. 274–5.
18 Thomas Shepherd, *Lectures on Landscape Gardening in New South Wales*, p. 79.
19 Peter Cunningham, *Two Years in New South Wales*, vol. 2, pp. 56–8; Chapman (ed.), *Diaries and Letters of G. T. W. B. Boyes*, p. 496.
20 Cunningham, *Two Years in New South Wales*, vol. 1, pp. 87, 230; vol. 2, p. 58. See similarly T. Betts, *An Account of the Colony of Van Diemen's Land*, p. 92.
21 *HRA*, series 1, vol. 3, p. 176; vol. 5, p. 586; Gilpin, *Remarks*, vol. 1, p. 210; vol. 2, p. 303; John White, *Journal of a Voyage to New South Wales*, p. 143; Watkin Tench, *A Complete Account of the Settlement at Port Jackson*, pp. 144–5, 163; Alan E. J. Andrews (ed.), *The*

Devil's Wilderness: George Caley's Journey to Mount Banks 1804, p. 94.

[22] *House of Commons Select Committee on Transportation*, 1812, p. 78; *Godwin's Emigrant's Guide to Van Diemen's Land*, pp. 2, 31; *Lachlan Macquarie, Governor of New South Wales: Journals of his Tours in New South Wales and Van Diemen's Land 1810–1822*, pp. 17, 131, 132, 147, 149, 150, 157–8, 163, 207, 243.

[23] James Atkinson, *An Account of the State of Agriculture and Grazing in New South Wales*, p. 5; Thomas Mitchell, *Three Expeditions*, vol. 1, p. 71; Charles Wilkes, *Narrative of the United States Exploring Expedition during the Years 1838, 1839, 1840, 1841, 1842*, vol. 2, p. 178.

[24] Hügel, *New Holland Journal*, p. 430; Alan E. J. Andrews (ed.), *Stapylton: With Major Mitchell's Australia Felix Expedition 1836*, pp. 125, 142, 144, 183–4, 204. For a variant on this theme, see Godfrey Charles Mundy, *Our Antipodes*, vol. 1, pp. 200–1.

[25] W. C. Wentworth, *Statistical, Historical and Political Description of the Colony of New South Wales*, pp. 14–15, 47–8, 58–9; Curr, *An Account of the Colony*, pp. 30–1; Robert Dawson, *The Present State of Australia*, p. 48; Lang, *An Historical and Statistical Account of New South Wales*, vol. 1, pp. 353–4; Wilkes, *Narrative*, vol. 2, p. 189; Hügel, *New Holland Journal*, p. 274.

[26] *HRNSW*, vol. 5, p. 224; Sydney Parkinson, *Journal of a Voyage to the South Seas in his Majesty's Ship the Endeavour*, p. 134; Hunter, *An Historical Journal*, pp. 77, 402, 403; Darwin, *Journal*, p. 525; Onslow, *Some Early Records*, pp. 48, 87; *Lachlan Macquarie*, p. 146; Worgan, *Journal*, p. 45.

[27] Curr, *An Account of the Colony*, p. 27; Mrs G. R. Porter, *Alfred Dudley*, p. 30.

[28] Gilpin, *Remarks*, vol. 1, p. 181; William Gilpin, *Observations relative to Picturesque Beauty made in the Year 1771*, vol. 1, p. 9.

[29] Atkinson, *An Account of the State of Agriculture*, p. 6; Catherine Parr Traill, *The Backwoods of Canada*, pp. 61, 86; Paul Shepherd, *English Reaction to the New Zealand Landscape before 1850*, pp. 3, 21–3; Thomas, *Man and the Natural World*, p. 286; Hügel, *New Holland Journal*, p. 430; Simon Ryan, *The Cartographic Eye: How Explorers Saw Australia*, pp. 10, 74.

[30] Onslow, *Some Early Records*, p. 48; John Manning Ward, *James Macarthur: Colonial Conservative 1798–1867*, pp. 8–9.

[31] Hunter, *An Historical Journal*, pp. 46–7; Lang, *An Historical and Statistical Account of New South Wales*, vol. 2, p. 144; Plomley, *Friendly Mission*, p. 54; Stephen J. Pyne, *Burning Bush: A Fire History of Australia*, p. 96. Cf Hügel, *New Holland Journal*, p. 439.

[32] Curr, *An Account of the Colony*, p. 27; Dawson, *The Present State of Australia*, p. 52; Mitchell, *Three Expeditions*, vol. 1, p. 90; Ryan, *Land Grants*, p. 73.

[33] Worgan, *Journal*, p. 8.

[34] Tench, *A Complete Account*, p. 77; Wentworth, *A Statistical Account of the British Settlements in Australasia*, vol. 2, p. 42; G. Paterson, *The History of New South Wales*, p. 149; J. F. Campbell, 'Rose Hill Government Farm and the Founding of Parramatta', p. 357; Bradley, *A Voyage*, p. 232; Ritchie (ed.), *The Evidence to the Bigge Reports*, vol. 1, p. 76.

[35] *HRA*, series 1, vol. 1, part 2, pp. 127, 306; vol. 10, pp. 723–4; vol. 11, pp. 323–4; Onslow, *Some Early Records*, p. 49; Atkinson, *An Account of the State of Agriculture*, pp. 87–8.

[36] *HRA*, series 1, vol. 7, pp. 551–2, 626; series 3, vol. 1, p. 645; *HRNSW*, vol. 7, p. 542; Curr, *An Account of the Colony*, pp. 164–5.

[37] Anne McKay (ed.), *Journals of the Land Commissioners for Van Diemen's Land 1826–28*, p. 9; Ritchie (ed.), *The Evidence to the Bigge Reports*, vol. 1, pp. 73–4; Robson, *A History of Tasmania*, vol. 1, p. 203.

[38] *Hobart Town Almanack for the Year 1829*, pp. 113, 120–1.

[39] Widowson, *Present State of Van Diemen's Land*, p. 80; Barrie Dyster, *Servant and Master: Building and Running the Grand Houses of Sydney 1788–1850*, p. 91.

[40] Traill, *The Backwoods of Canada*, p. 196; Marcia Fowler, *The Embroidered Tent: Five Gentlewomen in Early Canada*, pp. 70–2.

[41] *Hobart Town Almanack for the year 1830*, p. 91; Joseph Lycett, *Views in Australia*, text accompanying plates 5, 7; George Bennett, *Wanderings in New South Wales*, vol. 1, p. 199; Yarwood, *Samuel Marsden*, p. 88.

[42] Wentworth, *Statistical, Historical and Political Description of the Colony of New South Wales*, pp. 88–9; James Wallis, *An Historical Account of New South Wales*, p. 1; Robert Dixon, *The Course of Empire: Neo-classical Culture in New South Wales*, pp. 1, 61, 68.

[43] *Report of the Commissioner of Inquiry on the State of Agriculture and Trade in the Colony of New South Wales*, p. 7; Robert Gouger (ed.), *A Letter from Sydney: The Principal Town of Australasia*, pp. 6, 9–10.

[44] Cunningham, *Two Years in New South Wales*, vol. 2, pp. 172–4; Widowson, *Present State of Van Diemen's Land*, p. 81.

45 Atkinson, *An Account of the State of Agriculture,* p. 86; Cunningham, *Two Years in New South Wales*, vol. 2, p. 173; Shepherd, *Lectures on Landscape Gardening*, pp. 5–6; Hügel, *New Holland Journal*, p. 260.

46 Anna Jameson, *Winter Studies and Summer Rambles in Canada*, vol. 1, pp. 66, 96–7; vol. 2, pp. 102–3, 225; Michael Williams, *Americans and their Forests*, pp. 120–4.

47 *Godwin's Emigrant's Guide to Van Diemen's Land*, p. 38; Traill, *The Backwoods of Canada*, pp. 56–7, 132, 194, 311.

48 James Macarthur, *New South Wales: Its Present State and Future Prospects*, pp. 185–6.

49 W. Neate Chapman to his mother, 18 October 1792, A1974, p. 18, ML; Jane Lennon, 'Second Thoughts on First Views: The Port Jackson Circle 1788–1800', p. 37.

50 *HRA*, series 1, vol. 3, pp. 257–8; vol. 4, pp. 362–3; vol. 5, pp. 67–8; *SG*, 9 December 1815, p. 1.

51 Curr, *An Account of the Colony*, pp. 119–20; Chapman (ed.), *Diaries and Letters of G. T. W. B. Boyes*, pp. 169, 177.

52 Atkinson, *The Europeans*, pp. 83, 89, 93.

53 Widowson, *Present State of Van Diemen's Land*, pp. 81–2; *Hobart Town Almanack for 1832*, p. 119; Mrs Augustus Prinsep (ed.), *The Journal of a Voyage from Calcutta to Van Diemen's Land*, p. 62.

54 Graham Connah, 'Historical Reality, Archaeology Reality: Excavations at Regentville, Penrith, New South Wales, 1985', pp. 30–1; Hügel, *New Holland Journal*, pp. 259–60, 269–70, 274–5. See also Lang, *An Historical and Statistical Account of New South Wales*, vol. 2, p. 148.

55 Shepherd, *Lectures on Landscape Gardening*, pp. viii, 76, 90; James Broadbent, 'Introduction' to *Colonial Greek: The Greek Revival in New South Wales 1810–1850*; Broadbent, *The Australian Colonial House*, pp. 167–8.

56 Tench, *A Complete Account*, pp. 75–7.

57 Atkinson, *The Europeans*, vol. 1, pp. 89–90.

58 Traill, *The Backwoods of Canada*, pp. 197–9; Jameson, *Winter Studies and Summer Rambles*, vol. 1, p. 96.

59 Thomas Shepherd, *Lectures on the Horticulture of New South Wales*, p. 78; Shepherd, *Lectures on Landscape Gardening*, pp. 2, 4, 78.

60 Shepherd, *Lectures on Landscape Gardening*, pp. 2, 5–7, 87–8. See also Wilkes, *Narrative*, vol. 2, p. 191.

61 Shepherd, *Lectures on Landscape Gardening*, pp. 87–91

62 Shepherd, *Lectures on Landscape Gardening*, p. 2; Dyster, *Servant and Master*, p. 109.

63 John Glover to Emma Lord, 26 August 1831, pc; Tim Bonyhady, *Images in Opposition: Australian Landscape Painting 1801–1890*, pp. 5–6; Chapman (ed.), *Diaries and Letters of G. T. W. B. Boyes*, p. 421; Andrew Sayers, 'Transcendent Topography: J. M. W. Turner and Australian Painting', pp. 506–11.

64 John Glover, Sketchbook, Tasmanian Museum and Art Gallery; John McPhee, *The Art of John Glover*, p. 34.

65 Bonyhady, *Images in Opposition*, chs 2, 3.

66 John Glover to Emma Lord, 26 August 1831, pc; Chapman (ed.), *Diaries and Letters of G. T. W. B. Boyes*, p. 422.

67 John Glover to Emma Lord, 26 August 1831, pc; John McPhee, *The Art of John Glover*, pp. 42–3; Ian McLean, 'Your Own Land is the Best: The Limits of Redemption in Australian Colonial Art', pp. 128.

68 Press Cuttings from English Newspapers on Matters of Artistic Interest 1686–1835, vol. 6, p. 1649; McPhee, *The Art of John Glover*, p. 27

69 *Times*, 29 June 1835, p. 5; *Morning Post*, 4 July 1835, p. 5.

70 J. Massingberd Campbell, Diary, p. 58, MSS 1644, ML; George Augustus Robinson to John Glover, 25 March 1836, Robinson papers, vol. 22, ML; Chapman (ed.), *Diaries and Letters of G. T. W. B. Boyes*, p. 476.

71 Sharon Morgan, *Land Settlement in Early Tasmania: Creating an Antipodean England*, p. 93.

72 McPhee, *The Art of John Glover*, pp. 59–60

73 J. Massingberd Campbell, Diary, p. 57; McPhee, *The Art of John Glover*, p. 60.

74 James Backhouse, Journal, 9 May 1833, part 6, p. 41, B730, ML; McPhee, *The Art of John Glover*, p. 59; Ron Radford, *John Glover's House and Garden*; Trevor Nottle, 'John Glover', p. 24.

75 Nottle, 'John Glover', p. 24.

76 Curr, *An Account of the Colony*, pp. 11–12; McPhee, *The Art of John Glover*, p. 59; Paul Paffen, 'Forgotten Faces? Portraits and other Images of the Convict in Van Diemen's Land', pp. 75–7.

77 Bonyhady, *Images in Opposition*, pp. 73–4.

78 McPhee, *The Art of John Glover*, pp. 64, 66.

79 McPhee, *The Art of John Glover*, p. 66.

80 James Backhouse, Journal, 1833, part 6, p. 41, ML; McPhee, *The Art of John Glover*, p. 59; Morgan, *Land Settlement*, p. 107. The foreground of this painting appears to be based on a sketch from about 1835 (John Glover, Sketchbook, NK644/2, vol. 1, no. 6, NLA). That Glover used this sketch five years

later, when he easily could have made a new one, suggests that this part of his view remained more or less unchanged through these years.

CHAPTER 4: FERN FEVER

1 *ISN*, 15 June 1878, p. 6, 2 September 1881, pp. 18–19; *Australasian*, 22 November 1884, p. 967, 7 November 1885, p. 871; Terence Lane and Jessie Serle, *Australians at Home: A Documentary History of Australian Domestic Interiors from 1788 to 1914*, pp. 112, 175–6, 347–8.

2 William Woolls, *A Contribution to the Flora of Australia*, p. 36; F. M. Bailey, *Fern World of Australia*, preface; Plomley, *Friendly Mission*, p. 371.

3 Gilpin, *Remarks*, vol. 1, p. 219; David Elliston Allen, *The Victorian Fern Craze: A History of Pteridomania*, esp. pp. 19, 49, 56–61.

4 Bailey, *Fern World of Australia*, preface; Onslow, *Some Early Records*, p. 26; Graeme Davison, *The Rise and Fall of Marvellous Melbourne*, p. 140; Richard Barley, 'Plants from Old Nursery Catalogues', p. 19; John Foster, 'Natives in the Nineteenth Century Garden', p. 4; Yarwood, *Samuel Marsden*, p. 46.

5 Mundy, *Our Antipodes*, vol. 2, p. 27; Bonwick, *Western Victoria*, p. 64; Woolls, *A Contribution*, p. 40; Sophie C. Ducker (ed.), *The Contented Botanist: Letters of W. H. Harvey about Australia and the Pacific*, p. 153.

6 Cunningham, *Two Years in New South Wales*, vol. 1, p. 116; *Illustrated London News*, 15 November 1856, p. 491; *Argus*, supplement, 3 March 1866, p. 1, 18 February 1893, p. 4; *IMP*, 8 October 1868, p. 160.

7 *Argus*, 20 October 1854, p. 5, 25 October 1854, p. 5, supplement, 3 March 1866, p. 1; *Illustrated London News*, 15 November 1856, p. 491; *Age*, 16 October 1857, p. 5; *Australasian*, 22 December 1866, p. 1188; *Offical Catalogue of the Melbourne Exhibition, 1854*, pp. 45–6.

8 *Age*, 16 October 1857, p. 5, 8 December 1857, p. 5; *TPRSV*, vol. 8, 1867, p. 319; *DA*, 4 July 1889, p. 1; Tim Bonyhady, *Australian Colonial Paintings in the Australian National Gallery*, pp. 172–3.

9 *Argus*, 4 December 1857, p. 5; *H*, 5 December 1857, p. 5; *IJA*, vol. 4, 1858, p. 35.

10 *Argus*, 4 December 1857, p. 5; 29 December 1857, p. 4.

11 *IJA*, vol. 4, 1858, p. 95; *News Letter of Australasia*, February 1858, p. 4; *Argus*, 31 July 1858, p. 4, 11 March 1859, p. 6, 12 March 1859, p. 6; *H*, 4 February 1858, p. 5, 4 August 1858, p. 5, 16 April 1863, p. 2; *Age*, 13 January 1859, p. 5; *IMP*, 18 April 1863, p. 9.

12 A. W. Howitt to Anna Mary Howitt, 15 January 1858, LTL; *Argus*, 4 December 1857, p. 5, 13 August 1858, p. 6; *IJA*, March 1858, p. 120; *Melbourner Deutsche Zeitung*, 2 December 1859, p. 77; *Age*, 20 November 1860, p. 5; Marjorie Theobald, 'Julie Vieusseux: The Lady Principal and her School', in Marilyn Lake and Farley Kelly (eds), *Double Time: Women in Victoria—150 Years*, pp. 78–85.

13 A. W. Howitt to Anna Mary Howitt, 15 January 1858, LTL.

14 A. W. Howitt to Anna Mary Howitt, 15 January 1858, LTL.

15 Richard Twopeny, *Town Life in Australia*, esp. pp. 231, 238; Grove, *Green Imperialism*, p. 481; Grove, *Ecology, Climate and Empire*, p. 19.

16 *Argus*, 26 November 1861, p. 4; 29 November 1861, p. 4.

17 *TT*, 15 July 1887, p. 1.

18 James Smith, *Cyclopedia of Victoria*, vol. 1, p. 220. Compare Wright, *The Bureaucrats' Domain*, p. 130.

19 *Argus*, 29 November 1861, p. 4.

20 *Argus*, 29 November 1861, p. 4.

21 *Argus*, 22 November 1861, p. 5; 29 November 1861, p. 4.

22 *VGG*, 1857, p. 620; 1862, pp. 350–1; A. D. Hardy, 'John Hardy: Early Victorian Surveyor', p. 9.

23 *VGG*, vol. 33, 1867, p. 698; vol. 39, 1870, p. 221; Helen Coulson, *Story of the Dandenongs*, p. 26; Sandra Bardwell, *Ferntree Gully National Park: A Centenary History 1882–1982*, p. 4; Wright, *The Bureaucrats' Domain*, pp. 155, 192, 231, 247–9.

24 *IANHR*, 23 December 1865, pp. 8, 13.

25 *Argus*, supplement, 3 March 1866, p. 1; *Australasian*, 22 December 1866, p. 1188.

26 James Hingston, *Guide for Excursionists from Melbourne*, pp. 25–8; 1869, 2nd ed., p. 168; *Age*, 3 December 1869, p. 3; 4 December 1869, p. 3; *Visitors' Guide to the Upper Yarra and Fern Tree Gully District*, pp. 97–8; Coulson, *Story of the Dandenongs*, p. 26.

27 *Age*, 4 December 1869, p. 3; *Argus*, 4 December 1869, p. 6; Hingston, *Guide for Excursionists*, 1868, p. 24.

28 *VGG*, vol. 40, 1870, p. 1840.

29 *VGG*, vol. 45, 1873, p. 725; 'Papers Relating to Forest Conservancy', *VPP*, 1874, vol. 3, pp. 1–2, 8.

30 *The National Mutual Life Association's Guide*

to Melbourne, p. 30; Garnet Walch, *Victoria in 1880*, pp. 44–6; *Australasian*, 2 April 1881, p. 423; *AS*, 25 March 1882, p. 81, 13 February 1884, p. 19; *Age*, 5 July 1883, p. 7; *MB*, 21 November 1884, p. 6; *DA*, 13 January 1887, p. 2.

31 C. French, 'Victorian Ferns and their Habitats', *SSR*, no. 12, November 1881, p. 189; no. 13, December 1881, p. 207; Bailey, *Fern World of Australia*, preface; E. C. Spicer, 'A Holiday Ramble in Victoria', *SQM*, October 1883, pp. 66, 70; William Clarson, *The Flower Garden and Shrubbery*, n.p.

32 *Argus*, 30 November 1881, p. 10; *R v Rodd; ex parte Bucknall* [1881] 7 VLR 447; C. French, 'Victorian Ferns and their Habitats', *SSR*, no. 3, February 1881, p. 36; Alexander G. Hamilton, 'A Naturalist's Notes from Illawarra', p. 33; Alexander G. Hamilton, 'On the Effect which Settlement in Australia has produced upon Indigenous Vegetation', p. 184.

33 Land Act 1869 (Vic.), s. 94.

34 *Age*, 29 November 1881, p. 3; *Argus*, 29 November 1881, p. 5, 30 November 1881, p. 10; *R v Rodd; ex parte Bucknall* [1881]; Wright, *The Bureaucrats' Domain*, p. 232.

35 *Argus*, 29 November 1881, p. 5; *H*, 29 November 1881, p. 2; *DA*, 28 March 1883, p. 2, 4 April 1883, p. 2; *VGG*, vol. 55, 1878, p. 238, vol. 63, 1882, pp. 667, 1011; *VPD*, vol. 38, 1881, p. 975; Coulson, *Story of the Dandenongs*, p. 27; Sandra Bardwell, The National Park Movement in Victoria, p. 390; Bardwell, *Ferntree Gully National Park*, pp. 7–8; Wright, *The Bureaucrats' Domain*, p. 233.

36 *VGG*, vol. 65, 1883, p. 1678; Clarson, *The Flower Garden*, p. 104; *DA*, 13 January 1887, p. 2; 15 March 1888, p. 2; *Visitors' Guide to the Upper Yarra*, p. 10.

37 Archibald J. Campbell, 'A Day's Ferning on Mount Macedon', in his *Nests and Eggs of Australian Birds*, 1883, pp. xxiii–xxv; *Age*, 4 December 1889, p. 5; Paul Fox, 'The Simla of the South', p. 11; Francis Gilfedder, 'The Early Nursery Industry at Macedon Ranges', p. 20.

38 *Argus*, 24 July 1907, p. 7; *Bohemia*, 23 October 1890, p. 4; *Bulletin*, 25 July 1907, p. 9; *Lone Hand*, 2 September 1907, pp. 520–1; Francis Myers, *Irrigation or the New Australia*, p. 2.

39 *Australasian*, 5 April 1879, p. 434; *Argus*, 22 February 1888, p. 13, 3 March 1888, p. 11, 24 March 1888, p. 5, 27 March 1888, p. 4; *Visitors' Guide to the Upper Yarra*, p. 90; *VN*, vol. 4, 1887–88, pp. 66, 197–8; vol. 5, 1888–9, p. 2; *PRSV*, vol. 1, 1888–9, p. 118; Jane Lennon, 'Wilson's Promontory: Its Commercial Utilisation in the 19th Century', pp. 198–9.

40 *Argus*, 24 March 1888, p. 5; 15 December 1888, p. 13.

41 *Argus*, 24 March 1888, p. 5.

42 *Argus*, 24 March 1888, p. 5.

43 *DA*, 3 October 1889, p. 7; *Age*, 4 December 1889, p. 4; Inglis, *The Australian Colonists*, pp. 76–82; Geoffrey Serle, *The Rush to be Rich*, pp. 156–60.

44 *DA*, 14 January 1896, p. 2; Bardwell, *Ferntree Gully National Park*, pp. 9–10.

45 *Visitors' Guide to the Upper Yarra*, pp. 94–5, 101. See similarly *ISN*, 26 July 1888, p. 26.

46 *Age*, 4 December 1889, p. 5. See also *Argus*, 22 November 1890, p. 4.

47 L. E. Hervey, entry for 13 December 1889, 'Diary of a Tour Round the World 1889 and 1890', MS 12591, box 3420/2, LTL; *Age*, 4 December 1889, p. 5; *Visitors' Guide to the Upper Yarra*, p. 94.

48 *Age*, 10 November 1890, p. 5, 11 November 1890, p. 5; *Argus*, 11 November 1890, p. 5.

49 *Argus*, 11 November 1890, p. 5; 12 November 1890, p. 7.

50 *Argus*, 12 November 1890, p. 7; *DA*, 18 December 1890, p. 2.

51 *Argus*, 18 February 1893, p. 4.

52 *Argus*, 12 November 1890, p. 7; 20 February 1893, p. 6.

53 *Age*, 11 April 1893, p. 6; *Argus*, 11 April 1893, p. 7; Michael Cannon, *The Land Boomers*, pp. 21, 26–7.

54 *Age*, 11 April 1893, p. 6; *Argus*, 11 April 1893, p. 7.

55 *Argus*, 12 April 1893, p. 6, 17 April 1893, p. 5, 27 April 1893, pp. 5, 7, 4 May 1893, p. 7; Cannon, *Land Boomers*, pp. 192, 194; R. E. W. Kennedy, 'The Leongatha Labour Colony: Founding an Anti-Utopia', pp. 54–8; J. M. Powell, 'An Australian Utopia', p. 328.

56 *Argus*, 12 April 1893, p. 6, 17 April 1893, p. 5, 20 April 1893, p. 6; *VN*, vol. 9, 1892–93, p. 49; Coulson, *Story of the Dandenongs*, pp. 27, 29.

57 *Age*, 12 April 1893, p. 4; *Argus*, 13 April 1893, p. 4, 18 April 1893, p. 9, 20 April 1893, p. 6.

58 *Age*, 26 April 1893, p. 7. See also *Argus*, 20 April 1893, p. 4, 21 April 1893, p. 7, 24 April 1893, p. 6.

59 *Argus*, 19 April 1893, p. 9; Cannon, *Land Boomers*, p. 22.

60 *Argus*, 19 April 1893, p. 9; 20 April 1893, p. 9; 26 April 1893, p. 9; 2 March 1894, p. 6.

61 *Age*, 25 April 1893, p. 6, 4 May 1893, p. 3; *Argus*, 3 May 1893, p. 9, 4 May 1893, p. 7, 12 May 1893, p. 5; *DA*, 11 May 1893, p. 2; *VN*, vol. 10, 1893–4, p. 18; *PRSV*, vol. 6, 1893, p. 241.

62 *Age*, 27 April 1893, p. 4, 4 May 1893, p. 3;

Argus, 21 April 1893, p. 6, 4 May 1893, p. 7, 18 May 1893, p. 5.

63 R. S. Sugars, 'A Trip to Sassafras Gully', pp. 68–71; R. S. Sugars, 'Excursion to Sassafras Gully on 3rd November 1891', 116–19; *Argus*, 20 May 1893, p. 9.

64 *Argus*, 13 April 1893, p. 9; *DA*, 7 December 1893, p. 2.

65 *APJ*, 21 March 1898, p. 68; *DA*, 12 January 1899, p. 2; Bardwell, The National Park Movement in Victoria, p. 391.

66 *Age*, 7 August 1893, p. 6, 12 August 1893, p. 15; *VGG*, vol. 79, 1893, p. 1945; Campbell, *Nests and Eggs of Australian Birds*, 1901, part 1, pp. 519–20.

67 *DA*, 5 October 1893, supplement, p. 4; Coulson, *Story of the Dandenongs*, pp. 49, 343, 374; Kennedy, 'The Leongatha Labour Colony', p. 54; K. A. Patterson, 'Battlers of the 1890s', pp. 43–4.

68 *Age*, 3 March 1894, pp. 9–10, 7 March 1894, p. 6; *VPD*, vol. 74, 1894, p. 1137; L. J. Blake, 'Village Settlements', p. 198.

69 *DA*, 12 January 1899, p. 2; Coulson, *Story of the Dandenongs*, pp. 52–3.

70 *Argus*, 2 March 1894, p. 6; *DA*, 14 September 1905, p. 2; Coulson, *Story of the Dandenongs*, p. 53; Michael Jones, *Prolific in God's Gifts: A Social History of Knox and the Dandenongs*, pp. 122, 124.

CHAPTER FIVE: LOUISA

1 Louisa Anne Twamley, *Poems*, preface; Vivienne Rae Ellis, *Louisa Anne Meredith: A Tigress in Exile*, pp. 37–9.

2 *Athenaeum*, 1836, pp. 485–6, 501–2, 672–3; 1845, p. 66; Elizabeth Rigby, 'Lady Travellers', p. 106; Wilfred Blunt, *The Art of Botanical Illustration*, p. 220.

3 *SMH*, 1 March 1845, p. 3; *HTC*, 14 January 1846, p. 3; Margaret Swann, 'Mrs Meredith and Miss Atkinson: Writers and Naturalists', p. 5.

4 Mrs Charles Meredith, *My Home in Tasmania* [*MHT*], vol. 1, pp. viii–ix, 169; Vivienne Rae Ellis, 'Louisa Anne Meredith' in Joan Kerr (ed.), *The Dictionary of Australian Artists*, pp. 528–30.

5 Sara Maroske, '"The Whole Great Continent as a Present": Nineteenth-Century Australian Women Workers in Science', in Farley Kelly (ed.), *On the Edge of Discovery*, p. 29.

6 Louisa Anne Meredith to James Smith, 18 October 1868, 15 August 1884, 12 August 1891, MSS 212/2, ML; Louisa Anne Meredith, *Our Island Home: A Tasmanian Sketch Book* [*OIH*], pp. 8, 13, 20; Ellis, *Louisa Anne Meredith*, pp. 43, 217–18; Robson, *A History of Tasmania*, vol. 2, p. 18.

7 Louisa Anne Meredith, *Over the Straits: A Visit to Victoria* [*OS*], p. 44.

8 Louisa Anne Meredith, *Loved and Lost!* [*LL*], p. 12. See also *LE*, 17 July 1879, p. 2.

9 Patricia Clarke, *Pioneer Writer: The Life of Louisa Atkinson*, esp. pp. 190, 192; Elizabeth Lawson, *The Natural Art of Louisa Atkinson*, pp. 85–6.

10 See Judith Johnston, '"Women's Testimony": Imperialist Discourse in the Professional Colonial Travel Writing of Louisa Anne Meredith and Catherine Parr Traill', pp. 34–55.

11 Turner, *Reckoning with the Beast*, pp. 40, 44; Thomas, *Man and the Natural World*, p. 149. The only British legislation to excite an immediate response was the first comprehensive statute governing cruelty in 1849, which New South Wales copied within a year.

12 Thomas, *Man and the Natural World*, pp. 153, 180–2.

13 Meredith, *OS*, p. 206; Thomas, *Man and the Natural World*, pp. 153, 297.

14 Meredith, *Notes and Sketches of New South Wales during a Residence in the Colony from 1839 to 1844* [*NSNSW*], pp. 49, 111–2; Meredith, *MHT*, vol. 1, pp. 96, 113, 173, 176, 178; Thomas, *Man and the Natural World*, p. 153.

15 Meredith, *NSNSW*, p. 25; Meredith, *MHT*, vol. 1, pp. 33–4.

16 Meredith, *MHT*, vol. 1, p. 34; Meredith, *LL*, pp. 13, 18; Meredith, *OS*, pp. 189, 207; Louisa Anne Meredith, *Tasmanian Friends and Foes* [*TFF*], p. 181; Joan M. Buchanan, Mrs Charles Meredith: A Biography (1812–1895), p. 111.

17 Meredith, *NSNSW*, p. 63.

18 Field, *Geographical Memoirs*, pp. 447–8; Meredith, *NSNSW*, p. 112; Richard Darwin Keynes (ed.), *Charles Darwin's Beagle Diary*, pp. 401.

19 Field, *Geographical Memoirs*, pp. 447–8; Eric Rolls, *They All Ran Wild*, pp. 388–93; Keynes (ed.), *Charles Darwin's Beagle Diary*, p. 401.

20 Field, *Geographical Memoirs*, p. 448; Meredith, *NSNSW*, p. 112.

21 N. L. Kentish, *Work in the Bush*, p. 29; Meredith, *MHT*, vol. 1, pp. 244–6. Tasmania's Kangaroo Hunting Act 1846 was designed not to protect the kangaroos but simply to stop sheep and cattle thieves roaming the island under the pretence of being kangaroo hunters. See *HTC*, 14 July 1846, p. 2.

22 *HRA*, series 3, vol. 1, pp. 264–5; Meredith, *MHT*, vol. 1, p. 98; Meredith, *TFF*, p. 158.

23 Louisa Anne Meredith, *Walch's Tasmanian Guide Book* [*WTGB*], pp. 115–6.

24 Louisa Anne Twamley, *The Romance of Nature*, p. 191, republished in Louisa Anne Twamley, *Our Wild Flowers*, p. 249; Meredith, *MHT*, vol. 1, pp. 123, 125; vol. 2, pp. 161, 164–5; Meredith, *Some of My Bush Friends in Tasmania* [*SMBFT*], p. 49; Meredith, *TFF*, p. 219.

25 Meredith, *MHT*, vol. 2, p. 206; Meredith, *WTGB*, p. 60.

26 Meredith, *WTGB*, p. 60.

27 *Papers and Proceedings of the Royal Society of Tasmania*, 1876, pp. 8, 11, 24, 61.

28 Louisa Anne Meredith, *OIH*, pp. 9–11; Meredith, *TFF*, pp. 139–40; Meredith, *SMBFT*, p. 26.

29 Meredith, *SMBFT*, p. 54.

30 Meredith, *NSNSW*, pp. 40, 59–60, 74, 110, 121, 124; Meredith, *MHT*, vol. 1, pp. 26, 28.

31 Wilkes, *Narrative*, vol. 2, p. 190; Paul de Strzelecki, *Physical Description of New South Wales*, p. 242.

32 Meredith, *MHT*, vol. 1, pp. 27, 57–9, 66–7, 71–2, 88, 108; vol. 2, pp. 111, 126–7, 132, 137, 144.

33 Mundy, *Our Antipodes*, vol. 1, pp. 153, 190; vol. 2, p. 25; Meredith, *MHT*, vol. 1, pp. 72–3, 88, 108–9, 169; vol. 2, pp. 68, 126.

34 Sallyann Dakis, 'The Botanical Art of Mary Morton Allport', p. 13.

35 Meredith, *LL*, notes, p. 1.

36 Meredith, *SMBFT*, p. 54.

37 Meredith, *OIH*, preface, p. 26.

38 Louisa Anne Twamley, *The Annual of British Landscape Scenery 1839: An Autumn Ramble on the Wye*, preface, p. 10; Bernard Smith, *European Vision and the South Pacific*, p. 226.

39 *HRNSW*, vol. 2, p. 666.

40 John Hood, *Australia and the East*, pp. 91–2.

41 Woolls, *Miscellanies*, p. 87.

42 James Martin, *The Australian Sketch Book*, esp. pp. 45–6, 109; Elena Grainger, *Martin of Martin Place*, pp. 21–2.

Mundy, *Our Antipodes*, vol. 2, pp. 23–4; Elena Grainger, *The Remarkable Reverend Clarke*, p. 76.

44 Meredith, *NSNSW*, pp. 79–80.

45 Meredith, *OIH*, p. 16.

46 Turner, *Reckoning with the Beast*, pp. 35–6; Thomas, *Man and the Natural World*, p. 184.

47 Meredith, *MHT*, vol. 1, pp. 188, 190; N. J. B. Plomley (ed.), *Weep in Silence: A History of the Flinders Island Aboriginal Settlement*, p. 353; N. J. B. Plomley, *The Aboriginal/Settler Clash in Van Diemen's Land 1803–1831*, pp. 59, 67, 70, 74–6, 80, 93, 99.

48 J. S. Cumpston, *Kangaroo Island 1800–1836*, pp. 131, 145–7, 179; Plomley, *Weep in Silence*, pp. 353, 366, 405, 414, 654, 670–1, 677; Grimshaw, 'Writing the History of Aboriginal and White Women in Colonial Tasmania', pp. 1–11.

49 *South Australian Register*, 25 September 1844, p. 3; 28 September 1844, p. 3; Ellis, *Louisa Anne Meredith*, p. 58.

50 Meredith, *NSNSW*, pp. 92–4, 126. See also D. W. A. Baker, *The Civilised Surveyor: Thomas Mitchell and the Australian Aborigines*, p. 36.

51 Darwin, *Journal*, p. 553; John Lort Stokes, *Discoveries in Australia*, vol. 2, pp. 463–4; Mundy, *Our Antipodes*, vol. 3, p. 166; Meredith, *MHT*, vol. 1, pp. 190–2, 215; Lyndall Ryan, *The Aboriginal Tasmanians*, p. 86.

52 Meredith, *MHT*, vol. 1, p. 191; Ryan, *The Aboriginal Tasmanians*, p. 85; Henry Reynolds, *Fate of a Free People: A Radical Re-Examination of the Tasmanian Wars*, pp. 4, 31.

53 Meredith, *MHT*, vol. 1, pp. 191–2, 200; Ryan, *The Aboriginal Tasmanians*, pp. 79, 86–8.

54 Meredith, *MHT*, vol. 1, pp. 201–2; Reynolds, *Fate of a Free People*, p. 186.

55 Louisa Anne Meredith, *A Tasmanian Memory of 1834*, p. 21; J. E. Calder, *Some Account of the Wars, Extirpation, Habits &c. of the Native Tribes of Tasmania*, p. 8; Meredith, *TFF*, pp. 80–1.

56 R. Brough Smyth, *The Aborigines of Victoria*, vol. 2, pp. 383–4; Meredith, *BFT*, pp. 52–3.

57 Meredith, *MHT*, vol. 2, p. 23.

58 Meredith, *MHT*, vol. 1, pp. 125–6; vol. 2, p. 165; Meredith, *SMBFT*, p. 106; Meredith, *WTGB*, p. 54; Meredith, *TFF*, pp. 139, 219, 221.

59 Jameson, *Winter Studies and Summer Rambles*, vol. 1, p. 97, vol. 2, p. 102; Meredith, *NSNSW*, pp. 56–7.

60 Meredith, *MHT*, vol. 1, 161–2, 221–2.

61 Meredith, *MHT*, vol. 2, pp. 22, 46.

62 Stokes, *Discoveries in Australia*, vol. 1, pp. 315–16; Meredith, *MHT*, vol. 1, p. 162; vol. 2, p. 3; James Fenton, *Bush Life in Tasmania Fifty Years Ago*, p. 53.

63 Meredith, *MHT*, vol. 2, pp. 134–5, 178–9.

64 *JHA*, vol. 5, 1860, paper no. 72.

65 Undated letter, Louisa Anne Meredith to J. E. Calder, Calder papers, vol. 89, p. 311, LTL; *Mercury*, 29 August 1874, p. 3; Louisa Anne Meredith, 'The Hon. Charles Meredith', *Once a Month*, vol. 4, 1886, p. 282.

66 *LE*, 18 August 1860, p. 2.

67 *Mercury*, 6 August 1868, p. 2; 29 August 1874, p. 3; 3 September 1874, p. 2; 15 November 1877, p. 3; 17 November 1877, p. 3.
68 *Mercury*, 2 May 1879, p. 3.
69 'Preservation of Huon Pine and Blackwood', *JHA*, vol. 35, 1879, paper no. 132; *LE*, 21 May 1879, p. 2.
70 *Mercury*, 2 May 1879, p. 3; *LE*, 5 May 1879, p. 2. Black-backed and silver gulls were, however, included a few weeks later in the Game Protection Act 1879 (Tas.), s. 13 introduced by William Dobson.
71 *Mercury*, 5 May 1879, p. 2, 23 May 1879, p. 3; Prevention of Cruelty to Animals Act Amendment Act 1879 (Tas.), s. 2.
72 Ellis, *Louisa Anne Meredith*, pp. 39, 185.
73 *Australasian*, 26 October 1895, p. 799; Swann, 'Mrs Meredith and Miss Atkinson', p. 2; Ellis, *Louisa Anne Meredith*, p. 184.
74 *Mercury*, 29 August 1874, p. 2; 5 July 1879, p. 2; *ATCJ*, 3 April 1880, p. 641.
75 Undated letter, Louisa Anne Meredith to J. E. Calder, Calder papers, vol. 89, p. 311, LTL.
76 Ibid.; Meredith, 'The Hon. Charles Meredith', p. 282; Meredith, *TFF*, p. 158.
77 *Mercury*, 11 July 1878, p. 2.
78 *Mercury*, 15 July 1878, p. 2; 19 July 1878, p. 2.
79 *Mercury*, 20 July 1878, p. 2, 22 July 1878, p. 2, 19 July 1879, p. 3; Turner, *Reckoning with the Beast*, p. 58.
80 *Mercury*, 20 July 1878, p. 2; 23 July 1878, p. 3.
81 *Mercury*, 23 July 1878, p. 3; Thomas, *Man and the Natural World*, pp. 185–6; Harriet Ritvo, *The Animal Estate: The English and Other Creatures in the Victorian Age*, pp. 134–5.
82 *Mercury*, 26 July 1878, p. 3.
83 *Mercury*, 7 February 1879, supplement, p. 1; 5 April 1879, p. 3; 19 July 1879, p. 2.
84 *Mercury*, 8 January 1879, p. 3; 7 February 1879, supplement, p. 1; 21 February 1879, p. 2; 4 April 1879, p. 2; 19 July 1879, pp. 2–3.
85 *LE*, 7 March 1879, p. 3; 3 June 1879, p. 2; 5 June 1879, p. 2; 17 July 1879, p. 2; 21 August 1879, p. 3; *Mercury*, 8 May 1879, p. 2; 7 June 1879, p. 2.
86 *LE*, 26 June 1879, p. 3; 10 July 1879, p. 2; 21 August 1879, p. 3.
87 Louisa Anne Meredith to Henry Parkes, 29 October 1893, Parkes papers, vol. 24, A894, pp. 314–16, ML; *Mercury*, 27 October 1893, p. 3; 31 October 1893, p. 4; Swann, 'Mrs Meredith and Miss Atkinson', pp. 11–12.

CHAPTER 6: THE MASTER OF THE GUM TREE

1 R. B. Beckett (ed.), *John Constable's Correspondence VI: The Fishers*, pp. 117, 232; Walch, *Victoria in 1880*, p. 183; Twopeny, *Town Life in Australia*, p. 246.
2 Marjorie Hope Nicolson, *Mountain Gloom and Mountain Glory*; Raymond Williams, *The Country and the City*, p. 128; D. G. Charlton, *New Images of the Natural in France: A Study in European Cultural History 1750–1800*, ch. 3.
3 Hancock, *Australia*, p. 33.
4 *Brook v Bedford* (1856) 1 VLT 101.
5 *Brook v Bedford* (1856) 1 VLT 101.
6 *Bruce v Atkins* (1861) W and W 141, 143–5; *Turner v Jackson* (1856) 1 VLT 126.
7 *Brook v Bedford* (1856) 1 VLT 101, 102.
8 Morton J. Horwitz, *The Transformation of American Law 1780–1860*, pp. 54–5; Thomas R. Cox et al., *This Well-Wooded Land: Americans and Their Forests from Colonial Times to the Present*, pp. 33–4.
9 *Brook v Bedford* (1856) 1 VLT 101, 102.
10 Grove, *Green Imperialism*; Sue Rosen, *Losing Ground: An Environmental History of the Hawkesbury–Nepean Catchment*, p. 15.
11 Wentworth, *Statistical Account*, vol. 1, pp. 437–8; Field, *Geographical Memoirs*, p. 425; Strzelecki, *Physical Description*, p. 239; Hancock, *Australia*, pp. 57–9; Morgan, *Land Settlement*, p. 125.
12 *Argus*, 21 February 1860, p. 4, 25 April 1860, p. 4; Linden Gillbank, 'The Acclimatisation Society of Victoria', esp. pp. 259–60.
13 *Argus*, 5 August 1863, pp. 4–5; 25 February 1864, p. 5; *YAA*, 27 February 1864, p. 348, 19 March 1864, p. 395, 2 April 1864, p. 425; John Foster, 'Natives in the Nineteenth Century Garden', pp. 3–4.
14 *Australasian*, 28 October 1865, pp. 8, 9; *Age*, 7 November 1865, p. 6; R. L. J. Ellery, 'On the Relation between Forest Lands and Climate in Victoria', p. 1; Jenny Keating, *The Drought Walked Through: A History of Water Shortage in Victoria*, pp. 33–7.
15 *Age*, 3 October 1865, p. 5; George Perkins Marsh, *Man and Nature*, pp. 36, 49; Grove, *Green Imperialism*, pp. 441–61; Powell, *Environmental Management in Australia 1788–1914*, pp. 54–6.
16 'Report on the Advisableness of Establishing State Forests', *VPP*, 1864–5, vol. 4, pp. 1–6; *Argus*, 16 October 1865, p. 5; 13 November 1865, p. 4; Powell, *Environmental Management*, pp. 60, 62. Compare Wright, *The Bureaucrats' Domain*, p. 153.
17 *Argus*, 1 September 1866, p. 5; *Australasian*, 1 September 1866, p. 688; Wright, *The Bureaucrats' Domain*, p. 155.
18 *Argus*, 19 December 1874, p. 9; 31 May 1888,

p. 5; *AS*, 12 July 1888, p. 103; *TT*, 8 June 1888, p. 1; Bonyhady, *Images in Opposition*, p. 113.

19 *Argus*, 7 May 1867, p. 7; 11 April 1870, p. 5. See also, *AS*, 1 November 1873, p. 134; *TT* , 8 June 1888, p. 1.

20 *IANHR*, 7 October 1874, p. 170; *ISN*, 17 October 1874, pp. 16, 18; Walch, *Victoria in 1880*, p. 183.

21 *Australasian*, 21 October 1871, p. 533; *AS*, 1 November 1873, p. 129; 21 February 1874, p. 203; Thomas, *Man and the Natural World*, p. 213.

22 *Argus*, 27 October 1866, supplement, p. 4; *IANHR*, 2 November 1875, p. 11; *DT*, 7 October 1882, p. 5, 1 June 1888, p. 3; *Age*, 1 June 1888, p. 5.

23 *The Victorian Exhibition, opened 6th November 1872: Official Catalogue*, p. 2; *AS*, 1 November 1873, p. 134.

24 *Argus*, 31 May 1888, p. 5.

25 *Examiner and Melbourne Weekly News*, 26 May 1860, p. 8; *TT*, 8 June 1888, p. 1.

26 Anthony Trollope, *Australia and New Zealand*, vol. 1, p. 209.

27 Froude, *Oceana*, pp. 118, 121. Compare George Sala, *The Land of the Golden Fleece*, p. 57.

28 *Australasian*, 28 February 1885, supplement, p. 1; Howard Willoughby, *Australian Pictures drawn with Pen and Pencil*, pp. 194–5.

29 James Smith, *From Melbourne to Melrose*, preface, p. 313.

30 F. M. Bailey, 'A General Account of the Flora of Tropical Queensland', pp. 276–7.

31 Kenneth Thompson, 'The Australian Fever Tree in California: Eucalypts and Malaria Prophylaxis', pp. 230–44; Barley, 'Plants from Old Nursery Catalogues', p. 18; Ian Tyrrell, *The Gardens of the Gods: Californian–Australian Environmental Reform 1860–1930*, ch. 3.

32 *Edinburgh Medical Journal*, vol. 18, no. 5, 1872, pp. 470–7; Grove, *Ecology, Climate and Empire*, pp. 23, 118.

33 *Edinburgh Medical Journal*, vol. 18, no. 5, 1872, pp. 472–3, 475; *PPRRST*, 1875, p. 88; W. B. Clarke, *Effects of Forest Vegetation on Climate*, p. 35; *LE*, 8 July 1879, p, 2; 'Eucalyptus Globulus' in Ferdinand von Mueller, *Eucalyptographia*; Thompson, 'The Australian Fever Tree', p. 243.

34 *Australasian*, 3 August 1872, p. 146; *PPRRST*, 1877, p. 15; *Sydney University Magazine*, 1878, pp. 132–3; Barley, 'Plants from Old Nursery Catalogues', pp. 18–19.

35 Joseph Bosisto, 'Is the Eucalyptus a Fever-destroying Tree?', *TPRSV*, vol. 12, 1874–1875, pp. 10–23; *Argus*, 12 August 1874, pp. 4–5; Thompson, 'The Australian Fever Tree', p. 236; James Griffin, 'Joseph Bosisto', *Australian Dictionary of Biography*, vol. 3, p. 198; Barley, 'Plants from Old Nursery Catalogues', p. 19; Helen Cohn and Sara Maroske, 'Relief from Duties of Minor Importance: The Removal of Baron von Mueller from the Directorship of the Melbourne Botanic Gardens', p. 113.

36 *AS*, 5 September 1874, pp. 83, 91, 95.

37 *DT*, 16 July 1877, p. 2.

38 *DT*, 16 July 1877, p. 2.

39 *Australasian*, 21 October 1882, p. 530; 5 January 1884, pp. 16–17; 31 May 1884, p. 682; *SMH*, 16 July 1887, p. 111; F. E. H. W. Krichauff, 'Forest Conservancy and Timber Supply', in *South Australia Industries and Manufactures*, p. 269; William Woolls, *Lectures on the Vegetable Kingdom*, p. 92; *VPD*, vol. 57, 1888, p. 453; Angela Taylor, *A Forester's Log: The Story of John La Gerche and the Ballarat–Creswick State Forest 1882–1897*, p. 63.

40 Krichauff, 'Forest Conservancy and Timber Supply', pp. 258–9, 269–70; 'Annual Progress Report of the Forest Reserves of South Australia for 1879–80', *Proceedings of the Parliament of South Australia*, 1880, vol. 4, p. 35; David Jones, 'The Origins of the SA Woods and Forest Department: The Forest Board 1875–1878', pp. 42–3.

41 'Land Selection at Mount Macedon', *VPP*, 1899–1900, pp. 8–10; Chris McConville, 'A Forest at the Edge of the City', pp. 8–9; Fox, 'The Simla of the South', p. 10.

42 J. M. Powell, *The Public Lands of Australia Felix*,, esp. p. 188; Tony Dingle, *Settling*, pp. 63–7, 76.

43 Julian Tenison-Woods, 'Tasmanian Forests: Their Botany and Economical Value', p. 28.

44 *Australasian*, 18 January 1878, p. 81, 24 May 1879, p. 658; *Argus*, 3 May 1879, p. 7, 16 May 1879, p. 5, 19 May 1879, p. 5; *Age*, 8 May 1879, p. 3; Francis Gilfedder, 'The Early Nursery Industry at Macedon Ranges', p. 20; D. W. Meinig, *On the Margins of the Good Earth*, pp. 59–60, 70–2, 75, 84–9.

45 *Age*, 26 April 1879, pp. 4, 6, 30 April 1879, p. 2; *Argus*, 8 May 1879, p. 6, 9 May 1879, p. 6, 13 May 1879, pp. 4–5; Wright, *The Bureaucrats' Domain*, p. 245.

46 *Argus*, 18 April 1879, p. 4; Froude, *Oceana*, p. 247.

47 James Smith, 'Is the Earth Becoming Bald?', *VR*, vol. 1, 1 April 1880, pp. 876–93; *Important Auction Sale of a Valuable Library of*

Books . . . by Order of the Executors of the Late Mr James Smith, p. 28.

48 *Argus*, 17 March 1882, p. 5. 20 March 1882, p. 5; 'Papers Relating to Forest Conservancy', *VPP*, 1874, vol. 3, p. 10; David A. Crichton, 'State Forests and their Conservation', *VR*, 1 February 1882, p. 464.

49 *VPD*, vol. 35, 1880–81, p. 1268; Wright, *The Bureaucrats' Domain*, pp. 176–7, 191–2; Taylor, *A Forester's Log*, esp. ch. 4.

50 *Argus*, 15 August 1874, p. 4, 23 November 1881, p. 10, 8 June 1883, p. 4; *VPD*, vol. 33, 1880, p. 89; vol. 37, 1881, pp. 342, 397; vol. 38, 1881, p. 1281; vol. 44, 1883, p. 923; Wright, *The Bureaucrats' Domain*, p. 232.

51 *Australasian*, 26 August 1882, p. 273, 31 May 1884, p. 683; Crichton, 'State Forests', p. 458; Taylor, *A Forester's Log*, pp. 20–1.

52 Bonwick, *Western Victoria*, pp. 135–6; 'Report on the Waste Lands between the Mersey and Levien', pp. 3–4; Brett J. Stubbs, 'Land Improvement or Institutionalised Destruction? The Ringbarking Controversy, 1879–1884, and the Emergence of a Conservation Ethic in New South Wales', pp. 146–8.

53 *Australasian*, 25 February 1865, p. 8; 11 March 1865, p. 8; 30 June 1866, p. 409; Woolls, *Lectures on the Vegetable Kingdom*, p. 91; Gerald Walsh, *Pioneering Days: People and Innovations in Australia's Rural Past*, p. 41.

54 *SMH*, 1 November 1876, p. 5; W. A. Abbott, 'Ringbarking and its Effects', *JPRSNSW*, vol. 14, 1880, p. 97; Buxton, *The Riverina*, pp. 247–8.

55 William Farrer, *Grass and Sheep-Farming*, pp. 36–42, 64–5; Dingle, *Settling*, p. 133.

56 Ferdinand von Mueller, *Forest Culture in its Relation to Industrial Pursuits*, p. 8; Clarke, *Effects of Forest Vegetation*, pp. 2–3, 33, 35, 37; Woolls, *Lectures on the Vegetable Kingdom*, pp. 90–1.

57 *SMH*, 4 November 1876, p. 8; 8 November 1876, pp. 4–5; 13 November 1876, p. 5; 14 November 1876, p. 6; 20 November 1876, p. 7.

58 *JPRSNSW*, vol. 10, 1876, pp. 230–5; Tenison-Woods, 'Tasmanian Forests', pp. 27–8; Abbott, 'Ringbarking and its Effects', pp. 97–102; William Woolls, 'Species of Eucalypts in the County of Cumberland: Their Habits and Uses', *PLSNSW*, vol. 5, 1880–81, p. 507; William Woolls, 'Plants which have become naturalized in New South Wales', *PLSNSW*, vol. 9, 1884, p. 190.

59 Crown Land Regulations 1875 (NSW), reg. 66; *SMH*, 4 June 1881, pp. 5, 6; *ATCJ*, 11 June 1881, p. 1120; *NSWPD*, vol. 5, 1881, p. 1407.

60 Land Act Amendment Act 1880 (NSW), s. 15; *NSWPD*, vol. 4, 1880–81, pp. 1204–18, 1440; vol. 5, 1881, p. 48.

61 *Ex parte Thomas* (1881) 2 NSWR 39, 42–3 (L); Grainger, *Martin of Martin Place*, pp. 59–60; Sharon Beder, 'Early Environmentalists and the Battle against Sewers in Sydney', p. 28.

62 *NSWPD*, vol. 5, 1881, pp. 48–59, 438–69, 480–98, 573–92, 609–24, 670–82, 709–26, 920–40. 981–91, 1341–55.

63 Ringbarking on Crown Lands Regulation Act 1881 (NSW); Crown Lands Regulations 1884 (NSW), reg. 324; Land Act 1884 (Vic.), s. 27(6); *Argus*, 15 November 1886, p. 8; *VPD*, vol. 53, 1886, pp. 2306–7; vol. 57, 1888, pp. 418, 517; vol. 58, 1888, p. 1017; 'Ringbarking on Crown Lands', *NSWLAV&P*, 1887–88, p. 507; Stubbs, 'Land Improvement or Institutionalised Destruction?', pp. 159–60.

64 Edmund Marin la Meslée, *The New Australia*, p. 30; Donald Macdonald, *Gum Boughs and Wattle Blossom*, p. 126.

65 W. Frederick Morrison, *The Aldine Centennial History of New South Wales*, vol. 1, p. 58.

66 *Argus*, 10 July 1888, p. 9.

67 *NSWPD*, vol. 5, 1881, pp. 56–9, 488; Michael Ackland (ed.), *Henry Kendall: Poetry, Prose and Selected Correspondence*, pp. xxxi–xxxii; Michael Ackland, *Henry Kendall: The Man and the Myths*, pp. 232–4, 258, 272–4, 278–83.

68 *Argus*, 3 March 1888, p. 11, 23 March 1888, p. 4; David Young, Conservation Policy and Practice in Tasmanian Forests 1870–1900, pp. 45–7.

69 *LE*, 14 September 1887, p. 2; 'Woods and Forests of Tasmania: Report of the Conservator of Forests, 1886–87', *JPPPT*, vol. 12, 1887, paper no. 61, pp. 5, 9, 17; *Argus*, 30 January 1889, p. 4; *Age*, 30 January 1889, pp. 5, 6; Taylor, *A Forester's Log*, pp. 65, 116, 164.

70 *VPD*, vol. 58, 1888, p. 1671; *Australasian*, 9 June 1883, supplement, p. 6; *BA*, 27 August 1888, p. 2; 22 February 1889, p. 3; 23 February 1889, p. 4; *Argus*, 5 March 1889, p. 6.

71 *Argus*, 5 March 1889, p. 6.

72 *VPD*, vol. 57, 1888, pp. 3, 21, 640–1; vol. 58, 1888, p. 1704; vol. 59, 1888, pp. 1993, 2103.

73 *VPD*, vol. 57, 1888, pp. 418, 517; vol. 58, 1888, pp. 1017, 1704, 1855; *Argus*, 3 March 1888, p. 11, 3 August 1888, p. 5; *Australasian*, 11 August 1888, p. 308; Taylor, *A Forester's Log*, pp. 50, 92.

74 *Argus*, 3 August 1888, p. 5, 16 January 1889, p. 4, 26 January 1889, p. 13, 2 February 1889, p. 4, 9 February 1889, p. 4, 5 March 1890, p. 4; *Age*, 29 December 1888, p. 8; 'Report of the Conservator of Forests for the Year ending 30th June 1890', *VPP*, 1890, vol. 4, p. 1.

[75] *Argus*, 1 December 1888, p. 11, 4 December 1888, p. 6, 14 December 1888, p. 5, 28 December 1888, p. 5, 8 January 1889, p. 7, 9 January 1889, p. 4, 16 January 1889, p. 4, 9 February 1889, p. 4; Kevin J. Frawley, 'Rainforest Management in Queensland before 1900', pp. 13–14.

[76] *Argus*, 4 December 1888, p. 6, 28 December 1888, p. 5, 8 January 1889, p. 7, 9 January 1889, p. 4, 26 January 1889, p. 13, 9 February 1889, p. 4; *Age*, 29 December 1888, p. 8.

[77] *Argus*, 5 March 1889, p. 4.

[78] *BA*, supplement, 27 February 1889, p. 5, 16 March 1889, p. 3; *Argus*, 5 March 1889, p. 6, 12 March 1889, p. 5, 20 March 1889, p. 3.

[79] *VPD*, vol. 56, 1888, p. 2347; vol. 57, 1888, p. 640; *Argus*, 12 March 1889, p. 5.

[80] *Argus*, 22 November 1890, p. 13, 10 August 1893, p. 7; James Smith, *Cyclopedia of Victoria*, vol. 2, p. 85.

[81] *Argus*, 1 June 1889, p. 11.

[82] William Moore, 'Australian Art', pp. 74, 77.

[83] Nathan F. Spielvogel, *Our Gum Trees and Other Verses*, p. 7.

[84] *Bulletin*, 13 August 1908, p. 24.

CHAPTER SEVEN: ARTISTS WITH AXES

[1] *IAN*, 25 September 1865, p. 16; 12 June 1869, p. 133, 4 October 1869, p. 187, 31 December 1873, pp. 212–14, republished in *Illustrated Tasmanian News*, March 1874, pp. 12–13; *VN*, vol. 24, 1907, p. 110. See, more generally, Peter Quartermaine, '"Speaking to the Eye": Painting, Photography and the Popular Illustrated Press in Australia, 1850–1900', in Anthony Bradley and Terry Smith (eds), *Australian Art and Architecture: Essays Presented to Bernard Smith*, esp. pp. 64–8; Linden Gillbank, 'Charles Walter: Collector of Images and Plants in East Gippsland', pp. 3–10.

[2] *IAN*, 23 March 1868, p. 8; 31 December 1873, pp. 212–14.

[3] *IAN*, 27 October 1866, p. 8; 23 March 1868, p. 8; 12 June 1869, p. 133.

[4] J. E. M. Russell, *The Pictorial Guide to the Blue Mountains*, p. 9; *The Visitors' Guide to the Upper Yarra and Fern Tree Gully Districts*, p. 10.

[5] See Quartermaine, 'Speaking to the Eye', in Bradley and Smith, *Australian Art and Architecture*, pp. 68–70; Bonyhady, *Images in Opposition*, p. 100; Catherine Snowdon, 'The Take-Away Image: Photographing the Blue Mountains in the Nineteenth Century', in Peter Stanbury (ed.), *The Blue Mountains: Grand Adventure for All*, ch. 9.

[6] H. A. MacLeod Morgan, 'Eccleston du Faur', p. 19.

[7] Meinig, *On the Margins of the Good Earth*, esp. pp. 38, 41–2; Wright, *The Bureaucrats' Domain*, p. 153.

[8] *SMH*, 14 April 1900, p. 12; 22 September 1902, p. 5.

[9] Morgan, 'Eccleston du Faur', pp. 21–2.

[10] *SMH*, 11 November 1875, p. 5; undated newspaper cuttings in Eccleston du Faur, notebook, A1629, ML.

[11] 'Album of 20 albumen silver photographs of California by Carleton Watkins, 1861–1868', LTWEF 15, La Trobe Library; *Freeman's Journal*, 28 September 1872, p. 7; *IAN*, 7 August 1871, p. 128, 15 July 1873, pp. 122, 125; *ISN*, 2 August 1873, p. 8; John Smith, *Wayfaring Notes (Second Series): A Holiday Tour Round the World*, chaps 19, 20; Gael Newton, *Shades of Light: Photography and Australia 1839–1988*, pp. 184–5.

[12] *SMH*, 11 November 1875, p. 5.

[13] *SMH*, 15 April 1875, p. 5; 7 October 1875, p. 3.

[14] Eccleston du Faur, Notebook, A1629, ML; *SMH*, 4 October 1875, p. 2, 7 October 1875, p. 3, 11 November 1875, p. 5; *ATCJ*, 9 October 1875, p. 580; *AS*, 15 April 1876, p. 10; *Railway Guide to New South Wales*, p. 59.

[15] *SMH*, 7 October 1875, p. 3; *BJP*, 1876, pp. 309–10, 317–18.

[16] Joseph Bischoff, Album of Photographs of the Grose Valley, LTAF 340, esp. ff. 32–33, LTL; *SMH*, 7 October 1875, p. 3, 11 November 1875, p. 5; *ATCJ*, 9 October 1875, p. 580; *BJP*, 1876, p. 318; *Railway Guide of New South Wales*, p. 59.

[17] *BJP*, 1876, pp. 310, 317; Nicholas Caire, 'Scene from the Black Spur', in *Views of Victoria*, no. 27; Nicholas Caire, 'Scene at the Foot of Mt Strzeletzki',*Gippsland Scenery*, no. 7.

[18] *SMH*, 11 November 1875, p. 5; *ATCJ*, 9 October 1875, p. 580; *Railway Guide of New South Wales*, p. 59.

[19] *IAN*, 15 July 1873, pp. 122, 125.

[20] *BJP*, 1870–71, p. 150; Peter E. Palmquist, *Carleton E. Watkins: Photographer of the American West*, p. 59; James R. Ryan, *Picturing Empire: Photography and the Visualization of the British Empire*, p. 57.

[21] *Alta California*, 7 April 1872, quoted in *Eadward Muybridge: The Stanford Years 1872–1882*, p. 45; David Robertson, *West of Eden: A History of the Art and Literature of Yosemite*, p. xviii.

[22] J. H. Harvey, 'A Photographic Trip to the

Jenolan Caves and Kanangara Walls, N.S.W.', p. 147.

23 Harvey, 'A Photographic Trip', p. 148.

24 Nanette Sexton, 'Watkins' Style and Technique in the Early Photographs', pp. 246–7, 270.

25 A. H. Wall, *Artistic Landscape Photography*, p. 166; J. W. Beattie, 'The Picturesque West Coast of Tasmania', p. 191; Margaret Tassell and David Wood, *Tasmanian Photographer: From the John Watt Beattie Collection*, pp. 79, 86.

26 *IAN*, 17 June 1871, p. 125.

27 *Walch's Literary Intelligencer*, March 1863, p. 136; Ann-Marie Willis, *Picturing Australia: A History of Photography*, p. 34.

28 See Clarence S. Jackson, *William H. Jackson: Picture Maker of the Old West*, p. 57; James Alinder (ed.), *Carleton E. Watkins: Photographs of the Columbia River and Oregon*, plates 18, 20, 21. See also Palmquist, *Carleton E. Watkins*, p. 59.

29 William Gilpin, *Three Essays on Picturesque Beauty*, p. 68.

30 Barbara Novak, *Nature and Culture: American Landscape and Painting 1825–1875*, p. 160.

31 Kathryn Cave (ed.), *The Diary of Joseph Farington*, vol. 11, p. 3594.

32 Mary Howitt Walker, *Come Wind, Come Weather: A Biography of Alfred Howitt*, p. 95; Baker, *The Civilised Surveyor*, p. 29.

33 *Age*, 16 October 1857, p. 5.

34 *MP*, 15 July 1858, p. 204.

35 *Argus*, 4 December 1857, p. 5; *DA*, 4 July 1889, p. 1; Coulson, *Story of the Dandenongs*, pp. 24, 149–50.

36 Marjorie Tipping (ed.), *An Artist on the Goldfields: The Diary of Eugene von Guérard*, pp. 40, 56, 58, 60.

37 Tipping (ed.), *An Artist on the Goldfields*, p. 63.

38 Eugene von Guérard, *Eugène von Guérard's Australian Landscapes*, text accompanying plate 15.

39 *Argus*, 4 December 1857, p. 5.

40 *IJA*, January 1857, pp. 27–8.

41 Arthur Streeton, 'Personal Narrative', pp. 2–5.

42 Hingston, *Guide for Excursionists*, 1869, p. 167; *Argus*, 20 September 1884, p. 4; *SMH*, 4 October 1875, p. 2.

43 *HTC*, 10 January 1846, p. 3; *Argus*, 20 September 1884, p. 4.

44 *Visitors' Guide to the Upper Yarra*, pp. 96–7, 101–2; *Argus*, 24 March 1888, p. 5; *Argus*, 18 February 1893, p. 4.

45 *Argus*, 1 November 1890, p. 4; 21 March 1891, p. 4.

46 *Argus*, 25 June 1887, p. 13, 17 January 1891, p. 4, 7 March 1891, p. 4, 21 March 1891, p. 4; *Life*, 28 July 1887, p. 3; Humphrey McQueen, *Tom Roberts*, pp. 333–4.

47 *Argus*, 1 November 1890, p. 4; 8 November 1890, p. 4.

48 *Argus*, 1 November 1890, p. 4.

49 *Argus*, 16 June 1888, p. 5.

50 'National Park: Report of the Trustees for the year ended 31 December 1887', *NSWLAV&P*, 1888–89, vol. 3; 'National Park: Report of the Trustees for the year ended 31 December 1888', *NSWLAV&P*, second session 1888–89, vol. 2; Russell, *Pictorial Guide*, p. 39; *Blue Mountains Railway Tourist Guide*, pp. 10, 12, 14; William Dymock, *Dymock's Illustrated Guide to Sydney*, p. 122.

51 Alfred J. North, 'On Two Early Australian Ornithologists', p. 126; Rex and Thea Rienits, *Early Artists of Australia*, p. 125.

52 *The Original Water-Color Paintings by John James Audubon for the Birds of America*, vol. 1, notes to plate 54; John Chancellor, *Audubon*, p. 87; Ann Shelby Blum, *Picturing Nature: American Nineteenth-Century Zoological Illustration*, ch. 3.

53 John James Audubon, *Delineations of American Character and Scenery*, esp. pp. 68, 74, 253–8, 282, 286.

54 Audubon, *Delineations*, pp. 181, 189.

55 W. P. Adams, 'Deer Stalking with a Camera', *BJP*, 1889, p. 647; R. S. Sugars, 'A Trip to Sassafras Gully', p. 69; David Elliston Allen, *The Naturalist in Britain: a Social History*, pp. 232–4; David Knight, *Zoological Illustration: an Essay towards the History of Printed Zoological Pictures*, p. 67; Ryan, *Picturing Empire*, pp. 128–39.

56 R. S. Sugars, 'Notes on a Trip to South Gippsland', p. 69.

57 Campbell, *Nests and Eggs of Australian Birds*, 1883, pp. v, xiii; A. J. Marshall, 'Of the Plume Trade and Emu Oil', in Marshall (ed.), *The Great Extermination*, pp. 43–9.

58 Campbell, *Nests and Eggs of Australian Birds*, 1883, p. v; Archibald J. Campbell, 'Notes about Lyrebirds', pp. 105–8; Archibald J. Campbell, 'The Protection of Our Native Birds', pp. 161–4; Archibald J. Campbell, 'The Protection of Native Birds', pp. 187–9.

59 *Southern Sphere*, 1 July 1910, p. 8.

60 *Emu*, vol. 15, 1915–16, pp. 47, 160.

61 Charles Barrett (ed.), *Australian Nature Pictures; Gould League Songs and Poems*, p. 17.

62 Nancy K. Anderson, '"The Kiss of Enterprise": The Western Landscape as Symbol and Resource', in William Truettner (ed.), *The*

West as America: Reinterpreting Images of the Frontier 1820–1920, pp. 241–3.

63 Paul Fox with Jennifer Phipps, *Sweet Damper and Gossip: Colonial Sightings from the Goulburn and North-East*, pp. 7, 11. See also Simon Ryan, 'Exploring Aesthetics: the Picturesque Appropriation of Land in Journals of Australian Exploration', pp. 282–93.

64 Quoted by Eve Buscombe, 'A Discussion about Augustus Earle and Some of his Portraits', pp. 49–50.

CHAPTER EIGHT: THE KALIZOIC BROTHERHOOD

1 Twopeny, *Town Life in Australia*, pp. 243–6; W. S. Ramson (ed.), *The Australian National Dictionary*, esp. p. vi.

2 *Argus*, 4 January 1884, p. 3; Harold Love, *James Edward Neild: Victorian Virtuoso*, p. 184.

3 *Argus*, 5 January 1884, pp. 7, 9; Love, *James Edward Neild*, esp. p. 6.

4 *Argus*, 9 January 1884, p. 10; Love, *James Edward Neild*, pp. 93–9; Stuart, *James Smith*, pp. 31, 119–28.

5 *Argus*, 20 June 1877, pp. 5, 7, 29 August 1878, p. 5, 31 August 1878, p. 5, 31 October 1882, p. 10; James Smith, 'Nature's Scavengers', *VR*, vol. 3, 1880–81, pp. 42–53; *Australian Health Society, Melbourne: a Twenty-Five Years' Record of the Work and Progress of the Society*, pp. 6, 7, 9; Alan Mayne, *Fever, Squalor and Vice: Sanitation and Social Policy in Victorian Sydney*, pp. 28–9; David Dunstan, 'Dirt and Disease', in Graeme Davison, David Dunstan and Chris McConville (eds), *Outcasts of Melbourne: Essays in Social History*, pp. 159–63; Stuart, *James Smith*, pp. 59, 157.

6 *Argus*, 4 January 1884, p. 3, 11 January 1884, p. 6; *Australasian*, 9 February 1884, p. 178; *MP*, 22 May 1884, pp. 204, 205, 210.

7 *Herald*, 9 August 1919, p. 15.

8 Octavia Hill, 'Colour, Space and Music for the People', p. 745; F. K. Prochaska, *Women and Philanthropy in Nineteenth-Century England*, esp. pp. 130–3; H. L. Malchow, 'Public Gardens and Social Action in Late Victorian London', esp. p. 109; Gertude Himmelfarb, *Poverty and Compassion: The Moral Imagination of the Late Victorians*, esp. p. 217.

9 Anthony S. Wohl, *The Eternal Slum: Housing and Social Policy in Victorian London*, ch. 7.

10 Octavia Hill, 'Organized Work Among the Poor: Suggestions Founded on Four Years' Management of a London Court', p. 222; Wohl, *The Eternal Slum*, pp. 160–1, 164–78. Martin Gaskell, 'Gardens for the Working Class: Victorian Practical Pleasure', pp. 492–4.

11 Hill, 'Organized Work Among the Poor', pp. 741–52; Howard Erskine-Hill, *The Social Milieu of Alexander Pope*, pp. 27–8; Helen Ranlett, '"Checking Nature's Desecration": Late-Victorian Environmental Organization', pp. 200–2; Gillian Darley, *Octavia Hill: A Life*, p. 183.

12 *Australasian*, 27 September 1879, p. 390.

13 George A. Bicknell, 'A Plea for Sanitation', *VR*, vol. 7, 1882, p. 171.

14 Bicknell, 'A Plea for Sanitation', pp. 166–7, 171.

15 Bicknell, 'A Plea for Sanitation', pp. 172–3.

16 *Australasian*, 21 December 1871, p. 532.

17 *Argus*, 17 October 1872, p. 7; *Australasian*, 15 October 1881, p. 500; 11 November 1882, p. 628; H. d'E. Taylor, 'Health and Thrift', *VR*, vol. 5, 1 April 1882, pp. 653–4.

18 *Argus*, 16 October 1882, p. 9; 18 October 1882, p. 5; 19 October 1882, p. 9; 23 October 1882, p. 5; 24 October 1882, p. 10; 26 October 1882, p. 9; 30 October 1882, pp. 6–7; 31 October 1882, p. 5; 1 November 1882, p. 10; 3 November 1882, p. 10; 6 November 1882, pp. 9, 10.

19 *Argus*, 10 November 1882, p. 7, 11 November 1882, p. 4, 28 November 1882, p. 9; *Australasian*, 20 January 1883, p. 79, 27 January 1883, supplement, p. 10, 3 March 1883, p. 273, supplement, p. 9.

20 *Argus*, 4 January 1884, p. 3.

21 *Argus*, 4 January 1884, p. 3.

22 *Argus*, 4 January 1884, p. 3.

23 *Argus*, 5 January 1884, p. 7.

24 *Argus*, 4 January 1884, p. 3; 5 January 1884, p. 7.

25 River Yarra Pollution Act 1855 (Vic.), s. 1; Bernard Barrett, *The Inner Suburbs: The Evolution of an Industrial Area*, pp. 72–105; David Dunstan, *Governing the Metropolis: Politics, Technology and Social Change in a Victorian City, Melbourne 1850–1891*; John Lack, '"Worst Smelbourne": Melbourne's Noxious Trades', in Davison, Dunstan and McConville (eds), *Outcast Melbourne*, p. 173; Love, *James Edward Neild*, pp. 6–7, 88–91.

26 *Argus*, 9 January 1884, pp. 6, 10.

27 *Australasian*, 2 February 1884, p. 148; 9 February 1884, p. 178.

28 *Australasian*, 2 February 1884, p. 148; 9 February 1884, p. 178.

29 *Argus*, 14 March 1884, p. 5; *Australasian*, 8 March 1884, supplement, p. 6.

30 Nahum Barnet, 'Climatic Architecture', *VR*, vol. 7, 1 November 1882, pp. 37–43; *Argus*, 17 May 1884, p. 13.

31 Dunstan, *Governing the Metropolis*, esp. pp. 93, 104–6.

32 *Argus*, 12 January 1884, p. 10; *Australasian*, 8 March 1884, supplement, p. 6; Judith Godden, 'British Models and Colonial Experience: Women's Philanthropy in Late Nineteenth Century Sydney', esp. p. 48.

33 *MP*, 8 June 1882, p. 224.

34 See Lack, 'Worst Smelbourne', pp. 176–7.

35 *Australasian*, 24 February 1872, p. 231; *Argus*, 11 September 1879, p. 5.

36 *Argus*, 11 September 1879, p. 5. Compare Julian Ashton, *Now Came Still Evening On*, pp. 26–7.

37 Ashton, *Now Came Still Evening On*, p. 28; Dunstan, *Governing the Metropolis*, p. 261; Dunstan, 'Dirt and Disease', p. 144.

38 *Argus*, 15 January 1884, p. 6.

39 *Argus*, 15 January 1884, p. 6; *MP*, 17 January 1884, p. 27.

40 *MP*, 10 January 1884, p. 14, 17 January 1884, p. 27, 24 January 1884, pp. 24, 39, 7 February 1884, p. 58, 21 February 1884, p. 78, 27 March 1884, p. 124; *The Court*, 16 November 1898, p. 55.

41 *MP*, 7 February 1884, p. 58.

42 *MP*, 21 February 1884, pp. 77, 78, 22 May 1884, p. 204; *MB*, 7 March 1884, p. 8; *Australasian*, 5 July 1884, p. 7.

43 *Bulletin*, 19 January 1884, p. 11; *MB*, 22 February 1884, p. 9; Alan Mayne, *Representing the Slum: Popular Journalism in a late Nineteenth Century City*, pp. 29–31, 154–9.

44 *Argus*, 4 April 1884, p. 9, 7 April 1884, p. 10, 8 April 1884, p. 10, 9 April 1884, p. 6, 10 April 1884, p. 10, 21 May 1885, p. 10; *MP*, 17 April 1884, p. 152; Love, *James Edward Neild*, pp. 127, 146, 168, 187, 194, 196.

45 *Age*, 17 May 1884, p. 10; *Argus*, 17 May 1884, p. 10; *MB*, 16 May 1884, p. 9.

46 *Argus*, 17 May 1884, p. 13.

47 *Argus*, 17 May 1884, pp. 13–14; *MB*, 23 May 1884, pp. 1, 5; James Smith, *Presidential Address delivered at the Inauguration of the Kalizoic Society of Victoria*.

48 *Argus*, 20 June 1877, p. 7, 17 May 1884, p. 13; *MB*, 23 May 1884, p. 5; Gaskell, 'Gardens for the Working Class', p. 491.

49 *Argus*, 17 May 1884, p. 13.

50 James Smith, 'Some Social Aspects of England', *VR*, vol. 8, 1883, pp. 114, 120; *Argus*, 17 May 1884, pp. 13–14; 26 October 1885, p. 7; Malchow, 'Public Gardens and Social Action', p. 111.

51 *Argus*, 26 October 1885, p. 7.

52 *Argus*, 1 July 1882, p. 10, 3 July 1882, p. 4; *MP*, 6 July 1882, p. 9; *MB*, 7 July 1882, p. 3, 14 July 1882, p. 3, 28 July 1882, p. 9.

53 *Australasian Sketcher*, 22 April 1882, p. 1, 15 July 1882, p. 1; *MB*, 6 July 1882, p. 5, 27 July 1882, p. 31; *MP*, 22 May 1884, pp. 204, 210.

54 *Australasian*, 8 March 1884, supplement, p. 6, 12 July 1884, p. 55; *Argus*, 12 July 1884, p. 10.

55 *Argus*, 24 May 1884, p. 9, 12 July 1884, p. 10, 8 October 1884, p. 5, 23 March 1885, p. 5; *Australasian*, 14 June 1884, p. 775; *MB*, 25 July 1884, p. 1.

56 *Argus*, 18 June 1856, p. 4; W. A. Sanderson, 'The Alienation of Melbourne Park Lands'.

57 *VPD*, vol. 21, 1875–76, p. 426; *Palmer v Board of Land and Works* (1875) 1 VR 80; Wright, *The Bureaucrats' Domain*, pp. 203–4.

58 *Bland v Mosely* (1587) 77 ER 816, 817; *Palmer v Board of Land and Works* (1875) 1 VR 80, 86–9; *VPD*, vol. 21, 1875–76, pp. 398–410, 418–45; *Argus*, 1 June 1875, p. 4, 24 June 1875, p. 4, 29 June 1875, pp. 5, 7, 30 June 1875, p. 7; *Age*, 24 June 1875, p. 2; Sanderson, 'The Alienation of Melbourne Park Lands', p. 143; Tim Bonyhady, 'A Usable Past: The Public Trust in Australia', pp. 329–38.

59 *MP*, 1 July 1875, pp. 254, 258; *Argus*, 20 November 1882, p. 7, 14 March 1884, p. 6, 15 December 1884, p. 6, 3 January 1885, p. 9; *Australasian*, 27 December 1884, p. 1207. See generally Jill Barnard and Jenny Keating, *People's Playground: A History of Albert Park*, ch. 3.

60 *Argus*, 13 December 1884, p. 10, 20 December 1884, p. 9; *Australasian*, 27 December 1884, p. 1207; *MB*, 9 January 1885, p. 5.

61 *Argus*, 9 January 1884, p. 10; Smith, 'Some Social Aspects of England', pp. 112–13.

62 *Argus*, 3 January 1885, p. 9; *MB*, 26 December 1884, p. 4, 2 January 1885, p. 5, 9 January 1885, p. 5; *Australasian*, 27 December 1884, p. 1207.

63 Historical Press Clippings, LTL; *Argus*, 24 May 1884, p. 13, 7 June 1884, p. 13; Stuart, *James Smith*, pp. 59–60; Love, *James Edward Neild*, pp. 299–303.

64 *Argus*, 24 April 1885, p. 6; Love, *James Edward Neild*, p. 300.

65 *Argus*, 24 May 1884, p. 13; *Australian Tit-Bits*, 11 September 1884, p. 13; Love, *James Edward Neild*, p. 299.

66 *Argus*, 25 April 1893, p. 3; Stuart, *James Smith*, p. 184; Love, *James Edward Neild*, p. 302.

67 *Argus*, 9 September 1884, p. 6, 15 September 1884, p. 6, 17 September 1884, p. 7, 6 December 1884, p. 5; *MP*, 25 September 1884, p. 127; *Australasian*, 20 December 1884, p. 2.

68 *Australasian*, 20 December 1884, p. 2.

69 *Australasian*, 30 June 1883, p. 807, 15 September 1883, p. 327; *Argus*, 24 May 1884, p. 9, 3 June 1884, p. 3.

70 *Australasian*, 22 November 1884, pp. 966–7; *TT*, 20 November 1885, p. 7.

71 *Australasian*, 23 January 1886, p. 151; 30 January 1886, p. 199; McQueen, *Tom Roberts*, pp. 84–5.

72 *TT*, 10 December 1886, pp. 6, 12; 17 December 1886, p. 5.

73 *Argus*, 10 November 1882, p. 7, 21 May 1885, p. 10, 5 June 1885, p. 7; *MP*, 28 May 1885, p. 212.

74 Louis Henry to Hyndeman, 21 July 1887, Australian Artists' Association inward correspondence, box 583/1b, MS 7593, LTL; Australian Artists' Association minute book, box 554/4, MS 7593, LTL; *Argus*, 8 January 1887, p. 9, 8 March 1887, p. 7; McQueen, *Tom Roberts*, p. 178.

75 Australian Artists' Association minute book, 25 May 1887, 13 June 1887, 4 July 1887, box 554/4, MS 7593, LTL; *Argus*, 8 January 1887, p. 9; *Review of Reviews*, 20 November 1896, p. 517; McQueen, *Tom Roberts*, pp. 171, 178, 181.

76 Isobel Spencer, *Walter Crane*, p. 158.

77 *Argus*, 7 October 1887, p. 9.

78 *TT*, 27 April 1888, p. 12, 7 June 1889, p. 5; *Australian Health Society, Melbourne: A Twenty-Five Years' Record of the Work and Progress of the Society*; Ann Galbally and Anne Gray (eds), *Letters from Smike: The Letters of Arthur Streeton*, pp. 25, 32.

79 *TT*, 21 October 1887, p. 8, 25 November 1887, p. 8, 9 December 1887, p. 8, 4 January 1889, p. 6, 23 August 1889, p. 4; *Age*, 17 August 1889, p. 15; McQueen, *Tom Roberts*, p. 270.

80 *Australasian*, 21 June 1884, p. 823, 26 October 1889, p. 883; *TT*, 11 October 1889, p. 15; *Bohemia*, 18 September 1890, p. 11, 29 January 1891, p. 14.

81 *Bohemia*, 20 November 1890, p. 12; 29 January 1891, p. 14.

82 *SMH*, 18 November 1893, p. 5; *The Court*, 16 November 1898, pp. 54–5, 16 December 1898, pp. 73–4, 16 January 1899, pp. 88–90, 16 February 1899, pp. 103–5, 16 May 1899, pp. 152–4.

CHAPTER NINE: UNCLE SAM, THE BARON AND KING EDWARD VII

1 *Bulletin*, 21 February 1918, p. 14.

2 *Argus*, 30 January 1889, p. 8; N. J. Caire, 'Notes on the Giant Trees of Victoria', p. 127.

3 Caire, 'Notes on the Giant Trees of Victoria', p. 124.

4 *Australasian*, 16 July 1898, p. 138.

5 *Age*, 10 January 1872, p. 2; John Smith, *Wayfaring Notes (Second Series): A Holiday Tour Around the World*, p. 302.

6 *Australasian*, 22 July 1865, p. 9; 3 March 1866, p. 8; 2 June 1866, p. 264; 18 August 1866, p. 615; 24 November 1866, p. 1064; C. French, 'Victorian Ferns and their Habitats', *SSR*, no. 3, February 1881, p. 33, no. 4, March 1881, p. 68.

7 Ferdinand von Mueller to George Bentham, 1 January 1874, Mueller project; *Australasian*, 24 November 1866, p. 1064.

8 *Australasian*, 24 November 1866, p. 1064; Ferdinand von Mueller, *Intercolonial Exhibition 1866–67: Report on Vegetable Products*, pp. 1, 3–6; Ferdinand von Mueller, *Intercolonial Exhibition 1866–67: Australian Vegetation, Indigenous or Introduced*, pp. 16–17.

9 G. W. Robinson, 'In the Dandenong Ranges Sixty Years Ago', p. 30.

10 Ferdinand von Mueller to Ronald Gunn, 12 June 1867, MS 1104, NLA.

11 Mueller, *Intercolonial Exhibition 1866–67: Australian Vegetation, Indigenous or Introduced*, p. 17.

12 *Seventh Report of the Acclimatisation Society of Victoria*, 1870, p. 48; Ferdinand von Mueller, *Key to the System of Victorian Plants*, vol. 1, p. 236; James Moore, 'Green Gold: The Riches of Baron Ferdinand von Mueller', pp. 375–6, 379.

13 J. D. Whitney, *The Yosemite Guide-Book*, pp. 154–5; *Australasian*, 26 April 1884, p. 527; Willoughby, *Australian Pictures with Pen and Pencil*, p. 196; Schama, *Landscape and Memory*, pp. 187–8.

14 Trollope, *Australia and New Zealand*, vol. 1, pp. 442–3, 526–7; Froude, *Oceana*, pp. 144–6, 359–60.

15 *IANHR*, 23 April 1872, supplement, p. 101; Tom Griffiths, *Hunters and Collectors: The Antiquarian Imagination in Australia*, pp. 1, 152.

16 Bernard Smith (ed.), *Documents on Art and Taste in Australia*, pp. 133–6. See also John Foster, *Victorian Picturesque: The Gardens of William Sangster*, pp. 8, 80.

17 William Woolls, *A Contribution to the Flora of Australia*, p. 220; Woolls, *Lectures on the Vegetable Kingdom*, pp. 89, 92–3; Schama, *Landscape and Memory*, pp. 188, 190.

18 Woolls, *Lectures on the Vegetable Kingdom*, p. 93; Douglas Sladen, 'To the Fallen Gum-Tree on Mount Bawbaw, Gippsland', *VR*, 1 June 1882, pp. 160–1; Caire, 'Notes on the Giant

Trees of Victoria', pp. 122–3; Thomas, *Man and the Natural World*, p. 217.

19 *Australasian*, 24 November 1866, p. 1064; Mueller, *Intercolonial Exhibition 1866–7: Australian Vegetation, Indigenous or Introduced*, p. 17.

20 Ferdinand von Mueller, *On the Application of Phytology to the Industrial Purposes of Life*, pp. 9–10.

21 Mueller, *On the Application of Phytology*, pp. 10–11.

22 Mueller, *Forest Culture*, p. 51.

23 Mueller, *Forest Culture*, pp. 27, 52; Bonyhady, 'The Stuff of Heritage'.

24 *Argus*, 23 June 1871, pp. 6–7; *Australasian*, 1 July 1871, pp. 6–7; *Lectures delivered in the Lecture Room of the Museum during the Autumn Session of 1871*, pp. 45–96; Elwood Cooper, *Forest Culture and Eucalyptus Trees*, pp. 45–120; Ferdinand von Mueller, *Suggestions on the Maintenance, Creation and Enrichment of Forests*, pp. 6, 29–31; Ralph W. Emerson, *Agricultural Chemistry*, pp. 135–50; Linden Gillbank, 'Nineteenth Century Perceptions of Victorian Forests: Ideas and Concerns of Ferdinand Mueller', in John Dargavel and Sue Feary (eds), *Australia's Ever-Changing Forests II*, p. 9.

25 *Australasian*, 11 March 1882, supplement, p. 2.

26 *Argus*, 24 March 1888, p. 5; *Australasian*, 12 January 1889, p. 66; Froude, *Oceana*, p. 145.

27 *Australasian*, 23 November 1872, p. 647, 28 February 1885, supplement, p. 1; *Illustrated Australian News*, 10 June 1878, p. 102; *Argus*, 11 June 1889, p. 6; Caire, 'Notes on the Giant Trees of Victoria', pp. 122–3.

28 Willoughby, *Australian Pictures with Pen and Pencil*, pp. 196–7; Robinson, 'In the Dandenong Ranges Sixty Years Ago', pp. 30–2; A. D. Hardy, 'The Tall Trees of Australia', pp. 50–1.

29 *Argus*, 22 February 1872, p. 6; 12 January 1881, p. 6; Sladen, 'To the Fallen Gum-Tree', p. 160.

30 A. D. Hardy, 'John Hardy: Early Victorian Surveyor', p. 10.

31 *Argus*, 22 February 1872, p. 6; *Australasian*, 23 November 1872, p. 647, 20 June 1885, supplement, p. 1; Trollope, *Australia and New Zealand*, vol. 1, p. 527; Ferdinand von Mueller, *Eucalyptographia: A Descriptive Atlas of the Eucalypts of Australia*; Froude, *Oceana*, p. 145; Ferdinand von Mueller, *Select Extra-Tropical Plants Readily Eligible for Industrial Culture or Naturalisation*, p. 166; Robinson, 'In the Dandenong Ranges Sixty Years Ago', p. 32.

32 Mueller, *On the Application of Phytology*, p. 10; *Mercury*, 15 December 1880, p. 2; Lady Lefroy (ed.), *Autobiography of General Sir John Lefroy*, pp. 287–8; *Cyclopedia of Tasmania*, vol. 1, p. 466; *Australian Encyclopedia*, 2nd ed., vol. 9, p. 31; John F. Sears, *Sacred Places: American Tourist Attractions in the Nineteenth Century*, p. 147; Alfred Runte, *Yosemite: The Embattled Wilderness*, p. 164; Schama, *Landscape and Memory*, p. 191.

33 *The National Mutual Life Association's Guide to Melbourne*, c. 1880, pp. 29–30; *Australasian*, 13 June 1885, supplement, p. 1; 20 June 1885, supplement, p. 1; *Once a Month*, 15 March 1885, p. 234, 15 August 1885, pp. 103–113, 15 September 1885, pp. 184–91, 1 March 1886, p. 264; L. E. Hervey, 'Diary of a Tour round the World: 1889 and 1890', box 3420/2, MS12591, pp. 77–8, LTL.

34 'Christmas Day under "Uncle Sam"', *AS*, 21 December 1878, supplement; *Australasian*, 20 June 1885, supplement, p. 1; Nicholas Caire, 'Fernshawe', LTAF 302, ff. 12, 24, LTL; *The Visitors' Guide to the Upper Yarra*, p. 72; Caire, 'Notes on the Giant Trees of Victoria', p. 123; *Australasian*, 8 February 1908, p. 334.

35 Oliver Wendell Holmes, 'The Stereoscope and the Stereograph', *Atlantic Monthly*, vol. 3, June 1859, pp. 743–4; Oliver Wendell Holmes, *The Autocrat of the Breakfast-Table*, pp. 222–30; *Giant Trees of Victoria*, preface.

36 James Alinder (ed.), *Carleton E. Watkins: Photographs of the Columbia River and Oregon*, p. 19; Palmquist, *Carleton E. Watkins*, p. 18; Sears, *Sacred Places*, pp. 127–8.

37 Ferdinand von Mueller to Edward Bage, 31 March 1879, Mueller project, Melbourne; *California Horticulturist and Floral Magazine*, vol. 1, no. 2, December 1870, p. 52; *Gardeners' Chronicle*, 20 October 1877, p. 491; Ferdinand von Mueller, *Select Plants Readily Eligible for Industrial Culture or Naturalization in Victoria*, p. 76; Mueller, *Select Extra-Tropical Plants*, p. 114; Marianne North, *Recollections of a Happy Life*, vol. 2, pp. 144–5.

38 J. Duncan Peirce, *Photographs of the Broken Hill Silver Mine*; *Argus*, 4 June 1889, p. 9; *Giant Trees of Victoria*, preface; Colin Silcock, 'Tree Giants of Gippsland', pp. 35–40.

39 *Argus*, 3 July 1888, p. 5, 10 July 1888, p. 10; *Giant Trees of Victoria*, preface.

40 *Argus*, 9 August 1888, exhibition supplement, p. 14; 8 January 1889, exhibition supplement, p. 1.

41 *Argus*, 21 August 1888, p. 4, 29 August 1888, p. 4, 3 October 1888, p. 5, 11 October 1888, p. 11, 4 June 1889, p. 9; A. D. Hardy, 'The Measuring of Tall Trees', p. 172; Coulson, *Story of the Dandenongs*, p. 26.

[42] *The Visitors' Guide to the Upper Yarra*, p. 73; *MP*, 15 November 1888, p. 462; A. D. Hardy, 'Australia's Great Trees', pp. 231–2.

[43] *SMH*, 21 January 1889, p. 11; *Giant Trees of Victoria*, preface, plate 3.

[44] *Argus*, 18 January 1889, p. 9; *Official Record of the Centennial International Exhibition, Melbourne, 1888–1889*, p. 768.

[45] *Argus*, 30 January 1889, p. 8.

[46] *Argus*, 1 February 1889, p. 5; 7 February 1889, p. 8; *WN*, 22 February 1889, p. 2; *Australasian Builder and Contractors' News*, 23 February 1889, p. 176; *Australasian*, 16 March 1889, p. 556.

[47] *Argus*, 22 May 1889, p. 6; 6 June 1889, p. 8.

[48] *Argus*, 22 May 1889, p. 6.

[49] *Argus*, 22 May 1889, p. 6; Griffiths, *Hunters and Collectors*, pp. 32–3.

[50] 12, 28 May 1889, p. 10, 4 June 1889, p. 9; *Australasian*, 25 May 1889, p. 1089.

[51] *Argus*, 28 May 1889, p. 10; Caire, 'Notes on the Giant Trees of Victoria', p. 124.

[52] *Argus*, 4 June 1889, p. 9. Cf *Argus*, 6 June 1889, p. 8.

[53] *Argus*, 25 May 1889, p. 12; Ferdinand von Mueller, 'Inaugural Address', *Report of the Second Meeting of the Australasian Association for the Advancement of Science held at Melbourne, Victoria in January 1890*, pp. 10–11.

[54] *Australasian*, 22 December 1888, p. 1393.

[55] *VPD*, vol. 62, 1889, p. 2443; vol. 65, 1890, pp. 2114, 2120–1; 'Report of the Royal Commission on Gold Mining', *VPP*, 1890, vol. 5, p. 643; *Age*, 21 November 1889, p. 4; *Argus*, 21 November 1889, p. 7, 22 November 1889, pp. 6–7.

[56] *Argus*, 26 January 1889, p. 13, 21 November 1889, p. 7, 22 November 1889, pp. 6–7; *Age*, 21 November 1889, p. 4; *VPD*, vol. 62, 1889, pp. 2443, 2483; vol. 65, 1890, pp. 2114, 2120–1; 'Report from the Select Committee upon the Yea River Company', *VPP*, 1890, vol. 1; 'Report of the Conservator of Forests for the Year ending 30th June 1890', *VPP*, 1890, vol. 4, pp. 17–18; 'Report of the Royal Commission on Gold Mining', *VPP*, 1890, vol. 5, p. 643.

[57] *Argus*, 17 October 1890, p. 4; *VPD*, vol. 62, 1889, pp. 2441–4, 2482–6; vol. 64, 1890, pp. 1654–5, 1719; vol. 65, 1890, pp. 2110–32; Forests Commission of Victoria, *Empire Forestry Conference Australia and New Zealand 1928: Handbook of Forestry in Victoria*, pp. 43–4; Bardwell, The National Park Movement in Victoria, p. 324.

[58] *Age*, 21 November 1889, p. 4; *Argus*, 22 October 1890, p. 4.

[59] *VPD*, vol. 62, 1889, p. 2484; vol. 65, 1890, pp. 2114–15.

[60] *Argus*, 21 November 1889, p. 7.

[61] *Age*, 21 November 1889, p. 4; *VPD*, vol. 62, 1889, pp. 2443–4; vol. 65, 1890, pp. 2113–15.

[62] *Argus*, 7 December 1889, p. 4.

[63] *VPD*, vol. 62, 1889, p. 2484; vol. 65, 1890, p. 2121.

[64] *VPD*, vol. 65, 1890, pp. 2114.

[65] *VPD*, vol. 65, 1890, pp. 2114, 2116–17; *Argus*, 17 October 1890, p. 4.

[66] *VN*, vol. 18, August 1901, p. 54; Hardy, 'The Measuring of Tall Trees', pp. 171–3.

[67] F. G. A. Barnard, 'Excursion to Ferntree Gully', *VN*, vol. 13, 1896–97, p. 144.

[68] *WG*, 23 January 1894, p. 3; *Neerim News*, 9 February 1894, p. 2.

[69] *WG*, 29 January 1895, p. 3; *VN*, vol. 18, August 1901, p. 54; Caire, 'Notes on the Giant Trees of Victoria', p. 124.

[70] P. J. Ryan, 'John Muir and Tall Trees in Australia', p. 125; C. Michael Hall, 'John Muir's Travels in Australasia, 1903–1904: Their Significance for Conservation and Environmental Thought', in S. M. Miller (ed.), *John Muir: Life and Work*, p. 289.

[71] *PRSV*, vol. 3, 1890, pp. 128–9; Australasian Association for the Advancement of Science, *Excursions: Melbourne 1890 (Trip to the Black Spur)*, pp. 3–4; Francis Myers and Trant Chambers, *The Victorian Tourists Railway Guide*, pp. 66–7; *Glimpses of Australia: An Album of Photographic Scenes*, vol. 1, pp. 106, 332; vol. 2, pp. 14, 186, 212.

[72] John Muir, Diary, 21, 24 December 1903; John Muir to Robert Johnson, 18 June 1904; Ryan, 'John Muir and Tall Trees in Australia', pp. 125, 127–9; Hall, 'John Muir's Travels', pp. 290–1.

[73] J. W. Lindt,'Giant Eucalyptus "Uncle Sam" No. 1', 'Giant Eucalypti, Blacks Spur No. 3', *Views of Streets, Buildings and Gardens in Melbourne and Country*, LTAF 132, ff. 151, 152, LTL; Muir, Diary, 25 December 1904; Shar Jones, *J. W. Lindt: Master Photographer*, pp. 9, 16; Ryan, 'John Muir and Tall Trees in Australia', p. 129.

[74] Muir, Diary, 25 December 1903; Hardy, 'Australia's Great Trees', pp. 236, 239; Jones, *Lindt*, p. 18; Ryan, 'John Muir and Tall Trees in Australia', p. 129.

[75] Muir, Diary, 26 December 1903; John Muir to Louise Muir, 28 December 1903; Ryan, 'John Muir and Tall Trees in Australia', p. 130; Hall, 'John Muir's Travels', p. 292.

[76] Muir, Diary, 8 January 1904; *San Francisco Chronicle*, 28 May 1904, p. 9; J. H. Maiden,

The Useful Plants of Australia, p. 430; J. H. Maiden, *A Critical Revision of the Genus Eucalyptus*, vol. 1, p. 183; J. H. Maiden, *The Forest Flora of New South Wales*, vol. 2, pp. 159–63; Ryan, 'John Muir and Tall Trees in Australia', pp. 132–3; Hall, 'John Muir's Travels', pp. 294, 303.

77 *Leader*, 21 May 1904, p. 36, 4 June 1904, p. 22, 11 June 1904, pp. 33, 35; *Australasian*, 8 February 1908, p. 334; Hardy, 'Tall Trees of Australia', pp. 51–2; A. D. Hardy, 'Giant Eucalypts of Victoria', p. 16. *Leader*, 27 May 1905, p. 26 reported another 'giant tree', with a circumference of 78 feet six feet from the ground, at Mount Horsfall in the Upper Yarra catchment, which it claimed as the largest in Victoria.

78 *Leader*, 11 June 1904, p. 33.

79 Julian Tenison-Woods, 'Tasmanian Forests: Their Botany and Economical Value', pp. 21–2; *Australasian*, 22 February 1879, p. 230, 8 February 1908, p. 334; Caire, 'Notes on the Giant Trees of Victoria', pp. 122, 123, 125, 127.

80 Caire, 'Notes on the Giant Trees of Victoria', pp. 122, 124, 125. See also *Bulletin*, 21 February 1918, p. 14.

81 Caire, 'Notes on the Giant Trees of Victoria', pp. 125–6.

82 Caire, 'Notes on the Giant Trees of Victoria', pp. 123, 125, 127.

83 N. J. Caire and J. W. Lindt, *Companion Guide to Healesville, Blacks' Spur, Narbethong and Marysville: Historical, Descriptive and Pictorial*, esp. pp. 9–10, 26, 36, 61, 69–70.

CHAPTER TEN: THE FLOOD IN THE DARLING

1 W. C. Piguenit, Scrapbook, pp. 17, 46, 141, 144–6, PX D234, ML.

2 *Mercury*, 5 April 1871, pp. 2–3.

3 W. V. Legge, 'Protection of Tasmanian Owls', *PPRST*, 1889, pp. 40; 'Protection of the Cape Barren Goose', *PPRST*, 1889, pp. 41–2; *PPRST*, 1892, pp. ix–x; *PPRST*, 1894–5, pp. xiii–xv, xxxiv–xxxv, xxxvii–xxxviii; *Tasmanian Mail*, 6 May 1915, p. 4.

4 *Mercury*, 9 August 1871, p. 2; 17 August 1871, p. 2; 24 September 1887, p. 7. See, more generally, Bonyhady, *Images in Opposition*, pp. 100–2.

5 W. C. Piguenit, Scrapbook, p. 113, PX D234, ML.

6 H. C. Russell, 'Notes upon the History of Floods in the River Darling', *JPRSNSW*, vol. 20, 1886, pp. 155–210.

7 'Royal Commission on Conservation of Water: First Report', Minutes of Evidence, pp. 6, 39, 216; R. L. Heathcote, 'Drought in Australia: A Problem of Perception', pp. 175–94.

8 W. A. Dixon, 'On Salt-Bush and Native Fodder Plants of New South Wales', p. 133; Andrew Ross, 'On the Influence of the Australian Climate and Pastures upon the Growth of Wool', pp. 235–42.

9 R. L. Heathcote, *Back of Bourke: A Study of Land Appraisal and Settlement in Semi-Arid Australia*, pp. 166, 196–7, 199; Jeans, *An Historical Geography*, p. 288.

10 'Royal Commission on Conservation of Water: First Report', p. 23; *Argus*, 19 November 1887, p. 4.

11 *Argus*, 22 October 1887, p. 6; 19 November 1887, p. 4.

12 *Argus*, 22 April 1885, p. 9; J. W. H. Wyse, 'Water Supply for the Interior of New South Wales', *VR*, vol. 11, 1 April 1885, pp. 641–2; 'Royal Commission on Water Conservation: First Report', Minutes of Evidence, pp. 218–22; *JPRSNSW*, vol. 28, 1893, pp. 435–6.

13 *Bulletin*, 24 June 1882, p. 5; Edward B. Sanger, 'Waste in Nature', *VR*, vol. 7, 1883, pp. 280–6; Donald Worster, *Nature's Economy: The Roots of Ecology*, pp. 174–6; Paul Geoffrey Sinclair, Making the Deserts Bloom: Attitudes Towards Water and Nature in the Victorian Irrigation Debate 1880–1890, esp. pp. 58–9.

14 'Royal Commission on Conservation of Water: First Report', *NSWLAV&P*, 1885–86, vol. 6, Minutes of Evidence, p. 219.

15 *Bulletin*, 24 November 1888, p. 5; *Australasian*, 1 December 1888, p. 1209; C. J. Lloyd, *Either Drought or Plenty: Water Development and Management in New South Wales*, p. 175; Neville Nicholls, 'The Centennial Drought'. Cf McKinney, 'Irrigation', pp. 77, 92.

16 *ATCJ*, 29 March 1890, p. 14; *WHRDA*, 9 April 1890, p. 2; *DT*, 19 April 1890, p. 4; *SM*, 19 April 1890, p. 851, 26 April 1890, pp. 909–11; *Argus*, 25 April 1890, p. 6; *SMH*, 28 April 1890, p. 3, 29 April 1890, p. 4; *ISN*, 10 May 1890, p. 17; Russell, 'On Periodicity of Good and Bad Seasons', p. 160; Heathcote, *Back of Bourke*, p. 148.

17 *Argus*, 16 April 1890, p. 6; *SM*, 26 April 1890, pp. 921, 926–7; *ATCJ*, 19 April 1890, p. 12.

18 *ATCJ*, 29 March 1890, p. 13, 19 April 1890, p. 12; *DT*, 19 April 1890, p. 4; *Argus*, 21 April 1890, p. 8.

19 *Argus*, 16 April 1890, p. 6; *Australasian*, 19 April 1890, p. 774; *SM*, 19 April 1890, p. 851; *SMH*, 21 April 1890, pp. 7, 8, 28 April 1890, p. 3, 8 May 1890, p. 5; *DT*, 23 April 1890, p. 4, 10 May 1890, p. 4; *ISN*, 10 May 1890, p. 16.

20 *Argus*, 19 April 1890, p. 10, 21 April 1890,

p. 8, 22 April 1890, p. 5; *SMH*, 21 April 1890, p. 8, 28 April 1890, p. 3; *DT*, 24 April 1890, p. 5; *Australasian*, 26 April 1890, p. 817, 3 May 1890, p. 883; *ISN*, 10 May 1890, pp. 16–17.

21 *Argus*, 15 April 1890, p. 6, 19 April 1890, p. 9; *Australasian*, 19 April 1890, p. 769, 26 April 1890, p. 817; *DT*, 19 April 1890, p. 4; *Bulletin*, 26 April 1890, p. 1.

22 *SMH*, 29 April 1890, p. 4, 30 April 1890, p. 7, 3 May 1890, pp. 9, 11, 6 May 1890, p. 9; *SM*, 3 May 1890, p. 968.

23 *APR*, 15 May 1893, p. 125; Lloyd, *Either Drought or Plenty*, p. 176.

24 *SMH*, 21 January 1893, p. 5; McKinney, 'Irrigation', pp. 83–5; 'Report on Utilisation of the Waters of the River Darling', *NSWLAV&P*, 1892–93, part 2, esp. pp. 11, 20; H. G. McKinney, 'The Progress and Position of Irrigation in New South Wales', *JPRSNSW*, vol. 27, 1893, pp. 399–400; Lloyd, *Either Drought or Plenty*, pp. 119, 176–7; J. M. Powell, *The Emergence of Bioregionalism in the Murray–Darling Basin*, p. 80.

25 *SMH*, 6 May 1890, p. 9; 8 May 1890, p. 5; 24 January 1893, p. 6; 25 January 1893, p. 8; 5 February 1894, p. 5.

26 H. G. McKinney, 'Notes on the Experience of Other Countries in the Administration of their Water Supply', *JPRSNSW*, vol. 21, 1887, p. 60; H. G. McKinney, 'Water Conservation', *NSWLAV&P*, 1891–92, vol. 6, pp. 45–78; 'Report on Utilisation of the Waters of the River Darling', p. 4; H. G. McKinney, 'Irrigation', in Department of Agriculture, New South Wales, *Bulletin of the Conference of Delegates of Agricultural Societies*, p. 157. Compare *APR*, 15 May 1893, p. 125.

27 *SMH*, 2 April 1895, p. 4; *APR*, 17 April 1895, p. 57, 15 May 1895, pp. 112–13; E. A. Amphlett, 'The Bourke Lock and Weir', pp. 21–5; 28 March 1898, pp. 57–62; William Poole, 'The Locking of the Darling River: A Brief Review', *Australian Technical Journal*, 30 April 1898, pp. 99–101; 31 May 1898, pp. 139–42.

28 W. L. Higgins, 'The Possibilities of Irrigation in the West', Department of Agriculture, New South Wales, *Bulletin of the Conference of Delegates*, pp. 163; S. Svensen, *The Shearers' War*, p. 128; Heathcote, *Back of Bourke*, pp. 51, 155.

29 *APR*, 15 January 1895, p. 533; 15 February 1895, p. 575; 15 March 1895, p. 4; 17 April 1895, p. 55.

30 *APR*, 15 May 1895, p. 112.

31 *APR*, 15 June 1895, pp. 168, 199–200, 15 July 1895, pp. 217, 221, 15 August 1895, p. 286, 17 September 1895, p. 348; *Bulletin*, 31 August 1895, p. 9, 21 September 1895, pp. 6, 9; *DT*, 11 September 1895, p. 5; *SM*, 14 September 1895, p. 531; *Australasian*, 21 September 1895, p. 571. Cf Geoffrey Blainey, *A Land Half Won*, p. 353.

32 *APR*, 15 August 1891, pp. 199–200, 209, 15 October 1892, p. 848, 15 August 1895, p. 286; *SM*, 14 September 1895, p. 531; Thomas Heney, 'Unused National Resources', *Sydney Quarterly Magazine*, 1891, pp. 9–14; A. G. Hamilton, 'On the Effect which Settlement in Australia has produced upon Indigenous Vegetation', *JPRSNSW*, vol. 26, 1892, p. 211; McKinney, 'The Progress and Position of Irrigation in New South Wales', p. 395.

33 Frederick Turner, *A Census of Grasses of New South Wales*, p. vi; Frederick Turner, *The Forage Plants of Australia*, pp. ix–x; *SM*, 26 July 1902, p. 221; Jeans, *An Historical Geography*, p. 48.

34 *Freeman's Journal*, 7 September 1895, p. 14; *SMH*, 7 September 1895, p. 9; *NSWGG*, 1895, vol. 5, p. 5903.

35 *AS*, 11 March 1882, pp. 67, 78.

36 *Age*, 23 February 1882, p. 2; *Argus*, 23 February 1882, p. 4, 25 February 1882, p. 10, 27 February 1882, p. 5; Edith C. Rickards, *Bishop Moorhouse of Melbourne and Manchester*, pp. 118–20; T. W. H. Leavitt, *The Jubilee History of Victoria and Melbourne*, vol. 1, part IV, no. xxv; Serle, *Rush to be Rich*, p. 133; Stuart Macintyre, *A Colonial Liberalism: The Lost World of Three Victorian Visionaries*, pp. 122–3.

37 *Argus*, 27 February 1882, p. 5; *Age*, 28 February 1882, p. 2; F. B. Smith, Religion and Freethought in Melbourne, 1870 to 1890, pp. 222–4. Compare Macintyre, *A Colonial Liberalism*, pp. 123–4.

38 *Argus*, 20 March 1882, p. 9.

39 *Argus*, 23 March 1882, p. 10; *AS*, 8 April 1882, p. 98.

40 *Argus*, 20 March 1882, p. 9; *Leader*, 1 April 1882, p. 4.

41 *Argus*, 27 March 1882, p. 10, 30 March 1882, p. 4, 1 April 1882, p. 11, 3 April 1882, p. 9; *AS*, 8 April 1882, p. 99, 22 April 1882, pp. 114–15, 6 May 1882, p. 130, 20 May 1882, p. 147; *MB*, 4 April 1884, p. 9; E. C. Martin, 'A National Scheme of Water Conservation', *VR*, vol. 10, 1884, pp. 143–4; *SM*, 19 July 1902, p. 156; Smith, Religion and Freethought, p. 230; Macintyre, *A Colonial Liberalism*, p. 123.

42 *Australian Star*, 12 September 1895, p. 3; Macintyre, *A Colonial Liberalism*, p. 123.

43 *DT*, 7 September 1895, p. 5, 14 September

1895, p. 5, 16 September 1895, p. 6; *Australian Star*, 12 September 1895, p. 4, 16 September 1895, p. 3; *Bulletin*, 21 September 1895, p. 6.

44 *DT*, 14 September 1895, p. 3, 16 September 1895, p. 6, 18 September 1895, p. 6; *Australian Star*, 16 September 1895, p. 4.

45 *DT*, 16 September 1895, p. 6; *SMH*, 16 September 1895, p. 6.

46 *Australian Star*, 17 September 1895, p. 5.

47 *Australian Star*, 16 September 1895, p. 4, 18 September 1895, p. 5.

48 *SMH*, 28 September 1895, p. 10, 7 October 1895, p. 7; *NSWGG*, 1895, vol. 5, p. 6245; *Bulletin*, 5 October 1895, p. 1, 12 October 1895, pp. 1, 5, 6, 13, 14.

49 *SMH*, 5 September 1902, p. 4; *DT*, 8 September 1902, p. 6.

50 *Bulletin*, 12 December 1896, p. 10; A. B. Paterson, *Australia for the Australian*, p. 31; Colin Roderick, *Banjo Paterson: Poet by Accident*, pp. 142–3, 176–8.

51 *Albany Observer*, 24 May 1890, p. 3.

52 *Bulletin*, 9 July 1892, p. 21; 23 July 1892, p. 15, 6 August 1892, p. 5; Colin Roderick, *Henry Lawson: A Life*, p. 86; Roderick, *Banjo Paterson*, pp. 72–9.

53 Brian Kiernan (ed.), *The Essential Henry Lawson*, p. 101.

54 *APR*, 15 August 1892, pp. 767, 772, 790, 15 September 1892, p. 840, 15 October 1892, pp. 849, 887, 19 August 1893, p. 255. Compare Robyn Burrows and Alan Barton, *Henry Lawson: A Stranger on the Darling*, p. 170.

55 Colin Roderick (ed.), *Henry Lawson Letters 1890 to 1922*, p. 49.

56 *APR*, 15 September 1892, p. 840, 15 October 1892, pp. 849, 887, 14 January 1893, p. 1033, 15 March 1893, p. 44, 15 August 1893, pp. 275–6; Colin Roderick, *Henry Lawson Letters*, pp. 51, 54. Compare Burrows and Barton, *Henry Lawson*, pp. 169–70.

57 Burrows and Barton, *Henry Lawson*, pp. 20–1.

58 Roderick, *Henry Lawson Letters*, pp. 50–4.

59 *APR*, 15 June 1893, pp. 147, 155, 19 August 1893, p. 255, 15 September 1893, p. 310; Colin Roderick, *Henry Lawson: The Master Story-Teller*, p. 85.

60 Henry Lawson, 'The Darling River', *Worker*, 26 August 1893, p. 4; Henry Lawson, 'Some Popular Australian Mistakes', *Bulletin*, 18 November 1893, p. 20; Henry Lawson, *Autobiographical and Other Writings 1887–1922*, p. 31; Roderick, *Henry Lawson: A Life*, ch. 8; Burrows and Barton, *Henry Lawson*, p. 182.

61 Henry Lawson, 'The Song of the Darling River', *Bulletin*, 25 March 1899, p. 3; Lawson, *Autobiographical and other Writings*, pp. 31–2, 95.

62 Henry Lawson, 'The Heart of Australia', *Bulletin*, 13 October 1904, p. 11; Henry Lawson, 'Australian Engineers', *Bulletin*, 19 January 1905, p. 8; Henry Lawson, 'The Water', *Amateur Gardener*, 15 March 1905; Henry Lawson, 'Australia's Peril', *Worker*, 24 June 1905, p. 4; Lloyd, *Either Drought or Plenty*, pp. 187, 225; Roderick, *Henry Lawson: A Life*, p. 99.

63 Lawson, *Autobiographical and other Writings*, p. 316; Roderick, *Henry Lawson Letters*, p. 229; Roderick, *Henry Lawson: A Life*, p. 349.

64 Christa E. Johannes and Anthony V. Brown, *W. C. Piguenit 1836–1914 Retrospective*, pp. 22, 44, 79, 108.

65 'Locking of the River Darling', *NSWLAV&P*, 1890, vol. 8, pp. 634–5.

66 W. C. Piguenit to Fanny Piguenit, 21 January 1889, AGNSW; Neville Nicholls, 'Historical El Niño/Southern Oscillation Variability in the Australasian Region', in Henry F. Diaz and Vera Markgraf (eds), *El Niño: Historical and Paleoclimatic Aspects of the Southern Oscillation*, p. 159; Joyce Pryse-Jones and Marjorie Fitzgerald, *William Charles Piguenit 1836–1914: First Australian-Born Landscape Painter of any Note*, pp. 20–2.

67 W. C. Piguenit to Fanny Piguenit, October 1889 and 26 April 1890, AGNSW; Pryse-Jones and Fitzgerald, *William Charles Piguenit*, pp. 20–2.

68 W. C. Piguenit to Fanny Piguenit, 26 April 1890, AGNSW; Arvid Nilson, 'Aesthetics: 'The Beauty of Inorganic Nature', *VR*, vol. 6, 1882, p. 531.

69 *Australasian*, 19 April 1890, p. 773; *DT*, 26 April 1890, p. 6; *SMH*, 24 April 1890, p. 8, 26 April 1890, p. 12; *ISN*, 10 May 1890, p. 17.

70 *Argus*, 23 April 1890, p. 5.

71 *DT*, 6 September 1890, p. 9; *SMH*, 6 September 1890, p. 5, 27 September 1890, p. 5; *Bulletin*, 13 September 1890, p. 14.

72 *SMH*, 28 September 1895, p. 7, 30 August 1895, p. 5; *Australian Star*, 28 September 1895, p. 2; *Evening News*, 28 September 1895, p. 4, 5 October 1895, supplement, p. 1; *Bulletin*, 5 October 1895, p. 20.

73 DG D6 f. 27, State Library of New South Wales; W. C. Piguenit to Fanny Piguenit, October 1889, AGNSW; Pryse-Jones and Fitzgerald, *William Charles Piguenit*, p. 22.

74 D. H. Souter, 'William Charles Piguenit: An Australian Painter', p. 197; Roderick, *Henry Lawson: A Life*, p. 399.

75 *JPRSNSW*, vol. 30, 1896, pp. lxxxiv–v; *SMH*,

9 December 1902, p. 9. McKinney was more cautious. See his 'Projects for Water Conservation, Irrigation and Drainage in New South Wales', *JPRSNSW*, vol. 35, 1901, p. 242.

76 *SM*, 19 July 1902, p. 156.

77 *APR*, 15 October 1892, pp. 865–6; *NSWPD*, vol. 89, 1897, pp. 2886–7; E. D. Millen, *Our Western Lands: A Vanishing Asset.*

78 Millen, *Our Western Lands*, esp. pp. 11–13; 'Royal Commission to Inquire into the Condition of the Crown Tenants, Western Division of New South Wales', parts I and II, *Journal of the Legislative Council of New South Wales*, vol. 63, part, 2, 1901; J. H. Maiden, 'The Sand-Drift Problem in New South Wales', pp. 97–8.

79 Millen, *Our Western Lands*, pp. 5, 22–3; Michael Quinn, 'Committed to Conserve: The Western Lands Act 1901 and the Management of the Public Estate of the Western Division of New South Wales', esp. pp. 187, 191–2.

CHAPTER ELEVEN: CREMORNE PASTORAL

1 T. W. E. David and E. F. Pittman, 'Notes on the Cremorne Bore', *JPRSNSW*, vol. 27, 1893, pp. 450–2; Edward F. Pittman, *The Mineral Resources of New South Wales*, pp. 316–7; Eric Russell, *The Opposite Shore: North Sydney and its People*, pp. 182–4.

2 *DT*, 11 November 1893, p. 9, 13 November 1893, p. 5.

3 *SMH*, 11 November 1893, p. 7, 12 August 1895, p. 6, 31 August 1895, p. 6; H. C. Russell, 'Anniversary Address', *JPRSNSW*, vol. 26, 1892, p. 27; *NSWPD*, vol. 79, 1895, pp. 510, 517–18; Pittman, *Mineral Resources of New South Wales*, p. 318.

4 *SMH*, 11 November 1893, p. 7; 12 August 1895, p. 6; 31 August 1895, p. 6; David and Pittman, 'Notes on the Cremorne Bore', p. 444; *NSWPD*, vol. 67, 1893, pp. 723–4; vol. 79, 1895, pp. 510, 517–18.

5 *SMH*, 11 November 1893, p. 8, 14 November 1893, p. 5; *DT*, 13 November 1893, p. 5, 14 November 1893, p. 4, 18 November 1893, p. 8, 28 November 1893, p. 5; *Bulletin*, 18 November 1893, p. 7; *AMS*, 2 December 1893, p. 652.

6 Trollope, *Australia and New Zealand*, vol. 1, pp. 207–10; James Inglis, *Our Australian Cousins*, p. 141.

7 Twopeny, *Town Life in Australia*, p. 19; *MP*, 27 November 1884, p. 217; Francis Adams, *Australian Essays*, p. 37; W. Frederic Morrison, *The Aldine Centennial History of New South Wales*, vol. 1, p. 382; *SM*, 3 May 1890, p. 982; *SMH*, 11 November 1893, p. 8; Max Kelly, 'Nineteenth Century Sydney: "Beautiful Certainly; Not Bountiful"', in Jim Davidson (ed.), *The Sydney–Melbourne Book*, p. 48.

8 *SMH*, 11 November 1893, p. 8. See also *SMH*, 18 November 1893, p. 5.

9 *DT*, 13 November 1893, pp. 5–6.

10 Michael Roe, *Nine Australian Progressives*, ch. 8; Michael Roe, 'Albert Bathurst Piddington', in *Australian Dictionary of Biography: Volume 11*, pp. 224–6.

11 *DT*, 17 November 1893, p. 3.

12 *DT*, 17 November 1893, p. 3.

13 *SMH*, 17 May 1884, p. 7, 23 May 1884, pp. 6–7; *DT*, 17 November 1893, p. 3.

14 *DT*, 17 November 1893, p. 3.

15 *DT*, 18 November 1893, p. 8; *Bulletin*, 18 November 1893, pp. 4, 11.

16 Crown Lands Act 1884 (NSW), s. 91; *SMH*, 15 November 1893, p. 6; *Bulletin*, 18 November 1893, pp. 4, 7, 9.

17 *Bulletin*, 18 November 1893, p. 7; *DT*, 25 November 1893, p. 8; *NSWPD*, vol. 68, 1893, p. 1374.

18 *Illustrated Sydney News*, 25 November 1893, pp. 2, 3; 2 December 1893, p. 1; 16 December 1893, p. 4.

19 *Australian Star*, 11 November 1893, p. 5, 14 November 1893, p. 6; *SMH*, 14 November 1893, p. 5.

20 *Australian Star*, 11 November 1893, p. 5, 14 November 1893, p. 6; *SMH*, 11 November 1893, p. 8, 22 January 1896, p. 9; *DT*, 13 November 1893, p. 5, 18 November 1893, p. 10; *AMS*, 18 November 1893, p. 652, 2 December 1895, p. 680; David and Pittman, 'Notes on the Cremorne Bore', esp. pp. 443, 444, 460, 465.

21 Inglis, *Our Australian Cousins*, p. 141.

22 James Inglis, 'Recent Economic Developments of Australlian Enterprise', *New Zealand Country Journal*, vol. 18, no. 4, July 1894, pp. 351–2.

23 *DT*, 14 March 1894, p. 5; *SMH*, 31 August 1895, p. 6, 27 January 1896, p. 6; *AMS*, 26 October 1895, p. 563, 7 December 1895, p. 654; *NSWPD*, vol. 79, 1895, p. 529.

24 Mining Act 1874 (NSW), s. 56(5).

25 *SMH*, 16 April 1884, p. 5; *NSWPD*, vol. 27, 1887, pp. 2689–2712, 2756–95; P. B. Cabena, *Victoria's Water Frontage Reserves: An Historical Review and Resource Appreciation*, esp. pp. 14–16.

26 *NSWPD*, vol. 18, 1885–86, pp. 659, 1007; vol. 20, 1885–86, pp. 2784–5; vol. 21, 1885–86, pp. 3398–9; vol. 27, 1887, p. 2693; 'Water Frontages, Port Jackson', *NSWLAV&P*, 1885–86, vol. 4.

27 *SMH*, 14 July 1887, p. 4.

28 *NSWPD*, vol. 27, 1887, pp. 2340, 2383, 2689–2712, 2756, 2782–95.
29 *Attorney-General v Milson* (1891) 12 NSWR 121 (L); *SMH*, 13 June 1891, p. 8; *DT*, 13 November 1893, p. 6.
30 *SMH*, 31 August 1895, p. 8; 22 January 1896, p. 9.
31 *Australian Star*, 14 March 1894, p. 2; *SMH*, 16 March 1894, p. 6; *DT*, 13 November 1895, p. 6; Edmund Marin la Meslée, *The New Australia*, p. 65.
32 'Sydney Harbour Collieries Company (Particulars respecting Application by the Trustees of the Cooper Estate to Reclaim and purchase Certain Land at Kurraba Point, Neutral Bay)', *NSWLAV&P*, 1895, part 2; *Attorney-General v Milson* (1895) 16 NSWR 145 (L).
33 *SMH*, 9 June 1891, p. 4; 13 June 1891, pp. 8, 11.
34 H. E. Campbell, 'Our Mining Laws', *Sydney Quarterly Magazine*, March 1887, p. 44.
35 *DT*, 24 May 1895, p. 4; *SMH*, 24 May 1895, p. 5; *Australian Star*, 6 September 1895, p. 8.
36 Bede Nairn, *Civilising Capitalism: The Labor Movement in New South Wales 1870–1900*, p. 60.
37 *DT*, 24 May 1895, p. 4; *SMH*, 24 May 1895, p. 5, 31 May 1933, p. 15; *NSWPD*, vol. 79, 1895, p. 500.
38 *DT*, 10 June 1895, p. 4, 11 June 1895, p. 6; *SMH*, 11 June 1895, p. 6.
39 *SMH*, 12 June 1895, p. 5; *DT*, 13 June 1895, p. 7.
40 *SMH*, 13 June 1895, p. 6.
41 Campbell, p. 46; *DT*, 14 June 1895, p. 4; *SMH*, 14 June 1895, p. 4; *Australian Star*, 6 September 1895, p. 8; *NSWPD*, vol. 78, 1894–95, pp. 6765.
42 *Australasian*, 14 September 1895, p. 552; *SMH*, 11 June 1895, p. 6, 5 September 1895, p. 4; *DT*, 10 September 1895, p. 5; *NSWPD*, vol. 79, 1895, pp. 500, 502, 506, 790.
43 *SMH*, 11 June 1895, p. 6, 5 September 1895, p. 4; *DT*, 10 September 1895, p. 5; *NSWPD*, vol. 79, 1895, pp. 500, 506.
44 *NSWPD*, vol. 79, 1895, pp. 106, 163–4, 322, 498.
45 *SMH*, 30 August 1895, p. 6.
46 *Bulletin*, 31 August 1895, p. 9.
47 *SMH*, 20 August 1895, p. 20.
48 *Argus*, 3 December 1892, p. 13, 10 December 1892, p. 4, 30 September 1893, p. 14.
49 Streeton, 'Personal Narrative', p. 10; *Argus*, 2 December 1892, p. 7, 15 September 1934, p. 22; *SMH*, 28 November 1936, p. 13.
50 *Bulletin*, 11 August 1900, Red Page; Galbally and Gray, *Letters from Smike*, pp. 17, 34, 66–7; Albie Thoms, *Bohemians in the Bush: The Artists' Camps of Mosman*, ch. 5; Mary Eagle, *The Oil Paintings of Arthur Streeton in the National Gallery of Australia*, pp. 85–8.
51 D. J. Quinn, 'Artists and Artistic Taste in Australasia', *Review of Reviews*, 20 November 1896, p. 514; *SMH*, 2 September 1895, p. 7.
52 *SMH*, 2 September 1895, p. 7, 3 September 1895, p. 6, 4 September 1895, p. 7, 6 September 1895, p. 6; *DT*, 5 September 1895, p. 4; *Australian Star*, 5 September 1895, p. 4, 9 September 1895, p. 3; *EN*, 3 September 1895, p. 4, 5 September 1895, p. 4; *Bulletin*, 14 September 1895, p. 14; *NSWPD*, vol. 79, 1895, pp. 499–529.
53 *EN*, 20 August 1895, p. 4, 3 September 1895, p. 4; *SMH*, 31 August 1895, p. 6; *DT*, 5 September 1895, p. 4; *Australian Star*, 9 September 1895, p. 3, 26 September 1895, p. 4; *NSWPD*, vol. 79, 1895, pp. 502, 507, 510, 512–13, 528.
54 *EN*, 3 September 1895, p. 4; *SMH*, 3 September 1895, p. 6; *DT*, 5 September 1895, p. 4; *Australian Star*, 26 September 1895, p. 3; *NSWPD*, vol. 79, 1895, pp. 504, 510, 512.
55 *NSWPD*, vol. 79, 1895, p. 504; *SMH*, 6 September 1895, p. 6; *Australian Star*, 26 September 1895, p. 4.
56 Mark Twain, *Mark Twain in Australia and New Zealand*, p. 112.
57 *SMH*, 31 August 1895, p. 6.
58 *SMH*, 18 July 1887, p. 4, 9 September 1892, p. 6, 10 September 1892, p. 5, 15 June 1895, p. 5, 6 September 1895, p. 6, 5 February 1896, p. 6; *SM*, 23 July 1887, p. 176, 31 August 1895, p. 428; *NSWPD*, vol. 79, 1895, pp. 244–54.
59 *NSWPD*, vol. 79, 1895, p. 249; McQueen, *Tom Roberts*, pp. 400–4.
60 *SMH*, 6 September 1895, p. 6.
61 *NSWPD*, vol. 79, 1895, pp. 522, 528–9; *SMH*, 4 September 1895, p. 7, 5 September 1895, p. 4; *Bulletin*, 14 September 1895, p. 16.
62 *SMH*, 12 August 1895, p. 6; *DT*, 12 August 1895, p. 2, 13 August 1895, p. 6, 14 August 1895, p. 3, 20 August 1895, p. 7.
63 *DT*, 27 September 1895, p. 6; *SMH*, 27 September 1895, p. 2; *Bulletin*, 5 October 1895, p. 20; McQueen, *Tom Roberts*, pp. 386, 410–11. Compare Barry Pearce, 'Bailed Up 1895/1927', in *Tom Roberts*, pp. 116–22.
64 *Australian Star*, 26 September 1895, p. 5; *Bulletin*, 5 October 1895, p. 12; *Cosmos Magazine*, 31 October 1895, pp. 79, 84.
65 *DT*, 27 September 1895, p. 6.
66 *Australian Star*, 26 September 1895, p. 5; Lloyd Rees, *The Small Treasures of a Lifetime*, p. 48; Helen Topliss, *Tom Roberts 1856–1931: A Catalogue Raisonné*, vol. 1, pp. 132, 141, 148–9.
67 *SMH*, 28 September 1895, p. 10.
68 *In re Sydney Harbour Collieries Company* (1895) 5 Land Appeal Court Reports 243, 244–5, 251.

69 *In re Sydney Harbour Collieries Company* (1895) 5 Land Appeal Court Reports 243, 255–6.
70 *DT*, 23 October 1895, p. 3; *In re Sydney Harbour Collieries Company* (1895) 5 Land Appeal Court Reports 243, 246, 258–9.
71 *In re Sydney Harbour Collieries Company* (1895) 5 Land Appeal Court Reports 243, 259.
72 *DT*, 31 October 1895, p. 3; *In re Sydney Harbour Collieries Company* (1895) 5 Land Appeal Court Reports 243, 259–60.
73 *SMH*, 1 November 1895, p. 2; 22 January 1896, p. 9.
74 *NSWPD*, vol. 81, 1895, p. 3565; *DT*, 23 November 1895, p. 5, 5 February 1896, p. 4; *Bulletin*, 7 December 1895, p. 7; *SMH*, 5 February 1896, p. 4.
75 *SMH*, 22 January 1896, p. 9, 23 January 1896, p. 6, 27 January 1896, p. 6; *DT*, 23 January 1896, p. 4, 25 January 1896, p. 10, 27 January 1896, p. 5.
76 *DT*, 30 January 1896, p. 3; *SMH*, 6 February 1896, p. 6.
77 *DT*, 5 February 1896, p. 4, 11 February 1896, p. 4; *SMH*, 5 February 1896, p. 4, 6 February 1896, p. 6, 11 February 1896, p. 4; *NSWPD*, vol. 82, 1896, p. 217; vol. 83, 1896, p. 1433.
78 *SM*, 14 September 1895, p. 532.
79 *AMS*, 28 December 1895, p. 712; *SMH*, 2 January 1896, p. 9; 'Annual Report of the Department of Mines and Agriculture, New South Wales for the Year 1896', *NSWLAV&P*, 1897, vol. 3, p. 41; Shirley Fisher, 'The Pastoral Interest and Sydney's Public Health', p. 79; Shirley Fitzgerald, *Rising Damp: Sydney 1870–1890*, p. 32. The *Bulletin*, 1 February 1896, p. 12, appears to have been typically ill-informed when it reported that the company had bought a site on Taylor Bay, on the far side of Bradleys Head from Athol Bay.
80 Barrett, *The Inner Suburbs*, esp. pp. 11, 105–22; T. G. Parsons, 'Manufacturing on the Banks of the Yarra River, Melbourne: The Development of an Industrial Area', p. 22; Fisher, 'The Pastoral Interest', p. 81.
81 *SMH*, 26 September 1894, p. 5; *DT*, 27 September 1894, p. 6; *Australian Star*, 28 September 1895, p. 7; *AMS*, 28 December 1895, p. 712.
82 Morrison, *Aldine Centennial History*, vol. 2, p. 470; *DT*, 15 January 1896, p. 6.
83 A. J. C. Mayne, '"A Most Pernicious Principle": The Local Governmnt Franchise in Nineteenth-Century Sydney", pp. 160–71.
84 *Age*, 7 March 1872, p. 2; 14 April 1883, p. 6, 23 April 1883, supplement, p. 1; Parsons, 'Manufacturing on the Yarra', pp. 25–6; Lack,'Worst Smelbourne', pp. 190–1, 199.
85 *SMH*, 29 January 1896, p. 5, 5 February 1896, p. 5, 10 February 1896, p. 5; *Freeman's Journal*, 15 February 1896, p. 9; *AMS*, 2 April 1896, p. 942; 'Annual Report of the Department of Mines and Agriculture, New South Wales for the Year 1896', *NSWLAV&P*, vol. 3, p. 41; Pittman, *Mineral Resources of New South Wales*, pp. 319–20; Edward F. Pittman, *The Coal Resources of New South Wales*, pp. 18–19.
86 Pittman, *Coal Resources of New South Wales*, p. 19; *Cyclopedia of New South Wales*, p. 210; *NSWPD*, vol. 31, 1908, pp. 1474, 1671; McQueen, *Tom Roberts*, pp. 426, 508.

CHAPTER TWELVE: THE TEMPLATE

1 M. C. Downes, 'The History of Tower Hill to 1892', pp. 26–66; Bardwell, The National Park Movement in Victoria, pp. 375–6.
2 *Argus*, 4 October 1855, p. 5; *CC*, 2 April 1891, p. 2; *Standard*, 27 July 1896, p. 3; Bonwick, *Western Victoria*, p. 59; Christies Australia, *Australian Paintings and Books*, 7 October 1986, lot 275.
3 James Dawson to James Smith, 2 March 1881, Smith papers, MSS212/2, ML; James Dawson, *Australian Aborigines: The Language and Customs of Several Tribes of Aborigines of the Western District of Victoria*.
4 'Royal Commission on Aborigines', *VPP*, 1877–78, vol. 3, pp. 99–100, 105–6; Peter Corris, *Aborigines and Europeans in Western Victoria*, p. 18.
5 *Argus*, 9 September 1876, p. 10; 'Royal Commission on Aborigines', *VPP*, 1877–78, vol. 3, p. 100.
6 Jan Critchett, *A 'Distant Field of Murder': Western District Frontiers 1834–1848*, p. 191; Griffiths, *Hunters and Collectors*, pp. 112–13.
7 James Dawson, scrapbook, pp. 40–1, 50, LTL.
8 *Argus*, 23 March 1872, p. 6.
9 *CC*, 2 April 1891, p. 2; 24 February 1891, p. 4.
10 *KSTHA*, 7 March 1891, p. 2.
11 *CC*, 24 February 1891, p. 4; 10 March 1891, p. 4.
12 *KSTHA*, 6 May 1891, p. 2, 13 May 1891, p. 2; *Standard*, 27 July 1896, p. 3.
13 *KSTHA*, 22 August 1891, p. 2; 26 August 1891, p. 2; 7 November 1891, pp. 2, 3; 14 November 1891, p. 2.
14 *KSTHA*, 18 May 1892, p. 2; *Warrnambool Evening Echo*, 19 May 1892, p. 2; *VPD*, vol. 69, 1892–93, p. 589.
15 *KSTHA*, 29 July 1891, p. 3; 8 August 1891, p. 3; 2 September 1891, p. 2; 5 September 1891, p. 3; 12 March 1892, p. 2; 16 March 1892, p. 2.
16 *KSTHA*, 9 April 1892, p. 3, 8 June 1892, p. 2,

30 July 1892, p. 2, 6 August 1892, pp. 2, 3; *Argus*, 21 July 1892, pp. 4–5; *VPD*, vol. 69, 1892–93, pp. 589–91; Tower Hill National Park Act 1892 (Vic.), s. 2(1).

17 Tower Hill National Park Act 1892, second schedule.

18 J. J. Flahavin to J. Ros Garnet, 25 June 1948, VNPA file; *KS*, 4 February 1939, p. 4, 6 May 1939, p. 2, 4 November 1939, p. 2, 13 August 1960, p. 3; M. C. Downes, *What Happened at Tower Hill?*, p. 6; Ranald Anderson, 'The Tower Hill Experience', p. 98.

19 Agnes Taylor, 'Tower Hill: The Wonderland that Stands beside the Sea', p. 19; John Coto, 'Planting Six Hundred Pines on Tower Hill', p. 15; *KS*, 26 April 1924, p. 2, 10 May 1924, p. 3, 31 May 1924, p. 2, 14 June 1924, p. 2, 4 May 1940, p. 2, 31 May 1941, p. 2.

20 P. E. O'Grady to L. W. Cooper, 5 November 1937, 6 January 1938, VNPA file; *KS*, 29 July 1939, p. 2, 5 August 1939, p. 2, 23 September 1939, p. 2, 30 September 1939, p. 2, 4 May 1940, p. 2; Bill Phillips, *Koalas*, pp. 22, 38.

21 *KS*, 26 August 1939, p. 3; 7 October 1939, p. 2; 21 December 1940, p. 1; 1 February 1941, p. 2; 12 July 1941, p. 2; 19 July 1941, p. 3; 26 July 1941, p. 4.

22 *Age*, 29 August 1959, p. 20; *VN*, vol. 72, 1955, p. 58; J. L. Martin, 'Restoration of Vegetation at Tower Hill', p. 192; Eulalie Bennett, 'Port Fairy Excursion, Easter, 1964', pp. 40–1; *Tower Hill Guide*, 1966, pp. 2, 5, 6, 7; Catherine John and Helen Moore, *Redressing the Volcano: The Restoration of Tower Hill*, pp. 19, 22, 36, 37; D. M. d'Costa et al., 'Late Quarternary Palaeoecology of Tower Hill, Victoria, Australia', p. 480.

23 *Wild Life*, July 1947, p. 245, November 1950, p. 487, May 1952, p. 409; *VN*, vol. 67, 1951, pp. 189–90, 192, 195, vol. 69, April 1953, p. 148; *Wildlife and Outdoors*, August 1952, p. 158; *VPD*, vol. 248, 1956, p. 3747; vol. 249, p. 376.

24 *Walkabout*, 1 June 1950, p. 34; Graham Pizzey, *Crosbie Morrison: Voice of Nature*; Stephen Johnston, 'Profile of a Parks Pioneer', pp. 8–12.

25 Tower Hill file, VNPA; *Report of the State Development Committee on National Parks*, p. 37; Pizzey, *Crosbie Morrison*, ch. 12; John and Moore, *Redressing the Volcano*, p. 24.

26 Dewar W. Goode and J. Ros Garnet, 'National Parks', 30 August 1955.

27 *VPD*, vol. 250, 1956, pp. 5062–3, 5072.

28 Dewar Goode to Crosbie Morrison and Alex Wilkie, 22 July 1957; Dewar Goode to C. E. Isaac, 24 July 1957, Goode papers, box 14/41; National Parks Authority, 'First Annual Report for the Year ended 30th June 1957', *VPP*, 1956–58, vol. 2, p. 8; Pizzey, *Crosbie Morrison*, p. 252.

29 Dewar Goode to the Mayor of Koroit, 1 August 1957; 'Areas Proposed as National Parks and Additions as at 1.12.1957', Goode papers, box 14/41; *KS*, 4 May 1957, pp. 1, 2, 11 May 1957, pp. 1, 3, 16 November 1957, p. 2, 12 July 1958, p. 3, 16 January 1960, pp. 2, 4; *Age*, 9 May 1957, p. 7; National Parks Authority, 'First Annual Report', p. 8.

30 *KS*, 15 June 1957, p. 2.

31 *KS*, 6 July 1957, p. 3.

32 *KS*, 13 July 1957, p. 3; 3 August 1957, p. 1; 12 October 1957, p. 2.

33 *KS*, 3 August 1957, p. 1.

34 *KS*, 22 November 1958, p. 1; National Parks Authority, 'Annual Report for the Year Ended 30th June 1958', *VPP*, 1958–59, vol. 2, p. 6.

35 Aldo Leopold, *A Sand County Almanac*, p. 204; Worster, *Nature's Economy*, pp. 284, 286–7.

36 Worster, *Nature's Economy*, pp. 272, 284; Susan L. Flader, *Thinking like a Mountain: Aldo Leopold and the Evolution of an Ecological Attitude toward Deer, Wolves and Forests*, p. 23; Curt Meine, 'Aldo Leopold's Early Years', in J. Baird Callicott (ed.), *Companion to a Sand County Almanac*, pp. 30–4.

37 *Report of the 1954 Biennial Conference on Australian Fauna*, pp. 53–65. This section draws heavily on an interview with Max Downes, 9 November 1995.

38 M. C. Downes, 'Tower Hill as a State Game Reserve', p. 2; M. C. Downes, 'History of the Fisheries and Wildlife Division, Victoria 1934–84', in *Victorian Year Book 1984*, p. 325.

39 *Report of the 1954 Biennial Conference on Australian Fauna*, p. 58; *VPD*, vol. 259, 1959–60, pp. 1875, 2451; *KS*, 30 April 1960, p. 3, 3 June 1961, p. 3.

40 *Standard*, 17 February 1959, p. 10; *KS*, 7 March 1959, p. 3, 4 July 1859, p. 1; *VPD*, vol. 255, 1958–59, pp. 1681–2; A. J. Marshall, 'The Way Ahead', in Marshall (ed.), *The Great Extermination*, pp. 210–11; F. I. Norman and A. D. Young, 'Short-Sighted and Doubly Short-Sighted are They: A Brief Examination of the Game Laws of Victoria 1858–1958', esp. p. 16; Downes, 'History of the Fisheries and Wildlife Division', p. 327.

41 Reverend Shrader to J. Ros Garnet, 14 February 1959; Tom Connors to J. Ros Garnet, 26 February 1959, VNPA file.

42 J. Ros Garnet to Tom Connors, 11 February 1959, VNPA file; *KS*, 7 February 1959, p. 2; *Standard*, 17 February 1959, p. 10.

43 *KS*, 14 February 1959, p. 2; *Standard*, 14 February 1959, p. 6, 17 February 1959, p. 10.

[44] *Standard*, 23 February 1959, p. 3, 24 February 1959, p. 6; *KS*, 21 February 1959, p. 2, 7 March 1959, p. 3.

[45] *Standard*, 12 February 1959, p. 2, 24 February 1959, p. 6, 11 April 1959, p. 5, 2 April 1959, p. 2, 7 May 1959, p. 4, 13 May 1959, p. 2, 26 June 1959, p. 2, 27 June 1959, p. 3; *KS*, 7 March 1959, p. 2, 27 June 1959, p. 2; *Age*, 29 August 1959, p. 20; *Victorian National Parks Association Newsletter*, no. 30, July 1960; John and Moore, *Redressing the Volcano*, p. 32.

[46] *Standard*, 11 April 1959, p. 5; *KS*, 4 July 1959, p. 1, 11 July 1959, p. 2.

[47] *KS*, 10 October 1959, p. 4, 31 October 1959, p. 1; *Standard*, 10 October 1959, p. 5; Downes, 'Tower Hill as a State Game Reserve', pp. 5–6.

[48] *KS*, 4 April 1959, pp. 1, 3, 18 April 1959, pp. 2–3, 25 April 1959, p. 3; *Standard*, 15 April 1959, p. 2, 18 April 1959, p. 2, 21 April 1959, p. 2.

[49] Reverend Shrader to J. Ros Garnet, 23 October 1959, VNPA; Robert Billings to J. Ros Garnet, 17 December 1959, VNPA.

[50] *Standard*, 29 October 1959, p. 2; *KS*, 31 October 1959, p. 3.

[51] *Standard*, 4 May 1959, p. 2, 19 May 1959, p. 2, 19 June 1959, p. 3; *KS*, 16 January 1960, pp. 2–3, 6 February 1960, p. 2; *VPD*, vol. 262, 1960–61, p. 1386.

[52] *Herald*, 3 December 1966, p. 33; A. Dunbavin Butcher, *State Wildlife Reserves System*, p. 5; Keith McKenry, 'Parks for the People', p. 29.

[53] *KS*, 4 February 1961, p. 1, 4 March 1961, p. 1, 11 March 1961, p. 1; John and Moore, *Redressing the Volcano*, p. 44; Anderson, 'The Tower Hill Experience', p. 95.

[54] *KS*, 7 October 1961, p. 1, 14 October 1961, p. 1, 17 February 1962, p. 3; *Age*, 29 March 1980, p. 21.

[55] *KS*, 28 May 1960, p. 2, 4 June 1960, p. 2, 17 February 1962, p. 3; Downes, *What Happened at Tower Hill?*, pp. 1, 8; A. Dunbavin Butcher, 'Wildlife Reserves for Recreation', p. 100.

[56] *KS*, 7 November 1959, p. 3; 14 November 1959, p. 2.

[57] *Standard*, 19 March 1959, p. 2, 20 March 1959, p. 2; John and Moore, *Redressing the Volcano*, pp. 33–4.

[58] *Standard*, 19 March 1959, p. 2.

[59] Downes, 'A History of Tower Hill to 1892', p. 33; Daniel Thomas, 'Von Guérard's Reputation' in Candice Bruce, *Eugen von Guérard*, p. 131.

[60] Downes, 'A History of Tower Hill to 1892', p. 34; John and Moore, *Redressing the Volcano*, p. 34.

[61] Bruce, *Eugen von Guérard*, p. 134.

[62] Downes, 'A History of Tower Hill to 1892', appendix C.

[63] Mrs Charles Meredith, *Notes and Sketches of New South Wales*, p. 81; Mrs Charles Meredith, *My Home in Tasmania*, vol. 1, pp. 50–1; Wilkes, *Narrative*, vol. 2, p. 189.

[64] Downes, 'A History of Tower Hill to 1892', pp. 33–4; Robin Boyd, *Living in Australia*,, p. 140; John and Moore, *Redressing the Volcano*, pp. 8, 10, 34.

[65] Bonwick, *Western Victoria*, p. 64; Martin, 'Restoration of Vegetation at Tower Hill', p. 194; John and Moore, *Redressing the Volcano*, p. 36.

[66] *Herald*, 3 December 1966, p. 33; John and Moore, *Redressing the Volcano*, p. 36.

[67] *Tower Hill Guide*, 1966, p. 3; Anderson, 'The Tower Hill Experience', pp. 91–2.

[68] *Tower Hill Guide*, p. 2; M. C. Downes, *Tower Hill*, pp. 10–11.

[69] Gavin Cerini to J. Ros Garnet, 11 March 1970, VNPA file.

[70] Martin, 'Restoration of Vegetation at Tower Hill', p. 192.

[71] Michael Rosenthal, 'The Landscape of Nostalgia, The Landscape of Decline'.

[72] John and Moore, *Redressing the Volcano*, pp. 51–2.

[73] *KS*, 17 February 1962, p. 3, 13 October 1962, p. 2; *Herald*, 3 December 1966, p. 33; John and Moore, *Redressing the Volcano*, p. 41.

[74] Boyd, *Living in Australia*, pp. 142–3.

[75] David Hansen, *Tower Hill and its Artists*; Robyn McKenzie, 'Geoff Lowe and Tower Hill', pp. 19–22; Joan Kerr, 'Colonial Quotations', p. 380.

[76] *KS*, 4 July 1959, p. 1; 17 February 1962, p. 3.

[77] Anderson, 'The Tower Hill Experience', p. 94.

[78] John and Moore, *Redressing the Volcano*, pp. 36–7; Anderson, 'The Tower Hill Experience', p. 94.

[79] R. M. Warneke, 'The Status of the Koala in Victoria', in T. J. Bergin (ed.), *The Koala*, p. 111; A. K. Lee and R. W. Martin, *The Koala: A Natural History*, pp. 92–4; Phillips, *Koalas*, pp. 34–5, 40.

[80] Brett Anthony Bryan, 'A Generic Method for Identifying Regional Koala Habitat using GIS', pp. 125–6.

[81] Koala Management Task Force, *Final Report*, 1996.

[82] J. Sherwood et al., *Understorey Revegetation Project: Tower Hill State Game Reserve*, 1992.

SELECT BIBLIOGRAPHY

MANUSCRIPTS

Australian Artists' Association, Papers, LTL.
Backhouse, James, Journal, ML.
Calder, James, Papers, LTL.
Campbell, J. Massingberd, Diary, ML.
Dawson, James, Scrapbook, LTL.
Downes, M. C., 'The History of Tower Hill to 1892', Fisheries and Wildlife Department, Melbourne, 1961.
Downes, M. C., 'Tower Hill as a State Game Reserve', Fisheries and Wildlife Department, Melbourne, 1959.
du Faur, Eccleston, Notebook, ML.
Goode, Dewar W., Papers, Australian Science and Technology Heritage Centre, Melbourne.
King, Philip Gidley, Journal, NLA.
Hervey, L. E., 'Diary of a Tour round the World: 1889 and 1890', LTL.
Mueller, Ferdinand von, Letters, Mueller Project, National Herbarium, Melbourne.
Muir, John, Papers, Holt–Atherton Center for Western Studies, University of the Pacific, Stockton, California.
Nicholls, Neville, 'The Centennial Drought', 1988, private collection.
Parkes, Henry, Papers, ML.
Piguenit, W. C., Letters, AGNSW.
Piguenit, W. C., Scrapbook, ML.
Robinson, George Augustus, Papers, ML.
Rosenthal, Michael, 'The Landscape of Nostalgia, The Landscape of Decline', 1994, private collection.
Smith, James, Papers, ML.
Streeton, Arthur, 'Personal Narrative', private collection.
Tower Hill file, Victorian National Parks Association.

BOOKS, ARTICLES AND THESES

Abbott, W. A., 'Ringbarking and its Effects', *JPRSNSW*, vol. 14, 1880, pp. 97–102.
Ackland, Michael. *Henry Kendall: The Man and the Myths*. Melbourne University Press, Melbourne, 1995.
——— (ed.). *Henry Kendall: Poetry, Prose and Selected Correspondence*. University of Queensland Press, St Lucia, 1993.
Adams, Francis. *Australian Essays*. Inglis, Melbourne, 1886.
Adams, W. P., 'Deer Stalking with a Camera', *British Journal of Photography*, 1889, pp. 647–8.
Alinder, James (ed.). *Carleton E. Watkins: Photographs of the Columbia River and Oregon*. Friends of Photography, 1979.
Allen, David Elliston. *The Victorian Fern Craze: A History of Pteridomania*. Hutchinson, London, 1969.
——— *The Naturalist in Britain: a Social History*. Allen Lane, London, 1976.
Amphlett, E. A., 'The Bourke Lock and Weir', *Australian Technical Journal*, 28 February 1898, pp. 21–5; 28 March 1898, pp. 57–62.
Anderson, Ranald, 'The Tower Hill Experience', in *The Brilliance of Australian Plants: Association of Societies for Growing Australian Plants 18th Biennial Conference*, Ballarat, 1995, pp. 91–101.
Andrews, Alan E. J. (ed.). *The Devil's Wilderness: George Caley's Journey to Mount Banks 1804*. Blubber Head Press, Hobart, 1984.
——— *Stapylton: With Major Mitchell's Australia Felix Expedition 1836*. Blubber Head Press, Hobart, 1986.
'Annual Progress Report of the Forest Reserves of South Australia for 1879–80', *Proceedings of the Parliament of South Australia*, 1880, vol. 4.
'Annual Report of the Department of Mines and Agriculture, New South Wales for the Year 1896', *NSWLAV&P*, 1897, vol. 3.

Aplin, Graeme (ed.). *A Difficult Infant: Sydney before Macquarie*. University of New South Wales Press, Sydney, 1988.

Ashton, Julian. *Now Came Still Evening On*. Angus & Robertson, Sydney, 1941.

Atkinson, Alan, 'The British Whigs and the Rum Rebellion', *JRAHS*, vol. 66, 1980, pp. 73–90.

——— *The Europeans in Australia: A History Volume 1*. Oxford University Press, Melbourne, 1997.

Atkinson, James. *An Account of the State of Agriculture and Grazing in New South Wales*. Cross, London, 1826.

Audubon, John James. *Delineations of American Character and Scenery*. Baker, New York, 1926.

Australasian Association for the Advancement of Science. *Excursions: Melbourne 1890 (Trip to the Black Spur)*. Melbourne, 1890.

Australian Health Society, Melbourne: a Twenty-Five Years' Record of the Work and Progress of the Society. Australian Health Society, Melbourne, 1900.

Baalman, John, 'Gubernatorial Land Jobbing', *RAHSJP*, vol. 48, 1962, pp. 241–55.

Bailey, F. M. *Fern World of Australia*. Gordon & Gotch, Brisbane, 1881.

Baker, D. W. A. *The Civilised Surveyor: Thomas Mitchell and the Australian Aborigines*. Melbourne University Press, Melbourne, 1997.

Bardwell, Sandra. *Ferntree Gully National Park: A Centenary History 1882–1982*. National Parks Service, Melbourne, 1982.

——— The National Park Movement in Victoria, PhD, Monash University, 1974.

Barley, Richard, 'Plants from Old Nursery Catalogues', *Australian Garden History*, vol. 2, no. 3, November/December 1990, pp. 17–19.

Barnard, F. G. A., 'Excursion to Ferntree Gully', *Victorian Naturalist*, vol. 13, 1896–97, pp. 142–5.

Barnard, Jill and Keating, Jenny. *People's Playground: A History of Albert Park*. Chandos, Melbourne, 1996.

Barnet, Nahum, 'Climatic Architecture', *Victorian Review*, vol. 7, 1882, pp. 37–43.

Barrett, Bernard. *The Inner Suburbs: The Evolution of an Industrial Area*. Melbourne University Press, Melbourne, 1971.

Barrett, Charles (ed.). *Australian Nature Pictures*. Alexander McCubbin, Melbourne, 1920.

Bartrum, Mr. *Proceedings of a General Court-Martial . . . for the Trial of Lieut.-Col. Geo. Johnston . . . on a Charge of Mutiny*. Sherwood, Neely & Jones, London, 1811.

Beattie, J. W., 'The Picturesque West Coast of Tasmania', *Australian Photographic Journal*, 20 August 1897, pp. 191–2.

Beckett, R. B. (ed.). *John Constable's Correspondence VI: The Fishers*. Suffolk Records Society, Ipswich, vol. 12, 1968.

Beder, Sharon, 'Early Environmentalists and the Battle against Sewers in Sydney', *JRAHS*, vol. 76, 1990, pp. 27–43.

The Beginnings of Government in Australia. Library Committee of the Parliament of the Commonwealth, Sydney, 1913.

Bennett, Eulalie, 'Port Fairy Excursion, Easter, 1964', *Victorian Naturalist*, vol. 81, June 1964, pp. 40–2.

Bennett, George. *Wanderings in New South Wales*. Bentley, London, 1834, 2 vols.

Bennett, J. M., 'Richard Atkins: An Amateur Judge Jeffreys', *JRAHS*, vol. 52, 1966, pp. 261–92.

Bergin, T. J. (ed.). *The Koala*. John Sands, Sydney, 1978.

Betts, T. *An Account of the Colony of Van Diemen's Land*. Calcutta, Thacker, 1830.

Bicknell, George A., 'A Plea for Sanitation', *Victorian Review*, vol. 7, 1882, pp. 166–74.

Blackley, Roger. *The Art of Alfred Sharpe*. Auckland City Art Gallery, Auckland, 1992.

Blackstone, William. *Commentaries on the Laws of England*. Clarendon Press, Oxford, 1770, 4th ed., 4 vols.

Blainey, Geoffrey. *A Land Half Won*. Macmillan, Melbourne, 1980.

Blake, L. J., 'Village Settlements', *Victorian Historical Journal*, vol. 37, 1966, pp. 189–201.

Blue Mountains Railway Tourist Guide, Leigh, Sydney, c. 1895.
Blum, Ann Shelby. *Picturing Nature: American Nineteenth-Century Zoological Illustration*. Princeton University Press, Princeton, 1993.
Blunt, Wilfred. *The Art of Botanical Illustration*. Collins, London, 3rd ed., 1955.
Bolton, Geoffrey. *Spoils and Spoilers: Australians Make Their Environment 1788–1980*. Allen & Unwin, Sydney, 1982.
Bonwick, James. *Western Victoria: Its Geography, Geology and Social Condition*. Brown, Geelong, 1858.
Bonyhady, Tim, *Australian Colonial Paintings in the Australian National Gallery*. Australian National Gallery/ Oxford University Press, Melbourne, 1987.
——— *Images in Opposition: Australian Landscape Painting 1801–1890*, Oxford University Press, Melbourne, 1985.
——— 'Lake Pedder 1871', *Island*, no. 55, winter 1993, pp. 16–21.
——— *Places Worth Keeping: Conservationists, Politics and Law*, Allen & Unwin, Sydney, 1993.
——— 'A Usable Past: The Public Trust in Australia', *Environmental and Planning Law Journal*, vol. 12, 1995, pp. 329–38.
——— (ed.). *Environment Protection and Legal Change*. Federation Press, Sydney, 1992.
Bonyhady, Tim, and Griffiths, Tom (eds). *Prehistory to Politics: John Mulvaney, the Humanities and the Public Intellectual*. Melbourne University Press, Melbourne, 1996.
Bosisto, Joseph, 'Is the Eucalyptus a Fever-destroying Tree?', *Transactions and Proceedings of the Royal Society of Victoria*, vol. 12, 1874–75, pp. 10–23.
Boyd, Robin. *The Australian Ugliness*. Cheshire, Melbourne, 1960.
——— *Living in Australia*. Pergamon Press, Sydney, 1970.
Bradley, Anthony and Smith, Terry, (eds). *Australian Art and Architecture: Essays Presented to Bernard Smith*. Oxford University Press, Melbourne, 1980.
Bradley, William. *A Voyage to New South Wales*. Public Library of New South Wales/Ure Smith, Sydney, 1969.
Broadbent, James. *The Australian Colonial House*. Hordern House, Sydney, 1997.
——— 'Introduction' to *Colonial Greek: The Greek Revival in New South Wales 1810–1850*. Historic Houses Trust of New South Wales, Sydney, 1985.
Brown, Bob. *Lake Pedder*. Wilderness Society, Hobart, 1986.
Bruce, Candice. *Eugen von Guérard*. Australian Galleries Directors Council/ Australian National Gallery, Canberra, 1980.
Bryan, Brett Anthony, 'A Generic Method for Identifying Regional Koala Habitat using GIS', *Australian Geographic Studies*, vol. 35, 1997, pp. 125–39.
Buchanan, Joan M., Mrs Charles Meredith: A Biography (1812–1895), MA thesis, University of Melbourne, 1950.
Burroughs, Peter. *Britain and Australia 1831–1855*. Clarendon, Oxford, 1967.
Burrows, Robyn and Barton, Alan. *Henry Lawson: A Stranger on the Darling*. Angus & Robertson, Sydney, 1996.
Buscombe, Eve, 'A Discussion about Augustus Earle and some of his Portraits', *Art Bulletin of Victoria*, no. 19, 1978, pp. 46–59.
Butcher, A. Dunbavin. *State Wildlife Reserves System*. Fisheries and Wildlife Department, Melbourne, 1965.
——— 'Wildlife Reserves for Recreation', *Victoria's Resources*, vol. 76, no. 4, December 1964–February 1965, pp. 98–100.
Buxton, G. L. *The Riverina: An Australian Regional Study*. Melbourne University Press, Melbourne, 1967.
Cabena, P. B. *Victoria's Water Frontage Reserves: An Historical Review and Resource Appreciation*. Department of Crown Lands & Survey, Melbourne, 1983.
Caire, N. J., 'Notes on the Giant Trees of Victoria', *Victorian Naturalist*, vol. 21, 1904–05, pp. 122–8.
Caire, N. J., and Lindt, J. W. *Companion Guide to Healesville, Blacks' Spur, Narbethong and Marysville: Historical, Descriptive and Pictorial*. Atlas Press, Melbourne, 1904.

Calaby, John (ed.). *The Hunter Sketchbook*. National Library of Australia, Canberra, 1988.
Calder, J. E. *Some Accounts of the Wars, Extirpation, Habits &c. of the Native Tribes of Tasmania*. Henn, Hobart, 1875.
Callicott, J. Baird (ed.). *Companion to a Sand County Almanac*. University of Wisconsin Press, Madison, 1987, pp. 17–39.
Campbell, Archibald J. *Nests and Eggs of Australian Birds*. Campbell, Melbourne, 1883.
——— *Nests and Eggs of Australian Birds*. Pawson & Brailsford, Sheffield, 1901, 2 parts.
——— 'Notes about Lyrebirds', *Victorian Naturalist*, vol. 1, 1884–85, pp. 105–8.
——— 'The Protection of Native Birds', *Emu*, vol. 2, 1903, pp. 187–9.
——— 'The Protection of Our Native Birds', *Victorian Naturalist*, vol. 1, 1884–85, pp. 161–4.
Campbell, H. E., 'Our Mining Laws', *Sydney Quarterly Magazine*, March 1887, pp. 43–53.
Campbell, J. F., 'Historical Notes on Government House Domain, Sydney', *RAHSJP*, vol. 17, 1932, pp. 111–26.
——— 'Rose Hill Government Farm and the Founding of Parramatta', *RAHSJP*, vol. 12, 1926, pp. 353–77.
Cannon, Michael. *The Land Boomers*. Melbourne University Press, Melbourne, 1966.
Chancellor, John. *Audubon*. Weidenfeld & Nicholson, London, 1978.
Chapman, Peter (ed.). *The Diaries and Letters of G. T. W. B. Boyes: Volume 1, 1820–1832*. Oxford University Press, Melbourne, 1985.
Charlton, D. G. *New Images of the Natural in France: A Study in European Cultural History 1750–1800*. Cambridge University Press, Cambridge, 1984.
Christies Australia. *Australian Paintings and Books*. 7 October 1986.
Clark, C. M. H. *A History of Australia*. Melbourne University Press, Melbourne, 1962, vol. 1.
Clarke, Patricia. *Pioneer Writer: The Life of Louisa Atkinson*. Allen & Unwin, Sydney, 1990.
Clarke, W. B. *Effects of Forest Vegetation on Climate*. Sydney, 1876.
Clarson, William. *The Flower Garden and Shrubbery*. Gibbs, Shallard, Sydney, 1885.
Cohn, Helen and Maroske, Sara, 'Relief from Duties of Minor Importance: The Removal of Baron von Mueller from the Directorship of the Melbourne Botanic Gardens', *Victorian Historical Journal*, vol. 67, 1996, pp. 103–27.
Collins, David. *An Account of the English Colony of New South Wales*. Cadell & Davies, London, 1798. 2 vols.
Connah, Graham, 'Historical Reality, Archaeology Reality: Excavations at Regentville, Penrith, New South Wales, 1985', *Australian Historical Archaeology*, vol. 4, 1986, pp. 29–42.
Cooper, Elwood. *Forest Culture and Eucalyptus Trees*. Cobery, San Francisco, 1876.
Corris, Peter. *Aborigines and Europeans in Western Victoria*. Australian Institute of Aboriginal Studies, Canberra, 1968.
Cosgrove, Denis, and Daniels, Stephen (eds). *The Iconography of Landscape: Essays on the Symbolic Representation, Design and Use of Past Environments*. Cambridge University Press, Cambridge, 1988.
Coto, John, 'Planting Six Hundred Pines on Tower Hill', *The Link*, vol. 1, no. 7, September 1924, p. 15.
Coulson, Helen. *Story of the Dandenongs*. Cheshire, Melbourne, 1959.
Crichton, David A., 'State Forests and their Conservation', *Victorian Review*, vol. 5, 1882, pp. 458–66.
Critchett, Jan. *A 'Distant Field of Murder': Western District Frontiers 1834–1848*. Melbourne University Press, Melbourne, 1990.
Cumpston, J. S. *Kangaroo Island 1800–1836*. Roebuck, Canberra, 2nd ed., 1974.
Cunningham, Peter. *Two Years in New South Wales*. Colburn, London, 1827, 2 vols.
Curr, Edward. *An Account of the Colony of Van Diemen's Land*. Cowie, London, 1824.

Cyclopedia of New South Wales. McCarron, Stewart, Sydney, 1907.
Cyclopedia of Tasmania. Maitland & Krone, Hobart, 1899–1900, 2 vols.
Dakis, Sallyann, 'The Botanical Art of Mary Morton Allport', *Australian Garden History*, vol. 8, no. 5, March–April 1997, pp. 12–13.
Dalkin, R. N., 'Norfolk Isand: The First Settlement 1788-1814', *JRAHS*, vol. 57, 1971, pp. 189-212.
Dann, John C. (ed.). *The Nagle Journal*. Weidenfeld & Nicolson, New York, 1988.
Dargavel, John, and Feary, Sue (eds). *Australia's Ever-Changing Forests II*. Centre for Resource and Environmental Studies, ANU, Canberra, 1993.
Darley, Gillian. *Octavia Hill: A Life*. Constable, London, 1990.
Darwin, Charles. *Journal of Researches into the Geology and Natural History of the Various Countries visited by H.M.S. Beagle*. Colburn, London, 1839.
David, T. W. E., and Pittman, E. F., 'Notes on the Cremorne Bore', *JPRSNSW*, vol. 27, 1893, pp. 443–65.
Davidson, Jim (ed.). *The Sydney–Melbourne Book*. Allen & Unwin, Sydney, 1986.
Davison, Graeme. *The Rise and Fall of Marvellous Melbourne*. Melbourne University Press, Melbourne, 1979.
Davison, Graeme, Dunstan, David and McConville, Chris (eds). *The Outcasts of Melbourne: Essays in Social History*. Allen & Unwin, Sydney, 1985.
Dawson, James. *Australian Aborigines: The Language and Customs of Several Tribes of Aborigines of the Western District of Victoria*. Robertson, Melbourne, 1881.
Dawson, Robert. *The Present State of Australia*. Smith, Elder, London, 1830.
D'Costa, D. M., Edney, P., Kershaw, A. P., and Deckker, P. de, 'Late Quaternary Palaeoecology of Tower Hill, Victoria, Australia', *Journal of Biogeography*, vol. 16, 1989, pp. 461–82.
Diaz, Henry F. and Markgraf, Vera (eds). *El Nino: Historical and Paleoclimatic Aspects of the Southern Oscillation*. Cambridge University Press, Cambridge, 1992.
Dingle, Tony. *Settling*. Fairfax, Syme & Weldon, Sydney, 1984.
Dixon, Robert. *The Course of Empire: Neo-classical Culture in New South Wales*. Oxford University Press, Melbourne, 1985.
Dixon, W. A., 'On Salt-Bush and Native Fodder Plants of New South Wales', *JPRSNSW*, vol. 14, 1880, pp. 133-43.
Downes, M. C., 'History of the Fisheries and Wildlife Division, Victoria 1934–84', in *Victorian Year Book 1984*, Victorian Office of the Australian Bureau of Statistics, Melbourne, 1984, pp. 324–41.
——— *Tower Hill*, ICI/Fisheries and Wildlife Department of Victoria, Melbourne, 1967.
——— *What Happened at Tower Hill?* Fisheries and Wildlife Department, Melbourne, 1961.
Ducker, Sophie C. (ed.). *The Contented Botanist: Letters of W. H. Harvey about Australia and the Pacific*. Melbourne University Press, Melbourne, 1988.
Dunstan, David. *Governing the Metropolis: Politics, Technology and Social Change in a Victorian City, Melbourne 1850–1891*. Melbourne University Press, Melbourne, 1984.
Dymock, William. *Dymock's Illustrated Guide to Sydney*. Sydney, Dymock's Book Arcade, 1897.
Dysart, Dinah, 'William Charles Piguenit: Nineteenth Century Environmentalist', *Art and Australia*, vol. 29, 1991–92, pp. 480–8.
Dyster, Barrie. *Servant and Master: Building and Running the Grand Houses of Sydney 1788–1850*. University of New South Wales Press, Sydney, 1989.
Eadward Muybridge: The Stanford Years 1872–1882. Stanford University Press, Palo Alto, 1972.
Eagle, Mary. *The Oil Paintings of Arthur Streeton in the National Gallery of Australia*. National Gallery of Australia, Canberra, 1994.
Ellery, R. L. J., 'On the Relation between Forest Lands and Climate in Victoria', *Transactions and Proceedings of the Royal Society of Victoria*, vol. 16, 1879, pp. 1–6.
Ellis, Vivienne Rae. *Louisa Anne Meredith: A Tigress in Exile*. Blubber Head Press, Hobart, 1979.

Emerson, Ralph W. *Agricultural Chemistry*. Beal, Brisbane, 1879.
Erskine-Hill, Howard. *The Social Milieu of Alexander Pope*. Yale University Press, New Haven, 1975.
Evatt, H. V. *Rum Rebellion*. Angus & Robertson, Sydney, 1938.
Farrer, William. *Grass and Sheep-Farming*. Maddock, Sydney, 1873.
Fenton, James. *Bush Life in Tasmania Fifty Years Ago*. Hazell, Watson & Viney, London, 1891.
Fidlon, Paul G., and Ryan, R. J. (eds). *The Journal and Letters of Lieutenant Ralph Clark 1787–1792*. Australian Documents Library, Sydney, 1981.
Fidlon, Paul G., and Ryan, R. J. (eds). *The Journal of Philip Gidley King*. Australian Documents Library, Sydney, 1980.
Field, Barron. *Geographical Memoirs on New South Wales*. Murray, London, 1825.
Finney, C. M. *To Sail Beyond the Sunset: Natural History in Australia 1699–1829*. Rigby, Adelaide, 1984.
Fisher, Shirley, 'The Pastoral Interest and Sydney's Public Health', *Historical Studies*, vol. 20, 1982–83, pp. 73–89.
Fitzgerald, Ross, and Hearn, Mark. *Bligh, Macarthur and the Rum Rebellion*. Kangaroo Press, Sydney, 1988.
Fitzgerald, Shirley. *Rising Damp: Sydney 1870–1890*. Oxford University Press, Melbourne, 1987.
Flader, Susan L. *Thinking like a Mountain: Aldo Leopold and the Evolution of an Ecological Attitude toward Deer, Wolves and Forests*. University of Missouri Press, Columbia, 1974.
Flannery, Tim. *The Future Eaters: An Ecological History of the Australasian Lands and Peoples*. Reed, Sydney, 1994.
Fletcher, Brian H., 'The Hawkesbury Settlers and the Rum Rebellion', *JRAHS*, vol. 54, 1968, pp. 217–37.
Flinders, Matthew. *Observations on the Coast of Van Diemen's Land*. Nicol, London, 1801.
——— *A Voyage to Terra Australis*. Nicol, London, 1814, 2 vols.
Forests Commission of Victoria. *Empire Forestry Conference Australia and New Zealand 1928: Handbook of Forestry in Victoria*. Green, Melbourne, 1928.
Foster, John, 'Natives in the Nineteenth Century Garden', *Australian Garden History*, vol. 2, no. 4, January–February 1991, pp. 3–5.
——— *Victorian Picturesque: The Gardens of William Sangster*. History Department, University of Melbourne, Melbourne, 1989.
Fowler, Marcia. *The Embroidered Tent: Five Gentlewomen in Early Canada*. Anansi, Toronto, 1982.
Fox, Paul, 'The Simla of the South', *Australian Garden History*, vol. 6, no. 4, January–February 1995, pp. 10-14.
Fox, Paul, with Phipps, Jennifer. *Sweet Damper and Gossip: Colonial Sightings from the Goulburn and North-East*. Benalla Art Gallery, Benalla, 1994.
Frawley, Kevin J., 'Rainforest Management in Queensland before 1900', *Australian Historical Geography*, no. 4, January 1983, pp. 2–26.
French, C., 'Victorian Ferns and their Habitats', *Southern Scientific Record*, no. 3, February 1881, pp. 33-6.
——— 'Victorian Ferns and their Habitats', *Southern Scientific Record*, no. 4, March 1881, pp. 49-52.
——— 'Victorian Ferns and their Habitats', *Southern Scientific Record*, no. 12, November 1881, pp. 189-92.
Frost, Alan. *Arthur Phillip 1738–1814: His Voyaging*. Oxford University Press, Melbourne, 1987.
Froude, J. A. *Oceana or England and her Colonies*. Longman, Green, London, 1886.
Galbally, Ann, and Gray, Anne. *Letters from Smike: The Letters of Arthur Streeton 1890–1943*. Oxford University Press, Melbourne, 1989.
Gaskell, Martin S., 'Gardens for the Working Class: Victorian Practical Pleasure', *Victorian Studies*, vol. 23, 1980, pp. 479–501.

Giant Trees of Victoria. Victoria Crown and Lands Survey, Melbourne, c. 1890.

Gilfedder, Francine, 'Sowing the Seeds: The Early Nursery Industry at Macedon Ranges', *Australian Garden History*, vol. 6, no. 4, January–February 1995, pp. 18-21.

Gillbank, Linden, 'The Acclimatisation Society of Victoria', *Victorian Historical Journal*, vol. 51, no. 4, November 1980, pp. 255–70.

——— 'Charles Walter: Collector of Images and Plants in East Gippsland', *Gippsland Heritage Journal*, no. 13, December 1992, pp. 3–10.

Gilpin, William. *Observations relative to Picturesque Beauty made in the Year 1771*. Blamire, London, 1788, 2nd ed., 2 vols.

——— *Remarks on Forest Scenery*. Blamire, London, 1791, 2 vols.

——— *Three Essays on Picturesque Beauty*. Blamire, London, 1794, 2nd ed.

Glanz, David, 'Marvellous (Middle) Melbourne', *Eureka Street*, March 1995, pp. 14–17.

Godden, Judith, 'British Models and Colonial Experience: Women's Philanthropy in Late Nineteenth Century Sydney', *Journal of Australian Studies*, no. 19, November 1986, pp. 40–55.

Godwin's Emigrant's Guide to Van Diemen's Land. Sherwood, Jones, London, 1823.

Glimpses of Australia: An Album of Photographic Scenes. Gordon & Gotch, Melbourne, 1897, 2 vols.

Goody, Jack, 'Man and the Natural World', *Environment and History*, vol. 2, 1996, pp. 255–70.

Gouger, Robert (ed.). *A Letter from Sydney: The Principal Town of Australasia*. Cross, London, 1829.

Gould League Songs and Poems. New South Wales Gould League of Bird Lovers, Sydney, 1934.

Grainger, Elena. *Martin of Martin Place*. Alpha, Sydney, 1970.

——— *The Remarkable Reverend Clarke*. Oxford University Press, Melbourne, 1982.

Griffiths, Tom. *Hunters and Collectors: The Antiquarian Imagination in Australia*. Cambridge University Press, Cambridge, 1996.

Grimshaw, Patricia, 'Writing the History of Aboriginal and White Women in Colonial Tasmania', *Launceston Historical Society Papers and Proceedings*, 1994, pp. 1–11.

Grove, Richard. *Ecology, Climate and Empire: Colonialism and Global Environmental History 1400–1940*. Whitehorse Press, Cambridge, 1997.

——— *Green Imperialism: Colonial Expansion, Tropical Island Edens and the Origins of Environmentalism 1600–1860*. Cambridge University Press, New York, 1995.

Guérard, Eugene von. *Eugène von Guérard's Australian Landscapes*. Hamel & Ferguson, Melbourne, 1866–68.

Hainsworth, D. R. *The Sydney Traders: Simeon Lord and his Contemporaries*. Cassell, Sydney, 1972.

Halliday, T. R. *Vanishing Birds: Their Natural History and Conservation*. Sidgwick & Jackson, London, 1978.

Hamilton, Alexander G., 'A Naturalist's Notes from Illawarra', *Sydney Quarterly Magazine*, 1890, pp. 25–35.

——— 'On the Effect which Settlement in Australia has produced upon Indigenous Vegetation', *JPRSNSW*, vol. 26, 1892, pp. 178–239.

Hancock, W. K. *Australia*. Benn, London, 1930.

Hansen, David. *Tower Hill and its Artists*. Warrnambool Art Gallery, Warrnambool, 1985.

Hardy, A. D., 'Australia's Great Trees', *Victorian Naturalist*, vol. 41, 1935, pp. 231–41.

——— 'Giant Eucalypts of Victoria', *Gum Tree*, June 1921, vol. 6, no. 18, pp. 15-16.

——— 'John Hardy: Early Victorian Surveyor', *Victorian Historical Magazine*, vol. 20, 1943, pp. 1–14.

——— 'The Measuring of Tall Trees', *Victorian Naturalist*, vol. 39, 1923, pp. 166–75.

——— 'The Tall Trees of Australia', *Victorian Naturalist*, vol. 35, 1918, pp. 46–55.

Harvey, J. H., 'A Photographic Trip to the Jenolan Caves and Kanangara Walls, N.S.W.', *Australian Photographic Journal*, June 1894, pp. 147–8.

Hazzard, Margaret. *Punishment Short of Death: A History of the Penal Settlement at Norfolk Island*. Hyland House, Melbourne, 1984.
Headon, David and Williams, John (eds). *Makers of Miracles: The Cast of the Federation Story*. Melbourne University Press, Melbourne, 2000.
Heathcote, R. L. *Back of Bourke: A Study of Land Appraisal and Settlement in Semi-Arid Australia*. Melbourne University Press, Melbourne, 1965.
——— 'Drought in Australia: A Problem of Perception', *Geographical Review*, vol. 59, 1969, pp. 175–94.
Henderson, John. *Observations on the Colonies of New South Wales and Van Diemen's Land*. Baptist Mission, Calcutta, 1832.
Heney, Thomas, 'Unused National Resources', *Sydney Quarterly Magazine*, 1891, pp. 9–14.
Hermes, Neil. *Birds of Norfolk Island*. Wonderland Publications, Norfolk Island, 1985.
Higgins, W. L., 'The Possibilities of Irrigation in the West', *Bulletin of the Conference of Delegates of Agricultural Societies*, Potter, Sydney, 1895, pp. 162–5.
Hill, Octavia, 'Colour, Space and Music for the People', *Nineteenth Century*, vol. 15, 1884, pp. 741–52.
——— 'Organized Work Among the Poor: Suggestions founded on Four Years' Management of a London Court', *Macmillan's Magazine*, vol. 20, July 1869, pp. 219-26.
Hill-Reid, W. S. *John Grant's Journey: A Convict's Story 1803–1811*. Heinemann, London, 1957.
Himmelfarb, Gertude. *Poverty and Compassion: The Moral Imagination of the Late Victorians*. Knopf, New York, 1991.
Hindwood, K. A. *The Birds of Lord Howe Island*. Brown, Prior, Anderson, Sydney, 1940.
Hingston, James. *Guide for Excursionists from Melbourne*. Thomas, Melbourne, 1868.
——— *Guide for Excursionists from Melbourne*. Thomas, Melbourne, 2nd ed., 1869.
Hirst, J. B. *Convict Society and its Enemies: A History of Early New South Wales*. Allen & Unwin, Sydney, 1983.
Hobart Town Almanack for the Year 1829. Ross, Hobart, 1829.
Hobart Town Almanack for the Year 1830. Ross, Hobart, 1830.
Hobart Town Almanack for the Year 1832. Ross, Hobart, 1832.
Holmes, Oliver Wendell. *The Autocrat of the Breakfast-Table*. Dent, London, 1906.
——— 'The Stereoscope and the Stereograph', *Atlantic Monthly*, vol. 3, June 1859, pp. 738–48.
Hood, John. *Australia and the East*. Murray, London, 1843.
Horwitz, Morton J. *The Transformation of American Law 1780–1860*. Harvard University Press, Cambridge, 1977.
House of Commons Select Committee on Transportation. London, 1812.
Hügel, Carl. *New Holland Journal: November 1833–October 1834*. Melbourne University Press, Melbourne, 1994.
Hughes, Robert. *The Fatal Shore*. Collins Harvill, London, 1987.
Hull, A. F. Basset, 'The Birds of Lord Howe and Norfolk Islands', *Proceedings of the Linnean Society of New South Wales*, vol. 34, 1909, pp. 636–93.
——— 'Further Notes on the Birds of Lord Howe and Norfolk Islands', *Proceedings of the Linnean Society of New South Wales*, vol. 35, 1910, pp. 783–7.
Hunter, John. *An Historical Journal of the Transactions at Port Jackson and Norfolk Island*. Stockdale, London, 1793.
Huth, Hans, 'Nature and the American', *Journal of the Warburg and Courtauld Institutes*, vol. 13, 1950, pp. 101–49.
——— *Nature and the American: Three Centuries of Changing Attitudes*. University of California, Berkeley, 1957.
Important Auction Sale of a Valuable Library of Books . . . by Order of the Executors of the Late Mr James Smith. Melbourne, 1910.
Inglis, James. *Our Australian Cousins*. Macmillan, London, 1880.
——— 'Recent Economic Developments of Australian Enterprise', *New Zealand Country Journal*, vol. 18, no. 4, July 1894, pp. 336–53.

Inglis, K. S. *The Australian Colonists: An Exploration of Social History 1788–1870*. Melbourne University Press, Melbourne, 1974.
Iredale, Tom, 'Bird of Providence', *Australian Zoologist*, vol. 5, 1929, pp. 358–61.
Jackson, Clarence S. *William H. Jackson: Picture Maker of the Old West*. Charles Scribner's Sons, New York, 1947.
Jameson, Anna. *Winter Studies and Summer Rambles in Canada*. Saunders & Otley, London, 1838, 2 vols.
Jeans, D. N. *An Historical Geography of New South Wales to 1901*. Reed, Sydney, 1972.
Johannes, Christa E. and Brown, Anthony V. *W. C. Piguenit 1836–1914 Retrospective*. Tasmanian Museum and Art Gallery, Hobart, 1992.
John, Catherine and Moore, Helen. *Redressing the Volcano: The Restoration of Tower Hill*. Tower Hill Press, Woodford, 1992.
Johnston, Judith, '"Women's Testimony": Imperialist Discourse in the Professional Colonial Travel Writing of Louisa Anne Meredith and Catherine Parr Traill', *Australian and New Zealand Studies in Canada*, no. 11, June 1994, pp. 34–55.
Johnston, Stephen, 'Profile of a Parks Pioneer', *Park Watch*, no. 169, June 1992, pp. 8–12.
Jones, David, 'The Origins of the SA Woods and Forest Department: The Forest Board 1875–1878', *Journal of the Historical Society of South Australia*, no. 26, 1998, pp. 39–54.
Jones, Michael. *Prolific in God's Gifts: A Social History of Knox and the Dandenongs*. Allen & Unwin, Sydney, 1983.
Jones, Shar. *J. W. Lindt: Master Photographer*. Currey O'Neil, Melbourne, 1985.
Keating, Jenny. *The Drought Walked Through: A History of Water Shortage in Victoria*. Department of Water Resources, Melbourne, 1992.
Kelly, Farley (ed.). *On the Edge of Discovery*. Text, Melbourne, 1993.
Kennedy, R. E. W., 'The Leongatha Labour Colony: Founding an Anti-Utopia', *Labour History*, no. 14, May 1968, pp. 54–8.
Kentish, N. L. *Work in the Bush*. Rolwegan, Hobart, 1846.
Kercher, Bruce. *An Unruly Child: A History of Law in Australia*. Allen & Unwin, Sydney, 1995.
Kerr, Joan, 'Colonial Quotations', *Art and Australia*, vol. 33, 1996, pp. 376–87.
——— (ed.). *The Dictionary of Australian Artists*. Oxford University Press, Melbourne, 1992.
Keynes, Richard Darwin (ed.). *Charles Darwin's Beagle Diary*. Cambridge University Press, Cambridge, 1988.
Kiernan, Brian (ed.). *The Essential Henry Lawson*. Currey O'Neil, Melbourne, 1982.
King, Robert J. *The Secret History of the Convict Colony*. Angus & Robertson, Sydney, 1990.
Knight, David. *Zoological Illustration: An Essay towards the History of Printed Zoological Pictures*. Dawson, Folkestone, Kent, 1977.
Koala Management Task Force. *Final Report*. Adelaide, 1996.
La Nauze, J. A. *Alfred Deakin*. Melbourne University Press, Melbourne, 1965, 2 vols.
Lachlan Macquarie, Governor of New South Wales: Journals of his Tours in New South Wales and Van Diemen's Land 1810–1822. Public Library of New South Wales, Sydney, 1956.
Lake, Marilyn and Kelly, Farley (eds). *Double Time: Women in Victoria—150 Years*. Penguin, Melbourne, 1985.
'Land Selection at Mount Macedon', *Victorian Parliamentary Papers*, 1899–1900.
Lane, Terence, and Serle, Jessie. *Australians at Home: A Documentary History of Australian Domestic Interiors from 1788 to 1914*. Oxford University Press, Melbourne, 1990.
Lawson, Elizabeth. *The Natural Art of Louisa Atkinson*. State Library of New South Wales Press, Sydney, 1995.
Lawson, Henry, 'Australian Engineers', *Bulletin*, 19 January 1905, p. 8.
——— 'Australia's Peril', *Worker*, 24 June 1905, p. 4.
——— *Autobiographical and Other Writings*. Angus & Robertson, Sydney, 1972.

——— 'The Darling River', *Worker*, 26 August 1893, p. 4.
——— 'The Heart of Australia', *Bulletin*, 13 October 1904, p. 11.
——— 'Some Popular Australian Mistakes', *Bulletin*, 18 November 1893, p. 20.
——— 'The Song of the Darling River', *Bulletin*, 25 March 1899, p. 3.
——— 'The Water', *Amateur Gardener*, 15 March 1905.
Leavitt, T. W. H. *The Jubilee History of Victoria and Melbourne*. Melbourne, 1888, 2 vols.
Lectures delivered in the Lecture Room of the Museum during the Autumn Session of 1871. Industrial and Technical Museum, Melbourne, 1871.
Lee, A. K. and Martin, R. W. *The Koala: A Natural History*. University of New South Wales Press, Sydney, 1988.
Lefroy, Lady (ed.). *Autobiography of General Sir John Lefroy*. c. 1895.
Legge, W. V., 'Protection of Tasmanian Owls', *Papers and Proceedings of the Royal Society of Tasmania*, 1889, p. 40.
——— 'Protection of the Cape Barren Goose', *Papers and Proceedings of the Royal Society of Tasmania*, 1889, pp. 41–2.
Lennon, Jane, 'Second Thoughts on First Views: The Port Jackson Circle 1788–1800', *Australian Journal of Art*, vol. 14, no. 1, 1998, pp. 31–51.
——— 'Wilson's Promontory: Its Commercial Utilisation in the 19th Century', *Victorian Historical Magazine*, vol. 45, 1974, pp. 179–200.
Leopold, Aldo. *A Sand County Almanac*. Oxford University Press, Oxford, 1949.
'Letters of David Blackburn', *RAHSJP*, vol. 20, 1935, pp. 318–34.
Lindsay, Jack. *William Morris: His Life and Work*. Constable, London, 1975.
Lines, William J. *Taming the Great South Land*. Allen & Unwin, Sydney, 1991.
Lloyd, C. J. *Either Drought or Plenty: Water Development and Management in New South Wales*. Department of Water Resources (NSW), Sydney, 1988.
Love, Harold. *James Edward Neild: Victorian Virtuoso*. Melbourne University Press, Melbourne, 1989.
Lowenthal, David, and Binney, Marcus (eds). *Our Past Before Us: Why Do We Save It?* Temple Smith, London, 1981.
Lycett, Joseph. *Views in Australia*. Souter, London, 1824–25.
McConville, Chris, 'A Forest at the Edge of the City', *Australian Garden History*, vol. 6, no. 4, January–February 1995, pp. 8–9.
Macdonald, Donald. *Gum Boughs and Wattle Blossom*. Cassell, London, 1887.
Macintyre, Stuart. *A Colonial Liberalism: The Lost World of Three Victorian Visionaries*. Oxford University Press, Melbourne, 1991.
Mackaness, George. *The Life of Vice-Admiral William Bligh*. Angus & Robertson, Sydney, 1931, 2 vols.
——— (ed.). *Some Letters of Reverend Richard Johnson*. Sydney, 1954, 2 parts.
McKay, Anne (ed.). *Journals of the Land Commissioners for Van Diemen's Land 1826–28*. Tasmanian Historical Research Association, Hobart, 1962.
McKenzie, Robyn, 'Geoff Lowe and Tower Hill', *Parkett*, no. 45, 1995, pp. 19–22.
McKinney, H. G., 'Irrigation', in Department of Agriculture, New South Wales, *Bulletin of the Conference of Delegates of Agricultural Societies*, Potter, Sydney, 1895, pp. 155–62.
——— 'Irrigation in its Relation to the Pastoral Industry of New South Wales', *JPRSNSW*, vol. 23, 1889, pp. 75–96.
——— 'Notes on the Experience of Other Countries in the Administration of their Water Supply', *JPRSNSW*, vol. 21, 1887, pp. 60–73.
——— 'The Progress and Position of Irrigation in New South Wales', *JPRSNSW*, vol. 27, 1893, pp. 384–400.
——— 'Projects for Water Conservation, Irrigation and Drainage in New South Wales', *JPRSNSW*, vol. 35, 1901, pp. 223–42.
——— 'Water Conservation', *NSWLAV&P*, 1891–92, vol. 6, pp. 45–78.
McLean, Ian, 'Your Own Land is the Best: The Limits of Redemption in Australian Colonial Art', *Australian Journal of Art*, vol. 12, 1994–95, pp. 124–45.
McPhee, John. *The Art of John Glover*. Macmillan, Melbourne, 1980.

McQueen, Humphrey. *Tom Roberts*. Macmillan, Melbourne, 1996.
Maiden, J. H. *A Critical Revision of the Genus Eucalyptus*. Gullick, Sydney, vol. 1, 1905.
——— *The Forest Flora of New South Wales*. Gullick, Sydney, vol. 2, 1907.
——— 'The Sand-Drift Problem in New South Wales', *JPRSNSW*, vol. 37, 1903, pp. 82–106.
——— *The Useful Native Plants of Australia*. Turner & Henderson, Sydney, 1889.
Malchow, H. L., 'Public Gardens and Social Action in Late Victorian London', *Victorian Studies*, vol. 29, 1985, pp. 96–124.
Marsh, George Perkins. *Man and Nature*. Scribner, New York, 1864.
Marshall, A. J. (ed.). *The Great Extermination*. Heinemann, London, 1966.
Martin, E. C., 'A National Scheme of Water Conservation', *Victorian Review*, vol. 10, 1884, pp. 143–51.
Martin, J. L., 'Restoration of Vegetation at Tower Hill', *Victorian Naturalist*, vol. 79, November 1962, pp. 192–6.
Martin, James. *The Australian Sketch Book*. Tegg, Sydney, 1838.
Martin, Paul S. and Klein, Richard G. (eds). *Quaternary Extinctions: A Prehistoric Revolution*. University of Arizona Press, Tucson, 1984.
Mathews, Gregory M. *The Birds of Australia*. Witherby, London, 1910–27, 14 vols.
Mathews, Gregory M. and Iredale, Tom. *A Manual of the Birds of Australia*. Witherby, London, 1921.
Mayne, Alan. *Fever, Squalor and Vice: Sanitation and Social Policy in Victorian Sydney*. University of Queensland Press, St Lucia, 1982.
——— '"A Most Pernicious Principle": The Local Government Franchise in Nineteenth-Century Sydney', *Australian Journal of Politics and History*, vol. 27, 1981, pp. 160–71.
——— *Representing the Slum: Popular Journalism in a late Nineteenth Century City*. History Department, University of Melbourne, Melbourne, 1990.
Meinig, D. W. *On the Margins of the Good Earth: The South Australian Wheat Frontier 1869–1884*. Seal Books, Adelaide, 1970.
Meredith, Mrs Charles. *My Home in Tasmania*. Murray, London, 1852. 2 vols.
——— *Notes and Sketches of New South Wales during a Residence in the Colony from 1839 to 1844*. Murray, London, 1844.
Meredith, Louisa Anne, 'The Hon. Charles Meredith', *Once a Month*, vol. 4, 1886, pp. 178-83, 280-4.
——— *Loved and Lost!* Day, London, 1860.
——— *Our Island Home*. Walch, Hobart, 1879.
——— *Over the Straits: A Visit to Victoria*. Chapman & Hall, London, 1861.
——— *Some of My Bush Friends in Tasmania*. Day, London, 1860.
——— *Tasmanian Friends and Foes* . Walch, Hobart, 1880.
——— *A Tasmanian Memory of 1834*. Walch, Hobart, 1869.
——— *Walch's Tasmanian Guide Book*. Walch, Hobart, 1871.
Meslée, Edmund Marin la. *The New Australia*. Heinemann, London, 1973.
Millen, E. D. *Our Western Lands: A Vanishing Asset*. Less, Sydney, 1900.
Miller, S. M. (ed.). *John Muir: Life and Work*. University of New Mexico Press, Albuquerque, 1993.
Mitchell, Thomas. *Three Expeditions into the Interior of Eastern Australia*. Boone, London, 2nd ed., 1839, 2 vols.
Moore, James, 'Green Gold: The Riches of Baron Ferdinand von Mueller', *Historical Records of Australian Science*, vol. 11, 1997, pp. 371–88.
Moore, William, 'Australian Art', *Australia To-Day*, 1910, pp. 74–7.
Morgan, H. A. MacLeod, 'Eccleston du Faur', *JRAHS*, vol. 42, 1956, pp. 16–23.
Morgan, Sharon. *Land Settlement in Early Tasmania: Creating an Antipodean England*. Cambridge University Press, Cambridge, 1992.
Morrison, W. Frederick. *The Aldine Centennial History of New South Wales*. Aldine, Sydney, 1888, 2 vols.
Mueller, Ferdinand von. *Eucalyptographia*. Government Printer, Melbourne, 1880.
——— *Forest Culture in its Relation to Industrial Pursuits*. Melbourne, 1871.

——— 'Inaugural Address', *Report of the Second Meeting of the Australasian Association for the Advancement of Science held at Melbourne, Victoria in January 1890*, Melbourne, 1891.

——— *Intercolonial Exhibition 1866–67: Australian Vegetation, Indigenous or Introduced*. Blundell, Melbourne, 1867.

——— *Intercolonial Exhibition 1866–67: Report on Vegetable Products*. Blundell, Melbourne, 1867.

——— *Key to the System of Victorian Plants*. Brain, Melbourne, 1885–88, 2 vols.

——— *On the Application of Phytology to the Industrial Purposes of Life*. Mason, Firth & McCutcheon, Melbourne, 1870.

——— *Select Extra-Tropical Plants Readily Eligible for Industrial Culture or Naturalisation*. Richards, Sydney, 1881.

——— *Select Extra-Tropical Plants Readily Eligible for Industrial Culture or Naturalisation*. Goverment Printer, Melbourne, 8th ed., 1891.

——— *Select Plants Readily Eligible for Industrial Culture or Naturalization in Victoria*. McCarron, Bird, Melbourne, 1876.

——— *Suggestions on the Maintenance, Creation and Enrichment of Forests*. Stilwell, Melbourne, 1879.

Mulvaney, D. J. *Encounters in Place: Outsiders and Aboriginal Australians 1606–1985*. University of Queensland Press, St Lucia, 1989.

Mundy, Godfrey Charles. *Our Antipodes*. Bentley, London, 1852, 2nd ed., 2 vols.

Myers, Francis. *Irrigation or the New Australia*. Mildura, Chaffey Brothers, 1892.

Myers, Francis, and Chambers, Trant. *The Victorian Tourists Railway Guide*. Ferguson & Mitchell, Melbourne, 1892.

Nairn, Bede. *Civilising Capitalism: The Labor Movement in New South Wales 1870–1900*. ANU Press, Canberra, 1973.

Nash, Roderick (ed.). *The American Environment: Readings in the History of Conservation*. Addison-Wesley Publishing, Reading, 1968.

The National Mutual Life Association's Guide to Melbourne. National Mutual Life Association, Melbourne, c. 1880.

'National Park: Report of the Trustees for the year ended 31 December 1887', *Votes and Proceedings of the Legislative Assembly during the Session of 1888–89*(New South Wales), vol. 3.

'National Park: Report of the Trustees for the year ended 31 December 1888', *Votes and Proceedings of the Legislative Assembly during the Second Session of 1889* (New South Wales), vol. 2.

National Parks Authority, 'Annual Report for the Year Ended 30th June 1958', *Victorian Parliamentary Papers*, 1958–59, vol. 2.

——— 'First Annual Report for the Year ended 30th June 1957', *Victorian Parliamentary Papers*, 1956–58, vol. 2.

Neville, Richard. *A Rage for Curiosity: Visualising Australia 1788–1830*. State Library of New South Wales Press, Sydney, 1997.

New South Wales: Its Present State and Future Prospects. Walther, London, 1837.

New South Wales Pocket Almanack and Colonial Remembrancer for the Year of our Lord and Saviour 1806. Howe, Sydney, c. 1806.

Newton, Gael. *Shades of Light: Photography and Australia 1839–1988*. Australian National Gallery, Canberra, 1988.

Nicolson, Marjorie Hope. *Mountain Gloom and Mountain Glory*. Cornell University Press, Ithaca, 1959.

Nilson, Arvid, 'Aesthetics: 'The Beauty of Inorganic Nature', *Victorian Review*, vol. 6, 1882, pp. 520–33.

——— *The Timber Trees of New South Wales*. Department of Mines, Sydney, 1884.

Nobbs, Raymond (ed.). *Norfolk Island and its First Settlement 1788–1814*. Library of Australian History, Sydney, 1988.

Norman, F. I. and Young, A. D., 'Short-Sighted and Doubly Short-Sighted are They: A Brief Examination of the Game Laws of Victoria 1858–1958', *Journal of Australian Studies*, no. 7, November 1980, pp. 2–24.

North, Alfred J., 'On Two Early Australian Ornithologists', *Records of the Australian Museum*, vol. 6, 1906, pp. 121–8.

North, Marianne. *Recollections of a Happy Life*. Macmillan, London, 1892, 2 vols.

Nottle, Trevor, 'John Glover', *Australian Garden History*, vol. 11, no. 3, November–December 1999, p. 24.

Novak, Barbara. *Nature and Culture: American Landscape and Painting 1825–1875*. Oxford University Press, New York, 1980.

Official Catalogue of the Melbourne Exhibition, 1854. Sinnett, Melbourne, 1854.

Official Record of the Centennial International Exhibition, Melbourne, 1888–1889. Sands & McDougall, Melbourne, 1890.

Onslow, S. M. *Some Early Records of the Macarthurs*. Angus & Robertson, Sydney, 1914.

The Original Water-Color Paintings by John James Audubon for the Birds of America. American Heritage Publishing Co., New York, 1966.

Oxley, John. *Journal of Two Expeditions to the Interior of New South Wales*. Murray, London, 1820.

Paffen, Paul, 'Forgotten Faces? Portraits and other Images of the Convict in Van Diemen's Land', *Tasmanian Historical Research Association Papers and Proceedings*, vol. 46, 1999, pp. 57–95.

Palmquist, Peter E. *Carleton E. Watkins: Photographer of the American West*. University of New Mexico Press, Albuquerque, 1983.

'Papers Relating to Forest Conservancy', *Victorian Parliamentary Papers*, 1874, vol. 3.

Parkinson, Sydney. *Journal of a Voyage to the South Seas in his Majesty's Ship the Endeavour*. Parkinson, London, 1773.

Parsons, T. G., 'Manufacturing on the Banks of the Yarra River, Melbourne: The Development of an Industrial Area', *Journal of Australian Studies*, no. 11, 1982, pp. 21–35.

Paterson, A. B. *Australia for the Australian*. Gordon & Gotch, Sydney, 1889.

Paterson, G. *The History of New South Wales*. Mackenzie & Dent, Newcastle-upon-Tyne, 1811.

Patterson, K. A., 'Battlers of the 1890s', *Victorian Historical Journal*, vol. 51, 1980, pp. 42-7.

Pearce, Douglas G. and Richez, Gerard, 'Antipodean Contrasts: National Parks in New Zealand and Europe', *New Zealand Geographer*, vol. 43, 1987, pp. 53–9.

Peirce, J. Duncan. *Photographs of the Broken Hill Silver Mine*. Melbourne, 1887.

Péron, François. *King Island and the Sealing Trade 1802*. Roebuck, Canberra, 1971.

Perry, T. M. *Australia's First Frontier: The Spread of Settlement in New South Wales 1788–1825*. Melbourne University Press, Melbourne, 1963.

Phillip, Arthur. *The Voyage of Governor Phillip to Botany Bay*. Stockdale, London, 1789.

Phillips, Bill. *Koalas: The Little Australian We'd All Hate to Lose*. AGPS, Canberra, 1992.

Pittman, Edward F. *The Coal Resources of New South Wales*. Gullick, Sydney, 1912.

——— *The Mineral Resources of New South Wales*. Gullick, Sydney, 1901.

Pizzey, Graham. *Crosbie Morrison: Voice of Nature*. Victoria Press, Melbourne, 1992.

Plomley, N. J. B. *The Aboriginal/Settler Clash in Van Diemen's Land 1803–1831*. Queen Victorian Museum and Art Gallery, Launceston, 1992.

——— *Friendly Mission: The Tasmanian Journals and Papers of George Augustus Robinson*. Tasmanian Historical Research Association, Hobart, 1966.

——— *Weep in Silence: A History of the Flinders Island Aboriginal Settlement*. Blubber Head Press, Hobart, 1987.

Poole, William, 'The Locking of the Darling River: A Brief Review', *Australian Technical Journal*, 30 April 1898, pp. 99–101; 31 May 1898, pp. 139–42.

Porter, Mrs G. R. *Alfred Dudley*. Harvey & Darton, London, 1830.

Powell, J. M., 'An Australian Utopia', *Australian Geographer*, vol. 12, 1973, pp. 328–33.

——— *The Emergence of Bioregionalism in the Murray–Darling Basin.* Murray–Darling Basin Commission, Canberra, 1993.
——— *Environmental Management in Australia 1788–1914.* Oxford University Press, Melbourne, 1976.
——— *The Public Lands of Australia Felix.* Oxford University Press, Melbourne, 1970.
'Preservation of Huon Pine and Blackwood', *Journal of the House of Assembly* (Tasmania), vol. 35, 1879, paper no. 132.
Prinsep, Mrs Augustus. *The Journal of a Voyage from Calcutta to Van Diemen's Land.* Smith, Elder, London, 1833.
Prochaska, F. K. *Women and Philanthropy in Nineteenth-Century England.* Oxford University Press, Oxford, 1980.
Proudfoot, Helen, Bickford, Anne, Egloff, Brian, and Stocks, Robyn. *Australia's First Government House.* Allen & Unwin, Sydney, 1991.
Pryse-Jones, Joyce and Fitzgerald, Marjorie. *William Charles Piguenit 1836–1914: First Australian-Born Landscape Painter of any Note.* Sydney, 1992.
Pyne, Stephen J. *Burning Bush: A Fire History of Australia.* Holt, New York, 1991.
Quamman, David. *The Song of the Dodo: Island Biogeography in an Age of Extinctions.* Hutchinson, London, 1996.
Quincey, Elizabeth de. *The History of Mount Wellington: A Tasmanian Sketchbook.* De Quincey, Hobart, 1987.
Quinn, Michael, 'Committed to Conserve: The Western Lands Act 1901 and the Management of the Public Estate of the Western Division of New South Wales', *Australian Geographical Studies*, vol. 35, 1997, pp. 183–94.
Radford, Ron. *John Glover's House and Garden.* Art Gallery of South Australia, Adelaide, 1985.
Railway Guide to New South Wales. Richards, Sydney, 1879.
Ranken, George. *The Dry Country.* Cook, Sydney, 1884.
Ransom, W. S. (ed.). *The Australian National Dictionary.* Oxford University Press, Melbourne, 1988.
Ranlett, John, '"Checking Nature's Desecration": Late-Victorian Environmental Organization', *Victorian Studies*, vol. 26, 1983, pp. 197–222.
Rees, Lloyd. *Small Treasures of a Lifetime.* Ure Smith, Sydney, 1969.
'Report from the Select Committee upon the Yea River Company', *Victorian Parliamentary Papers*, 1890, vol. 1.
Report of the Commissioner of Inquiry on the State of Agriculture and Trade in the Colony of New South Wales, HMSO, London, 1823.
'Report of the Conservator of Forests for the Year ending 30th June 1890', *Victorian Parliamentary Papers*, 1890, vol. 4.
Report of the 1954 Biennial Conference on Australian Fauna, Fisheries & Game Department, Melbourne, 1954.
'Report of the Royal Commission on Gold Mining', *Victorian Parliamentary Papers*, 1890, vol. 5.
Report of the State Development Committee on National Parks, Government Printer, Melbourne, 1951.
'Report on the Advisableness of Establishing State Forests', *Victorian Parliamentary Papers*, 1864–65, vol. 4.
'Report on the Waste Lands between the Mersey and Levien', *Journal of the House of Assembly* (Tasmania), vol. 5, 1860.
Reynolds, Henry. *Fate of a Free People: A Radical Re-Examination of the Tasmanian Wars.* Penguin, Ringwood, 1995.
——— *This Whispering in Our Hearts.* Allen & Unwin, Sydney, 1998.
Rickards, Edith C. *Bishop Moorhouse of Melbourne and Manchester.* Murray, London, 1920.
Rienits, Rex and Thea. *Early Artists of Australia.* Angus & Robertson, Sydney, 1963.
Rigby, Elizabeth, 'Lady Travellers', *Quarterly Review*, vol. 76, 1845, pp. 98–137.
'Ringbarking on Crown Lands', *NSWLAV&P*, 1887–88.

Ritchie, John, 'Introduction' to *A Charge of Mutiny: The Court Martial of Lieutenant Colonel George Johnston for Deposing Governor William Bligh in the Rebellion of 26 January 1808*. National Library of Australia, Canberra, 1988.
——— *The Wentworths: Father and Son*. Melbourne University Press, Melbourne, 1997.
——— (ed.). *The Evidence to the Bigge Reports*. Heinemann, Melbourne, 1971, 2 vols.
Ritvo, Harriet. *The Animal Estate: The English and Other Creatures in the Victorian Age*. Harvard University Press, Cambridge, Mass., 1987.
Robertson, David. *West of Eden: A History of the Art and Literature of Yosemite*. Yosemite Natural History Association/Wilderness Press, c. 1984.
Robinson, G. W., 'In the Dandenong Ranges Sixty Years Ago', *Victorian Naturalist*, vol. 28, 1911, pp. 30–2.
Robson, Lloyd. *A History of Tasmania: Volume 1*. Oxford University Press, Melbourne, 1983.
——— *A History of Tasmania: Volume II*. Oxford University Press, Melbourne, 1991.
Roderick, Colin. *Banjo Paterson: Poet by Accident*. Allen & Unwin, Sydney, 1993.
——— *Henry Lawson: A Life*. Angus & Robertson, Sydney, 1991.
——— *Henry Lawson: The Master Story-Teller*. Angus & Robertson, Sydney, 1984.
——— (ed.). *Henry Lawson Letters 1890 to 1922*. Angus & Robertson, Sydney, 1970.
Roe, Michael. *Nine Australian Progressives*. University of Queensland Press, St Lucia, 1984.
Rolls, Eric. *They All Ran Wild*. Angus & Robertson, Sydney, 1969.
Rosen, Sue. *Losing Ground: An Environmental History of the Hawkesbury–Nepean Catchment*. Hale & Iremonger, Sydney, 1995.
Ross, Andrew, 'On the Influence of the Australian Climate and Pastures upon the Growth of Wool', *JPRSNSW*, vol. 16, 1882, pp. 235–42.
'Royal Commission on Aborigines', *Victorian Parliamentary Papers*, 1877–78, vol. 3.
'Royal Commission on Conservation of Water: First Report', *NSWLAV&P*, 1885–86, vol. 6.
'Royal Commission to Inquire into the Condition of the Crown Tenants in the Western Division of New South Wales', parts I & II, *Journal of the Legislative Council of New South Wales*, vol. 63, part 2, 1901.
Runte, Alfred. *Yosemite: The Embattled Wilderness*. University of Nebraska Press, Lincoln, 1988.
Russell, Eric. *The Opposite Shore: North Sydney and its People*. North Shore Historical Society/ Council of the Municipality of Sydney, Sydney, 1990.
Russell, H. C., 'Anniversary Address', *JPRSNSW*, vol. 26, 1892, pp. 1–51.
——— 'Notes upon the History of Floods in the River Darling', *JPRSNSW*, vol. 20, 1886, pp. 155–210.
——— 'On Periodicity of Good and Bad Seasons', *JPRSNSW*, vol. 30, 1896, pp. 70–115.
Russell, J. E. M. *The Pictorial Guide to the Blue Mountains*. Gibbs, Shallard, Sydney, 1885, 3rd ed.
Ryan, James R. *Picturing Empire: Photography and the Visualization of the British Empire*. University of Chicago Press, Chicago, 1997.
Ryan, Lyndall. *The Aboriginal Tasmanians*. University of Queensland Press, St Lucia, 1981.
Ryan, P. J., 'John Muir and Tall Trees in Australia', *Pacific Historian*, vol. 29, 1985, pp. 124–35.
Ryan, R. J. *Land Grants 1788–1809*. Australian Documents Library, Sydney, 1974.
Ryan, Simon. *The Cartographic Eye: How Explorers Saw Australia*. Cambridge University Press, Cambridge, 1996.
——— 'Exploring Aesthetics: the Picturesque Appropriation of Land in Journals of Australian Exploration', *Australian Literary Studies*, vol. 15, no. 4, October 1992, pp. 282–93.

Sala, George. *The Land of the Golden Fleece*. Mulini, Canberra, 1995.
Sanderson, W. A., 'The Alienation of Melbourne Park Lands', *Victorian Historical Magazine*, vol. 14, December 1932, pp. 141–65.
Sanger, Edward B., 'Waste in Nature', *Victorian Review*, vol. 7, 1883, pp. 280–6.
Sayers, Andrew, 'Transcendent Topography: J. M. W. Turner and Australian Painting', *Art and Australia*, vol. 33, 1995–96, pp. 506–11.
Schama, Simon. *Landscape and Memory*. Harper Collins, London, 1995.
Schodde, R., Fullagar, P. and Hermes, N. *A Review of Norfolk Island Birds: Past and Present*. Australian National Parks and Wildlife Service Special Publication 8, Canberra, 1981.
Sears, John F. *Sacred Places: American Tourist Attractions in the Nineteenth Century*. Oxford University Press, New York, 1989.
Serle, Geoffrey. *The Rush to be Rich*. Melbourne University Press, Melbourne, 1971.
Serventy, Vincent. *A Continent in Danger*. André Deutsch, London, 1966.
Seventh Report of the Acclimatisation Society of Victoria. Melbourne, 1870.
Sexton, Nanette, 'Watkins' Style and Technique in the Early Photographs', *California History*, vol. 57, 1978, pp. 242–51.
Shepherd, Paul. *English Reaction to the New Zealand Landscape before 1850*. Victoria University, Wellington, 1969.
Shepherd, Thomas. *Lectures on Landscape Gardening in New South Wales*. McGarvie, Sydney, 1836.
——— *Lectures on the Horticulture of New South Wales*. McGarvie, Sydney, 1835.
Sherwood, J., Cumming, K., Stagnitti, F. and Anderson, R. *Understorey Revegetation Project: Tower Hill State Game Reserve*. Winsearch, Warrnambool, 1992.
Silcock, Colin, 'Tree Giants of Gippsland', *Gippsland Heritage Journal*, no. 19, March 1996, pp. 35–40.
Sinclair, Paul Geoffrey, Making the Deserts Bloom: Attitudes Towards Water and Nature in the Victorian Irrigation Debate 1880–1890, MA thesis, University of Melbourne, 1994.
Sladen, Douglas, 'To the Fallen Gum-Tree on Mount Bawbaw, Gippsland', *Victorian Review*, 1 June 1882, pp. 160–1.
Smith, Bernard. *European Vision and the South Pacific*. Oxford University Press, Oxford, 1960.
——— (ed.). *Documents on Art and Taste in Australia*. Oxford University Press, Melbourne, 1975.
Smith, Bernard, and Wheeler, Alwnne (eds). *The Art of the First Fleet*. Oxford University Press, Melbourne, 1988.
Smith, F. B., Religion and Freethought in Melbourne, 1870 to 1890, MA thesis, University of Melbourne, 1960.
Smith, James. *Cyclopedia of Victoria*. Cyclopedia Co., Melbourne, 1903–04, 3 vols.
——— *From Melbourne to Melrose*. Centennial Publishing, Melbourne, 1888.
——— 'Is the Earth Becoming Bald?', *Victorian Review*, vol. 1, 1880, pp. 876–93.
——— 'Nature's Scavengers', *Victorian Review*, vol. 3, 1880–81, pp. 42–53.
——— *Presidential Address delivered at the inauguration of the Kalizoic Society of Victoria*. Stilwell, Melbourne, 1884.
——— 'Some Social Aspects of England', *Victorian Review*, vol. 8, 1883, pp. 109–120.
Smith, John. *Wayfaring Notes (Second Series): A Holiday Tour Round the World*. Brown, Aberdeen, 1876.
Smyth, R. Brough. *The Aborigines of Victoria*. Government Printer, Melbourne, 1878, 2 vols.
Souter, D. H., 'William Charles Piguenit: An Australian Painter', *Art and Architecture*, September–October 1905, pp. 194–200.
South Australia Industries and Manufactures. Cox, Adelaide, 1875.
Spicer, E. C., 'A Holiday Ramble in Victoria', *Sydney Quarterly Magazine*, October 1883, pp. 64–73.
Spielvogel, Nathan F. *Our Gum Trees and Other Verses*. Paterson, Melbourne, 1913.

Stanbury, Peter (ed.). *The Blue Mountains: Grand Adventure for All*. Macleay Museum/Second Back Row Press, Sydney, 1988.
Steven, Margaret, 'Robert Campbell and the Bligh Rebellion', *RAHSJP*, vol. 48, 1962, pp. 344–60.
Stokes, John Lort. *Discoveries in Australia*. Boone, London, 1846, 2 vols.
Strzelecki, Paul. *Physical Description of New South Wales and Van Diemen's Land*. Longman, Brown & Green, London, 1845.
Stuart, Lurline. *James Smith: The Making of a Colonial Culture*. Allen & Unwin, Sydney, 1989.
Stubbs, Brett J., 'Land Improvement or Institutionalised Destruction? The Ringbarking Controversy, 1879–1884, and the Emergence of a Conservation Ethic in New South Wales', *Environment and History*, vol. 4, 1998, pp. 145–68.
Sugars, R. S., 'Excursion to Sassafras Gully on 3rd November 1891', *Victorian Naturalist*, vol. 8, 1891–92, pp. 116–19.
——— 'Notes on a Trip to South Gippsland', *Victorian Naturalist*, vol. 9, 1892–93, pp. 68–74.
——— 'A Trip to Sassafras Gully', *Victorian Naturalist*, vol. 8, 1891–92, pp. 68–72.
Svensen, S. *The Shearers' War*. University of Queensland Press, St Lucia, 1989.
Swann, Margaret, 'Mrs Meredith and Miss Atkinson: Writers and Naturalists', *RAHSJP*, vol. 15, 1929, pp. 1–29.
'Sydney Habour Collieries Company (Particulars respecting Application by the Trustees of the Cooper Estate to Reclaim and purchase Certain Land at Kurraba Point, Neutral Bay)', *NSWLAV&P*, 1895, part 2.
Tassell, Margaret, and Wood, David. *Tasmanian Photographer: From the John Watt Beattie Collection*. Macmillan, Melbourne, 1981.
Taylor, Agnes, 'Tower Hill: The Wonderland that Stands beside the Sea', *The Link*, vol. 1, no. 3, May 1922, p. 19.
Taylor, Angela. *A Forester's Log: The Story of John La Gerche and the Ballarat-Creswick State Forest 1882–1897*. Melbourne University Press, Melbourne, 1998.
Taylor, H. d'E., 'Health and Thrift', *Victorian Review*, vol. 5, 1 April 1882, pp. 650–7.
Tench, Watkin. *A Complete Account of the Settlement at Port Jackson*. Nicol, London, 1793.
——— *A Narrative of the Expedition to Botany Bay*. Debrett, London, 1789.
Tenison-Woods, Julian, 'Tasmanian Forests: Their Botany and Economical Value', *JPRSNSW*, vol. 12, 1878, pp. 17–28.
Thomas, Keith. *Man and the Natural World: Changing Attitudes in England 1500–1800*. Allen Lane, London, 1983.
Thompson, Kenneth, 'The Australian Fever Tree in California: Eucalypts and Malaria Prophylaxis', *Annals of the Association of American Geographers*, vol. 60, 1970, pp. 230–44.
Thoms, Albie. *Bohemians in the Bush: The Artists' Camps of Mosman*. Art Gallery of New South Wales, Sydney, 1991.
Tipping, Marjorie (ed.). *An Artist on the Goldfields: The Diary of Eugene von Guérard*. Curry O'Neil, Melbourne, 1982.
Tom Roberts. Art Gallery of South Australia, Adelaide, 1996.
Topliss, Helen. *Tom Roberts 1856–1931: A Catalogue Raisonné*. Oxford University Press, Melbourne, 1985, 2 vols.
Tower Hill Guide. Melbourne, 1966.
Traill, Catherine Parr. *The Backwoods of Canada*. Knight, London, 1836.
Treadgold, M.L. *Bounteous Bestowal: The Economic History of Norfolk Island*. National Centre for Development Studies, ANU, Canberra, 1988.
Trollope, Anthony. *Australia and New Zealand*. Chapman & Hall, London, 1873, 2 vols.
Troy, P. N. (ed.). *Equity, Environment and Efficiency*. Melbourne University Press, Melbourne, 2000.
Truettner, William (ed.). *The West as America: Reinterpreting Images of the Frontier 1820–1920*. Smithsonian Institution Press, Washington, 1991.

Turner, Frederick. *A Census of Grasses of New South Wales*. Potter, Sydney, 1890.
——— *The Forage Plants of Australia*. Chapman, Sydney, 1891.
Turner, James. *Reckoning with the Beast: Animals, Pain and Humanity in the Victorian Mind*. Johns Hopkins University Press, Baltimore, 1980.
Twain, Mark. *Mark Twain in Australia and New Zealand*. Penguin, Melbourne, 1973.
Twamley, Louisa Anne. *The Annual of British Landscape Scenery 1839: An Autumn Ramble on the Wye*. Orr, London, 1839.
——— *Our Wild Flowers*. Tilt, London, 1839.
——— *Poems*. Tilt, London, 1835.
——— *The Romance of Nature*. Tilt, London, 1836.
Twopeny, Richard. *Town Life in Australia*. Stock, London, 1883.
Tyrrell, Ian. *True Gardens of the Gods: Californian-Australian Environmental Reform 1860–1930*. University of California Press, Berkeley, 1999.
The Victorian Exhibition, opened 6th November 1872: Official Catalogue. Melbourne, 1872.
The Visitors' Guide to the Upper Yarra and Fern Tree Gully Districts. Massina, Melbourne, 1888.
Walch, Garnet. *Victoria in 1880*. George Robertson, Melbourne, 1881.
Walker, Mary Howitt. *Come Wind, Come Weather: A Biography of Alfred Howitt*. Melbourne University Press, Melbourne, 1971.
Wall, A. H. *Artistic Landscape Photography*. Percy Lund, Bradford, 1896.
Wallis, James. *An Historical Account of New South Wales*. Ackermann, London, 1821.
Walsh, Gerald. *Pioneering Days: People and Innovations in Australia's Rural Past*. Allen & Unwin, Sydney, 1993.
Ward, John Manning. *James Macarthur: Colonial Conservative 1798–1867*. Sydney University Press, Sydney, 1981.
Watling, Thomas. *Letters from an Exile at Botany Bay to his Aunt in Dumfries*. Bell, Penrith, 1794.
Wentworth, William Charles. *Statistical Account of the British Settlement in Australasia*. Whittaker, London, 1824, 2 vols.
———- *Statistical, Historical and Political Description of the Colony of New South Wales*. Whittaker, London, 1819.
Whitaker, Anne-Maree, 'Joseph Foveaux: "A Gentleman of High Reputation"', *JRAHS*, vol. 83, 1997, pp. 17–30.
White, John. *Journal of a Voyage to New South Wales*. Debrett, London, 1790.
Whitley, Gilbert, 'The Doom of the Bird of Providence', *Australian Zoologist*, vol. 8, 1934, pp. 42–9.
Whitney, J. D. *The Yosemite Guide-Book*. California State Legislature, Sacramento, 1869.
Widowson, Henry. *Present State of Van Diemen's Land*. Robinson, London, 1829.
Wilkes, Charles. *Narrative of the United States Exploring Expedition during the Years 1838, 1839, 1840, 1841, 1842*. Sherman, Philadelphia, 1844, 5 vols.
Williams, Michael. *Americans and their Forests*. Cambridge University Press, Cambridge, 1989.
Williams, Raymond. *The Country and the City*. Chatto & Windus, London, 1973.
Willis, Ann-Marie. *Picturing Australia: A History of Photography*. Angus & Robertson, Sydney, 1988.
Willoughby, Howard. *Australian Pictures drawn with Pen and Pencil*. Religious Tract Society, London, 1886.
Wohl, Anthony S. *The Eternal Slum: Housing and Social Policy in Victorian London*. Edward Arnold, London, 1977.
'Woods and Forests of Tasmania: Report of the Conservator of Forests, 1886–87', *Journal and Printed Papers of the Parliament of Tasmania*, vol. 12, 1887, paper no. 61.
Woolls, William. *A Contribution to the Flora of Australia*. White, Sydney, 1867.
——— *Lectures on the Vegetable Kingdom*. Fuller, Sydney, 1879.
——— *Miscellanies in Prose and Verse*. Evans, Sydney, 1838.

——— 'Plants Which Have Become Naturalized in New South Wales', *Proceedings of the Linnean Society of New South Wales*, vol. 9, 1884, pp. 185–205.

——— 'Species of Eucalypts in the County of Cumberland: Their Habits and Uses', *Proceedings of the Linnean Society of New South Wales*, vol. 5, 1880–81, pp. 488–510.

Worgan, George B. *Journal of a First Fleet Surgeon*. Library Council of New South Wales, Sydney, 1978.

Worster, Donald. *Nature's Economy: The Roots of Ecology*. Sierra Club Books, San Francisco, 1977.

Wright, Raymond. *The Bureaucrats' Domain: Space and the Public Interest in Victoria 1836–84*. Oxford University Press, Melbourne, 1989.

Wright, Reg. *The Forgotten Generations of Norfolk Island and Van Diemen's Land*. Library of Australian History, Sydney, 1986.

Wyse, J. W. H., 'Water Supply for the Interior of New South Wales', *Victorian Review*, vol. 11, 1885, pp. 641–65.

Yarwood, A. T. *Samuel Marsden: The Great Survivor*. Melbourne University Press, Melbourne, 1996.

Young, David, Conservation Policy and Practice in Tasmanian Forests 1870–1900, Graduate Diploma in Environmental Studies, University of Tasmania, 1991.

INDEX

THE MIEGUNYAH PRESS
MELBOURNE UNIVERSITY PRESS

THIS BOOK WAS DESIGNED AND TYPESET BY SANDRA NOBES
THE TEXT WAS SET IN 10 POINT STEMPEL GARAMOND
WITH 14 POINTS OF LEADING
THE TEXT IS PRINTED ON EURO SATIN 115 GSM

THE TEXT WAS EDITED BY JENNY LEE